W9-DEW-223

Student Quick Tips

Use this Student Quick Tips guide for a quick and easy start with McGraw-Hill Connect. You'll get valuable tips on registering, doing assignments, and accessing resources, as well as information about the support center hours.

Getting Started

TIP: To get started in Connect, you will need the following:

- Your instructor's Connect Web Address

  Sample of Connect Web Address:

  http://www.mcgrawhillconnect.com/class/instructorname_section_name

- Connect Access Code

TIP: If you do not have an access code or have not yet secured your tuition funds, you can click "Free Trial" during registration. This trial will provide temporary Connect access (typically three weeks) and will remind you to purchase online access before the end of your trial.

Registration and Sign In

1. Go to the Connect Web Address provided by your instructor
2. Click on **Register Now**
3. Enter your email address

TIP: If you already have a McGraw-Hill account, you will be asked for your password and will not be required to create a new account.

4. Enter a registration code or choose **Buy Online** to purchase access online

5. Follow the on-screen directions

TIP: Please choose your Security Question and Answer carefully. We will ask you for this information if you forget your password.

6. When registration is complete, click on **Go to Connect Now**

7. You are now ready to use **Connect**

Trouble Logging In?

- Ensure you are using the same email address you used during registration

- If you have forgotten your password, click on the "Forgot Password?" link at your Instructor's Connect Course Web Address

- When logged into Connect, you can update your account information (e.g. email address, password, and security question/answer) by clicking on the *"My Account"* link located at the top-right corner

Home (Assignments)

TIP: If you are unable to begin an assignment, verify the following:

- The assignment is available (start and due dates)

- That you have not exceeded the maximum number of attempts

- That you have not achieved a score of 100%

- If your assignment contains questions that require manual grading, you will not be able to begin your next attempt until your instructor has graded those questions

TIP: Based on the assignment policy settings established by your Instructor, you may encounter the following limitations when working on your assignment(s):

- Ability to Print Assignment

- Timed assignments – once you begin a "*timed assignment*," the timer will not stop by design

TIP: "*Save & Exit*" vs. "*Submit*" button

- If you are unable to complete your assignment in one sitting, utilize the "*Save & Exit*" button to save your work and complete it at a later time

- Once you have completed your assignment, utilize the "*Submit*" button in order for your assignment to be graded

Library

TIP: The *Library* section of your Connect account provides shortcuts to various resources.

- If you purchased ConnectPlus, you will see an *eBook* link, which can also be accessed from the section information widget of the *Home* tab

- *Recorded Lectures* can be accessed if your instructor is using *Tegrity Campus* to capture lectures. You may also access recorded lectures when taking an assignment by clicking on the projector icon in the navigation bar

- Many McGraw-Hill textbooks offer additional resources such as narrated slides and additional problems, which are accessible through the *Student Resources* link

Reports

TIP: Once you submit your assignment, you can view your available results in the *Reports* tab.

- If you see a dash (-) as your score, your instructor has either delayed or restricted your ability to see the assignment feedback

- Your instructor has the ability to limit the amount of information (e.g. questions, answers, scores) you can view for each submitted assignment

Need More Help?

CONTACT US ONLINE

Visit us at:

www.mcgrawhillconnect.com/support

Browse our support materials including tutorial videos and our searchable Connect knowledge base. If you cannot find an answer to your question, click on "Contact Us" button to send us an email.

GIVE US A CALL

Call us at:

1-800-331-5094

Our live support is available:

Mon-Thurs: 8 am – 11 pm CT
Friday: 8 am – 6 pm CT
Sunday: 6 pm – 11 pm CT

Financial Accounting Fundamentals

4th edition

John J. Wild

University of Wisconsin at Madison

Custom Value Edition for Bryant University

Mc Graw Hill Education

Copyright © 2013 by McGraw-Hill Education. All rights reserved. Printed in the United States of America. Except as permitted under the United States Copyright Act of 1976, no part of this publication may be reproduced or distributed in any form or by any means, or stored in a data base retrieval system, without prior written permission of the publisher.

2 3 4 5 6 7 8 9 0 BRP BRP 15 14 13

ISBN-13: 978-0-07-809649-5
ISBN-10: 0-07-809649-9

Learning Solutions Consultant: Anthony Mansella
Associate Project Manager: Alyssa Gantzert

Financial Accounting Fundamentals, 4e

Enhancements in technology have changed the spectrum of how we live and learn in the world today. Being able to download and work with learning tools on smart phones, tablets, or laptop computers empowers students to drive their own learning by putting increasingly intelligent technology into their hands.

No two students are alike, and whether the goal is to become an accountant or a businessperson or simply to be an informed consumer of accounting information, *Financial Accounting Fundamentals (FAF)* has helped generations of students succeed by giving them support in the form of leading-edge accounting content that engages students, paired with state-of-the-art technology that elevates their understanding of key accounting principles.

With *FAF* on your side, you'll be provided with **engaging content** in a **motivating style** to help students see the relevance of accounting. Students are motivated when reading materials that are clear and pertinent. *FAF* excels at engaging students. Its chapter-opening vignettes showcase dynamic, successful entrepreneurial individuals and companies guaranteed to **interest and excite students, and highlights the usefulness of accounting to those business owners**. This edition's featured companies—**Polaris, Arctic Cat, KTM,** and **Piaggio**—captivate students with their products and annual reports, which are a pathway for learning financial statements. Further, this book's coverage of the accounting cycle fundamentals is widely praised for its clarity and effectiveness.

FAF also delivers innovative technology to help student performance. ***Connect Accounting*** provides students with instant grading and feedback for assignments that are completed online. With our new **Intelligent Response Technology**, we are taking our accounting content to the next level, delivering assessment material in a **more intuitive, less restrictive** format that adapts to the needs of today's students.

Our new content features:

- a **general journal interface** that looks and feels more like that found in practice.
- an **auto-calculation** feature that allows students to focus on concepts rather than rote tasks.
- a **smart (auto-fill) drop-down design**.

The end result is content that better prepares students for the real world. *Connect Accounting* also includes digitally based, interactive adaptive learning tools that provide an opportunity to engage students more effectively by offering varied instructional methods and more personalized learning paths that build on different learning styles, interests, and abilities, allowing students to work at their own pace.

McGraw-Hill LearnSmart™ is an intelligent learning system that uses a series of adaptive questions to pinpoint each student's knowledge gaps. LearnSmart then provides an optimal learning path for each student, so that they spend less time in areas they already know and more time in areas they don't. The result is LearnSmart's adaptive learning path that helps students retain more knowledge, learn faster, and study more efficiently.

Our **Interactive Presentations** teach each chapter's core learning objectives in a rich multimedia format, bringing the content to life. Your students will come to class prepared when you assign Interactive Presentations. Students can also review the Interactive Presentations as they study.

Guided Examples provide students with narrated, animated, step-by-step walkthroughs of algorithmic versions of assigned exercises. Students appreciate the Guided Examples because they can help students learn accounting and complete assignments when outside of class.

Connect Plus Accounting integrates a media-rich online version of the textbook with *Connect Accounting*.

"This is an excellent book that is well-written and contains excellent illustrations. It has the best online supplements of any of the texts that I have reviewed. . . . This is an excellent book that I would recommend to all of my colleagues."

— **KAREN CRISONINO, County College of Morris**

About the Author

JOHN J. WILD is a distinguished professor of accounting at the University of Wisconsin at Madison. He previously held appointments at Michigan State University and the University of Manchester in England. He received his BBA, MS, and PhD from the University of Wisconsin.

Professor Wild teaches accounting courses at both the undergraduate and graduate levels. He has received numerous teaching honors, including the Mabel W. Chipman Excellence-in-Teaching Award, the departmental Excellence-in-Teaching Award, and the Teaching Excellence Award from the 2003 and 2005 business graduates at the University of Wisconsin. He also received the Beta Alpha Psi and Roland F. Salmonson Excellence-in-Teaching Award from Michigan State University. Professor Wild has received several research honors and is a past KPMG Peat Marwick National Fellow and is a recipient of fellowships from the American Accounting Association and the Ernst and Young Foundation.

Professor Wild is an active member of the American Accounting Association and its sections. He has served on several committees of these organizations, including the Outstanding Accounting Educator Award, Wildman Award, National Program Advisory, Publications, and Research Committees. Professor Wild is author of *Fundamental Accounting Principles, Financial and Managerial Accounting, Financial Accounting, Managerial Accounting,* and *College Accounting*, each published by McGraw-Hill/Irwin. His research articles on accounting and analysis appear in *The Accounting Review, Journal of Accounting Research, Journal of Accounting and Economics, Contemporary Accounting Research, Journal of Accounting, Auditing and Finance, Journal of Accounting and Public Policy*, and other journals. He is past associate editor of *Contemporary Accounting Research* and has served on several editorial boards including *The Accounting Review*.

In his leisure time, Professor Wild enjoys hiking, sports, travel, people, and spending time with family and friends.

Dear Colleagues/Friends,

As we roll out the new edition of *Financial Accounting Fundamentals,* I thank each of you who provided suggestions to improve the textbook. As teachers, we know how important it is to select the right book for our course. This new edition reflects the advice and wisdom of many dedicated reviewers, symposium and workshop participants, students, and instructors. This book consistently rates number one in customer loyalty because of you. Together, we have created the most readable, concise, current, accurate, and innovative accounting book available today.

Throughout the writing process, I steered this book in the manner you directed. Reviewers, instructors, and students say this book's enhanced presentation, graphics, and technology cater to different learning styles and helps students better understand accounting. *Connect Plus Accounting* offers new features to improve student learning and to assist instructor teaching and grading. You and your students will find all these tools easy to apply.

I owe the success of this book to you and other instructors who graciously took time to help me focus on the changing demands of today's students and their learning needs. I feel fortunate to have witnessed our profession's extraordinary devotion to teaching. Your feedback and suggestions are reflected in everything I write. Please accept my heartfelt thanks for your dedication in helping today's students learn, understand, and appreciate accounting.

With kindest regards,

John J. Wild

Adapting to the Needs of

McGraw-Hill *Connect Plus Accounting* is a complete online assignment, learning, and textbook assessment solution that connects your students with the tools and resources needed to achieve success through faster learning, more efficient studying, and higher retention of knowledge. Key features found in *Connect Plus Accounting* include:

Intelligent Response Technology Intelligent Response Technology is *Connect Accounting's* new student interface for end-of-chapter assessment content. Intelligent Response Technology provides a general journal application that looks and feels more like what you would find in a general ledger software package, improves answer acceptance to reduce student frustration with formatting issues (such as rounding), and, for select questions, provides an expanded table that guides students through the process of solving the problem.

> "I like that this system was formatted like real-world accounting is."
>
> **—Student, Rose State College**

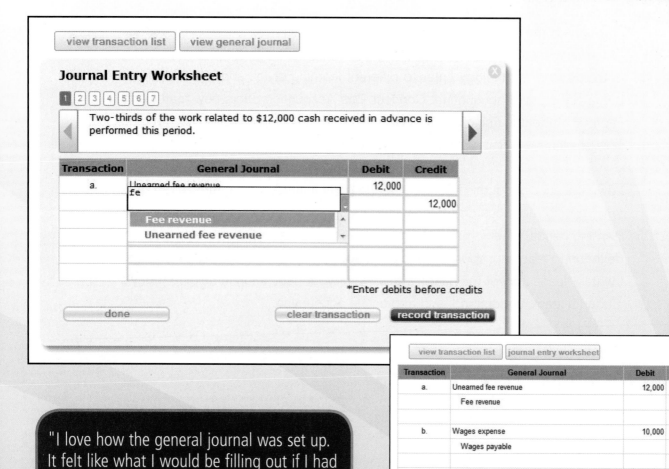

> "I love how the general journal was set up. It felt like what I would be filling out if I had an accounting job."
>
> **—Student, Chabot Community College**

Today's Students!

1. Complete the table to determine the cost assigned to ending inventory and cost of goods sold using specific identification.

Specific Identification

	Available for Sale			Cost of Goods Sold			Ending Inventory		
Date	Activity	Units	Unit Cost	Units Sold	Unit Cost	COGS	Ending Inventory-Units	Cost Per Unit	Ending Inventory-Cost
Mar. 1	Beginning Inventory	150							
Mar. 20	Purchase	220							
Mar. 30	Purchase	90							
		460				$ 0			$ 0

contact MH Publishing   check my work   💡 View Hint #1   ⊗ references   ⊗ ebook & resources

BIZKID COMPANY
Income Statement
For Year Ended August 31, 2011

Sales	✓		$ 218,880 ✓
Less: Sales discounts	✓	$ 3,349 ✓	
Less: Sales returns and allowances	✓	14,446 ✓	17,795
Net sales	✓		201,085
Cost of goods sold	✓		85,312 ✓
Gross profit	✓		115,773
Expenses			
Selling expenses			
Sales salaries expense	✓	29,987 ✓	
Rent expense-selling space	✓	10,287 ✓	
Store supplies expense	✓	2,627 ✓	
Advertising expense	✓	18,605 ✓	
Total selling expenses			61,506
General and administrative expenses			
Accounts payable	✗	876 ✓	
Accum-depreciation - store equipment	✗	9,785 ✗	
Total general and administrative expenses			10,661
Total expenses			72,167

BIZKID COMPANY
Income Statement
For Year Ended August 31, 2011

Sales		$ 218,880
Less: Sales discounts	$ 3,349	
Less: Sales returns and allowances	14,446	17,795
Net sales		201,085
Cost of goods sold		85,312
Gross profit		115,773
Expenses		
Selling expenses		
Sales salaries expense	29,987	
Rent expense-selling space	10,287	
Store supplies expense	2,627	
Advertising expense	18,605	
Total selling expenses		61,506
General and administrative expenses		
Office salaries expense	876	
Rent expense-office space	2,627	
of		
Cost of goods sold		3,503
Office salaries expense		65,009
Office supplies expense		
Rent expense-office space		

ask your instructor a question   report a content issue   check my work   ⊗ references

Connect Accounting helps students learn more efficiently by providing feedback and practice material when they need it, where they need it. *Connect* grades homework automatically and gives immediate feedback on any questions students may have missed.

"This system has improved the journal entry and T-account set-up processes to more accurately resemble the way it is done in class."

—**Student, Tallahassee Community College**

Adapting to the Needs of

Interactive Presentations *Connect Accounting's* Interactive Presentations teach each chapter's core learning objectives and concepts through an engaging, hands-on presentation, bringing the text content to life. Interactive Presentations harness the full power of technology to truly engage and appeal to all learning styles. Interactive Presentations are ideal in all class formats—online, face-to-face, or hybrid.

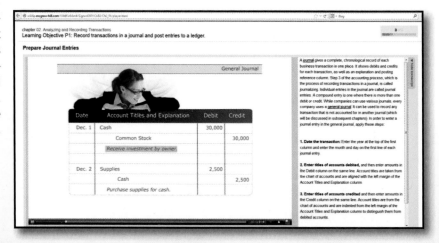

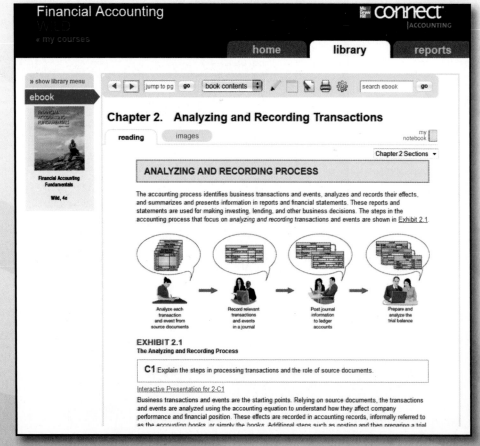

Integrated eBooks *Connect Plus* includes a media-rich eBook. With it, you can share your notes with your students, and they can insert their own notes, highlight the text, search for specific information, and review their materials. Using an eBook with *Connect* gives your students a complete digital solution that allows them to access their materials from any computer. And over time, as more and more students use mobile devices, our eBooks will even enable them to learn on the go.

Today's Students!

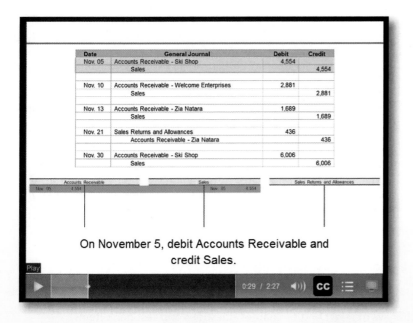

Guided Examples Guided Examples provide narrated, animated, and step-by-step walkthroughs of algorithmic versions of assigned exercises in *Connect Accounting*, allowing the student to identify, review, or reinforce the concepts and activities covered in class. Guided Examples provide immediate feedback and focus on the areas where students need the most guidance.

LearnSmart No two students are alike. McGraw-Hill LearnSmart™ is an intelligent learning system that uses a series of adaptive questions to pinpoint each student's knowledge gaps. LearnSmart then provides an optimal learning path for each student, so that they spend less time in areas they already know and more time in areas they don't. The result is that LearnSmart's adaptive learning path helps students retain more knowledge, learn faster, and study more efficiently.

Student Resource Library The *Connect Accounting* Student Study Center gives access to additional resources such as recorded lectures, online practice materials, an eBook, and more.

Adapting to the Needs of

McGraw-Hill's solutions are proven to improve student performance. With *Connect Accounting*, students can access a wealth of engaging resources to help them study more effectively and perform at a higher level on homework and exams. *Connect Accounting* also allows instructors to assign McGraw-Hill's world class content and assess student performance.

The integrated solutions for *Financial Accounting Fundamentals* have been specifically designed to help you achieve your course goals of improving student readiness, enhancing student engagement, and increasing their comprehension of content. McGraw-Hill's adaptive learning component, LearnSmart, provides assignable modules that help students master chapter core content and come to class more prepared.
In addition, Interactive Presentations deliver learning objectives in an interactive environment, giving students access to course-critical content anytime, anywhere. Known for its engaging style, the *FAF* solution employs the use of current companies, LearnSmart, and our instant feedback on practice problems to help students engage with our materials, comprehend the content, and achieve higher outcomes in the course.

Simple Assignment Management and Smart Grading
With *Connect Plus Accounting,* creating assignments is easier than ever, so you can spend more time teaching and less time managing. *Connect Accounting* enables you to:

- Create and deliver assignments easily with select end-of-chapter questions and test bank items.
- Go paperless with the eBook and online submission and grading of student assignments.
- Have assignments scored automatically, giving students immediate feedback on their work and side-by-side comparisons with correct answers.
- Reinforce classroom concepts with practice tests and instant quizzes.

"Connect certainly offers so much for the students and at the same time helps the professors. The professors can offer more learning opportunities to the students without intensive time investment."

—Constance Hylton, George Mason University

Today's Instructors

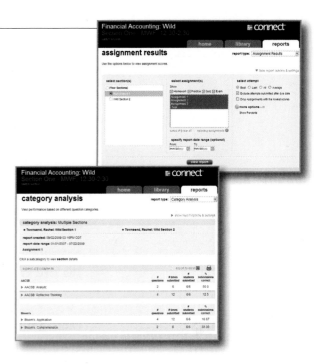

Student Reporting

Connect Accounting keeps instructors informed about how each student, section, and class is performing, allowing for more productive use of lecture and office hours. The reporting function enables you to:

- View scored work immediately and track individual or group performance with assignment and grade reports.
- Access an instant view of student or class performance relative to learning objectives.
- Collect data and generate reports required by many accreditation organizations, such as AACSB and AICPA.
- Identify low-performance students with the "At Risk" student report.

Instructor Library

The *Connect Accounting* Instructor Library is your repository for additional resources to improve student engagement in and out of class. You can select and use any asset that enhances your lecture. The *Connect Accounting* Instructor Library includes: access to the eBook version of the text, PowerPoint files, Solutions Manual, Instructor Resource Manual, and Test Bank.

Tegrity: Lectures 24/7

Make your classes available anytime, anywhere. With simple one-click recording, instructors can record lectures, presentations, and step-by-step problem solutions with Tegrity. Using Tegrity with *Connect Accounting*, instructors can post recordings directly to *Connect* for student viewing. Students can also search for a word or phrase and be taken to the exact place in your lecture that they need to review.

To learn more about Tegrity watch a two-minute Flash demo at **http://tegritycampus.mhhe.com**.

McGraw-Hill Customer Experience Group Contact Information

At McGraw-Hill, we understand that getting the most from new technology can be challenging. That's why our services don't stop after you purchase our products. You can e-mail our Product Specialists 24 hours a day to get product training online. Or you can search our knowledge bank of Frequently Asked Questions on our support Website. For Customer Support, call 800-331-5094 or visit **www.mhhe.com/support**. One of our Technical Support Analysts will be able to assist you in a timely fashion.

How Can Text-Related Web Resources Enrich My Course?

Online Learning Center (OLC)

We offer an Online Learning Center (OLC) that follows *Financial Accounting Fundamentals* chapter by chapter. It doesn't require any building or maintenance on your part. It's ready to go the moment you and your students type in the URL: *www.mhhe.com/wildFAF4e*

As students study and learn from *Financial Accounting Fundamentals*, they can visit the Student Edition of the OLC Website to work with a multitude of helpful tools:

- Generic Template Working Papers
- Chapter Learning Objectives
- Interactive Chapter Quizzes
- PowerPoint® Presentations
- Excel Template Assignments

A secured Instructor Edition stores essential course materials to save you prep time before class. Everything you need to run a lively classroom and an efficient course is included. All resources available to students, plus . . .

- Instructor's Resource Manual
- Solutions Manual
- Solutions to Excel Template Assignments
- Test Bank
- Solutions to Sage 50 Complete Accounting and QuickBooks templates

The OLC Website also serves as a doorway to other technology solutions, like course management systems.

Online Course Management

The Best of Both Worlds

McGraw-Hill Higher Education and Blackboard have teamed up. What does this mean for you?

1. Single sign-on. Now you and your students can access McGraw-Hill's *Connect*™ and Create™ right from within your Blackboard course—all with one single sign-on.

2. Deep integration of content and tools. You get single sign-on with *Connect* and Create, you also get integration of McGraw-Hill content and content engines right in Blackboard. Whether you're choosing a book for your course or building *Connect* assignments, all the tools you need are right where you want them—inside Blackboard.

3. One grade book. Keeping several grade books and manually synchronizing grades in Blackboard is no longer necessary. When a student completes an integrated *Connect* assignment, the grade for that assignment automatically (and instantly) feeds your Blackboard grade center.

4. A solution for everyone. Whether your institution is already using Blackboard or you just want to try Blackboard on your own, we have a solution for you. McGraw-Hill and Blackboard can now offer you easy access to industry-leading technology and content, whether your campus hosts it, or we do. Be sure to ask your local McGraw-Hill representative for details.

McGraw-Hill Campus™

McGraw-Hill Campus™ is a new one-stop teaching and learning experience available to users of any learning management system. This complimentary integration allows faculty and students to enjoy single sign-on (SSO) access to all McGraw-Hill Higher Education materials and synchronized grade-book with our award-winning McGraw-Hill Connect platform. McGraw-Hill Campus provides faculty with instant access to all McGraw-Hill Higher Education teaching materials (eTextbooks, test banks, PowerPoint slides, animations and learning objects, and so on), allowing them to browse, search, and use any instructor ancillary content in our vast library at no additional cost to instructor or students. Students enjoy SSO access to a variety of free (quizzes, flash cards, narrated presentations, and so on) and subscription-based products (McGraw-Hill Connect). With this integration enabled, faculty and students will never need to create another account to access McGraw-Hill products and services. For more information on McGraw-Hill Campus please visit our website at **www.mhcampus.com**.

CourseSmart

CourseSmart is a new way to find and buy eTextbooks. CourseSmart has the largest selection of eTextbooks available anywhere, offering thousands of the most commonly adopted textbooks from a wide variety of higher education publishers. CourseSmart eTextbooks are available in one standard online reader with full text search, notes, highlighting, and email tools for sharing between classmates. Visit **www.CourseSmart.com** for more information on ordering.

Instructor Supplements

Instructor's Resource CD-ROM
ISBN13: 9780077584108
ISBN10: 0077584104

This is your all-in-one resource. It allows you to create custom presentations from your own materials or from the following text-specific materials provided in the CD's asset library:

- **Instructor's Resource Manual**
  Written by April Mohr, Jefferson Community and Technical College, SW.

This manual contains (for each chapter) a Lecture Outline, a chart linking all assignment materials to Learning Objectives, and additional visuals with transparency masters.

- **Solutions Manual**
  Written by John J. Wild, and Anita Kroll, University of Wisconsin–Madison.

- **Test Bank**
  Revised by Laurie Hays, Western Michigan University.

- **PowerPoint® Presentations**
  Prepared by Anna Boulware, St. Charles Community College.

  Presentations allow for revision of lecture slides, and includes a viewer, allowing screens to be shown with or without the software.

Student Supplements

Working Papers
Available through Create. Contact your publisher representative for details.

Written by John J. Wild.

Connect Accounting with LearnSmart One Semester Access Code Card
ISBN13: 9780077584078
ISBN10: 0077584074

Connect Plus Accounting with LearnSmart One Semester Access Code Card
ISBN13: 9780077584092
ISBN10: 0077584090

Carol Yacht's Sage 50 Complete Accounting 2013 Student Guide and Templates
ISBN13: 9780077796860
ISBN10: 0077796861

Prepared by Carol Yacht.

To better prepare students for accounting in the real world, selected end-of-chapter material in the text is tied to Sage 50 Complete Accounting 2013 software (formerly Peachtree). The accompanying student guide provides a step-by-step walkthrough for students on how to complete the problem in the software.

QuickBooks Pro 2013 Student Guide and Templates
ISBN13: 9780077598686
ISBN10: 0077598687

Prepared by Carol Yacht.

To better prepare students for accounting in the real world, selected end-of-chapter material in the text is tied to QuickBooks software. The accompanying student guide provides a step-by-step walkthrough for students on how to complete the problem in the software.

Innovative Textbook Features

Using Accounting for Decisions

Whether we prepare, analyze, or apply accounting information, one skill remains essential: decision-making. To help develop good decision-making habits and to illustrate the relevance of accounting, our book uses a unique pedagogical framework we call the Decision Center. This framework is comprised of a variety of approaches and subject areas, giving students insight into every aspect of business decision-making; see three examples to the right and one below. Answers to Decision Maker and Ethics boxes are at the end of each chapter.

Decision Insight

Women Entrepreneurs The Center for Women's Business Research reports that women-owned businesses, such as **Nom Nom Truck**, are growing and that they:

- Total approximately 11 million and employ nearly 20 million workers.
- Generate $2.5 trillion in annual sales and tend to embrace technology.
- Are philanthropic—70% of owners volunteer at least once per month.
- Are more likely funded by individual investors (73%) than venture firms (15%).

Decision Ethics

Payables Manager As a new accounts payable manager, you are being trained by the outgoing manager. She explains that the system prepares checks for amounts net of favorable cash discounts, and the checks are dated the last day of the discount period. She also tells you that checks are not mailed until five days later, adding that "the company gets free use of cash for an extra five days, and our department looks better. When a supplier complains, we blame the computer system and the mailroom." Do you continue this payment policy? [Answer—p. 208]

Decision Maker

Entrepreneur You purchase a batch of products on terms of 3/10, n/90, but your company has limited cash and you must borrow funds at an 11% annual rate if you are to pay within the discount period. Is it to your advantage to take the purchase discount? Explain. [Answer—p. 208]

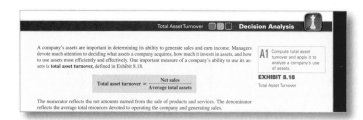

Total Asset Turnover — **Decision Analysis**

A company's assets are important in determining its ability to generate sales and earn income. Managers devote much attention to deciding what assets a company acquires, how much it invests in assets, and how to use assets most efficiently and effectively. One important measure of a company's ability to use its assets is **total asset turnover**, defined in Exhibit 8.18.

$$\text{Total asset turnover} = \frac{\text{Net sales}}{\text{Average total assets}}$$

A1 Compute total asset turnover and apply it to analyze a company's use of assets.

EXHIBIT 8.18
Total Asset Turnover

The numerator reflects the net amounts earned from the sale of products and services. The denominator reflects the average total resources devoted to operating the company and generating sales.

CAP Model

The Conceptual/Analytical/Procedural (CAP) Model allows courses to be specially designed to meet your teaching needs or those of a diverse faculty. This model identifies learning objectives, textual materials, assignments, and test items by C, A, or P, allowing different instructors to teach from the same materials, yet easily customize their courses toward a conceptual, analytical, or procedural approach (or a combination thereof) based on personal preferences.

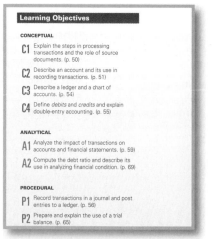

Learning Objectives

CONCEPTUAL

C1 Explain the steps in processing transactions and the role of source documents. (p. 50)

C2 Describe an account and its use in recording transactions. (p. 51)

C3 Describe a ledger and a chart of accounts. (p. 54)

C4 Define *debits* and *credits* and explain double-entry accounting. (p. 55)

ANALYTICAL

A1 Analyze the impact of transactions on accounts and financial statements. (p. 59)

A2 Compute the debt ratio and describe its use in analyzing financial condition. (p. 69)

PROCEDURAL

P1 Record transactions in a journal and post entries to a ledger. (p. 56)

P2 Prepare and explain the use of a trial balance. (p. 65)

GLOBAL VIEW

We explained that accounting under U.S. GAAP is similar, but n... tion discusses differences in adjusting accounts, preparing fina... liabilities on a balance sheet.

Adjusting Accounts Both U.S. GAAP and IFRS includ... ing accounts. Although some variations exist in revenue and ... all of the adjustments in this chapter are accounted for identica... ters we describe how certain assets and liabilities can result... value measurements.

Preparing Financial Statements Both U.S. GAAP a... cial statements following the same process discussed in this ch... GAAP and IFRS require current items to be separated from nonc... a classified balance sheet). U.S. GAAP balance sheets report cur... liquid to least liquid, where liquid refers to the ease of converting... nearest to maturity to furthest from maturity, maturity refers to th... balance sheets normally present noncurrent items first (and equity... ment. Other differences with financial statements exist, which we... the following example of IFRS reporting for its assets, liabilities,...

PIAGGIO

PIAGGIO
Balance Sheet (in thousands of...
December 31, 2011

Assets

Noncurrent assets   Total equity

Global View

This section explains international accounting practices relating to the material covered in that chapter. This section is purposefully located at the end of each chapter so that each instructor can decide what emphasis, if at all, is to be assigned to it. The aim of this Global View section is to describe accounting practices and to identify the similarities and differences in international accounting practices versus that in the United States. As we move toward global convergence in accounting practices, and as we witness the likely conversion of U.S. GAAP to IFRS, the importance of student familiarity with international accounting grows. This innovative section—helps us begin down that path of learning and teaching global accounting practices.

"We are very impressed with the text itself. The updated look, colors, illustrations, . . . the inclusion of IFRS information will help the transition in the future—which is a good thing. We have the flexibility to pick and choose for now with the way you have laid out the information."

—Bob Urell, Irvine Valley College

Bring Accounting To Life

Chapter Preview With Flowchart

This feature provides a handy textual/visual guide at the start of every chapter. Students can now begin their reading with a clear understanding of what they will learn and when, allowing them to stay more focused and organized along the way.

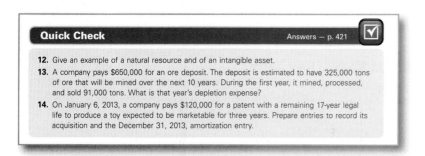

Quick Check

These short question/answer features reinforce the material immediately preceding them. They allow the reader to pause and reflect on the topics described, then receive immediate feedback before going on to new topics. Answers are provided at the end of each chapter.

"I like the layout of the text and the readability. The illustrations and comics in the book make the text seem less intimidating and boring for students. The PowerPoint slides are easy to understand and use, the pictorials are great, and the text has great coverage of accounting material. The addition of IFRS information and the updates to the opening stories are great. I like that the decision insights are about businesses the students can relate to (i.e., Facebook, women start-up businesses, etc)."

—**Jeannie Liu, Chaffey College**

Point: Prepaid accounts that apply to current and future periods are assets. These assets are adjusted at the end of each period to reflect only those amounts that have not yet expired, and to record as expenses those amounts that have expired.

when an insurance fee, called a *premium,* is pai account Prepaid Insurance. Over time, the ex this asset account and reported in expenses on in Prepaid Insurance and is reported on the bala accounts that will expire or be used before the statements are prepared. In this case, the prepa

Marginal Student Annotations

These annotations provide students with additional hints, tips, and examples to help them more fully understand the concepts and retain what they have learned. The annotations also include notes on global implications of accounting and further examples.

Outstanding Assignment Material

Once a student has finished reading the chapter, how well he or she retains the material can depend greatly on the questions, exercises, and problems that reinforce it. This book leads the way in comprehensive, accurate assignments.

Demonstration Problems present both a problem and a complete solution, allowing students to review the entire problem-solving process and achieve success.

Chapter Summaries provide students with a review organized by learning objectives. Chapter Summaries are a component of the CAP model (see page xvi), which recaps each conceptual, analytical, and procedural objective.

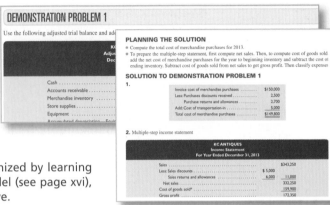

Key Terms are bolded in the text and repeated at the end of the chapter with page numbers indicating their location. The book also includes a complete Glossary of Key Terms.

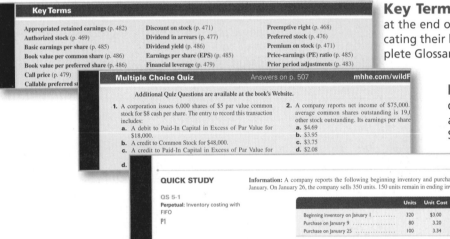

Multiple Choice Quiz questions quickly test chapter knowledge before a student moves on to complete Quick Studies, Exercises, and Problems.

Quick Study assignments are short exercises that often focus on one learning objective. Most are included in *Connect Accounting*. There are usually 8-10 Quick Study assignments per chapter.

Exercises are one of this book's many strengths and a competitive advantage. There are about 10-15 per chapter and most are included in *Connect Accounting*.

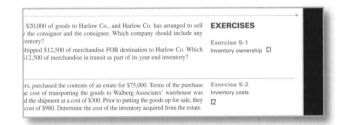

Problem Sets A & B are proven problems that can be assigned as homework or for in-class projects. All problems are coded according to the CAP model (see page xvi), and Set A is included in *Connect Accounting*.

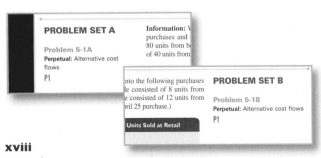

Helps Students Master Key Concepts

Beyond the Numbers exercises ask students to use accounting figures and understand their meaning. Students also learn how accounting applies to a variety of business situations. These creative and fun exercises are all new or updated, and are divided into sections:

- Reporting in Action
- Comparative Analysis
- Ethics Challenge
- Communicating in Practice
- Taking It To The Net
- Teamwork in Action
- Hitting the Road
- Entrepreneurial Decision
- Global Decision

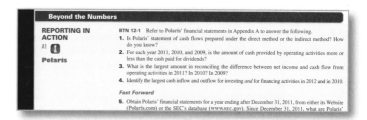

Serial Problem uses a continuous running case study to illustrate chapter concepts in a familiar context. The Serial Problem can be followed continuously from the first chapter or picked up at any later point in the book; enough information is provided to ensure students can get right to work.

> "The serial problems are excellent.... I like the continuation of the same problem to the next chapters if applicable. I use the Quick Studies as practice problems. . . . Students have commented that this really works for them if they work (these questions) before attempting the assigned exercises and problems. I also like the discussion (questions) and make this an assignment. You have done an outstanding job presenting accounting to our students."
>
> **—Jerri Tittle, Rose State College**

The End of the Chapter Is Only the Beginning Our valuable and proven assignments aren't just confined to the book. From problems that require technological solutions to materials found exclusively online, this book's end-of-chapter material is fully integrated with its technology package.

- Quick Studies, Exercises, and Problems available in *Connect* are marked with an icon.

- Problems supported by the Sage 50 Complete Accounting or Quickbooks are marked with an icon.

mhhe.com/wildFAF4e
- Problems supported with Microsoft Excel template assignments are marked with an icon.

- Assignments that focus on global accounting practices and companies are often identified with an icon.

Enhancements in This Edition

This edition's revisions are driven by instructors and students. General revisions to the entire book follow (including chapter-by-chapter revisions):

- Revised and updated assignments throughout
- Updated ratio/tool analysis and data for each chapter
- New material on International Financial Reporting Standards (IFRS) in most chapters, including global examples
- New and revised entrepreneurial examples and elements
- Revised serial problem through nearly all chapters
- New art program, visual info-graphics, and text layout

- New Polaris (maker of ATVs, snowmobiles, motorcycles, and electric vehicles) annual report with comparisons to competitors, including Arctic Cat, KTM (IFRS), and Piaggio (IFRS) with new assignments
- Updated graphics added to each chapter's analysis section
- New technology content integrated and referenced in the book
- Updated Global View section in each chapter
- New innovative assignments sprinkled throughout the book

Chapter 1

Twitter NEW opener with new entrepreneurial assignment
Streamlined and reorganized discussion of the users of accounting information
Updated salary information and new margin notes on the value of education
New presentation on the 'fraud triangle' and its relevance to accounting and internal control
New discussion on the joint role of the FASB and IASB in standard setting
Revised layout for accounting principles and assumptions
New information on the Dodd-Frank act and its relevance to accounting
New survey data from executives on the impact of fraud in the economic downturn
New world map on the adoption of IFRS or a variant of IFRS across countries
New company (Dell) for the return on assets section of Decision Analysis

Chapter 2

Nom Nom Truck NEW opener with new entrepreneurial assignment
Reorganized discussion and presentation of assets, liabilities, and equity accounts
Revised description of journalizing and posting of transactions
New headings on each general journal for this chapter's major illustration introducing our unique four-step transaction analysis
Revised global view and new Piaggio's (abbreviated) balance sheet
Updated debt ratio discussion using recent Skechers's information

Chapter 3

ash&dans NEW opener with new entrepreneurial assignment
New layout for the types of adjustments

New example of unearned revenues using USA Today
Enhanced and emphasized the innovative three-step process for adjusting accounts
Updated IFRS and FASB revenue recognition convergence
Added six new Quick Studies to directly apply the three-step adjustment process
Expanded explanation of temporary and permanent accounts
Revised visual display of four-step closing process
Enhanced display of general ledger for ease in learning

Chapter 4

Faithful Fish NEW opener with new entrepreneurial assignment
Enhanced exhibit on transportation costs and FOB terms, with inclusion of entries
New discussion of online ordering, tracking numbers, RFID, and FOB
Revised the two-step explanation of recording merchandise sales
New discussion on the importance and risks of accounting for sales returns
Revised visual display of a sales invoice
Revised discussion of merchandising purchases and sales
New Volkswagen example of IFRS income statement

Chapter 5

Feverish Ice Cream NEW opener with new entrepreneurial assignment
Enhanced exhibit that visually shows cost flows from inventory to financial statements, with superior info-graphics
Added new discussion on inventory controls
New explanatory boxes added to selected exhibits as learning aids

Expanded assignments covering perpetual and periodic inventory measurement
New material on IFRS and inventory methods

Chapter 6

CHEESEBOY NEW opener with new entrepreneurial assignment
New discussion of payroll controls
Expanded presentation of 'Hacker's Guide'
New discussion of the lock box and its purpose
New data on sources of fraud complaints
New evidence on methods to override controls
New visual on document to bond (insure) an employee
New example of MLB controls, or lack thereof

Chapter 7

Under Armour NEW opener with new entrepreneurial assignment
Added explanation of credit card sales
New discussion of mobile payment systems using mini-card-readers and iPads
New illustration comparing bad debts recognition under the allowance method versus the direct write-off method
Revised exhibit on aging of accounts receivable, including all detailed accounts
New illustration on why the banker's rule is commonly applied

Chapter 8

BizChair.com NEW opener with new entrepreneurial assignment
New learning boxes added to selected exhibits identifying salvage value
New explanation on how asset purchases

For Better Learning

occurring on different days of the month are commonly processed
New example of extraordinary repairs applied to the stealth bomber
New notes added to emphasize that depreciation is cost allocation, and not valuation
New explanation on how drugmakers fight patent expirations
New information on the Mickey Mouse Protection Act for intangibles
New goodwill example using Google's purchase of YouTube

Chapter 9
SmartIT Staffing NEW opener with new entrepreneurial assignment
Revised unearned revenues example based on Rihanna ticket sales
Added explanation on the role of sellers as tax collection 'agents' for the government
New information on franchise costs and how they are accounted for
Added select formulas to enhance the exhibit on payroll deductions
Updated payroll rates to 2012 with discussion on likely adjustments for 2013 and 2014
Added discussion on maximum withholding allowances claimed
New discussion on IRS actions against companies that fail to pay employment taxes
New evidence on payroll fraud, its median loss, and time taken to uncover such frauds

Chapter 10
barley & birch NEW opener with new entrepreneurial assignment
New explanation on why debt (credit) financing is less costly than equity financing
New margin graphics (four) illustrating how a debt's carrying value is periodically adjusted until it equals maturity value at the end of its life
New margin boxes on calculator functions to compute the price of bonds

New explanation of what is investment grade debt
New discussion on the role of unreported liabilities and the 2008–2009 financial crisis
Reference to changes in lease accounting
New discussion of collateral and its role in debt financing
New separate appendix learning objectives on amortizing a discount or a premium using effective interest

Chapter 11
Groupon NEW opener with new entrepreneurial assignment
New discussion of Facebook's IPO and the role of accounting information
New reference to corporate governance
New reference to state laws and where companies incorporate
New examples using Target for stock quotes and Google for stock splits
New discussion of fraudulent information dissemination and stock prices
Updated the global view on equity accounting

Chapter 12
TOMS NEW opener with new entrepreneurial assignment
Revised graphics to better illustrate cash inflows and outflows for operating, investing, and financing activities
Revised graphic to better reflect cash and cash equivalents
Added discussion on the use of T-accounts for reconstructing transactions impacting cash
New margin clarification for computing free cash flow
New discussion on the potential for IASB and FASB to issue guidance for the statement of cash flow that would require the direct method... stay tuned

Chapter 13
Motley Fool REVISED opener with new entrepreneurial assignment
New companies—Polaris, Arctic Cat, KTM and Piaggio—data throughout the chapter, exhibits, and illustrations
New boxed discussion on the role of financial statement analysis to fight and prevent fraud
Enhanced horizontal, vertical, ratio analysis using new companies and industry data
Streamlined global view section

Appendix C
myYearbook (MeetMe Inc.) NEW opener with new entrepreneurial assignment
New discussion of the two optional presentations for comprehensive income per FASB guidance in 2012
Revised discussion of accounting for securities
New reference to Greek debt in the context of international operations

Appendix D
New examples of LLPs and their prevalence among professional services
New discussion of the potential for multiple drawing accounts in practice
Revised and streamlined three-step process to liquidate a partnership

Appendix E
Expanded discussion and examples of hackers and internal controls
New pneumonic tool for system principles
Enhanced exhibit on system components
New discussion on voice recognition controls
New discussion on cloud computing, its implications to accounting, and its risks
New references to XBRL, Great Plains, and QuickBooks in accounting
Updated discussion and examples for ERP

Assurance of Learning Ready

Many educational institutions today are focused on the notion of assurance of learning, an important element of some accreditation standards. *Financial Accounting Fundamentals* is designed specifically to support your assurance of learning initiatives with a simple, yet powerful solution. Each test bank question for *Financial Accounting Fundamentals* maps to a specific chapter learning objective listed in the text. You can use our test bank software, EZ Test Online or *Connect Accounting* to easily query for learning objectives that directly relate to the learning objectives for your course. You can then use the reporting features of EZ Test to aggregate student results in similar fashion, making the collection and presentation of assurance of learning data simple and easy.

> "This textbook does address many learning styles and at the same time allows for many teaching styles ... our faculty have been very pleased with the continued revisions and supplements. From paper working papers ... to continually improved homework sites and e-books. I'm a 'Wild' fan!"
>
> —**Rita Hays, Southwestern Oklahoma State University**

AACSB Statement

The McGraw-Hill Companies is a proud corporate member of AACSB International. Understanding the importance and value of AACSB accreditation, *Financial Accounting Fundamentals* recognizes the curricula guidelines detailed in the AACSB standards for business accreditation by connecting selected questions in the test bank to the six general knowledge and skill guidelines in the AACSB standards. The statements contained in *Financial Accounting Fundamentals* are provided only as a guide for the users of this textbook. The AACSB leaves content coverage and assessment within the purview of individual schools, the mission of the school, and the faculty. While *Financial Accounting Fundamentals* and the teaching package make no claim of any specific AACSB qualification or evaluation, we have within *Financial Accounting Fundamentals* labeled select questions according to the six general knowledge and skills areas.

Acknowledgments

John J. Wild and McGraw-Hill/Irwin would like to recognize the following instructors for their valuable feedback and involvement in the development of *Financial Accounting Fundamentals,* 4e. We are thankful for their suggestions, counsel, and encouragement.

Thomas Arcuri, Florida State University

Sidney Askew, Borough of Manhattan Community College

Richard Barnhart, Grand Rapids Community College

Jaswinder Bhangal, Chabot College

Patrick Borja, Citrus College

Anna Boulware, St. Charles Community College

Billy Brewster, University of Texas at Arlington

Marci Butterfield, University of Utah

Colleen Chung, Miami Dade College- Kendall

Robert Churchman, Harding University

Marilyn Ciolino, Delgado Community College

Ken Couvillion, Delta College

Karen Crisonino, County College of Morris

Stan Davis, University of Tennessee at Chattanooga

Walter DeAguero, Saddleback College

Mike Deschamps, MiraCosta College

Ron Dustin, Fresno City College

Albert Fisher, College of Southern Nevada

Linda Flowers, Houston Community College

Jeannie Folk, College of DuPage

Ernesto Gonzalez, Florida National College

Ann Gregory, South Plains College

Rebecca Hancock, El Paso Community College-Valley Verde

Laurie Hays, Western Michigan University

Rita Hays, Southwestern Oklahoma State University

Constance Hylton, George Mason University

Todd Jensen, Sierra College

Gina M. Jones, Aims Community College

Jeff Jones, College of Southern Nevada

Sandra Jordan, Florida State College at Jacksonville

Dmitriy Kalyagin, Chabot College

Thomas Kam, Hawaii Pacific University

Shirly A. Kleiner, Johnson County Community College

Anita Kroll, University of Wisconsin-Madison

David Krug, Johnson County Community College

Christopher Kwak, DeAnza College

David Laurel, South Texas College

Charles Lewis, Houston Community College

Jeannie Liu, Chaffey College

Thomas S. Marsh, Northern Virginia Community College-Annandale

Stacie Mayes, Rose State College

Donald McWilliams, Jackson State University

Jeanine Metzler, Northampton Community College

Edna C. Mitchell, Polk State College

Kathleen O'Donnell, Onondaga Community College

Yvonne Phang, Borough of Manhattan Community College

James Racic, Lakeland Community College

Ruthie Reynolds, Howard University

Helen Roybark, Radford University

Richard Sarkisian, Camden County College

Tracy Schmeltzer, Wayne Community College

Debbie Schmidt, Cerritos College

Geeta Shankhar, University of Dayton

Regina Shea, Community College of Baltimore County—Essex

Jaye Simpson, Tarrant County College

Erik Slayter, California Polytechnic State University San Luis Obispo

Gerald Smith, University of Northern Iowa

Dominique Svarc, William Rainey Harper College

Ulysses Taylor, Fayetteville State University

Anthony Teng, Saddleback College

Teresa Thompson, Chaffey Community College

Jerri Tittle, Rose State College

Bob Urell, Irvine Valley College

Adam Vitalis, University of Wisconsin-Madison

Patricia Walczak, Lansing Community College

Dave Welch, Franklin University

Jean Wells-Jessup, Howard University

Christopher Widmer, Tidewater Community College

Gayle Williams, Sacramento City College

Kenneth L. Wild, University of London

Jonathan M. Wild, University of Wisconsin

John Woodward, Polk State College

Wanda Wong, Chabot College

Judy Zander, Grossmont College

The author extends a special thank you to our contributing and technology supplement authors:

Contributing Authors: Anita Kroll, University of Wisconsin; Kathleen O'Donnell, Onondaga Community College

Accuracy Checkers: Dave Krug, Johnson County Community College; Albert Fisher, College of Southern Nevada; Judy Zander, Grossmont College; Ann McCarthy, Eastern Carolina University; Mark McCarthy, East Carolina University; Helen Roybark, Radford University; and Barbara Schnathorst

LearnSmart Authors: April Mohr, Jefferson Community and Technical College, SW; Anna Boulware, St. Charles Community College; and Dominique Svarc, William Rainey Harper College

Online Quizzes: Constance Hylton, George Mason University

Interactive Presentations: Jeannie Folk, College of DuPage

PowerPoint: Anna Boulware, St. Charles Community College

Instructor Resource Manual: April Mohr, Jefferson Community and Technical College, SW

Test Bank: Laurie Hays, Western Michigan University

QuickBooks and Sage 50 Complete Accounting: Carol Yacht

Excel Templates: Jack Terry

In addition to the helpful and generous colleagues listed above, I thank the entire McGraw-Hill/Irwin *Financial Accounting Fundamentals,* 4e team, including Tim Vertovec, Steve Schuetz, Christina Sanders, Aaron Downey of Matrix Productions, Lori Koetters, Matthew Baldwin, Carol Bielski, Patricia Plumb, Jeremy Cheshareck, Ron Nelms, Xin Lin, Julie Hankins, and Brian Nacik. I also thank the great marketing and sales support staff, including Michelle Heaster and Kathleen Klehr. Many talented educators and professionals worked hard to create the supplements for this book, and for their efforts I'm grateful. Finally, many more people I either did not meet or whose efforts I did not personally witness nevertheless helped to make this book everything that it is, and I thank them all.

John J. Wild

Brief Contents

* Appendices D&E are available on the book's Website, **mhhe.com/wildFAF4e**, and as print copy from a McGraw-Hill representative.

Contents

---

* Appendices D&E are available on the book's Website, **mhhe.com/wildFAF4e**, and as print copy from a McGraw-Hill representative.

Financial Accounting Fundamentals

Introducing Financial Accounting

1

Learning Objectives are classified as conceptual, analytical, or procedural.

A Look at This Chapter

Accounting is crucial in our information age. In this chapter, we discuss the importance of accounting to different types of organizations and describe its many users and uses. We explain that ethics are essential to accounting. We also explain business transactions and how they are reflected in financial statements.

A Look Ahead

Chapter 2 describes and analyzes business transactions. We explain the analysis and recording of transactions, the ledger and trial balance, and the double-entry system. More generally, Chapters 2 and 3 use the accounting cycle to show how financial statements reflect business activities.

*A **Decision Feature** launches each chapter showing the relevance of accounting for a real entrepreneur. An **Entrepreneurial Decision** problem at the end of the assignments returns to this feature with a mini-case.*

Accounting for Twitter

"There is so much going on here . . ."
—BIZ STONE (CENTER)

SAN FRANCISCO—"We came across the word 'twitter,' and it was just perfect," recalls Jack Dorsey (right of photo). "The definition was 'a short burst of inconsequential information,' and 'chirps from birds,' and that's exactly what the product was." Today, Twitter boasts over 200 million users. Founded by Jack, along with Biz Stone and Evan Williams (left), **Twitter** (**Twitter.com**) is "facilitating connections between businesses and individuals in meaningful and relevant ways," says Jack. Along the way, the young entrepreneurs had to learn accounting and the details of preparing and interpreting financial statements.

"There is so much going on here," explains Biz when describing Twitter's business model. However, admits Evan, "We did a poor job of communicating." Important questions involving business formation, transaction analysis, and financial reporting arose. The entrepreneurs eventually met those challenges and, in the process, set Twitter apart. "If you stand pat," says Evan, "you risk being stagnant."

Information is the focus within Twitter's accounting records and systems. Jack recalls that when they launched Twitter, there were all these reasons why they would not succeed. He applied their similar "can-do" approach to accounting information. "My whole philosophy is making tech [and accounting] more accessible and human," says Jack. This includes using accounting information to make key business decisions.

Twitter is the language of micro-blogging, and accounting is the language of business. "Twitter is so many things: a messaging service, a customer-service tool, a real-time search," explains Biz, and the accounting system had to capture those things. Biz adds that Twitter is exploring additional "interesting ways to generate revenue." That revenue-stream is reflected in its financial statements, which are based on transaction analysis and accounting concepts.

Twitter's revenues exhibit growth and reflect what experts call the *monetizing* of its business. A recent study by the marketing firm SocialTwist found that the click-through rate was 19 for Twitter, which is the number of clicks on an embedded link. This compares with 3 clicks for Facebook links. Twitter's revenues in the recent year were estimated at $45 million, which are projected to exceed $100 million next year. Twitter also tracks its expenses and asset purchases. Twitter owners have an estimated valuation of between $5 and $10 billion!

The three entrepreneurs emphasize that accounting records must be in order for Twitter to realize its full potential. Many experts predict a public offering of its stock within the next two years, which could generate untold wealth. Still, Evan recognizes that "so many people here [at Twitter] contribute to that success." He also emphasizes that learning is a key to their business success. "I realized," insists Evan, "I could buy accounting books and learn something that people spent years learning."

[Sources: Twitter Website, January 2013; *Entrepreneur,* December 2010; *USA Today,* May 2009; Smedio.com, June 2011; *San Francisco Chronicle,* March 2011; SocialTwist.com, October 2010; *The Wall Street Journal,* February 2011]

*A **Preview** opens each chapter with a summary of topics covered.*

Today's world is one of information—its preparation, communication, analysis, and use. Accounting is at the core of this information age. Knowledge of accounting gives us career opportunities and the insight to take advantage of them. This book introduces concepts, procedures, and analyses that help us make better decisions, including career choices. In this chapter we describe accounting, the users and uses of accounting information, the forms and activities of organizations, and several accounting principles. We also introduce transaction analysis and financial statements.

Introducing Financial Accounting

Importance of Accounting	Fundamentals of Accounting	Transaction Analysis	Financial Statements
• Accounting information users • Opportunities in accounting	• Ethics—key concept • Generally accepted accounting principles • International standards	• Accounting equation • Transaction analysis—illustrated	• Income statement • Statement of retained earnings • Balance sheet • Statement of cash flows

IMPORTANCE OF ACCOUNTING

C1 Explain the purpose and importance of accounting.

Why is accounting so popular on campus? Why are there so many openings for accounting jobs? Why is accounting so important to companies? Why do politicians and business leaders focus on accounting regulations? The answer is that we live in an information age, where that information, and its reliability, impacts us all.

Accounting is an information and measurement system that identifies, records, and communicates relevant, reliable, and comparable information about an organization's business activities. *Identifying* business activities requires that we select relevant transactions and events. Examples are the sale of iPhones by **Apple** and the receipt of ticket money by **TicketMaster**. *Recording* business activities requires that we keep a chronological log of transactions and events measured in dollars. *Communicating* business activities requires that we prepare accounting reports such as financial statements, which we analyze and interpret. (The financial statements and notes of **Polaris** are shown in Appendix A near the end of this book. This appendix also shows the financial statements of **Arctic Cat**, **KTM**, and **Piaggio**.) Exhibit 1.1 summarizes accounting activities.

Real company names are printed in bold magenta.

Accounting is part of our everyday lives. Our most common contact with accounting is through credit approvals, checking accounts, tax forms, and payroll. These experiences tend to focus on the recordkeeping parts of accounting. **Recordkeeping,** or **bookkeeping,** is the recording of transactions and events, either manually or electronically. This is just one part of accounting. Accounting also identifies and communicates information on transactions and events, and it includes the crucial processes of analysis and interpretation.

Technology is a key part of modern business and plays a major role in accounting. Technology reduces the time, effort, and cost of recordkeeping while improving clerical accuracy. Some small organizations continue to perform various accounting tasks manually, but even they are impacted

EXHIBIT 1.1

Accounting Activities

Identifying	Recording	Communicating
Select transactions and events	Input, measure, and log	Prepare, analyze, and interpret

by technology. As technology makes more information available, the demand for accounting increases and so too the skills for applying that information. Consulting, planning, and other financial services are now closely linked to accounting. These services require sorting through data, interpreting their meaning, identifying key factors, and analyzing their implications.

Users of Accounting Information

Accounting is called the *language of business* because all organizations set up an accounting information system to communicate data to help people make better decisions. Exhibit 1.2 shows that accounting serves many users (this is a partial listing) who can be divided into two groups: external users and internal users.

Point: Technology is only as useful as the accounting data available, and users' decisions are only as good as their understanding of accounting. The best software and recordkeeping cannot make up for lack of accounting knowledge.

Margin notes further enhance the textual material.

External users	Internal users

• Lenders • Consumer groups • Shareholders • External auditors • Governments • Customers	• Officers • Sales staff • Managers • Budget officers • Internal auditors • Controllers

EXHIBIT 1.2

Users of Accounting Information

Infographics reinforce key concepts through visual learning.

External Information Users   **External users** of accounting information are *not* directly involved in running the organization. They include shareholders (investors), lenders, directors, customers, suppliers, regulators, lawyers, brokers, and the press. External users have limited access to an organization's information. Yet their business decisions depend on information that is reliable, relevant, and comparable. **Financial accounting** is the area of accounting aimed at serving external users by providing them with *general-purpose financial statements*. The term *general-purpose* refers to the broad range of purposes for which external users rely on these statements. Following is a partial list of external users and some decisions they make with accounting information.

C2   Identify users and uses of, and opportunities in, accounting.

- *Lenders* (creditors) loan money or other resources to an organization. Banks, savings and loans, co-ops, and mortgage and finance companies are lenders. Lenders look for information to help them assess whether an organization is likely to repay its loans with interest.
- *Shareholders* (*investors*) are the owners of a corporation. They use accounting reports in deciding whether to buy, hold, or sell stock.
- *Directors* are typically elected to a *board of directors* to oversee their interests in an organization. Since directors are responsible to shareholders, their information needs are similar.
- *External* (independent) *auditors* examine financial statements to verify that they are prepared according to generally accepted accounting principles.
- *Nonexecutive employees* and *labor unions* use financial statements to judge the fairness of wages, assess job prospects, and bargain for better wages.
- *Regulators* often have legal authority over certain activities of organizations. For example, the Internal Revenue Service (IRS) and other tax authorities require organizations to file accounting reports in computing taxes. Other regulators include utility boards that use accounting information to set utility rates and securities regulators that require reports for companies that sell their stock to the public.
- *Voters, legislators,* and *government officials* use accounting information to monitor and evaluate government receipts and expenses.
- *Contributors* to nonprofit organizations use accounting information to evaluate the use and impact of their donations.

● *Suppliers* use accounting information to judge the soundness of a customer before making sales on credit.

● *Customers* use financial reports to assess the staying power of potential suppliers.

Internal Information Users   **Internal users** of accounting information are those directly involved in managing and operating an organization. They use the information to help improve the efficiency and effectiveness of an organization. **Managerial accounting** is the area of accounting that serves the decision-making needs of internal users. Internal reports are not subject to the same rules as external reports and instead are designed with the special needs of internal users in mind. Following is a partial list of internal users and some decisions they make with accounting information.

● *Research and development managers* need information about projected costs and revenues of any proposed changes in products and services.

● *Purchasing managers* need to know what, when, and how much to purchase.

● *Human resource managers* need information about employees' payroll, benefits, performance, and compensation.

● *Production managers* depend on information to monitor costs and ensure quality.

● *Distribution managers* need reports for timely, accurate, and efficient delivery of products and services.

● *Marketing managers* use reports about sales and costs to target consumers, set prices, and monitor consumer needs, tastes, and price concerns.

● *Service managers* require information on the costs and benefits of looking after products and services.

Opportunities in Accounting

Accounting information is in all aspects of our lives. When we earn money, pay taxes, invest savings, budget earnings, and plan for the future, we use accounting. Accounting has four broad areas of opportunities: financial, managerial, taxation, and accounting-related. Exhibit 1.3 lists selected opportunities in each area.

EXHIBIT 1.3

Accounting Opportunities

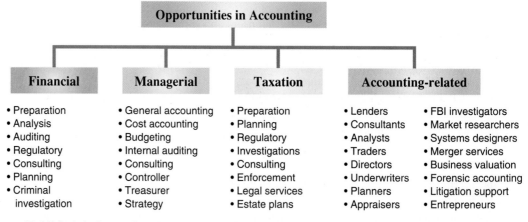

Exhibit 1.4 shows that the majority of opportunities are in *private accounting,* which are employees working for businesses. *Public accounting* offers the next largest number of opportunities, which involve services such as auditing and tax advice. Still other opportunities exist in government and not-for-profit agencies, including business regulation and investigation of law violations.

EXHIBIT 1.4

Accounting Jobs by Area

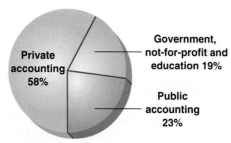

Accounting specialists are highly regarded and their professional standing is often denoted by a certificate. Certified public accountants (CPAs) must meet education and experience requirements, pass an examination, and exhibit ethical character. Many accounting specialists hold certificates in addition to or instead of the CPA. Two of the most common are the certificate in management accounting (CMA) and the certified internal auditor (CIA). Employers also look for specialists with designations such as certified bookkeeper (CB), certified payroll professional (CPP), personal financial specialist (PFS), certified fraud examiner (CFE), and certified forensic accountant (CrFA).

Demand for accounting specialists is strong. Exhibit 1.5 reports average annual salaries for several accounting positions. Salary variation depends on location, company size, professional designation, experience, and other factors. For example, salaries for chief financial officers (CFO) range from under $100,000 to more than $1 million per year. Likewise, salaries for bookkeepers range from under $30,000 to more than $80,000.

Point: The largest accounting firms are Deloitte, Ernst & Young, KPMG, and PricewaterhouseCoopers.

Point: Census Bureau (2011) reports that for workers 25 and over, higher education yields higher average pay:
Advanced degree $81,568
Bachelor's degree   57,326
High school degree   36,876
No high school degree   26,124

Field	Title (experience)	2011 Salary	2016 Estimate*
Public Accounting	Partner	$202,000	$223,000
	Manager (6–8 years)	97,500	107,500
	Senior (3–5 years)	75,000	83,000
	Junior (0–2 years)	57,500	63,500
Private Accounting	CFO	242,000	267,000
	Controller/Treasurer	157,500	174,000
	Manager (6–8 years)	91,500	101,000
	Senior (3–5 years)	74,500	82,000
	Junior (0–2 years)	53,000	58,500
Recordkeeping	Full-charge bookkeeper	59,500	65,500
	Accounts manager	52,000	57,500
	Payroll manager	55,500	61,000
	Accounting clerk (0–2 years)	38,500	42,500

EXHIBIT 1.5

Accounting Salaries for Selected Fields

Point: For updated salary information:
Abbott-Langer.com
www.AICPA.org
Kforce.com

* Estimates assume a 2% compounded annual increase over current levels (rounded to nearest $500).

Quick Check

Answers — p. 29

1. What is the purpose of accounting?
2. What is the relation between accounting and recordkeeping?
3. Identify some advantages of technology for accounting.
4. Who are the internal and external users of accounting information?
5. Identify at least five types of managers who are internal users of accounting information.

Quick Check is a chance to stop and reflect on key points.

Point: U.S. Bureau of Labor (June 2011) reports higher education is associated with a lower unemployment rate:
Bachelor's degree or more 4.4%
High school degree 10.0%
No high school degree 14.3%

FUNDAMENTALS OF ACCOUNTING

Accounting is guided by principles, standards, concepts, and assumptions. This section describes several of these key fundamentals of accounting.

Ethics—A Key Concept

The goal of accounting is to provide useful information for decisions. For information to be useful, it must be trusted. This demands ethics in accounting. **Ethics** are beliefs that distinguish right from wrong. They are accepted standards of good and bad behavior.

Identifying the ethical path is sometimes difficult. The preferred path is a course of action that avoids casting doubt on one's decisions. For example, accounting users are less likely to trust an auditor's report if the auditor's pay depends on the client's success . To avoid such concerns, ethics rules are often set. For example, auditors are banned from direct investment in their

C3 Explain why ethics are crucial to accounting.

Point: Sarbanes-Oxley Act requires each issuer of securities to disclose whether it has adopted a code of ethics for its senior officers and the contents of that code.

EXHIBIT 1.6

Guidelines for Ethical
Decision Making

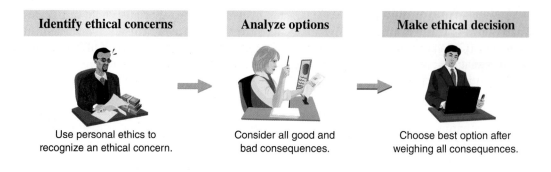

Identify ethical concerns	Analyze options	Make ethical decision
Use personal ethics to recognize an ethical concern.	Consider all good and bad consequences.	Choose best option after weighing all consequences.

client and cannot accept pay that depends on figures in the client's reports. Exhibit 1.6 gives guidelines for making ethical decisions.

Accountants face many ethical choices as they prepare financial reports. These choices can affect the price a buyer pays and the wages paid to workers. They can even affect the success of products and services. Misleading information can lead to a wrongful closing of a division that harms workers, customers, and suppliers. There is an old saying: *Good ethics are good business.*

Some people extend ethics to *social responsibility,* which refers to a concern for the impact of actions on society. An organization's social responsibility can include donations to hospitals, colleges, community programs, and law enforcement. It also can include programs to reduce pollution, increase product safety, improve worker conditions, and support continuing education. These programs are not limited to large companies. For example, many small businesses offer discounts to students and senior citizens. Still others help sponsor events such as the Special Olympics and summer reading programs.

Point: The American Institute of Certified Public Accountants' *Code of Professional Conduct* is available at **www.AICPA.org**.

Decision Insight boxes highlight → relevant items from practice.

▧ **Decision** Insight ♟

Virtuous Returns   Virtue is not always its own reward. Compare the S&P 500 with the Domini Social Index (DSI), which covers 400 companies that have especially good records of social responsibility. We see that returns for companies with socially responsible behavior are roughly on par with those of the S&P 500 for the past 10-year period (Domini.com, 2011 Annual Report). Copyright © 2005 by KLD Research & Analytics, Inc. The "Domini 400 Social Index" is a service mark of KLD Research & Analytics. ■

Fraud Triangle

The fraud triangle is a model created by a criminologist that asserts the following *three* factors must exist for a person to commit fraud: opportunity, pressure, and rationalization.

Opportunity is one side of the fraud triangle. A person must envision a way to commit fraud with a low perceived risk of getting caught. Employers can directly reduce this risk. An example of some control on opportunity is a pre-employment background check. *Pressure,* or incentive, is another side of the fraud triangle. A person must have some pressure to commit fraud. Examples are unpaid bills and addictions. *Rationalization,* or attitude, is the third side of the fraud triangle. A person who rationalizes fails to see the criminal nature of the fraud or justifies the action.

It is important to recognize that all three factors of the fraud triangle must usually exist for fraud to occur. The absence of one or more factors suggests fraud is unlikely.

The key to dealing with fraud is to focus on prevention. It is less expensive and more effective to prevent fraud from happening than it is to try to detect the crime. By the time the fraud is discovered, the money is gone and chances are slim that it will be recovered. Additionally, it is costly and time-consuming to investigate a fraud.

Both internal and external users rely on internal controls to reduce the likelihood of fraud. *Internal controls* are procedures set up to protect company property and equipment, ensure reliable accounting reports, promote efficiency, and encourage adherence to company policies. Examples are good records, physical controls (locks, passwords, guards), and independent reviews.

◼ **Decision** Insight

They Fought the Law Our economic and social welfare depends on reliable accounting. Some individuals forgot that and are now paying their dues. They include Raj Rajaratnam (in photo), an investor, convicted of trading stocks using inside information; Bernard Madoff of **Madoff Investment Securities**, convicted of falsifying securities records; Bernard Ebbers of **WorldCom**, convicted of an $11 billion accounting scandal; Andrew Fastow of **Enron**, guilty of hiding debt and inflating income; and Ramalinga Raju of **Satyam Computers**, accused of overstating assets by $1.5 billion. ◼

Generally Accepted Accounting Principles

Financial accounting is governed by concepts and rules known as **generally accepted accounting principles (GAAP).** We must understand these principles to best use accounting data. GAAP aims to make information *relevant, reliable,* and *comparable.* Relevant information affects decisions of users. Reliable information is trusted by users. Comparable information is helpful in contrasting organizations.

In the United States, the **Securities and Exchange Commission (SEC),** a government agency, has the legal authority to set GAAP. The SEC also oversees proper use of GAAP by companies that raise money from the public through issuances of their stock and debt. Those companies that issue their stock on U.S. exchanges include both *U.S. SEC registrants* (companies incorporated in the United States) and *non-U.S. SEC registrants* (companies incorporated under non-U.S. laws). The SEC has largely delegated the task of setting U.S. GAAP to the **Financial Accounting Standards Board (FASB),** which is a private-sector group that sets both broad and specific principles.

> **C4** Explain generally accepted accounting principles and define and apply several accounting principles.

Point: State ethics codes require CPAs who audit financial statements to disclose areas where those statements fail to comply with GAAP. If CPAs fail to report noncompliance, they can lose their licenses and be subject to criminal and civil actions and fines.

International Standards

In today's global economy, there is increased demand by external users for comparability in accounting reports. This demand often arises when companies wish to raise money from lenders and investors in different countries. To that end, the **International Accounting Standards Board (IASB),** an independent group (consisting of individuals from many countries), issues **International Financial Reporting Standards (IFRS)** that identify preferred accounting practices.

If standards are harmonized, one company can potentially use a single set of financial statements in all financial markets. Differences between U.S. GAAP and IFRS are decreasing as the FASB and IASB pursue a *convergence* process aimed to achieve a single set of accounting standards for global use. More than 115 countries now require or permit companies to prepare financial reports following IFRS. Further, non-U.S. SEC registrants can use IFRS in financial reports filed with the SEC (with no reconciliation to U.S. GAAP). This means there are *two* sets of accepted accounting principles in the United States: (1) U.S. GAAP for U.S. SEC registrants and (2) either IFRS or U.S. GAAP for non-U.S. SEC registrants.

The SEC is encouraging the FASB to change U.S. GAAP over a period of several years by endorsing, and thereby incorporating, individual IFRS standards into U.S. GAAP. This endorsement process would still allow the FASB to modify IFRS when necessary. The SEC would:

● Maintain its statutory oversight of the FASB, including authority to prescribe accounting principles and standards for U.S. issuers.

● Contribute to oversight and governance of the IASB through its involvement on the IFRS Foundation Monitoring Board.

The FASB would continue, but its role would be to provide input and support to the IASB in crafting high-quality, global standards. The FASB is to develop a transition plan to effect these changes over the next five years or so. For updates on this roadmap, we can check with the AICPA (IFRS.com), FASB (FASB.org), and IASB (ifrs.org).

 IFRS _____

Like the FASB, the IASB uses a conceptual framework to aid in revising or drafting new standards. However, unlike the FASB, the IASB's conceptual framework is used as a reference when specific guidance is lacking. The IASB also requires that transactions be accounted for according to their substance (not only their legal form), and that financial statements give a fair presentation, whereas the FASB narrows that scope to fair presentation *in accordance with U.S. GAAP.* ■

Conceptual Framework and Convergence

The FASB and IASB are attempting to converge and enhance the **conceptual framework** that guides standard setting. The FASB framework consists broadly of the following:

● **Objectives**—to provide information useful to investors, creditors, and others.

● **Qualitative Characteristics**—to require information that is *relevant, reliable,* and *comparable.*

● **Elements**—to define items that financial statements can contain.

● **Recognition and Measurement**—to set criteria that an item must meet for it to be recognized as an element; and how to measure that element.

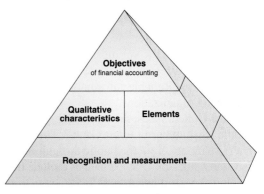

For updates on this joint FASB and IASB conceptual framework convergence we can check with FASB.org or ifrs.org Websites. We must remember that U.S. GAAP and IFRS are two similar, but not identical, systems. However, their similarities greatly outweigh any differences. The remainder of this section describes key principles and assumptions of accounting.

■ **Decision** Insight ═══════════════════════════════

Principles and Scruples   Auditors, directors, and lawyers are using principles to improve accounting reports. Examples include accounting restatements at **Navistar**, financial restatements at **Nortel**, accounting reviews at **Echostar**, and expense adjustments at **Electronic Data Systems**. Principles-based accounting has led accounting firms to drop clients deemed too risky. Examples include **Grant Thornton**'s resignation as auditor of **Fremont General** due to alleged failures in providing information when promised, and **Ernst and Young**'s resignation as auditor of **Catalina Marketing** due to alleged accounting errors. ■

Principles and Assumptions of Accounting   Accounting principles (and assumptions) are of two types. *General principles* are the basic assumptions, concepts, and guidelines for preparing financial statements. *Specific principles* are detailed rules used in reporting business transactions and events. General principles stem from long-used accounting practices. Specific principles arise more often from the rulings of authoritative groups.

We need to understand both general and specific principles to effectively use accounting information. Several general principles are described in this section that are relied on in later chapters. General principles (in purple font with white shading) and assumptions (in red font with white shading) are portrayed

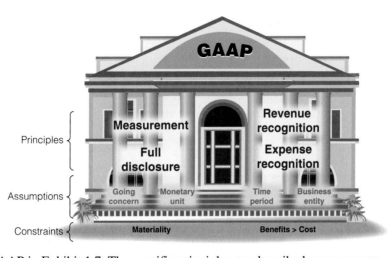

EXHIBIT 1.7

Building Blocks for GAAP

as building blocks of GAAP in Exhibit 1.7. The specific principles are described as we encounter them in the book.

Accounting Principles   General principles consist of at least four basic principles, four assumptions, and two constraints.

- *Measurement*   The **measurement principle,** also called the **cost principle,** usually prescribes that accounting information is based on actual cost (with a potential for subsequent adjustments to market). Cost is measured on a cash or equal-to-cash basis. This means if cash is given for a service, its cost is measured as the amount of cash paid. If something besides cash is exchanged (such as a car traded for a truck), cost is measured as the cash value of what is given up or received. The cost principle emphasizes reliability and verifiability, and information based on cost is considered objective. *Objectivity* means that information is supported by independent, unbiased evidence; it demands more than a person's opinion. To illustrate, suppose a company pays $5,000 for equipment. The cost principle requires that this purchase be recorded at $5,000. It makes no difference if the owner thinks this equipment is worth $7,000. Later in the book we introduce *fair value* measures.

  Point: The cost principle is also called the *historical cost principle.*

- *Revenue recognition*   Revenue (sales) is the amount received from selling products and services. The **revenue recognition principle** provides guidance on when a company must recognize revenue. To *recognize* means to record it. If revenue is recognized too early, a company would look more profitable than it is. If revenue is recognized too late, a company would look less profitable than it is. Three concepts are important to revenue recognition. (1) *Revenue is recognized when earned.* The earnings process is normally complete when services are performed or a seller transfers ownership of products to the buyer. (2) *Proceeds from selling products and services need not be in cash.* A common noncash proceed received by a seller is a customer's promise to pay at a future date, called *credit sales.* (3) *Revenue is measured by the cash received plus the cash value of any other items received.*

  Example: When a bookstore sells a textbook on credit is its earnings process complete? *Answer:* A bookstore can record sales for these books minus an amount expected for returns.

- *Expense recognition*   The **expense recognition principle,** also called the **matching principle,** prescribes that a company record the expenses it incurred to generate the revenue reported. The principles of matching and revenue recognition are key to modern accounting.

- *Full disclosure*   The **full disclosure principle** prescribes that a company report the details behind financial statements that would impact users' decisions. Those disclosures are often in footnotes to the statements.

Decision Insight

Revenues for the Green Bay Packers, New England Patriots, New York Giants, and other professional football teams include ticket sales, television and cable broadcasts, radio rights, concessions, and advertising. Revenues from ticket sales are earned when the NFL team plays each game. Advance ticket sales are not revenues; instead, they represent a liability until the NFL team plays the game for which the ticket was sold. At that point, the liability is removed and revenues are reported. ∎

Accounting Assumptions   There are four accounting assumptions: the going-concern assumption, the monetary unit assumption, the time period assumption, and the business entity assumption.

- *Going concern*   The **going-concern assumption** means that accounting information reflects a presumption that the business will continue operating instead of being closed or sold. This implies, for example, that property is reported at cost instead of, say, liquidation values that assume closure.

Point: For currency conversion: xe.com

- *Monetary unit*   The **monetary unit assumption** means that we can express transactions and events in monetary, or money, units. Money is the common denominator in business. Examples of monetary units are the dollar in the United States, Canada, Australia, and Singapore; and the peso in Mexico, the Philippines, and Chile. The monetary unit a company uses in its accounting reports usually depends on the country where it operates, but many companies today are expressing reports in more than one monetary unit.

- *Time period*   The **time period assumption** presumes that the life of a company can be divided into time periods, such as months and years, and that useful reports can be prepared for those periods.

Point: Abuse of the entity assumption was a main culprit in **Enron's** collapse.

- *Business entity*   The **business entity assumption** means that a business is accounted for separately from other business entities, including its owner. The reason for this assumption is that separate information about each business is necessary for good decisions. A business entity can take one of three legal forms: *proprietorship, partnership,* or *corporation.*

1. A **sole proprietorship,** or simply **proprietorship,** is a business owned by one person in which that person and the company are viewed as one entity for tax and liability purposes. No special legal requirements must be met to start a proprietorship. It is a separate entity for accounting purposes, but it is *not* a separate legal entity from its owner. This means, for example, that a court can order an owner to sell personal belongings to pay a proprietorship's debt. This *unlimited liability* of a proprietorship is a disadvantage. However, an advantage is that a proprietorship's income is not subject to a business income tax but is instead reported and taxed on the owner's personal income tax return. Proprietorship attributes are summarized in Exhibit 1.8, including those for partnerships and corporations.

EXHIBIT 1.8

Attributes of Businesses

Attribute Present	Proprietorship	Partnership	Corporation
One owner allowed............	yes	no	yes
Business taxed	no	no	yes
Limited liability...............	no*	no*	yes
Business entity	yes	yes	yes
Legal entity..................	no	no	yes
Unlimited life	no	no	yes

* Proprietorships and partnerships that are set up as LLCs provide limited liability.

2. A **partnership** is a business owned by two or more people, called *partners,* which are jointly liable for tax and other obligations. Like a proprietorship, no special legal requirements must be met in starting a partnership. The only requirement is an agreement between partners to run a business together. The agreement can be either oral or written and usually indicates how income and losses are to be shared. A partnership, like a proprietorship, is *not* legally separate from its owners. This means that each partner's share of profits is reported and taxed on that partner's tax return. It also means *unlimited liability* for its partners. However, at least three types of partnerships limit liability. A *limited partnership* (*LP*) includes a general partner(s) with unlimited liability and a limited partner(s) with liability restricted to the amount invested. A *limited liability partnership* (*LLP*) restricts partners' liabilities to their own acts and the acts of individuals under their control. This protects an innocent partner from the negligence of another partner, yet all partners remain responsible for partnership debts. A *limited liability company* (*LLC*) offers the limited liability of a corporation and the tax treatment of a partnership (and proprietorship). Most proprietorships and partnerships are now organized as LLCs.

Point: Proprietorships and partnerships are usually managed by their owners. In a corporation, the owners (shareholders) elect a board of directors who appoint managers to run the business.

3. A **corporation,** also called *C corporation,* is a business legally separate from its owner or owners, meaning it is responsible for its own acts and its own debts. Separate legal status

means that a corporation can conduct business with the rights, duties, and responsibilities of a person. A corporation acts through its managers, who are its legal agents. Separate legal status also means that its owners, who are called **shareholders** (or **stockholders**), are not personally liable for corporate acts and debts. This limited liability is its main advantage. A main disadvantage is what's called *double taxation*—meaning that (1) the corporation income is taxed and (2) any distribution of income to its owners through dividends is taxed as part of the owners' personal income, usually at the 15% rate. (For lower income taxpayers, the dividend tax is less than 15%, and in some cases zero.) An *S corporation,* a corporation with special attributes, does not owe corporate income tax. Owners of S corporations report their share of corporate income with their personal income. Ownership of all corporations is divided into units called **shares** or **stock.** When a corporation issues only one class of stock, we call it **common stock** (or *capital stock*).

Decision Ethics

Decision Ethics boxes are role-playing exercises that stress ethics in accounting and business.

Entrepreneur   You and a friend develop a new design for in-line skates that improves speed by 25% to 30%. You plan to form a business to manufacture and market those skates. You and your friend want to minimize taxes, but your prime concern is potential lawsuits from individuals who might be injured on these skates. What form of organization do you set up? ■   [Answer—p. 28]

Accounting Constraints   There are two basic constraints on financial reporting.

- *Materiality* The **materiality constraint** prescribes that only information that would influence the decisions of a reasonable person need be disclosed. This constraint looks at both the importance and relative size of an amount.
- *Benefit exceeds cost* The **cost-benefit constraint** prescribes that only information with benefits of disclosure greater than the costs of providing it need be disclosed.

Conservatism and *industry practices* are also sometimes referred to as accounting constraints.

Sarbanes–Oxley (SOX)

Congress passed the **Sarbanes–Oxley Act,** also called *SOX,* to help curb financial abuses at companies that issue their stock to the public. SOX requires that these public companies apply both accounting oversight and stringent internal controls. The desired results include more transparency, accountability, and truthfulness in reporting transactions.

Point: An audit examines whether financial statements are prepared using GAAP. It does *not* attest to absolute accuracy of the statements.

Compliance with SOX requires documentation and verification of internal controls and increased emphasis on internal control effectiveness. Failure to comply can yield financial penalties, stock market delisting, and criminal prosecution of executives. Management must issue a report stating that internal controls are effective. CEOs and CFOs who knowingly sign off on bogus accounting reports risk millions of dollars in fines and years in prison. **Auditors** also must verify the effectiveness of internal controls.

Point: *BusinessWeek* reports that external audit costs run about $35,000 for start-ups, up from $15,000 pre-SOX.

A listing of some of the more publicized accounting scandals in recent years follows.

Company	Alleged Accounting Abuses
Enron	Inflated income, hid debt, and bribed officials
WorldCom	Understated expenses to inflate income and hid debt
Fannie Mae	Inflated income
Adelphia Communications	Understated expenses to inflate income and hid debt
AOL Time Warner.	Inflated revenues and income
Xerox.	Inflated income
Bristol-Myers Squibb	Inflated revenues and income
Nortel Networks	Understated expenses to inflate income
Global Crossing.	Inflated revenues and income
Tyco	Hid debt, and CEO evaded taxes
Halliburton	Inflated revenues and income
Qwest Communications	Inflated revenues and income

To reduce the risk of accounting fraud, companies set up *governance systems.* A company's governance system includes its owners, managers, employees, board of directors, and other important stakeholders, who work together to reduce the risk of accounting fraud and increase confidence in accounting reports.

The impact of SOX regulations for accounting and business is discussed throughout this book. Ethics and investor confidence are key to company success. Lack of confidence in accounting numbers impacts company value as evidenced by huge stock price declines for Enron, WorldCom, Tyco, and ImClone after accounting misconduct was uncovered.

Decision Insight

Economic Downturn, Fraud Upturn? Executives polled show that 80% believe that the economic downturn has or will have a significant impact on fraud control in their companies (Deloitte 2010). The top three responses to the question "What activity would best counter this increased fraud risk?" are tallied in the graphic to the right. ▪

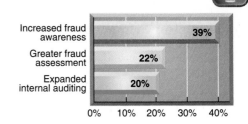

Dodd-Frank

Congress passed the **Dodd-Frank Wall Street Reform and Consumer Protection Act**, or *Dodd-Frank*, in a desire to (1) promote accountability and transparency in the financial system, (2) put an end to the notion of "too big to fail," (3) protect the taxpayer by ending bailouts, and (4) protect consumers from abusive financial services. It includes provisions whose impacts are unknown until regulators set detailed rules. However, a few proposals are notable and include the following:

- Exemption from Section 404(b) of SOX for smaller public entities (whose public value is less than $75 million) from the requirement to obtain an external audit on the effectiveness of internal control over financial reporting.
- Independence for all members of the compensation committee (including additional disclosures); in the event of an accounting restatement, an entity must set policies mandating recovery ("clawback") of excess incentive compensation.
- Requires the SEC, when sanctions exceed $1 million, to pay whistle-blowers between 10% and 30% of the sanction.

Quick Check   Answers — p. 29

6. What are internal controls and why are they important?
7. What three-step guidelines can help people make ethical decisions?
8. Why are ethics and social responsibility valuable to organizations?
9. Why are ethics crucial in accounting?
10. Who sets U.S. accounting rules?
11. How are U.S. companies affected by international accounting standards?
12. How are the objectivity concept and cost principle related?
13. Why is the business entity assumption important?
14. Why is the revenue recognition principle important?
15. What are the three basic forms of business organization?
16. Identify the owners of corporations and the terminology for ownership units.

TRANSACTION ANALYSIS AND THE ACCOUNTING EQUATION

To understand accounting information, we need to know how an accounting system captures relevant data about transactions, and then classifies, records, and reports data.

Accounting Equation

The accounting system reflects two basic aspects of a company: what it owns and what it owes. *Assets* are resources a company owns or controls. Examples are cash, supplies, equipment, and land, where each carries expected benefits. The claims on a company's assets—what it owes—are separated into owner and nonowner claims. *Liabilities* are what a company owes its nonowners (creditors) in future payments, products, or services. *Equity* (also called owner's equity or capital) refers to the claims of its owner(s). Together, liabilities and equity are the source of funds to acquire assets. The relation of assets, liabilities, and equity is reflected in the following **accounting equation:**

$$\text{Assets} = \text{Liabilities} + \text{Equity}$$

Liabilities are usually shown before equity in this equation because creditors' claims must be paid before the claims of owners. (The terms in this equation can be rearranged; for example, Assets − Liabilities = Equity.) The accounting equation applies to all transactions and events, to all companies and forms of organization, and to all points in time. For example, **Apple**'s assets equal $116,371, its liabilities equal $39,756, and its equity equals $76,615 ($ in millions). Let's now look at the accounting equation in more detail.

Assets Assets are resources a company owns or controls. These resources are expected to yield future benefits. Examples are Web servers for an online services company, musical instruments for a rock band, and land for a vegetable grower. The term *receivable* is used to refer to an asset that promises a future inflow of resources. A company that provides a service or product on credit is said to have an account receivable from that customer.

Liabilities Liabilities are creditors' claims on assets. These claims reflect company obligations to provide assets, products or services to others. The term *payable* refers to a liability that promises a future outflow of resources. Examples are wages payable to workers, accounts payable to suppliers, notes payable to banks, and taxes payable to the government.

Equity Equity is the owner's claim on assets, and is equal to assets minus liabilities. This is the reason equity is also called *net assets* or *residual equity*.

A corporation's equity—often called stockholders' or shareholders' equity—has two parts: contributed capital and retained earnings. **Contributed capital** refers to the amount that stockholders invest in the company—included under the title **common stock. Retained earnings** refer to **income** (revenues less expenses) that has *not* been distributed to its stockholders. The distribution of assets to stockholders is called **dividends,** which reduce retained earnings. **Revenues** increase retained earnings (via net income) and are resources generated from a company's earnings activities. Examples are consulting services provided, sales of products, facilities rented to others, and commissions from services. **Expenses** decrease retained earnings and are the cost of assets or services used to earn revenues. Examples are costs of employee time, use of supplies, and advertising, utilities, and insurance services from others. In sum, retained earnings is the accumulated revenues less the accumulated expenses and dividends since the company began.

This breakdown of equity yields the following **expanded accounting equation:**

$$\begin{array}{c} \overbrace{\qquad\qquad\qquad\qquad\text{Equity}\qquad\qquad\qquad\qquad} \\ \text{Assets} = \text{Liabilities} + \overbrace{\text{Contributed Capital} + \text{Retained Earnings}} \\ = \text{Liabilities} + \text{Common Stock} - \underbrace{\text{Dividends} + \text{Revenues} - \text{Expenses}} \end{array}$$

Net income occurs when revenues exceed expenses. Net income increases equity. A **net loss** occurs when expenses exceed revenues, which decreases equity.

A1 Define and interpret the accounting equation and each of its components.

Assets = Liabilities + Equity

Point: The phrases "on credit" and "on account" imply that cash payment will occur at a future date.

Key **terms** *are printed in bold and defined again in the end-of-book glossary.*

Decision Insight

Web Info   Most organizations maintain Websites that include accounting data—see Polaris Industries (<u>Polaris.com</u>) as an example. Polaris makes off-road vehicles such as all-terrain vehicles (ATV) and snowmobiles; it also makes on-road vehicles such as motorcycles and small electric vehicles. The SEC keeps an online database called **EDGAR** (<u>www.sec.gov/edgar.shtml</u>), which has accounting information for thousands of companies that issue stock to the public. The annual report filing for most publicly traded U.S. companies is known as Form 10-K, and the quarterly filing is Form 10-Q. Information services such as <u>Finance.Google.com</u> and <u>Finance.Yahoo.com</u> offer online data and analysis. ■

Transaction Analysis

P1   Analyze business transactions using the accounting equation.

Business activities can be described in terms of transactions and events. **External transactions** are exchanges of value between two entities, which yield changes in the accounting equation. An example is the sale of ad space by **Twitter**. **Internal transactions** are exchanges within an entity, which may or may not affect the accounting equation. An example is Twitter's use of its supplies, which are reported as expenses when used. **Events** refer to happenings that affect the accounting equation *and* are reliably measured. They include business events such as changes in the market value of certain assets and liabilities and natural events such as floods and fires that destroy assets and create losses. They do not include, for example, the signing of service or product contracts, which by themselves do not impact the accounting equation.

This section uses the accounting equation to analyze 11 selected transactions and events of FastForward, a start-up consulting (service) business, in its first month of operations. Remember that each transaction and event leaves the equation in balance and that assets *always* equal the sum of liabilities and equity.

Point: There are 3 basic types of company operations: (1) **Services**—providing customer services for profit, (2) **Merchandisers**—buying products and re-selling them for profit, and (3) **Manufacturers**—creating products and selling them for profit.

Transaction 1: Investment by Owner   On December 1, Chas Taylor forms a consulting business, named FastForward and set up as a corporation, that focuses on assessing the performance of footwear and accessories. Taylor owns and manages the business. The marketing plan for the business is to focus primarily on publishing online reviews and consulting with clubs, athletes, and others who place orders for footwear and accessories with manufacturers. Taylor personally invests $30,000 cash in the new company and deposits the cash in a bank account opened under the name of FastForward. After this transaction, the cash (an asset) and the stockholders' equity each equal $30,000. The source of increase in equity is the owner's investment (stock issuance), which is included in the column titled Common Stock. The effect of this transaction on FastForward is reflected in the accounting equation as follows (we label the equity entries):

	Assets	=	Liabilities	+	Equity
	Cash	**=**			**Common Stock**
(1)	+$30,000	=			+$30,000 owner investment

Transaction 2: Purchase Supplies for Cash   FastForward uses $2,500 of its cash to buy supplies of brand name footwear for performance testing over the next few months. This transaction is an exchange of cash, an asset, for another kind of asset, supplies. It merely changes the form of assets from cash to supplies. The decrease in cash is exactly equal to the increase in supplies. The supplies of footwear are assets because of the expected future benefits from the test results of their performance. This transaction is reflected in the accounting equation as follows:

	Assets			=	Liabilities	+	Equity
	Cash	**+**	**Supplies**	**=**			**Common Stock**
Old Bal.	$30,000			=			$30,000
(2)	−2,500	+	$2,500				
New Bal.	$27,500	+	$ 2,500	=			$30,000
		$30,000				$30,000	

Transaction 3: Purchase Equipment for Cash
FastForward spends $26,000 to acquire equipment for testing footwear. Like transaction 2, transaction 3 is an exchange of one asset, cash, for another asset, equipment. The equipment is an asset because of its expected future benefits from testing footwear. This purchase changes the makeup of assets but does not change the asset total. The accounting equation remains in balance.

	Assets				=	Liabilities	+	Equity
	Cash	+	Supplies	+	Equipment	=		Common Stock
Old Bal.	$27,500	+	$2,500			=		$30,000
(3)	−26,000			+	$26,000			
New Bal.	$ 1,500	+	$2,500	+	$ 26,000	=		$30,000

$30,000 $30,000

Transaction 4: Purchase Supplies on Credit
Taylor decides more supplies of footwear and accessories are needed. These additional supplies total $7,100, but as we see from the accounting equation in transaction 3, FastForward has only $1,500 in cash. Taylor arranges to purchase them on credit from CalTech Supply Company. Thus, FastForward acquires supplies in exchange for a promise to pay for them later. This purchase increases assets by $7,100 in supplies, and liabilities (called *accounts payable* to CalTech Supply) increase by the same amount. The effects of this purchase follow:

Example: If FastForward pays $500 cash in transaction 4, how does this partial payment affect the liability to CalTech? What would be FastForward's cash balance? *Answers:* The liability to CalTech would be reduced to $6,600 and the cash balance would be reduced to $1,000.

	Assets				=	Liabilities	+	Equity
	Cash	+	Supplies	+	Equipment	=	Accounts Payable	+	Common Stock
Old Bal.	$1,500	+	$2,500	+	$26,000	=			$30,000
(4)		+	7,100				+$7,100		
New Bal.	$1,500	+	$9,600	+	$26,000	=	$ 7,100	+	$30,000

$37,100 $37,100

Transaction 5: Provide Services for Cash
FastForward earns revenues by selling online ad space to manufacturers and by consulting with clients about test results on footwear and accessories. It earns net income only if its revenues are greater than its expenses incurred in earning them. In one of its first jobs, FastForward provides consulting services to a power-walking club and immediately collects $4,200 cash. The accounting equation reflects this increase in cash of $4,200 and in equity of $4,200. This increase in equity is identified in the far right column under Revenues because the cash received is earned by providing consulting services.

	Assets						=	Liabilities	+		Equity	
	Cash	+	Supplies	+	Equipment		=	Accounts Payable	+	Common Stock	+	Revenues
Old Bal.	$1,500	+	$9,600	+	$26,000		=	$7,100	+	$30,000		
(5)	+4,200										+	$4,200 consulting
New Bal.	$5,700	+	$9,600	+	$26,000		=	$7,100	+	$30,000	+	$ 4,200

$41,300 $41,300

Transactions 6 and 7: Payment of Expenses in Cash
FastForward pays $1,000 rent to the landlord of the building where its facilities are located. Paying this amount allows FastForward to occupy the space for the month of December. The rental payment is reflected in the following accounting equation as transaction 6. FastForward also pays the biweekly $700 salary of the company's only employee. This is reflected in the accounting equation as transaction 7. Both transactions 6 and 7 are December expenses for FastForward. The costs of both rent and salary are expenses, as opposed to assets, because their benefits are used in December (they

By definition, increases in expenses yield decreases in equity.

have no future benefits after December). These transactions also use up an asset (cash) in carrying out FastForward's operations. The accounting equation shows that both transactions reduce cash and equity. The far right column identifies these decreases as Expenses.

	Assets				=	Liabilities	+			Equity		
	Cash	+	Supplies	+	Equipment	=	Accounts Payable	+	Common Stock	+	Revenues	−	Expenses
Old Bal.	$5,700	+	$9,600	+	$26,000	=	$7,100	+	$30,000	+	$4,200		
(6)	−1,000											−	$1,000 rent
Bal.	4,700	+	9,600	+	26,000	=	7,100	+	30,000	+	4,200	−	1,000
(7)	− 700											−	700 salaries
New Bal.	$4,000	+	$9,600	+	$26,000	=	$7,100	+	$30,000	+	$4,200	−	$ 1,700
			$39,600							$39,600			

Transaction 8: Provide Services and Facilities for Credit   FastForward provides consulting services of $1,600 and rents its test facilities for $300 to a podiatric services center. The rental involves allowing members to try recommended footwear and accessories at FastForward's testing area. The center is billed for the $1,900 total. This transaction results in a new asset, called *accounts receivable,* from this client. It also yields an increase in equity from the two revenue components reflected in the Revenues column of the accounting equation:

	Assets								=	Liabilities	+			Equity		
	Cash	+	Accounts Receivable	+	Supplies	+	Equipment	=	Accounts Payable	+	Common Stock	+	Revenues	−	Expenses
Old Bal.	$4,000	+		+	$9,600	+	$26,000	=	$7,100	+	$30,000	+	$4,200	−	$1,700
(8)		+	$1,900									+	1,600 consulting		
												+	300 rental		
New Bal.	$4,000	+	$ 1,900	+	$9,600	+	$26,000	=	$7,100	+	$30,000	+	$6,100	−	$1,700
			$41,500									$41,500			

Transaction 9: Receipt of Cash from Accounts Receivable   The client in transaction 8 (the podiatric center) pays $1,900 to FastForward 10 days after it is billed for consulting services. This transaction 9 does not change the total amount of assets and does not affect liabilities or equity. It converts the receivable (an asset) to cash (another asset). It does not create new revenue. Revenue was recognized when FastForward rendered the services in transaction 8, not when the cash is now collected. This emphasis on the earnings process instead of cash flows is a goal of the revenue recognition principle and yields useful information to users. The new balances follow:

Point: Receipt of cash is not always a revenue.

	Assets								=	Liabilities	+			Equity		
	Cash	+	Accounts Receivable	+	Supplies	+	Equipment	=	Accounts Payable	+	Common Stock	+	Revenues	−	Expenses
Old Bal.	$4,000	+	$1,900	+	$9,600	+	$26,000	=	$7,100	+	$30,000	+	$6,100	−	$1,700
(9)	+1,900	−	1,900												
New Bal.	$5,900	+	$ 0	+	$9,600	+	$26,000	=	$7,100	+	$30,000	+	$6,100	−	$1,700
			$41,500									$41,500			

Transaction 10: Payment of Accounts Payable   FastForward pays CalTech Supply $900 cash as partial payment for its earlier $7,100 purchase of supplies (transaction 4), leaving $6,200 unpaid. The accounting equation shows that this transaction decreases FastForward's cash by $900 and decreases its liability to CalTech Supply by $900. Equity does not change. This event does not create an expense even though cash flows out of FastForward (instead the expense is recorded when FastForward derives the benefits from these supplies).

	Assets						=	Liabilities	+			Equity			
	Cash	+	Accounts Receivable	+	Supplies	+	Equipment	=	Accounts Payable	+	Common Stock	+	Revenues	−	Expenses
Old Bal.	$5,900	+	$ 0	+	$9,600	+	$26,000	=	$7,100	+	$30,000	+	$6,100	−	$1,700
(10)	− 900								− 900						
New Bal.	$5,000	+	$ 0	+	$9,600	+	$26,000	=	$6,200	+	$30,000	+	$6,100	−	$1,700
				$40,600							$40,600				

Transaction 11: Payment of Cash Dividend   FastForward declares and pays a $200 cash dividend to its owner (the sole shareholder). Dividends (decreases in equity) are not reported as expenses because they are not part of the company's earnings process. Since dividends are not company expenses, they are not used in computing net income.

By definition, increases in dividends yield decreases in equity.

	Assets						=	Liabilities	+			Equity				
	Cash	+	Accounts Receivable	+	Supplies	+	Equipment	=	Accounts Payable	+	Common Stock	−	Dividends	+	Revenues	−	Expenses
Old Bal.	$5,000	+	$ 0	+	$9,600	+	$26,000	=	$6,200	+	$30,000			+	$6,100	−	$1,700
(11)	− 200											−	$200 dividend				
New Bal.	$4,800	+	$ 0	+	$9,600	+	$26,000	=	$6,200	+	$30,000	−	$200	+	$6,100	−	$1,700
				$40,400								$40,400					

Summary of Transactions

We summarize in Exhibit 1.9 the effects of these 11 transactions of FastForward using the accounting equation. First, we see that the accounting equation remains in balance after each transaction. Second, transactions can be analyzed by their effects on components of the

EXHIBIT 1.9

Summary of Transactions Using the Accounting Equation

	Assets						=	Liabilities	+		Equity				
	Cash	+	Accounts Receivable	+	Supplies	+	Equipment	=	Accounts Payable	+	Common Stock	− Dividends	+	Revenues	− Expenses
(1)	$30,000							=			$30,000				
(2)	− 2,500			+	$2,500										
Bal.	27,500			+	2,500			=			30,000				
(3)	−26,000					+	$26,000								
Bal.	1,500			+	2,500	+	26,000	=			30,000				
(4)				+	7,100				+$7,100						
Bal.	1,500			+	9,600	+	26,000	=	7,100	+	30,000				
(5)	+ 4,200												+	$4,200	
Bal.	5,700			+	9,600	+	26,000	=	7,100	+	30,000			+	4,200	
(6)	− 1,000														− $1,000
Bal.	4,700			+	9,600	+	26,000	=	7,100	+	30,000			+	4,200	− 1,000
(7)	− 700														− 700
Bal.	4,000			+	9,600	+	26,000	=	7,100	+	30,000			+	4,200	− 1,700
(8)		+	$1,900											+	1,600	
														+	300	
Bal.	4,000	+	1,900	+	9,600	+	26,000	=	7,100	+	30,000			+	6,100	− 1,700
(9)	+ 1,900	−	1,900												
Bal.	5,900	+	0	+	9,600	+	26,000	=	7,100	+	30,000			+	6,100	− 1,700
(10)	− 900								− 900						
Bal.	5,000	+	0	+	9,600	+	26,000	=	6,200	+	30,000			+	6,100	− 1,700
(11)	− 200											− $200			
Bal.	$ 4,800	+	$ 0	+	$ 9,600	+	$ 26,000	=	$ 6,200	+	$ 30,000	− $ 200		+	$6,100	− $ 1,700

Point: Knowing how financial statements are prepared improves our analysis of them. We develop the skills for analysis of financial statements throughout the book. Chapter 13 focuses on financial statement analysis.

accounting equation. For example, in transactions 2, 3, and 9, one asset increased while another asset decreased by equal amounts.

Quick Check   Answers — p. 29

17. When is the accounting equation in balance, and what does that mean?
18. How can a transaction not affect any liability and equity accounts?
19. Describe a transaction increasing equity and one decreasing it.
20. Identify a transaction that decreases both assets and liabilities.

FINANCIAL STATEMENTS

P2 Identify and prepare basic financial statements and explain how they interrelate.

This section introduces us to how financial statements are prepared from the analysis of business transactions. The four financial statements and their purposes are:

1. **Income statement**—describes a company's revenues and expenses along with the resulting net income or loss over a period of time due to earnings activities.
2. **Statement of retained earnings**—explains changes in equity from net income (or loss) and from any dividends over a period of time.
3. **Balance sheet**—describes a company's financial position (types and amounts of assets, liabilities, and equity) at a point in time.
4. **Statement of cash flows**—identifies cash inflows (receipts) and cash outflows (payments) over a period of time.

We prepare these financial statements, in this order, using the 11 selected transactions of FastForward. (These statements are technically called *unadjusted*—we explain this in Chapters 2 and 3.)

Income Statement

FastForward's income statement for December is shown at the top of Exhibit 1.10. Information about revenues and expenses is conveniently taken from the Equity columns of Exhibit 1.9. Revenues are reported first on the income statement. They include consulting revenues of $5,800 from transactions 5 and 8 and rental revenue of $300 from transaction 8. Expenses are reported after revenues. (For convenience in this chapter, we list larger amounts first, but we can sort expenses in different ways.) Rent and salary expenses are from transactions 6 and 7. Expenses reflect the costs to generate the revenues reported. Net income (or loss) is reported at the bottom of the statement and is the amount earned in December. Stockholders' investments and dividends are *not* part of income.

Point: Net income is sometimes called *earnings* or *profit*.

Statement of Retained Earnings

Point: The statement of retained earnings is also called the *statement of changes in retained earnings*. Note: Beg. Retained Earnings + Net Income − Dividends = End. Retained Earnings

The statement of retained earnings reports information about how retained earnings changes over the reporting period. This statement shows beginning retained earnings, events that increase it (net income), and events that decrease it (dividends and net loss). Ending retained earnings is computed in this statement and is carried over and reported on the balance sheet. FastForward's statement of retained earnings is the second report in Exhibit 1.10. The beginning balance is measured as of the start of business on December 1. It is zero because FastForward did not exist before then. An existing business reports the beginning balance equal to that as of the end of the prior reporting period (such as from November 30). FastForward's statement shows the $4,400 of net income earned during the period. This links the income statement to the statement of retained earnings (see line ①). The statement also reports the $200 cash dividend and FastForward's end-of-period retained earnings balance.

Balance Sheet

FastForward's balance sheet is the third report in Exhibit 1.10. This statement refers to FastForward's financial condition at the close of business on December 31. The left side of the balance

EXHIBIT 1.10

Financial Statements and
Their Links

FASTFORWARD
Income Statement
For Month Ended December 31, 2013

Revenues		
Consulting revenue ($4,200 + $1,600).................	$ 5,800	
Rental revenue.......................................	300	
Total revenues		$ 6,100
Expenses		
Rent expense	1,000	
Salaries expense	700	
Total expenses		1,700
Net income		$ 4,400

Point: A statement's heading identifies the company, the statement title, and the date or time period.

FASTFORWARD
Statement of Retained Earnings
For Month Ended December 31, 2013

Retained earnings, December 1, 2013............................	$ 0	
Plus: Net income.......................................	4,400	
	4,400	
Less: Dividends	200	
Retained earnings, December 31, 2013...........................	$ 4,200	

Point: Arrow lines show how the statements are linked. ① Net income is used to compute equity. ② Retained earnings is used to prepare the balance sheet. ③ Cash from the balance sheet is used to reconcile the statement of cash flows.

FASTFORWARD
Balance Sheet
December 31, 2013

Assets		Liabilities	
Cash	$ 4,800	Accounts payable.............	$ 6,200
Supplies	9,600	Total liabilities	6,200
Equipment........	26,000	**Equity**	
		Common stock	30,000
		Retained earnings	4,200
		Total equity	34,200
Total assets	$ 40,400	Total liabilities and equity	$ 40,400

Point: The income statement, the statement of retained earnings, and the statement of cash flows are prepared for a *period* of time. The balance sheet is prepared as of a *point* in time.

FASTFORWARD
Statement of Cash Flows
For Month Ended December 31, 2013

Cash flows from operating activities		
Cash received from clients ($4,200 + $1,900)..........	$ 6,100	
Cash paid for supplies ($2,500 + $900)...............	(3,400)	
Cash paid for rent	(1,000)	
Cash paid to employee	(700)	
Net cash provided by operating activities		$ 1,000
Cash flows from investing activities		
Purchase of equipment	(26,000)	
Net cash used by investing activities		(26,000)
Cash flows from financing activities		
Investments by stockholder.......................	30,000	
Dividends to stockholder	(200)	
Net cash provided by financing activities		29,800
Net increase in cash		$ 4,800
Cash balance, December 1, 2013		0
Cash balance, December 31, 2013		$ 4,800

Point: A single ruled line denotes an addition or subtraction. Final totals are double underlined. Negative amounts are often in parentheses.

sheet lists FastForward's assets: cash, supplies, and equipment. The upper right side of the balance sheet shows that FastForward owes $6,200 to creditors. Any other liabilities (such as a bank loan) would be listed here. The equity balance is $34,200. Line ② shows the link between the ending balance of the statement of retained earnings and the retained earnings balance on the balance sheet. (This presentation of the balance sheet is called the *account form:* assets on the left and liabilities and equity on the right. Another presentation is the *report form:* assets on top, followed by liabilities and then equity at the bottom. Either presentation is acceptable.) As always, we see the accounting equation applies: Assets of $40,400 = Liabilities of $6,200 + Equity of $34,200.

Statement of Cash Flows

Point: Statement of cash flows has three main sections: operating, investing, and financing.

Point: Payment for supplies is an operating activity because supplies are expected to be used up in short-term operations (typically less than one year).

Point: Investing activities refer to long-term asset investments by the company, *not* to owner investments.

FastForward's statement of cash flows is the final report in Exhibit 1.10. The first section reports cash flows from *operating activities*. It shows the $6,100 cash received from clients and the $5,100 cash paid for supplies, rent, and employee salaries. Outflows are in parentheses to denote subtraction. Net cash provided by operating activities for December is $1,000. If cash paid exceeded the $5,100 cash received, we would call it "cash used by operating activities." The second section reports *investing activities,* which involve buying and selling assets such as land and equipment that are held for *long-term use* (typically more than one year). The only investing activity is the $26,000 purchase of equipment. The third section shows cash flows from *financing activities,* which include the *long-term* borrowing and repaying of cash from lenders and the cash investments from, and dividends to, stockholders. FastForward reports $30,000 from the owner's initial investment and the $200 cash dividend. The net cash effect of all financing transactions is a $29,800 cash inflow. The final part of the statement shows FastForward increased its cash balance by $4,800 in December. Since it started with no cash, the ending balance is also $4,800—see line ③. We see that cash flow numbers are different from income statement (*accrual*) numbers, which is common.

Quick Check	Answers — p. 29

21. Explain the link between the income statement and the statement of retained earnings.
22. Describe the link between the balance sheet and the statement of retained earnings.
23. Discuss the three major sections of the statement of cash flows.

GLOBAL VIEW

Accounting according to U.S. GAAP is similar, but not identical, to IFRS. Throughout the book we use this last section to identify major similarities and differences between IFRS and U.S. GAAP for the materials in each chapter.

Basic Principles   Both U.S. GAAP and IFRS include broad and similar guidance for accounting. However, neither system specifies particular account names nor the detail required. (A typical *chart of accounts* is shown near the end of this book.) IFRS does require certain minimum line items be reported in the balance sheet along with other minimum disclosures that U.S. GAAP does not. On the other hand, U.S. GAAP requires disclosures for the current and prior two years for the income statement, statement of cash flows, and statement of retained earnings (equity), while IFRS requires disclosures for the current and prior year. Still, the basic principles behind these two systems are similar.

Transaction Analysis   Both U.S. GAAP and IFRS apply transaction analysis identically as shown in this chapter. Although some variations exist in revenue and expense recognition and other principles, all of the transactions in this chapter are accounted for identically under these two systems. It is often said that U.S. GAAP is more *rules-based* whereas IFRS is more *principles-based*. The main difference on the rules versus principles focus is with the approach in deciding how to account for certain transactions. Under U.S. GAAP, the approach is more focused on strictly following the accounting rules; under IFRS, the approach is more focused on a review of the situation and how accounting can best reflect it. This difference typically impacts advanced topics beyond the introductory course.

PIAGGIO   **Financial Statements**   Both U.S. GAAP and IFRS prepare the same four basic financial statements. To illustrate, a condensed version of Piaggio's income statement follows (numbers are in Euros thousands).

Piaggio manufactures two-, three- and four-wheel vehicles, and is Europe's leading manufacturer of motorcycles and scooters. Similar condensed versions can be prepared for the other three statements (see Appendix A).

PIAGGIO **Income Statement (in € thousands)** **For Year Ended December 31, 2011**	
Net revenues	1,516,463
Cost for materials	904,060
Cost for services, leases, employees, depreciation, and other expenses	533,045
Taxes	32,305
Net income (profit)	47,053

Status of IFRS   Accounting impacts companies across the world, which requires us to take a global view. IFRS is now adopted or accepted in over 115 countries, including over 30 member-states of the EU (see gold and light tan shading in the map below). Teal shading in the map reflects a system other than IFRS. The FASB and IASB continue to work on the convergence of IFRS and U.S. GAAP. Further, the SEC has a "roadmap" for ultimate use of IFRS by U.S. companies. Currently, the roadmap extends out over the next several years.

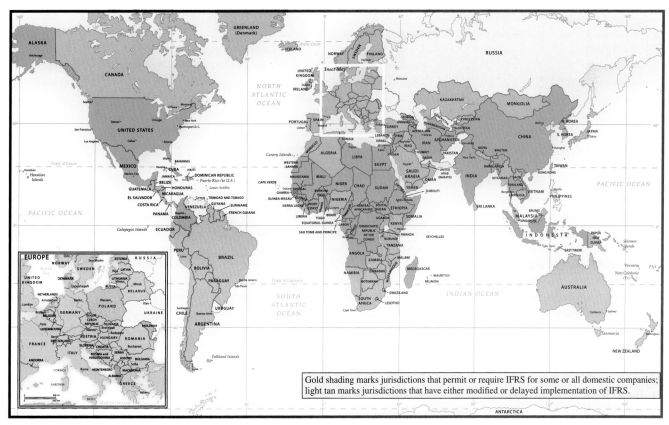

Gold shading marks jurisdictions that permit or require IFRS for some or all domestic companies; light tan marks jurisdictions that have either modified or delayed implementation of IFRS.

Decision Analysis (a section at the end of each chapter) introduces and explains ratios helpful in decision making using real company data. Instructors can skip this section and cover all ratios in Chapter 13.

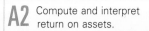
Return on Assets   **Decision Analysis**

A *Decision Analysis* section at the end of each chapter is devoted to financial statement analysis. We organize financial statement analysis into four areas: (1) liquidity and efficiency, (2) solvency, (3) profitability, and (4) market prospects—Chapter 13 has a ratio listing with definitions and groupings by area. When analyzing ratios, we need benchmarks to identify good, bad, or average levels. Common benchmarks include the company's prior levels and those of its competitors.

A2 Compute and interpret return on assets.

This chapter presents a profitability measure: return on assets. Return on assets is useful in evaluating management, analyzing and forecasting profits, and planning activities. **Dell** has its marketing department compute return on assets for *every* order. **Return on assets (ROA),** also called *return on investment* (*ROI*), is defined in Exhibit 1.11.

EXHIBIT 1.11

Return on Assets

$$\text{Return on assets} = \frac{\text{Net income}}{\text{Average total assets}}$$

Net income is from the annual income statement, and average total assets is computed by adding the beginning and ending amounts for that same period and dividing by 2. To illustrate, **Dell** reports net income of $3,492 million for fiscal year 2012. At the beginning of fiscal 2012, its total assets are $38,599 million and at the end of fiscal 2012, they total $44,533 million. Dell's return on assets for fiscal 2012 is:

$$\text{Return on assets} = \frac{\$3,492 \text{ million}}{(\$38,599 \text{ million} + \$44,533 \text{ million})/2} = 8.4\%$$

Is an 8.4% return on assets good or bad for Dell? To help answer this question, we compare (benchmark) Dell's return with its prior performance, the returns of competitors (such as **Hewlett-Packard**, **IBM**, and **Lenovo**), and the returns from alternative investments. Dell's return for each of the prior five years is in the second column of Exhibit 1.12, which ranges from 4.8% to 11.1%.

EXHIBIT 1.12

Dell and Industry Returns

	Return on Assets	
Fiscal Year	**Dell**	**Industry**
2012	8.4%	6.9%
2011	7.3	6.5
2010	4.8	4.7
2009	9.2	7.2
2008	11.1	8.1

Dell shows a fairly stable pattern of good returns that reflect its productive use of assets. There is a decline in its 2009–2010 returns reflecting the recessionary period. We compare Dell's return to the normal return for similar manufacturers of computers (third column). Industry averages are available from services such as **Dun & Bradstreet**'s *Industry Norms and Key Ratios* and **The Risk Management Association** *Annual Statement Studies*. When compared to the industry, Dell performs slightly above average.

*Each **Decision Analysis** section ends with a role-playing scenario to show the usefulness of ratios.*

■ **Decision Maker** ━━━━━━━━━━━━━━━━━━━━━━━━━━━━━━━━

Business Owner   You own a small winter ski resort that earns a 21% return on its assets. An opportunity to purchase a winter ski equipment manufacturer is offered to you. This manufacturer earns a 19% return on its assets. The industry return for this manufacturer is 14%. Do you purchase this manufacturer? ■   [Answer—p. 29]

*The **Demonstration Problem** is a review of key chapter content. The Planning the Solution offers strategies in solving the problem.*

DEMONSTRATION PROBLEM

After several months of planning, Jasmine Worthy started a haircutting business called Expressions. The following events occurred during its first month of business.

a. On August 1, Worthy invested $3,000 cash and $15,000 of equipment in Expressions in exchange for its common stock.

b. On August 2, Expressions paid $600 cash for furniture for the shop.

c. On August 3, Expressions paid $500 cash to rent space in a strip mall for August.

d. On August 4, it purchased $1,200 of equipment on credit for the shop (using a long-term note payable).

e. On August 5, Expressions opened for business. Cash received from haircutting services in the first week and a half of business (ended August 15) was $825.

f. On August 15, it provided $100 of haircutting services on account.

g. On August 17, it received a $100 check for services previously rendered on account.

h. On August 17, it paid $125 cash to an assistant for hours worked during the grand opening.

i. Cash received from services provided during the second half of August was $930.

j. On August 31, it paid a $400 installment toward principal on the note payable entered into on August 4.

k. On August 31, it paid $900 cash in dividends to Worthy (sole shareholder).

Required

1. Arrange the following asset, liability, and equity titles in a table similar to the one in Exhibit 1.9: Cash; Accounts Receivable; Furniture; Store Equipment; Note Payable; Common Stock; Dividends; Revenues; and Expenses. Show the effects of each transaction using the accounting equation.

2. Prepare an income statement for August.

3. Prepare a statement of retained earnings for August.

4. Prepare a balance sheet as of August 31.

5. Prepare a statement of cash flows for August.

6. Determine the return on assets ratio for August.

PLANNING THE SOLUTION

- Set up a table like Exhibit 1.9 with the appropriate columns for accounts.
- Analyze each transaction and show its effects as increases or decreases in the appropriate columns. Be sure the accounting equation remains in balance after each transaction.
- Prepare the income statement, and identify revenues and expenses. List those items on the statement, compute the difference, and label the result as *net income* or *net loss*.
- Use information in the Equity columns to prepare the statement of retained earnings.
- Use information in the last row of the transactions table to prepare the balance sheet.
- Prepare the statement of cash flows; include all events listed in the Cash column of the transactions table. Classify each cash flow as operating, investing, or financing.
- Calculate return on assets by dividing net income by average assets.

SOLUTION TO DEMONSTRATION PROBLEM

1.

	Assets					=	Liabilities	+		Equity				
	Cash	+	Accounts Receivable	+	Furniture	+	Store Equipment	=	Note Payable	+	Common Stock	−	Dividends	+	Revenues	−	Expenses
a.	$3,000						$15,000				$18,000					
b.	− 600				+ $600											
Bal.	2,400	+		+	600	+	15,000	=			18,000					
c.	− 500															− $500
Bal.	1,900	+		+	600	+	15,000	=			18,000					− 500
d.						+	1,200		+$1,200							
Bal.	1,900	+		+	600	+	16,200	=	1,200	+	18,000					− 500
e.	+ 825													+	$ 825	
Bal.	2,725	+		+	600	+	16,200	=	1,200	+	18,000			+	825	− 500
f.		+	$100											+	100	
Bal.	2,725	+	100	+	600	+	16,200	=	1,200	+	18,000			+	925	− 500
g.	+ 100	−	100													
Bal.	2,825	+	0	+	600	+	16,200	=	1,200	+	18,000			+	925	− 500
h.	− 125															− 125
Bal.	2,700	+	0	+	600	+	16,200	=	1,200	+	18,000			+	925	− 625
i.	+ 930													+	930	
Bal.	3,630	+	0	+	600	+	16,200	=	1,200	+	18,000			+	1,855	− 625
j.	− 400								− 400							
Bal.	3,230	+	0	+	600	+	16,200	=	800	+	18,000			+	1,855	− 625
k.	− 900											−	$900			
Bal.	$ 2,330	+	0	+	$600	+	$ 16,200	=	$ 800	+	$ 18,000	−	$900	+	$1,855	− $625

2.

EXPRESSIONS
Income Statement
For Month Ended August 31

Revenues		
Haircutting services revenue		$1,855
Expenses		
Rent expense	$500	
Wages expense	125	
Total expenses		625
Net Income		$1,230

3.

EXPRESSIONS
Statement of Retained Earnings
For Month Ended August 31

Retained earnings, August 1*	$ 0
Plus: Net income	1,230
	1,230
Less: Dividend to owner	900
Retained earnings, August 31	$ 330

* If Expressions had been an existing business from a prior period, the beginning retained earnings balance would equal the retained earnings balance from the end of the prior period.

4.

EXPRESSIONS
Balance Sheet
August 31

Assets		**Liabilities**	
Cash	$ 2,330	Note payable	$ 800
Furniture	600	**Equity**	
Store equipment	16,200	Common stock	18,000
		Retained earnings................	330
		Total equity	18,330
Total assets	$19,130	Total liabilities and equity	$19,130

5.

EXPRESSIONS
Statement of Cash Flows
For Month Ended August 31

Cash flows from operating activities		
Cash received from customers	$1,855	
Cash paid for rent	(500)	
Cash paid for wages	(125)	
Net cash provided by operating activities		$1,230
Cash flows from investing activities		
Cash paid for furniture		(600)
Cash flows from financing activities		
Cash investments from stockholders	3,000	
Cash dividends to stockholders	(900)	
Partial repayment of (long-term) note payable	(400)	
Net cash provided by financing activities		1,700
Net increase in cash.............................		$2,330
Cash balance, August 1		0
Cash balance, August 31..........................		$2,330

Required

1. Arrange the following asset, liability, and equity titles in a table like Exhibit 1.9: Cash; Accounts Receivable; Equipment; Accounts Payable; Common Stock; Dividends; Revenues; and Expenses.

2. Show the effects of the transactions on the accounts of the accounting equation by recording increases and decreases in the appropriate columns. Do not determine new account balances after each transaction. Determine the final total for each account and verify that the equation is in balance.

3. Prepare a June income statement, a June statement of retained earnings, a June 30 balance sheet, and a June statement of cash flows.

Check   (2) Ending balances: Cash, $130,060; Expenses, $9,790

(3) Net income, $7,135; Total assets, $133,135

Truro Excavating Co., owned by Raul Truro, began operations in July and completed these transactions during that first month of operations.

Problem 1-8B
Analyzing transactions and preparing financial statements
C4 P1 P2

July	1	R. Truro invested $80,000 cash in the company in exchange for its common stock.
	2	The company rented office space and paid $700 cash for the July rent.
	3	The company purchased excavating equipment for $5,000 by paying $1,000 cash and agreeing to pay the $4,000 balance in 30 days.
	6	The company purchased office supplies for $600 cash.
	8	The company completed work for a customer and immediately collected $7,600 cash for the work.
	10	The company purchased $2,300 of office equipment on credit.
	15	The company completed work for a customer on credit in the amount of $8,200.
	17	The company purchased $3,100 of office supplies on credit.
	23	The company paid $2,300 cash for the office equipment purchased on July 10.
	25	The company billed a customer $5,000 for work completed; the balance is due in 30 days.
	28	The company received $8,200 cash for the work completed on July 15.
	30	The company paid an assistant's salary of $1,560 cash for this month.
	31	The company paid $295 cash for this month's utility bill.
	31	The company paid $1,800 cash in dividends to the owner (sole shareholder).

Required

1. Arrange the following asset, liability, and equity titles in a table like Exhibit 1.9: Cash; Accounts Receivable; Office Supplies; Office Equipment; Excavating Equipment; Accounts Payable; Common Stock; Dividends; Revenues; and Expenses.

2. Use additions and subtractions to show the effects of each transaction on the accounts in the accounting equation. Show new balances after each transaction.

3. Use the increases and decreases in the columns of the table from part 2 to prepare an income statement, a statement of retained earnings, and a statement of cash flows—each of these for the current month. Also prepare a balance sheet as of the end of the month.

Check   (2) Ending balances: Cash, $87,545; Accounts Payable, $7,100

(3) Net income, $18,245; Total assets, $103,545

Analysis Component

4. Assume that the $5,000 purchase of excavating equipment on July 3 was financed from an owner investment of another $5,000 cash in the business in exchange for more common stock (instead of the purchase conditions described in the transaction). Explain the effect of this change on total assets, total liabilities, and total equity.

Nico Mitchell started a new business, Nico's Solutions, and completed the following transactions during its first year of operations.

Problem 1-9B
Analyzing effects of transactions
C4 P1 P2 A1

a. N. Mitchell invests $90,000 cash and office equipment valued at $20,000 in the company in exchange for its common stock.

b. The company purchased a $150,000 building to use as an office. It paid $40,000 in cash and signed a note payable promising to pay the $110,000 balance over the next ten years.

c. The company purchased office equipment for $25,000 cash.

d. The company purchased $1,200 of office supplies and $1,700 of office equipment on credit.

e. The company paid a local newspaper $750 cash for printing an announcement of the office's opening.

f. The company completed a financial plan for a client and billed that client $2,800 for the service.

g. The company designed a financial plan for another client and immediately collected a $4,000 cash fee.

h. The company paid $11,500 cash in dividends to the owner (sole shareholder).

i. The company received $1,800 cash from the client described in transaction *f*.

j. The company made a payment of $700 cash on the equipment purchased in transaction *d*.

k. The company paid $2,500 cash for the office secretary's wages.

Required

1. Create a table like the one in Exhibit 1.9, using the following headings for the columns: Cash; Accounts Receivable; Office Supplies; Office Equipment; Building; Accounts Payable; Notes Payable; Common Stock; Dividends; Revenues; and Expenses.

Check (2) Ending balances: Cash, $15,350; Expenses, $3,250; Notes Payable, $110,000

(3) Net income, $3,550

2. Use additions and subtractions within the table created in part *1* to show the dollar effects of each transaction on individual items of the accounting equation. Show new balances after each transaction.

3. Once you have completed the table, determine the company's net income.

Problem 1-10B
Computing and interpreting return on assets

A2

AT&T and Verizon produce and market telecommunications products and are competitors. Key financial figures (in $ millions) for these businesses over the past year follow.

Key Figures ($ millions)	AT&T	Verizon
Sales	$126,723	$110,875
Net income	4,184	10,198
Average assets	269,868	225,233

Required

Check (1a) 1.6%; (1b) 4.5%

1. Compute return on assets for (*a*) AT&T and (*b*) Verizon.

2. Which company is more successful in the total amount of sales to consumers?

3. Which company is more successful in returning net income from its assets invested?

Analysis Component

4. Write a one-paragraph memorandum explaining which company you would invest your money in and why. (Limit your explanation to the information provided.)

Problem 1-11B
Determining expenses, liabilities, equity, and return on assets

A1 A2

Carbondale Company manufactures, markets, and sells snowmobile and snowmobile equipment and accessories. The average total assets for Carbondale is $3,000,000. In its most recent year, Carbondale reported net income of $201,000 on revenues of $1,400,000.

Required

1. What is Carbondale Company's return on assets?

2. Does return on assets seem satisfactory for Carbondale given that its competitors average a 9.5% return on assets?

Check (3) $1,199,000

(4) $3,000,000

3. What are the total expenses for Carbondale Company in its most recent year?

4. What is the average total amount of liabilities plus equity for Carbondale Company?

All business decisions involve aspects of risk and return.

Problem 1-12B[A]
Identifying risk and return
A3

Required

Identify both the risk and the return in each of the following activities:

1. Stashing $500 cash under your mattress.

2. Placing a $250 bet on a horse running in the Kentucky Derby.

3. Investing $20,000 in Nike stock.

4. Investing $35,000 in U.S. Savings Bonds.

A start-up company often engages in the following activities during its first year of operations. Classify each of the following activities into one of the three major activities of an organization.

Problem 1-13B[B]
Describing organizational activities
C5

F. Financing   **I.** Investing   **O.** Operating

_____ **1.** Providing client services.   _____ **5.** Supervising workers.

_____ **2.** Obtaining a bank loan.   _____ **6.** Owner investing money in business.

_____ **3.** Purchasing machinery.   _____ **7.** Renting office space.

_____ **4.** Research for its products.   _____ **8.** Paying utilities expenses.

Identify in outline format the three major business activities of an organization. For each of these activities, identify at least two specific transactions or events normally undertaken by the business's owners or its managers.

Problem 1-14B[B]
Describing organizational activities C5

This serial problem starts in this chapter and continues throughout most chapters of the book. It is most readily solved if you use the Working Papers that accompany this book (but working papers are not required).

SP 1   On October 1, 2013, Adria Lopez launched a computer services company, **Success Systems,** that is organized as a corporation and provides consulting services, computer system installations, and custom program development. Lopez adopts the calendar year for reporting purposes and expects to prepare the company's first set of financial statements on December 31, 2013.

SERIAL PROBLEM
Success Systems
C4 P1

Required

Create a table like the one in Exhibit 1.9 using the following headings for columns: Cash; Accounts Receivable; Computer Supplies; Computer System; Office Equipment; Accounts Payable; Common Stock; Dividends; Revenues; and Expenses. Then use additions and subtractions within the table created to show the dollar effects for each of the following October transactions for Success Systems on the individual items of the accounting equation. Show new balances after each transaction.

Oct. 1   A. Lopez invested $55,000 cash, a $20,000 computer system, and $8,000 of office equipment in the company in exchange for its common stock.

 3   The company purchased $1,420 of computer supplies on credit from Harris Office Products.

 6   The company billed Easy Leasing $4,800 for services performed in installing a new Web server.

 8   The company paid $1,420 cash for the computer supplies purchased from Harris Office Products on October 3.

 10   The company hired Lyn Addie as a part-time assistant for $125 per day, as needed.

 12   The company billed Easy Leasing another $1,400 for services performed.

 15   The company received $4,800 cash from Easy Leasing as partial payment toward its account.

 17   The company paid $805 cash to repair computer equipment damaged when moving it.

 20   The company paid $1,940 cash for advertisements published in the local newspaper.

Check Ending balances: Cash, $52,560; Revenues, $11,408; Expenses, $3,620

22 The company received $1,400 cash from Easy Leasing toward its account.
28 The company billed IFM Company $5,208 for services performed.
31 The company paid $875 cash for Lyn Addie's wages for seven days of work this month.
31 The company paid $3,600 cash in dividends to the owner (sole shareholder).

Beyond the Numbers (BTN) is a special problem section aimed to refine communication, conceptual, analysis, and research skills. It includes many activities helpful in developing an active learning environment.

Beyond the Numbers

REPORTING IN ACTION

A1 A2 A3

Polaris

BTN 1-1 Key financial figures for Polaris's fiscal year ended December 31, 2011, follow.

Key Figure	In Thousands
Liabilities + Equity.........	$1,228,024
Net income	227,575
Revenues	2,656,949

Required

Check (2) 19.9%

1. What is the total amount of assets invested in Polaris?
2. What is Polaris's return on assets for 2011? Its assets at December 31, 2010, equal $1,061,647 (in thousands).
3. How much are total expenses for Polaris for the year ended December 31, 2011?
4. Does Polaris's return on assets for 2011 seem satisfactory if competitors average an 18% return?

Fast Forward

5. Access Polaris's financial statements (Form 10-K) for years ending after December 31, 2011, from its Website (Polaris.com) or from the SEC Website (www.SEC.gov) and compute its return on assets for those years. Compare the December 31, 2011, year-end return on assets to any subsequent years' returns you are able to compute, and interpret the results.

COMPARATIVE ANALYSIS

A1 A2 A3

Polaris
Arctic Cat

BTN 1-2 Key comparative figures ($ thousands) for both Polaris and Arctic Cat follow.

Key Figure	Polaris	Arctic Cat
Liabilities + Equity..........	$1,228,024	$272,906
Net income	227,575	13,007
Revenues and sales	2,656,949	464,651

Required

Check (2b) 5.0%

1. What is the total amount of assets invested in (*a*) Polaris and (*b*) Arctic Cat?
2. What is the return on assets for (*a*) Polaris and (*b*) Arctic Cat? Polaris's beginning-year assets equal $1,061,647 (in thousands) and Arctic Cat's beginning-year assets equal $246,084 (in thousands).
3. How much are expenses for (*a*) Polaris and (*b*) Arctic Cat?
4. Is return on assets satisfactory for (*a*) Polaris and (*b*) Arctic Cat? (Assume competitors average an 18% return.)
5. What can you conclude about Polaris and Arctic Cat from these computations?

BTN 1-3   Craig Thorne works in a public accounting firm and hopes to eventually be a partner. The management of Allnet Company invites Thorne to prepare a bid to audit Allnet's financial statements. In discussing the audit fee, Allnet's management suggests a fee range in which the amount depends on the reported profit of Allnet. The higher its profit, the higher will be the audit fee paid to Thorne's firm.

ETHICS CHALLENGE

C3 C4

Required

1. Identify the parties potentially affected by this audit and the fee plan proposed.
2. What are the ethical factors in this situation? Explain.
3. Would you recommend that Thorne accept this audit fee arrangement? Why or why not?
4. Describe some ethical considerations guiding your recommendation.

BTN 1-4   Refer to this chapter's opening feature about Twitter. Assume that the owners desire to expand their online services to meet people's demands regarding online services. They eventually decide to meet with their banker to discuss a loan to allow Twitter to expand.

COMMUNICATING IN PRACTICE

A1 C2

Required

1. Prepare a half-page report outlining the information you would request from the owners if you were the loan officer.
2. Indicate whether the information you request and your loan decision are affected by the form of business organization for Twitter.

BTN 1-5   Visit the EDGAR database at (www.sec.gov). Access the Form 10-K report of Rocky Mountain Chocolate Factory (ticker RMCF) filed on May 24, 2011, covering its 2011 fiscal year.

TAKING IT TO THE NET

A2

Required

1. Item 6 of the 10-K report provides comparative financial highlights of RMCF for the years 2007–2011. How would you describe the revenue trend for RMCF over this five-year period?
2. Has RMCF been profitable (see net income) over this five-year period? Support your answer.

BTN 1-6   Teamwork is important in today's business world. Successful teams schedule convenient meetings, maintain regular communications, and cooperate with and support their members. This assignment aims to establish support/learning teams, initiate discussions, and set meeting times.

TEAMWORK IN ACTION

C1

Required

1. Form teams and open a team discussion to determine a regular time and place for your team to meet between each scheduled class meeting. Notify your instructor via a memorandum or e-mail message as to when and where your team will hold regularly scheduled meetings.
2. Develop a list of telephone numbers and/or e-mail addresses of your teammates.

ENTREPRENEURIAL DECISION

A1 P1

BTN 1-7   Refer to this chapter's opening feature about Twitter. Assume that the owners decide to open a new Website devoted to micro-blogging for accountants and those studying accounting. This new company will be called **AccounTwit**.

Required

1. AccounTwit obtains a $500,000 loan and the three owners contribute $250,000 in total from their own savings in exchange for common stock in the new company.
   a. What is the new company's total amount of liabilities plus equity?
   b. What is the new company's total amount of assets?

Check   (2) 10.7%

2. If the new company earns $80,250 in net income in the first year of operation, compute its return on assets (assume average assets equal $750,000). Assess its performance if competitors average a 10% return.

HITTING THE ROAD

C2

BTN 1-8   You are to interview a local business owner. (This can be a friend or relative.) Opening lines of communication with members of the business community can provide personal benefits of business networking. If you do not know the owner, you should call ahead to introduce yourself and explain your position as a student and your assignment requirements. You should request a 30-minute appointment for a face-to-face or phone interview to discuss the form of organization and operations of the business. Be prepared to make a good impression.

Required

1. Identify and describe the main operating activities and the form of organization for this business.
2. Determine and explain why the owner(s) chose this particular form of organization.
3. Identify any special advantages and/or disadvantages the owner(s) experiences in operating with this form of business organization.

GLOBAL DECISION

A1 A2 A3

KTM
Polaris
Arctic Cat

BTN 1-9   KTM (KTM.com) is a leading manufacturer of offroad and street motorcycles, and it competes to some extent with both **Polaris** and **Arctic Cat**. Key financial figures for KTM follow.

Key Figure*	Euro in Thousands
Average assets.................	465,550
Net income	20,818
Revenue......................	526,801
Return on assets	4.5%

* Figures prepared in accordance with International Financial Reporting Standards.

Required

1. Identify any concerns you have in comparing KTM's income and revenue figures to those of Polaris and Arctic Cat (in BTN 1-2) for purposes of making business decisions.
2. Identify any concerns you have in comparing KTM's return on assets ratio to those of Polaris and Arctic Cat (computed for BTN 1-2) for purposes of making business decisions.

ANSWERS TO MULTIPLE CHOICE QUIZ

1. c; $450,000 is the actual cost incurred.

2. b; revenue is recorded when earned.

3. d;

Assets	=	Liabilities	+	Equity
+$100,000	=	+35,000	+	?

Change in equity = $100,000 − $35,000 = $65,000

4. a

5. a

Accounting for Transactions

A Look Back

Chapter 1 defined accounting and introduced financial statements. We described forms of organizations and identified users and uses of accounting. We defined the accounting equation and applied it to transaction analysis.

A Look at This Chapter

This chapter focuses on the accounting process. We describe transactions and source documents, and we explain the analysis and recording of transactions. The accounting equation, T-account, general ledger, trial balance, and debits and credits are key tools in the accounting process.

A Look Ahead

Chapter 3 extends our focus on processing information. We explain the importance of adjusting accounts and the procedures in preparing financial statements.

Learning Objectives

CONCEPTUAL

C1 Explain the steps in processing transactions and the role of source documents. (p. 52)

C2 Describe an account and its use in recording transactions. (p. 53)

C3 Describe a ledger and a chart of accounts. (p. 56)

C4 Define *debits* and *credits* and explain double-entry accounting. (p. 57)

ANALYTICAL

A1 Analyze the impact of transactions on accounts and financial statements. (p. 61)

A2 Compute the debt ratio and describe its use in analyzing financial condition. (p. 71)

PROCEDURAL

P1 Record transactions in a journal and post entries to a ledger. (p. 58)

P2 Prepare and explain the use of a trial balance. (p. 67)

P3 Prepare financial statements from business transactions. (p. 68)

Decision Insight

Some Like It Hot

"You can still excel if you work really hard and follow your dreams!"

—MISA CHIEN (ON LEFT)

LOS ANGELES—"We call our customers Nomsters!" exclaims Misa. "There's an entire Nom Nom movement." **Nom Nom Truck (NomNomTruck.com)** is a mobile food business and the brainchild of Misa Chien and Jennifer Green. (Nom Nom is drawn from the sound "nom nom nom" when eating something "oh so tasty.") Their specialty is the Vietnamese baguette sandwich, called *banh mi*, a sort of Vietnamese subsandwich. "It's portable, it's fast, and has a fresh taste that you can't get from a burrito or hamburger," states Jennifer.

To pursue their business ambitions, Misa and Jennifer took business courses. They learned about recordkeeping processes, transaction analysis, inventory accounting, and financial statement reporting. "We did lose a lot of money initially," explains Misa. "We didn't have the right pricing structure." With careful analysis of their accounting reports, Misa and Jennifer solved the problem. Their business is now profitable and they have a reliable accounting system to help them make good business decisions.

"We had to account for product expenses, trucking expenses, supplier payments, and other expenses such as salaries, rent and insurance," explains Misa. At the same time, the

two have grown sales and expanded their food offerings. "Sales have definitely increased," says Misa. "People totally embraced us!"

The two insist that it is crucial to track and account for all revenues and expenses, including what is invested in the business. They maintain that success requires proper accounting for and analysis of the financial side. "There was a point when we couldn't keep up," recounts Misa. Given the importance of accounting, "we [now] have a bookkeeper and an accountant!" The women emphasize the value of a great business model along with a sound accounting system. "It's really easy to balance both now that we've been in the business for awhile," explains Misa.

"The bigger message of our company", says Jennifer, "is that each of us can succeed no matter what our starting point". "You have to be responsible for yourself," adds Misa. "We want to make people happy through our food!"

[Sources: *Nom Nom Truck Website,* January 2013; *Inc.,* June 2011; *Bundle.com,* October 2010; *VirgoBlue.net,* September 2011; *CNNMone* October 2011.]

Financial statements report on the financial performance and condition of an organization. Knowledge of their preparation, organization, and analysis is important. A main goal of this chapter is to illustrate how transactions are recorded, how they are reflected in financial statements, and how they impact analysis of financial statements. Debits and credits are introduced and identified as a tool in helping analyze and process transactions.

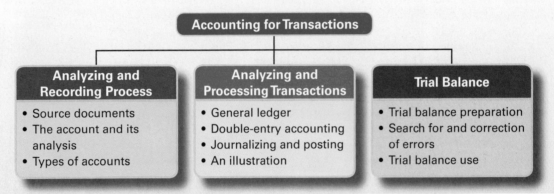

Accounting for Transactions		
Analyzing and Recording Process	**Analyzing and Processing Transactions**	**Trial Balance**
• Source documents • The account and its analysis • Types of accounts	• General ledger • Double-entry accounting • Journalizing and posting • An illustration	• Trial balance preparation • Search for and correction of errors • Trial balance use

ANALYZING AND RECORDING PROCESS

The accounting process identifies business transactions and events, analyzes and records their effects, and summarizes and presents information in reports and financial statements. These reports and statements are used for making investing, lending, and other business decisions. The steps in the accounting process that focus on *analyzing and recording* transactions and events are shown in Exhibit 2.1.

EXHIBIT 2.1

The Analyzing and Recording Process

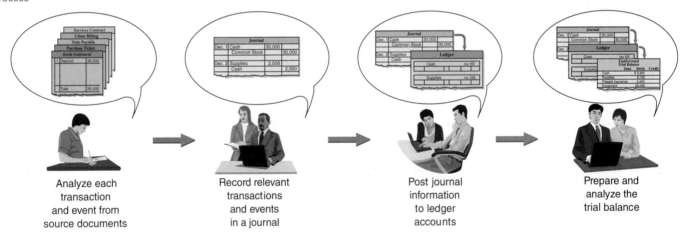

| Analyze each transaction and event from source documents | Record relevant transactions and events in a journal | Post journal information to ledger accounts | Prepare and analyze the trial balance |

C1 Explain the steps in processing transactions and the role of source documents.

Business transactions and events are the starting points. Relying on source documents, the transactions and events are analyzed using the accounting equation to understand how they affect company performance and financial position. These effects are recorded in accounting records, informally referred to as the *accounting books,* or simply the *books*. Additional steps such as posting and then preparing a trial balance help summarize and classify the effects of transactions and events. Ultimately, the accounting process provides information in useful reports or financial statements to decision makers.

Source Documents

Source documents identify and describe transactions and events entering the accounting process. They are the sources of accounting information and can be in either hard copy or electronic form. Examples are sales tickets, checks, purchase orders, bills from suppliers, employee earnings records, and bank statements. To illustrate, when an item is purchased on credit, the seller usually prepares at least two copies of a sales invoice. One copy is given to the buyer. Another copy, often sent electronically, results in an entry in the seller's information system to record the sale. Sellers use invoices for recording sales and for control; buyers use them for recording purchases and for monitoring purchasing activity. Many cash registers record information for each sale on a tape or electronic file locked inside the register. This record can be used as a source document for recording sales in the accounting records. Source documents, especially if obtained from outside the organization, provide objective and reliable evidence about transactions and events and their amounts.

Point: To ensure that all sales are rung up on the register, most sellers require customers to have their receipts to exchange or return purchased items.

■ Decision Ethics

Cashier Your manager requires that you, as cashier, immediately enter each sale. Recently, lunch hour traffic has increased and the assistant manager asks you to avoid delays by taking customers' cash and making change without entering sales. The assistant manager says she will add up cash and enter sales after lunch. She says that, in this way, the register will always match the cash amount when the manager arrives at three o'clock. What do you do? ■ [Answer—p. 76]

The Account and Its Analysis

An **account** is a record of increases and decreases in a specific asset, liability, equity, revenue, or expense item. Information from an account is analyzed, summarized, and presented in reports and financial statements. The **general ledger,** or simply **ledger,** is a record containing all accounts used by a company. The ledger is often in electronic form. While most companies' ledgers contain similar accounts, a company often uses one or more unique accounts because of its type of operations. As shown in Exhibit 2.2, accounts are classified into three general categories based on the accounting equation: asset, liability, or equity.

C2 Describe an account and its use in recording transactions.

EXHIBIT 2.2

Accounts Organized by the Accounting Equation

Asset Accounts Assets are resources owned or controlled by a company, and those resources have expected future benefits. Most accounting systems include (at a minimum) separate accounts for the assets described here.

Cash A *Cash* account reflects a company's cash balance. All increases and decreases in cash are recorded in the Cash account. It includes money and any medium of exchange that a bank accepts for deposit (coins, checks, money orders, and checking account balances).

Accounts Receivable *Accounts receivable* are held by a seller and refer to promises of payment from customers to sellers. These transactions are often called *credit sales* or *sales on account* (or *on credit*). Accounts receivable are increased by credit sales and are decreased by customer payments. A company needs a separate record for each customer, but for now, we use the simpler practice of recording all increases and decreases in receivables in a single account called Accounts Receivable.

Point: Customers and others who owe a company are called its **debtors.**

Note Receivable A *note receivable,* or promissory note, is a written promise of another entity to pay a definite sum of money on a specified future date to the holder of the note. A company holding a promissory note signed by another entity has an asset that is recorded in a Note (or Notes) Receivable account.

Prepaid Accounts *Prepaid accounts* (also called *prepaid expenses*) are assets that represent prepayments of future expenses (*not* current expenses). When the expenses are later incurred, the amounts in prepaid accounts are transferred to expense accounts. Common examples of prepaid accounts include prepaid insurance, prepaid rent, and prepaid services (such as club memberships). Prepaid accounts expire with the passage of time (such as with rent) or through use (such as with prepaid meal tickets). When financial statements are prepared, prepaid accounts are adjusted so that (1) all expired and used prepaid accounts are recorded as regular expenses and (2) all unexpired and unused prepaid accounts are recorded as assets (reflecting future use in future periods). To illustrate,

Point: A college parking fee is a prepaid account from the student's standpoint. At the beginning of the term, it represents an asset that entitles a student to park on or near campus. The benefits of the parking fee expire as the term progresses. At term-end, prepaid parking (asset) equals zero as it has been entirely recorded as parking expense.

Point: Prepaid accounts that apply to current and future periods are assets. These assets are adjusted at the end of each period to reflect only those amounts that have not yet expired, and to record as expenses those amounts that have expired.

when an insurance fee, called a *premium,* is paid in advance, the cost is typically recorded in the asset account Prepaid Insurance. Over time, the expiring portion of the insurance cost is removed from this asset account and reported in expenses on the income statement. Any unexpired portion remains in Prepaid Insurance and is reported on the balance sheet as an asset. (An exception exists for prepaid accounts that will expire or be used before the end of the current accounting period when financial statements are prepared. In this case, the prepayments *can* be recorded immediately as expenses.)

Supplies Accounts   *Supplies* are assets until they are used. When they are used up, their costs are reported as expenses. The costs of unused supplies are recorded in a Supplies asset account. Supplies are often grouped by purpose—for example, office supplies and store supplies. *Office supplies* include stationery, paper, toner, and pens. *Store supplies* include packaging materials, plastic and paper bags, gift boxes and cartons, and cleaning materials. The costs of these unused supplies can be recorded in an Office Supplies or a Store Supplies asset account. When supplies are used, their costs are transferred from the asset accounts to expense accounts.

Point: Some assets are described as *intangible* because they do not have physical existence or their benefits are highly uncertain. A recent balance sheet for **Coca-Cola Company** shows nearly $1 billion in intangible assets.

Equipment Accounts   *Equipment* is an asset. When equipment is used and gets worn down, its cost is gradually reported as an expense (called depreciation). Equipment is often grouped by its purpose—for example, office equipment and store equipment. *Office equipment* includes computers, printers, desks, chairs, and shelves. Costs incurred for these items are recorded in an Office Equipment asset account. The Store Equipment account includes the costs of assets used in a store, such as counters, showcases, ladders, hoists, and cash registers.

Buildings Accounts   *Buildings* such as stores, offices, warehouses, and factories are assets because they provide expected future benefits to those who control or own them. Their costs are recorded in a Buildings asset account. When several buildings are owned, separate accounts are sometimes kept for each of them.

Land   The cost of *land* owned by a business is recorded in a Land account. The cost of buildings located on the land is separately recorded in one or more building accounts.

Decision Insight

Women Entrepreneurs   The Center for Women's Business Research reports that women-owned businesses, such as **Nom Nom Truck**, are growing and that they:

- Total approximately 11 million and employ nearly 20 million workers.
- Generate $2.5 trillion in annual sales and tend to embrace technology.
- Are philanthropic—70% of owners volunteer at least once per month.
- Are more likely funded by individual investors (73%) than venture firms (15%). ∎

Liability Accounts   Liabilities are claims (by creditors) against assets, which means they are obligations to transfer assets or provide products or services to others. **Creditors** are individuals and organizations that have rights to receive payments from a company. If a company fails to pay its obligations, the law gives creditors a right to force the sale of that company's assets to obtain the money to meet creditors' claims. When assets are sold under these conditions, creditors are paid first, but only up to the amount of their claims. Any remaining money, the residual, goes to the owners of the company. Creditors often use a balance sheet to help decide whether to loan money to a company. A loan is less risky if the borrower's liabilities are small in comparison to assets because this means there are more resources than claims on resources. Common liability accounts are described here.

Point: Accounts payable are also called *trade payables*.

Accounts Payable   *Accounts payable* refer to oral or implied promises to pay later, which usually arise from purchases of merchandise. Payables can also arise from purchases of supplies, equipment, and services. Accounting systems keep separate records about each creditor. We describe these individual records in Chapter 4.

Note Payable   A *note payable* refers to a formal promise, usually denoted by the signing of a promissory note, to pay a future amount. It is recorded in either a short-term Note Payable account or a long-term Note Payable account, depending on when it must be repaid. We explain details of short- and long-term classification in Chapter 3.

Unearned Revenue Accounts   **Unearned revenue** refers to a liability that is settled in the future when a company delivers its products or services. When customers pay in advance for products or services (before revenue is earned), the revenue recognition principle requires that the seller consider this payment as unearned revenue. Examples of unearned revenue include magazine subscriptions collected in advance by a publisher, sales of gift certificates by stores, and season ticket sales by sports teams. The seller would record these in liability accounts such as Unearned Subscriptions, Unearned Store Sales, and Unearned Ticket Revenue. When products and services are later delivered, the earned portion of the unearned revenue is transferred to revenue accounts such as Subscription Fees, Store Sales, and Ticket Sales.[1]

Point: If a subscription is canceled, the publisher is expected to refund the unused portion to the subscriber.

Accrued Liabilities   *Accrued liabilities* are amounts owed that are not yet paid. Examples are wages payable, taxes payable, and interest payable. These are often recorded in separate liability accounts by the same title. If they are not large in amount, one or more ledger accounts can be added and reported as a single amount on the balance sheet. (Financial statements often have amounts reported that are a summation of several ledger accounts.)

Decision Insight

Revenue Spread   The **New York Giants** have *Unearned Revenues* of about $100 million in advance ticket sales. When the team plays its home games, it settles this liability to its ticket holders and then transfers the amount earned to *Ticket Revenues*. ▪

Equity Accounts   The owner's claim on a company's assets is called *equity,* or *stockholders' equity,* or *shareholders' equity.* Equity is the owners' *residual interest* in the assets of a business after deducting liabilities. Equity is impacted by four types of accounts: common stock, dividends, revenues, and expenses. We show this visually in Exhibit 2.3 by expanding the accounting equation. (As Chapter 1 explains, the accounts for dividends, revenues, and expenses are reflected in the retained earnings account, and that account is reported in the balance sheet.)

Point: Equity is also called *net assets.*

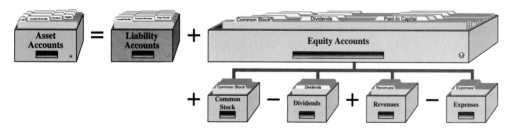

EXHIBIT 2.3

Expanded Accounting Equation

Common Stock   When an owner invests in a company in exchange for common stock, the invested amount is recorded in an account titled **Common Stock.** Any further owner investments are recorded in this account.

Point: The Dividends account is sometimes referred to as a *contra equity* account because it reduces the normal balance of equity.

Dividends   When the company pays any cash dividends, it decreases both the company's assets and its total equity. Dividends are not expenses of the business. They are simply the opposite of owner investments. A **Dividends** account is used in recording asset distributions to stockholders (owners).

Point: The withdrawal of assets by the owners of a corporation is called a *dividend.*

Revenue Accounts   Revenues and expenses also impact equity. Examples of revenue accounts are Sales, Commissions Earned, Professional Fees Earned, Rent Revenue, and Interest Revenue. *Revenues increase equity* and result from products and services provided to customers.

---

[1] In practice, account titles vary. As one example, Subscription Fees is sometimes called Subscription Fees Revenue, Subscription Fees Earned, or Earned Subscription Fees. As another example, Rent Earned is sometimes called Rent Revenue, Rental Revenue, or Earned Rent Revenue. We must use good judgment when reading financial statements because titles can differ even within the same industry. For example, product sales are called *sales* at **Polaris**, *net sales* at **Arctic Cat**, and *net revenues* at **Piaggio**. Generally, the term *revenues* or *fees* is more commonly used with service businesses, and *net sales* or *sales* with product businesses.

Expense Accounts   Examples of expense accounts are Advertising Expense, Store Supplies Expense, Office Salaries Expense, Office Supplies Expense, Rent Expense, Utilities Expense, and Insurance Expense. *Expenses decrease equity* and result from assets and services used in a company's operations. The variety of revenues and expenses can be seen by looking at the *chart of accounts* that follows the index at the back of this book. (Different companies sometimes use different account titles than those in this book's chart of accounts. For example, some might use Interest Revenue instead of Interest Earned, or Rental Expense instead of Rent Expense. It is important only that an account title describe the item it represents.)

Decision Insight

Sporting Accounts   The **Miami Heat, Los Angeles Lakers,** and the other NBA teams have the following major revenue and expense accounts:

Revenues	Expenses
Basketball ticket sales	Team salaries
TV & radio broadcast fees	Game costs
Advertising revenues	NBA franchise costs
Basketball playoff receipts	Promotional costs ■

ANALYZING AND PROCESSING TRANSACTIONS

This section explains several tools and processes that comprise an accounting system. These include a ledger, T-account, debits and credits, double-entry accounting, journalizing, and posting.

Ledger and Chart of Accounts

C3 Describe a ledger and a chart of accounts.

The collection of all accounts and their balances for an information system is called a *ledger* (or *general ledger*). If accounts are in files on a hard drive, the sum of those files is the ledger. If the accounts are pages in a file, that file is the ledger. A company's size and diversity of operations affect the number of accounts needed. A small company can get by with as few as 20 or 30 accounts; a large company can require several thousand. The **chart of accounts** is a list of all ledger accounts and includes an identification number assigned to each account. A small business might use the following numbering system for its accounts:

Chart of Accounts	
101–199	Asset accounts
201–299	Liability accounts
301–399	Equity accounts
401–499	Revenue accounts
501–699	Expense accounts

These numbers provide a three-digit code that is useful in recordkeeping. In this case, the first digit assigned to asset accounts is a 1, the first digit assigned to liability accounts is a 2, and so on. The second and third digits relate to the accounts' subcategories. Exhibit 2.4 shows a partial

EXHIBIT 2.4

Partial Chart of Accounts for FastForward

Chart of Accounts							
Acct. No.	**Account Name**		**Acct. No.**	**Account Name**		**Acct. No.**	**Account Name**
101	Cash		236	Unearned consulting revenue		406	Rental revenue
106	Accounts receivable					622	Salaries expense
126	Supplies		307	Common stock		637	Insurance expense
128	Prepaid insurance		318	Retained earnings		640	Rent expense
167	Equipment		319	Dividends		652	Supplies expense
201	Accounts payable		403	Consulting revenue		690	Utilities expense

chart of accounts for FastForward, the focus company of Chapter 1. (Please review the more complete chart of accounts that follows the index at the back of this book.)

Debits and Credits

A **T-account** represents a ledger account and is a tool used to understand the effects of one or more transactions. Its name comes from its shape like the letter **T**. The layout of a T-account, shown in Exhibit 2.5, is (1) the account title on top, (2) a left, or debit side, and (3) a right, or credit, side.

The left side of an account is called the **debit** side, often abbreviated *Dr.* The right side is called the **credit** side, abbreviated *Cr.*[2] To enter amounts on the left side of an account is to *debit* the account. To enter amounts on the right side is to *credit* the account. Do not make the error of thinking that the terms *debit* and *credit* mean increase or decrease. Whether a debit or a credit is an increase or decrease depends on the account. For an account where a debit is an increase, the credit is a decrease; for an account where a debit is a decrease, the credit is an increase. The difference between total debits and total credits for an account, including any beginning balance, is the **account balance.** When the sum of debits exceeds the sum of credits, the account has a *debit balance*. It has a *credit balance* when the sum of credits exceeds the sum of debits. When the sum of debits equals the sum of credits, the account has a *zero balance.*

Account Title	
(Left side) **Debit**	(Right side) **Credit**

C4 Define *debits* and *credits* and explain double-entry accounting.

EXHIBIT 2.5
The T-Account

Point: Think of *debit* and *credit* as accounting directions for left and right.

Double-Entry Accounting

Double-entry accounting requires that for each transaction:

- At least two accounts are involved, with at least one debit and one credit.
- The total amount debited must equal the total amount credited.
- The accounting equation must not be violated.

This means the sum of the debits for all entries must equal the sum of the credits for all entries, and the sum of debit account balances in the ledger must equal the sum of credit account balances.

The system for recording debits and credits follows from the usual accounting equation—see Exhibit 2.6. Two points are important here. First, like any simple mathematical relation, net increases or decreases on one side have equal net effects on the other side. For example, a net increase in assets must be accompanied by an identical net increase on the liabilities and equity

"Total debits equal total credits for each entry."

Assets		=	Liabilities		+	Equity	
Debit for increases	Credit for decreases		Debit for decreases	Credit for increases		Debit for decreases	Credit for increases
+	**−**		**−**	**+**		**−**	**+**
Normal				Normal			Normal

EXHIBIT 2.6
Debits and Credits in the Accounting Equation

side. Recall that some transactions affect only one side of the equation, meaning that two or more accounts on one side are affected, but their net effect on this one side is zero. Second, the left side is the *normal balance* side for assets, and the right side is the *normal balance* side for liabilities and equity. This matches their layout in the accounting equation where assets are on the left side of this equation, and liabilities and equity are on the right.

Recall that equity increases from revenues and stock issuances, and it decreases from expenses and dividends. These important equity relations are conveyed by expanding the accounting equation to include debits and credits in double-entry form as shown in Exhibit 2.7.

Increases (credits) to common stock and revenues *increase* equity; increases (debits) to dividends and expenses *decrease* equity. The normal balance of each account (asset, liability, common stock, dividends, revenue, or expense) refers to the left or right (debit or credit) side

Point: Debits and credits do not mean favorable or unfavorable. A debit to an asset increases it, as does a debit to an expense. A credit to a liability increases it, as does a credit to a revenue.

---

[2] These abbreviations are remnants of 18th-century English recordkeeping practices where the terms *debitor* and *creditor* were used instead of *debit* and *credit.* The abbreviations use the first and last letters of these terms, just as we still do for Saint (St.) and Doctor (Dr.).

EXHIBIT 2.7

Debit and Credit Effects for
Component Accounts

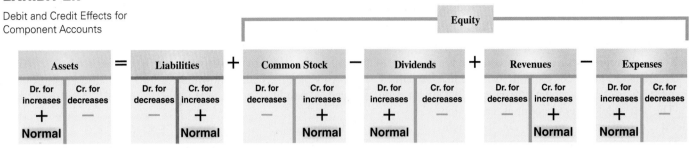

where *increases* are recorded. Understanding these diagrams and rules is required to prepare, analyze, and interpret financial statements.

The T-account for FastForward's Cash account, reflecting its first 11 transactions (from Exhibit 1.9), is shown in Exhibit 2.8. The total increases in its Cash account are $36,100, the total decreases are $31,300, and the account's debit balance is $4,800. (We illustrate use of T-accounts later in this chapter.)

EXHIBIT 2.8

Computing the Balance for
a T-Account

Cash				
Receive investment by owner for stock	30,000	Purchase of supplies	2,500
Consulting services revenue earned	4,200	Purchase of equipment	26,000
Collection of account receivable	1,900	Payment of rent	1,000
		Payment of salary	700
		Payment of account payable	900
		Payment of cash dividend	200
Balance	4,800		

Point: The ending balance is on the side with the larger dollar amount. Also, a plus (+) and minus (−) are not used in a T-account.

Quick Check   Answers — p. 77

1. Identify examples of accounting source documents.
2. Explain the importance of source documents.
3. Identify each of the following as either an asset, a liability, or equity: *(a)* Prepaid Rent, *(b)* Unearned Fees, *(c)* Building, *(d)* Wages Payable, and *(e)* Office Supplies.
4. What is an account? What is a ledger?
5. What determines the number and types of accounts a company uses?
6. Does *debit* always mean increase and *credit* always mean decrease?
7. Describe a chart of accounts.

Journalizing and Posting Transactions

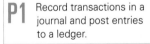

Processing transactions is a crucial part of accounting. The four usual steps of this process are depicted in Exhibit 2.9. Steps 1 and 2—involving transaction analysis and the accounting equation—were introduced in prior sections. This section extends that discussion and focuses on steps 3 and 4 of the accounting process. Step 3 is to record each transaction chronologically in a journal. A **journal** gives a complete record of each transaction in one place. It also shows debits and credits for each transaction. The process of recording transactions in a journal is called **journalizing.** Step 4 is to transfer (or *post*) entries from the journal to the ledger. The process of transferring journal entry information to the ledger is called **posting.**

Journalizing Transactions   The process of journalizing transactions requires an understanding of a journal. While companies can use various journals, every company uses a **general journal.** It can be used to record any transaction and includes the following information about each transaction: ⓐ date of transaction, ⓑ titles of affected accounts, ⓒ dollar amount of each

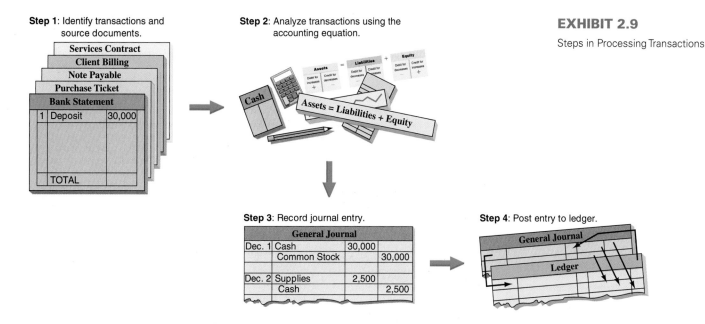

EXHIBIT 2.9

Steps in Processing Transactions

debit and credit, and ⓓ explanation of the transaction. Exhibit 2.10 shows how the first two transactions of FastForward are recorded in a general journal. This process is similar for manual and computerized systems. Computerized journals are often designed to look like a manual journal page, and also include error-checking routines that ensure debits equal credits for each entry. Shortcuts allow recordkeepers to select account names and numbers from pull-down menus.

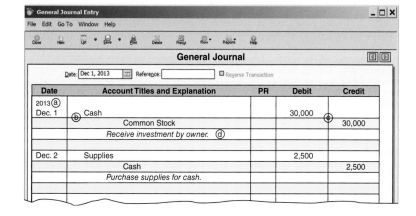

EXHIBIT 2.10

Partial General Journal for FastForward

To record entries in a general journal, apply these steps; refer to the entries in Exhibit 2.10 when reviewing these steps.

a. Date the transaction: Enter the year at the top of the first column and the month and day on the first line of each journal entry.

b. Enter titles of accounts debited and then enter amounts in the Debit column on the same line. Account titles are taken from the chart of accounts and are aligned with the left margin of the Account Titles and Explanation column.

c. Enter titles of accounts credited and then enter amounts in the Credit column on the same line. Account titles are from the chart of accounts and are indented from the left margin of the Account Titles and Explanation column to distinguish them from debited accounts.

d. Enter a brief explanation of the transaction on the line below the entry (it often references a source document). This explanation is indented about half as far as the credited account titles to avoid confusing it with accounts, and it is italicized.

Point: There are no exact rules for writing journal entry explanations. An explanation should be short yet describe why an entry is made.

A blank line is left between each journal entry for clarity. When a transaction is first recorded, the **posting reference (PR) column** is left blank (in a manual system). Later, when posting entries to the ledger, the identification numbers of the individual ledger accounts are entered in the PR column.

 IFRS _____

IFRS requires that companies report the following four basic financial statements with explanatory notes:

- Balance sheet
- Income statement
- Statement of changes in equity (or statement of recognized revenue and expense)
- Statement of cash flows

IFRS does not prescribe specific formats; and comparative information is required for the preceding period only. ∎

Balance Column Account   T-accounts are simple and direct means to show how the accounting process works. However, actual accounting systems need more structure and therefore use **balance column accounts,** such as that in Exhibit 2.11.

EXHIBIT 2.11

Cash Account in Balance
Column Format

General Ledger					
			Cash		Account No. 101
Date	Explanation	PR	Debit	Credit	Balance
2013 Dec. 1		G1	30,000		30,000
Dec. 2		G1		2,500	27,500
Dec. 3		G1		26,000	1,500
Dec. 10		G1	4,200		5,700

The balance column account format is similar to a T-account in having columns for debits and credits. It is different in including transaction date and explanation columns. It also has a column with the balance of the account after each entry is recorded. To illustrate, FastForward's Cash account in Exhibit 2.11 is debited on December 1 for the $30,000 owner investment, yielding a $30,000 debit balance. The account is credited on December 2 for $2,500, yielding a $27,500 debit balance. On December 3, it is credited again, this time for $26,000, and its debit balance is reduced to $1,500. The Cash account is debited for $4,200 on December 10, and its debit balance increases to $5,700; and so on.

Point: Explanations are typically included in ledger accounts only for unusual transactions or events.

EXHIBIT 2.12

Posting an Entry to the Ledger

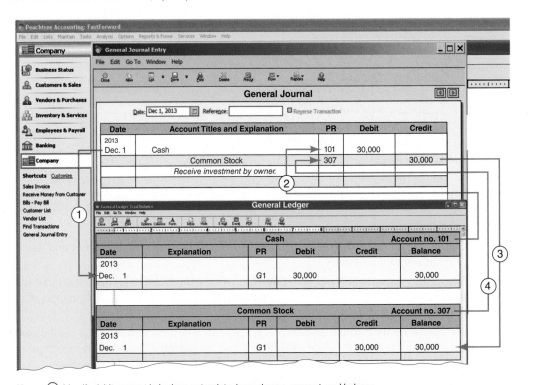

Point: The fundamental concepts of a manual (pencil-and-paper) system are identical to those of a computerized information system.

Key: ① Identify debit account in Ledger: enter date, journal page, amount, and balance.
② Enter the debit account number from the Ledger in the PR column of the journal.
③ Identify credit account in Ledger: enter date, journal page, amount, and balance.
④ Enter the credit account number from the Ledger in the PR column of the journal.

The heading of the Balance column does not show whether it is a debit or credit balance. Instead, an account is assumed to have a *normal balance*. Unusual events can sometimes temporarily give an account an abnormal balance. An *abnormal balance* refers to a balance on the side where decreases are recorded. For example, a customer might mistakenly overpay a bill. This gives that customer's account receivable an abnormal (credit) balance. An abnormal balance is often identified by circling it or by entering it in red or some other unusual color. A zero balance for an account is usually shown by writing zeros or a dash in the Balance column to avoid confusion between a zero balance and one omitted in error.

Posting Journal Entries   Step 4 of processing transactions is to post journal entries to ledger accounts (see Exhibit 2.9). To ensure that the ledger is up-to-date, entries are posted as soon as possible. This might be daily, weekly, or when time permits. All entries must be posted to the ledger before financial statements are prepared to ensure that account balances are up-to-date. When entries are posted to the ledger, the debits in journal entries are transferred into ledger accounts as debits, and credits are transferred into ledger accounts as credits. Exhibit 2.12 shows the *four steps to post a journal entry*. First, identify the ledger account that is debited in the entry; then, in the ledger, enter the entry date, the journal and page in its PR column, the debit amount, and the new balance of the ledger account. (The letter *G* shows it came from the General Journal.) Second, enter the ledger account number in the PR column of the journal. Steps 3 and 4 repeat the first two steps for credit entries and amounts. The posting process creates a link between the ledger and the journal entry. This link is a useful cross-reference for tracing an amount from one record to another.

Analyzing Transactions — An Illustration

We return to the activities of FastForward to show how double-entry accounting is useful in analyzing and processing transactions. Analysis of each transaction follows the four steps of Exhibit 2.9.

| Step 1 | Identify the transaction and any source documents. |

| Step 2 | Analyze the transaction using the accounting equation. |

| Step 3 | Record the transaction in journal entry form applying double-entry accounting. |

| Step 4 | Post the entry (for simplicity, we use T-accounts to represent ledger accounts). |

Study each transaction thoroughly before proceeding to the next. The first 11 transactions are from Chapter 1, and we analyze five additional December transactions of FastForward (numbered 12 through 16) that were omitted earlier.

Point: Computerized systems often provide a code beside a balance such as *dr.* or *cr.* to identify its balance. Posting is automatic and immediate with accounting software.

Point: A journal is often referred to as the *book of original entry.* The ledger is referred to as the *book of final entry* because financial statements are prepared from it.

> **A1** Analyze the impact of transactions on accounts and financial statements.

Point: In the Demonstration Problem at the chapter end we show how to use "balance column accounts" for the ledger.

I. Receive investment by Owner

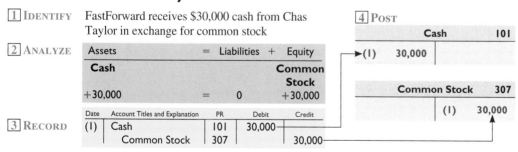

2. Purchase Supplies for Cash

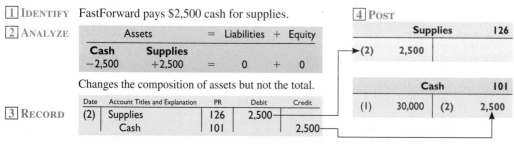

3. Purchase Equipment for Cash

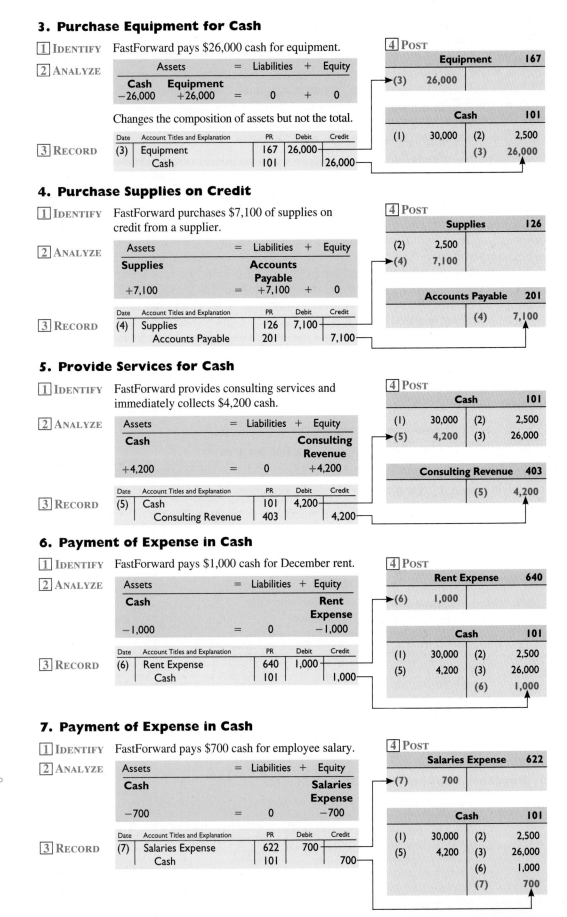

1 IDENTIFY FastForward pays $26,000 cash for equipment.

2 ANALYZE

Assets		=	Liabilities	+	Equity
Cash	**Equipment**				
−26,000	+26,000	=	0	+	0

Changes the composition of assets but not the total.

3 RECORD

Date	Account Titles and Explanation	PR	Debit	Credit
(3)	Equipment	167	26,000	
	Cash	101		26,000

4 POST

Equipment		167
(3)	26,000	

Cash		101
(1)	30,000	(2) 2,500
		(3) 26,000

4. Purchase Supplies on Credit

1 IDENTIFY FastForward purchases $7,100 of supplies on credit from a supplier.

2 ANALYZE

Assets	=	Liabilities	+	Equity
Supplies		**Accounts Payable**		
+7,100	=	+7,100	+	0

3 RECORD

Date	Account Titles and Explanation	PR	Debit	Credit
(4)	Supplies	126	7,100	
	Accounts Payable	201		7,100

4 POST

Supplies		126
(2)	2,500	
(4)	7,100	

Accounts Payable		201
		(4) 7,100

5. Provide Services for Cash

1 IDENTIFY FastForward provides consulting services and immediately collects $4,200 cash.

2 ANALYZE

Assets	=	Liabilities	+	Equity
Cash				**Consulting Revenue**
+4,200	=	0		+4,200

3 RECORD

Date	Account Titles and Explanation	PR	Debit	Credit
(5)	Cash	101	4,200	
	Consulting Revenue	403		4,200

4 POST

Cash		101
(1)	30,000	(2) 2,500
(5)	4,200	(3) 26,000

Consulting Revenue		403
		(5) 4,200

6. Payment of Expense in Cash

1 IDENTIFY FastForward pays $1,000 cash for December rent.

2 ANALYZE

Assets	=	Liabilities	+	Equity
Cash				**Rent Expense**
−1,000	=	0		−1,000

3 RECORD

Date	Account Titles and Explanation	PR	Debit	Credit
(6)	Rent Expense	640	1,000	
	Cash	101		1,000

4 POST

Rent Expense		640
(6)	1,000	

Cash		101
(1)	30,000	(2) 2,500
(5)	4,200	(3) 26,000
		(6) 1,000

7. Payment of Expense in Cash

1 IDENTIFY FastForward pays $700 cash for employee salary.

Point: *Salary* usually refers to compensation for an employee who receives a fixed amount for a given time period, whereas *wages* usually refers to compensation based on time worked.

2 ANALYZE

Assets	=	Liabilities	+	Equity
Cash				**Salaries Expense**
−700	=	0		−700

3 RECORD

Date	Account Titles and Explanation	PR	Debit	Credit
(7)	Salaries Expense	622	700	
	Cash	101		700

4 POST

Salaries Expense		622
(7)	700	

Cash		101
(1)	30,000	(2) 2,500
(5)	4,200	(3) 26,000
		(6) 1,000
		(7) 700

TRIAL BALANCE

Double-entry accounting requires the sum of debit account balances to equal the sum of credit account balances. A trial balance is used to confirm this. A **trial balance** is a list of accounts and their balances at a point in time. Account balances are reported in their appropriate debit or credit columns of a trial balance. A trial balance can be used to confirm this and to follow up on any abnormal or unusual balances. Exhibit 2.14 shows the trial balance for FastForward after its 16 entries have been posted to the ledger. (This is an *unadjusted* trial balance—Chapter 3 explains the necessary adjustments.)

EXHIBIT 2.14

Trial Balance (Unadjusted)

Peachtree Accounting: FastForward

File Edit Lists Maintain Tasks Analysis Options Reports & Forms Services Window Help

FASTFORWARD
Trial Balance
December 31, 2013

	Debit	Credit
Cash	$ 4,350	
Accounts receivable	0	
Supplies	9,720	
Prepaid insurance	2,400	
Equipment	26,000	
Accounts payable		$ 6,200
Unearned consulting revenue		3,000
Common stock		30,000
Dividends	200	
Consulting revenue		5,800
Rental revenue		300
Salaries expense	1,400	
Rent expense	1,000	
Utilities expense	230	
Totals	$ 45,300	$ 45,300

Point: The ordering of accounts in a trial balance typically follows their identification number from the chart of accounts.

Preparing a Trial Balance

Preparing a trial balance involves three steps:

P2 Prepare and explain the use of a trial balance.

1. List each account title and its amount (from ledger) in the trial balance. If an account has a zero balance, list it with a zero in its normal balance column (or omit it entirely).
2. Compute the total of debit balances and the total of credit balances.
3. Verify (*prove*) total debit balances equal total credit balances.

The total of debit balances equals the total of credit balances for the trial balance in Exhibit 2.14. Equality of these two totals does not guarantee that no errors were made. For example, the column totals still will be equal when a debit or credit of a correct amount is made to a wrong account. Another error that does not cause unequal column totals occurs when equal debits and credits of an incorrect amount are entered.

Searching for and Correcting Errors   If the trial balance does not balance (when its columns are not equal), the error (or errors) must be found and corrected. An efficient way to search for an error is to check the journalizing, posting, and trial balance preparation

Point: A trial balance is *not* a financial statement but a mechanism for checking equality of debits and credits in the ledger. Financial statements do not have debit and credit columns.

Example: If a credit to Unearned Revenue was incorrectly posted from the journal as a credit to the Revenue ledger account, would the ledger still balance? Would the financial statements be correct? *Answers:* The ledger would balance, but liabilities would be understated, equity would be overstated, and income would be overstated (all because of overstated revenues).

Point: The IRS requires companies to keep records that can be audited.

in *reverse order.* Step 1 is to verify that the trial balance columns are correctly added. If step 1 fails to find the error, step 2 is to verify that account balances are accurately entered from the ledger. Step 3 is to see whether a debit (or credit) balance is mistakenly listed in the trial balance as a credit (or debit). A clue to this error is when the difference between total debits and total credits equals twice the amount of the incorrect account balance. If the error is still undiscovered, Step 4 is to recompute each account balance in the ledger. Step 5 is to verify that each journal entry is properly posted. Step 6 is to verify that the original journal entry has equal debits and credits. At this point, the errors should be uncovered.[3]

If an error in a journal entry is discovered before the error is posted, it can be corrected in a manual system by drawing a line through the incorrect information. The correct information is written above it to create a record of change for the auditor. Many computerized systems allow the operator to replace the incorrect information directly.

If an error in a journal entry is not discovered until after it is posted, we do not strike through both erroneous entries in the journal and ledger. Instead, we correct this error by creating a *correcting entry* that removes the amount from the wrong account and records it to the correct account. As an example, suppose a $100 purchase of supplies is journalized with an incorrect debit to Equipment, and then this incorrect entry is posted to the ledger. The Supplies ledger account balance is understated by $100, and the Equipment ledger account balance is overstated by $100. The correcting entry is: debit Supplies and credit Equipment (both for $100).

Using a Trial Balance to Prepare Financial Statements

P3   Prepare financial statements from business transactions.

This section shows how to prepare *financial statements* from the trial balance in Exhibit 2.14 and from information on the December transactions of FastForward. These statements differ from those in Chapter 1 because of several additional transactions. These statements are also more precisely called *unadjusted statements* because we need to make some further accounting adjustments (described in Chapter 3).

EXHIBIT 2.15

Links between Financial Statements across Time

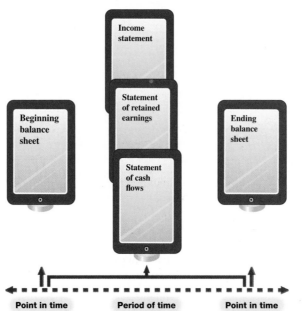

How financial statements are linked in time is illustrated in Exhibit 2.15. A balance sheet reports on an organization's financial position at a *point in time.* The income statement, statement of retained earnings, and statement of cash flows report on financial performance over a *period of time.* The three statements in the middle column of Exhibit 2.15 link balance sheets from the beginning to the end of a reporting period. They explain how financial position changes from one point to another.

Preparers and users (including regulatory agencies) determine the length of the reporting period. A one-year, or annual, reporting period is common, as are semiannual, quarterly, and monthly periods. The one-year reporting period

[3] *Transposition* occurs when two digits are switched, or transposed, within a number. If transposition is the only error, it yields a difference between the two trial balance totals that is evenly divisible by 9. For example, assume that a $691 debit in an entry is incorrectly posted to the ledger as $619. Total credits in the trial balance are then larger than total debits by $72 ($691 − $619). The $72 error is *evenly* divisible by 9 (72/9 = 8). The first digit of the quotient (in our example it is 8) equals the difference between the digits of the two transposed numbers (the 9 and the 1). The number of digits in the quotient also tells the location of the transposition, starting from the right. The quotient in our example had only one digit (8), so it tells us the transposition is in the first digit. Consider another example where a transposition error involves posting $961 instead of the correct $691. The difference in these numbers is $270, and its quotient is 30 (270/9). The quotient has two digits, so it tells us to check the second digit from the right for a transposition of two numbers that have a difference of 3.

is known as the *accounting,* or *fiscal, year.* Businesses whose accounting year begins on January 1 and ends on December 31 are known as *calendar-year* companies. **Polaris** is a calendar-year company. Many companies choose a fiscal year ending on a date other than December 31. **Arctic Cat** is a *noncalendar-year* company as reflected in the headings of its March 31 year-end financial statements in Appendix A near the end of the book.

Point: A statement's heading lists the 3 W's: **Who**—name of organization, **What**—name of statement, **When**—statement's point in time or period of time.

Income Statement An income statement reports the revenues earned less the expenses incurred by a business over a period of time. FastForward's income statement for December is shown at the top of Exhibit 2.16. Information about revenues and expenses is conveniently taken from the trial balance in Exhibit 2.14. Net income of $3,470 is reported at the bottom of the statement. Owner investments and dividends are *not* part of income.

Statement of Retained Earnings The statement of retained earnings reports information about how retained earnings change over the reporting period. FastForward's statement of retained earnings is the second report in Exhibit 2.16. It shows the $3,470 of net income, the

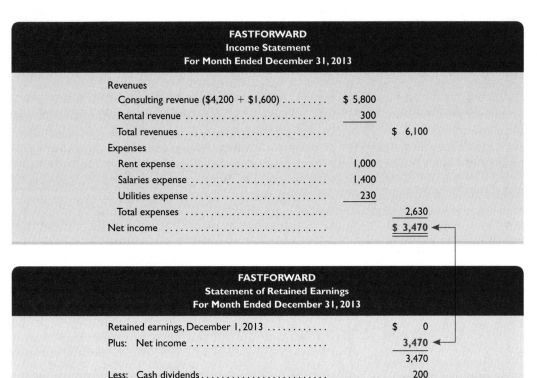

EXHIBIT 2.16

Financial Statements and Their Links

Point: Arrow lines show how the statements are linked.

FASTFORWARD
Income Statement
For Month Ended December 31, 2013

Revenues		
Consulting revenue ($4,200 + $1,600)	$ 5,800	
Rental revenue	300	
Total revenues		$ 6,100
Expenses		
Rent expense	1,000	
Salaries expense	1,400	
Utilities expense	230	
Total expenses		2,630
Net income		$ 3,470

FASTFORWARD
Statement of Retained Earnings
For Month Ended December 31, 2013

Retained earnings, December 1, 2013	$ 0	
Plus: Net income	3,470	
	3,470	
Less: Cash dividends	200	
Retained earnings, December 31, 2013	$ 3,270	

FASTFORWARD
Balance Sheet
December 31, 2013

Assets		Liabilities	
Cash	$ 4,350	Accounts payable	$ 6,200
Supplies	9,720	Unearned revenue	3,000
Prepaid insurance . .	2,400	Total liabilities	9,200
Equipment	26,000	**Equity**	
		Common stock	30,000
		Retained earnings	3,270
		Total equity	33,270
Total assets	$42,470	Total liabilities and equity . .	$42,470

Point: To *foot* a column of numbers is to add them.

$200 dividend, and the $3,270 end-of-period balance. (The beginning balance in the statement of retained earnings is rarely zero; an exception is for the first period of operations. The beginning balance in January 2014 is $3,270, which is December's ending balance.)

Balance Sheet   The balance sheet reports the financial position of a company at a point in time, usually at the end of a month, quarter, or year. FastForward's balance sheet is the third report in Exhibit 2.16. This statement refers to financial condition at the close of business on December 31. The left side of the balance sheet lists its assets: cash, supplies, prepaid insurance, and equipment. The upper right side of the balance sheet shows that it owes $6,200 to creditors and $3,000 in services to customers who paid in advance. The equity section shows an ending balance of $33,270. Note the link between the ending balance of the statement of retained earnings and the retained earnings balance. (Recall that this presentation of the balance sheet is called the *account form:* assets on the left and liabilities and equity on the right. Another presentation is the *report form:* assets on top, followed by liabilities and then equity. Either presentation is acceptable.)

Point: An income statement is also called an *earnings statement, a statement of operations,* or a *P&L* (profit and loss) statement. A balance sheet is also called a *statement of financial position.*

Point: While revenues increase equity, and expenses decrease equity, the amounts are not reported in detail in the statement of retained earnings. Instead, their effects are reflected through net income.

Point: Knowing how financial statements are prepared improves our analysis of them.

Decision Maker

Entrepreneur You open a wholesale business selling entertainment equipment to retail outlets. You find that most of your customers demand to buy on credit. How can you use the balance sheets of these customers to decide which ones to extend credit to? ■   [Answer—p. 76]

Presentation Issues   Dollar signs are not used in journals and ledgers. They do appear in financial statements and other reports such as trial balances. The usual practice is to put dollar signs beside only the first and last numbers in a column. **Polaris**'s financial statements in Appendix A show this. When amounts are entered in a journal, ledger, or trial balance, commas are optional to indicate thousands, millions, and so forth. However, commas are always used in financial statements. Companies also commonly round amounts in reports to the nearest dollar, or even to a higher level. Polaris is typical of many companies in that it rounds its financial statement amounts to the nearest thousand (or million). This decision is based on the perceived impact of rounding for users' business decisions.

off the mark .com   by Mark Parisi
                         offthemark.com

HE CONTINUED ACCOUNTING RIGHT THROUGH HIS COFFEE BREAK...THEN HIS LUNCH BREAK. CLEARLY, MYRON WAS "IN THE ZONE."

Quick Check   Answers — p. 77

14. Where are dollar signs typically entered in financial statements?
15. If a $4,000 debit to Equipment in a journal entry is incorrectly posted to the ledger as a $4,000 credit, and the ledger account has a resulting debit balance of $20,000, what is the effect of this error on the Trial Balance column totals?
16. Describe the link between the income statement and the statement of retained earnings.
17. Explain the link between the balance sheet and the statement of retained earnings.
18. Define and describe revenues and expenses.
19. Define and describe assets, liabilities, and equity.

GLOBAL VIEW

Financial accounting according to U.S. GAAP is similar, but not identical, to IFRS. This section discusses differences in analyzing and recording transactions, and with the preparation of financial statements.

Analyzing and Recording Transactions   Both U.S. GAAP and IFRS include broad and similar guidance for financial accounting. As the FASB and IASB work toward a common conceptual framework over the next few years, even those differences will fade. Further, both U.S. GAAP and IFRS apply transaction analysis and recording as shown in this chapter—using the same debit and credit system and accrual account-ing. Although some variations exist in revenue and expense recognition and other accounting principles, all of the transactions in this chapter are accounted for identically under these two systems.

Financial Statements   Both U.S. GAAP and IFRS prepare the same four basic financial state-ments. A few differences within each statement do exist and we will discuss those throughout the book. For example, both U.S. GAAP and IFRS require balance sheets to separate current items from noncurrent items. However, while U.S. GAAP balance sheets report current items first, IFRS balance sheets normally (but are not required to) present noncurrent items first, and equity before liabilities. To illustrate, a con-densed version of **Piaggio**'s balance sheet follows (numbers using Euros in thousands).

PIAGGIO

PIAGGIO Balance Sheet (in thousands of Euros) December 31, 2011			
Assets		**Equity and Liabilities**	
Noncurrent assets	1,010,476	Total equity	446,218
Current assets	509,708	Noncurrent liabilities	429,689
		Current liabilities	644,277
Total assets	1,520,184	Total equity and liabilities	1,520,184

Accounting Controls and Assurance   Accounting systems depend on control procedures that assure the proper principles were applied in processing accounting information. The passage of SOX leg-islation strengthened U.S. control procedures in recent years. However, global standards for control are diverse and so are enforcement activities. Consequently, while global accounting standards are converg-ing, their application in different countries can yield different outcomes depending on the quality of their auditing standards and enforcement.

Decision Insight

Accounting Control Recording valid transactions, and not recording fraudulent transactions, enhances the quality of financial statements. The graph here shows the percentage of employ-ees in information technology that report observing specific types of misconduct within the past year [Source: KPMG 2009]. ■

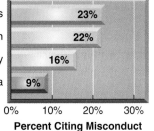

Breaching database controls 23%
Mishandling private information 22%
Breaching customer privacy 16%
Falsifying accounting data 9%

0%   10%   20%   30%

Percent Citing Misconduct

Debt Ratio   **Decision Analysis**

An important business objective is gathering information to help assess a company's risk of failing to pay its debts. Companies finance their assets with either liabilities or equity. A company that finances a rela-tively large portion of its assets with liabilities is said to have a high degree of *financial leverage*. Higher financial leverage involves greater risk because liabilities must be repaid and often require regular interest payments (equity financing does not). The risk that a company might not be able to meet such required payments is higher if it has more liabilities (is more highly leveraged). One way to assess the risk associ-ated with a company's use of liabilities is to compute the **debt ratio** as in Exhibit 2.17.

A2 Compute the debt ratio and describe its use in analyzing financial condition.

$$\text{Debt ratio} = \frac{\text{Total liabilities}}{\text{Total assets}}$$

EXHIBIT 2.17

Debt Ratio

Point: Compare the equity amount to the liability amount to assess the extent of owner versus nonowner financing.

To see how to apply the debt ratio, let's look at Skechers's liabilities and assets. The company designs, markets, and sells footwear for men, women, and children under the Skechers brand. Exhibit 2.18 computes and reports its debt ratio at the end of each year from 2006 to 2011.

EXHIBIT 2.18

Computation and Analysis of Debt Ratio

$ in millions	2011	2010	2009	2008	2007	2006
Total liabilities	$ 389	$ 359	$246	$204	$201	$288
Total assets	$1,282	$1,305	$996	$876	$828	$737
Debt ratio	0.30	0.28	0.25	0.23	0.24	0.39
Industry debt ratio	0.47	0.49	0.51	0.50	0.46	0.48

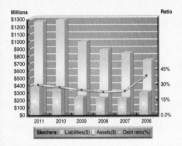

Skechers's debt ratio ranges from a low of 0.23 to a high of 0.39—also, see graph in margin. Its ratio is lower, compared with the industry ratio. This analysis implies a low risk from its financial leverage. Is financial leverage good or bad for Skechers? To answer that question we need to compare the company's return on the borrowed money to the rate it is paying creditors. If the company's return is higher, it is successfully borrowing money to make more money. A company's success with making money from borrowed money can quickly turn unprofitable if its own return drops below the rate it is paying creditors.

■ **Decision Maker** ━━━━━━━━━━━━━━━━━━━━━━━━━

Investor   You consider buying stock in Converse. As part of your analysis, you compute its debt ratio for 2011, 2012, and 2013 as: 0.35, 0.74, and 0.94, respectively. Based on the debt ratio, is Converse a low-risk investment? Has the risk of buying Converse stock changed over this period? (The industry debt ratio averages 0.40.) ■   [Answer—p. 76]

DEMONSTRATION PROBLEM

(This problem extends the demonstration problem of Chapter 1.) After several months of planning, Jasmine Worthy started a haircutting business called Expressions. The following events occurred during its first month.

a. On August 1, Worthy invested $3,000 cash and $15,000 of equipment in Expressions in exchange for common stock.

b. On August 2, Expressions paid $600 cash for furniture for the shop.

c. On August 3, Expressions paid $500 cash to rent space in a strip mall for August.

d. On August 4, it purchased $1,200 of equipment on credit for the shop (using a long-term note payable).

e. On August 5, Expressions opened for business. Cash received from haircutting services in the first week and a half of business (ended August 15) was $825.

f. On August 15, it provided $100 of haircutting services on account.

g. On August 17, it received a $100 check for services previously rendered on account.

h. On August 17, it paid $125 to an assistant for hours worked during the grand opening.

i. Cash received from services provided during the second half of August was $930.

j. On August 31, it paid a $400 installment toward principal on the note payable entered into on August 4.

k. On August 31, it paid $900 cash in dividends to Worthy (sole shareholder).

Required

1. Open the following ledger accounts in balance column format (account numbers are in parentheses): Cash (101); Accounts Receivable (102); Furniture (161); Store Equipment (165); Note Payable (240); Common Stock (307); Dividends (319); Haircutting Services Revenue (403); Wages Expense (623); and Rent Expense (640). Prepare general journal entries for the transactions.

2. Post the journal entries from (1) to the ledger accounts.

3. Prepare a trial balance as of August 31.

4. Prepare an income statement for August.

5. Prepare a statement of retained earnings for August.

6. Prepare a balance sheet as of August 31.

7. Determine the debt ratio as of August 31.

Extended Analysis

8. In the coming months, Expressions will experience a greater variety of business transactions. Identify which accounts are debited and which are credited for the following transactions. (*Hint:* We must use some accounts not opened in part 1.)

a. Purchase supplies with cash.

b. Pay cash for future insurance coverage.

c. Receive cash for services to be provided in the future.

d. Purchase supplies on account.

PLANNING THE SOLUTION

- Analyze each transaction and use the debit and credit rules to prepare a journal entry for each.
- Post each debit and each credit from journal entries to their ledger accounts and cross-reference each amount in the posting reference (PR) columns of the journal and ledger.
- Calculate each account balance and list the accounts with their balances on a trial balance.
- Verify that total debits in the trial balance equal total credits.
- To prepare the income statement, identify revenues and expenses. List those items on the statement, compute the difference, and label the result as *net income* or *net loss*.
- Use information in the ledger to prepare the statement of retained earnings.
- Use information in the ledger to prepare the balance sheet.
- Calculate the debt ratio by dividing total liabilities by total assets.
- Analyze the future transactions to identify the accounts affected and apply debit and credit rules.

SOLUTION TO DEMONSTRATION PROBLEM

1. General journal entries:

General Journal   `_ □ ✕`

Page 1

Date	Account Titles and Explanation	PR	Debit	Credit
Aug. 1	Cash	101	3,000	
	Store Equipment	165	15,000	
	Common Stock	307		18,000
	Owner's investment for stock.			
2	Furniture	161	600	
	Cash	101		600
	Purchased furniture for cash.			
3	Rent Expense	640	500	
	Cash	101		500
	Paid rent for August.			
4	Store Equipment	165	1,200	
	Note Payable	240		1,200
	Purchased additional equipment on credit.			
15	Cash	101	825	
	Haircutting Services Revenue	403		825
	Cash receipts from first half of August.			

[continued on next page]

[continued from previous page]

15	Accounts Receivable	102	100	
	Haircutting Services Revenue	403		100
	To record revenue for services provided on account.			
17	Cash	101	100	
	Accounts Receivable	102		100
	To record cash received as payment on account.			
17	Wages Expense	623	125	
	Cash	101		125
	Paid wages to assistant.			
31	Cash	101	930	
	Haircutting Services Revenue	403		930
	Cash receipts from second half of August.			
31	Note Payable	240	400	
	Cash	101		400
	Paid an installment on the note payable.			
31	Dividends	319	900	
	Cash	101		900
	Paid cash dividend.			

2. Post journal entries from part 1 to the ledger accounts:

General Ledger

Cash   **Account No. 101**

Date	PR	Debit	Credit	Balance
Aug. 1	G1	3,000		3,000
2	G1		600	2,400
3	G1		500	1,900
15	G1	825		2,725
17	G1	100		2,825
17	G1		125	2,700
31	G1	930		3,630
31	G1		400	3,230
31	G1		900	2,330

Accounts Receivable   **Account No. 102**

Date	PR	Debit	Credit	Balance
Aug. 15	G1	100		100
17	G1		100	0

Furniture   **Account No. 161**

Date	PR	Debit	Credit	Balance
Aug. 2	G1	600		600

Store Equipment   **Account No. 165**

Date	PR	Debit	Credit	Balance
Aug. 1	G1	15,000		15,000
4	G1	1,200		16,200

Note Payable   **Account No. 240**

Date	PR	Debit	Credit	Balance
Aug. 4	G1		1,200	1,200
31	G1	400		800

Common Stock   **Account No. 307**

Date	PR	Debit	Credit	Balance
Aug. 1	G1		18,000	18,000

Dividends   **Account No. 319**

Date	PR	Debit	Credit	Balance
Aug. 31	G1	900		900

Haircutting Services Revenue   **Account No. 403**

Date	PR	Debit	Credit	Balance
Aug. 15	G1		825	825
15	G1		100	925
31	G1		930	1,855

Wages Expense   **Account No. 623**

Date	PR	Debit	Credit	Balance
Aug. 17	G1	125		125

Rent Expense   **Account No. 640**

Date	PR	Debit	Credit	Balance
Aug. 3	G1	500		500

3. Prepare a trial balance from the ledger:

EXPRESSIONS Trial Balance August 31		
	Debit	**Credit**
Cash	$ 2,330	
Accounts receivable	0	
Furniture	600	
Store equipment	16,200	
Note payable		$ 800
Common stock...................		18,000
Dividends	900	
Haircutting services revenue		1,855
Wages expense	125	
Rent expense	500	
Totals	$20,655	$20,655

4.

EXPRESSIONS Income Statement For Month Ended August 31		
Revenues		
Haircutting services revenue		$1,855
Operating expenses		
Rent expense	$500	
Wages expense	125	
Total operating expenses		625
Net income		$1,230

5.

EXPRESSIONS Statement of Retained Earnings For Month Ended August 31	
Retained earnings, August 1	$ 0
Plus: Net income	1,230
	1,230
Less: Cash dividends	900
Retained earnings, August 31	$ 330

6.

EXPRESSIONS Balance Sheet August 31			
Assets		**Liabilities**	
Cash	$ 2,330	Note payable	$ 800
Furniture	600	**Equity**	
Store equipment	16,200	Common stock.................	18,000
		Retained earnings	330
		Total equity	18,330
Total assets	$19,130	Total liabilities and equity	$19,130

7. Debt ratio $= \dfrac{\text{Total liabilities}}{\text{Total assets}} = \dfrac{\$800}{\$19,130} = \mathbf{4.18\%}$

8a. Supplies *debited*
        Cash *credited*

8b. Prepaid Insurance *debited*
        Cash *credited*

8c. Cash *debited*
        Unearned Services Revenue *credited*

8d. Supplies *debited*
        Accounts Payable *credited*

Summary

C1 Explain the steps in processing transactions and the role of source documents. The accounting process identifies business transactions and events, analyzes and records their effects, and summarizes and prepares information useful in making decisions. Transactions and events are the starting points in the accounting process. Source documents identify and describe transactions and events. Examples are sales tickets, checks, purchase orders, bills, and bank statements. Source documents provide objective and reliable evidence, making information more useful. The effects of transactions and events are recorded in journals. Posting along with a trial balance helps summarize and classify these effects.

C2 Describe an account and its use in recording transactions. An account is a detailed record of increases and decreases in a specific asset, liability, equity, revenue, or expense. Information from accounts is analyzed, summarized, and presented in reports and financial statements for decision makers.

C3 Describe a ledger and a chart of accounts. The ledger (or general ledger) is a record containing all accounts used by a company and their balances. It is referred to as the *books*. The chart of accounts is a list of all accounts and usually includes an identification number assigned to each account.

C4 Define *debits* and *credits* and explain double-entry accounting. *Debit* refers to left, and *credit* refers to right. Debits increase assets, expenses, and dividends while credits decrease them. Credits increase liabilities, common stock, and revenues; debits decrease them. Double-entry accounting means each transaction affects at least two accounts and has at least one debit and one credit. The system for recording debits and credits follows from the accounting equation. The left side of an account is the normal balance for assets, dividends, and expenses, and the right side is the normal balance for liabilities, common stock, and revenues.

A1 Analyze the impact of transactions on accounts and financial statements. We analyze transactions using concepts of double-entry accounting. This analysis is performed by determining a transaction's effects on accounts. These effects are recorded in journals and posted to ledgers.

A2 Compute the debt ratio and describe its use in analyzing financial condition. A company's debt ratio is computed as total liabilities divided by total assets. It reveals how much of the assets are financed by creditor (nonowner) financing. The higher this ratio, the more risk a company faces because liabilities must be repaid at specific dates.

P1 Record transactions in a journal and post entries to a ledger. Transactions are recorded in a journal. Each entry in a journal is posted to the accounts in the ledger. This provides information that is used to produce financial statements. Balance column accounts are widely used and include columns for debits, credits, and the account balance.

P2 Prepare and explain the use of a trial balance. A trial balance is a list of accounts from the ledger showing their debit or credit balances in separate columns. The trial balance is a summary of the ledger's contents and is useful in preparing financial statements and in revealing recordkeeping errors.

P3 Prepare financial statements from business transactions. The balance sheet, the statement of retained earnings, the income statement, and the statement of cash flows use data from the trial balance (and other financial statements) for their preparation.

Guidance Answers to Decision Maker and Decision Ethics

Cashier The advantages to the process proposed by the assistant manager include improved customer service, fewer delays, and less work for you. However, you should have serious concerns about internal control and the potential for fraud. In particular, the assistant manager could steal cash and simply enter fewer sales to match the remaining cash. You should reject her suggestion without the manager's approval. Moreover, you should have an ethical concern about the assistant manager's suggestion to ignore store policy.

Entrepreneur We can use the accounting equation (Assets = Liabilities + Equity) to help us identify risky customers to whom we would likely not want to extend credit. A balance sheet provides amounts for each of these key components. The lower a customer's equity is relative to liabilities, the less likely you would extend credit. A low equity means the business has little value that does not already have creditor claims to it.

Investor The debt ratio suggests the stock of Converse is of higher risk than normal and that this risk is rising. The average industry ratio of 0.40 further supports this conclusion. The 2013 debt ratio for Converse is twice the industry norm. Also, a debt ratio approaching 1.0 indicates little to no equity.

Guidance Answers to Quick Checks

1. Examples of source documents are sales tickets, checks, purchase orders, charges to customers, bills from suppliers, employee earnings records, and bank statements.

2. Source documents serve many purposes, including record-keeping and internal control. Source documents, especially if obtained from outside the organization, provide objective and reliable evidence about transactions and their amounts.

3.

Assets	Liabilities	Equity
a,c,e	b,d	—

4. An account is a record in an accounting system that records and stores the increases and decreases in a specific asset, liability, equity, revenue, or expense. The ledger is a collection of all the accounts of a company.

5. A company's size and diversity affect the number of accounts in its accounting system. The types of accounts depend on information the company needs to both effectively operate and report its activities in financial statements.

6. No. Debit and credit both can mean increase or decrease. The particular meaning in a circumstance depends on the *type of account*. For example, a debit increases the balance of asset, dividends, and expense accounts, but it decreases the balance of liability, common stock, and revenue accounts.

7. A chart of accounts is a list of all of a company's accounts and their identification numbers.

8. Equity is increased by revenues and by owner investments. Equity is decreased by expenses and dividends.

9. The name *double-entry* is used because all transactions affect at least two accounts. There must be at least one debit in one account and at least one credit in another account.

10. The answer is (*c*).

11.

Cash	15,000	
Equipment	23,000	
Common Stock		38,000
Investment by owner of cash and equipment.		

12. A compound journal entry affects three or more accounts.

13. Posting reference numbers are entered in the journal when posting to the ledger as a cross-reference that allows the record-keeper or auditor to trace debits and credits from one record to another.

14. At a minimum, dollar signs are placed beside the first and last numbers in a column. It is also common to place dollar signs beside any amount that appears after a ruled line to indicate that an addition or subtraction has occurred.

15. The Equipment account balance is incorrectly reported at $20,000—it should be $28,000. The effect of this error understates the trial balance's Debit column total by $8,000. This results in an $8,000 difference between the column totals.

16. An income statement reports a company's revenues and expenses along with the resulting net income or loss. A statement of retained earnings reports changes in retained earnings, including that from net income or loss. Both statements report transactions occurring over a period of time.

17. The balance sheet describes a company's financial position (assets, liabilities, and equity) at a point in time. The retained earnings amount in the balance sheet is obtained from the statement of retained earnings.

18. Revenues are inflows of assets in exchange for products or services provided to customers as part of the main operations of a business. Expenses are outflows or the using up of assets that result from providing products or services to customers.

19. Assets are the resources a business owns or controls that carry expected future benefits. Liabilities are the obligations of a business, representing the claims of others against the assets of a business. Equity reflects the owner's claims on the assets of the business after deducting liabilities.

Key Terms

Account (p. 53)

Account balance, or Balance (p. 60)

Balance column account (p. 60)

Chart of accounts (p. 56)

Compound journal entry (p. 63)

Credit (p. 57)

Creditors (p. 54)

Debit (p. 57)

Debt ratio (p. 71)

Dividends (p. 55)

Double-entry accounting (p. 57)

General journal (p. 58)

General ledger (p. 53)

Journal (p. 58)

Journalizing (p. 58)

Posting (p. 58)

Posting reference (PR) column (p. 60)

Source documents (p. 52)

T-accounts (p. 57)

Trial balance (p. 67)

Unearned revenue (p. 55)

Additional Quiz Questions are available at the book's Website.

1. Amalia Company received its utility bill for the current period of $700 and immediately paid it. Its journal entry to record this transaction includes a
   a. Credit to Utility Expense for $700.
   b. Debit to Utility Expense for $700.
   c. Debit to Accounts Payable for $700.
   d. Debit to Cash for $700.
   e. Credit to Common Stock for $700.

2. On May 1, Mattingly Lawn Service collected $2,500 cash from a customer in advance of five months of lawn service. Mattingly's journal entry to record this transaction includes a
   a. Credit to Unearned Lawn Service Fees for $2,500.
   b. Debit to Lawn Service Fees Earned for $2,500.
   c. Credit to Cash for $2,500.
   d. Debit to Unearned Lawn Service Fees for $2,500.
   e. Credit to Common Stock for $2,500.

3. Liang Shue contributed $250,000 cash and land worth $500,000 to open his new business, Shue Consulting Corporation. Which of the following journal entries does Shue Consulting make to record this transaction?

a. Cash Assets	750,000	
Common Stock		750,000
b. Common Stock	750,000	
Assets		750,000
c. Cash	250,000	
Land	500,000	
Common Stock		750,000
d. Common Stock	750,000	
Cash		250,000
Land		500,000

4. A trial balance prepared at year-end shows total credits exceed total debits by $765. This discrepancy could have been caused by
   a. An error in the general journal where a $765 increase in Accounts Payable was recorded as a $765 decrease in Accounts Payable.
   b. The ledger balance for Accounts Payable of $7,650 being entered in the trial balance as $765.
   c. A general journal error where a $765 increase in Accounts Receivable was recorded as a $765 increase in Cash.
   d. The ledger balance of $850 in Accounts Receivable was entered in the trial balance as $85.
   e. An error in recording a $765 increase in Cash as a credit.

5. Bonaventure Company has total assets of $1,000,000, liabilities of $400,000, and equity of $600,000. What is its debt ratio (rounded to a whole percent)?
   a. 250%
   b. 167%
   c. 67%
   d. 150%
   e. 40%

I Icon denotes assignments that involve decision making.

Discussion Questions

1. Provide the names of two (a) asset accounts, (b) liability accounts, and (c) equity accounts.
2. What is the difference between a note payable and an account payable?
3. **I** Discuss the steps in processing business transactions.
4. What kinds of transactions can be recorded in a general journal?
5. Are debits or credits typically listed first in general journal entries? Are the debits or the credits indented?
6. Should a transaction be recorded first in a journal or the ledger? Why?
7. If assets are valuable resources and asset accounts have debit balances, why do expense accounts also have debit balances?
8. **I** Why does the recordkeeper prepare a trial balance?
9. If an incorrect amount is journalized and posted to the accounts, how should the error be corrected?
10. Identify the four financial statements of a business.
11. **I** What information is reported in a balance sheet?
12. **I** What information is reported in an income statement?

13. **I** Why does the user of an income statement need to know the time period that it covers?
14. Define (a) assets, (b) liabilities, (c) equity, and (d) net assets.
15. Which financial statement is sometimes called the statement of financial position?
16. **I** Review the **Polaris** balance sheet in Appendix A. Identify three accounts on its balance sheet that carry debit balances and three accounts on its balance sheet that carry credit balances. **Polaris**
17. Review the **Arctic Cat** balance sheet in Appendix A. Identify an asset with the word receivable in its account title and a liability with the word payable in its account title. **Arctic Cat**
18. Locate **KTM**'s income statement in Appendix A. What is the title of its revenue account? **KTM**
19. Refer to **Piaggio**'s balance sheet in Appendix A. What does Piaggio title its current asset referring to merchandise available for sale? **PIAGGIO**

connect

Identify the items from the following list that are likely to serve as source documents.

a. Sales ticket	**d.** Telephone bill	**g.** Balance sheet
b. Income statement	**e.** Invoice from supplier	**h.** Prepaid insurance
c. Trial balance	**f.** Company revenue account	**i.** Bank statement

QUICK STUDY

QS 2-1
Identifying source documents
C1

Identify the financial statement(s) where each of the following items appears. Use I for income statement, E for statement of retained earnings, and B for balance sheet.

a. Office equipment	**d.** Prepaid insurance	**g.** Cash
b. Cash dividends	**e.** Office supplies	**h.** Unearned rent revenue
c. Revenue	**f.** Rent expense	**i.** Accounts payable

QS 2-2
Identifying financial statement items
C2 P3

Identify the normal balance (debit or credit) for each of the following accounts.

a. Office Supplies	**d.** Wages Expense	**g.** Wages Payable
b. Dividends	**e.** Accounts Receivable	**h.** Building
c. Fees Earned	**f.** Prepaid Rent	**i.** Common Stock

QS 2-3
Identifying normal balance
C4

Indicate whether a debit or credit *decreases* the normal balance of each of the following accounts.

a. Service Revenue	**e.** Common Stock	**i.** Dividends
b. Interest Payable	**f.** Prepaid Insurance	**j.** Unearned Revenue
c. Accounts Receivable	**g.** Buildings	**k.** Accounts Payable
d. Salaries Expense	**h.** Interest Revenue	**l.** Land

QS 2-4
Linking debit or credit with normal balance
C4

Identify whether a debit or credit yields the indicated change for each of the following accounts.

a. To increase Land	**f.** To decrease Prepaid Rent
b. To decrease Cash	**g.** To increase Notes Payable
c. To increase Office Expense	**h.** To decrease Accounts Receivable
d. To increase Fees Earned	**i.** To increase Common Stock
e. To decrease Unearned Revenue	**j.** To increase Store Equipment

QS 2-5
Analyzing debit or credit by account
A1

Prepare journal entries for each of the following selected transactions.

a. On May 15, DeShawn Tyler opens a landscaping company called Elegant Lawns by investing $70,000 cash along with equipment having a $30,000 value in exchange for common stock.

b. On May 21, Elegant Lawns purchases office supplies on credit for $280.

c. On May 25, Elegant Lawns receives $7,800 cash for performing landscaping services.

d. On May 30, Elegant Lawns receives $1,000 cash in advance of providing landscaping services to a customer.

QS 2-6
Preparing journal entries
P1

A trial balance has total debits of $20,000 and total credits of $24,500. Which one of the following errors would create this imbalance? Explain.

a. A $2,250 debit to Utilities Expense in a journal entry is incorrectly posted to the ledger as a $2,250 credit, leaving the Utilities Expense account with a $3,000 debit balance.

b. A $4,500 debit to Salaries Expense in a journal entry is incorrectly posted to the ledger as a $4,500 credit, leaving the Salaries Expense account with a $750 debit balance.

c. A $2,250 credit to Consulting Fees Earned in a journal entry is incorrectly posted to the ledger as a $2,250 debit, leaving the Consulting Fees Earned account with a $6,300 credit balance.

d. A $2,250 debit posting to Accounts Receivable was posted mistakenly to Land.

e. A $4,500 debit posting to Equipment was posted mistakenly to Cash.

f. An entry debiting Cash and crediting Accounts Payable for $4,500 was mistakenly not posted.

QS 2-7
Identifying a posting error
P2

QS 2-8

Classifying accounts in
financial statements

P3

Indicate the financial statement on which each of the following items appears. Use I for income statement,
E for statement of retained earnings, and B for balance sheet.

a. Services Revenue	**e.** Equipment	**i.** Dividends
b. Interest Payable	**f.** Prepaid Insurance	**j.** Office Supplies
c. Accounts Receivable	**g.** Buildings	**k.** Interest Expense
d. Salaries Expense	**h.** Rental Revenue	**l.** Insurance Expense

---

QS 2-9

International accounting
standards

C4

Answer each of the following questions related to international accounting standards.

a. What type of entry system is applied when accounting follows IFRS?

b. Identify the number and usual titles of the financial statements prepared under IFRS.

c. How do differences in accounting controls and enforcement impact accounting reports prepared across
different countries?

---

connect

EXERCISES

Exercise 2-1

Steps in analyzing and recording
transactions   **C1**

Order the following steps in the accounting process that focus on analyzing and recording transactions.

_____ **a.** Analyze each transaction from source documents.

_____ **b.** Prepare and analyze the trial balance.

_____ **c.** Record relevant transactions in a journal.

_____ **d.** Post journal information to ledger accounts.

Exercise 2-2

Identifying and classifying
accounts

C2

Enter the number for the item that best completes each of the descriptions below.

1. Asset   **3.** Account   **5.** Three

2. Equity   **4.** Liability

a. An _____ is a record of increases and decreases in a specific asset, liability, equity, revenue, or
expense item.

b. Accounts payable, unearned revenue, and note payable are examples of _____ accounts.

c. Accounts receivable, prepaid accounts, supplies, and land are examples of _____ accounts.

d. Accounts are arranged into _____ general categories.

e. Common stock and dividends are examples of _____ accounts.

Exercise 2-3

Identifying a ledger and chart
of accounts

C3

Enter the number for the item that best completes each of the descriptions below.

1. Chart   **2.** General ledger

a. The _____ is a record containing all accounts used by a company.

b. A _____ of accounts is a list of all accounts a company uses.

Exercise 2-4

Identifying type and normal
balances of accounts

C4

For each of the following (1) identify the type of account as an asset, liability, equity, revenue, or expense,
(2) identify the normal balance of the account, and (3) enter *debit* (*Dr.*) or *credit* (*Cr.*) to identify the kind of
entry that would increase the account balance.

a. Cash	**e.** Accounts Receivable	**i.** Fees Earned
b. Legal Expense	**f.** Dividends	**j.** Equipment
c. Prepaid Insurance	**g.** License Fee Revenue	**k.** Notes Payable
d. Land	**h.** Unearned Revenue	**l.** Common Stock

Exercise 2-5

Analyzing account entries
and balances

A1

Use the information in each of the following separate cases to calculate the unknown amount.

a. Corentine Co. had $152,000 of accounts payable on September 30 and $132,500 on October 31. Total
purchases on account during October were $281,000. Determine how much cash was paid on accounts
payable during October.

b. On September 30, Valerian Co. had a $102,500 balance in Accounts Receivable. During October, the
company collected $102,890 from its credit customers. The October 31 balance in Accounts Receivable was $89,000. Determine the amount of sales on account that occurred in October.

c. During October, Alameda Company had $102,500 of cash receipts and $103,150 of cash disbursements. The October 31 Cash balance was $18,600. Determine how much cash the company had at the
close of business on September 30.

Groro Co. bills a client $62,000 for services provided and agrees to accept the following three items in full payment: (1) $10,000 cash, (2) computer equipment worth $80,000, and (3) to assume responsibility for a $28,000 note payable related to the computer equipment. The entry Groro makes to record this transaction includes which one or more of the following?

a. $28,000 increase in a liability account

b. $10,000 increase in the Cash account

c. $10,000 increase in a revenue account

d. $62,000 increase in an asset account

e. $62,000 increase in a revenue account

f. $62,000 increase in an equity account

Exercise 2-6
Analyzing effects of transactions on accounts
A1

Prepare general journal entries for the following transactions of a new company called Pose-for-Pics.

Aug. 1   Madison Harris, the owner, invested $6,500 cash and $33,500 of photography equipment in the company in exchange for common stock.
    2   The company paid $2,100 cash for an insurance policy covering the next 24 months.
    5   The company purchased office supplies for $880 cash.
    20   The company received $3,331 cash in photography fees earned.
    31   The company paid $675 cash for August utilities.

Exercise 2-7
Preparing general journal entries
P1

Use the information in Exercise 2-7 to prepare an August 31 trial balance for Pose-for-Pics. Begin by opening these T-accounts: Cash; Office Supplies; Prepaid Insurance; Photography Equipment; Common Stock; Photography Fees Earned; and Utilities Expense. Then, post the general journal entries to these T-accounts (which will serve as the ledger), and prepare the trial balance.

Exercise 2-8
Preparing T-accounts (ledger) and a trial balance   P2

Prepare general journal entries to record the transactions below for Spade Company by using the following accounts: Cash; Accounts Receivable; Office Supplies; Office Equipment; Accounts Payable; Common Stock; Dividends; Fees Earned; and Rent Expense. Use the letters beside each transaction to identify entries. After recording the transactions, post them to T-accounts, which serves as the general ledger for this assignment. Determine the ending balance of each T-account.

a. Kacy Spade, owner, invested $100,750 cash in the company in exchange for common stock.

b. The company purchased office supplies for $1,250 cash.

c. The company purchased $10,050 of office equipment on credit.

d. The company received $15,500 cash as fees for services provided to a customer.

e. The company paid $10,050 cash to settle the payable for the office equipment purchased in transaction c.

f. The company billed a customer $2,700 as fees for services provided.

g. The company paid $1,225 cash for the monthly rent.

h. The company collected $1,125 cash as partial payment for the account receivable created in transaction f.

i. The company paid $10,000 cash in dividends to Spade (sole shareholder).

Exercise 2-9
Recording effects of transactions in T-accounts
A1

Check   Cash ending balance, $94,850

After recording the transactions of Exercise 2-9 in T-accounts and calculating the balance of each account, prepare a trial balance. Use May 31, 2013, as its report date.

Exercise 2-10
Preparing a trial balance   P2

Examine the following transactions and identify those that create revenues for Valdez Services, a company owned by Brina Valdez. Prepare general journal entries to record those revenue transactions and explain why the other transactions did not create revenues.

a. Brina Valdez invests $39,350 cash in the company in exchange for common stock.

b. The company provided $2,300 of services on credit.

c. The company provided services to a client and immediately received $875 cash.

d. The company received $10,200 cash from a client in payment for services to be provided next year.

e. The company received $3,500 cash from a client in partial payment of an account receivable.

f. The company borrowed $120,000 cash from the bank by signing a promissory note.

Exercise 2-11
Analyzing and journalizing revenue transactions
A1 P1

Exercise 2-12

Analyzing and journalizing
expense transactions

A1 P1

Examine the following transactions and identify those that create expenses for Valdez Services. Prepare general journal entries to record those expense transactions and explain why the other transactions did not create expenses.

  a. The company paid $12,200 cash for payment on a 16-month old liability for office supplies.

  b. The company paid $1,233 cash for the just completed two-week salary of the receptionist.

  c. The company paid $39,200 cash for equipment purchased.

  d. The company paid $870 cash for this month's utilities.

  e. The company paid $4,500 cash in dividends.

Exercise 2-13

Preparing an income
statement

C3 P3

Carmen Camry operates a consulting firm called Help Today, which began operations on August 1. On August 31, the company's records show the following accounts and amounts for the month of August. Use this information to prepare an August income statement for the business.

Cash	$ 25,360	Dividends	$ 6,000
Accounts receivable	22,360	Consulting fees earned	27,000
Office supplies	5,250	Rent expense	9,550
Land	44,000	Salaries expense.	5,600
Office equipment	20,000	Telephone expense	860
Accounts payable	10,500	Miscellaneous expenses.	520
Common stock	102,000		

Check   Net income, $10,470

Exercise 2-14

Preparing a statement
of retained earnings   P3

Use the information in Exercise 2-13 to prepare an August statement of retained earnings for Help Today. (The owner invested a total of $102,000 in the company in exchange for common stock on August 1.)

Exercise 2-15

Preparing a balance sheet   P3

Use the information in Exercise 2-13 (if completed, you can also use your solution to Exercise 2-14) to prepare an August 31 balance sheet for Help Today.

Exercise 2-16

Computing net income

A1

A corporation had the following assets and liabilities at the beginning and end of this year.

	Assets	Liabilities
Beginning of the year	$ 60,000	$20,000
End of the year	105,000	36,000

Determine the net income earned or net loss incurred by the business during the year for each of the following *separate* cases:

  a. Owner made no investments in the business and no dividends were paid during the year.

  b. Owner made no investments in the business but dividends were $1,250 cash per month.

  c. No dividends were paid during the year but the owner did invest an additional $55,000 cash in exchange for common stock.

  d. Dividends were $1,250 cash per month and the owner invested an additional $35,000 cash in exchange for common stock.

Exercise 2-17

Analyzing changes in a
company's equity

P3

Compute the missing amount for each of the following separate companies *a* through *d*.

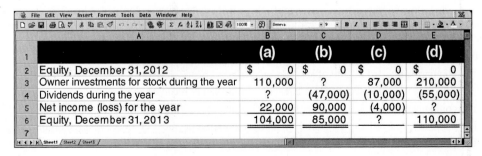

	A	(a)	(b)	(c)	(d)
1					
2	Equity, December 31, 2012	$ 0	$ 0	$ 0	$ 0
3	Owner investments for stock during the year	110,000	?	87,000	210,000
4	Dividends during the year	?	(47,000)	(10,000)	(55,000)
5	Net income (loss) for the year	22,000	90,000	(4,000)	?
6	Equity, December 31, 2013	104,000	85,000	?	110,000
7					

Business transactions completed by Hannah Venedict during the month of September are as follows.

a. Venedict invested $60,000 cash along with office equipment valued at $25,000 in exchange for common stock of a new company named HV Consulting.

b. The company purchased land valued at $40,000 and a building valued at $160,000. The purchase is paid with $30,000 cash and a long-term note payable for $170,000.

c. The company purchased $2,000 of office supplies on credit.

d. Venedict invested her personal automobile in the company in exchange for more common stock. The automobile has a value of $16,500 and is to be used exclusively in the business.

e. The company purchased $5,600 of additional office equipment on credit.

f. The company paid $1,800 cash salary to an assistant.

g. The company provided services to a client and collected $8,000 cash.

h. The company paid $635 cash for this month's utilities.

i. The company paid $2,000 cash to settle the account payable created in transaction *c*.

j. The company purchased $20,300 of new office equipment by paying $20,300 cash.

k. The company completed $6,250 of services for a client, who must pay within 30 days.

l. The company paid $1,800 cash salary to an assistant.

m. The company received $4,000 cash in partial payment on the receivable created in transaction *k*.

n. The company paid $2,800 cash in dividends.

Required

1. Prepare general journal entries to record these transactions (use account titles listed in part 2).

2. Open the following ledger accounts—their account numbers are in parentheses (use the balance column format): Cash (101); Accounts Receivable (106); Office Supplies (108); Office Equipment (163); Automobiles (164); Building (170); Land (172); Accounts Payable (201); Notes Payable (250); Common Stock (307); Dividends (319); Fees Earned (402); Salaries Expense (601); and Utilities Expense (602). Post the journal entries from part 1 to the ledger accounts and enter the balance after each posting.

3. Prepare a trial balance as of the end of September.

Problem 2-6A
Recording transactions; posting to ledger; preparing a trial balance
C3 A1 P1 P2

Check (2) Ending balances: Cash, $12,665; Office Equipment, $50,900

(3) Trial balance totals, $291,350

At the beginning of April, Bernadette Grechus launched a custom computer solutions company called Softworks. The company had the following transactions during April.

a. Bernadette Grechus invested $65,000 cash, office equipment with a value of $5,750, and $30,000 of computer equipment in the company in exchange for common stock.

b. The company purchased land worth $22,000 for an office by paying $5,000 cash and signing a long-term note payable for $17,000.

c. The company purchased a portable building with $34,500 cash and moved it onto the land acquired in *b*.

d. The company paid $5,000 cash for the premium on a two-year insurance policy.

e. The company provided services to a client and immediately collected $4,600 cash.

f. The company purchased $4,500 of additional computer equipment by paying $800 cash and signing a long-term note payable for $3,700.

g. The company completed $4,250 of services for a client. This amount is to be received within 30 days.

h. The company purchased $950 of additional office equipment on credit.

i. The company completed client services for $10,200 on credit.

j. The company received a bill for rent of a computer testing device that was used on a recently completed job. The $580 rent cost must be paid within 30 days.

k. The company collected $5,100 cash in partial payment from the client described in transaction *i*.

l. The company paid $1,800 cash for wages to an assistant.

m. The company paid $950 cash to settle the payable created in transaction *h*.

n. The company paid $608 cash for minor maintenance of the company's computer equipment.

o. The company paid $6,230 cash in dividends.

p. The company paid $1,800 cash for wages to an assistant.

q. The company paid $750 cash for advertisements on the Web during April.

PROBLEM SET B

Problem 2-1B
Preparing and posting journal entries; preparing a trial balance
C3 C4 A1 P1 P2

Required

1. Prepare general journal entries to record these transactions (use account titles listed in part 2).

2. Open the following ledger accounts—their account numbers are in parentheses (use the balance column format): Cash (101); Accounts Receivable (106); Prepaid Insurance (108); Office Equipment (163); Computer Equipment (164); Building (170); Land (172); Accounts Payable (201); Notes Payable (250); Common Stock (307); Dividends (319); Fees Earned (402); Wages Expense (601); Computer Rental Expense (602); Advertising Expense (603); and Repairs Expense (604). Post the journal entries from part 1 to the accounts and enter the balance after each posting.

3. Prepare a trial balance as of the end of April.

Check   (2) Ending balances: Cash, $17,262; Accounts Receivable, $9,350; Accounts Payable, $580

(3) Trial balance totals, $141,080

Problem 2-2B
Preparing and posting journal entries; preparing a trial balance
C3 C4 A1 P1 P2

Zucker Management Services opens for business and completes these transactions in November.

Nov. 1 Matt Zucker, the owner, invested $30,000 cash along with $15,000 of office equipment in the company in exchange for common stock.
  2 The company prepaid $4,500 cash for six months' rent for an office. (*Hint:* Debit Prepaid Rent for $4,500.)
  4 The company made credit purchases of office equipment for $2,500 and of office supplies for $600. Payment is due within 10 days.
  8 The company completed work for a client and immediately received $3,400 cash.
  12 The company completed a $10,200 project for a client, who must pay within 30 days.
  13 The company paid $3,100 cash to settle the payable created on November 4.
  19 The company paid $1,800 cash for the premium on a 24-month insurance policy.
  22 The company received $5,200 cash as partial payment for the work completed on November 12.
  24 The company completed work for another client for $1,750 on credit.
  28 The company paid $5,300 cash in dividends.
  29 The company purchased $249 of additional office supplies on credit.
  30 The company paid $831 cash for this month's utility bill.

Required

1. Prepare general journal entries to record these transactions (use account titles listed in part 2).

2. Open the following ledger accounts—their account numbers are in parentheses (use the balance column format): Cash (101); Accounts Receivable (106); Office Supplies (124); Prepaid Insurance (128); Prepaid Rent (131); Office Equipment (163); Accounts Payable (201); Common Stock (307); Dividends (319); Services Revenue (403); and Utilities Expense (690). Post the journal entries from part 1 to the ledger accounts and enter the balance after each posting.

3. Prepare a trial balance as of the end of November.

Check   (2) Ending balances: Cash, $23,069; Accounts Receivable, $6,750; Accounts Payable, $249

(3) Total debits, $60,599

Problem 2-3B
Preparing and posting journal entries; preparing a trial balance
C3 C4 A1 P1 P2

Humble Management Services opens for business and completes these transactions in September.

Sept. 1 Henry Humble, the owner, invests $38,000 cash along with office equipment valued at $15,000 in the company in exchange for common stock.
  2 The company prepaid $9,000 cash for 12 months' rent for office space. (*Hint:* Debit Prepaid Rent for $9,000.)
  4 The company made credit purchases for $8,000 in office equipment and $2,400 in office supplies. Payment is due within 10 days.
  8 The company completed work for a client and immediately received $3,280 cash.
  12 The company completed a $15,400 project for a client, who must pay within 30 days.
  13 The company paid $10,400 cash to settle the payable created on September 4.
  19 The company paid $1,900 cash for the premium on an 18-month insurance policy. (*Hint:* Debit Prepaid Insurance for $1,900.)

22 The company received $7,700 cash as partial payment for the work completed on September 12.

24 The company completed work for another client for $2,100 on credit.

28 The company paid $5,300 cash in dividends.

29 The company purchased $550 of additional office supplies on credit.

30 The company paid $860 cash for this month's utility bill.

Required

1. Prepare general journal entries to record these transactions (use account titles listed in part 2).

2. Open the following ledger accounts—their account numbers are in parentheses (use the balance column format): Cash (101); Accounts Receivable (106); Office Supplies (124); Prepaid Insurance (128); Prepaid Rent (131); Office Equipment (163); Accounts Payable (201); Common Stock (307); Dividends (319); Service Fees Earned (401); and Utilities Expense (690). Post journal entries from part 1 to the ledger accounts and enter the balance after each posting.

3. Prepare a trial balance as of the end of September.

Check (2) Ending balances: Cash, $21,520; Accounts Receivable, $9,800; Accounts Payable, $550

(3) Total debits, $74,330

The accounting records of Tama Co. show the following assets and liabilities as of December 31, 2012 and 2013.

Problem 2-4B
Computing net income from equity analysis, preparing a balance sheet, and computing the debt ratio

C2 A1 A2 P3

December 31	2012	2013
Cash	$20,000	$ 5,000
Accounts receivable	35,000	25,000
Office supplies	8,000	13,500
Office equipment	40,000	40,000
Machinery	28,500	28,500
Building	0	250,000
Land	0	50,000
Accounts payable	4,000	12,000
Note payable	0	250,000

Late in December 2013, the business purchased a small office building and land for $300,000. It paid $50,000 cash toward the purchase and a $250,000 note payable was signed for the balance. Joe Tama, the owner, had to invest an additional $15,000 cash (in exchange for common stock) to enable it to pay the $50,000 cash toward the purchase. The business also pays $250 cash per month for dividends.

Required

1. Prepare balance sheets for the business as of December 31, 2012 and 2013. (*Hint:* Report only total equity on the balance sheet and remember that total equity equals the difference between assets and liabilities.)

2. By comparing equity amounts from the balance sheets and using the additional information presented in the problem, prepare a calculation to show how much net income was earned by the business during 2013.

3. Calculate the December 31, 2013, debt ratio (in percent and rounded to one decimal).

Check (2) Net income, $10,500

(3) Debt ratio, 63.6%

Roshaun Gould started a Web consulting firm called Gould Solutions. He began operations and completed seven transactions in April that resulted in the following accounts, which all have normal balances.

Problem 2-5B
Analyzing account balances and reconstructing transactions

C1 C3 A1 P2

Cash	$19,982
Office supplies	760
Prepaid rent	1,800
Office equipment	12,250
Accounts payable	12,250
Common stock	15,000
Dividends...................	5,200
Consulting fees earned	20,400
Operating expenses	7,658

Required

Check (1) Trial balance total, $47,650

1. Prepare a trial balance for this business as of the end of April.

Analysis Component

2. Analyze the accounts and their balances and prepare a list that describes each of the seven most likely transactions and their amounts.

(3) Cash paid, $15,418

3. Prepare a report of cash received and cash paid showing how the seven transactions in part 2 yield the $19,982 ending Cash balance.

Problem 2-6B

Recording transactions; posting to ledger; preparing a trial balance

C3 A1 P1 P2

Nuncio Consulting completed the following transactions during June.

a. Armand Nuncio, the owner, invested $35,000 cash along with office equipment valued at $11,000 in the new company in exchange for common stock.

b. The company purchased land valued at $7,500 and a building valued at $40,000. The purchase is paid with $15,000 cash and a long-term note payable for $32,500.

c. The company purchased $500 of office supplies on credit.

d. A. Nuncio invested his personal automobile in the company in exchange for more common stock. The automobile has a value of $8,000 and is to be used exclusively in the business.

e. The company purchased $1,200 of additional office equipment on credit.

f. The company paid $1,000 cash salary to an assistant.

g. The company provided services to a client and collected $3,200 cash.

h. The company paid $540 cash for this month's utilities.

i. The company paid $500 cash to settle the payable created in transaction *c*.

j. The company purchased $3,400 of new office equipment by paying $3,400 cash.

k. The company completed $4,200 of services for a client, who must pay within 30 days.

l. The company paid $1,000 cash salary to an assistant.

m. The company received $2,200 cash in partial payment on the receivable created in transaction *k*.

n. The company paid $1,100 cash in dividends.

Required

1. Prepare general journal entries to record these transactions (use account titles listed in part 2).

Check (2) Ending balances: Cash, $17,860; Office Equipment, $15,600

2. Open the following ledger accounts—their account numbers are in parentheses (use the balance column format): Cash (101); Accounts Receivable (106); Office Supplies (108); Office Equipment (163); Automobiles (164); Building (170); Land (172); Accounts Payable (201); Notes Payable (250); Common Stock (307); Dividends (319); Fees Earned (402); Salaries Expense (601); and Utilities Expense (602). Post the journal entries from part 1 to the ledger accounts and enter the balance after each posting.

(3) Trial balance totals, $95,100

3. Prepare a trial balance as of the end of June.

SERIAL PROBLEM

Success Systems

A1 P1 P2

(This serial problem started in Chapter 1 and continues through most of the chapters. If the Chapter 1 segment was not completed, the problem can begin at this point. It is helpful, but not necessary, to use the Working Papers that accompany this book.)

SP 2   On October 1, 2013, Adria Lopez launched a computer services company called **Success Systems,** which provides consulting services, computer system installations, and custom program development. Adria adopts the calendar year for reporting purposes and expects to prepare the company's first set of financial statements on December 31, 2013. The company's initial chart of accounts follows.

Sage 50

Account	No.	Account	No.
Cash...................	101	Common Stock...................	307
Accounts Receivable.........	106	Dividends..........................	319
Computer Supplies..........	126	Computer Services Revenue.........	403
Prepaid Insurance...........	128	Wages Expense...................	623
Prepaid Rent...............	131	Advertising Expense...............	655
Office Equipment...........	163	Mileage Expense...................	676
Computer Equipment........	167	Miscellaneous Expenses.............	677
Accounts Payable..........	201	Repairs Expense—Computer........	684

Required

1. Prepare journal entries to record each of the following transactions for Success Systems.

Oct.   1   Adria Lopez invested $55,000 cash, a $20,000 computer system, and $8,000 of office equip-ment in the company in exchange for its common stock.

      2   The company paid $3,300 cash for four months' rent. (*Hint:* Debit Prepaid Rent for $3,300.)

      3   The company purchased $1,420 of computer supplies on credit from Harris Office Products.

      5   The company paid $2,220 cash for one year's premium on a property and liability insurance policy. (*Hint:* Debit Prepaid Insurance for $2,220.)

      6   The company billed Easy Leasing $4,800 for services performed in installing a new Web server.

      8   The company paid $1,420 cash for the computer supplies purchased from Harris Office Prod-ucts on October 3.

    10   The company hired Lyn Addie as a part-time assistant for $125 per day, as needed.

    12   The company billed Easy Leasing another $1,400 for services performed.

    15   The company received $4,800 cash from Easy Leasing as partial payment on its account.

    17   The company paid $805 cash to repair computer equipment that was damaged when mov-ing it.

    20   The company paid $1,940 cash for advertisements published in the local newspaper.

    22   The company received $1,400 cash from Easy Leasing on its account.

    28   The company billed IFM Company $5,208 for services performed.

    31   The company paid $875 cash for Lyn Addie's wages for seven days' work.

    31   The company paid $3,600 cash in dividends.

Nov.   1   The company reimbursed Adria Lopez in cash for business automobile mileage allowance (Lopez logged 1,000 miles at $0.32 per mile).

      2   The company received $4,633 cash from Liu Corporation for computer services performed.

      5   The company purchased computer supplies for $1,125 cash from Harris Office Products.

      8   The company billed Gomez Co. $5,668 for services performed.

    13   The company received notification from Alex's Engineering Co. that Success Systems' bid of $3,950 for an upcoming project is accepted.

    18   The company received $2,208 cash from IFM Company as partial payment of the October 28 bill.

    22   The company donated $250 cash to the United Way in the company's name.

    24   The company completed work for Alex's Engineering Co. and sent it a bill for $3,950.

    25   The company sent another bill to IFM Company for the past-due amount of $3,000.

    28   The company reimbursed Adria Lopez in cash for business automobile mileage (1,200 miles at $0.32 per mile).

    30   The company paid $1,750 cash for Lyn Addie's wages for 14 days' work.

    30   The company paid $2,000 cash in dividends.

2. Open ledger accounts (in balance column format) and post the journal entries from part 1 to them.

3. Prepare a trial balance as of the end of November.

Check   (2) Cash, Nov. 30 bal., $48,052

          (3) Trial bal. totals, $108,659

Beyond the Numbers

REPORTING IN ACTION

A1 A2

Polaris

BTN 2-1   Refer to Polaris's financial statements in Appendix A for the following questions.

Required

1. What amount of total liabilities does it report for each of the fiscal years ended December 31, 2011 and 2010?
2. What amount of total assets does it report for each of the fiscal years ended December 31, 2011 and 2010?
3. Compute its debt ratio for each of the fiscal years ended December 31, 2011 and 2010. (Report ratio in percent and round it to one decimal.)
4. In which fiscal year did it employ more financial leverage (December 31, 2011 or 2010)? Explain.

Fast Forward

5. Access its financial statements (10-K report) for a fiscal year ending after December 31, 2011, from its Website (Polaris.com) or the SEC's EDGAR database (www.SEC.gov). Recompute its debt ratio for any subsequent year's data and compare it with the debt ratio for 2010 and 2011.

COMPARATIVE ANALYSIS

A1 A2

Polaris

Arctic Cat

BTN 2-2   Key comparative figures for Polaris and Arctic Cat follow.

($ thousands)	Polaris		Arctic Cat	
	Current Year	Prior Year	Current Year	Prior Year
Total liabilities	$ 727,968	$ 690,656	$ 89,870	$ 78,745
Total assets	1,228,024	1,061,647	272,906	246,084

1. What is the debt ratio for Polaris in the current year and for the prior year?
2. What is the debt ratio for Arctic Cat in the current year and for the prior year?
3. Which of the two companies has the higher degree of financial leverage? What does this imply?

ETHICS CHALLENGE

C1 ◢

BTN 2-3   Review the *Decision Ethics* case from the first part of this chapter involving the cashier. The guidance answer suggests that you should not comply with the assistant manager's request.

Required

Propose and evaluate two other courses of action you might consider, and explain why.

COMMUNICATING IN PRACTICE

C1 C2 A1 P3

BTN 2-4   Lila Corentine is an aspiring entrepreneur and your friend. She is having difficulty understanding the purposes of financial statements and how they fit together across time.

Required

Write a one-page memorandum to Corentine explaining the purposes of the four financial statements and how they are linked across time.

BTN 2-5 Access EDGAR online (www.sec.gov) and locate the 2011 year 10-K report of Amazon.com (ticker AMZN) filed on February 1, 2012. Review its financial statements reported for years ended 2011, 2010, and 2009 to answer the following questions.

TAKING IT TO THE NET

A1

Required

1. What are the amounts of its net income or net loss reported for each of these three years?
2. Does Amazon's operating activities provide cash or use cash for each of these three years?
3. If Amazon has a 2011 net income of more than $600 million and 2011 operating cash flows of nearly $4,000 million, how is it possible that its cash balance at December 31, 2011, increases by less than $1,500 million relative to its balance at December 31, 2010?

BTN 2-6 The expanded accounting equation consists of assets, liabilities, common stock, dividends, revenues, and expenses. It can be used to reveal insights into changes in a company's financial position.

TEAMWORK IN ACTION

C1 C2 C4 A1

Required

1. Form *learning teams* of six (or more) members. Each team member must select one of the six components and each team must have at least one expert on each component: (*a*) assets, (*b*) liabilities, (*c*) common stock, (*d*) dividends, (*e*) revenues, and (*f*) expenses.
2. Form *expert teams* of individuals who selected the same component in part 1. Expert teams are to draft a report that each expert will present to his or her learning team addressing the following:
   a. Identify for its component the (i) increase and decrease side of the account and (ii) normal balance side of the account.
   b. Describe a transaction, with amounts, that increases its component.
   c. Using the transaction and amounts in (*b*), verify the equality of the accounting equation and then explain any effects on the income statement and statement of cash flows.
   d. Describe a transaction, with amounts, that decreases its component.
   e. Using the transaction and amounts in (*d*), verify the equality of the accounting equation and then explain any effects on the income statement and statement of cash flows.
3. Each expert should return to his/her learning team. In rotation, each member presents his/her expert team's report to the learning team. Team discussion is encouraged.

BTN 2-7 Assume Misa Chien and Jennifer Green of Nom Nom Truck plan on expanding their business to accommodate more product lines. They are considering financing their expansion in one of two ways: (1) contributing more of their own funds to the business or (2) borrowing the funds from a bank.

ENTREPRENEURIAL DECISION

A1 A2 P3

Required

Identify at least two issues that Misa and Jennifer should consider when trying to decide on the method for financing their expansion.

ENTREPRENEURIAL DECISION

A1 A2 P3

BTN 2-8 Angel Martin is a young entrepreneur who operates Martin Music Services, offering singing lessons and instruction on musical instruments. Martin wishes to expand but needs a $30,000 loan. The bank requests Martin to prepare a balance sheet and key financial ratios. Martin has not kept formal records but is able to provide the following accounts and their amounts as of December 31, 2013.

Cash	$ 3,600	Accounts Receivable	$ 9,600	Prepaid Insurance	$ 1,500
Prepaid Rent	9,400	Store Supplies	6,600	Equipment	50,000
Accounts Payable	2,200	Unearned Lesson Fees ...	15,600	Total Equity*	62,900
Annual net income ...	40,000				

* The total equity amount reflects all owner investments, dividends, revenues, and expenses as of December 31, 2013.

Required

1. Prepare a balance sheet as of December 31, 2013, for Martin Music Services. (Report only the total equity amount on the balance sheet.)
2. Compute Martin's debt ratio and its return on assets (the latter ratio is defined in Chapter 1). Assume average assets equal its ending balance.
3. Do you believe the prospects of a $30,000 bank loan are good? Why or why not?

HITTING THE ROAD

C1

BTN 2-9 Obtain a recent copy of the most prominent newspaper distributed in your area. Research the classified section and prepare a report answering the following questions (attach relevant classified clippings to your report). Alternatively, you may want to search the Web for the required information. One suitable Website is **CareerOneStop** (<u>www.CareerOneStop.org</u>). For documentation, you should print copies of Websites accessed.

1. Identify the number of listings for accounting positions and the various accounting job titles.
2. Identify the number of listings for other job titles, with examples, that require or prefer accounting knowledge/experience but are not specifically accounting positions.
3. Specify the salary range for the accounting and accounting-related positions if provided.
4. Indicate the job that appeals to you, the reason for its appeal, and its requirements.

GLOBAL DECISION

A2

KTM

Polaris

Arctic Cat

BTN 2-10 KTM (www.KTM.com) is a leading manufacturer of offroad and street motorcycles, and it competes to some extent with both **Polaris** and **Arctic Cat**. Key financial ratios for the current fiscal year follow.

Key Figure	KTM	Polaris	Arctic Cat
Return on assets	4.3%	18.5%	4.8%
Debt ratio	54.8%	59.3%	32.9%

Required

1. Which company is most profitable according to its return on assets?
2. Which company is most risky according to the debt ratio?
3. Which company deserves increased investment based on a joint analysis of return on assets and the debt ratio? Explain.

EXHIBIT 3.17

General Ledger after the Closing Process for FastForward

Asset Accounts

Cash — Acct. No. 101

Date	Explan.	PR	Debit	Credit	Balance
2013					
Dec. 1	(1)	G1	30,000		30,000
2	(2)	G1		2,500	27,500
3	(3)	G1		26,000	1,500
5	(5)	G1	4,200		5,700
6	(13)	G1		2,400	3,300
12	(6)	G1		1,000	2,300
12	(7)	G1		700	1,600
22	(9)	G1	1,900		3,500
24	(10)	G1		900	2,600
24	(11)	G1		200	2,400
26	(12)	G1	3,000		5,400
26	(14)	G1		120	5,280
26	(15)	G1		230	5,050
26	(16)	G1		700	4,350

Accounts Receivable — Acct. No. 106

Date	Explan.	PR	Debit	Credit	Balance
2013					
Dec. 12	(8)	G1	1,900		1,900
22	(9)	G1		1,900	0
31	Adj.(f)	G1	1,800		1,800

Supplies — Acct. No. 126

Date	Explan.	PR	Debit	Credit	Balance
2013					
Dec. 2	(2)	G1	2,500		2,500
6	(4)	G1	7,100		9,600
26	(14)	G1	120		9,720
31	Adj.(b)	G1		1,050	8,670

Prepaid Insurance — Acct. No. 128

Date	Explan.	PR	Debit	Credit	Balance
2013					
Dec. 6	(13)	G1	2,400		2,400
31	Adj.(a)	G1		100	2,300

Equipment — Acct. No. 167

Date	Explan.	PR	Debit	Credit	Balance
2013					
Dec. 3	(3)	G1	26,000		26,000

Accumulated Depreciation— Equipment — Acct. No. 168

Date	Explan.	PR	Debit	Credit	Balance
2013					
Dec. 31	Adj.(c)	G1		375	375

Liability and Equity Accounts

Accounts Payable — Acct. No. 201

Date	Explan.	PR	Debit	Credit	Balance
2013					
Dec. 6	(4)	G1		7,100	7,100
24	(10)	G1	900		6,200

Salaries Payable — Acct. No. 209

Date	Explan.	PR	Debit	Credit	Balance
2013					
Dec. 31	Adj.(e)	G1		210	210

Unearned Consulting Revenue — Acct. No. 236

Date	Explan.	PR	Debit	Credit	Balance
2013					
Dec. 26	(12)	G1		3,000	3,000
31	Adj.(d)	G1	250		2,750

Common Stock — Acct. No. 307

Date	Explan.	PR	Debit	Credit	Balance
2013					
Dec. 1	(1)	G1		30,000	30,000

Retained Earnings — Acct. No. 318

Date	Explan.	PR	Debit	Credit	Balance
2013					
Dec. 31	Clos.(3)	G1		3,785	3,785
31	Clos.(4)	G1	200		3,585

Dividends — Acct. No. 319

Date	Explan.	PR	Debit	Credit	Balance
2013					
Dec. 24	(11)	G1	200		200
31	Clos.(4)	G1		200	0

Revenue and Expense Accounts (Including Income Summary)

Consulting Revenue — Acct. No. 403

Date	Explan.	PR	Debit	Credit	Balance
2013					
Dec. 5	(5)	G1		4,200	4,200
12	(8)	G1		1,600	5,800
31	Adj.(d)	G1		250	6,050
31	Adj.(f)	G1		1,800	7,850
31	Clos.(1)	G1	7,850		0

Rental Revenue — Acct. No. 406

Date	Explan.	PR	Debit	Credit	Balance
2013					
Dec. 12	(8)	G1		300	300
31	Clos.(1)	G1	300		0

Depreciation Expense— Equipment — Acct. No. 612

Date	Explan.	PR	Debit	Credit	Balance
2013					
Dec. 31	Adj.(c)	G1	375		375
31	Clos.(2)	G1		375	0

Salaries Expense — Acct. No. 622

Date	Explan.	PR	Debit	Credit	Balance
2013					
Dec. 12	(7)	G1	700		700
26	(16)	G1	700		1,400
31	Adj.(e)	G1	210		1,610
31	Clos.(2)	G1		1,610	0

Insurance Expense — Acct. No. 637

Date	Explan.	PR	Debit	Credit	Balance
2013					
Dec. 31	Adj.(a)	G1	100		100
31	Clos.(2)	G1		100	0

Rent Expense — Acct. No. 640

Date	Explan.	PR	Debit	Credit	Balance
2013					
Dec. 12	(6)	G1	1,000		1,000
31	Clos.(2)	G1		1,000	0

Supplies Expense — Acct. No. 652

Date	Explan.	PR	Debit	Credit	Balance
2013					
Dec. 31	Adj.(b)	G1	1,050		1,050
31	Clos.(2)	G1		1,050	0

Utilities Expense — Acct. No. 690

Date	Explan.	PR	Debit	Credit	Balance
2013					
Dec. 26	(15)	G1	230		230
31	Clos.(2)	G1		230	0

Income Summary — Acct. No. 901

Date	Explan.	PR	Debit	Credit	Balance
2013					
Dec. 31	Clos.(1)	G1		8,150	8,150
31	Clos.(2)	G1	4,365		3,785
31	Clos.(3)	G1	3,785		0

(1) total debits equal total credits for permanent accounts and (2) all temporary accounts have zero balances. FastForward's post-closing trial balance is shown in Exhibit 3.18. The post-closing trial balance usually is the last step in the accounting process.

EXHIBIT 3.18

Post-Closing Trial Balance

FASTFORWARD **Post-Closing Trial Balance** **December 31, 2013**		
	Debit	**Credit**
Cash	$ 4,350	
Accounts receivable	1,800	
Supplies	8,670	
Prepaid insurance	2,300	
Equipment	26,000	
Accumulated depreciation—Equipment		$ 375
Accounts payable		6,200
Salaries payable		210
Unearned consulting revenue		2,750
Common stock		30,000
Retained earnings.		3,585
Totals	$43,120	$43,120

Accounting Cycle

C3 Identify steps in the accounting cycle.

The term **accounting cycle** refers to the steps in preparing financial statements. It is called a *cycle* because the steps are repeated each reporting period. Exhibit 3.19 shows the 10 steps in the cycle, beginning with analyzing transactions and ending with a post-closing trial balance or

EXHIBIT 3.19

Steps in the Accounting Cycle*

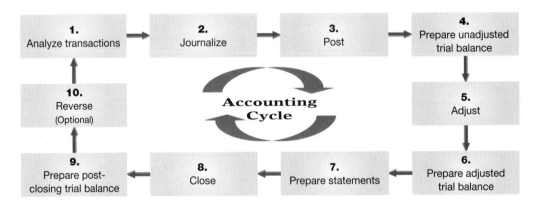

Explanations

1. Analyze transactions	Analyze transactions to prepare for journalizing.
2. Journalize	Record accounts, including debits and credits, in a journal.
3. Post	Transfer debits and credits from the journal to the ledger.
4. Prepare unadjusted trial balance	Summarize unadjusted ledger accounts and amounts.
5. Adjust	Record adjustments to bring account balances up to date; journalize and post adjustments.
6. Prepare adjusted trial balance	Summarize adjusted ledger accounts and amounts.
7. Prepare statements	Use adjusted trial balance to prepare financial statements.
8. Close	Journalize and post entries to close temporary accounts.
9. Prepare post-closing trial balance	Test clerical accuracy of the closing procedures.
10. Reverse (optional)	Reverse certain adjustments in the next period—optional step; see Appendix 3C.

* Steps 4, 6, and 9 can be done on a work sheet. A work sheet is useful in planning adjustments, but adjustments (step 5) must always be journalized and posted. Steps 3, 4, 6, and 9 are automatic with a computerized system.

reversing entries. Steps 1 through 3 usually occur regularly as a company enters into transactions. Steps 4 through 9 are done at the end of a period. *Reversing entries* in step 10 are optional and are explained in Appendix 3C.

Quick Check   Answers — p. 133

14. What are the major steps in preparing closing entries?
15. Why are revenue and expense accounts called *temporary?* Identify and list the types of temporary accounts.
16. What accounts are listed on the post-closing trial balance?

CLASSIFIED BALANCE SHEET

Our discussion to this point has been limited to unclassified financial statements. This section describes a classified balance sheet. The next chapter describes a classified income statement. An **unclassified balance sheet** is one whose items are broadly grouped into assets, liabilities, and equity. One example is FastForward's balance sheet in Exhibit 3.14. A **classified balance sheet** organizes assets and liabilities into important subgroups that provide more information to decision makers.

C4 | Explain and prepare a classified balance sheet.

Classification Structure

A classified balance sheet has no required layout, but it usually contains the categories in Exhibit 3.20. One of the more important classifications is the separation between current and noncurrent items for both assets and liabilities. Current items are those expected to come due (either collected or owed) within one year or the company's operating cycle, whichever is longer. The **operating cycle** is the time span from when *cash is used* to acquire goods and services until *cash is received* from the sale of goods and services. "Operating" refers to company operations and "cycle" refers to the circular flow of cash used for company inputs and then cash received from its outputs. The length of a company's operating cycle depends on its activities. For a service company, the operating cycle is the time span between (1) paying employees who perform the services and (2) receiving cash from customers. For a merchandiser selling products, the operating cycle is the time span between (1) paying suppliers for merchandise and (2) receiving cash from customers.

Point: Current and Noncurrent are also referred to as Short-Term and Long-Term, respectively.

Assets	Liabilities and Equity
Current assets	Current liabilities
Noncurrent assets	Noncurrent liabilities
Long-term investments	Equity
Plant assets	
Intangible assets	

EXHIBIT 3.20

Typical Categories in a Classified Balance Sheet

Most operating cycles are less than one year. This means most companies use a one-year period in deciding which assets and liabilities are current. A few companies have an operating cycle longer than one year. For instance, producers of certain beverages (wine) and products (ginseng) that require aging for several years have operating cycles longer than one year. A balance sheet lists current assets before noncurrent assets and current liabilities before noncurrent liabilities. This consistency in presentation allows users to quickly identify current assets that are most easily converted to cash and current liabilities that are shortly coming due. Items in current assets and current liabilities are listed in the order of how quickly they will be converted to, or paid in, cash.

EXHIBIT 3.21

Example of a Classified
Balance Sheet

SNOWBOARDING COMPONENTS Balance Sheet January 31, 2013		
Assets		
Current assets		
Cash	$ 6,500	
Short-term investments	2,100	
Accounts receivable, net	4,400	
Merchandise inventory	27,500	
Prepaid expenses	2,400	
Total current assets		$ 42,900
Long-term investments		
Notes receivable	1,500	
Investments in stocks and bonds	18,000	
Land held for future expansion	48,000	
Total long-term investments		67,500
Plant assets		
Equipment and buildings	203,200	
Less accumulated depreciation	53,000	
Equipment and buildings, net		150,200
Land		73,200
Total plant assets		223,400
Intangible assets		10,000
Total assets		$343,800
Liabilities		
Current liabilities		
Accounts payable	$ 15,300	
Wages payable	3,200	
Notes payable	3,000	
Current portion of long-term liabilities	7,500	
Total current liabilities		$ 29,000
Long-term liabilities (net of current portion)		150,000
Total liabilities		179,000
Equity		
Common stock		50,000
Retained earnings		114,800
Total equity		164,800
Total liabilities and equity		$343,800

Classification Categories

This section describes the most common categories in a classified balance sheet. The balance sheet for Snowboarding Components in Exhibit 3.21 shows the typical categories. Its assets are classified as either current or noncurrent. Its noncurrent assets include three main categories: long-term investments, plant assets, and intangible assets. Its liabilities are classified as either current or long-term. Not all companies use the same categories of assets and liabilities for their balance sheets. **K2 Sports**, a manufacturer of snowboards, reported a balance sheet with only three asset classes: current assets; property, plant and equipment; and other assets.

Current Assets   **Current assets** are cash and other resources that are expected to be sold, collected, or used within one year or the company's operating cycle, whichever is longer. Examples are cash, short-term investments, accounts receivable, short-term notes receivable, goods for sale (called *merchandise* or *inventory*), and prepaid expenses. The individual prepaid expenses of a company are usually small in amount compared to many other assets and are often combined and shown as a single item. The prepaid expenses likely include items such as prepaid insurance, prepaid rent, office supplies, and store supplies. Prepaid expenses are usually listed last because they will not be converted to cash (instead, they are used).

Long-Term Investments   A second major balance sheet classification is **long-term** (or *noncurrent*) **investments.** Notes receivable and investments in stocks and bonds are long-term assets when they are expected to be held for more than the longer of one year or the operating cycle. Land held for future expansion is a long-term investment because it is *not* used in operations.

Plant Assets   Plant assets are tangible assets that are both *long-lived* and *used to produce* or *sell products and services.* Examples are equipment, machinery, buildings, and land that are used to produce or sell products and services. The order listing for plant assets is usually from most liquid to least liquid such as equipment and machinery to buildings and land.

Point: Plant assets are also called *fixed assets; property, plant and equipment;* or *long-lived assets.*

Intangible Assets   **Intangible assets** are long-term resources that benefit business operations, usually lack physical form, and have uncertain benefits. Examples are patents, trademarks, copyrights, franchises, and goodwill. Their value comes from the privileges or rights granted to or held by the owner. **K2 Sports**, reported intangible assets of $228 million, which is nearly 20 percent of its total assets. Its intangibles included trademarks, patents, and licensing agreements.

Point: Furniture and fixtures are referred to as F&F, which are classified as noncurrent assets.

Current Liabilities   **Current liabilities** are obligations due to be paid or settled within one year or the operating cycle, whichever is longer. They are usually settled by paying out current assets such as cash. Current liabilities often include accounts payable, notes payable, wages payable, taxes payable, interest payable, and unearned revenues. Also, any portion of a long-term liability due to be paid within one year or the operating cycle, whichever is longer, is a current liability. Unearned revenues are current liabilities when they will be settled by delivering products or services within one year or the operating cycle, whichever is longer. Current liabilities are reported in the order of those to be settled first.

Point: Many financial ratios are distorted if accounts are not classified correctly.

Long-Term Liabilities   **Long-term liabilities** are obligations *not* due within one year or the operating cycle, whichever is longer. Notes payable, mortgages payable, bonds payable, and lease obligations are common long-term liabilities. If a company has both short- and long-term items in each of these categories, they are commonly separated into two accounts in the ledger.

Point: Only assets and liabilities are classified as current or noncurrent.

Equity   Equity is the owner's claim on assets. The equity section for a corporation is divided into two main subsections, common stock and retained earnings.

Quick Check   Answers — p. 133

17. Classify the following assets as (1) current assets, (2) plant assets, or (3) intangible assets: (*a*) land used in operations, (*b*) office supplies, (*c*) receivables from customers due in 10 months, (*d*) insurance protection for the next 9 months, (*e*) trucks used to provide services to customers, (*f*) trademarks.

18. Cite at least two examples of assets classified as investments on the balance sheet.

19. Explain the operating cycle for a service company.

GLOBAL VIEW

We explained that accounting under U.S. GAAP is similar, but not identical, to that under IFRS. This section discusses differences in adjusting accounts, preparing financial statements, and reporting assets and liabilities on a balance sheet.

Adjusting Accounts   Both U.S. GAAP and IFRS include broad and similar guidance for adjusting accounts. Although some variations exist in revenue and expense recognition and other principles, all of the adjustments in this chapter are accounted for identically under the two systems. In later chapters we describe how certain assets and liabilities can result in different adjusted amounts using fair value measurements.

Preparing Financial Statements   Both U.S. GAAP and IFRS prepare the same four basic financial statements following the same process discussed in this chapter. Chapter 2 explained how both U.S. GAAP and IFRS require current items to be separated from noncurrent items on the balance sheet (yielding a classified balance sheet). U.S. GAAP balance sheets report current items first. Assets are listed from most liquid to least liquid, where liquid refers to the ease of converting an asset to cash. Liabilities are listed from nearest to maturity to furthest from maturity, maturity refers to the nearness of paying off the liability. IFRS balance sheets normally present noncurrent items first (and equity before liabilities), but this is not a requirement. Other differences with financial statements exist, which we identify in later

PIAGGIO   chapters. Piaggio provides the following example of IFRS reporting for its assets, liabilities, and equity within the balance sheet:

Point: IASB and FASB are working to improve financial statements. One proposal would reorganize the balance sheet to show assets and liabilities classified as operating, investing, or financing.

PIAGGIO Balance Sheet (in thousands of Euro) December 31, 2011				
Assets		**Equity and Liabilities**		
Noncurrent assets		Total equity		446,218
Intangible assets..............	649,420	Noncurrent liabilities		
Property, plant and equipment....	274,871	Financial liabilities falling due after one year......		329,200
Other noncurrent assets	86,185	Other long-term liabilities		100,489
Total noncurrent assets	1,010,476	Total noncurrent liabilities		429,689
Current assets		Current liabilities		
Trade receivables..............	65,560	Financial liabilities falling due within one year		170,261
Other receivables	28,028	Trade payables............................		375,263
Short-term tax receivables	27,245	Tax payables		20,920
Inventories	236,988	Other short-term payables		64,718
Cash and cash equivalents	151,887	Current portion of other long-term provisions ...		13,115
Total current assets	509,708	Total current liabilities		644,277
Total assets	1,520,184	Total equity and liabilities		1,520,184

Closing Process   The closing process is identical under U.S. GAAP and IFRS. Although unique accounts can arise under either system, the closing process remains the same.

IFRS: New revenue recognition rules proposed by the FASB and the IASB reduce variation between U.S. GAAP and IFRS when accounting for revenue.

Financial Pressure

IFRS

Revenue and expense recognition are key to recording accounting adjustments. IFRS tends to be more *principles-based* relative to U.S. GAAP, which is viewed as more *rules-based*. A principles-based system depends heavily on control procedures to reduce the potential for fraud or misconduct. Failure in judgment led to improper accounting adjustments at **Fannie Mae**, **Xerox**, **WorldCom**, and others. A KPMG survey of accounting and finance employees found that more than 10% of them had witnessed falsification or manipulation of accounting data within the past year. Internal controls and governance processes are directed at curtailing such behavior. Yet, a 2011 KPMG fraud survey found that one in seven frauds was uncovered by chance, which emphasizes our need to improve internal controls and governance. ∎

Profit Margin

A useful measure of a company's operating results is the ratio of its net income to net sales. This ratio is called **profit margin,** or *return on sales,* and is computed as in Exhibit 3.22.

$$\text{Profit margin} = \frac{\text{Net income}}{\text{Net sales}}$$

| A2 | Compute profit margin and describe its use in analyzing company performance. |

EXHIBIT 3.22

Profit Margin

This ratio is interpreted as reflecting the percent of profit in each dollar of sales. To illustrate how we compute and use profit margin, let's look at the results of **Limited Brands, Inc.,** in Exhibit 3.23 for its fiscal years 2007 through 2011.

EXHIBIT 3.23

Limited Brands' Profit Margin

$ in millions	2011	2010	2009	2008	2007
Net income	$ 805	$ 448	$ 220	$ 718	$ 676
Net sales	$9,613	$8,632	$9,043	$10,134	$10,671
Profit margin	8.4%	5.2%	2.4%	7.1%	6.3%
Industry profit margin	2.1%	0.9%	0.3%	1.1%	1.6%

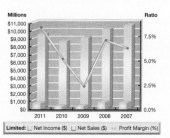

The Limited's average profit margin is 5.9% during this 5-year period. This favorably compares to the average industry profit margin of 1.2%. However, Limited's profit margin has rebounded in the most recent two years—from 2.4% in 2009 to 5.2% and 8.4% for the recent recovery periods (see margin graph). Future success depends on Limited maintaining its market share and increasing its profit margin.

Current Ratio

An important use of financial statements is to help assess a company's ability to pay its debts in the near future. Such analysis affects decisions by suppliers when allowing a company to buy on credit. It also affects decisions by creditors when lending money to a company, including loan terms such as interest rate, due date, and collateral requirements. It can also affect a manager's decisions about using cash to pay debts when they come due. The **current ratio** is one measure of a company's ability to pay its short-term obligations. It is defined in Exhibit 3.24 as current assets divided by current liabilities.

| A3 | Compute the current ratio and describe what it reveals about a company's financial condition. |

$$\text{Current ratio} = \frac{\text{Current assets}}{\text{Current liabilities}}$$

EXHIBIT 3.24

Current Ratio

Using financial information from **Limited Brands, Inc.,** we compute its current ratio for the recent five-year period. The results are in Exhibit 3.25.

EXHIBIT 3.25

Limited Brands' Current Ratio

$ in millions	2012	2011	2010	2009	2008	2007
Current assets	$2,368	$2,592	$3,250	$2,867	$2,919	$2,771
Current liabilities	$1,526	$1,504	$1,322	$1,255	$1,374	$1,709
Current ratio	1.6	1.7	2.5	2.3	2.1	1.6
Industry current ratio	1.6	1.7	1.9	2.0	2.1	2.3

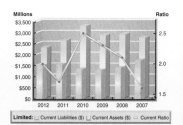

Limited Brands' current ratio averaged 2.0 for its fiscal years 2007 through 2012. The current ratio for each of these years suggests that the company's short-term obligations can be covered with its short-term assets. However, if its ratio would approach 1.0, Limited would expect to face challenges in covering liabilities. If the ratio were *less* than 1.0, current liabilities would exceed current assets, and the company's ability to pay short-term obligations could be in doubt. Limited Brand's liquidity, as evidenced by its current ratio, declines in 2011 and 2012, after growing steadily from 2008–2010.

Decision Maker

Analyst   You are analyzing the financial condition of a company to assess its ability to meet upcoming loan payments. You compute its current ratio as 1.2. You also find that a major portion of accounts receivable is due from one client who has not made any payments in the past 12 months. Removing this receivable from current assets lowers the current ratio to 0.7. What do you conclude? ■   [Answer—p. 132]

DEMONSTRATION PROBLEM 1

The following information relates to Fanning's Electronics on December 31, 2013. The company, which uses the calendar year as its annual reporting period, initially records prepaid and unearned items in balance sheet accounts (assets and liabilities, respectively).

a. The company's weekly payroll is $8,750, paid each Friday for a five-day workweek. Assume December 31, 2013, falls on a Monday, but the employees will not be paid their wages until Friday, January 4, 2014.

b. Eighteen months earlier, on July 1, 2012, the company purchased equipment that cost $20,000. Its useful life is predicted to be five years, at which time the equipment is expected to be worthless (zero salvage value).

c. On October 1, 2013, the company agreed to work on a new housing development. The company is paid $120,000 on October 1 in advance of future installation of similar alarm systems in 24 new homes. That amount was credited to the Unearned Services Revenue account. Between October 1 and December 31, work on 20 homes was completed.

d. On September 1, 2013, the company purchased a 12-month insurance policy for $1,800. The transaction was recorded with an $1,800 debit to Prepaid Insurance.

e. On December 29, 2013, the company completed a $7,000 service that has not been billed and not recorded as of December 31, 2013.

Required

1. Prepare any necessary adjusting entries on December 31, 2013, in relation to transactions and events *a* through *e*.

2. Prepare T-accounts for the accounts affected by adjusting entries, and post the adjusting entries. Determine the adjusted balances for the Unearned Revenue and the Prepaid Insurance accounts.

3. Complete the following table and determine the amounts and effects of your adjusting entries on the year 2013 income statement and the December 31, 2013, balance sheet. Use up (down) arrows to indicate an increase (decrease) in the Effect columns.

Entry	Amount in the Entry	Effect on Net Income	Effect on Total Assets	Effect on Total Liabilities	Effect on Total Equity

PLANNING THE SOLUTION

- Analyze each situation to determine which accounts need to be updated with an adjustment.
- Calculate the amount of each adjustment and prepare the necessary journal entries.
- Show the amount of each adjustment in the designated accounts, determine the adjusted balance, and identify the balance sheet classification of the account.
- Determine each entry's effect on net income for the year and on total assets, total liabilities, and total equity at the end of the year.

SOLUTION TO DEMONSTRATION PROBLEM 1

1. Adjusting journal entries.

(a) Dec. 31	Wages Expense	1,750	
	Wages Payable		1,750
	To accrue wages for the last day of the year		
	($8,750 × 1/5).		
(b) Dec. 31	Depreciation Expense—Equipment	4,000	
	Accumulated Depreciation—Equipment		4,000
	To record depreciation expense for the year		
	($20,000/5 years = $4,000 per year).		
(c) Dec. 31	Unearned Services Revenue	100,000	
	Services Revenue		100,000
	To recognize services revenue earned		
	($120,000 × 20/24).		
(d) Dec. 31	Insurance Expense	600	
	Prepaid Insurance		600
	To adjust for expired portion of insurance		
	($1,800 × 4/12).		
(e) Dec. 31	Accounts Receivable	7,000	
	Services Revenue		7,000
	To record services revenue earned.		

2. T-accounts for adjusting journal entries *a* through *e*.

Wages Expense			
(a)	1,750		

Wages Payable			
		(a)	1,750

Depreciation Expense—Equipment			
(b)	4,000		

Accumulated Depreciation—Equipment			
		(b)	4,000

Unearned Services Revenue			
		Unadj. Bal.	120,000
(c)	100,000		
		Adj. Bal.	20,000

Services Revenue			
		(c)	100,000
		(e)	7,000
		Adj. Bal.	107,000

Insurance Expense			
(d)	600		

Prepaid Insurance			
Unadj. Bal.	1,800		
		(d)	600
Adj. Bal.	1,200		

Accounts Receivable			
(e)	7,000		

3. Financial statement effects of adjusting journal entries.

Entry	Amount in the Entry	Effect on Net Income	Effect on Total Assets	Effect on Total Liabilities	Effect on Total Equity
a	$ 1,750	$ 1,750 ↓	No effect	$ 1,750 ↑	$ 1,750 ↓
b	4,000	4,000 ↓	$4,000 ↓	No effect	4,000 ↓
c	100,000	100,000 ↑	No effect	$100,000 ↓	100,000 ↑
d	600	600 ↓	$ 600 ↓	No effect	600 ↓
e	7,000	7,000 ↑	$7,000 ↑	No effect	7,000 ↑

DEMONSTRATION PROBLEM 2

Use the following adjusted trial balance to answer questions 1–3.

CHOI COMPANY Adjusted Trial Balance December 31	Debit	Credit
Cash	$ 3,050	
Accounts receivable	400	
Prepaid insurance	830	
Supplies	80	
Equipment	217,200	
Accumulated depreciation—Equipment		$ 29,100
Wages payable		880
Interest payable		3,600
Unearned rent		460
Long-term notes payable		150,000
Common stock		10,000
Retained earnings..........................		30,340
Dividends	21,000	
Rent earned		57,500
Wages expense	25,000	
Utilities expense	1,900	
Insurance expense	3,200	
Supplies expense	250	
Depreciation expense—Equipment	5,970	
Interest expense	3,000	
Totals	$281,880	$281,880

1. Prepare the annual income statement from the adjusted trial balance of Choi Company.

Answer:

CHOI COMPANY Income Statement For Year Ended December 31		
Revenues		
Rent earned		$57,500
Expenses		
Wages expense	$25,000	
Utilities expense	1,900	
Insurance expense	3,200	
Supplies expense	250	
Depreciation expense—Equipment	5,970	
Interest expense	3,000	
Total expenses		39,320
Net income		$18,180

2. Prepare a statement of retained earnings from the adjusted trial balance of Choi Company.

Answer:

CHOI COMPANY	
Statement of Retained Earnings	
For Year Ended December 31	
Retained earnings, December 31 prior year-end	$30,340
Plus: Net income	18,180
	48,520
Less: Dividends	21,000
Retained earnings, December 31 current year-end	$27,520

3. Prepare a balance sheet from the adjusted trial balance of Choi Company.

Answer:

CHOI COMPANY		
Balance Sheet		
December 31		
Assets		
Cash		$ 3,050
Accounts receivable		400
Prepaid insurance		830
Supplies		80
Equipment	$217,200	
Less accumulated depreciation	29,100	188,100
Total assets		$192,460
Liabilities		
Wages payable		$ 880
Interest payable		3,600
Unearned rent		460
Long-term notes payable		150,000
Total liabilities		154,940
Equity		
Common stock		10,000
Retained earnings		27,520
Total equity		37,520
Total liabilities and equity		$192,460

APPENDIX

Alternative Accounting for Prepayments   3A

This appendix explains an alternative in accounting for prepaid expenses and unearned revenues.

RECORDING PREPAYMENT OF EXPENSES <u>IN EXPENSE ACCOUNTS</u>

An alternative method is to record *all* prepaid expenses with debits to expense accounts. If any prepaids remain unused or unexpired at the end of an accounting period, then adjusting entries must transfer the cost of the unused portions from expense accounts to prepaid expense (asset) accounts. This alternative method is acceptable. The financial statements are identical under either method, but the adjusting entries

P6	Explain the alternatives in accounting for prepaids.

are different. To illustrate the differences between these two methods, let's look at FastForward's cash payment of December 6 for 24 months of insurance coverage beginning on December 1. FastForward recorded that payment with a debit to an asset account, but it could have recorded a debit to an expense account. These alternatives are shown in Exhibit 3A.1.

EXHIBIT 3A.1

Alternative Initial Entries for Prepaid Expenses

			Payment Recorded as Asset	Payment Recorded as Expense
Dec. 6	Prepaid Insurance		2,400	
	Cash		2,400	
Dec. 6	Insurance Expense			2,400
	Cash			2,400

At the end of its accounting period on December 31, insurance protection for one month has expired. This means $100 ($2,400/24) of insurance coverage expired and is an expense for December. The adjusting entry depends on how the original payment was recorded. This is shown in Exhibit 3A.2.

EXHIBIT 3A.2

Adjusting Entry for Prepaid Expenses for the Two Alternatives

			Payment Recorded as Asset	Payment Recorded as Expense
Dec. 31	Insurance Expense		100	
	Prepaid Insurance		100	
Dec. 31	Prepaid Insurance			2,300
	Insurance Expense			2,300

When these entries are posted to the accounts in the ledger, we can see that these two methods give identical results. The December 31 adjusted account balances in Exhibit 3A.3 show Prepaid Insurance of $2,300 and Insurance Expense of $100 for both methods.

EXHIBIT 3A.3

Account Balances under Two Alternatives for Recording Prepaid Expenses

Payment Recorded as Asset			
Prepaid Insurance			128
Dec. 6	2,400	Dec. 31	100
Balance	2,300		

Insurance Expense			637
Dec. 31	100		

Payment Recorded as Expense			
Prepaid Insurance			128
Dec. 31	2,300		

Insurance Expense			637
Dec. 6	2,400	Dec. 31	2,300
Balance	100		

RECORDING PREPAYMENT OF REVENUES IN REVENUE ACCOUNTS

As with prepaid expenses, an alternative method is to record *all* unearned revenues with credits to revenue accounts. If any revenues are unearned at the end of an accounting period, then adjusting entries must transfer the unearned portions from revenue accounts to unearned revenue (liability) accounts. This alternative method is acceptable. The adjusting entries are different for these two alternatives, but the financial statements are identical. To illustrate the accounting differences between these two methods, let's look at FastForward's December 26 receipt of $3,000 for consulting services covering the period December 27 to February 24. FastForward recorded this transaction with a credit to a liability account. The alternative is to record it with a credit to a revenue account, as shown in Exhibit 3A.4.

EXHIBIT 3A.4

Alternative Initial Entries for Unearned Revenues

			Receipt Recorded as Liability	Receipt Recorded as Revenue
Dec. 26	Cash		3,000	
	Unearned Consulting Revenue		3,000	
Dec. 26	Cash			3,000
	Consulting Revenue			3,000

By the end of its accounting period on December 31, FastForward has earned $250 of this revenue. This means $250 of the liability has been satisfied. Depending on how the initial receipt is recorded, the adjusting entry is as shown in Exhibit 3A.5.

		Receipt Recorded as Liability	Receipt Recorded as Revenue
Dec. 31	Unearned Consulting Revenue	250	
	Consulting Revenue	250	
Dec. 31	Consulting Revenue		2,750
	Unearned Consulting Revenue		2,750

EXHIBIT 3A.5

Adjusting Entry for Unearned Revenues for the Two Alternatives

After adjusting entries are posted, the two alternatives give identical results. The December 31 adjusted account balances in Exhibit 3A.6 show unearned consulting revenue of $2,750 and consulting revenue of $250 for both methods.

Receipt Recorded as Liability		Receipt Recorded as Revenue	

Unearned Consulting Revenue 236

Dec. 31	250	Dec. 26	3,000
		Balance	2,750

Unearned Consulting Revenue 236

Dec. 31	2,750

Consulting Revenue 403

Dec. 31	250

Consulting Revenue 403

Dec. 31	2,750	Dec. 26	3,000
		Balance	250

EXHIBIT 3A.6

Account Balances under Two Alternatives for Recording Unearned Revenues

---

APPENDIX

Work Sheet as a Tool

3B

Information preparers use various analyses and internal documents when organizing information for internal and external decision makers. Internal documents are often called **working papers.** One widely used working paper is the **work sheet,** which is a useful tool for preparers in working with accounting information. It is usually not available to external decision makers.

Benefits of a Work Sheet (Spreadsheet)   A work sheet is *not* a required report, yet using a manual or electronic work sheet has several potential benefits. Specifically, a work sheet:

P7 Prepare a work sheet and explain its usefulness.

- Aids the preparation of financial statements.
- Reduces the possibility of errors when working with many accounts and adjustments.
- Links accounts and adjustments to their impacts in financial statements.
- Assists in planning and organizing an audit of financial statements—as it can be used to reflect any adjustments necessary.
- Helps in preparing interim (monthly and quarterly) financial statements when the journalizing and posting of adjusting entries are postponed until the year-end.
- Shows the effects of proposed or "what if" transactions.

Use of a Work Sheet (Spreadsheet)   When a work sheet is used to prepare financial statements, it is constructed at the end of a period before the adjusting process. The complete work sheet includes a list of the accounts, their balances and adjustments, and their sorting into financial statement columns. It provides two columns each for the unadjusted trial balance, the adjustments, the adjusted trial balance, the income statement, and the balance sheet. To describe and interpret the work sheet, we

Point: Since a work sheet is *not* a required report or an accounting record, its format is flexible and can be modified by its user to fit his/her preferences.

use the information from FastForward. Preparing the work sheet has five important steps. Each step, 1 through 5, is color-coded and explained with reference to Exhibit 3B.1.

① Step 1. Enter Unadjusted Trial Balance

The first step in preparing a work sheet is to list the title of every account and its account number that is expected to appear on its financial statements. This includes all accounts in the ledger plus any new ones from adjusting entries. Most adjusting entries—including expenses from salaries, supplies, depreciation, and insurance—are predictable and recurring. The unadjusted balance for each account is then entered in the appropriate Debit or Credit column of the unadjusted trial balance columns. The totals of these two columns must be equal. Exhibit 3B.1 shows FastForward's work sheet after completing this first step. Sometimes blank lines are left on the work sheet based on past experience to indicate where lines will be needed for adjustments to certain accounts. Exhibit 3B.1 shows Consulting Revenue as one example. An alternative is to squeeze adjustments on one line or to combine the effects of two or more adjustments in one amount. In the unusual case when an account is not predicted, we can add a new line for such an account following the *Totals* line.

② Step 2. Enter Adjustments

The second step in preparing a work sheet is to enter adjustments in the Adjustments columns. The adjustments shown are the same ones shown in Exhibit 3.13. An identifying letter links the debit and credit of each adjusting entry. This is called *keying* the adjustments. After preparing a work sheet, adjusting entries must still be entered in the journal and posted to the ledger. The Adjustments columns provide the information for those entries.

③ Step 3. Prepare Adjusted Trial Balance

Point: To avoid omitting the transfer of an account balance, start with the first line (cash) and continue in account order.

The adjusted trial balance is prepared by combining the adjustments with the unadjusted balances for each account. As an example, the Prepaid Insurance account has a $2,400 debit balance in the Unadjusted Trial Balance columns. This $2,400 debit is combined with the $100 credit in the Adjustments columns to give Prepaid Insurance a $2,300 debit in the Adjusted Trial Balance columns. The totals of the Adjusted Trial Balance columns confirm the equality of debits and credits.

④ Step 4. Sort Adjusted Trial Balance Amounts to Financial Statements

This step involves sorting account balances from the adjusted trial balance to their proper financial statement columns. Expenses go to the Income Statement Debit column and revenues to the Income Statement Credit column. Assets and Dividends go to the Balance Sheet Debit column. Liabilities, Retained Earnings, and Common Stock go to the Balance Sheet Credit column.

⑤ Step 5. Total Statement Columns, Compute Income or Loss, and Balance Columns

Each financial statement column (from Step 4) is totaled. The difference between the totals of the Income Statement columns is net income or net loss. This occurs because revenues are entered in the Credit column and expenses in the Debit column. If the Credit total exceeds the Debit total, there is net income. If the Debit total exceeds the Credit total, there is a net loss. For FastForward, the Credit total exceeds the Debit total, giving a $3,785 net income.

   The net income from the Income Statement columns is then entered in the Balance Sheet Credit column. Adding net income to the last Credit column implies that it is to be added to retained earnings. If a loss occurs, it is added to the Debit column. This implies that it is to be subtracted from retained earnings. The ending balance of retained earnings does not appear in the last two columns as a single amount, but it is computed in the statement of retained earnings using these account balances. When net income or net loss is added to the proper Balance Sheet column, the totals of the last two columns must balance. If they do not, one or more errors have been made. The error can either be mathematical or involve sorting one or more amounts to incorrect columns.

Work Sheet Applications and Analysis   A work sheet does not substitute for financial statements. It is a tool we can use at the end of an accounting period to help organize data and prepare financial statements. FastForward's financial statements are shown in Exhibit 3.14. Its income statement amounts are taken from the Income Statement columns of the work sheet. Similarly, amounts for its balance sheet and its statement of retained earnings are taken from the Balance Sheet columns of the work sheet.

   Work sheets are also useful in analyzing the effects of proposed, or what-if, transactions. This is done by entering financial statement amounts in the Unadjusted (what-if) columns. Proposed transactions are then entered in the Adjustments columns. We then compute "adjusted" amounts from these proposed transactions. The extended amounts in the financial statement columns show the effects of these proposed transactions. These financial statement columns yield **pro forma financial statements** because they show the statements *as if* the proposed transactions occurred.

EXHIBIT 3B.1

Work Sheet

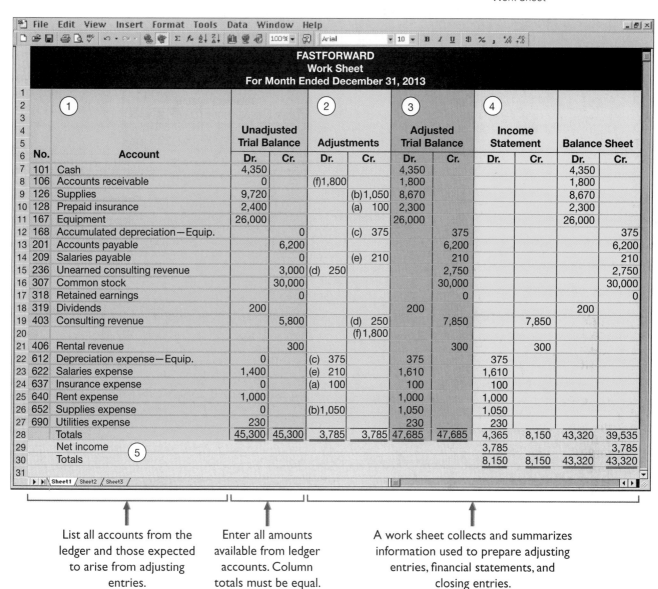

List all accounts from the ledger and those expected to arise from adjusting entries.

Enter all amounts available from ledger accounts. Column totals must be equal.

A work sheet collects and summarizes information used to prepare adjusting entries, financial statements, and closing entries.

APPENDIX

Reversing Entries

3C

Reversing entries are optional. They are recorded in response to accrued assets and accrued liabilities that were created by adjusting entries at the end of a reporting period. The purpose of reversing entries is to simplify a company's recordkeeping. Exhibit 3C.1 shows an example of FastForward's reversing entries. The top of the exhibit shows the adjusting entry FastForward recorded on December 31 for its employee's earned but unpaid salary. The entry recorded three days' salary of $210, which increased December's total salary expense to $1,610. The entry also recognized a liability of $210. The expense is reported on December's income statement. The expense account is then closed. The ledger on January 1, 2014, shows a $210 liability and a zero balance in the Salaries Expense account. At this point, the choice is made between using or not using reversing entries.

Point: As a general rule, adjusting entries that create new asset or liability accounts are likely candidates for reversing.

EXHIBIT 3C.1

Reversing Entries for an
Accrued Expense

Accrue salaries expense on December 31, 2013

Salaries Expense	210	
Salaries Payable		210

Salaries Expense

Date	Expl.	Debit	Credit	Balance
2013				
Dec. 12	(7)	700		700
26	(16)	700		1,400
31	(e)	210		1,610

Salaries Payable

Date	Expl.	Debit	Credit	Balance
2013				
Dec. 31	(e)		210	210

WITHOUT Reversing Entries	— OR —	**WITH Reversing Entries**

No reversing entry recorded on January 1, 2014	*Reversing entry recorded on January 1, 2014*

WITHOUT Reversing Entries

NO ENTRY

Salaries Expense

Date	Expl.	Debit	Credit	Balance
2014				

Salaries Payable

Date	Expl.	Debit	Credit	Balance
2013				
Dec. 31	(e)		210	210
2014				

WITH Reversing Entries

Salaries Payable	210	
Salaries Expense		210

Salaries Expense*

Date	Expl.	Debit	Credit	Balance
2014				
Jan. 1			210	(210)

Salaries Payable

Date	Expl.	Debit	Credit	Balance
2013				
Dec. 31	(e)		210	210
2014				
Jan. 1		210		0

Pay the accrued and current salaries on January 9, the first payday in 2014

WITHOUT Reversing Entries

Salaries Expense	490	
Salaries Payable	210	
Cash		700

Salaries Expense

Date	Expl.	Debit	Credit	Balance
2014				
Jan. 9		490		490

Salaries Payable

Date	Expl.	Debit	Credit	Balance
2013				
Dec. 31	(e)		210	210
2014				
Jan. 9		210		0

WITH Reversing Entries

Salaries Expense	700	
Cash		700

Salaries Expense*

Date	Expl.	Debit	Credit	Balance
2014				
Jan. 1			210	(210)
Jan. 9		700		490

Salaries Payable

Date	Expl.	Debit	Credit	Balance
2013				
Dec. 31	(e)		210	210
2014				
Jan. 1		210		0

Under both approaches, the expense and liability accounts have
identical balances after the cash payment on January 9.

Salaries Expense	$490
Salaries Payable	$ 0

*Circled numbers in the *Balance* column indicate abnormal balances.

Accounting *without* Reversing Entries The path down the left side of Exhibit 3C.1 is described in the chapter. To summarize here, when the next payday occurs on January 9, we record payment with a compound entry that debits both the expense and liability accounts and credits Cash. Posting that entry creates a $490 balance in the expense account and reduces the liability account balance to zero because the debt has been settled. The disadvantage of this approach is the slightly more complex entry required on January 9. Paying the accrued liability means that this entry differs from the routine entries made on all other paydays. To construct the proper entry on January 9, we must recall the effect of the December 31 adjusting entry. Reversing entries overcome this disadvantage.

For each separate case below, follow the 3-step process for adjusting the supplies asset account: Step 1: Determine what the current account balance equals. Step 2: Determine what the current account balance should equal. Step 3: Record an adjusting entry to get from step 1 to step 2. *Assume no other adjusting entries are made during the year.*

a. Supplies. The Supplies account has a $300 debit balance to start the year. No supplies were purchased during the current year. A December 31 physical count shows $110 of supplies remaining.

b. Supplies. The Supplies account has an $800 debit balance to start the year. Supplies of $2,100 were purchased during the current year and debited to the Supplies account. A December 31 physical count shows $650 of supplies remaining.

c. Supplies. The Supplies account has a $4,000 debit balance to start the year. During the current year, supplies of $9,400 were purchased and debited to the Supplies account. The inventory of supplies available at December 31 totaled $2,660.

QS 3-15
Prepaid (deferred) expenses
adjustments
P1

For each separate case below, follow the 3-step process for adjusting the accumulated depreciation account: Step 1: Determine what the current account balance equals. Step 2: Determine what the current account balance should equal. Step 3: Record an adjusting entry to get from step 1 to step 2. *Assume no other adjusting entries are made during the year.*

a. Accumulated Depreciation. The Krug Company's Accumulated Depreciation account has a $13,500 balance to start the year. A review of depreciation schedules reveals that $14,600 of depreciation expense must be recorded for the year.

b. Accumulated Depreciation. The company has only one fixed asset (truck) that it purchased at the start of this year. That asset had cost $44,000, had an estimated life of 5 years, and is expected to have zero value at the end of the 5 years.

c. Accumulated Depreciation. The company has only one fixed asset (equipment) that it purchased at the start of this year. That asset had cost $32,000, had an estimated life of 7 years, and is expected to be valued at $4,000 at the end of the 7 years.

QS 3-16
Accumulated depreciation
adjustments
P1

For each separate case below, follow the 3-step process for adjusting the unearned revenue liability account: Step 1: Determine what the current account balance equals. Step 2: Determine what the current account balance should equal. Step 3: Record an adjusting entry to get from step 1 to step 2. *Assume no other adjusting entries are made during the year.*

a. Unearned Rent Revenue. The Krug Company collected $6,000 rent in advance on November 1, debiting Cash and crediting Unearned Rent Revenue. The tenant was paying twelve months rent in advance and occupancy began November 1.

b. Unearned Services Revenue. The company charges $75 per month to spray a house for insects. A customer paid $300 on October 1 in advance for four treatments, which was recorded with a debit to Cash and a credit to Unearned Services Revenue. At year-end, the company has applied three treatments for the customer.

c. Unearned Rent Revenue. On September 1, a client paid the company $24,000 cash for six months of rent in advance (the client leased a building and took occupancy immediately). The company recorded the cash as Unearned Rent Revenue.

QS 3-17
Unearned (deferred) revenues
adjustments
P1

For each separate case below, follow the 3-step process for adjusting the accrued expense account: Step 1: Determine what the current account balance equals. Step 2: Determine what the current account balance should equal. Step 3: Record an adjusting entry to get from step 1 to step 2. *Assume no other adjusting entries are made during the year.*

a. Salaries Payable. At year-end, salaries expense of $15,500 has been incurred by the company, but is not yet paid to employees.

b. Interest Payable. At its December 31 year-end, the company owes $250 of interest on a line-of-credit loan. That interest will not be paid until sometime in January of the next year.

c. Interest Payable. At its December 31 year-end, the company holds a mortgage payable that has incurred $875 in annual interest that is neither recorded nor paid. The company intends to pay the interest on January 7 of the next year.

QS 3-18
Accrued expenses adjustments
P1

QS 3-19

Accrued revenues adjustments

P1

For each separate case below, follow the 3-step process for adjusting the accrued revenue account: Step 1: Determine what the current account balance equals. Step 2: Determine what the current account balance should equal. Step 3: Record an adjusting entry to get from step 1 to step 2. *Assume no other adjusting entries are made during the year.*

a. **Accounts Receivable.** At year-end, the Krug Company has completed services of $19,000 for a client, but the client has not yet been billed for those services.

b. **Interest Receivable.** At year-end, the company has earned, but not yet recorded, $390 of interest earned from its investments in government bonds.

c. **Accounts Receivable.** A painting company collects fees when jobs are complete. The work for one customer, whose job was bid at $1,300, has been completed, but the customer has not yet been billed.

QS 3-20

Identifying the accounting cycle

C3

List the following steps of the accounting cycle in their proper order.

a. Posting the journal entries.

b. Journalizing and posting adjusting entries.

c. Preparing the adjusted trial balance.

d. Journalizing and posting closing entries.

e. Analyzing transactions and events.

f. Preparing the financial statements.

g. Preparing the unadjusted trial balance.

h. Journalizing transactions and events.

i. Preparing the post-closing trial balance.

QS 3-21

Classifying balance sheet items

C4

The following are common categories on a classified balance sheet.

A. Current assets

B. Long-term investments

C. Plant assets

D. Intangible assets

E. Current liabilities

F. Long-term liabilities

For each of the following items, select the letter that identifies the balance sheet category where the item typically would appear.

_____ 1. Land not currently used in operations

_____ 2. Notes payable (due in five years)

_____ 3. Accounts receivable

_____ 4. Trademarks

_____ 5. Accounts payable

_____ 6. Store equipment

_____ 7. Wages payable

_____ 8. Cash

QS 3-22

Identifying current accounts and computing the current ratio

A3

Compute Chavez Company's current ratio using the following information.

Accounts receivable	$18,000	Long-term notes payable	$21,000
Accounts payable	11,000	Office supplies	2,800
Buildings	45,000	Prepaid insurance	3,560
Cash	7,000	Unearned services revenue	3,000

QS 3-23

Prepare closing entries from the ledger   P4

The ledger of Mai Company includes the following accounts with normal balances: Common Stock $9,000; Dividends $800; Services Revenue $13,000; Wages Expense $8,400; and Rent Expense $1,600. Prepare the necessary closing entries from the available information at December 31.

QS 3-24

Identify post-closing accounts   P5

Identify the accounts listed in QS 3-23 that would be included in a post-closing trial balance.

QS 3-25[B]

Preparing a partial work sheet

P7

The ledger of Claudell Company includes the following unadjusted normal balances: Prepaid Rent $1,000, Services Revenue $55,600, and Wages Expense $5,000. Adjusting entries are required for (a) prepaid rent expired, $200; (b) accrued services revenue $900; and (c) accrued wages expense $700. Enter these unadjusted balances and the necessary adjustments on a work sheet and complete the work sheet for these accounts. *Note:* Also include the following accounts: Accounts Receivable, Wages Payable, and Rent Expense.

QS 3-26[C]

Reversing entries

P8

On December 31, 2012, Yates Co. prepared an adjusting entry for $12,000 of earned but unrecorded management fees. On January 16, 2013, Yates received $26,700 cash in management fees, which included the accrued fees earned in 2012. Assuming the company uses reversing entries, prepare the January 1, 2013, reversing entry and the January 16, 2013, cash receipt entry.

connect

Prepare adjusting journal entries for the year ended (date of) December 31, 2013, for each of these separate situations. Assume that prepaid expenses are initially recorded in asset accounts. Also assume that fees collected in advance of work are initially recorded as liabilities.

a. Depreciation on the company's equipment for 2013 is computed to be $18,000.

b. The Prepaid Insurance account had a $6,000 debit balance at December 31, 2013, before adjusting for the costs of any expired coverage. An analysis of the company's insurance policies showed that $1,100 of unexpired insurance coverage remains.

c. The Office Supplies account had a $700 debit balance on December 31, 2012; and $3,480 of office supplies were purchased during the year. The December 31, 2013, physical count showed $298 of supplies available.

d. Two-thirds of the work related to $15,000 of cash received in advance was performed this period.

e. The Prepaid Insurance account had a $6,800 debit balance at December 31, 2013, before adjusting for the costs of any expired coverage. An analysis of insurance policies showed that $5,800 of coverage had expired.

f. Wage expenses of $3,200 have been incurred but are not paid as of December 31, 2013.

EXERCISES

Exercise 3-1
Preparing adjusting entries
P1

Check (c) Dr. Office Supplies Expense, $3,882; (e) Dr. Insurance Expense, $5,800

For each of the following separate cases, prepare adjusting entries required of financial statements for the year ended (date of) December 31, 2013. (Assume that prepaid expenses are initially recorded in asset accounts and that fees collected in advance of work are initially recorded as liabilities.)

a. One-third of the work related to $15,000 cash received in advance is performed this period.

b. Wages of $8,000 are earned by workers but not paid as of December 31, 2013.

c. Depreciation on the company's equipment for 2013 is $18,531.

d. The Office Supplies account had a $240 debit balance on December 31, 2012. During 2013, $5,239 of office supplies are purchased. A physical count of supplies at December 31, 2013, shows $487 of supplies available.

e. The Prepaid Insurance account had a $4,000 balance on December 31, 2012. An analysis of insurance policies shows that $1,200 of unexpired insurance benefits remain at December 31, 2013.

f. The company has earned (but not recorded) $1,050 of interest from investments in CDs for the year ended December 31, 2013. The interest revenue will be received on January 10, 2014.

g. The company has a bank loan and has incurred (but not recorded) interest expense of $2,500 for the year ended December 31, 2013. The company must pay the interest on January 2, 2014.

Exercise 3-2
Preparing adjusting entries
P1

Check (e) Dr. Insurance Expense, $2,800; (f) Cr. Interest Revenue, $1,050

Pablo Management has five part-time employees, each of whom earns $250 per day. They are normally paid on Fridays for work completed Monday through Friday of the same week. Assume that December 28, 2013, was a Friday, and that they were paid in full on that day. The next week, the five employees worked only four days because New Year's Day was an unpaid holiday. (a) Assuming that December 31, 2013, was a Monday, prepare the adjusting entry that would be recorded at the close of that day. (b) Assuming that January 4, 2014, was a Friday, prepare the journal entry that would be made to record payment of the employees' wages.

Exercise 3-3
Adjusting and paying accrued wages
C1 P1

The following three separate situations require adjusting journal entries to prepare financial statements as of April 30. For each situation, present both the April 30 adjusting entry and the subsequent entry during May to record the payment of the accrued expenses.

a. On April 1, the company retained an attorney for a flat monthly fee of $3,500. Payment for April legal services was made by the company on May 12.

b. A $900,000 note payable requires 10% annual interest, or $9,000 to be paid at the 20th day of each month. The interest was last paid on April 20 and the next payment is due on May 20. As of April 30, $3,000 of interest expense has accrued.

c. Total weekly salaries expense for all employees is $10,000. This amount is paid at the end of the day on Friday of each five-day workweek. April 30 falls on Tuesday of this year, which means that the employees had worked two days since the last payday. The next payday is May 3.

Exercise 3-4
Adjusting and paying accrued expenses
A1

Check (b) May 20 Dr. Interest Expense, $6,000

Exercise 3-5

Determining cost flows
through accounts

C1   A1

Determine the missing amounts in each of these four separate situations *a* through *d*.

	a	b	c	d
Supplies available—prior year-end	$ 400	$1,200	$1,260	?
Supplies purchased during the current year	2,800	6,500	?	$3,000
Supplies available—current year-end	650	?	1,350	700
Supplies expense for the current year	?	1,200	8,400	4,588

Exercise 3-6

Analyzing and preparing
adjusting entries

A1   P3

Following are two income statements for Alexis Co. for the year ended December 31. The left column is prepared before any adjusting entries are recorded, and the right column includes the effects of adjusting entries. The company records cash receipts and payments related to unearned and prepaid items in balance sheet accounts. Analyze the statements and prepare the eight adjusting entries that likely were recorded. (*Note:* 30% of the $7,000 adjustment for Fees Earned has been earned but not billed, and the other 70% has been earned by performing services that were paid for in advance.)

ALEXIS CO.
Income Statements
For Year Ended December 31

	Unadjusted	Adjusted
Revenues		
Fees earned	$18,000	$25,000
Commissions earned	36,500	36,500
Total revenues	$54,500	61,500
Expenses		
Depreciation expense—Computers	0	1,600
Depreciation expense—Office furniture	0	1,850
Salaries expense	13,500	15,750
Insurance expense	0	1,400
Rent expense	3,800	3,800
Office supplies expense	0	580
Advertising expense	2,500	2,500
Utilities expense	1,245	1,335
Total expenses	21,045	28,815
Net income	$33,455	$32,685

Exercise 3-7

Computing and interpreting
profit margin

A2

Use the following information to compute profit margin for each separate company *a* through *e*.

		Net Income	Net Sales			Net Income	Net Sales
a.		$ 4,361	$ 44,500	**d.**		$65,646	$1,458,800
b.		97,706	398,800	**e.**		80,142	435,500
c.		111,281	257,000				

Which of the five companies is the most profitable according to the profit margin ratio? Interpret that company's profit margin ratio.

Exercise 3-8ᴬ

Adjusting for prepaids recorded
as expenses and unearned
revenues recorded as revenues

P6

Ricardo Construction began operations on December 1. In setting up its accounting procedures, the company decided to debit expense accounts when it prepays its expenses and to credit revenue accounts when customers pay for services in advance. Prepare journal entries for items *a* through *d* and the adjusting entries as of its December 31 period-end for items *e* through *g*.

a. Supplies are purchased on December 1 for $2,000 cash.

b. The company prepaid its insurance premiums for $1,540 cash on December 2.

c. On December 15, the company receives an advance payment of $13,000 cash from a customer for remodeling work.

d. On December 28, the company receives $3,700 cash from another customer for remodeling work to be performed in January.

e. A physical count on December 31 indicates that the Company has $1,840 of supplies available.

f. An analysis of the insurance policies in effect on December 31 shows that $340 of insurance coverage had expired.

g. As of December 31, only one remodeling project has been worked on and completed. The $5,570 fee for this project had been received in advance and recorded as remodeling fees earned.

Check   (f) Cr. Insurance Expense, $1,200; (g) Dr. Remodeling Fees Earned, $11,130

Costanza Company experienced the following events and transactions during July.

July 1   Received $3,000 cash in advance of performing work for Vivian Solana.
      6   Received $7,500 cash in advance of performing work for Iris Haru.
     12   Completed the job for Solana.
     18   Received $8,500 cash in advance of performing work for Amina Jordan.
     27   Completed the job for Haru.
     31   None of the work for Jordan has been performed.

a. Prepare journal entries (including any adjusting entries as of the end of the month) to record these events using the procedure of initially crediting the Unearned Fees account when payment is received from a customer in advance of performing services.

b. Prepare journal entries (including any adjusting entries as of the end of the month) to record these events using the procedure of initially crediting the Fees Earned account when payment is received from a customer in advance of performing services.

c. Under each method, determine the amount of earned fees reported on the income statement for July and the amount of unearned fees reported on the balance sheet as of July 31.

Exercise 3-9[A]
Recording and reporting
revenues received in advance
P6

Check   (c) Fees Earned—using entries from part b, $10,500

---

adidas AG reports the following balance sheet accounts for the year ended December 31, 2011 (euros in millions). Prepare the balance sheet for this company as of December 31, 2011, following usual IFRS practices.

Exercise 3-10
Preparing a balance sheet
following IFRS
P3

Tangible and other assets	€ 255		Intangible assets	€ 154
Total equity	2,322		Total current liabilities	345
Receivables and other assets	1,767		Inventories	30
Total noncurrent liabilities	3,379		Total liabilities	3,724
Cash and cash equivalents	383		Other current assets	28
Total current assets	2,208		Total noncurrent assets	3,838
Other noncurrent assets	3,429			

Use the following adjusted trial balance of Wilson Trucking Company to prepare the (1) income statement and (2) statement of retained earnings, for the year ended December 31, 2013. The retained earnings account balance is $145,000 at December 31, 2012.

Exercise 3-11
Preparing financial statements
C3 P3

Account Title	Debit	Credit
Cash	$ 8,000	
Accounts receivable	17,500	
Office supplies	3,000	
Trucks	172,000	
Accumulated depreciation—Trucks		$ 36,000
Land	85,000	
Accounts payable		12,000
Interest payable		4,000
Long-term notes payable		53,000
Common stock		30,000
Retained earnings		145,000
Dividends	20,000	
Trucking fees earned		130,000
Depreciation expense—Trucks	23,500	
Salaries expense	61,000	
Office supplies expense	8,000	
Repairs expense—Trucks	12,000	
Totals	$410,000	$410,000

Exercise 3-12

Preparing a classified balance sheet **C4**

Check Total assets, $249,500

Use the information in the adjusted trial balance reported in Exercise 3-11 to prepare Wilson Trucking Company's classified balance sheet as of December 31, 2013.

Exercise 3-13

Computing the current ratio

A3

Use the information in the adjusted trial balance reported in Exercise 3-11 to compute the current ratio as of the balance sheet date (round the ratio to two decimals). Interpret the current ratio for the Wilson Trucking Company. (Assume that the industry average for the current ratio is 1.5.)

Exercise 3-14

Computing and analyzing the current ratio

A3

Calculate the current ratio in each of the following separate cases (round the ratio to two decimals). Identify the company case with the strongest liquidity position. (These cases represent competing companies in the same industry.)

	Current Assets	Current Liabilities
Case 1	$ 79,040	$ 32,000
Case 2	104,880	76,000
Case 3	45,080	49,000
Case 4	85,680	81,600
Case 5	61,000	100,000

Exercise 3-15[A]

Preparing reversing entries

P8

The following two events occurred for Trey Co. on October 31, 2013, the end of its fiscal year.

a. Trey rents a building from its owner for $2,800 per month. By a prearrangement, the company delayed paying October's rent until November 5. On this date, the company paid the rent for both October and November.

b. Trey rents space in a building it owns to a tenant for $850 per month. By prearrangement, the tenant delayed paying the October rent until November 8. On this date, the tenant paid the rent for both October and November.

Required

1. Prepare adjusting entries that the company must record for these events as of October 31.

2. Assuming Trey does *not* use reversing entries, prepare journal entries to record Trey's payment of rent on November 5 and the collection of the tenant's rent on November 8.

3. Assuming that the company uses reversing entries, prepare reversing entries on November 1 and the journal entries to record Trey's payment of rent on November 5 and the collection of the tenant's rent on November 8.

Exercise 3-16

Preparing closing entries

P4

Following are Nintendo's revenue and expense accounts for a recent calendar year (yen in millions). Prepare the company's closing entries for its revenues and its expenses.

Net sales	¥1,014,345
Cost of sales	626,379
Advertising expense	96,359
Other expense, net	213,986

Exercise 3-17

Completing a worksheet

P7

The following data are taken from the unadjusted trial balance of the Westcott Company at December 31, 2013. Each account carries a normal balance and the accounts are shown here in alphabetical order.

Accounts Payable	$ 6	Prepaid Insurance	$18	Retained earnings	$32
Accounts Receivable..............	12	Revenue	75	Dividends	6
Accumulated Depreciation—Equip.	15	Salaries Expense	18	Unearned Revenue	12
Cash........................	21	Supplies	24	Utilities Expense	12
Equipment.....................	39	Common stock	10		

1. Use the data above to prepare a worksheet. Enter the accounts in proper order and enter their balances in the correct debit or credit column.

2. Use the following adjustment information to complete the worksheet.

    a. Depreciation on equipment, $3

    b. Accrued salaries, $6

    c. The $12 of unearned revenue has been earned

    d. Supplies available at December 31, 2013, $15

    e. Expired insurance, $15

▥ connect

For each of the following entries, enter the letter of the explanation that most closely describes it in the space beside each entry. (You can use letters more than once.)

A. To record receipt of unearned revenue.

B. To record this period's earning of prior unearned revenue.

C. To record payment of an accrued expense.

D. To record receipt of an accrued revenue.

E. To record an accrued expense.

F. To record an accrued revenue.

G. To record this period's use of a prepaid expense.

H. To record payment of a prepaid expense.

I. To record this period's depreciation expense.

PROBLEM SET A

Problem 3-1A
Identifying adjusting entries with explanations

P1

		Debit	Credit
____	**1.** Interest Expense	1,000	
	Interest Payable		1,000
____	**2.** Depreciation Expense	4,000	
	Accumulated Depreciation		4,000
____	**3.** Unearned Professional Fees	3,000	
	Professional Fees Earned		3,000
____	**4.** Insurance Expense	4,200	
	Prepaid Insurance		4,200
____	**5.** Salaries Payable	1,400	
	Cash		1,400
____	**6.** Prepaid Rent	4,500	
	Cash		4,500
____	**7.** Salaries Expense	6,000	
	Salaries Payable		6,000
____	**8.** Interest Receivable	5,000	
	Interest Revenue		5,000
____	**9.** Cash	9,000	
	Accounts Receivable (from consulting)		9,000
____	**10.** Cash	7,500	
	Unearned Professional Fees		7,500
____	**11.** Cash	2,000	
	Interest Receivable		2,000
____	**12.** Rent Expense	2,000	
	Prepaid Rent		2,000

Arnez Co. follows the practice of recording prepaid expenses and unearned revenues in balance sheet accounts. The company's annual accounting period ends on December 31, 2013. The following information concerns the adjusting entries to be recorded as of that date.

a. The Office Supplies account started the year with a $4,000 balance. During 2013, the company purchased supplies for $13,400, which was added to the Office Supplies account. The inventory of supplies available at December 31, 2013, totaled $2,554.

Problem 3-2A
Preparing adjusting and subsequent journal entries

C1 A1 P1

b. An analysis of the company's insurance policies provided the following facts.

Policy	Date of Purchase	Months of Coverage	Cost
A	April 1, 2011	24	$14,400
B	April 1, 2012	36	12,960
C	August 1, 2013	12	2,400

The total premium for each policy was paid in full (for all months) at the purchase date, and the Prepaid Insurance account was debited for the full cost. (Year-end adjusting entries for Prepaid Insurance were properly recorded in all prior years.)

c. The company has 15 employees, who earn a total of $1,960 in salaries each working day. They are paid each Monday for their work in the five-day workweek ending on the previous Friday. Assume that December 31, 2013, is a Tuesday, and all 15 employees worked the first two days of that week. Because New Year's Day is a paid holiday, they will be paid salaries for five full days on Monday, January 6, 2014.

d. The company purchased a building on January 1, 2013. It cost $960,000 and is expected to have a $45,000 salvage value at the end of its predicted 30-year life. Annual depreciation is $30,500.

e. Since the company is not large enough to occupy the entire building it owns, it rented space to a tenant at $3,000 per month, starting on November 1, 2013. The rent was paid on time on November 1, and the amount received was credited to the Rent Earned account. However, the tenant has not paid the December rent. The company has worked out an agreement with the tenant, who has promised to pay both December and January rent in full on January 15. The tenant has agreed not to fall behind again.

f. On November 1, the company rented space to another tenant for $2,800 per month. The tenant paid five months' rent in advance on that date. The payment was recorded with a credit to the Unearned Rent account.

Check (1*b*) Dr. Insurance Expense, $7,120 (1*d*) Dr. Depreciation Expense, $30,500

Required

1. Use the information to prepare adjusting entries as of December 31, 2013.

2. Prepare journal entries to record the first subsequent cash transaction in 2014 for parts *c* and *e*.

Problem 3-3A
Preparing adjusting entries, adjusted trial balance, and financial statements

A1 P1 P2 P3

mhhe.com/wildFAF4e

Wells Technical Institute (WTI), a school owned by Tristana Wells, provides training to individuals who pay tuition directly to the school. WTI also offers training to groups in off-site locations. Its unadjusted trial balance as of December 31, 2013, follows. WTI initially records prepaid expenses and unearned revenues in balance sheet accounts. Descriptions of items *a* through *h* that require adjusting entries on December 31, 2013, follow.

Additional Information Items

a. An analysis of WTI's insurance policies shows that $2,400 of coverage has expired.

b. An inventory count shows that teaching supplies costing $2,800 are available at year-end 2013.

c. Annual depreciation on the equipment is $13,200.

d. Annual depreciation on the professional library is $7,200.

e. On November 1, WTI agreed to do a special six-month course (starting immediately) for a client. The contract calls for a monthly fee of $2,500, and the client paid the first five months' fees in advance. When the cash was received, the Unearned Training Fees account was credited. The fee for the sixth month will be recorded when it is collected in 2014.

f. On October 15, WTI agreed to teach a four-month class (beginning immediately) for an individual for $3,000 tuition per month payable at the end of the class. The class started on October 15, but no payment has yet been received. (WTI's accruals are applied to the nearest half-month; for example, October recognizes one-half month accrual.)

g. WTI's two employees are paid weekly. As of the end of the year, two days' salaries have accrued at the rate of $100 per day for each employee.

h. The balance in the Prepaid Rent account represents rent for December.

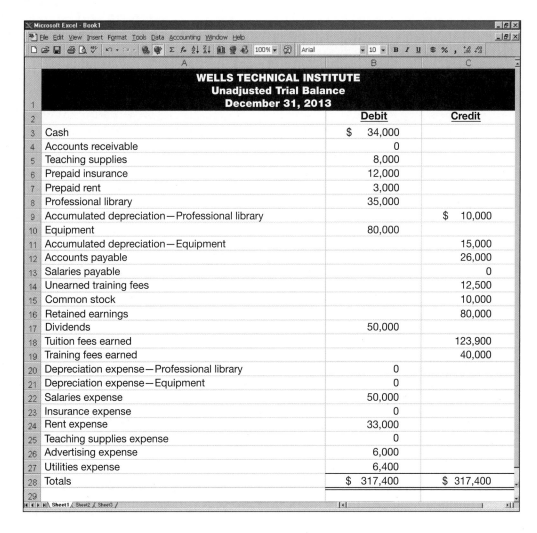

WELLS TECHNICAL INSTITUTE Unadjusted Trial Balance December 31, 2013		
	Debit	**Credit**
3 Cash	$ 34,000	
4 Accounts receivable	0	
5 Teaching supplies	8,000	
6 Prepaid insurance	12,000	
7 Prepaid rent	3,000	
8 Professional library	35,000	
9 Accumulated depreciation—Professional library		$ 10,000
10 Equipment	80,000	
11 Accumulated depreciation—Equipment		15,000
12 Accounts payable		26,000
13 Salaries payable		0
14 Unearned training fees		12,500
15 Common stock		10,000
16 Retained earnings		80,000
17 Dividends	50,000	
18 Tuition fees earned		123,900
19 Training fees earned		40,000
20 Depreciation expense—Professional library	0	
21 Depreciation expense—Equipment	0	
22 Salaries expense	50,000	
23 Insurance expense	0	
24 Rent expense	33,000	
25 Teaching supplies expense	0	
26 Advertising expense	6,000	
27 Utilities expense	6,400	
28 Totals	$ 317,400	$ 317,400

Required

1. Prepare T-accounts (representing the ledger) with balances from the unadjusted trial balance.

2. Prepare the necessary adjusting journal entries for items *a* through *h* and post them to the T-accounts. Assume that adjusting entries are made only at year-end.

3. Update balances in the T-accounts for the adjusting entries and prepare an adjusted trial balance.

4. Prepare Wells Technical Institute's income statement and statement of retained earnings for the year 2013 and prepare its balance sheet as of December 31, 2013.

Check (2*e*) Cr. Training Fees Earned, $5,000; (2*f*) Cr. Tuition Fees Earned, $7,500; (3) Adj. Trial balance totals, $345,700; (4) Net income, $49,600

A six-column table for JKL Company follows. The first two columns contain the unadjusted trial balance for the company as of July 31, 2013. The last two columns contain the adjusted trial balance as of the same date.

Required

Analysis Component

1. Analyze the differences between the unadjusted and adjusted trial balances to determine the eight adjustments that likely were made. Show the results of your analysis by inserting these adjustment amounts in the table's two middle columns. Label each adjustment with a letter *a* through *h* and provide a short description of it at the bottom of the table.

Preparation Component

2. Use the information in the adjusted trial balance to prepare the company's (*a*) income statement and its statement of retained earnings for the year ended July 31, 2013 (*Note:* retained earnings at July 31, 2012, was $25,000, and the current-year dividends were $5,000), and (*b*) the balance sheet as of July 31, 2013.

Problem 3-4A
Interpreting unadjusted and adjusted trial balances, and preparing financial statements

A1 P1 P2 P3

mhhe.com/wildFAF4e

Check (2) Net income, $4,960; Total assets, $124,960

	Unadjusted Trial Balance		Adjustments		Adjusted Trial Balance	
Cash	$ 34,000				$ 34,000	
Accounts receivable	14,000				22,000	
Office supplies	16,000				2,000	
Prepaid insurance	8,540				2,960	
Office equipment	84,000				84,000	
Accum. depreciation—						
Office equip.		$ 14,000				$ 20,000
Accounts payable		9,100				10,000
Interest payable		0				1,000
Salaries payable		0				7,000
Unearned consulting fees		18,000				15,000
Long-term notes payable		52,000				52,000
Common stock		15,000				15,000
Retained earnings.............		25,000				25,000
Dividends	5,000				5,000	
Consulting fees earned		123,240				134,240
Depreciation expense—						
Office equip.	0				6,000	
Salaries expense	67,000				74,000	
Interest expense	1,200				2,200	
Insurance expense	0				5,580	
Rent expense	14,500				14,500	
Office supplies expense	0				14,000	
Advertising expense	12,100				13,000	
Totals	$256,340	$256,340			$279,240	$279,240

Problem 3-5A

Preparing financial statements from the adjusted trial balance and calculating profit margin

P3 A1 A2

The adjusted trial balance for Chiara Company as of December 31, 2013, follows.

	Debit	Credit
Cash	$ 30,000	
Accounts receivable	52,000	
Interest receivable	18,000	
Notes receivable (due in 90 days)	168,000	
Office supplies	16,000	
Automobiles	168,000	
Accumulated depreciation—Automobiles		$ 50,000
Equipment	138,000	
Accumulated depreciation—Equipment		18,000
Land	78,000	
Accounts payable		96,000
Interest payable		20,000
Salaries payable		19,000
Unearned fees		30,000
Long-term notes payable		138,000
Common stock		20,000
Retained earnings............................		235,800
Dividends	46,000	
Fees earned		484,000
Interest earned		24,000
Depreciation expense—Automobiles	26,000	
Depreciation expense—Equipment	18,000	
Salaries expense	188,000	
Wages expense	40,000	
Interest expense	32,000	
Office supplies expense	34,000	
Advertising expense	58,000	
Repairs expense—Automobiles	24,800	
Totals	$1,134,800	$1,134,800

Required

1. Prepare the income statement and the statement of retained earnings for the calendar year 2013 and the classified balance sheet at December 31, 2013.

2. Prepare the necessary closing entries at December 31, 2013.

3. Use the information in the financial statements to calculate these ratios: (*a*) return on assets (total assets at December 31, 2012, were $160,000), (*b*) debt ratio, (*c*) profit margin ratio (use total revenues as the denominator), and (*d*) current ratio. Round ratios to three decimals for parts *a* and *c*, and to two decimals for parts *b* and *d*.

Check (1) Total assets (12/31/2013), $164,700; Net income, $28,890

This serial problem began in Chapter 1 and continues through most of the book. If previous chapter segments were not completed, the serial problem can still begin at this point. It is helpful, but not necessary, to use the Working Papers that accompany the book.

SERIAL PROBLEM
Success Systems
P1 P2 P3 P4 P5

Sage 50

SP 3 After the success of the company's first two months, Adria Lopez continues to operate Success Systems. (Transactions for the first two months are described in the serial problem of Chapter 2.) The November 30, 2013, unadjusted trial balance of Success Systems (reflecting its transactions for October and November of 2013) follows.

No.	Account Title	Debit	Credit
101	Cash	$ 48,052	
106	Accounts receivable	12,618	
126	Computer supplies	2,545	
128	Prepaid insurance	2,220	
131	Prepaid rent	3,300	
163	Office equipment	8,000	
164	Accumulated depreciation—Office equipment		$ 0
167	Computer equipment	20,000	
168	Accumulated depreciation—Computer equipment		0
201	Accounts payable		0
210	Wages payable		0
236	Unearned computer services revenue		0
307	Common stock		83,000
318	Retained earnings		0
319	Dividends	5,600	
403	Computer services revenue		25,659
612	Depreciation expense—Office equipment	0	
613	Depreciation expense—Computer equipment	0	
623	Wages expense	2,625	
637	Insurance expense	0	
640	Rent expense	0	
652	Computer supplies expense	0	
655	Advertising expense	1,940	
676	Mileage expense	704	
677	Miscellaneous expenses	250	
684	Repairs expense—Computer	805	
	Totals	$108,659	$108,659

Success Systems had the following transactions and events in December 2013.

Dec. 2 Paid $1,025 cash to Hillside Mall for Success Systems' share of mall advertising costs.
  3 Paid $500 cash for minor repairs to the company's computer.
  4 Received $3,950 cash from Alex's Engineering Co. for the receivable from November.
  10 Paid cash to Lyn Addie for six days of work at the rate of $125 per day.
  14 Notified by Alex's Engineering Co. that Success Systems' bid of $7,000 on a proposed project has been accepted. Alex's paid a $1,500 cash advance to Success Systems.
  15 Purchased $1,100 of computer supplies on credit from Harris Office Products.
  16 Sent a reminder to Gomez Co. to pay the fee for services recorded on November 8.
  20 Completed a project for Liu Corporation and received $5,625 cash.

22–26   Took the week off for the holidays.
   28   Received $3,000 cash from Gomez Co. on its receivable.
   29   Reimbursed A. Lopez for business automobile mileage (600 miles at $0.32 per mile).
   31   The business paid $1,500 cash for dividends.

The following additional facts are collected for use in making adjusting entries prior to preparing financial statements for the company's first three months:

a. The December 31 inventory count of computer supplies shows $580 still available.

b. Three months have expired since the 12-month insurance premium was paid in advance.

c. As of December 31, Lyn Addie has not been paid for four days of work at $125 per day.

d. The computer system, acquired on October 1, is expected to have a four-year life with no salvage value.

e. The office equipment, acquired on October 1, is expected to have a five-year life with no salvage value.

f. Three of the four months' prepaid rent has expired.

Required

1. Prepare journal entries to record each of the December transactions and events for Success Systems. Post those entries to the accounts in the ledger.

2. Prepare adjusting entries to reflect *a* through *f*. Post those entries to the accounts in the ledger.

Check   (3) Adjusted trial balance totals, $119,034

3. Prepare an adjusted trial balance as of December 31, 2013.

4. Prepare an income statement for the three months ended December 31, 2013.

5. Prepare a statement of retained earnings for the three months ended December 31, 2013.

(6) Total assets, $93,248

6. Prepare a balance sheet as of December 31, 2013.

Check   Post-closing trial balance totals, $94,898

7. Record and post the necessary closing entries for Success Systems.

8. Prepare a post-closing trial balance as of December 31, 2013.

Beyond the Numbers

REPORTING IN ACTION

C1 C2 A1 A2 P4

Polaris

BTN 3-1   Refer to Polaris's financial statements in Appendix A to answer the following.

1. Identify and write down the revenue recognition principle as explained in the chapter.

2. Review Polaris's footnotes to discover how it applies the revenue recognition principle and when it recognizes revenue. Report what you discover.

3. What is Polaris's profit margin for fiscal years ended December 31, 2011 and 2010.

4. For the year ended December 31, 2011, what amount is credited to Income Summary to summarize its revenues earned?

5. For the year ended December 31, 2011, what amount is debited to Income Summary to summarize its expenses incurred?

6. For the year ended December 31, 2011, what is the balance of its Income Summary account before it is closed?

Fast Forward

7. Access Polaris's annual report (10-K) for fiscal years ending after December 31, 2011, at its Website (Polaris.com) or the SEC's EDGAR database (www.SEC.gov). Assess and compare the December 31, 2011, fiscal year profit margin to any subsequent year's profit margin that you compute.

COMPARATIVE ANALYSIS

A2 A3

Polaris
Arctic Cat

BTN 3-2   Key figures for the recent two years of both Polaris and Arctic Cat follow.

($ thousands)	Polaris		Arctic Cat	
	Current Year	Prior Year	Current Year	Prior Year
Net income	$ 227,575	$ 147,138	$ 13,007	$ 1,875
Net sales	2,656,949	1,991,139	363,015	350,871
Current assets	878,676	808,145	232,040	201,015
Current liabilities	615,531	584,210	87,444	75,320

Required

1. Compute profit margins for (a) Polaris and (b) Arctic Cat for the two years of data shown.
2. Which company is more successful on the basis of profit margin? Explain.
3. Compute the current ratio for both years for both companies.
4. Which company has the better ability to pay short-term obligations according to the current ratio?
5. Analyze and comment on each company's current ratios for the past two years.
6. How do Polaris's and Arctic Cat's current ratios compare to their industry (assumed) average ratio of 2.4?

BTN 3-3   Jessica Boland works for Sea Biscuit Co. She and Farah Smith, her manager, are preparing adjusting entries for annual financial statements. Boland computes depreciation and records it as

ETHICS CHALLENGE

C1 C2 A1

| Depreciation Expense—Equipment . . . . | 123,000 | |
| Accumulated Depreciation—Equipment . . . . | | 123,000 |

Smith agrees with her computation but says the credit entry should be directly to the Equipment account. Smith argues that while accumulated depreciation is technically correct, "it is less hassle not to use a contra account and just credit the Equipment account directly. And besides, the balance sheet shows the same amount for total assets under either method."

Required

1. How should depreciation be recorded? Do you support Boland or Smith?
2. Evaluate the strengths and weaknesses of Smith's reasons for preferring her method.
3. Indicate whether the situation Boland faces is an ethical problem. Explain.

BTN 3-4   Assume that one of your classmates states that a company's books should be ongoing and therefore not closed until that business is terminated. Write a half-page memo to this classmate explaining the concept of the closing process by drawing analogies between (1) a scoreboard for an athletic event and the revenue and expense accounts of a business or (2) a sports team's record book and retained earnings. (*Hint:* Think about what would happen if the scoreboard is not cleared before the start of a new game.)

COMMUNICATING IN PRACTICE

P4

BTN 3-5   Access EDGAR online (www.sec.gov) and locate the 10-K report of The Gap, Inc., (ticker GPS) filed on March 26, 2012. Review its financial statements reported for the year ended January 28, 2012, to answer the following questions.

TAKING IT TO THE NET

C1 A2

Required

1. What are Gap's main brands?
2. What is Gap's fiscal year-end?
3. What is Gap's net sales for the period ended January 28, 2012?
4. What is Gap's net income for the period ended January 28, 2012?
5. Compute Gap's profit margin for the year ended January 28, 2012.
6. Do you believe Gap's decision to use a year-end of late January or early February relates to its natural business year? Explain.

TEAMWORK IN ACTION

A1 P1

BTN 3-6   Four types of adjustments are described in the chapter: (1) prepaid expenses, (2) unearned revenues, (3) accrued expenses, and (4) accrued revenues.

Required

1. Form *learning teams* of four (or more) members. Each team member must select one of the four adjustments as an area of expertise (each team must have at least one expert in each area).
2. Form *expert teams* from the individuals who have selected the same area of expertise. Expert teams are to discuss and write a report that each expert will present to his or her learning team addressing the following:
   a. Description of the adjustment and why it's necessary.
   b. Example of a transaction or event, with dates and amounts, that requires adjustment.
   c. Adjusting entry(ies) for the example in requirement *b*.
   d. Status of the affected account(s) before and after the adjustment in requirement *c*.
   e. Effects on financial statements of not making the adjustment.
3. Each expert should return to his or her learning team. In rotation, each member should present his or her expert team's report to the learning team. Team discussion is encouraged.

ENTREPRENEURIAL DECISION

A2

BTN 3-7   Review the opening feature of this chapter dealing with **ash&dans** and the entrepreneurial owners, Ashley Cook and Danielle Dankner.

Required

1. Assume that ash&dans sells a $300 gift certificate to a customer, collecting the $300 cash in advance. Prepare the journal entry for the (*a*) collection of the cash for delivery of the gift certificate to the customer and (*b*) revenue from the subsequent delivery of merchandise when the gift certificate is used.
2. How can keeping less inventory help to improve ash&dans's profit margin?
3. Ashley Cook and Danielle Dankner understand that many companies carry considerable inventory, and they are thinking of carrying additional inventory of merchandise for sale. Ashley and Danielle desire your advice on the pros and cons of carrying such inventory. Provide at least one reason for and one reason against carrying additional inventory.

HITTING THE ROAD

C1

BTN 3-8   Select a company that you can visit in person or interview on the telephone. Call ahead to the company to arrange a time when you can interview an employee (preferably an accountant) who helps prepare the annual financial statements. Inquire about the following aspects of its *accounting cycle:*

1. Does the company prepare interim financial statements? What time period(s) is used for interim statements?
2. Does the company use the cash or accrual basis of accounting?
3. Does the company use a work sheet in preparing financial statements? Why or why not?
4. Does the company use a spreadsheet program? If so, which software program is used?
5. How long does it take after the end of its reporting period to complete annual statements?

GLOBAL DECISION

A2 A3 C1 C2

PIAGGIO

BTN 3-9   Piaggio (Piaggio.com) manufactures two-, three- and four-wheel vehicles and is Europe's leading manufacturer of motorcycles and scooters. The following selected information is available from Piaggio's financial statements.

(Euro thousands)	Current Year	Prior Year
Current assets	509,708	575,897
Current liabilities	644,277	616,166

Required

1. Locate the notes to its December 31, 2011, financial statements at the company's Website, and read note *2.2 Accounting Principles—Recognition of Revenues,* first paragraph only. When is revenue recognized by Piaggio?

2. Refer to Piaggio's financials in Appendix A. What is Piaggio's profit margin for the year ended December 31, 2011?

3. Compute Piaggio's current ratio for both the current year and the prior year.

4. Comment on any change from the prior year to the current year for the current ratio.

ANSWERS TO MULTIPLE CHOICE QUIZ

1. b; the forgotten adjusting entry is: *dr.* Wages Expense, *cr.* Wages Payable.

2. c; Supplies used = $450 − $125 = $325

3. b; Insurance expense = $24,000 × (8/24) = $8,000; adjusting entry is: *dr.* Insurance Expense for $8,000, *cr.* Prepaid Insurance for $8,000.

4. a; Consulting fees earned = $3,600 × (2/6) = $1,200; adjusting entry is: *dr.* Unearned Consulting Fee for $1,200, *cr.* Consulting Fees Earned for $1,200.

5. e; Profit margin = $15,000/$300,000 = 5%

6. b

Accounting for Merchandising Operations

A Look Back

Chapter 3 focused on the final steps of the accounting process. We explained the importance of proper revenue and expense recognition and described the adjusting and closing processes. We also prepared financial statements.

A Look at This Chapter

This chapter emphasizes merchandising activities. We explain how reporting merchandising activities differs from reporting service activities. We also analyze and record merchandise purchases and sales transactions, and explain the adjustments and closing process for merchandisers.

A Look Ahead

Chapter 5 extends our analysis of merchandising activities and focuses on the valuation of inventory. Topics include the items in inventory, costs assigned, costing methods used, and inventory estimation techniques.

Learning Objectives

CONCEPTUAL

C1 Describe merchandising activities and identify income components for a merchandising company. (p. 162)

C2 Identify and explain the inventory asset and cost flows of a merchandising company. (p. 163)

ANALYTICAL

A1 Compute the acid-test ratio and explain its use to assess liquidity. (p. 178)

A2 Compute the gross margin ratio and explain its use to assess profitability. (p. 178)

PROCEDURAL

P1 Analyze and record transactions for merchandise purchases using a perpetual system. (p. 164)

P2 Analyze and record transactions for merchandise sales using a perpetual system. (p. 169)

P3 Prepare adjustments and close accounts for a merchandising company. (p. 172)

P4 Define and prepare multiple-step and single-step income statements. (p. 174)

P5 *Appendix 4A*—Record and compare merchandising transactions using both periodic and perpetual inventory systems. (p. 183)

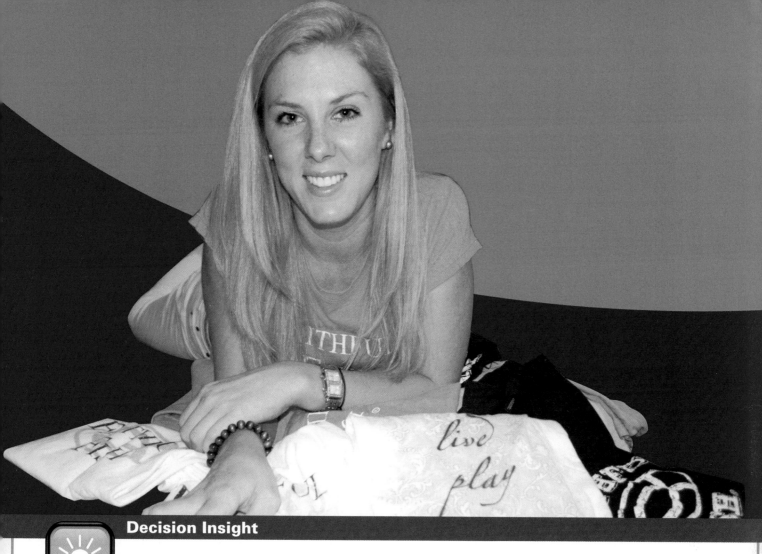

Faithful Business

"I have a vision, a BIG vision, a HUGE vision!"
—**CHELSEA EUBANK**

ATLANTA—"I have a learning disability," explains Chelsea Eubank. "I went to LD schools and attend Beacon College, the only accredited LD college in America. It will always be with me." However, Chelsea uses her LD as an opportunity. "It [LD] has made me take risks and focus on what my gifts are." Explains Chelsea, "I always tell them that everyone has a talent and everyone has a disability. They just need to figure out what their talent is!"

For Chelsea, her "goal is to create a clothing line that gives to charity and to become a role model for students with challenges." That goal has led her to launch **Faithful Fish (FaithfulFish.com)**. Our mission, explains Chelsea, is to develop a "clothing line that expresses the customers positive values and lifestyle." She adds, "We are offering something that is not in the marketplace."

Still, her start-up was a struggle. "We had to go through our business plan and then . . . give a summary of the company," explains Chelsea. She recalls how the business required a merchandising accounting system to account for purchases and sales transactions and to effectively track merchandise. Inventory was especially important to account for and monitor.

Chelsea admits, "I don't really know what I am doing, so I have made mistakes."

To succeed, Chelsea made smart business decisions. She set up an accounting system to capture and communicate costs and sales information. Tracking merchandising activities was necessary to set prices and to manage discounts, allowances, and returns of both sales and purchases. A perpetual inventory system enabled her to stock the right kind and amount of merchandise and to avoid the costs of out-of-stock and excess inventory. Chelsea stresses that one must "ask people for advice." To help with the accounting for merchandise, Chelsea admits, "I have a financial manager."

Mastering accounting for merchandising is about more than profits and losses—it is a means to an end for Chelsea. "Faithful Fish gives a portion of all sales to charities." Adds Chelsea, "I want Faithful Fish to get big enough that I will be able to give over $1,000,000 a year away!"

[Sources: *Faithful Fish Website*, January 2013; *YHP,* October 2009; *FBEnow.com*, August 2009; *Entrepreneur Girl*, January 2012; *EmbracingBeauty.com*, March 2011]

Buyers of merchandise expect many products, discount prices, inventory on demand, and high quality. This chapter introduces the accounting practices used by companies engaged in merchandising. We show how financial statements reflect merchandising activities and explain the new financial statement items created by merchandising activities. We also analyze and record merchandise purchases and sales, and explain the adjustments and the closing process for these companies.

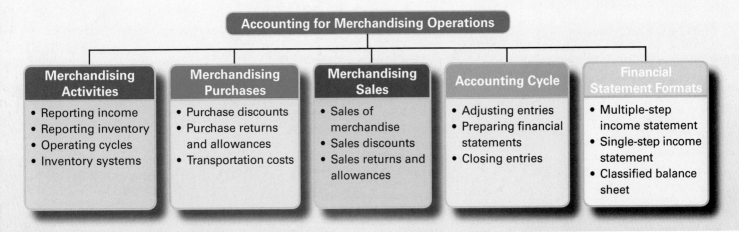

Accounting for Merchandising Operations

Merchandising Activities	Merchandising Purchases	Merchandising Sales	Accounting Cycle	Financial Statement Formats
• Reporting income • Reporting inventory • Operating cycles • Inventory systems	• Purchase discounts • Purchase returns and allowances • Transportation costs	• Sales of merchandise • Sales discounts • Sales returns and allowances	• Adjusting entries • Preparing financial statements • Closing entries	• Multiple-step income statement • Single-step income statement • Classified balance sheet

MERCHANDISING ACTIVITIES

C1 Describe merchandising activities and identify income components for a merchandising company.

Previous chapters emphasized the accounting and reporting activities of service companies. A merchandising company's activities differ from those of a service company. **Merchandise** consists of products, also called *goods,* that a company acquires to resell to customers. A **merchandiser** earns net income by buying and selling merchandise. Merchandisers are often identified as either wholesalers or retailers. A **wholesaler** is an *intermediary* that buys products from manufacturers or other wholesalers and sells them to retailers or other wholesalers. A **retailer** is an intermediary that buys products from manufacturers or wholesalers and sells them to consumers. Many retailers sell both products and services.

Reporting Income for a Merchandiser

Net income for a merchandiser equals revenues from selling merchandise minus both the cost of merchandise sold to customers and the cost of other expenses for the period, see Exhibit 4.1. The

EXHIBIT 4.1

Computing Income for a Merchandising Company versus a Service Company

Service Company

Revenues —— *Minus* —→ Expenses —— Equals —→ Net income

Merchandiser

Net sales —*Minus*→ Cost of goods sold —Equals→ Gross profit —*Minus*→ Expenses —Equals→ Net income

usual accounting term for revenues from selling merchandise is *sales,* and the term used for the expense of buying and preparing the merchandise is **cost of goods sold.** (Some service companies use the term *sales* instead of revenues; and cost of goods sold is also called *cost of sales.*)

The income statement for Z-Mart in Exhibit 4.2 illustrates these key components of a merchandiser's net income. The first two lines show that products are acquired at a cost of $230,400 and sold for $314,700. The third line shows an $84,300 **gross profit,** also called

Point: Fleming, SuperValu, and **SYSCO** are wholesalers. **Aeropostale, Coach, Target,** and **Walmart** are retailers.

EXHIBIT 4.2

Merchandiser's Income Statement

Z-MART
Income Statement
For Year Ended December 31, 2013

Net sales	$314,700
Cost of goods sold	230,400
Gross profit	84,300
Expenses	71,400
Net income	$ 12,900

gross margin, which equals net sales less cost of goods sold. Additional expenses of $71,400 are reported, which leaves $12,900 in net income.

Reporting Inventory for a Merchandiser

A merchandiser's balance sheet includes a current asset called *merchandise inventory,* an item not on a service company's balance sheet. **Merchandise inventory,** or simply *inventory,* refers to products that a company owns and intends to sell. The cost of this asset includes the cost incurred to buy the goods, ship them to the store, and make them ready for sale.

C2 Identify and explain the inventory asset and cost flows of a merchandising company.

Operating Cycle for a Merchandiser

A merchandising company's operating cycle begins by purchasing merchandise and ends by collecting cash from selling the merchandise. The length of an operating cycle differs across the types of businesses. Department stores often have operating cycles of two to five months. Operating cycles for grocery merchants usually range from two to eight weeks. A grocer has more operating cycles in a year than, say, clothing or electronics retailers.

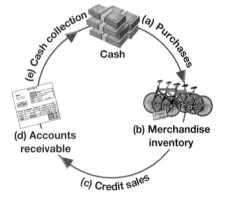

EXHIBIT 4.3

Merchandiser's Operating Cycle

Exhibit 4.3 illustrates an operating cycle for a merchandiser with credit sales. The cycle moves from (*a*) cash purchases of merchandise to (*b*) inventory for sale to (*c*) credit sales to (*d*) accounts receivable to (*e*) cash. Companies try to keep their operating cycles short because assets tied up in inventory and receivables are not productive. Cash sales shorten operating cycles.

Inventory Systems

Cost of goods sold is the cost of merchandise sold to customers during a period. It is often the largest single expense on a merchandiser's income statement. **Inventory** refers to products a company owns and expects to sell in its normal operations. Exhibit 4.4 shows that a company's merchandise available for sale consists of what it begins with (beginning inventory) and what it

EXHIBIT 4.4

Merchandiser's Cost Flow for a Single Time Period

Point: Mathematically, Exhibit 4.4 says

BI + NP = MAS,

where BI is beginning inventory, NP is net purchases, and MAS is merchandise available for sale. Exhibit 4.4 also says

MAS = EI + COGS,

which can be rewritten as MAS − EI = COGS or MAS − COGS = EI, where EI is ending inventory and COGS is cost of goods sold. In both equations above, if we know two of the three values, we can solve for the third.

purchases (net purchases). The merchandise available is either sold (cost of goods sold) or kept for future sales (ending inventory).

Two alternative inventory accounting systems can be used to collect information about cost of goods sold and cost of inventory: *perpetual system* or *periodic system*. The **perpetual inventory system** continually updates accounting records for merchandising transactions—specifically, for those records of inventory available for sale and inventory sold. The **periodic inventory system** updates the accounting records for merchandise transactions only at the *end of a period*. Technological advances and competitive pressures have dramatically increased the use of the perpetual system. It gives managers immediate access to detailed information on sales and inventory levels, where they can strategically react to sales trends, cost changes, consumer tastes, and so forth, to increase gross profit. (Some companies use a *hybrid* system where the perpetual system is used for tracking units available and the periodic system is used to compute cost of sales.)

Point: Growth of superstores such as **Costco** and **Sam's** is fueled by efficient use of perpetual inventory. Such large stores evolved only after scannable UPC codes to help control inventory were invented.

Quick Check
Answers — p. 189

1. Describe a merchandiser's cost of goods sold.
2. How do we compute gross profit for a merchandising company?
3. Explain why use of the perpetual inventory system has dramatically increased.

The following sections, consisting of the next 10 pages on purchasing, selling, and adjusting merchandise, use the perpetual system. Appendix 4A uses the periodic system (with the perpetual results on the side). An instructor can choose to cover either one or both inventory systems.

ACCOUNTING FOR MERCHANDISE PURCHASES

P1 Analyze and record transactions for merchandise purchases using a perpetual system.

The cost of merchandise purchased for resale is recorded in the Merchandise Inventory asset account. To illustrate, Z-Mart records a $1,200 cash purchase of merchandise on November 2 as follows:

Assets = Liabilities + Equity
+1,200
−1,200

Nov. 2	Merchandise Inventory	1,200	
	Cash		1,200
	Purchased merchandise for cash.		

The invoice for this merchandise is shown in Exhibit 4.5. The buyer usually receives the original invoice, and the seller keeps a copy. This *source document* serves as the purchase invoice of Z-Mart (buyer) and the sales invoice for Trex (seller). The amount recorded for merchandise inventory includes its purchase cost, shipping fees, taxes, and any other costs necessary to make it ready for sale. This section explains how we compute the recorded cost of merchandise purchases.

Point: The Merchandise Inventory account reflects the cost of goods available for resale. Costs recorded in Merchandise Inventory are sometimes called *inventoriable costs.*

■ Decision Insight

Trade Discounts When a manufacturer or wholesaler prepares a catalog of items it has for sale, it usually gives each item a **list price,** also called a *catalog price.* However, an item's intended *selling price* equals list price minus a given percent called a **trade discount.** The amount of trade discount usually depends on whether a buyer is a wholesaler, retailer, or final consumer. A wholesaler buying in large quantities is often granted a larger discount than a retailer buying in smaller quantities. A buyer records the net amount of list price minus trade discount. For example, in the November 2 purchase of merchandise by Z-Mart, the merchandise was listed in the seller's catalog at $2,000 and Z-Mart received a 40% trade discount. This meant that Z-Mart's purchase price was $1,200, computed as $2,000 − (40% × $2,000). ■

Point: Lowes and **Home Depot** offer trade discounts to construction companies and contractors. Trade discounts help create loyalty among customers.

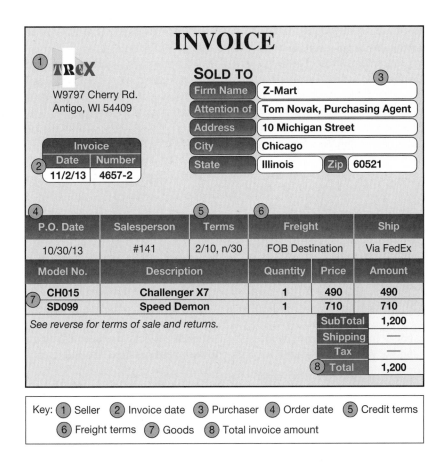

EXHIBIT 4.5

Invoice

Purchase Discounts

The purchase of goods on credit requires a clear statement of expected future payments and dates to avoid misunderstandings. **Credit terms** for a purchase include the amounts and timing of payments from a buyer to a seller. Credit terms usually reflect an industry's practices. To illustrate, when sellers require payment within 10 days after the end of the month of the invoice date, the invoice will show credit terms as "n/10 EOM," which stands for net 10 days after end of month (**EOM**). When sellers require payment within 30 days after the invoice date, the invoice shows credit terms of "n/30," which stands for *net 30 days*.

Exhibit 4.6 portrays credit terms. The amount of time allowed before full payment is due is called the **credit period.** Sellers can grant a **cash discount** to encourage buyers to pay earlier. A buyer views a cash discount as a **purchase discount.** A seller views a cash discount as a **sales discount.** Any cash discounts are described in the credit terms on the invoice. For example, credit terms of "2/10, n/60" mean that full payment is due within a 60-day credit period, but the buyer can deduct 2% of the invoice amount if payment is made within 10 days of the invoice date. This reduced payment applies only for the **discount period.**

Point: Since both the buyer and seller know the invoice date, this date is used in setting the discount and credit periods.

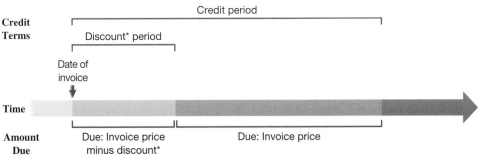

EXHIBIT 4.6

Credit Terms

Point: Appendix 4A repeats journal entries *a* through *f* using a periodic inventory system.

Assets = Liabilities + Equity
+1,200   +1,200

To illustrate how a buyer accounts for a purchase discount, assume that Z-Mart's $1,200 purchase of merchandise is on credit with terms of 2/10, n/30. Its entry is

(a) Nov. 2	Merchandise Inventory	1,200	
	Accounts Payable		1,200
	Purchased merchandise on credit, invoice		
	dated Nov. 2, terms 2/10, n/30.		

If Z-Mart pays the amount due on (or before) November 12, the entry is

Assets = Liabilities + Equity
−24   −1,200
−1,176

(b) Nov. 12	Accounts Payable	1,200	
	Merchandise Inventory		24
	Cash		1,176
	Paid for the $1,200 purchase of Nov. 2 less the		
	discount of $24 (2% × $1,200).		

Point: These entries illustrate what is called the *gross method* of accounting for purchases with discount terms.

The Merchandise Inventory account after these entries reflects the net cost of merchandise purchased, and the Accounts Payable account shows a zero balance. Both ledger accounts, in T-account form, follow:

Merchandise Inventory					Accounts Payable			
Nov. 2	1,200	Nov. 12	24		Nov. 12	1,200	Nov. 2	1,200
Balance	1,176						Balance	0

A buyer's failure to pay within a discount period can be expensive. To illustrate, if Z-Mart does not pay within the 10-day 2% discount period, it can delay payment by 20 more days. This delay costs Z-Mart $24, computed as 2% × $1,200. Most buyers take advantage of a purchase discount because of the usually high interest rate implied from not taking it.[1] Also, good cash management means that no invoice is paid until the last day of the discount or credit period.

 **Decision** Maker

Entrepreneur You purchase a batch of products on terms of 3/10, n/90, but your company has limited cash and you must borrow funds at an 11% annual rate if you are to pay within the discount period. Is it to your advantage to take the purchase discount? Explain. ■ [Answer—p. 188]

Purchase Returns and Allowances

Purchase returns refer to merchandise a buyer acquires but then returns to the seller. A *purchase allowance* is a reduction in the cost of defective or unacceptable merchandise that a buyer acquires. Buyers often keep defective but still marketable merchandise if the seller grants an acceptable allowance. When a buyer returns or takes an allowance on merchandise, the buyer issues a **debit memorandum** to inform the seller of a debit made to the seller's account payable in the buyer's records.

Point: The sender (maker) of a *debit memorandum* will debit the account payable of the memo's receiver. The memo's receiver will credit the sender's account receivable.

---

[1] The *implied annual interest rate* formula is:

$$[365 \text{ days} \div (\text{Credit period} - \text{Discount period})] \times \text{Cash discount rate}.$$

For terms of 2/10, n/30, missing the 2% discount for an additional 20 days is equal to an annual interest rate of 36.5%, computed as [365 days/(30 days − 10 days)] × 2% discount rate. *Favorable purchase discounts* are those with implied annual interest rates that exceed the purchaser's annual rate for borrowing money.

Purchase Allowances   To illustrate purchase allowances, assume that on November 15, Z-Mart (buyer) issues a $300 debit memorandum for an allowance from Trex for defective merchandise. Z-Mart's November 15 entry to update its Merchandise Inventory account to reflect the purchase allowance is

(c) Nov. 15	Accounts Payable	300	
	Merchandise Inventory		300
	Allowance for defective merchandise.		

Assets = Liabilities + Equity
−300   −300

The buyer's allowance for defective merchandise is usually offset against the buyer's current account payable balance to the seller. When cash is refunded, the Cash account is debited instead of Accounts Payable.

Purchase Returns   Returns are recorded at the net costs charged to buyers. To illustrate the accounting for returns, suppose Z-Mart purchases $1,000 of merchandise on June 1 with terms 2/10, n/60. Two days later, Z-Mart returns $100 of goods before paying the invoice. When Z-Mart later pays on June 11, it takes the 2% discount only on the $900 remaining balance. When goods are returned, a buyer can take a purchase discount on only the remaining balance of the invoice. The resulting discount is $18 (2% × $900) and the cash payment is $882 ($900 − $18). The following entries reflect this illustration.

Point: In the perpetual system, all purchases, purchase discounts, purchase returns, and cost of sales are recorded in the Merchandise Inventory account. This is different from the periodic system as explained in Appendix 4A.

June 1	Merchandise Inventory	1,000	
	Accounts Payable		1,000
	Purchased merchandise, invoice dated June 1,		
	terms 2/10, n/60.		
June 3	Accounts Payable.............................	100	
	Merchandise Inventory		100
	Returned merchandise to seller.		
June 11	Accounts Payable.............................	900	
	Merchandise Inventory		18
	Cash		882
	Paid for $900 merchandise ($1,000 − $100)		
	less $18 discount (2% × $900).		

Example: Assume Z-Mart pays $980 cash for $1,000 of merchandise purchased within its 2% discount period. Later, it returns $100 of the original $1,000 merchandise. The return entry is
Cash 98
      Merchandise Inventory 98

Decision Ethics

Payables Manager   As a new accounts payable manager, you are being trained by the outgoing manager. She explains that the system prepares checks for amounts net of favorable cash discounts, and the checks are dated the last day of the discount period. She also tells you that checks are not mailed until five days later, adding that "the company gets free use of cash for an extra five days, and our department looks better. When a supplier complains, we blame the computer system and the mailroom." Do you continue this payment policy? ■ [Answer—p. 188]

Transportation Costs and Ownership Transfer

The buyer and seller must agree on who is responsible for paying any freight costs and who bears the risk of loss during transit for merchandising transactions. This is essentially the same as asking at what point ownership transfers from the seller to the buyer. The point of transfer is called the **FOB** (*free on board*) point, which determines who pays transportation costs (and often other incidental costs of transit such as insurance).

   Exhibit 4.7 identifies two alternative points of transfer. (1) *FOB shipping point*, also called *FOB factory*, means the buyer accepts ownership when the goods depart the seller's place of business. The buyer is then responsible for paying shipping costs and bearing the risk of damage or loss when goods are in transit. The goods are part of the buyer's inventory when they are in transit since ownership has transferred to the buyer. **1-800-FLOWERS.COM**, a floral and gift

EXHIBIT 4.7

Ownership Transfer and
Transportation Costs

Shipping Terms	Ownership Transfers When Goods Passed to	Transportation Costs Paid by	
FOB shipping point	Carrier	**Buyer**	Merchandise Inventory... # Cash.............. #
FOB destination	Buyer	**Seller**	Delivery Expense........ # Cash.............. #

Point: If we place an order online and receive free shipping, we have terms FOB destination.

Point: The party not responsible for shipping costs sometimes pays the carrier. In these cases, the party paying these costs either bills the party responsible or, more commonly, adjusts its account payable or account receivable with the other party. For example, a buyer paying a carrier when terms are FOB destination can decrease its account payable to the seller by the amount of shipping cost.

merchandiser, and **Bare Escentuals**, a cosmetic manufacturer, both use FOB shipping point. (2) *FOB destination* means ownership of goods transfers to the buyer when the goods arrive at the buyer's place of business. The seller is responsible for paying shipping charges and bears the risk of damage or loss in transit. The seller does not record revenue from this sale until the goods arrive at the destination because this transaction is not complete before that point. **Kyocera**, a manufacturer, uses FOB destination.

Z-Mart's $1,200 purchase on November 2 is on terms of FOB destination. This means Z-Mart is not responsible for paying transportation costs. When a buyer is responsible for paying transportation costs, the payment is made to a carrier or directly to the seller depending on the agreement. The cost principle requires that any necessary transportation costs of a buyer (often called *transportation-in* or *freight-in*) be included as part of the cost of purchased merchandise. To illustrate, Z-Mart's entry to record a $75 freight charge from an independent carrier for merchandise purchased FOB shipping point is

Assets = Liabilities + Equity
+75
−75

(d) Nov. 24	Merchandise Inventory		75	
	Cash			75
	Paid freight costs on purchased merchandise.			

A seller records the costs of shipping goods to customers in a Delivery Expense account when the seller is responsible for these costs. Delivery Expense, also called *transportation-out* or *freight-out,* is reported as a selling expense in the seller's income statement.

In summary, purchases are recorded as debits to Merchandise Inventory. Any later purchase discounts, returns, and allowances are credited (decreases) to Merchandise Inventory. Transportation-in is debited (added) to Merchandise Inventory. Z-Mart's itemized costs of merchandise purchases for year 2013 are in Exhibit 4.8.

Point: With *tracking numbers* it is possible to know the exact time shipped goods arrive at their destination.

EXHIBIT 4.8

Itemized Costs of
Merchandise Purchases

Z-MART **Itemized Costs of Merchandise Purchases** **For Year Ended December 31, 2013**	
Invoice cost of merchandise purchases	$ 235,800
Less: Purchase discounts received	(4,200)
Purchase returns and allowances	(1,500)
Add: Costs of transportation-in	2,300
Total cost of merchandise purchases	**$232,400**

Point: Some companies have separate accounts for purchase discounts, returns and allowances, and transportation-in. These accounts are then transferred to Merchandise Inventory at period-end. This is a *hybrid system* of perpetual and periodic. That is, Merchandise Inventory is updated on a perpetual basis but only for purchases and cost of goods sold.

The accounting system described here does not provide separate records (accounts) for total purchases, total purchase discounts, total purchase returns and allowances, and total transportation-in. Yet nearly all companies collect this information in supplementary records because managers need this information to evaluate and control each of these cost elements. **Supplementary records,** also called *supplemental records,* refer to information outside the usual general ledger accounts.

Quick Check   Answers — p. 189

4. How long are the credit and discount periods when credit terms are 2/10, n/60?

5. Identify which items are subtracted from the *list* amount and not recorded when computing purchase price: (a) freight-in; (b) trade discount; (c) purchase discount; (d) purchase return.

6. What does *FOB* mean? What does *FOB destination* mean?

ACCOUNTING FOR MERCHANDISE SALES

Merchandising companies also must account for sales, sales discounts, sales returns and allowances, and cost of goods sold. A merchandising company such as Z-Mart reflects these items in its gross profit computation, as shown in Exhibit 4.9. This section explains how this information is derived from transactions.

P2 Analyze and record transactions for merchandise sales using a perpetual system.

EXHIBIT 4.9

Gross Profit Computation

Z-MART Computation of Gross Profit For Year Ended December 31, 2013		
Sales.		$321,000
Less: Sales discounts	$4,300	
Sales returns and allowances	2,000	6,300
Net sales		314,700
Cost of goods sold		230,400
Gross profit		$ 84,300

Sales of Merchandise

Each sales transaction for a seller of merchandise involves two parts.

1. Revenue received in the form of an asset from the customer.
2. Cost recognized for the merchandise sold to the customer.

Accounting for a sales transaction under the perpetual system requires recording information about both parts. This means that each sales transaction for merchandisers, whether for cash or on credit, requires *two entries:* one for revenue and one for cost. To illustrate, Z-Mart sold $2,400 of merchandise on credit on November 3. The revenue part of this transaction is recorded as

(e) Nov. 3	Accounts Receivable	2,400	
	Sales		2,400
	Sold merchandise on credit.		

Assets = Liabilities + Equity
+2,400   +2,400

This entry reflects an increase in Z-Mart's assets in the form of accounts receivable. It also shows the increase in revenue (Sales). If the sale is for cash, the debit is to Cash instead of Accounts Receivable.

The cost part of each sales transaction ensures that the Merchandise Inventory account under a perpetual inventory system reflects the updated cost of the merchandise available for sale. For example, the cost of the merchandise Z-Mart sold on November 3 is $1,600, and the entry to record the cost part of this sales transaction is

(e) Nov. 3	Cost of Goods Sold	1,600	
	Merchandise Inventory		1,600
	To record the cost of Nov. 3 sale.		

Assets = Liabilities + Equity
−1,600   −1,600

■ **Decision** Insight ══════════════════════════════════════

Suppliers and Demands   Large merchandising companies often bombard suppliers with demands. These include discounts for bar coding and technology support systems, and fines for shipping errors. Merchandisers' goals are to reduce inventories, shorten lead times, and eliminate errors. Many colleges now offer programs in supply chain management and logistics to train future employees that can help merchandisers meet such goals. ■

Sales Discounts

Point: Radio-frequency identification (RFID) tags attach to objects for tracking purposes. Such tags help find items in a store, monitor shipments, and help check on production progress.

Sales discounts on credit sales can benefit a seller by decreasing the delay in receiving cash and reducing future collection efforts. At the time of a credit sale, a seller does not know whether a customer will pay within the discount period and take advantage of a discount. This means the seller usually does not record a sales discount until a customer actually pays within the discount period. To illustrate, Z-Mart completes a credit sale for $1,000 on November 12 with terms of 2/10, n/60. The entry to record the revenue part of this sale is

Assets = Liabilities + Equity
+1,000   +1,000

Nov. 12	Accounts Receivable	1,000	
	Sales		1,000
	Sold merchandise under terms of 2/10, n/60.		

This entry records the receivable and the revenue as if the customer will pay the full amount. The customer has two options, however. One option is to wait 60 days until January 11 and pay the full $1,000. In this case, Z-Mart records that payment as

Assets = Liabilities + Equity
+1,000
−1,000

Jan. 11	Cash	1,000	
	Accounts Receivable		1,000
	Received payment for Nov. 12 sale.		

The customer's second option is to pay $980 within a 10-day period ending November 22. If the customer pays on (or before) November 22, Z-Mart records the payment as

Assets = Liabilities + Equity
+980   −20
−1,000

Nov. 22	Cash	980	
	Sales Discounts	20	
	Accounts Receivable		1,000
	Received payment for Nov. 12 sale less discount.		

Sales Discounts is a contra revenue account, meaning the Sales Discounts account is deducted from the Sales account when computing a company's net sales (see Exhibit 4.9). Management monitors Sales Discounts to assess the effectiveness and cost of its discount policy.

Sales Returns and Allowances

Point: Published income statements rarely disclose sales discounts, returns and allowances.

Sales returns refer to merchandise that customers return to the seller after a sale. Many companies allow customers to return merchandise for a full refund. *Sales allowances* refer to reductions in the selling price of merchandise sold to customers. This can occur with damaged or defective merchandise that a customer is willing to purchase with a decrease in selling price. Sales returns and allowances usually involve dissatisfied customers and the possibility of lost future sales, and managers monitor information about returns and allowances.

Sales Returns   To illustrate, recall Z-Mart's sale of merchandise on November 3 for $2,400 that had cost $1,600. Assume that the customer returns part of the merchandise on

November 6, and the returned items sell for $800 and cost $600. The revenue part of this transaction must reflect the decrease in sales from the customer's return of merchandise as follows:

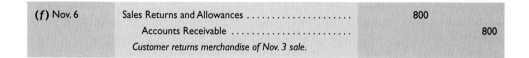

(f) Nov. 6	Sales Returns and Allowances	800	
	Accounts Receivable		800
	Customer returns merchandise of Nov. 3 sale.		

Assets = Liabilities + Equity
−800   −800

If the merchandise returned to Z-Mart is not defective and can be resold to another customer, Z-Mart returns these goods to its inventory. The entry to restore the cost of such goods to the Merchandise Inventory account is

Nov. 6	Merchandise Inventory	600	
	Cost of Goods Sold		600
	Returned goods added to inventory.		

Assets = Liabilities + Equity
+600   +600

This entry changes if the goods returned are defective. In this case the returned inventory is recorded at its estimated value, not its cost. To illustrate, if the goods (costing $600) returned to Z-Mart are defective and estimated to be worth $150, the following entry is made: Dr. Merchandise Inventory for $150, Dr. Loss from Defective Merchandise for $450, and Cr. Cost of Goods Sold for $600.

Point: Some sellers charge buyers a re-stocking fee for returns.

Decision Insight

Reversing Returns. On May 3, 2011, Green Mountain Coffee Roasters beat analysts' earnings estimates by $0.10 per share for the 13-week period ended March 26, 2011. The next day the stock price rose $11.91 per share to close at $75.98 per share, an 18.5% increase over the prior day's closing price. In the weeks that followed, some analysts raised questions about the quality of Green Mountain's earnings because of its accounting for sales returns. They allege that a large part of that earnings increase was due to an accounting adjustment that reversed much of a reserve that was set up for sales returns in prior periods. ■

Sales Allowances To illustrate sales allowances, assume that $800 of the merchandise Z-Mart sold on November 3 is defective but the buyer decides to keep it because Z-Mart offers a $100 price reduction. Z-Mart records this allowance as follows:

Nov. 6	Sales Returns and Allowances	100	
	Accounts Receivable		100
	To record sales allowance on Nov. 3 sale.		

Assets = Liabilities + Equity
−100   −100

The seller usually prepares a credit memorandum to confirm a buyer's return or allowance. A seller's **credit memorandum** informs a buyer of the seller's credit to the buyer's Account Receivable (on the seller's books).

Point: The sender (maker) of a credit memorandum will *credit* the account of the receiver. The receiver of a credit memorandum will *debit* the sender's account.

Quick Check
Answers – p. 189

7. Why are sales discounts and sales returns and allowances recorded in contra revenue accounts instead of directly in the Sales account?

8. Under what conditions are two entries necessary to record a sales return?

9. When merchandise is sold on credit and the seller notifies the buyer of a price allowance, does the seller create and send a credit memorandum or a debit memorandum?

COMPLETING THE ACCOUNTING CYCLE

Exhibit 4.10 shows the flow of merchandising costs during a period and where these costs are reported at period-end. Specifically, beginning inventory plus the net cost of purchases is the merchandise available for sale. As inventory is sold, its cost is recorded in cost of goods sold on the income statement; what remains is ending inventory on the balance sheet. A period's ending inventory is the next period's beginning inventory.

EXHIBIT 4.10

Merchandising Cost Flow in the Accounting Cycle

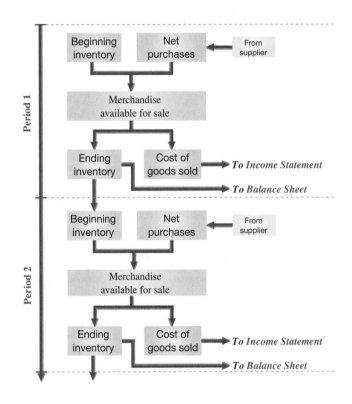

Adjusting Entries for Merchandisers

P3 Prepare adjustments and close accounts for a merchandising company.

Each of the steps in the accounting cycle described in the prior chapter for a service company applies to a merchandiser. This section and the next two further explain three steps of the accounting cycle for a merchandiser—adjustments, statement preparation, and closing.

Adjusting entries are generally the same for merchandising companies and service companies, including those for prepaid expenses (including depreciation), accrued expenses, unearned revenues, and accrued revenues. However, a merchandiser using a perpetual inventory system is usually required to make another adjustment to update the Merchandise Inventory account to reflect any loss of merchandise, including theft and deterioration. **Shrinkage** is the term used to refer to the loss of inventory and it is computed by comparing a physical count of inventory with recorded amounts. A physical count is usually performed at least once annually.

To illustrate, Z-Mart's Merchandise Inventory account at the end of year 2013 has a balance of $21,250, but a physical count reveals that only $21,000 of inventory exists. The adjusting entry to record this $250 shrinkage is

Point: About two-thirds of shoplifting losses are thefts by employees.

Assets = Liabilities + Equity
−250   −250

Dec. 31	Cost of Goods Sold	250	
	Merchandise Inventory		250
	To adjust for $250 shrinkage revealed by a		
	physical count of inventory.		

Preparing Financial Statements

The financial statements of a merchandiser, and their preparation, are similar to those for a service company described in Chapters 2 and 3. The income statement mainly differs by the inclusion of *cost of goods sold* and *gross profit.* Also, net sales is affected by discounts, returns, and allowances, and some additional expenses are possible such as delivery expense and loss from defective merchandise. The balance sheet mainly differs by the inclusion of *merchandise inventory* as part of current assets. The statement of retained earnings is unchanged. A work sheet can be used to help prepare these statements, and one is illustrated in Appendix 4B for Z-Mart.

Point: Staples's costs of shipping merchandise to its stores is included in its costs of inventories as required by the cost principle.

Closing Entries for Merchandisers

Closing entries are similar for service companies and merchandising companies using a perpetual system. The difference is that we must close some new temporary accounts that arise from merchandising activities. Z-Mart has several temporary accounts unique to merchandisers: Sales (of goods), Sales Discounts, Sales Returns and Allowances, and Cost of Goods Sold. Their existence in the ledger means that the first two closing entries for a merchandiser are slightly different from the ones described in the prior chapter for a service company. These differences are set in **red boldface** in the closing entries of Exhibit 4.11.

Point: The Inventory account is not affected by the closing process under a perpetual system.

EXHIBIT 4.11

Closing Entries for a Merchandiser

Step 1: Close Credit Balances in Temporary Accounts to Income Summary.

Dec. 31	**Sales**	**321,000**	
	Income Summary		321,000
	To close credit balances in temporary accounts.		

Step 2: Close Debit Balances in Temporary Accounts to Income Summary.

Dec. 31	Income Summary	308,100	
	Sales Discounts		**4,300**
	Sales Returns and Allowances		**2,000**
	Cost of Goods Sold		**230,400**
	Depreciation Expense		3,700
	Salaries Expense		43,800
	Insurance Expense		600
	Rent Expense		9,000
	Supplies Expense		3,000
	Advertising Expense		11,300
	To close debit balances in temporary accounts.		

Step 3: Close Income Summary to Retained Earnings.

The third closing entry is identical for a merchandising company and a service company. The $12,900 amount is net income reported on the income statement.

Dec. 31	Income Summary	12,900	
	Retained Earnings		12,900
	To close the Income Summary account.		

Step 4: Close Dividends Account to Retained Earnings.

The fourth closing entry is identical for a merchandising company and a service company. It closes the Dividends account and adjusts the Retained Earnings account to the amount shown on the balance sheet.

Dec. 31	Retained Earnings	4,000	
	Dividends		4,000
	To close the Dividends account.		

Summary of Merchandising Entries

Exhibit 4.12 summarizes the key adjusting and closing entries of a merchandiser (using a perpetual inventory system) that are different from those of a service company described in prior chapters (the Demonstration Problem 2 illustrates these merchandising entries).

EXHIBIT 4.12

Summary of Merchandising Entries

	Merchandising Transactions	Merchandising Entries	Dr.	Cr.
Purchases	Purchasing merchandise for resale.	Merchandise Inventory	#	
		Cash or Accounts Payable		#
	Paying freight costs on purchases; FOB shipping point.	Merchandise Inventory	#	
		Cash		#
	Paying within discount period.	Accounts Payable	#	
		Merchandise Inventory		#
		Cash		#
	Recording purchase returns or allowances.	Cash or Accounts Payable	#	
		Merchandise Inventory		#
Sales	Selling merchandise.	Cash or Accounts Receivable	#	
		Sales		#
		Cost of Goods Sold	#	
		Merchandise Inventory		#
	Receiving payment within discount period.	Cash	#	
		Sales Discounts	#	
		Accounts Receivable		#
	Granting sales returns or allowances.	Sales Returns and Allowances	#	
		Cash or Accounts Receivable		#
		Merchandise Inventory	#	
		Cost of Goods Sold		#
	Paying freight costs on sales; FOB destination.	Delivery Expense	#	
		Cash		#

	Merchandising Events	Adjusting and Closing Entries		
Adjusting	Adjusting due to shrinkage (occurs when recorded amount larger than physical inventory).	Cost of Goods Sold	#	
		Merchandise Inventory		#
Closing	Closing temporary accounts with credit balances.	Sales	#	
		Income Summary		#
	Closing temporary accounts with debit balances.	Income Summary	#	
		Sales Returns and Allowances		#
		Sales Discounts		#
		Cost of Goods Sold		#
		Delivery Expense		#
		"Other Expenses"		#

Quick Check   Answers — p. 189

10. When a merchandiser uses a perpetual inventory system, why is it sometimes necessary to adjust the Merchandise Inventory balance with an adjusting entry?

11. What temporary accounts do you expect to find in a merchandising business but not in a service business?

12. Describe the closing entries normally made by a merchandising company.

FINANCIAL STATEMENT FORMATS

P4 Define and prepare multiple-step and single-step income statements.

Generally accepted accounting principles do not require companies to use any one presentation format for financial statements so we see many different formats in practice. This section describes two common income statement formats: multiple-step and single-step. The classified balance sheet of a merchandiser is also explained.

Multiple-Step Income Statement

A **multiple-step income statement** format shows detailed computations of net sales and other costs and expenses, and reports subtotals for various classes of items. Exhibit 4.13 shows a multiple-step income statement for Z-Mart. The statement has three main parts: (1) *gross profit,* determined by net sales less cost of goods sold, (2) *income from operations,* determined by gross profit less operating expenses, and (3) *net income,* determined by income from operations adjusted for nonoperating items.

EXHIBIT 4.13

Multiple-Step Income Statement

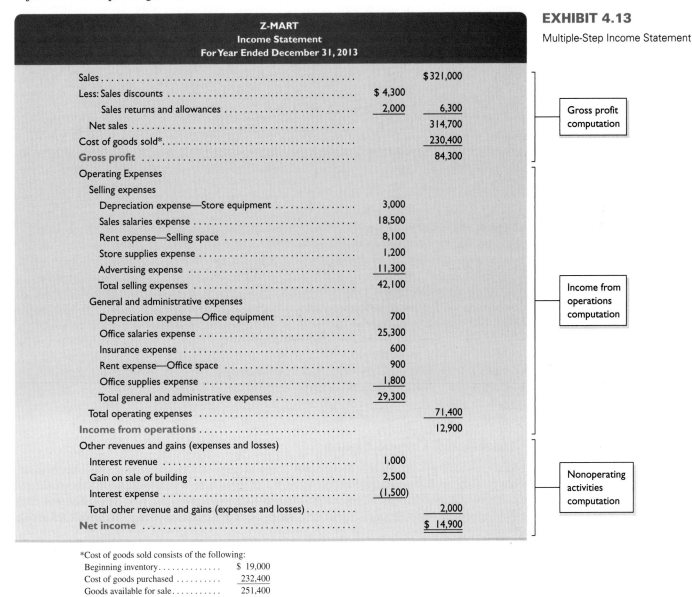

Z-MART			
Income Statement			
For Year Ended December 31, 2013			
Sales			$321,000
Less: Sales discounts		$ 4,300	
Sales returns and allowances		2,000	6,300
Net sales			314,700
Cost of goods sold*			230,400
Gross profit			84,300
Operating Expenses			
Selling expenses			
Depreciation expense—Store equipment	3,000		
Sales salaries expense	18,500		
Rent expense—Selling space	8,100		
Store supplies expense	1,200		
Advertising expense	11,300		
Total selling expenses	42,100		
General and administrative expenses			
Depreciation expense—Office equipment	700		
Office salaries expense	25,300		
Insurance expense	600		
Rent expense—Office space	900		
Office supplies expense	1,800		
Total general and administrative expenses	29,300		
Total operating expenses		71,400	
Income from operations		12,900	
Other revenues and gains (expenses and losses)			
Interest revenue	1,000		
Gain on sale of building	2,500		
Interest expense	(1,500)		
Total other revenue and gains (expenses and losses)		2,000	
Net income		$ 14,900	

Gross profit computation

Income from operations computation

Nonoperating activities computation

*Cost of goods sold consists of the following:

Beginning inventory	$ 19,000
Cost of goods purchased	232,400
Goods available for sale	251,400
Less ending inventory	21,000
Cost of goods sold	$230,400

Operating expenses are classified into two sections. **Selling expenses** include the expenses of promoting sales by displaying and advertising merchandise, making sales, and delivering goods to customers. **General and administrative expenses** support a company's overall operations and include expenses related to accounting, human resource management, and financial management. Expenses are allocated between sections when they contribute to more than one. Z-Mart allocates rent expense of $9,000 from its store building between two sections: $8,100 to selling expense and $900 to general and administrative expense.

Nonoperating activities consist of other expenses, revenues, losses, and gains that are unrelated to a company's operations. *Other revenues and gains* commonly include interest revenue,

Point: Z-Mart did not have any nonoperating activities; however, Exhibit 4.13 includes some for illustrative purposes.

dividend revenue, rent revenue, and gains from asset disposals. *Other expenses and losses* commonly include interest expense, losses from asset disposals, and casualty losses. When a company has no reportable nonoperating activities, its income from operations is simply labeled net income.

Single-Step Income Statement

A **single-step income statement** is another widely used format and is shown in Exhibit 4.14 for Z-Mart. It lists cost of goods sold as another expense and shows only one subtotal for total expenses. Expenses are grouped into very few, if any, categories. Many companies use formats that combine features of both the single- and multiple-step statements. Provided that income statement items are shown sensibly, management can choose the format. (In later chapters, we describe some items, such as extraordinary gains and losses, that must be reported in certain locations on the income statement.) Similar presentation options are available for the statement of retained earnings and statement of cash flows.

Point: Many companies report interest expense and interest revenue in separate categories after operating income and before subtracting income tax expense. As one example, see **Arctic Cat**'s and **KTM**'s income statements in Appendix A.

Example: Sometimes interest revenue and interest expense are reported on the income statement as *interest, net*. To illustrate, if a company has $1,000 of interest expense and $600 of interest revenue, it might report $400 as *interest, net*.

EXHIBIT 4.14

Single-Step Income Statement

Z-MART		
Income Statement		
For Year Ended December 31, 2013		
Revenues		
Net sales		$314,700
Interest revenue		1,000
Gain on sale of building		2,500
Total revenues		318,200
Expenses		
Cost of goods sold	$230,400	
Selling expenses	42,100	
General and administrative expenses	29,300	
Interest expense	1,500	
Total expenses		303,300
Net income		$ 14,900

Classified Balance Sheet

The merchandiser's classified balance sheet reports merchandise inventory as a current asset, usually after accounts receivable according to an asset's nearness to liquidity. Inventory is usually less liquid than accounts receivable because inventory must first be sold before cash can be received; but it is more liquid than supplies and prepaid expenses. Exhibit 4.15 shows the current asset section of Z-Mart's classified balance sheet (other sections are as shown in Chapter 3).

EXHIBIT 4.15

Classified Balance Sheet (partial) of a Merchandiser

Z-MART	
Balance Sheet (partial)	
December 31, 2013	
Current assets	
Cash	$ 8,200
Accounts receivable	11,200
Merchandise inventory	21,000
Office supplies	550
Store supplies	250
Prepaid insurance	300
Total current assets	$ 41,500

Decision Insight

Merchandising Shenanigans Accurate invoices are important to both sellers and buyers. Merchandisers rely on invoices to make certain they receive all monies for products provided—no more, no less. To achieve this, controls are set up. Still, failures arise. A survey reports that 9% of employees in sales and marketing witnessed false or misleading invoices sent to customers. Another 14% observed employees violating contract terms with customers (KPMG 2009). ■

GLOBAL VIEW

This section discusses similarities and differences between U.S. GAAP and IFRS in accounting and reporting for merchandise purchases and sales, and for the income statement.

Accounting for Merchandise Purchases and Sales Both U.S. GAAP and IFRS include broad and similar guidance for the accounting of merchandise purchases and sales. Specifically, all of the transactions presented and illustrated in this chapter are accounted for identically under the two systems. The closing process for merchandisers also is identical for U.S. GAAP and IFRS. In the next chapter we describe how inventory valuation can, in some cases, be different for the two systems.

Income Statement Presentation We explained that net income, profit, and earnings refer to the same (*bottom line*) item. However, IFRS tends to use the term *profit* more than any other term, whereas U.S. statements tend to use *net income* more than any other term. Both U.S. GAAP and IFRS income statements begin with the net sales or net revenues (*top line*) item. For merchandisers and manufacturers, this is followed by cost of goods sold. The presentation is similar for the remaining items with the following differences.

- U.S. GAAP offers little guidance about the presentation or order of expenses. IFRS requires separate disclosures for financing costs (interest expense), income tax expense, and some other special items.
- Both systems require separate disclosure of items when their size, nature, or frequency are important.
- IFRS permits expenses to be presented by their function or their nature. U.S. GAAP provides no direction but the SEC requires presentation by function.
- Neither U.S. GAAP nor IFRS define *operating* income, which results in latitude in reporting.
- IFRS permits alternative income measures on the income statement; U.S. GAAP does not.

Volkswagen Group provides the following example of income statement reporting. We see the separate disclosure of finance costs, taxes, and other items. We also see the unusual practice of using the minus symbol in an income statement.

VOLKSWAGEN

VOLKSWAGEN GROUP Income Statement (in Euros million) For Year Ended December 31, 2011	
Sales revenue	159,337
Cost of sales	−131,371
Gross profit	27,966
Distribution expenses	−14,582
Administrative expenses	−4,384
Other operating income (net of other expenses)	2,271
Operating profit	11,271
Finance costs	−2,047
Other financial results (including equity investments)	9,702
Profit before tax	18,926
Income tax	−3,127
Profit	15,799

Balance Sheet Presentation Chapters 2 and 3 explained how both U.S. GAAP and IFRS require current items to be separated from noncurrent items on the balance sheet (yielding a *classified balance sheet*). As discussed, U.S. GAAP balance sheets report current items first. Assets are listed from most liquid to least liquid, whereas liabilities are listed from nearest to maturity to furthest from maturity. IFRS balance sheets normally present noncurrent items first (and equity before liabilities), but this is *not* a requirement. **Piaggio** provides an example of IFRS reporting for the balance sheet in Appendix A.

PIAGGIO

Decision Analysis Acid-Test and Gross Margin Ratios

Acid-Test Ratio

A1 Compute the acid-test ratio and explain its use to assess liquidity.

For many merchandisers, inventory makes up a large portion of current assets. Inventory must be sold and any resulting accounts receivable must be collected before cash is available. Chapter 3 explained that the current ratio, defined as current assets divided by current liabilities, is useful in assessing a company's ability to pay current liabilities. Because it is sometimes unreasonable to assume that inventories are a source of payment for current liabilities, we look to other measures.

One measure of a merchandiser's ability to pay its current liabilities (referred to as its *liquidity*) is the acid-test ratio. It differs from the current ratio by excluding less liquid current assets such as inventory and prepaid expenses that take longer to be converted to cash. The **acid-test ratio,** also called *quick ratio,* is defined as *quick assets* (cash, short-term investments, and current receivables) divided by current liabilities—see Exhibit 4.16.

EXHIBIT 4.16

Acid-Test (Quick) Ratio

$$\text{Acid-test ratio} = \frac{\text{Cash and cash equivalents + Short-term investments + Current receivables}}{\text{Current liabilities}}$$

Exhibit 4.17 shows both the acid-test and current ratios of retailer **JCPenney** for fiscal years 2008 through 2012—also see margin graph. JCPenney's acid-test ratio reveals a general increase from 2008 through 2011 that exceeds the industry average, and then a marked decline in 2012. Further, JCPenney's current ratio shows a marked decline in 2012 to 1.84, which suggests that its short-term obligations are less confidently covered with short-term assets compared with prior years.

EXHIBIT 4.17

JCPenney's Acid-Test and Current Ratios

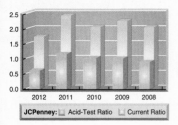

($ millions)	2012	2011	2010	2009	2008
Total quick assets	$1,920	$2,956	$3,406	$2,704	$2,845
Total current assets	5,081	$6,370	$6,652	$6,220	$6,751
Total current liabilities	2,756	$2,647	$3,249	$2,794	$3,338
Acid-test ratio	0.70	1.12	1.05	0.97	0.85
Current ratio	1.84	2.41	2.05	2.23	2.02
Industry acid-test ratio	0.54	0.61	0.59	0.63	0.62
Industry current ratio	2.01	2.27	2.15	2.31	2.39

Point: Successful use of a just-in-time inventory system can narrow the gap between the acid-test ratio and the current ratio.

An acid-test ratio less than 1.0 means that current liabilities exceed quick assets. A rule of thumb is that the acid-test ratio should have a value near, or higher than, 1.0 to conclude that a company is unlikely to face near-term liquidity problems. A value much less than 1.0 raises liquidity concerns unless a company can generate enough cash from inventory sales or if much of its liabilities are not due until late in the next period. Similarly, a value slightly larger than 1.0 can hide a liquidity problem if payables are due shortly and receivables are not collected until late in the next period. Analysis of JCPenney shows some need for concern regarding its liquidity as its acid-test ratio is less than one. However, retailers such as JCPenney pay many current liabilities from inventory sales and in all years, JCPenney's acid-test ratios exceed the industry norm (and its inventory is fairly liquid).

Decision Maker

Supplier A retailer requests to purchase supplies on credit from your company. You have no prior experience with this retailer. The retailer's current ratio is 2.1, its acid-test ratio is 0.5, and inventory makes up most of its current assets. Do you extend credit? ■ [Answer—p. 188]

Gross Margin Ratio

A2 Compute the gross margin ratio and explain its use to assess profitability.

The cost of goods sold makes up much of a merchandiser's expenses. Without sufficient gross profit, a merchandiser will likely fail. Users often compute the gross margin ratio to help understand this relation. It differs from the profit margin ratio in that it excludes all costs except cost of goods sold. The **gross margin ratio** (also called *gross profit ratio*) is defined as *gross margin* (net sales minus cost of goods sold) divided by net sales—see Exhibit 4.18.

EXHIBIT 4.18

Gross Margin Ratio

$$\text{Gross margin ratio} = \frac{\text{Net sales} - \text{Cost of goods sold}}{\text{Net sales}}$$

Exhibit 4.19 shows the gross margin ratio of JCPenney for fiscal years 2008 through 2012. For JCPenney, each $1 of sales in 2012 yielded about 36.0¢ in gross margin to cover all other expenses and still produce a net income. This 36.0¢ margin is down from 38.6¢ in 2008. This decrease is not a favorable development. Success for merchandisers such as JCPenney depends on adequate gross margin. For example, the 2.60¢ decrease in the gross margin ratio, computed as 36.0¢ − 38.6¢, means that JCPenney has $448.76 million less in gross margin! (This is computed as net sales of $17,260 million multiplied by the 2.6% decrease in gross margin.) Management's discussion in its annual report attributes this decline to "softer than expected selling environment and the resulting increased promotional activity and the costs associated with implementing our new pricing strategy."

Point: The power of a ratio is often its ability to identify areas for more detailed analysis.

($ millions)	2012	2011	2010	2009	2008
Gross margin	$ 6,218	$ 6,960	$ 6,910	$ 6,915	$ 7,671
Net sales	$17,260	$17,759	$17,556	$18,486	$19,860
Gross margin ratio	36.0%	39.2%	39.4%	37.4%	38.6%

EXHIBIT 4.19
JCPenney's Gross Margin Ratio

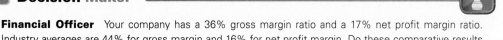

Decision Maker

Financial Officer Your company has a 36% gross margin ratio and a 17% net profit margin ratio. Industry averages are 44% for gross margin and 16% for net profit margin. Do these comparative results concern you? ■ [Answer—p. 189]

DEMONSTRATION PROBLEM 1

Use the following adjusted trial balance and additional information to complete the requirements.

KC ANTIQUES
Adjusted Trial Balance
December 31, 2013

	Debit	Credit
Cash	$ 7,000	
Accounts receivable	13,000	
Merchandise inventory	60,000	
Store supplies	1,500	
Equipment	45,600	
Accumulated depreciation—Equipment		$ 16,600
Accounts payable		9,000
Salaries payable		2,000
Common Stock		20,000
Retained Earnings		59,000
Dividends	10,000	
Sales		343,250
Sales discounts	5,000	
Sales returns and allowances	6,000	
Cost of goods sold	159,900	
Depreciation expense—Store equipment	4,100	
Depreciation expense—Office equipment	1,600	
Sales salaries expense	30,000	
Office salaries expense	34,000	
Insurance expense	11,000	
Rent expense (70% is store, 30% is office)	24,000	
Store supplies expense	5,750	
Advertising expense	31,400	
Totals	$449,850	$449,850

KC Antiques' *supplementary records* for 2013 reveal the following itemized costs for merchandising activities:

Invoice cost of merchandise purchases	$150,000
Purchase discounts received	2,500
Purchase returns and allowances	2,700
Cost of transportation-in	5,000

Required

1. Use the supplementary records to compute the total cost of merchandise purchases for 2013.

2. Prepare a 2013 multiple-step income statement. (Inventory at December 31, 2012, is $70,100.)

3. Prepare a single-step income statement for 2013.

4. Prepare closing entries for KC Antiques at December 31, 2013.

5. Compute the acid-test ratio and the gross margin ratio. Explain the meaning of each ratio and interpret them for KC Antiques.

PLANNING THE SOLUTION

● Compute the total cost of merchandise purchases for 2013.

● To prepare the multiple-step statement, first compute net sales. Then, to compute cost of goods sold, add the net cost of merchandise purchases for the year to beginning inventory and subtract the cost of ending inventory. Subtract cost of goods sold from net sales to get gross profit. Then classify expenses as selling expenses or general and administrative expenses.

● To prepare the single-step income statement, begin with net sales. Then list and subtract the expenses.

● The first closing entry debits all temporary accounts with credit balances and opens the Income Summary account. The second closing entry credits all temporary accounts with debit balances. The third entry closes the Income Summary account to the retained earnings account, and the fourth entry closes the dividends account to the retained earnings account.

● Identify the quick assets on the adjusted trial balance. Compute the acid-test ratio by dividing quick assets by current liabilities. Compute the gross margin ratio by dividing gross profit by net sales.

SOLUTION TO DEMONSTRATION PROBLEM 1

1.

Invoice cost of merchandise purchases	$150,000
Less: Purchases discounts received	2,500
Purchase returns and allowances	2,700
Add: Cost of transportation-in	5,000
Total cost of merchandise purchases	$149,800

2. Multiple-step income statement

KC ANTIQUES		
Income Statement		
For Year Ended December 31, 2013		
Sales		$343,250
Less: Sales discounts	$ 5,000	
Sales returns and allowances	6,000	11,000
Net sales		332,250
Cost of goods sold*		159,900
Gross profit		172,350
Expenses		
Selling expenses		
Depreciation expense—Store equipment	4,100	
Sales salaries expense	30,000	
Rent expense—Selling space	16,800	
Store supplies expense	5,750	
Advertising expense	31,400	
Total selling expenses	88,050	

[continued on next page]

[continued from previous page]

General and administrative expenses		
Depreciation expense—Office equipment	1,600	
Office salaries expense	34,000	
Insurance expense	11,000	
Rent expense—Office space	7,200	
Total general and administrative expenses	53,800	
Total operating expenses		141,850
Net income		$ 30,500

* Cost of goods sold can also be directly computed (applying concepts from Exhibit 4.4):

Merchandise inventory, December 31, 2012	$ 70,100
Total cost of merchandise purchases (from part 1)	149,800
Goods available for sale	219,900
Merchandise inventory, December 31, 2013	60,000
Cost of goods sold	$159,900

3. Single-step income statement

KC ANTIQUES
Income Statement
For Year Ended December 31, 2013

Net sales		$332,250
Expenses		
Cost of goods sold	$159,900	
Selling expenses	88,050	
General and administrative expenses	53,800	
Total expenses		301,750
Net income		$ 30,500

4.

Dec. 31	Sales	343,250	
	Income Summary		343,250
	To close credit balances in temporary accounts.		
Dec. 31	Income Summary	312,750	
	Sales Discounts		5,000
	Sales Returns and Allowances		6,000
	Cost of Goods Sold		159,900
	Depreciation Expense—Store Equipment		4,100
	Depreciation Expense—Office Equipment		1,600
	Sales Salaries Expense		30,000
	Office Salaries Expense		34,000
	Insurance Expense		11,000
	Rent Expense		24,000
	Store Supplies Expense		5,750
	Advertising Expense		31,400
	To close debit balances in temporary accounts.		
Dec. 31	Income Summary	30,500	
	Retained Earnings		30,500
	To close the Income Summary account.		
Dec. 31	Retained Earnings	10,000	
	Dividends		10,000
	To close the Dividends account.		

5. Acid-test ratio = (Cash and equivalents + Short-term investments + Current receivables)/
Current liabilities

= (Cash + Accounts receivable/(Accounts payable + Salaries payable)

= ($7,000 + $13,000)/($9,000 + $2,000) = $20,000/$11,000 = 1.82

Gross margin ratio = Gross profit/Net sales = $172,350/$332,250 = 0.52 (or 52%)

KC Antiques has a healthy acid-test ratio of 1.82. This means it has more than $1.80 in liquid assets to satisfy each $1.00 in current liabilities. The gross margin of 0.52 shows that KC Antiques spends 48¢ ($1.00 − $0.52) of every dollar of net sales on the costs of acquiring the merchandise it sells. This leaves 52¢ of every dollar of net sales to cover other expenses incurred in the business and to provide a net profit.

DEMONSTRATION PROBLEM 2

Prepare journal entries to record the following merchandising transactions for both the seller (BMX) and buyer (Sanuk).

May 4   BMX sold $1,500 of merchandise on account to Sanuk, terms FOB shipping point, n/45, invoice dated May 4. The cost of the merchandise was $900.

May 6   Sanuk paid transportation charges of $30 on the May 4 purchase from BMX.

May 8   BMX sold $1,000 of merchandise on account to Sanuk, terms FOB destination, n/30, invoice dated May 8. The cost of the merchandise was $700.

May 10   BMX paid transportation costs of $50 for delivery of merchandise sold to Sanuk on May 8.

May 16   BMX issued Sanuk a $200 credit memorandum for merchandise returned. The merchandise was purchased by Sanuk on account on May 8. The cost of the merchandise returned was $140.

May 18   BMX received payment from Sanuk for purchase of May 8.

May 21   BMX sold $2,400 of merchandise on account to Sanuk, terms FOB shipping point, 2/10, n/EOM. BMX prepaid transportation costs of $100, which were added to the invoice. The cost of the merchandise was $1,440.

May 31   BMX received payment from Sanuk for purchase of May 21, less discount (2% × $2,400).

SOLUTION TO DEMONSTRATION PROBLEM 2

	BMX (Seller)			Sanuk (Buyer)		
May 4	Accounts Receivable—Sanuk	1,500		Merchandise Inventory	1,500	
	Sales		1,500	Accounts Payable—BMX		1,500
	Cost of Goods Sold	900				
	Merchandise Inventory		900			
6	No entry.			Merchandise Inventory	30	
				Cash		30
8	Accounts Receivable—Sanuk	1,000		Merchandise Inventory	1,000	
	Sales		1,000	Accounts Payable—BMX		1,000
	Cost of Goods Sold	700				
	Merchandise Inventory		700			
10	Delivery Expense	50		No entry.		
	Cash		50			
16	Sales Returns & Allowances	200		Accounts Payable—BMX	200	
	Accounts Receivable—Sanuk		200	Merchandise Inventory		200
	Merchandise Inventory	140				
	Cost of Goods Sold		140			
18	Cash	800		Accounts Payable—BMX	800	
	Accounts Receivable—Sanuk		800	Cash		800
21	Accounts Receivable—Sanuk	2,400		Merchandise Inventory	2,500	
	Sales		2,400	Accounts Payable—BMX		2,500
	Accounts Receivable—Sanuk	100				
	Cash		100			
	Cost of Goods Sold	1,440				
	Merchandise Inventory		1,440			
31	Cash	2,452		Accounts Payable—BMX	2,500	
	Sales Discounts	48		Merchandise Inventory		48
	Accounts Receivable—Sanuk		2,500	Cash		2,452

13. What account is used (for journalizing entries) in a perpetual inventory system but not in a periodic system?

14. Which of the following accounts are temporary accounts under a periodic system?
(*a*) Merchandise Inventory; (*b*) Purchases; (*c*) Transportation-In.

15. How is cost of goods sold computed under a periodic inventory system?

16. Do reported amounts of ending inventory and net income differ if the adjusting entry method of recording the change in inventory is used instead of the closing entry method?

APPENDIX

Work Sheet—Perpetual System

4B

Exhibit 4B.1 shows the work sheet for preparing financial statements of a merchandiser. It differs slightly from the work sheet layout in Chapter 3—the differences are in **red boldface**. Also, the adjustments in the work sheet reflect the following: (*a*) Expiration of $600 of prepaid insurance. (*b*) Use of $3,000 of supplies. (*c*) Depreciation of $3,700 for equipment. (*d*) Accrual of $800 of unpaid salaries. (*e*) Inventory shrinkage of $250. Once the adjusted amounts are extended into the financial statement columns, the information is used to develop financial statements.

EXHIBIT 4B.1

Work Sheet for Merchandiser (using a perpetual system)

No.	Account	Unadjusted Trial Balance Dr.	Cr.	Adjustments Dr.	Cr.	Adjusted Trial Balance Dr.	Cr.	Income Statement Dr.	Cr.	Balance Sheet Dr.	Cr.
101	Cash	8,200				8,200				8,200	
106	Accounts receivable	11,200				11,200				11,200	
119	Merchandise Inventory	21,250			(e) 250	21,000				21,000	
126	Supplies	3,800			(b) 3,000	800				800	
128	Prepaid insurance	900			(a) 600	300				300	
167	Equipment	34,200				34,200				34,200	
168	Accumulated depr.—Equip.		3,700		(c) 3,700		7,400				7,400
201	Accounts payable		16,000				16,000				16,000
209	Salaries payable				(d) 800		800				800
307	Common stock		10,000				10,000				10,000
318	Retained earnings		32,600				32,600				32,600
319	Dividends	4,000				4,000				4,000	
413	Sales		321,000				321,000		321,000		
414	Sales returns and allowances	2,000				2,000		2,000			
415	Sales discounts	4,300				4,300		4,300			
502	Cost of goods sold	230,150		(e) 250		230,400		230,400			
612	Depreciation expense—Equip.			(c) 3,700		3,700		3,700			
622	Salaries expense	43,000		(d) 800		43,800		43,800			
637	Insurance expense			(a) 600		600		600			
640	Rent expense	9,000				9,000		9,000			
652	Supplies expense			(b) 3,000		3,000		3,000			
655	Advertising expense	11,300				11,300		11,300			
	Totals	383,300	383,300	8,350	8,350	387,800	387,800	308,100	321,000	79,700	66,800
	Net income							12,900			12,900
	Totals							321,000	321,000	79,700	79,700

Summary

C1 **Describe merchandising activities and identify income components for a merchandising company.** Merchandisers buy products and resell them. Examples of merchandisers include Walmart, Home Depot, The Limited, and Barnes & Noble. A merchandiser's costs on the income statement include an amount for cost of goods sold. Gross profit, or gross margin, equals sales minus cost of goods sold.

C2 **Identify and explain the inventory asset and cost flows of a merchandising company.** The current asset section of a merchandising company's balance sheet includes *merchandise inventory,* which refers to the products a merchandiser sells and are available for sale at the balance sheet date. Cost of merchandise purchases flows into Merchandise Inventory and from there to Cost of Goods Sold on the income statement. Any remaining inventory is reported as a current asset on the balance sheet.

A1 **Compute the acid-test ratio and explain its use to assess liquidity.** The acid-test ratio is computed as quick assets (cash, short-term investments, and current receivables) divided by current liabilities. It indicates a company's ability to pay its current liabilities with its existing quick assets. An acid-test ratio equal to or greater than 1.0 is often adequate.

A2 **Compute the gross margin ratio and explain its use to assess profitability.** The gross margin ratio is computed as gross margin (net sales minus cost of goods sold) divided by net sales. It indicates a company's profitability before considering other expenses.

P1 **Analyze and record transactions for merchandise purchases using a perpetual system.** For a perpetual inventory system, purchases of inventory (net of trade discounts) are added to the Merchandise Inventory account. Purchase discounts and purchase returns and allowances are subtracted from Merchandise Inventory, and transportation-in costs are added to Merchandise Inventory.

P2 **Analyze and record transactions for merchandise sales using a perpetual system.** A merchandiser records sales at list price less any trade discounts. The cost of items sold is transferred from Merchandise Inventory to Cost of Goods Sold. Refunds or credits given to customers for unsatisfactory merchandise are recorded in Sales Returns and Allowances, a contra account to Sales. If merchandise is returned and restored to inventory, the cost of this merchandise is removed from Cost of Goods Sold and transferred back to Merchandise Inventory. When cash discounts from the sales price are offered and customers pay within the discount period, the seller records Sales Discounts, a contra account to Sales.

P3 **Prepare adjustments and close accounts for a merchandising company.** With a perpetual system, it is often necessary to make an adjustment for inventory shrinkage. This is computed by comparing a physical count of inventory with the Merchandise Inventory balance. Shrinkage is normally charged to Cost of Goods Sold. Temporary accounts closed to Income Summary for a merchandiser include Sales, Sales Discounts, Sales Returns and Allowances, and Cost of Goods Sold.

P4 **Define and prepare multiple-step and single-step income statements.** Multiple-step income statements include greater detail for sales and expenses than do single-step income statements. They also show details of net sales and report expenses in categories reflecting different activities.

P5A **Record and compare merchandising transactions using both periodic and perpetual inventory systems.** A perpetual inventory system continuously tracks the cost of goods available for sale and the cost of goods sold. A periodic system accumulates the cost of goods purchased during the period and does not compute the amount of inventory or the cost of goods sold until the end of a period. Transactions involving the sale and purchase of merchandise are recorded and analyzed under both the periodic and perpetual inventory systems. Adjusting and closing entries for both inventory systems are illustrated and explained.

Guidance Answers to Decision Maker and Decision Ethics

Entrepreneur For terms of 3/10, n/90, missing the 3% discount for an additional 80 days equals an implied annual interest rate of 13.69%, computed as (365 days ÷ 80 days) × 3%. Since you can borrow funds at 11% (assuming no other processing costs), it is better to borrow and pay within the discount period. You save 2.69% (13.69% − 11%) in interest costs by paying early.

Payables Manager Your decision is whether to comply with prior policy or to create a new policy and not abuse discounts offered by suppliers. Your first step should be to meet with your superior to find out if the late payment policy is the actual policy and, if so, its rationale. If it is the policy to pay late, you must apply your own sense of ethics. One point of view is that the late payment policy is unethical. A deliberate plan to make late payments means the company lies when it pretends to make payment within the discount period. Another view is that the late payment policy is acceptable. In some markets, attempts to take discounts through late payments are accepted as a continued phase of "price negotiation." Also, your company's suppliers can respond by billing your company for the discounts not accepted because of late payments. However, this is a dubious viewpoint, especially since the prior manager proposes that you dishonestly explain late payments as computer or mail problems and since some suppliers have complained.

Supplier A current ratio of 2.1 suggests sufficient current assets to cover current liabilities. An acid-test ratio of 0.5 suggests, however, that quick assets can cover only about one-half of current liabilities. This implies that the retailer depends on money from sales of inventory to pay current liabilities. If sales of inventory decline or profit margins decrease, the likelihood that this retailer will default on its payments increases. Your decision is probably not to extend credit. If you do extend credit, you are likely to closely monitor the retailer's financial condition. (It is better to hold unsold inventory than uncollectible receivables.)

Answer each of the following questions related to international accounting standards.

a. Explain how the accounting for merchandise purchases and sales is different between accounting under IFRS versus U.S. GAAP.

b. Income statements prepared under IFRS usually report an item titled *finance costs*. What do finance costs refer to?

c. U.S. GAAP prohibits alternative measures of income reported on the income statement. Does IFRS permit such alternative measures on the income statement?

QS 4-15
International accounting standards

C1

On August 1, Gilmore Company purchased merchandise from Hendren with an invoice price of $60,000 and credit terms of 2/10, n/30. Gilmore Company paid Hendren on August 11. Prepare any required journal entry(ies) for Gilmore Company (the purchaser) on: (*a*) August 1, and (*b*) August 11. Assume Gilmore uses the perpetual inventory method.

QS 4-16
Recording discounts taken—perpetual P1

On September 15, Krug Company purchased merchandise inventory from Makarov with an invoice price of $35,000 and credit terms of 2/10, n/30. Krug Company paid Makarov on September 28. Prepare any required journal entry(ies) for Krug Company (the purchaser) on: (*a*) September 15, and (*b*) September 28. Assume Krug uses the perpetual inventory method.

QS 4-17
Recording discounts missed—perpetual P1

Use the following information (in random order) from a service company and from a merchandiser to compute net income. For the merchandiser, also compute gross profit, the goods available for sale, and the cost of goods sold. *Hint:* Not all information may be necessary.

QS 4-18
Merchandise equations and flows

C2

Krug Service Company		Kleiner Merchandising Company	
Expenses................	$ 8,500	Accumulated depreciation..........	$ 700
Revenues	14,000	Beginning inventory	5,000
Dividends	1,600	Common stock	50
Cash	700	Retained earnings................	900
Prepaid rent	800	Ending inventory	1,700
Accounts payable........	200	Operating expenses..............	1,450
Common stock	500	Purchases.....................	3,900
Retained earnings........	2,500	Sales	9,500
Equipment	1,300	Dividends.....................	1,600

---

connect

The operating cycle of a merchandiser with credit sales includes the following five activities. Starting with merchandise acquisition, identify the chronological order of these five activities.

a. _____ inventory made available for sale.
b. _____ cash collections from customers.
c. _____ credit sales to customers.
d. _____ purchases of merchandise.
e. _____ accounts receivable accounted for.

EXERCISES

Exercise 4-1
Operating cycle for merchandiser

C2

Prepare journal entries to record the following transactions for a retail store. Assume a perpetual inventory system.

Apr. 2   Purchased merchandise from Lyon Company under the following terms: $4,600 price, invoice dated April 2, credit terms of 2/15, n/60, and FOB shipping point.
    3   Paid $300 for shipping charges on the April 2 purchase.
    4   Returned to Lyon Company unacceptable merchandise that had an invoice price of $600.
    17   Sent a check to Lyon Company for the April 2 purchase, net of the discount and the returned merchandise.
    18   Purchased merchandise from Frist Corp. under the following terms: $8,500 price, invoice dated April 18, credit terms of 2/10, n/30, and FOB destination.
    21   After negotiations, received from Frist a $1,100 allowance on the April 18 purchase.
    28   Sent check to Frist paying for the April 18 purchase, net of the discount and allowance.

Exercise 4-2
Recording entries for merchandise purchases

P1

Check April 28, Cr. Cash $7,252

Exercise 4-3

Analyzing and recording merchandise transactions—both buyer and seller

P1 P2

Check (3) $465 savings

Santa Fe Company purchased merchandise for resale from Mesa Company with an invoice price of $24,000 and credit terms of 3/10, n/60. The merchandise had cost Mesa $16,000. Santa Fe paid within the discount period. Assume that both buyer and seller use a perpetual inventory system.

1. Prepare entries that the buyer should record for (*a*) the purchase and (*b*) the cash payment.
2. Prepare entries that the seller should record for (*a*) the sale and (*b*) the cash collection.
3. Assume that the buyer borrowed enough cash to pay the balance on the last day of the discount period at an annual interest rate of 8% and paid it back on the last day of the credit period. Compute how much the buyer saved by following this strategy. (Assume a 365-day year and round dollar amounts to the nearest cent, including computation of interest per day.)

Exercise 4-4

Recording sales returns and allowances P2

Check (c) Dr. Merchandise Inventory $400

Allied Parts was organized on May 1, 2013, and made its first purchase of merchandise on May 3. The purchase was for 2,000 units at a price of $10 per unit. On May 5, Allied Parts sold 1,500 of the units for $14 per unit to Baker Co. Terms of the sale were 2/10, n/60. Prepare entries for Allied Parts to record the May 5 sale and each of the following separate transactions *a* through *c* using a perpetual inventory system.

a. On May 7, Baker returns 200 units because they did not fit the customer's needs. Allied Parts restores the units to its inventory.
b. On May 8, Baker discovers that 300 units are damaged but are still of some use and, therefore, keeps the units. Allied Parts sends Baker a credit memorandum for $600 to compensate for the damage.
c. On May 15, Baker discovers that 100 units are the wrong color. Baker keeps 60 of these units because Allied Parts sends a $120 credit memorandum to compensate. Baker returns the remaining 40 units to Allied Parts. Allied Parts restores the 40 returned units to its inventory.

Exercise 4-5

Recording purchase returns and allowances P1

Refer to Exercise 4-4 and prepare the appropriate journal entries for Baker Co. to record the May 5 purchase and each of the three separate transactions *a* through *c*. Baker is a retailer that uses a perpetual inventory system and purchases these units for resale.

Exercise 4-6

Sales returns and allowances

C1

Business decision makers desire information on sales returns and allowances. (1) Explain why a company's manager wants the accounting system to record customers' returns of unsatisfactory goods in the Sales Returns and Allowances account instead of the Sales account. (2) Explain whether this information would be useful for external decision makers.

Exercise 4-7

Analyzing and recording merchandise transactions—both buyer and seller

P1 P2

Check (1) May 20, Cr. Cash $37,442

On May 11, Sydney Co. accepts delivery of $40,000 of merchandise it purchases for resale from Troy Corporation. With the merchandise is an invoice dated May 11, with terms of 3/10, n/90, FOB shipping point. The goods cost Troy $30,000. When the goods are delivered, Sydney pays $345 to Express Shipping for delivery charges on the merchandise. On May 12, Sydney returns $1,400 of goods to Troy, who receives them one day later and restores them to inventory. The returned goods had cost Troy $800. On May 20, Sydney mails a check to Troy Corporation for the amount owed. Troy receives it the following day. (Both Sydney and Troy use a perpetual inventory system.)

1. Prepare journal entries that Sydney Co. records for these transactions.
2. Prepare journal entries that Troy Corporation records for these transactions.

Exercise 4-8

Recording effects of merchandising activities

P1 P2

Check Year-End Merchandise Inventory Dec. 31, $20,000

The following supplementary records summarize Tosca Company's merchandising activities for year 2013. Set up T-accounts for Merchandise Inventory and Cost of Goods Sold. Then record the summarized activities in those T-accounts and compute account balances.

Cost of merchandise sold to customers in sales transactions	$196,000
Merchandise inventory, December 31, 2012	25,000
Invoice cost of merchandise purchases	192,500
Shrinkage determined on December 31, 2013	800
Cost of transportation-in	2,900
Cost of merchandise returned by customers and restored to inventory	2,100
Purchase discounts received	1,700
Purchase returns and allowances	4,000

The following list includes selected permanent accounts and all of the temporary accounts from the December 31, 2013, unadjusted trial balance of Emiko Co., a business owned by Kumi Emiko. Use these account balances along with the additional information to journalize (*a*) adjusting entries and (*b*) closing entries. Emiko Co. uses a perpetual inventory system.

Exercise 4-9
Preparing adjusting and closing entries for a merchandiser
P3

	Debit	Credit
Merchandise inventory	$ 30,000	
Prepaid selling expenses	5,600	
Dividends	33,000	
Sales		$529,000
Sales returns and allowances	17,500	
Sales discounts	5,000	
Cost of goods sold	212,000	
Sales salaries expense	48,000	
Utilities expense	15,000	
Selling expenses	36,000	
Administrative expenses	105,000	

Additional Information

Accrued sales salaries amount to $1,700. Prepaid selling expenses of $3,000 have expired. A physical count of year-end merchandise inventory shows $28,450 of goods still available.

Check   Entry to close Income Summary: Cr. Retained Earnings $84,250

Using your accounting knowledge, fill in the blanks in the following separate income statements *a* through *e*. Identify any negative amount by putting it in parentheses.

Exercise 4-10
Computing revenues, expenses, and income
C1 C2

	a	b	c	d	e
Sales	$62,000	$43,500	$46,000	$?	$25,600
Cost of goods sold					
Merchandise inventory (beginning)	8,000	17,050	7,500	8,000	4,560
Total cost of merchandise purchases	38,000	?	?	32,000	6,600
Merchandise inventory (ending)	?	(3,000)	(9,000)	(6,600)	?
Cost of goods sold	34,050	16,000	?	?	7,000
Gross profit	?	?	3,750	45,600	?
Expenses	10,000	10,650	12,150	3,600	6,000
Net income (loss)	$?	$16,850	$ (8,400)	$42,000	$?

A retail company recently completed a physical count of ending merchandise inventory to use in preparing adjusting entries. In determining the cost of the counted inventory, company employees failed to consider that $3,000 of incoming goods had been shipped by a supplier on December 31 under an FOB shipping point agreement. These goods had been recorded in Merchandise Inventory as a purchase, but they were not included in the physical count because they were in transit. Explain how this overlooked fact affects the company's financial statements and the following ratios: return on assets, debt ratio, current ratio, and acid-test ratio.

Exercise 4-11
Interpreting a physical count error as inventory shrinkage
A1

Refer to the information in Exercise 4-11 and explain how the error in the physical count affects the company's gross margin ratio and its profit margin ratio.

Exercise 4-12
Physical count error and profits
A2

Exercise 4-13
Computing and analyzing
acid-test and current ratios

A1

Compute the current ratio and acid-test ratio for each of the following separate cases. (Round ratios to two decimals.) Which company case is in the best position to meet short-term obligations? Explain.

	Case X	Case Y	Case Z
Cash	$2,000	$ 110	$1,000
Short-term investments	0	0	600
Current receivables	350	590	700
Inventory	2,650	2,300	4,100
Prepaid expenses	200	500	900
Total current assets	$5,200	$3,500	$7,300
Current liabilities	$2,200	$1,200	$3,750

Exercise 4-14
Preparing journal entries—
perpetual system

P1 P2

Journalize the following merchandising transactions for Chilton Systems assuming it uses a perpetual inventory system.

1. On November 1, Chilton Systems purchases merchandise for $1,500 on credit with terms of 2/5, n/30, FOB shipping point; invoice dated November 1.
2. On November 5, Chilton Systems pays cash for the November 1 purchase.
3. On November 7, Chilton Systems discovers and returns $200 of defective merchandise purchased on November 1 for a cash refund.
4. On November 10, Chilton Systems pays $90 cash for transportation costs with the November 1 purchase.
5. On November 13, Chilton Systems sells merchandise for $1,600 on credit. The cost of the merchandise is $800.
6. On November 16, the customer returns merchandise from the November 13 transaction. The returned items would sell for $300 and cost $130; the items were not damaged and were returned to inventory.

Exercise 4-15
Multiple-step income statement

P4

A company reports the following sales related information: Sales (gross) of $200,000; Sales discounts of $4,000; Sales returns and allowances of $16,000; Sales salaries expense of $10,000. Prepare the net sales portion only of this company's multiple-step income statement.

Exercise 4-16^A
Recording purchases—
periodic system   P5

Refer to Exercise 4-2 and prepare journal entries to record each of the merchandising transactions assuming that the periodic inventory system is used.

Exercise 4-17^A
Recording purchases and sales—
periodic system   P5

Refer to Exercise 4-3 and prepare journal entries to record each of the merchandising transactions assuming that the periodic inventory system is used by both the buyer and the seller. (Skip the part 3 requirement.)

Exercise 4-18^A
Buyer and seller transactions—
periodic system   P5

Refer to Exercise 4-7 and prepare journal entries to record each of the merchandising transactions assuming that the periodic inventory system is used by both the buyer and the seller.

Exercise 4-19^A
Recording purchases—
periodic system   P5

Refer to Exercise 4-14 and prepare journal entries to record each of the merchandising transactions assuming that the periodic inventory system is used.

L'Oréal reports the following income statement accounts for the year ended December 31, 2011 (euros in millions). Prepare the income statement for this company for the year ended December 31, 2011, following usual IFRS practices.

Exercise 4-20
Preparing an income statement following IFRS

P4

Net profit	€ 2,440.9	Income tax expense	€1,025.8
Finance costs	19.6	Profit before tax expense	3,466.7
Net sales	20,343.1	Research and development expense	720.5
Gross profit	14,491.6	Selling, general and administrative expense	4,186.9
Other income	193.7	Advertising and promotion expense	6,291.6
Cost of sales	5,851.5		

connect

Prepare journal entries to record the following merchandising transactions of Blink Company, which applies the perpetual inventory system. (*Hint:* It will help to identify each receivable and payable; for example, record the purchase on July 1 in Accounts Payable—Boden.)

PROBLEM SET A

Problem 4-1A
Preparing journal entries for merchandising activities—perpetual system

P1 P2 Sage 50

July 1 Purchased merchandise from Boden Company for $6,000 under credit terms of 1/15, n/30, FOB shipping point, invoice dated July 1.
   2 Sold merchandise to Creek Co. for $900 under credit terms of 2/10, n/60, FOB shipping point, invoice dated July 2. The merchandise had cost $500.
   3 Paid $125 cash for freight charges on the purchase of July 1.
   8 Sold merchandise that had cost $1,300 for $1,700 cash.
   9 Purchased merchandise from Leight Co. for $2,200 under credit terms of 2/15, n/60, FOB destination, invoice dated July 9.
   11 Received a $200 credit memorandum from Leight Co. for the return of part of the merchandise purchased on July 9.
   12 Received the balance due from Creek Co. for the invoice dated July 2, net of the discount.
   16 Paid the balance due to Boden Company within the discount period.
   19 Sold merchandise that cost $800 to Art Co. for $1,200 under credit terms of 2/15, n/60, FOB shipping point, invoice dated July 19.
   21 Issued a $200 credit memorandum to Art Co. for an allowance on goods sold on July 19.
   24 Paid Leight Co. the balance due after deducting the discount.
   30 Received the balance due from Art Co. for the invoice dated July 19, net of discount.
   31 Sold merchandise that cost $4,800 to Creek Co. for $7,000 under credit terms of 2/10, n/60, FOB shipping point, invoice dated July 31.

Check July 12, Dr. Cash $882
July 16, Cr. Cash $5,940

July 24, Cr. Cash $1,960
July 30, Dr. Cash $980

Prepare journal entries to record the following merchandising transactions of Sheng Company, which applies the perpetual inventory system. (*Hint:* It will help to identify each receivable and payable; for example, record the purchase on August 1 in Accounts Payable—Arotek.)

Problem 4-2A
Preparing journal entries for merchandising activities—perpetual system

P1 P2

Aug. 1 Purchased merchandise from Arotek Company for $7,500 under credit terms of 1/10, n/30, FOB destination, invoice dated August 1.
   4 At Arotek's request, Sheng paid $200 cash for freight charges on the August 1 purchase, reducing the amount owed to Arotek.
   5 Sold merchandise to Laird Corp. for $5,200 under credit terms of 2/10, n/60, FOB destination, invoice dated August 5. The merchandise had cost $4,000.
   8 Purchased merchandise from Waters Corporation for $5,400 under credit terms of 1/10, n/45, FOB shipping point, invoice dated August 8. The invoice showed that at Sheng's request, Waters paid the $140 shipping charges and added that amount to the bill. (*Hint:* Discounts are not applied to freight and shipping charges.)
   9 Paid $125 cash for shipping charges related to the August 5 sale to Laird Corp.
   10 Laird returned merchandise from the August 5 sale that had cost Sheng $400 and been sold for $600. The merchandise was restored to inventory.
   12 After negotiations with Waters Corporation concerning problems with the merchandise purchased on August 8, Sheng received a credit memorandum from Waters granting a price reduction of $700.

Check Aug. 9, Dr. Delivery Expense, $125

Aug. 18, Cr. Cash $4,793

15 Received balance due from Laird Corp. for the August 5 sale less the return on August 10.

18 Paid the amount due Waters Corporation for the August 8 purchase less the price reduction granted.

19 Sold merchandise to Tux Co. for $4,800 under credit terms of 1/10, n/30, FOB shipping point, invoice dated August 19. The merchandise had cost $2,400.

22 Tux requested a price reduction on the August 19 sale because the merchandise did not meet specifications. Sheng sent Tux a $500 credit memorandum to resolve the issue.

Aug. 29, Dr. Cash $4,257

29 Received Tux's cash payment for the amount due from the August 19 sale.

30 Paid Arotek Company the amount due from the August 1 purchase.

Problem 4-3A
Preparing adjusting entries and income statements; and computing gross margin, acid-test, and current ratios

A1 A2 P3 P4

mhhe.com/wildFAF4e

The following unadjusted trial balance is prepared at fiscal year-end for Nelson Company.

	Debit	Credit
NELSON COMPANY		
Unadjusted Trial Balance		
January 31, 2013		
Cash	$ 1,000	
Merchandise inventory	12,500	
Store supplies	5,800	
Prepaid insurance	2,400	
Store equipment	42,900	
Accumulated depreciation—Store equipment		$ 15,250
Accounts payable		10,000
Common stock		5,000
Retained earnings		27,000
Dividends	2,200	
Sales		111,950
Sales discounts	2,000	
Sales returns and allowances	2,200	
Cost of goods sold	38,400	
Depreciation expense—Store equipment	0	
Salaries expense	35,000	
Insurance expense	0	
Rent expense	15,000	
Store supplies expense	0	
Advertising expense	9,800	
Totals	$169,200	$169,200

Rent expense and salaries expense are equally divided between selling activities and the general and administrative activities. Nelson Company uses a perpetual inventory system.

Required

1. Prepare adjusting journal entries to reflect each of the following:

   a. Store supplies still available at fiscal year-end amount to $1,750.

   b. Expired insurance, an administrative expense, for the fiscal year is $1,400.

   c. Depreciation expense on store equipment, a selling expense, is $1,525 for the fiscal year.

   d. To estimate shrinkage, a physical count of ending merchandise inventory is taken. It shows $10,900 of inventory is still available at fiscal year-end.

Check   (2) Gross profit, $67,750; (3) Total expenses, $106,775; Net income, $975

2. Prepare a multiple-step income statement for fiscal year 2013.

3. Prepare a single-step income statement for fiscal year 2013.

4. Compute the current ratio, acid-test ratio, and gross margin ratio as of January 31, 2013. (Round ratios to two decimals.)

BTN 4-8 Arrange an interview (in person or by phone) with the manager of a retail shop in a mall or in the downtown area of your community. Explain to the manager that you are a student studying merchandising activities and the accounting for sales returns and sales allowances. Ask the manager what the store policy is regarding returns. Also find out if sales allowances are ever negotiated with customers. Inquire whether management perceives that customers are abusing return policies and what actions management takes to counter potential abuses. Be prepared to discuss your findings in class.

 HITTING THE ROAD

C1

Point: This activity complements the Ethics Challenge assignment.

BTN 4-9 KTM (www.KTM.com), Polaris, and Arctic Cat are competitors in the global marketplace. Key comparative figures for each company follow.

GLOBAL DECISION

A2 P4

KTM

Polaris

Arctic Cat

	Net Sales	Cost of Sales
KTM*.............	526,801	371,752
Polaris†	$2,656,949	$1,916,366
Arctic Cat†	$ 464,651	$ 363,142

* EUR thousands for KTM.

† $ thousands for Polaris and Arctic Cat.

Required

1. Rank the three companies (highest to lowest) based on the gross margin ratio.
2. Which of the companies uses a multiple-step income statement format? (These companies' income statements are in Appendix A.)

ANSWERS TO MULTIPLE CHOICE QUIZ

1. c; Gross profit = $550,000 − $193,000 = $357,000
2. d; ($4,500 − $250) × (100% − 2%) = $4,165
3. b; Net sales = $75,000 + $320,000 − $13,700 − $6,000 = $375,300

4. b; Acid-test ratio = $37,500/$50,000 = 0.750
5. a; Gross margin ratio = ($675,000 − $459,000)/$675,000 = 32%

Accounting for Inventories

5

A Look Back

Chapter 4 focused on merchandising activities and how they are reported. We analyzed and recorded purchases and sales and explained accounting adjustments and closing for merchandisers.

A Look at This Chapter

This chapter emphasizes accounting for inventory. We describe methods for assigning costs to inventory and we explain the items and costs making up merchandise inventory. We also discuss methods of estimating and measuring inventory.

A Look Ahead

Chapter 6 focuses on internal controls and accounting for cash and cash equivalents. We explain good internal control procedures and their importance to accounting.

Learning Objectives

CONCEPTUAL

C1 Identify the items making up merchandise inventory. (p. 210)

C2 Identify the costs of merchandise inventory. (p. 211)

ANALYTICAL

A1 Analyze the effects of inventory methods for both financial and tax reporting. (p. 218)

A2 Analyze the effects of inventory errors on current and future financial statements. (p. 220)

A3 Assess inventory management using both inventory turnover and days' sales in inventory. (p. 223)

PROCEDURAL

P1 Compute inventory in a perpetual system using the methods of specific identification, FIFO, LIFO, and weighted average. (p. 213)

P2 Compute the lower of cost or market amount of inventory. (p. 219)

P3 *Appendix 5A*—Compute inventory in a periodic system using the methods of specific identification, FIFO, LIFO, and weighted average. (p. 229)

P4 *Appendix 5B*—Apply both the retail inventory and gross profit methods to estimate inventory. (p. 234)

Cool Company

"We had to be really creative."

—FELECIA HATCHER

MIAMI—"America is, and will always be, a place of unlimited opportunity for all who dream," insists Derick Pearson. Derick, along with his soon-to-be-wife Felecia Hatcher, launched **Feverish Ice Cream (FeverishIceCream.com)** after losing their jobs. Their company sells gourmet ice pops and ice cream concocted in their production facility, and the two sell them using ecofriendly, acid green carts and a Scion. Felecia explains that they focus on venues that attract young adults such as music events, campuses, skate parks, and farmers' markets. Their travels are posted on Twitter and Facebook.

The company launch, however, was a challenge. "We purchased two tricycle carts that we found on Craigslist," explains Felecia. "As the business grew, we were able to reinvest more money into it, buy more equipment." The couple also had to confront inventory production and sales planning, and had to deal with discounts and allowances.

A major challenge was identifying the appropriate inventories while controlling costs. "In the beginning it was just a lot of trial and error," says Felecia. "We had a lot of melted ice cream!" Applying inventory management, and old fashioned trial-and-error, Felecia and Derick learned to fill orders, collect money, and maintain the right level and mix of inventory. To help, they set up an inventory system to account for sales and purchases in real time.

The two insist that while it is important to serve customers' needs, business success demands sound inventory management. Further, that success requires more than good products and perpetual inventory management. Felecia explains that it requires commitment, patience, energy, faith, and maybe some luck. "It was a crazy idea but we really didn't have anything to lose," recalls Felecia. "Loving ice cream fueled a lot of our madness!"

While Derick and Felecia continue to measure, monitor, and manage inventories and costs, their success and growth are pushing them into new products and opportunities. "[We are] always about growing as organically as possible," asserts Felecia. "[Including] sustaining that growth." Their inventory procedures and accounting systems contribute to their lean business model. "[We] budget every cent, along with saving for future expenses," explains Derick. "There's nothing wrong with living simple," says Felecia. "Spend money on things that will last, and make do with what you have." Adds Derick, "We are living examples that dreams do come true!"

[Sources: Feverish Ice Cream Website, January 2013; *South Florida Times,* November 2011; *Palm Beach Post,* July 2011; Graves Publishing Company, February 2010; *Miami New Times,* November 2011]

Merchandisers' activities include the purchasing and reselling of merchandise. We explained accounting for merchandisers in Chapter 4, including that for purchases and sales. In this chapter, we extend the study and analysis of inventory by explaining the methods used to assign costs to merchandise inventory *and* to cost of goods sold. Retailers, wholesalers, and other merchandising companies that purchase products for resale use the principles and methods described here. Understanding inventory accounting helps in the analysis and interpretation of financial statements and helps people run their businesses.

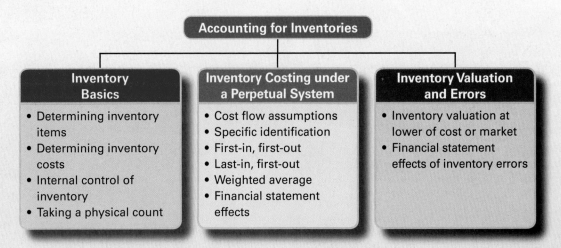

INVENTORY BASICS

This section identifies the items and costs making up merchandise inventory. It also describes the importance of internal controls in taking a physical count of inventory.

Determining Inventory Items

C1 Identify the items making up merchandise inventory.

Merchandise inventory includes all goods that a company owns and holds for sale. This rule holds regardless of where the goods are located when inventory is counted. Certain inventory items require special attention, including goods in transit, goods on consignment, and goods that are damaged or obsolete.

Goods in Transit   Does a purchaser's inventory include goods in transit from a supplier? The answer is that if ownership has passed to the purchaser, the goods are included in the purchaser's inventory. We determine this by reviewing the shipping terms: *FOB destination* or *FOB shipping point.* If the purchaser is responsible for paying freight, ownership passes when goods are loaded on the transport vehicle. If the seller is responsible for paying freight, ownership passes when goods arrive at their destination.

Point: FOB shipping point is also called *FOB origin* or *FOB supplier's warehouse.*

Goods on Consignment   Goods on consignment are goods shipped by the owner, called the **consignor,** to another party, the **consignee.** A consignee sells goods for the owner. The consignor continues to own the consigned goods and reports them in its inventory. **Upper Deck**, for instance, pays sports celebrities such as Aaron Rodgers of the Green Bay Packers to sign memorabilia, which are offered to shopping networks on consignment. Upper Deck, the consignor, must report these items in its inventory until sold.

Goods Damaged or Obsolete   Damaged and obsolete (and deteriorated) goods are not counted in inventory if they cannot be sold. If these goods can be sold at a reduced price, they are included in inventory at a conservative estimate of their **net realizable value.** Net realizable value is sales price minus the cost of making the sale. The period when damage or obsolescence (or deterioration) occurs is the period when the loss in value is reported.

Decision Insight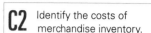

A wireless portable device with a two-way radio allows clerks to quickly record inventory by scanning bar codes and to instantly send and receive inventory data. It gives managers access to up-to-date information on inventory and its location. ∎

Determining Inventory Costs

Merchandise inventory includes costs of expenditures necessary, directly or indirectly, to bring an item to a salable condition and location. This means that the cost of an inventory item includes its invoice cost minus any discount, and plus any incidental costs necessary to put it in a place and condition for sale. Incidental costs can include import tariffs, freight, storage, insurance, and costs incurred in an aging process (for example, aging wine or cheese).

Accounting principles prescribe that incidental costs be added to inventory. Also, the *matching (expense recognition) principle* states that inventory costs should be recorded against revenue in the period when inventory is sold. However, some companies use the *materiality constraint (cost-to-benefit constraint)* to avoid assigning some incidental costs of acquiring merchandise to inventory. Instead, they expense them to cost of goods sold when incurred. These companies argue either that those incidental costs are immaterial or that the effort in assigning them outweighs the benefit.

C2 Identify the costs of merchandise inventory.

Internal Controls and Taking a Physical Count

Events can cause the Inventory account balance to differ from the actual inventory available. Such events include theft, loss, damage, and errors. Thus, nearly all companies take a *physical count of inventory* at least once each year—informally called *taking an inventory*. This often occurs at the end of a fiscal year or when inventory amounts are low. This physical count is used to adjust the Inventory account balance to the actual inventory available.

A company applies internal controls when taking a physical count of inventory that usually include the following procedures to minimize fraud and to increase reliability:

- *Prenumbered inventory tickets* are prepared and distributed to the *counters*—each ticket must be accounted for.
- Counters of inventory are assigned and do not include those responsible for inventory.
- Counters confirm the validity of inventory, including its existence, amount, and quality.
- A second count is taken by a different counter.
- A manager confirms that all inventories are ticketed once, and only once.

Fraud: Auditors commonly observe employees as they take a physical inventory. Auditors take their own test counts to monitor the accuracy of a company's count.

Point: The Inventory account is a controlling account for the inventory subsidiary ledger. This *subsidiary ledger* contains a separate record (units and costs) for each separate product, and it can be in electronic or paper form. Subsidiary records assist managers in planning and monitoring inventory.

Quick Check   Answers — p. 237

1. What accounting principle most guides the allocation of cost of goods available for sale between ending inventory and cost of goods sold?
2. If **Skechers** sells goods to **Famous Footwear** with terms FOB shipping point, which company reports these goods in its inventory while they are in transit?
3. An art gallery purchases a painting for $11,400 on terms FOB shipping point. Additional costs in obtaining and offering the artwork for sale include $130 for transportation-in, $150 for import tariffs, $100 for insurance during shipment, $180 for advertising, $400 for framing, and $800 for office salaries. In computing inventory, what cost is assigned to the painting?

INVENTORY COSTING UNDER A PERPETUAL SYSTEM

Accounting for inventory affects both the balance sheet and the income statement. A major goal in accounting for inventory is to properly match costs with sales. We use the *expense recognition* (or *matching*) *principle* to decide how much of the cost of the goods available for sale is deducted from sales and how much is carried forward as inventory and matched against future sales.

Management decisions in accounting for inventory involve the following:

- Items included in inventory and their costs.
- Costing method (specific identification, FIFO, LIFO, or weighted average).
- Inventory system (perpetual or periodic).
- Use of market values or other estimates.

The first point was explained on the prior two pages. The second and third points will be addressed now. The fourth point is the focus at the end of this chapter. Decisions on these points affect the reported amounts for inventory, cost of goods sold, gross profit, income, current assets, and other accounts.

One of the most important issues in accounting for inventory is determining the per unit costs assigned to inventory items. When all units are purchased at the same unit cost, this process is simple. When identical items are purchased at different costs, however, a question arises as to which amounts to record in cost of goods sold and which amounts remain in inventory.

Four methods are commonly used to assign costs to inventory and to cost of goods sold: (1) specific identification; (2) first-in, first-out; (3) last-in, first-out; and (4) weighted average. Exhibit 5.1 shows the frequency in the use of these methods.

EXHIBIT 5.1

Frequency in Use of Inventory Methods

Other* 3%

FIFO 50%

Weighted Average 20%

LIFO 27%

*Includes specific identification.

Each method assumes a particular pattern for how costs flow through inventory. Each of these four methods is acceptable whether or not the actual physical flow of goods follows the cost flow assumption. Physical flow of goods depends on the type of product and the way it is stored. (Perishable goods such as fresh fruit demand that a business attempt to sell them in a first-in, first-out physical flow. Other products such as crude oil and minerals such as coal, gold, and decorative stone can be sold in a last-in, first-out physical flow.) **Physical flow and cost flow need not be the same.**

Inventory Cost Flow Assumptions

This section introduces inventory cost flow assumptions. For this purpose, assume that three identical units are purchased separately at the following three dates and costs: May 1 at $45, May 3 at $65, and May 6 at $70. One unit is then sold on May 7 for $100. Exhibit 5.2 gives a visual layout of the flow of costs to either the gross profit section of the income statement or the inventory reported on the balance sheet for FIFO, LIFO, and weighted average.

(1) *FIFO assumes costs flow in the order incurred.* The unit purchased on May 1 for $45 is the earliest cost incurred—it is sent to cost of goods sold on the income statement first. The remaining two units ($65 and $70) are reported in inventory on the balance sheet.

(2) *LIFO assumes costs flow in the reverse order incurred.* The unit purchased on May 6 for $70 is the most recent cost incurred—it is sent to cost of goods sold on the income statement. The remaining two units ($45 and $65) are reported in inventory on the balance sheet.

(3) *Weighted average assumes costs flow at an average of the costs available.* The units available at the May 7 sale average $60 in cost, computed as ($45 + $65 + $70)/3. One unit's $60 average cost is sent to cost of goods sold on the income statement. The remaining two units' average costs are reported in inventory at $120 on the balance sheet.

Cost flow assumptions can markedly impact gross profit and inventory numbers. Exhibit 5.2 shows that gross profit as a percent of net sales ranges from 30% to 55% due to nothing else but the cost flow assumption.

Point: It is helpful to recall the cost flow of inventory from Exhibit 4.4.

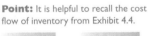

Beginning inventory + Net purchases

= Merchandise available for sale

Ending inventory + Cost of goods sold

The following sections on inventory costing use the perpetual system. Appendix 5A uses the periodic system. An instructor can choose to cover either one or both systems. If the perpetual system is skipped, then read Appendix 5A and return to the Decision Maker box (on page 218) titled "Cost Analyst."

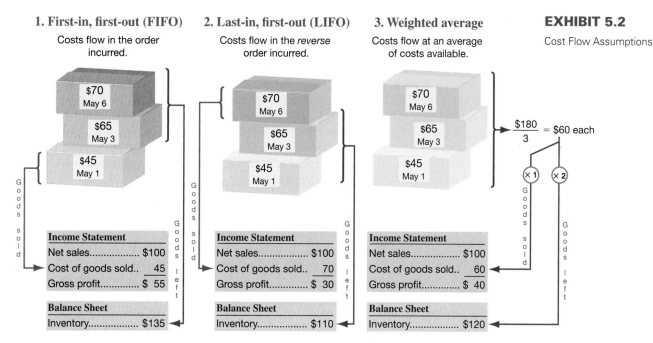

EXHIBIT 5.2

Cost Flow Assumptions

Inventory Costing Illustration

This section provides a comprehensive illustration of inventory costing methods. We use information from Trekking, a sporting goods store. Among its many products, Trekking carries one type of mountain bike whose sales are directed at resorts that provide inexpensive mountain bikes for complimentary guest use. Its customers usually purchase in amounts of 10 or more bikes. We use Trekking's data from August. Its mountain bike (unit) inventory at the beginning of August and its purchases and sales during August are shown in Exhibit 5.3. It ends August with 12 bikes remaining in inventory.

P1 Compute inventory in a perpetual system using the methods of specific identification, FIFO, LIFO, and weighted average.

Date	Activity	Units Acquired at Cost	Units Sold at Retail	Unit Inventory
Aug. 1	Beginning inventory	10 units @ $ 91 = $ 910		10 units
Aug. 3	Purchases	15 units @ $106 = $1,590		25 units
Aug. 14	Sales		20 units @ $130	5 units
Aug. 17	Purchases	20 units @ $115 = $2,300		25 units
Aug. 28	Purchases	10 units @ $119 = $1,190		35 units
Aug. 31	Sales		23 units @ $150	12 units
	Totals	55 units $5,990	43 units	

Units available for sale • Goods available for sale • Units sold • Units left

EXHIBIT 5.3

Purchases and Sales of Goods

Trekking uses the perpetual inventory system, which means that its merchandise inventory account is continually updated to reflect purchases and sales. (**Appendix 5A describes the assignment of costs to inventory using a periodic system.**) Regardless of what inventory method or system is used, cost of goods available for sale must be allocated between cost of goods sold and ending inventory.

Point: The perpetual inventory system is the most dominant system for U.S. businesses.

Point: Beginning inventory units plus purchased units equals units available for sale (UAFS).

Specific Identification

When each item in inventory can be identified with a specific purchase and invoice, we can use **specific identification** (also called *specific invoice inventory pricing*) to assign costs. We also need sales records that identify exactly which items were sold and when. Trekking's internal documents reveal the following specific unit sales:

August 14   Sold 8 bikes costing $91 each and 12 bikes costing $106 each

August 31   Sold 2 bikes costing $91 each, 3 bikes costing $106 each, 15 bikes costing $115 each, and 3 bikes costing $119 each

Point: Three key variables determine the value assigned to ending inventory: (1) inventory quantity, (2) unit costs of inventory, and (3) cost flow assumption.

Applying specific identification, and using the information above and from Exhibit 5.3, we prepare Exhibit 5.4. This exhibit starts with 10 bikes at $91 each in beginning inventory. On August 3, 15 more bikes are purchased at $106 each for $1,590. Inventory available now consists of 10 bikes at $91 each and 15 bikes at $106 each, for a total of $2,500. On August 14 (see sales data on previous page), 20 bikes costing $2,000 are sold—leaving 5 bikes costing $500 in inventory. On August 17, 20 bikes costing $2,300 are purchased, and on August 28, another 10 bikes costing $1,190 are purchased, for a total of 35 bikes costing $3,990 in inventory. On August 31 (see sales data on previous page), 23 bikes costing $2,582 are sold, which leaves 12 bikes costing $1,408 in ending inventory. Carefully study this exhibit and the boxed explanations to see the flow of costs both in and out of inventory. Each unit, whether sold or remaining in inventory, has its own specific cost attached to it.

EXHIBIT 5.4

Specific Identification Computations

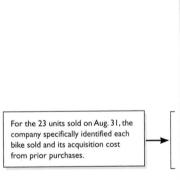

For the 20 units sold on Aug. 14, the company specifically identified that 8 of those had cost $91 and 12 had cost $106.

For the 23 units sold on Aug. 31, the company specifically identified each bike sold and its acquisition cost from prior purchases.

			"goods in"		"goods out"		"what's left"
Date	**Goods Purchased**		**Cost of Goods Sold**		**Inventory Balance**		
Aug. 1	Beginning balance				10 @ $ 91 = $ 910		
Aug. 3	15 @ $106 = $1,590				10 @ $ 91 ⎫ = $2,500 15 @ $106 ⎭		
Aug. 14			8 @ $ 91 = $ 728 ⎫ = $2,000* 12 @ $106 = $1,272 ⎭		2 @ $ 91 ⎫ = $ 500 3 @ $106 ⎭		
Aug. 17	20 @ $115 = $2,300				2 @ $ 91 ⎫ 3 @ $106 ⎬ = $2,800 20 @ $115 ⎭		
Aug. 28	10 @ $119 = $1,190				2 @ $ 91 ⎫ 3 @ $106 ⎪ 20 @ $115 ⎬ = $3,990 10 @ $119 ⎭		
Aug. 31			2 @ $ 91 = $ 182 ⎫ 3 @ $106 = $ 318 ⎪ = $2,582* 15 @ $115 = $1,725 ⎬ 3 @ $119 = $ 357 ⎭ $4,582		5 @ $115 ⎫ = $1,408 7 @ $119 ⎭		

* Identification of items sold (and their costs) is obtained from internal documents that track each unit from its purchase to its sale.

When using specific identification, Trekking's cost of goods sold reported on the income statement totals $4,582, the sum of $2,000 and $2,582 from the third column of Exhibit 5.4. Trekking's ending inventory reported on the balance sheet is $1,408, which is the final inventory balance from the fourth column of Exhibit 5.4.

The purchases and sales entries for Exhibit 5.4 follow (the colored boldface numbers are those impacted by the cost flow assumption):

Point: Specific identification is usually practical for companies with expensive or custom-made inventory. Examples include car dealerships, implement dealers, jewelers, and fashion designers.

Point: The assignment of costs to the goods sold and to inventory using specific identification is the same for both the perpetual and periodic systems.

Purchases

Aug. 3	Merchandise Inventory	1,590	
	Accounts Payable		1,590
17	Merchandise Inventory	2,300	
	Accounts Payable		2,300
28	Merchandise Inventory	1,190	
	Accounts Payable		1,190

Sales

Aug. 14	Accounts Receivable	2,600	
	Sales		2,600
14	Cost of Goods Sold	2,000	
	Merchandise Inventory		2,000
31	Accounts Receivable	3,450	
	Sales		3,450
31	Cost of Goods Sold	2,582	
	Merchandise Inventory		2,582

First-In, First-Out

The **first-in, first-out (FIFO)** method of assigning costs to both inventory and cost of goods sold assumes that inventory items are sold in the order acquired. When sales occur, the costs of the earliest units acquired are charged to cost of goods sold. This leaves the costs from the most recent purchases in ending inventory. Use of FIFO for computing the cost of inventory and cost of goods sold is shown in Exhibit 5.5.

This exhibit starts with beginning inventory of 10 bikes at $91 each. On August 3, 15 more bikes costing $106 each are bought for $1,590. Inventory now consists of 10 bikes at $91 each and 15 bikes at $106 each, for a total of $2,500. On August 14, 20 bikes are sold—applying FIFO, the first 10 sold cost $91 each and the next 10 sold cost $106 each, for a total cost of $1,970. This leaves 5 bikes costing $106 each, or $530, in inventory. On August 17, 20 bikes costing $2,300 are purchased, and on August 28, another 10 bikes costing $1,190 are purchased, for a total of 35 bikes costing $4,020 in inventory. On August 31, 23 bikes are sold—applying FIFO, the first 5 bikes sold cost $530 and the next 18 sold cost $2,070, which leaves 12 bikes costing $1,420 in ending inventory.

Point: The "Goods Purchased" column is identical for all methods. Data are taken from Exhibit 5.3.

Date	Goods Purchased	Cost of Goods Sold	Inventory Balance
Aug. 1	Beginning balance		10 @ $ 91 = $ 910
Aug. 3	15 @ $106 = $1,590		10 @ $ 91 } 15 @ $106 } = $2,500
Aug. 14		10 @ $ 91 = $ 910 } 10 @ $106 = $1,060 } = $1,970	5 @ $106 = $ 530
Aug. 17	20 @ $115 = $2,300		5 @ $106 } 20 @ $115 } = $2,830
Aug. 28	10 @ $119 = $1,190		5 @ $106 } 20 @ $115 } = $4,020 10 @ $119 }
Aug. 31		5 @ $106 = $ 530 } 18 @ $115 = $2,070 } = $2,600 $4,570	2 @ $115 } = $1,420 10 @ $119 }

EXHIBIT 5.5

FIFO Computations— Perpetual System

> For the 20 units sold on Aug. 14, the first 10 sold are assigned the earliest cost of $91 (from beg. bal.). The next 10 sold are assigned the next earliest cost of $106.

> For the 23 units sold on Aug. 31, the first 5 sold are assigned the earliest available cost of $106 (from Aug. 3 purchase). The next 18 sold are assigned the next earliest cost of $115 (from Aug. 17 purchase).

Trekking's FIFO cost of goods sold reported on its income statement (reflecting the 43 units sold) is **$4,570** ($1,970 + $2,600), and its ending inventory reported on the balance sheet (reflecting the 12 units unsold) is **$1,420**.

The purchases and sales entries for Exhibit 5.5 follow (the colored boldface numbers are those affected by the cost flow assumption).

Point: Under FIFO, a unit sold is assigned the earliest (oldest) cost from inventory. This leaves the most recent costs in ending inventory.

Point: *LOSH (last ones still here)* can help remember what costs are in FIFO ending inventory.

Purchases

Aug. 3	Merchandise Inventory 1,590	
	Accounts Payable	1,590
17	Merchandise Inventory 2,300	
	Accounts Payable	2,300
28	Merchandise Inventory 1,190	
	Accounts Payable	1,190

Sales

Aug. 14	Accounts Receivable 2,600	
	Sales	2,600
14	Cost of Goods Sold 1,970	
	Merchandise Inventory	1,970
31	Accounts Receivable 3,450	
	Sales	3,450
31	Cost of Goods Sold 2,600	
	Merchandise Inventory	2,600

Last-In, First-Out

The **last-in, first-out (LIFO)** method of assigning costs assumes that the most recent purchases are sold first. These more recent costs are charged to the goods sold, and the costs of the earliest purchases are assigned to inventory. As with other methods, LIFO is acceptable even when the

Point: Under LIFO, a unit sold is assigned the most recent (latest) cost from inventory. This leaves the oldest costs in inventory.

Point: FOSH (first ones still here) can help remember what costs are in LIFO ending inventory.

physical flow of goods does not follow a last-in, first-out pattern. One appeal of LIFO is that by assigning costs from the most recent purchases to cost of goods sold, LIFO comes closest to matching current costs of goods sold with revenues (compared to FIFO or weighted average).

Exhibit 5.6 shows the LIFO computations. It starts with beginning inventory of 10 bikes at $91 each. On August 3, 15 more bikes costing $106 each are bought for $1,590. Inventory now consists of 10 bikes at $91 each and 15 bikes at $106 each, for a total of $2,500. On August 14, 20 bikes are sold—applying LIFO, the first 15 sold are from the most recent purchase costing $106 each, and the next 5 sold are from the next most recent purchase costing $91 each, for a total cost of $2,045. This leaves 5 bikes costing $91 each, or $455, in inventory. On August 17, 20 bikes costing $2,300 are purchased, and on August 28, another 10 bikes costing $1,190 are purchased, for a total of 35 bikes costing $3,945 in inventory. On August 31, 23 bikes are sold—applying LIFO, the first 10 bikes sold are from the most recent purchase costing $1,190, and the next 13 sold are from the next most recent purchase costing $1,495, which leaves 12 bikes costing $1,260 in ending inventory.

EXHIBIT 5.6

LIFO Computations—
Perpetual System

For the 20 units sold on Aug. 14, the first 15 sold are assigned the most recent cost of $106. The next 5 sold are assigned the next most recent cost of $91.

For the 23 units sold on Aug. 31, the first 10 sold are assigned the most recent cost of $119. The next 13 sold are assigned the next most recent cost of $115.

Date	Goods Purchased	Cost of Goods Sold	Inventory Balance
Aug. 1	Beginning balance		10 @ $ 91 = $ 910
Aug. 3	15 @ $106 = $1,590		10 @ $ 91 } = $ 2,500 15 @ $106 }
Aug. 14		15 @ $106 = $1,590 } 5 @ $ 91 = $ 455 } = $2,045	5 @ $ 91 = $ 455
Aug. 17	20 @ $115 = $2,300		5 @ $ 91 } = $ 2,755 20 @ $115 }
Aug. 28	10 @ $119 = $1,190		5 @ $ 91 } 20 @ $115 } = $ 3,945 10 @ $119 }
Aug. 31		10 @ $119 = $1,190 } 13 @ $115 = $1,495 } = $2,685 $4,730	5 @ $ 91 } = $1,260 7 @ $115 }

Trekking's LIFO cost of goods sold reported on the income statement is **$4,730** ($2,045 + $2,685), and its ending inventory reported on the balance sheet is **$1,260**.

The purchases and sales entries for Exhibit 5.6 follow (the colored boldface numbers are those affected by the cost flow assumption).

Point: Grocers prefer a FIFO physical flow of milk cartons. Consumers prefer a LIFO flow as they desire a long refrigerator life and reach for recently stocked milk. However, the cost flow in accounting need not match the physical flow in the store.

	Purchases		
Aug. 3	Merchandise Inventory	1,590	
	Accounts Payable		1,590
17	Merchandise Inventory	2,300	
	Accounts Payable		2,300
28	Merchandise Inventory	1,190	
	Accounts Payable		1,190

	Sales		
Aug. 14	Accounts Receivable	2,600	
	Sales		2,600
14	Cost of Goods Sold	2,045	
	Merchandise Inventory		2,045
31	Accounts Receivable	3,450	
	Sales		3,450
31	Cost of Goods Sold	2,685	
	Merchandise Inventory		2,685

Weighted Average

The **weighted average** (also called **average cost**) method of assigning cost requires that we use the weighted average cost per unit of inventory at the time of each sale. Weighted average cost per unit at the time of each sale equals the cost of goods available for sale divided by the units available. The results using weighted average (WA) for Trekking are shown in Exhibit 5.7.

This exhibit starts with beginning inventory of 10 bikes at $91 each. On August 3, 15 more bikes costing $106 each are bought for $1,590. Inventory now consists of 10 bikes at $91 each and 15 bikes at $106 each, for a total of $2,500. The average cost per bike for that inventory is $100, computed as $2,500/(10 bikes + 15 bikes). On August 14, 20 bikes are sold—applying

EXHIBIT 5.7

Weighted Average
Computations—Perpetual System

Date	Goods Purchased	Cost of Goods Sold	Inventory Balance
Aug. 1	Beginning balance		10 @ $ 91 = $ 910
Aug. 3	15 @ $106 = $1,590		10 @ $ 91 } = $2,500 (or $100 per unit)[a] 15 @ $106 }
Aug. 14		20 @ $100 = **$2,000**	5 @ $100 = $ 500 (or $100 per unit)[b]
Aug. 17	20 @ $115 = $2,300		5 @ $100 } = $2,800 (or $112 per unit)[c] 20 @ $115 }
Aug. 28	10 @ $119 = $1,190		5 @ $100 } 20 @ $115 } = $3,990 (or $114 per unit)[d] 10 @ $119 }
Aug. 31		23 @ $114 = **$2,622**	12 @ $114 = $1,368 (or $114 per unit)[e]
		$4,622	

> For the 20 units sold on Aug. 14, the cost assigned is the $100 *average cost* per unit from the inventory balance column at the time of sale.

> For the 23 units sold on Aug. 31, the cost assigned is the $114 *average cost* per unit from the inventory balance column at the time of sale.

[a] $100 per unit = ($2,500 inventory balance ÷ 25 units in inventory).
[b] $100 per unit = ($500 inventory balance ÷ 5 units in inventory).
[c] $112 per unit = ($2,800 inventory balance ÷ 25 units in inventory).
[d] $114 per unit = ($3,990 inventory balance ÷ 35 units in inventory).
[e] $114 per unit = ($1,368 inventory balance ÷ 12 units in inventory).

WA, the 20 sold are assigned the $100 average cost, for a total cost of $2,000. This leaves 5 bikes with an average cost of $100 each, or $500, in inventory. On August 17, 20 bikes costing $2,300 are purchased, and on August 28, another 10 bikes costing $1,190 are purchased, for a total of 35 bikes costing $3,990 in inventory at August 28. The average cost per bike for the August 28 inventory is $114, computed as $3,990/(5 bikes + 20 bikes + 10 bikes). On August 31, 23 bikes are sold—applying WA, the 23 sold are assigned the $114 average cost, for a total cost of $2,622. This leaves 12 bikes costing $1,368 in ending inventory.

Trekking's cost of goods sold reported on the income statement (reflecting the 43 units sold) is **$4,622** ($2,000 + $2,622), and its ending inventory reported on the balance sheet (reflecting the 12 units unsold) is **$1,368**.

The purchases and sales entries for Exhibit 5.7 follow (the colored boldface numbers are those affected by the cost flow assumption).

> **Point:** Under weighted average, a unit sold is assigned the average cost of all items currently available for sale at the date of each sale. This means a new average cost is computed after each purchase.

Purchases

Aug. 3	Merchandise Inventory	1,590	
	Accounts Payable		1,590
17	Merchandise Inventory	2,300	
	Accounts Payable		2,300
28	Merchandise Inventory	1,190	
	Accounts Payable		1,190

Sales

Aug. 14	Accounts Receivable	2,600	
	Sales		2,600
14	Cost of Goods Sold	**2,000**	
	Merchandise Inventory		**2,000**
31	Accounts Receivable	3,450	
	Sales		3,450
31	Cost of Goods Sold	**2,622**	
	Merchandise Inventory		**2,622**

This completes computations under the four most common perpetual inventory costing methods. Advances in technology have greatly reduced the cost of a perpetual inventory system. Many companies now ask whether they can afford *not* to have a perpetual inventory system because timely access to inventory information is a competitive advantage and it can help reduce the amount of inventory, which reduces costs.

> **Point:** Cost of goods available for sale (COGAFS), units available for sale (UAFS), and units in ending inventory are identical for all methods.

Decision Insight

Inventory Control Inventory safeguards include restricted access, use of authorized requisitions, security measures, and controlled environments to prevent damage. Proper accounting includes matching inventory received with purchase order terms and quality requirements, preventing misstatements, and controlling access to inventory records. A study reports that 23% of employees in purchasing and procurement observed inappropriate kickbacks or gifts from suppliers. Another study reports that submission of fraudulent supplier invoices is now common, and perpetrators are often employees (KPMG 2011). ■

A1   Analyze the effects of inventory methods for both financial and tax reporting.

Financial Statement Effects of Costing Methods

When purchase prices do not change, each inventory costing method assigns the same cost amounts to inventory and to cost of goods sold. When purchase prices are different, however, the methods nearly always assign different cost amounts. We show these differences in Exhibit 5.8 using Trekking's data.

EXHIBIT 5.8

Financial Statement Effects of Inventory Costing Methods

TREKKING COMPANY For Month Ended August 31				
	Specific Identification	FIFO	LIFO	Weighted Average
Income Statement				
Sales	$ 6,050	$ 6,050	$ 6,050	$ 6,050
Cost of goods sold	4,582	4,570	4,730	4,622
Gross profit	1,468	1,480	1,320	1,428
Expenses	450	450	450	450
Income before taxes	1,018	1,030	870	978
Income tax expense (30%)	305	309	261	293
Net income	$ 713	$ 721	$ 609	$ 685
Balance Sheet				
Inventory	$1,408	$1,420	$1,260	$1,368

This exhibit reveals two important results. First, when purchase costs *regularly rise,* as in Trekking's case, the following occurs:

- FIFO assigns the lowest amount to cost of goods sold—yielding the highest gross profit and net income.

Point: Managers prefer FIFO when costs are rising *and* incentives exist to report higher income for reasons such as bonus plans, job security, and reputation.

- LIFO assigns the highest amount to cost of goods sold—yielding the lowest gross profit and net income, which also yields a temporary tax advantage by postponing payment of some income tax.
- Weighted average yields results between FIFO and LIFO.
- Specific identification always yields results that depend on which units are sold.

Second, when costs *regularly decline,* the reverse occurs for FIFO and LIFO. Namely, FIFO gives the highest cost of goods sold—yielding the lowest gross profit and income. However, LIFO then gives the lowest cost of goods sold—yielding the highest gross profit and income.

Point: LIFO inventory is often less than the inventory's replacement cost because LIFO inventory is valued using the oldest inventory purchase costs.

All four inventory costing methods are acceptable. However, a company must disclose the inventory method it uses in its financial statements or notes. Each method offers certain advantages as follows:

- FIFO assigns an amount to inventory on the balance sheet that approximates its current cost; it also mimics the actual flow of goods for most businesses.
- LIFO assigns an amount to cost of goods sold on the income statement that approximates its current cost; it also better matches current costs with revenues in computing gross profit.
- Weighted average tends to smooth out erratic changes in costs.
- Specific identification exactly matches the costs of items with the revenues they generate.

■ Decision Maker

Cost Analyst   Your supervisor says she finds managing product costs easier if the balance sheet reflects inventory values that closely reflect replacement cost. Which inventory costing method do you advise adopting? ■ [Answer—p. 236]

Tax Effects of Costing Methods   Trekking's segment income statement in Exhibit 5.8 includes income tax expense (at a rate of 30%) because it was formed as a corporation. Since inventory costs affect net income, they have potential tax effects. Trekking gains a temporary tax advantage by using LIFO. Many companies use LIFO for this reason.

Companies can and often do use different costing methods for financial reporting and tax reporting. *The only exception is when LIFO is used for tax reporting; in this case, the IRS requires that it also be used in financial statements*—called the **LIFO conformity rule.**

Point: *LIFO conformity rule* may be revised if IFRS is adopted for U.S. companies as IFRS currently does not permit LIFO (see Global View).

Consistency in Using Costing Methods

The **consistency concept** prescribes that a company use the same accounting methods period after period so that financial statements are comparable across periods—the only exception is when a change from one method to another will improve its financial reporting. The *full-disclosure principle* prescribes that the notes to the statements report this type of change, its justification, and its effect on income.

The consistency concept does *not* require a company to use one method exclusively. For example, it can use different methods to value different categories of inventory.

■ Decision **Ethics**

Inventory Manager Your compensation as inventory manager includes a bonus plan based on gross profit. Your superior asks your opinion on changing the inventory costing method from FIFO to LIFO. Since costs are expected to continue to rise, your superior predicts that LIFO would match higher current costs against sales, thereby lowering taxable income (and gross profit). What do you recommend? ■ [Answer—p. 236]

Quick Check	Answers – p. 237

4. Describe one advantage for each of the inventory costing methods: specific identification, FIFO, LIFO, and weighted average.

5. When costs are rising, which method reports higher net income—LIFO or FIFO?

6. When costs are rising, what effect does LIFO have on a balance sheet compared to FIFO?

7. A company takes a physical count of inventory at the end of 2012 and finds that ending inventory is understated by $10,000. Would this error cause cost of goods sold to be overstated or understated in 2012? In year 2013? If so, by how much?

VALUING INVENTORY AT LCM AND THE EFFECTS OF INVENTORY ERRORS

This section examines the role of market costs in determining inventory on the balance sheet and also the financial statement effects of inventory errors.

Lower of Cost or Market

We explained how to assign costs to ending inventory and cost of goods sold using one of four costing methods (FIFO, LIFO, weighted average, or specific identification). However, *accounting principles require that inventory be reported at the market value (cost) of replacing inventory when market value is lower than cost*. Merchandise inventory is then said to be reported on the balance sheet at the **lower of cost or market (LCM).**

P2 Compute the lower of cost or market amount of inventory.

Computing the Lower of Cost or Market   *Market* in the term *LCM* is defined as the current replacement cost of purchasing the same inventory items in the usual manner. A decline in replacement cost reflects a loss of value in inventory. When the recorded cost of inventory is higher than the replacement cost, a loss is recognized. When the recorded cost is lower, no adjustment is made.

LCM is applied in one of three ways: (1) to each individual item separately, (2) to major categories of items, or (3) to the whole of inventory. The less similar the items that make up inventory, the more likely companies are to apply LCM to individual items or categories. With the increasing application of technology and inventory tracking, companies increasingly apply

EXHIBIT 5.9

Lower of Cost or Market
Computations

$140,000 is the lower of $160,000
or $140,000

Market amount of $265,000 is lower
than the $295,000 recorded cost

Inventory Items	Units	Per Unit		Total Cost	Total Market	LCM Applied to Items
		Cost	Market			
Cycles						
Roadster	20	$8,000	$7,000	$160,000	$140,000	$ 140,000
Sprint	10	5,000	6,000	50,000	60,000	50,000
Off-Road						
Trax-4	8	5,000	6,500	40,000	52,000	40,000
Blazer	5	9,000	7,000	45,000	35,000	35,000
Totals				$295,000		$265,000

LCM to each individual item separately. Accordingly, we show that method only; however, advanced courses cover the other two methods. To illustrate LCM, we apply it to the ending inventory of a motorsports retailer in Exhibit 5.9.

LCM Applied to Individual Items   When LCM is applied to individual *items* of inventory, the number of comparisons equals the number of items. For Roadster, $140,000 is the lower of the $160,000 cost and the $140,000 market. For Sprint, $50,000 is the lower of the $50,000 cost and the $60,000 market. For Trax-4, $40,000 is the lower of the $40,000 cost and the $52,000 market. For Blazer, $35,000 is the lower of the $45,000 cost and the $35,000 market. This yields a $265,000 reported inventory, computed from $140,000 for Roadster plus $50,000 for Sprint plus $40,000 for Trax-4 plus $35,000 for Blazer.

Point: Advances in technology encourage the individual-item approach for LCM.

The retailer **The Buckle** applies LCM and reports that its "inventory is stated at the lower of cost or market. Cost is determined using the average cost method."

Global: IFRS requires LCM applied to individual items; this results in the most conservative inventory amount.

Recording the Lower of Cost or Market   Inventory must be adjusted downward when market is less than cost. To illustrate, if LCM is applied to the individual items of inventory in Exhibit 5.9, the Merchandise Inventory account must be adjusted from the $295,000 recorded cost down to the $265,000 market amount as follows.

Cost of Goods Sold	30,000	
Merchandise Inventory		30,000
To adjust inventory cost to market.		

Accounting rules require that inventory be adjusted to market when market is less than cost, but inventory normally cannot be written up to market when market exceeds cost. If recording inventory down to market is acceptable, why are companies not allowed to record inventory up to market? One view is that a gain from a market increase should not be realized until a sales transaction verifies the gain. However, this view also applies when market is less than cost. A second and primary reason is the **conservatism constraint,** which prescribes the use of the less optimistic amount when more than one estimate of the amount to be received or paid exists and these estimates are about equally likely.

Financial Statement Effects of Inventory Errors

A2 Analyze the effects of inventory errors on current and future financial statements.

Companies must take care in both taking a physical count of inventory and in assigning a cost to it. An inventory error causes misstatements in cost of goods sold, gross profit, net income, current assets, and equity. It also causes misstatements in the next period's statements because ending inventory of one period is the beginning inventory of the next. As we consider the financial statement effects in this section, it is helpful if we recall the following *inventory relation.*

Beginning inventory	+	Net purchases	−	Ending inventory	=	Cost of goods sold

Income Statement Effects   Exhibit 5.10 shows the effects of inventory errors on key amounts in the current and next periods' income statements. Let's look at row 1 and year 1. We see that understating ending inventory overstates cost of goods sold. This can be seen from the above inventory relation where we subtract a smaller ending inventory amount in computing cost of goods sold. Then a higher cost of goods sold yields a lower income.

To understand year 2 of row 1, remember that an understated ending inventory for year 1 becomes an understated beginning inventory for year 2. Using the above inventory relation, we see that if beginning inventory is understated, then cost of goods sold is understated (because we are starting with a smaller amount). A lower cost of goods sold yields a higher income.

Turning to overstatements, let's look at row 2 and year 1. If ending inventory is overstated, we use the inventory relation to see that cost of goods sold is understated. A lower cost of goods sold yields a higher income.

For year 2 of row 2, we again recall that an overstated ending inventory for year 1 becomes an overstated beginning inventory for year 2. If beginning inventory is overstated, we use the inventory relation to see that cost of goods sold is overstated. A higher cost of goods sold yields a lower income.

EXHIBIT 5.10

Effects of Inventory Errors on the Income Statement

	Year 1		Year 2	
Ending Inventory	**Cost of Goods Sold**	**Net Income**	**Cost of Goods Sold**	**Net Income**
Understated ↓	Overstated ↑	Understated ↓	Understated ↓	Overstated ↑
Overstated* ↑	Understated ↓	Overstated ↑	Overstated ↑	Understated ↓

* This error is less likely under a perpetual system versus a periodic because it implies more inventory than is recorded (or less shrinkage than expected). Management will normally follow up and discover and correct this error before it impacts any accounts.

To illustrate, consider an inventory error for a company with $100,000 in sales for each of the years 2012, 2013, and 2014. If this company maintains a steady $20,000 inventory level during this period and makes $60,000 in purchases in each of these years, its cost of goods sold is $60,000 and its gross profit is $40,000 each year.

Ending Inventory Understated—Year 1   Assume that this company errs in computing its 2012 ending inventory and reports $16,000 instead of the correct amount of $20,000. The effects of this error are shown in Exhibit 5.11. The $4,000 understatement of 2012 ending inventory causes a $4,000 overstatement in 2012 cost of goods sold and a $4,000 understatement in both gross profit and net income for 2012. We see that these effects match the effects predicted in Exhibit 5.10.

EXHIBIT 5.11

Effects of Inventory Errors on Three Periods' Income Statements

Income Statements			
	2012	**2013**	**2014**
Sales	$100,000	$100,000	$100,000
Cost of goods sold			
Beginning inventory	$20,000	→ $16,000*	→ $20,000
Cost of goods purchased	60,000	60,000	60,000
Goods available for sale	80,000	76,000	80,000
Ending inventory	16,000*	20,000	20,000
Cost of goods sold	64,000†	56,000†	60,000
Gross profit	36,000	44,000	40,000
Expenses	10,000	10,000	10,000
Net income	$ 26,000	$ 34,000	$ 30,000

Correct income is $30,000 for each year

* Correct amount is $20,000.   † Correct amount is $60,000.

Ending Inventory Understated—Year 2   The 2012 understated ending inventory becomes the 2013 understated *beginning* inventory. We see in Exhibit 5.11 that this error causes an understatement in 2013 cost of goods sold and a $4,000 overstatement in both gross profit and net income for 2013.

Ending Inventory Understated—Year 3   Exhibit 5.11 shows that the 2012 ending inventory error affects only that period and the next. It does not affect 2014 results or any period thereafter. An inventory error is said to be *self-correcting* because it always yields an offsetting error in the next period. This does not reduce the severity of inventory errors. Managers, lenders, owners, and others make important decisions from analysis of income and costs.

Example: If 2012 ending inventory in Exhibit 5.11 is overstated by $3,000 (not understated by $4,000), what is the effect on cost of goods sold, gross profit, assets, and equity? *Answer:* Cost of goods sold is understated by $3,000 in 2012 and overstated by $3,000 in 2013. Gross profit and net income are overstated in 2012 and understated in 2013. Assets and equity are overstated in 2012.

Point: A former internal auditor at **Coca-Cola** alleges that just before midnight at a prior calendar year-end, fully loaded Coke trucks were ordered to drive about 2 feet away from the loading dock so that Coke could record millions of dollars in extra sales.

We can also do an analysis of beginning inventory errors. The income statement effects are the opposite of those for ending inventory.

Balance Sheet Effects   Balance sheet effects of an inventory error can be seen by considering the accounting equation: Assets = Liabilities + Equity. For example, understating ending inventory understates both current and total assets. An understatement in ending inventory also yields an understatement in equity because of the understatement in net income. Exhibit 5.12 shows the effects of inventory errors on the current period's balance sheet amounts. Errors in *beginning* inventory do not yield misstatements in the end-of-period balance sheet, but they do affect that current period's income statement.

EXHIBIT 5.12

Effects of Inventory Errors on Current Period's Balance Sheet

Ending Inventory	Assets	Equity
Understated ⬇	Understated ⬇	Understated ⬇
Overstated ⬆	Overstated ⬆	Overstated ⬆

Quick Check

Answers — p. 237

8. Use LCM applied separately to the following individual items to compute ending inventory.

Product	Units	Unit Recorded Cost	Unit Market Cost
A	20	$ 6	$ 5
B	40	9	8
C	10	12	15

GLOBAL VIEW

This section discusses differences between U.S. GAAP and IFRS in the items and costs making up merchandise inventory, in the methods to assign costs to inventory, and in the methods to estimate inventory values.

Items and Costs Making Up Inventory   Both U.S. GAAP and IFRS include broad and similar guidance for the items and costs making up merchandise inventory. Specifically, under both accounting systems, merchandise inventory includes all items that a company owns and holds for sale. Further, merchandise inventory includes costs of expenditures necessary, directly or indirectly, to bring those items to a salable condition and location.

Assigning Costs to Inventory   Both U.S. GAAP and IFRS allow companies to use specific identification in assigning costs to inventory. Further, both systems allow companies to apply a *cost flow assumption*. The usual cost flow assumptions are: FIFO, Weighted Average, and LIFO. However, IFRS does not (currently) allow use of LIFO. As the convergence project progresses, this prohibition may or may not persist.

Estimating Inventory Costs   The value of inventory can change while it awaits sale to customers. That value can decrease or increase.

Decreases in Inventory Value   Both U.S. GAAP and IFRS require companies to write down (reduce the cost recorded for) inventory when its value falls below the cost recorded. This is referred to as the *lower of cost or market* method explained in this chapter. U.S. GAAP prohibits any later increase in the recorded value of that inventory even if that decline in value is reversed through value increases in later periods. However, IFRS allows reversals of those write downs up to the original acquisition cost. For example, if **Polaris** wrote down its 2011 inventory from $298 million to $250 million, it could not reverse this in future periods even if its value increased to more than $298 million. However, if Polaris applied IFRS, it could reverse that previous loss. (Another difference is that value refers to *replacement cost* under U.S. GAAP, but *net realizable value* under IFRS.)

Polaris

Increases in Inventory Value   Neither U.S. GAAP nor IFRS allow inventory to be adjusted upward beyond the original cost. (One exception is that IFRS requires agricultural assets such as animals, forests, and plants to be measured at fair value less point-of-sale costs.)

5 bikes costing $500 in inventory. On August 17, 20 bikes costing $2,300 are purchased, and on August 28, another 10 bikes costing $1,190 are purchased, for a total of 35 bikes costing $3,990 in inventory. On August 31 (see sales data above), 23 bikes costing $2,582 are sold, which leaves 12 bikes costing $1,408 in ending inventory. Carefully study Exhibit 5A.2 to see the flow of costs both in and out of inventory. Each unit, whether sold or remaining in inventory, has its own specific cost attached to it.

When using specific identification, Trekking's cost of goods sold reported on the income statement totals **$4,582**, the sum of $2,000 and $2,582 from the third column of Exhibit 5A.2. Trekking's ending inventory reported on the balance sheet is **$1,408**, which is the final inventory balance from the fourth column. The purchases and sales entries for Exhibit 5A.2 follow (the colored boldface numbers are those impacted by the cost flow assumption):

Point: The assignment of costs to the goods sold and to inventory using specific identification is the same for both the perpetual and periodic systems.

Point: Specific identification is usually practical only for companies with expensive, custom-made inventory. Examples include car dealerships, implement dealers such as John Deere, jewelers, and fashion designers.

Purchases

Aug. 3	Purchases 1,590	
	Accounts Payable	1,590
17	Purchases 2,300	
	Accounts Payable	2,300
28	Purchases 1,190	
	Accounts Payable	1,190

Sales

Aug. 14	Accounts Receivable 2,600	
	Sales....................	2,600
31	Accounts Receivable 3,450	
	Sales....................	3,450

Adjusting Entry

31	Merchandise Inventory 1,408	
	Income Summary.........	498
	Merchandise Inventory	910

First-In, First-Out   The first-in, first-out (FIFO) method of assigning costs to both inventory and cost of goods sold assumes that inventory items are sold in the order acquired. When sales occur, the costs of the earliest units acquired are charged to cost of goods sold. This leaves the costs from the most recent purchases in ending inventory. Use of FIFO for computing the cost of inventory and cost of goods sold is shown in Exhibit 5A.3.

This exhibit starts with computing $5,990 in total units available for sale—this is from Exhibit 5A.1. Applying FIFO, we know that the 12 units in ending inventory will be reported at the cost of the most recent 12 purchases. Reviewing purchases in reverse order, we assign costs to the 12 bikes in ending inventory as follows: $119 cost to 10 bikes and $115 cost to 2 bikes. This yields 12 bikes costing $1,420 in ending inventory. We then subtract this $1,420 in ending inventory from $5,990 in cost of goods available to get $4,570 in cost of goods sold.

Total cost of 55 units available for sale (from Exhibit 5A.1)		$5,990
Less ending inventory priced using FIFO		
10 units from August 28 purchase at $119 each	$1,190	
2 units from August 17 purchase at $115 each	230	
Ending inventory		**1,420**
Cost of goods sold		**$4,570**

EXHIBIT 5A.3

FIFO Computations— Periodic System

Exhibit 5A.1 shows that the 12 units in ending inventory consist of 10 units from the latest purchase on Aug. 28 and 2 units from the next latest purchase on Aug. 17.

Point: The assignment of costs to the goods sold and to inventory using FIFO is the same for both the perpetual and periodic systems.

Trekking's ending inventory reported on the balance sheet is **$1,420**, and its cost of goods sold reported on the income statement is **$4,570**. These amounts are the same as those computed using the perpetual system. This always occurs because the most recent purchases are in ending inventory under both systems. The purchases and sales entries for Exhibit 5A.3 follow (the colored boldface numbers are those affected by the cost flow assumption).

Purchases

Aug. 3	Purchases..................... 1,590	
	Accounts Payable..........	1,590
17	Purchases..................... 2,300	
	Accounts Payable..........	2,300
28	Purchases..................... 1,190	
	Accounts Payable..........	1,190

Sales

Aug. 14	Accounts Receivable 2,600	
	Sales....................	2,600
31	Accounts Receivable 3,450	
	Sales....................	3,450

Adjusting Entry

31	Merchandise Inventory 1,420	
	Income Summary	510
	Merchandise Inventory	910

Last-In, First-Out The last-in, first-out (LIFO) method of assigning costs assumes that the most recent purchases are sold first. These more recent costs are charged to the goods sold, and the costs of the earliest purchases are assigned to inventory. LIFO results in costs of the most recent purchases being assigned to cost of goods sold, which means that LIFO comes close to matching current costs of goods sold with revenues. Use of LIFO for computing cost of inventory and cost of goods sold is shown in Exhibit 5A.4.

This exhibit starts with computing $5,990 in total units available for sale—this is from Exhibit 5A.1. Applying LIFO, we know that the 12 units in ending inventory will be reported at the cost of the earliest 12 purchases. Reviewing the earliest purchases in order, we assign costs to the 12 bikes in ending inventory as follows: $91 cost to 10 bikes and $106 cost to 2 bikes. This yields 12 bikes costing $1,122 in ending inventory. We then subtract this $1,122 in ending inventory from $5,990 in cost of goods available to get $4,868 in cost of goods sold.

EXHIBIT 5A.4

LIFO Computations—
Periodic System

Exhibit 5A.1 shows that the 12 units in ending inventory consist of 10 units from the earliest purchase (beg. inv.) and 2 units from the next earliest purchase on Aug. 3.

Total cost of 55 units available for sale (from Exhibit 5A.1)		$5,990
Less ending inventory priced using LIFO		
10 units in beginning inventory at $91 each	$910	
2 units from August 3 purchase at $106 each	212	
Ending inventory		1,122
Cost of goods sold		$4,868

Trekking's ending inventory reported on the balance sheet is $1,122, and its cost of goods sold reported on the income statement is $4,868. When LIFO is used with the periodic system, cost of goods sold is assigned costs from the most recent purchases for the period. With a perpetual system, cost of goods sold is assigned costs from the most recent purchases at the point of *each sale*. The purchases and sales entries for Exhibit 5A.4 follow (the colored boldface numbers are those affected by the cost flow assumption).

Purchases			
Aug. 3	Purchases	1,590	
	Accounts Payable		1,590
17	Purchases	2,300	
	Accounts Payable		2,300
28	Purchases	1,190	
	Accounts Payable		1,190

Sales			
Aug. 14	Accounts Receivable	2,600	
	Sales		2,600
31	Accounts Receivable	3,450	
	Sales		3,450
	Adjusting Entry		
31	Merchandise Inventory	1,122	
	Income Summary		212
	Merchandise Inventory		910

Weighted Average The **weighted average** or **WA** (also called **average cost**) method of assigning cost requires that we use the average cost per unit of inventory at the end of the period. Weighted average cost per unit equals the cost of goods available for sale divided by the units available. The weighted average method of assigning cost involves three important steps. The first two steps are shown in Exhibit 5A.5. First, multiply the per unit cost for beginning inventory and each particular purchase by the corresponding number of units (from Exhibit 5A.1). Second, add these amounts and divide by the total number of units available for sale to find the weighted average cost per unit.

EXHIBIT 5A.5

Weighted Average Cost per Unit

Example: In Exhibit 5A.5, if 5 more units had been purchased at $120 each, what would be the weighted average cost per unit?
Answer: $109.83 ($6,590/60)

Step 1:	10 units @ $ 91 =	$ 910
	15 units @ $106 =	1,590
	20 units @ $115 =	2,300
	10 units @ $119 =	1,190
	55	$5,990
Step 2:	$5,990/55 units = **$108.91** weighted average cost per unit	

The third step is to use the weighted average cost per unit to assign costs to inventory and to the units sold as shown in Exhibit 5A.6.

EXHIBIT 5A.6
Weighted Average
Computations—Periodic

Step 3:	Total cost of 55 units available for sale (from Exhibit 5A.1)..........	$5,990
	Less **ending inventory** priced on a weighted average	
	cost basis: 12 units at $108.91 each (from Exhibit 5A.5)...........	1,307
	Cost of goods sold	$4,683

Trekking's ending inventory reported on the balance sheet is $1,307, and its cost of goods sold reported on the income statement is $4,683 when using the weighted average (periodic) method. The purchases and sales entries for Exhibit 5A.6 follow (the colored boldface numbers are those affected by the cost flow assumption).

Point: Weighted average usually yields different results for the perpetual and the periodic systems because under a perpetual system it recomputes the per unit cost prior to each sale, whereas under a periodic system, the per unit cost is computed only at the end of a period.

Purchases		
Aug. 3 Purchases.....................	1,590	
Accounts Payable..........		1,590
17 Purchases.....................	2,300	
Accounts Payable..........		2,300
28 Purchases.....................	1,190	
Accounts Payable..........		1,190

Sales		
Aug. 14 Accounts Receivable	2,600	
Sales....................		2,600
31 Accounts Receivable	3,450	
Sales....................		3,450
Adjusting Entry		
31 Merchandise Inventory	**1,307**	
Income Summary		397
Merchandise Inventory		910

Point: LIFO inventory is often less than the inventory's replacement cost because LIFO inventory is valued using the oldest inventory purchase costs.

Financial Statement Effects When purchase prices do not change, each inventory costing method assigns the same cost amounts to inventory and to cost of goods sold. When purchase prices are different, however, the methods nearly always assign different cost amounts. We show these differences in Exhibit 5A.7 using Trekking's data.

EXHIBIT 5A.7
Financial Statement Effects of
Inventory Costing Methods

TREKKING COMPANY For Month Ended August 31	Specific Identification	FIFO	LIFO	Weighted Average
Income Statement				
Sales	$6,050	$6,050	$6,050	$6,050
Cost of goods sold	4,582	4,570	4,868	4,683
Gross profit	1,468	1,480	1,182	1,367
Expenses......................	450	450	450	450
Income before taxes..............	1,018	1,030	732	917
Income tax expense (30%).........	305	309	220	275
Net income	$ 713	$ 721	$ 512	$ 642
Balance Sheet				
Inventory	$1,408	$1,420	$1,122	$1,307

This exhibit reveals two important results. First, when purchase costs *regularly rise,* as in Trekking's case, observe the following:

● FIFO assigns the lowest amount to cost of goods sold—yielding the highest gross profit and net income.
● LIFO assigns the highest amount to cost of goods sold—yielding the lowest gross profit and net income, which also yields a temporary tax advantage by postponing payment of some income tax.
● Weighted average yields results between FIFO and LIFO.
● Specific identification always yields results that depend on which units are sold.

Second, when costs *regularly decline,* the reverse occurs for FIFO and LIFO. FIFO gives the highest cost of goods sold—yielding the lowest gross profit and income. And LIFO gives the lowest cost of goods sold—yielding the highest gross profit and income.

All four inventory costing methods are acceptable in practice. A company must disclose the inventory method it uses. Each method offers certain advantages as follows:

- FIFO assigns an amount to inventory on the balance sheet that approximates its current cost; it also mimics the actual flow of goods for most businesses.
- LIFO assigns an amount to cost of goods sold on the income statement that approximates its current cost; it also better matches current costs with revenues in computing gross profit.
- Weighted average tends to smooth out erratic changes in costs.
- Specific identification exactly matches the costs of items with the revenues they generate.

APPENDIX

5B

Inventory Estimation Methods

P4 Apply both the retail inventory and gross profit methods to estimate inventory.

Inventory sometimes requires estimation for two reasons. First, companies often require **interim statements** (financial statements prepared for periods of less than one year), but they only annually take a physical count of inventory. Second, companies may require an inventory estimate if some casualty such as fire or flood makes taking a physical count impossible. Estimates are usually only required for companies that use the periodic system. Companies using a perpetual system would presumably have updated inventory data.

This appendix describes two methods to estimate inventory.

Retail Inventory Method   To avoid the time-consuming and expensive process of taking a physical inventory each month or quarter, some companies use the **retail inventory method** to estimate cost of goods sold and ending inventory. Some companies even use the retail inventory method to prepare the annual statements. **Home Depot,** for instance, says in its annual report: "Inventories are stated at the lower of cost (first-in, first-out) or market, as determined by the retail inventory method." A company may also estimate inventory for audit purposes or when inventory is damaged or destroyed.

The retail inventory method uses a three-step process to estimate ending inventory. We need to know the amount of inventory a company had at the beginning of the period in both *cost* and *retail* amounts. We already explained how to compute the cost of inventory. The *retail amount of inventory* refers to its dollar amount measured using selling prices of inventory items. We also need to know the net amount of goods purchased (minus returns, allowances, and discounts) in the period, both at cost and at retail. The amount of net sales at retail is also needed. The process is shown in Exhibit 5B.1.

The reasoning behind the retail inventory method is that if we can get a good estimate of the cost-to-retail ratio, we can multiply ending inventory at retail by this ratio to estimate ending inventory at cost. We show in Exhibit 5B.2 how these steps are applied to estimate ending inventory for a typical company. First, we find that $100,000 of goods (at retail selling prices) were available for sale. We see that $70,000 of these goods were sold, leaving $30,000 (retail value) of merchandise in ending inventory. Second, the cost of these goods is 60% of the $100,000 retail value. Third, since cost for these goods is 60% of retail, the estimated cost of ending inventory is $18,000.

Point: When a retailer takes a physical inventory, it can restate the retail value of inventory to a cost basis by applying the cost-to-retail ratio. It can also estimate the amount of shrinkage by comparing the inventory computed with the amount from a physical inventory.

EXHIBIT 5B.1

Retail Inventory Method of Inventory Estimation

Step 1   Goods available for sale at retail   −   Net sales at retail   =   Ending inventory at retail

Step 2   Goods available for sale at cost   ÷   Goods available for sale at retail   =   Cost-to-retail ratio

Step 3   Ending inventory at retail   ×   Cost-to-retail ratio   =   Estimated ending inventory at cost

Example: What is the cost of ending inventory in Exhibit 5B.2 if the cost of beginning inventory is $22,500 and its retail value is $34,500? *Answer:* $30,000 × 62% = $18,600

	At Cost	At Retail
Goods available for sale		
Beginning inventory	$ 20,500	$ 34,500
Cost of goods purchased.....................................	39,500	65,500
Goods available for sale	60,000	100,000
Step 1: Deduct net sales at retail		70,000
Ending inventory at retail		$ 30,000
Step 2: Cost-to-retail ratio: ($60,000 ÷ $100,000) = 60%		
Step 3: Estimated ending inventory at cost ($30,000 × 60%)	$18,000	

EXHIBIT 5B.2

Estimated Inventory Using the Retail Inventory Method

Point: A retailer such as Target can speed up its year-end physical count by using the retail inventory method. Inventory counters can record the item's retail price without having to look up the cost of each item.

Gross Profit Method The **gross profit method** estimates the cost of ending inventory by applying the gross profit ratio to net sales (at retail). This type of estimate often is needed when inventory is destroyed, lost, or stolen. These cases require an inventory estimate so that a company can file a claim with its insurer. Users also apply this method to see whether inventory amounts from a physical count are reasonable. This method uses the historical relation between cost of goods sold and net sales to estimate the proportion of cost of goods sold making up current sales. This cost of goods sold estimate is then subtracted from cost of goods available for sale to estimate the ending inventory at cost. These two steps are shown in Exhibit 5B.3.

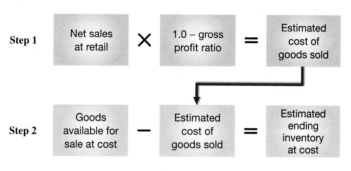

EXHIBIT 5B.3

Gross Profit Method of Inventory Estimation

To illustrate, assume that a company's inventory is destroyed by fire in March 2013. When the fire occurs, the company's accounts show the following balances for January through March: sales, $31,500; sales returns, $1,500; inventory (January 1, 2013), $12,000; and cost of goods purchased, $20,500. If this company's gross profit ratio is 30%, then 30% of each net sales dollar is gross profit and 70% is cost of goods sold. We show in Exhibit 5B.4 how this 70% is used to estimate lost inventory of $11,500. To understand this exhibit, think of subtracting the cost of goods sold from the goods available for sale to get the ending inventory.

Point: A fire or other catastrophe can result in an insurance claim for lost inventory or income. Backup and off-site storage of data help ensure coverage for such losses.

Point: Reliability of the gross profit method depends on an accurate and stable estimate of the gross profit ratio.

EXHIBIT 5B.4

Estimated Inventory Using the Gross Profit Method

Goods available for sale	
Inventory, January 1, 2013	$12,000
Cost of goods purchased	20,500
Goods available for sale (at cost)	32,500
Net sales at retail ($31,500 − $1,500)	$30,000
Step 1: Estimated cost of goods sold ($30,000 × 70%)	(21,000) ← × 0.70
Step 2: Estimated March inventory at cost	$11,500

Quick Check   Answer — p. 237

9. Using the retail method and the following data, estimate the cost of ending inventory.

	Cost	Retail
Beginning inventory	$324,000	$530,000
Cost of goods purchased	195,000	335,000
Net sales		320,000

Summary

C1   **Identify the items making up merchandise inventory.** Merchandise inventory refers to goods owned by a company and held for resale. Three special cases merit our attention. Goods in transit are reported in inventory of the company that holds ownership rights. Goods on consignment are reported in the consignor's inventory. Goods damaged or obsolete are reported in inventory at their net realizable value.

C2   **Identify the costs of merchandise inventory.** Costs of merchandise inventory include expenditures necessary to bring an item to a salable condition and location. This includes its invoice cost minus any discount plus any added or incidental costs necessary to put it in a place and condition for sale.

A1   **Analyze the effects of inventory methods for both financial and tax reporting.** When purchase costs are rising or falling, the inventory costing methods are likely to assign different costs to inventory. Specific identification exactly matches costs and revenues. Weighted average smooths out cost changes. FIFO assigns an amount to inventory closely approximating current replacement cost. LIFO assigns the most recent costs incurred to cost of goods sold and likely better matches current costs with revenues.

A2   **Analyze the effects of inventory errors on current and future financial statements.** An error in the amount of ending inventory affects assets (inventory), net income (cost of goods sold), and equity for that period. Since ending inventory is next period's beginning inventory, an error in ending inventory affects next period's cost of goods sold and net income. Inventory errors in one period are offset in the next period.

A3   **Assess inventory management using both inventory turnover and days' sales in inventory.** We prefer a high inventory turnover, provided that goods are not out of stock and customers are not turned away. We use days' sales in inventory to assess the likelihood of goods being out of stock. We prefer a small number of days' sales in inventory if we can serve customer needs and provide a buffer for uncertainties.

P1   **Compute inventory in a perpetual system using the methods of specific identification, FIFO, LIFO, and weighted average.** Costs are assigned to the cost of goods sold account *each time* a

sale occurs in a perpetual system. Specific identification assigns a cost to each item sold by referring to its actual cost (for example, its net invoice cost). Weighted average assigns a cost to items sold by dividing the current balance in the inventory account by the total items available for sale to determine cost per unit. We then multiply the number of units sold by this cost per unit to get the cost of each sale. FIFO assigns cost to items sold assuming that the earliest units purchased are the first units sold. LIFO assigns cost to items sold assuming that the most recent units purchased are the first units sold.

P2   **Compute the lower of cost or market amount of inventory.** Inventory is reported at market cost when market is *lower* than recorded cost, called the *lower of cost or market (LCM) inventory.* Market is typically measured as replacement cost. Lower of cost or market can be applied separately to each item, to major categories of items, or to the entire inventory.

P3^A   **Compute inventory in a periodic system using the methods of specific identification, FIFO, LIFO, and weighted average.** Periodic inventory systems allocate the cost of goods available for sale between cost of goods sold and ending inventory *at the end of a period.* Specific identification and FIFO give identical results whether the periodic or perpetual system is used. LIFO assigns costs to cost of goods sold assuming the last units purchased for the period are the first units sold. The weighted average cost per unit is computed by dividing the total cost of beginning inventory and net purchases for the period by the total number of units available. Then, it multiplies cost per unit by the number of units sold to give cost of goods sold.

P4^B   **Apply both the retail inventory and gross profit methods to estimate inventory.** The retail inventory method involves three steps: (1) goods available at retail minus net sales at retail equals ending inventory at retail, (2) goods available at cost divided by goods available at retail equals the cost-to-retail ratio, and (3) ending inventory at retail multiplied by the cost-to-retail ratio equals estimated ending inventory at cost. The gross profit method involves two steps: (1) net sales at retail multiplied by 1 minus the gross profit ratio equals estimated cost of goods sold, and (2) goods available at cost minus estimated cost of goods sold equals estimated ending inventory at cost.

Guidance Answers to Decision Maker and Decision Ethics

Cost Analyst   Explain to your supervisor that when inventory costs are increasing, FIFO results in an inventory valuation that approximates replacement cost. The most recently purchased goods are assigned to ending inventory under FIFO and are likely closer to replacement values than earlier costs that would be assigned to inventory if LIFO were used.

Inventory Manager   It seems your company can save (or at least postpone) taxes by switching to LIFO, but the switch is likely to reduce bonus money that you think you have earned and deserve. Since the U.S. tax code requires companies that use LIFO for tax reporting also to use it for financial reporting, your options are further constrained. Your best decision is to tell your superior about the tax savings with

LIFO. You also should discuss your bonus plan and how this is likely to hurt you unfairly. You might propose to compute inventory under the LIFO method for reporting purposes but use the FIFO method for your bonus calculations. Another solution is to revise the bonus plan to reflect the company's use of the LIFO method.

Entrepreneur   Your inventory turnover is markedly higher than the norm, whereas days' sales in inventory approximates the norm. Since your turnover is already 14% better than average, you are probably best served by directing attention to days' sales in inventory. You should see whether you can reduce the level of inventory while maintaining service to customers. Given your higher turnover, you should be able to hold less inventory.

Guidance Answers to Quick Checks

1. The matching principle.

2. Famous Footwear reports these goods in its inventory.

3. Total cost assigned to the painting is $12,180, computed as $11,400 + $130 + $150 + $100 + $400.

4. Specific identification exactly matches costs and revenues. Weighted average tends to smooth out cost changes. FIFO assigns an amount to inventory that closely approximates current replacement cost. LIFO assigns the most recent costs incurred to cost of goods sold and likely better matches current costs with revenues.

5. FIFO—it gives a lower cost of goods sold, a higher gross profit, and a higher net income when costs are rising.

6. When costs are rising, LIFO gives a lower inventory figure on the balance sheet as compared to FIFO. FIFO's inventory amount approximates current replacement costs.

7. Cost of goods sold would be overstated by $10,000 in 2012 and understated by $10,000 in year 2013.

8. The reported LCM inventory amount (using items) is $540, computed as [(20 × $5) + (40 × $8) + (10 × $12)].

9.[B] Estimated ending inventory (at cost) is $327,000. It is computed as follows:

Step 1:   ($530,000 + $335,000) − $320,000 = $545,000

Step 2: $\dfrac{\$324,000 + \$195,000}{\$530,000 + \$335,000} = 60\%$

Step 3: $545,000 × 60% = \underline{\$327,000}$

Key Terms

Average cost (p. 216, 232)
Conservatism constraint (p. 220)
Consignee (p. 210)
Consignor (p. 210)
Consistency concept (p. 219)
Days' sales in inventory (p. 223)

First-in, first-out (FIFO) (p. 215)
Gross profit method (p. 235)
Interim statements (p. 234)
Inventory turnover (p. 223)
Last-in, first-out (LIFO) (p. 215)
Lower of cost or market (LCM) (p. 219)

Net realizable value (p. 210)
Retail inventory method (p. 234)
Specific identification (p. 213, 230)
Weighted average (p. 216, 232)

Multiple Choice Quiz

Answers on p. 254   mhhe.com/wildFAF4e

Additional Quiz Questions are available at the book's Website.

Use the following information from Marvel Company for the month of July to answer questions 1 through 4.

July 1	Beginning inventory	75 units @ $25 each
July 3	Purchase	348 units @ $27 each
July 8	Sale	300 units
July 15	Purchase	257 units @ $28 each
July 23	Sale	275 units

1. **Perpetual:** Assume that Marvel uses a *perpetual* FIFO inventory system. What is the dollar value of its ending inventory?
   a. $2,940   d. $2,852
   b. $2,685   e. $2,705
   c. $2,625

2. **Perpetual:** Assume that Marvel uses a *perpetual* LIFO inventory system. What is the dollar value of its ending inventory?
   a. $2,940   d. $2,852
   b. $2,685   e. $2,705
   c. $2,625

3. **Perpetual:** Assume that Marvel uses a perpetual specific identification inventory system. Its ending inventory consists of 20 units from beginning inventory, 40 units from the July 3 purchase, and 45 units from the July 15 purchase. What is the dollar value of its ending inventory?
   a. $2,940   d. $2,852
   b. $2,685   e. $2,840
   c. $2,625

4. **Periodic:** Assume that Marvel uses a *periodic* FIFO inventory system. What is the dollar value of its ending inventory?
   a. $2,940   d. $2,852
   b. $2,685   e. $2,705
   c. $2,625

5. **Periodic:** A company reports the following beginning inventory and purchases, and it ends the period with 30 units in inventory.

Beginning inventory	100 units at $10 cost per unit
Purchase 1	40 units at $12 cost per unit
Purchase 2	20 units at $14 cost per unit

   a. Compute ending inventory using the FIFO *periodic* system.
   b. Compute cost of goods sold using the LIFO *periodic* system.

6. A company has cost of goods sold of $85,000 and ending inventory of $18,000. Its days' sales in inventory equals:
   a. 49.32 days   d. 77.29 days
   b. 0.21 days   e. 1,723.61 days
   c. 4.72 days

B   *Superscript letter A (B) denotes assignments based on Appendix 5A (5B).*

🔲 Icon denotes assignments that involve decision making.

Discussion Questions

1. Describe how costs flow from inventory to cost of goods sold for the following methods: (*a*) FIFO and (*b*) LIFO.

2. Where is the amount of merchandise inventory disclosed in the financial statements?

3. Why are incidental costs sometimes ignored in inventory costing? Under what accounting constraint is this permitted?

4. 🔲 If costs are declining, will the LIFO or FIFO method of inventory valuation yield the lower cost of goods sold? Why?

5. What does the full-disclosure principle prescribe if a company changes from one acceptable accounting method to another?

6. Can a company change its inventory method each accounting period? Explain.

7. 🔲 Does the accounting concept of consistency preclude any changes from one accounting method to another?

8. 🔲 If inventory errors are said to correct themselves, why are accounting users concerned when such errors are made?

9. Explain the following statement: "Inventory errors correct themselves."

10. What is the meaning of *market* as it is used in determining the lower of cost or market for inventory?

11. 🔲 What guidance does the accounting constraint of conservatism offer?

12. What factors contribute to (or cause) inventory shrinkage?

13.ᴮ When preparing interim financial statements, what two methods can companies utilize to estimate cost of goods sold and ending inventory?

14. Refer to **Polaris**' financial statements in Appendix A. On December 31, 2011, what percent of current assets are represented by inventory?   **Polaris**

15. Refer to **Arctic Cat**'s financial statements in Appendix A and compute its cost of goods available for sale for the year ended March 31, 2011.   **Arctic Cat**

16. Refer to **KTM**'s financial statements in Appendix A. Compute its cost of goods available for sale for the year ended December 31, 2011.   **KTM**

17. Refer to **Piaggio**'s financial statements in Appendix A. What percent of its current assets are inventory as of December 31, 2011 and 2010?   **PIAGGIO**

🄼 **connect**

QUICK STUDY

QS 5-1

Perpetual: Inventory costing with FIFO

P1

Information: A company reports the following beginning inventory and purchases for the month of January. On January 26, the company sells 350 units. 150 units remain in ending inventory at January 31.

	Units	Unit Cost
Beginning inventory on January 1	320	$3.00
Purchase on January 9	80	3.20
Purchase on January 25	100	3.34

Required

Assume the perpetual inventory system is used and then determine the costs assigned to ending inventory when costs are assigned based on the FIFO method. (Round per unit costs and inventory amounts to cents.)

QS 5-2

Perpetual: Inventory costing with LIFO **P1**

Refer to the information in QS 5-1 and assume the perpetual inventory system is used. Determine the costs assigned to ending inventory when costs are assigned based on LIFO. (Round per unit costs and inventory amounts to cents.)

QS 5-3

Perpetual: Inventory costing with weighted average **P1**

Check $465

Refer to the information in QS 5-1 and assume the perpetual inventory system is used. Determine the costs assigned to ending inventory when costs are assigned based on the weighted average method. (Round per unit costs and inventory amounts to cents.)

QS 5-4ᴬ

Periodic: Inventory costing with FIFO **P3**

Refer to the **information** in QS 5-1 and assume the periodic inventory system is used. Determine the costs assigned to ending inventory when costs are assigned based on the FIFO method. (Round per unit costs and inventory amounts to cents.)

Refer to the **information** in QS 5-1 and assume the periodic inventory system is used. Determine the costs assigned to ending inventory when costs are assigned based on the LIFO method. (Round per unit costs and inventory amounts to cents.)

QS 5-5[A]
Periodic: Inventory costing with LIFO P3

Refer to the **information** in QS 5-1 and assume the periodic inventory system is used. Determine the costs assigned to ending inventory when costs are assigned based on the weighted average method. (Round per unit costs and inventory amounts to cents.)

QS 5-6[A]
Periodic: Inventory costing with weighted average P3

Wattan Company reports beginning inventory of 10 units at $60 each. Every week for four weeks it purchases an additional 10 units at respective costs of $61, $62, $65 and $70 per unit for weeks 1 through 4. Calculate the cost of goods available for sale and the units available for sale for this four-week period. Assume that no sales occur during those four weeks.

QS 5-7
Computing goods available for sale P1

Information: Trey Monson starts a merchandising business on December 1 and enters into the following three inventory purchases. During December, Monson sells 15 units for $20 each on December 15.

QS 5-8
Perpetual: Assigning costs with FIFO

P1

Purchases on December 7	10 units @ $ 6.00 cost
Purchases on December 14	20 units @ $12.00 cost
Purchases on December 21	15 units @ $14.00 cost

Required

Monson uses a perpetual inventory system. Determine the costs assigned to the December 31 ending inventory based on the FIFO method. (Round per unit costs and inventory amounts to cents.)

Refer to the information in QS 5-8 and assume the perpetual inventory system is used. Determine the costs assigned to ending inventory when costs are assigned based on the LIFO method. (Round per unit costs and inventory amounts to cents.)

QS 5-9
Perpetual: Inventory costing with LIFO P1

Refer to the information in QS 5-8 and assume the perpetual inventory system is used. Determine the costs assigned to ending inventory when costs are assigned based on the weighted average method. (Round per unit costs and inventory amounts to cents.)

QS 5-10
Perpetual: Inventory costing with weighted average P1

Check End. Inv. = $360

Refer to the information in QS 5-8 and assume the perpetual inventory system is used. Determine the costs assigned to ending inventory when costs are assigned based on specific identification. Of the units sold, eight are from the December 7 purchase and seven are from the December 14 purchase. (Round per unit costs and inventory amounts to cents.)

QS 5-11
Perpetual: Inventory costing with specific identification P1

Refer to the **information** in QS 5-8 and assume the periodic inventory system is used. Determine the costs assigned to ending inventory when costs are assigned based on the FIFO method. (Round per unit costs and inventory amounts to cents.)

QS 5-12[A]
Periodic: Inventory costing with FIFO P3

Refer to the **information** in QS 5-8 and assume the periodic inventory system is used. Determine the costs assigned to ending inventory when costs are assigned based on the LIFO method. (Round per unit costs and inventory amounts to cents.)

QS 5-13
Periodic: Inventory costing with LIFO P3

Refer to the **information** in QS 5-8 and assume the periodic inventory system is used. Determine the costs assigned to ending inventory when costs are assigned based on the weighted average method. (Round per unit costs and inventory amounts to cents.)

QS 5-14[A]
Periodic: Inventory costing with weighted average P3

Refer to the **information** in QS 5-8 and assume the periodic inventory system is used. Determine the costs assigned to ending inventory when costs are assigned based on specific identification. Of the units sold, eight are from the December 7 purchase and seven are from the December 14 purchase. (Round per unit costs and inventory amounts to cents.)

QS 5-15[A]
Periodic: Inventory costing with specific identification P3

QS 5-16

Contrasting inventory
costing methods

A1

Identify the inventory costing method best described by each of the following separate statements. Assume a period of increasing costs.

1. Yields a balance sheet inventory amount often markedly less than its replacement cost.

2. Results in a balance sheet inventory amount approximating replacement cost.

3. Provides a tax advantage (deferral) to a corporation when costs are rising.

4. Recognizes (matches) recent costs against net sales.

5. The preferred method when each unit of product has unique features that markedly affect cost.

QS 5-17

Inventory ownership

C1

Homestead Crafts, a distributor of handmade gifts, operates out of owner Emma Finn's house. At the end of the current period, Emma reports she has 1,300 units (products) in her basement, 20 of which were damaged by water and cannot be sold. She also has another 350 units in her van, ready to deliver per a customer order, terms FOB destination, and another 80 units out on consignment to a friend who owns a retail store. How many units should Emma include in her company's period-end inventory?

QS 5-18

Inventory costs

C2

A car dealer acquires a used car for $14,000, terms FOB shipping point. Additional costs in obtaining and offering the car for sale include $250 for transportation-in, $900 for import duties, $300 for insurance during shipment, $150 for advertising, and $1,250 for sales staff salaries. For computing inventory, what cost is assigned to the used car?

QS 5-19

Applying LCM to inventories

P2

Ames Trading Co. has the following products in its ending inventory. Compute lower of cost or market for inventory applied separately to each product.

Product	Quantity	Cost per Unit	Market per Unit
Mountain bikes	11	$600	$550
Skateboards	13	350	425
Gliders	26	800	700

QS 5-20

Inventory errors

A2

In taking a physical inventory at the end of year 2013, Grant Company forgot to count certain units. Explain how this error affects the following: (*a*) 2013 cost of goods sold, (*b*) 2013 gross profit, (*c*) 2013 net income, (*d*) 2014 net income, (*e*) the combined two-year income, and (*f*) income for years after 2014.

QS 5-21

Analyzing inventory   A3

Endor Company begins the year with $150,000 of goods in inventory. At year-end, the amount in inventory has increased to $180,000. Cost of goods sold for the year is $1,200,000. Compute Endor's inventory turnover and days' sales in inventory. Assume that there are 365 days in the year.

QS 5-22^B

Estimating inventories—gross
profit method

P4

Kauai Store's inventory is destroyed by a fire on September 5, 2013. The following data for year 2013 are available from the accounting records. Estimate the cost of the inventory destroyed.

Jan. 1 inventory	$190,000
Jan. 1 through Sept. 5 purchases (net)	$352,000
Jan. 1 through Sept. 5 sales (net)	$685,000
Year 2013 estimated gross profit rate	44%

QS 5-23

International accounting
standards

C1 C2 P2

Answer each of the following questions related to international accounting standards.

a. Explain how the accounting for items and costs making up merchandise inventory is different between IFRS and U.S. GAAP.

b. Can companies reporting under IFRS apply a cost flow assumption in assigning costs to inventory? If yes, identify at least two acceptable cost flow assumptions.

c. Both IFRS and U.S. GAAP apply the lower of cost or market method for reporting inventory values. If inventory is written down from applying the lower of cost or market method, explain in general terms how IFRS and U.S. GAAP differ in accounting for any subsequent period reversal of that reported decline in inventory value.

connect

1. Harris Company has shipped $20,000 of goods to Harlow Co., and Harlow Co. has arranged to sell the goods for Harris. Identify the consignor and the consignee. Which company should include any unsold goods as part of its inventory?

2. At year-end, Harris Co. had shipped $12,500 of merchandise FOB destination to Harlow Co. Which company should include the $12,500 of merchandise in transit as part of its year-end inventory?

EXERCISES

Exercise 5-1
Inventory ownership C1

Walberg Associates, antique dealers, purchased the contents of an estate for $75,000. Terms of the purchase were FOB shipping point, and the cost of transporting the goods to Walberg Associates' warehouse was $2,400. Walberg Associates insured the shipment at a cost of $300. Prior to putting the goods up for sale, they cleaned and refurbished them at a cost of $980. Determine the cost of the inventory acquired from the estate.

Exercise 5-2
Inventory costs
C2

Information: Laker Company reported the following January purchases and sales data for its only product.

Date	Activities	Units Acquired at Cost	Units Sold at Retail
Jan. 1	Beginning inventory	140 units @ $6.00 = $ 840	
Jan. 10	Sales		100 units @ $15
Jan. 20	Purchase	60 units @ $5.00 = 300	
Jan. 25	Sales		80 units @ $15
Jan. 30	Purchase	180 units @ $4.50 = 810	
	Totals	380 units $1,950	180 units

Exercise 5-3
Perpetual: Inventory costing methods
P1

Required

The Company uses a perpetual inventory system. Determine the cost assigned to ending inventory and to cost of goods sold using (a) specific identification, (b) weighted average, (c) FIFO, and (d) LIFO. (Round per unit costs and inventory amounts to cents.) For specific identification, ending inventory consists of 200 units, where 180 are from the January 30 purchase, 5 are from the January 20 purchase, and 15 are from beginning inventory.

Check Ending inventory: LIFO, $930; WA, $918

Use the data in Exercise 5-3 to prepare comparative income statements for the month of January for Laker Company similar to those shown in Exhibit 5.8 for the four inventory methods. Assume expenses are $1,250, and that the applicable income tax rate is 40%. (Round amounts to cents.)

1. Which method yields the highest net income?
2. Does net income using weighted average fall between that using FIFO and LIFO?
3. If costs were rising instead of falling, which method would yield the highest net income?

Exercise 5-4
Perpetual: Income effects of inventory methods
A1

Refer to the information in Exercise 5-3 and assume the periodic inventory system is used. Determine the costs assigned to ending inventory and to cost of goods sold using (a) specific identification, (b) weighted average, (c) FIFO, and (d) LIFO. (Round per unit costs and inventory amounts to cents.)

Exercise 5-5ᴬ
Periodic: Inventory costing P3

Use the data in Exercise 5-5 to prepare comparative income statements for the month of January for the company similar to those shown in Exhibit 5.8 for the four inventory methods. Assume expenses are $1,250, and that the applicable income tax rate is 40%. (Round amounts to cents.)

Exercise 5-6ᴬ
Periodic: Income effects of inventory methods
A1

Required

1. Which method yields the highest net income?
2. Does net income using weighted average fall between that using FIFO and LIFO?
3. If costs were rising instead of falling, which method would yield the highest net income?

Exercise 5-7

Perpetual: Inventory costing methods—FIFO and LIFO

P1

Information: Hemming Co. reported the following current-year purchases and sales for its only product.

Date	Activities	Units Acquired at Cost	Units Sold at Retail
Jan. 1	Beginning inventory	200 units @ $10 = $ 2,000	
Jan. 10	Sales		150 units @ $40
Mar. 14	Purchase	350 units @ $15 = 5,250	
Mar. 15	Sales		300 units @ $40
July 30	Purchase	450 units @ $20 = 9,000	
Oct. 5	Sales		430 units @ $40
Oct. 26	Purchase	100 units @ $25 = 2,500	
	Totals	1,100 units $18,750	880 units

Required

Check Ending inventory: LIFO, $4,150

Hemming uses a perpetual inventory system. Determine the costs assigned to ending inventory and to cost of goods sold using (*a*) FIFO and (*b*) LIFO. Compute the gross margin for each method. (Round amounts to cents.)

Exercise 5-8

Specific identification **P1**

Refer to the information in Exercise 5-7. Ending inventory consists of 45 units from the March 14 purchase, 75 units from the July 30 purchase, and all 100 units from the October 26 purchase. Using the specific identification method, calculate (*a*) the cost of goods sold and (*b*) the gross profit. (Round amounts to cents.)

Exercise 5-9ᴬ

Periodic: Inventory costing

P3

Refer to the **information** in Exercise 5-7 and assume the periodic inventory system is used. Determine the costs assigned to ending inventory and to cost of goods sold using (*a*) FIFO and (*b*) LIFO. Then (*c*) compute the gross margin for each method.

Exercise 5-10

Lower of cost or market

P2

Martinez Company's ending inventory includes the following items. Compute the lower of cost or market for ending inventory applied separately to each product.

		Per Unit	
Product	Units	Cost	Market
Helmets	24	$50	$54
Bats	17	78	72
Shoes	38	95	91
Uniforms	42	36	36

Check LCM = $7,394

Exercise 5-11

Comparing LIFO numbers to FIFO numbers; ratio analysis

A1 A3

Cruz Company uses LIFO for inventory costing and reports the following financial data. It also recomputed inventory and cost of goods sold using FIFO for comparison purposes.

	2013	2012
LIFO inventory	$160	$110
LIFO cost of goods sold	740	680
FIFO inventory	240	110
FIFO cost of goods sold	660	645
Current assets (using LIFO)	220	180
Current liabilities	200	170

Check (1) FIFO: Current ratio, 1.5; Inventory turnover, 3.8 times

1. Compute its current ratio, inventory turnover, and days' sales in inventory for 2013 using (*a*) LIFO numbers and (*b*) FIFO numbers. (Round answers to one decimal.)

2. Comment on and interpret the results of part 1.

Vibrant Company had $850,000 of sales in each of three consecutive years 2012–2014, and it purchased merchandise costing $500,000 in each of those years. It also maintained a $250,000 physical inventory from the beginning to the end of that three-year period. In accounting for inventory, it made an error at the end of year 2012 that caused its year-end 2012 inventory to appear on its statements as $230,000 rather than the correct $250,000.

1. Determine the correct amount of the company's gross profit in each of the years 2012–2014.
2. Prepare comparative income statements as in Exhibit 5.11 to show the effect of this error on the company's cost of goods sold and gross profit for each of the years 2012–2014.

Exercise 5-12
Analysis of inventory errors
A2

Check 2012 reported gross profit, $330,000

Use the following information for Palmer Co. to compute inventory turnover for 2013 and 2012, and its days' sales in inventory at December 31, 2013 and 2012. (Round answers to one decimal.) Comment on Palmer's efficiency in using its assets to increase sales from 2012 to 2013.

Exercise 5-13
Inventory turnover and days' sales in inventory
A3

	2013	2012	2011
Cost of goods sold	$643,825	$426,650	$391,300
Ending inventory	97,400	87,750	92,500

Martinez Co. reported the following current-year data for its only product. The company uses a periodic inventory system, and its ending inventory consists of 150 units—50 from each of the last three purchases. Determine the cost assigned to ending inventory and to cost of goods sold using (a) specific identification, (b) weighted average, (c) FIFO, and (d) LIFO. (Round per unit costs and inventory amounts to cents.) Which method yields the highest net income?

Exercise 5-14ᴬ
Periodic: Cost flow assumptions
P3

Jan. 1	Beginning inventory	96 units @ $2.00 = $	192
Mar. 7	Purchase	220 units @ $2.25 =	495
July 28	Purchase	544 units @ $2.50 =	1,360
Oct. 3	Purchase	480 units @ $2.80 =	1,344
Dec. 19	Purchase	160 units @ $2.90 =	464
	Totals	1,500 units	$3,855

Check Inventory; LIFO, $313.50; FIFO, $435.00

Flora's Gifts reported the following current-monthly data for its only product. The company uses a periodic inventory system, and its ending inventory consists of 60 units—50 units from the January 6 purchase, and 10 units from the January 25 purchase. Determine the cost assigned to ending inventory and to cost of goods sold using (a) specific identification, (b) weighted average, (c) FIFO, and (d) LIFO. (Round per unit costs and inventory amounts to cents.) Which method yields the lowest net income?

Exercise 5-15
Periodic: Cost flow assumptions
P3

Jan. 1	Beginning inventory	138 units @ $3.00 = $	414
Jan. 6	Purchase	300 units @ $2.80 =	840
Jan. 17	Purchase	540 units @ $2.30 =	1,242
Jan. 25	Purchase	22 units @ $2.00 =	44
	Totals	1,000 units	$2,540

Check Inventory: LIFO, $180.00; FIFO, $131.40

In 2013, Dakota Company had net sales (at retail) of $260,000. The following additional information is available from its records at the end of 2013. Use the retail inventory method to estimate Dakota's 2013 ending inventory at cost.

Exercise 5-16ᴮ
Estimating ending inventory— retail method
P4

	At Cost	At Retail
Beginning inventory	$ 63,800	$128,400
Cost of goods purchased	115,060	196,800

Check End. Inventory, $35,860

Exercise 5-17[B]

Estimating ending inventory—gross profit method

P4

On January 1, JKR Shop had $225,000 of inventory at cost. In the first quarter of the year, it purchased $795,000 of merchandise, returned $11,550, and paid freight charges of $18,800 on purchased merchandise, terms FOB shipping point. The company's gross profit averages 30%, and the store had $1,000,000 of net sales (at retail) in the first quarter of the year. Use the gross profit method to estimate its cost of inventory at the end of the first quarter.

Exercise 5-18

Accounting for inventory following IFRS

P2

Samsung Electronics reports the following regarding its accounting for inventories.

> Inventories are stated at the lower of cost or net realizable value. Cost is determined using the average cost method, except for materials-in-transit. Inventories are reduced for the estimated losses arising from excess, obsolescence, and the decline in value. This reduction is determined by estimating market value based on future customer demand. The losses on inventory obsolescence are recorded as a part of cost of sales.

1. What cost flow assumption(s) does Samsung apply in assigning costs to its inventories?
2. If at year-end 2011 there was an increase in the value of its inventories such that there was a reversal of ₩550 (₩ is Korean won) million for the 2010 write-down, how would Samsung account for this under IFRS? Would Samsung's accounting be different for this reversal if it reported under U.S. GAAP? Explain.

PROBLEM SET A

Problem 5-1A

Perpetual: Alternative cost flows

P1

Information: Warnerwoods Company uses a perpetual inventory system. It entered into the following purchases and sales transactions for March. (For specific identification, the March 9 sale consisted of 80 units from beginning inventory and 340 units from the March 5 purchase; the March 29 sale consisted of 40 units from the March 18 purchase and 120 units from the March 25 purchase.)

Date	Activities	Units Acquired at Cost	Units Sold at Retail
Mar. 1	Beginning inventory	100 units @ $50.00 per unit	
Mar. 5	Purchase	400 units @ $55.00 per unit	
Mar. 9	Sales		420 units @ $85.00 per unit
Mar. 18	Purchase	120 units @ $60.00 per unit	
Mar. 25	Purchase	200 units @ $62.00 per unit	
Mar. 29	Sales		160 units @ $95.00 per unit
	Totals	820 units	580 units

Required

1. Compute cost of goods available for sale and the number of units available for sale.
2. Compute the number of units in ending inventory.
3. Compute the cost assigned to ending inventory using (*a*) FIFO, (*b*) LIFO, (*c*) weighted average, and (*d*) specific identification. (Round all amounts to cents.)
4. Compute gross profit earned by the company for each of the four costing methods in part 3.

Check (3) Ending Inventory: FIFO, $14,800; LIFO, $13,680, WA, $14,352
(4) LIFO gross profit, $17,980

Problem 5-2A[A]

Periodic: Alternative cost flows

P1

Refer to the **information** in Problem 5-1A and assume the periodic inventory system is used.

Required

1. Compute cost of goods available for sale and the number of units available for sale.
2. Compute the number of units in ending inventory.
3. Compute the cost assigned to ending inventory using (*a*) FIFO, (*b*) LIFO, (*c*) weighted average, and (*d*) specific identification. (Round all amounts to cents.)
4. Compute gross profit earned by the company for each of the four costing methods in part 3.

Problem 5-3A

Perpetual: Alternative cost flows

P1

Information: Montoure Company uses a perpetual inventory system. It entered into the following calendar-year 2013 purchases and sales transactions. (For specific identification, units sold consist of 600 units from beginning inventory, 300 from the February 10 purchase, 200 from the March 13 purchase, 50 from the August 21 purchase, and 250 from the September 5 purchase.)

Date	Activities	Units Acquired at Cost	Units Sold at Retail
Jan. 1	Beginning inventory	600 units @ $45.00 per unit	
Feb. 10	Purchase..................	400 units @ $42.00 per unit	
Mar. 13	Purchase..................	200 units @ $27.00 per unit	
Mar. 15	Sales		800 units @ $75.00 per unit
Aug. 21	Purchase..................	100 units @ $50.00 per unit	
Sept. 5	Purchase..................	500 units @ $46.00 per unit	
Sept. 10	Sales		600 units @ $75.00 per unit
	Totals	1,800 units	1,400 units

Required

1. Compute cost of goods available for sale and the number of units available for sale.
2. Compute the number of units in ending inventory.
3. Compute the cost assigned to ending inventory using (*a*) FIFO, (*b*) LIFO, (*c*) weighted average, and (*d*) specific identification. (Round all amounts to cents.)
4. Compute gross profit earned by the company for each of the four costing methods in part 3.

Analysis Component

5. If the company's manager earns a bonus based on a percent of gross profit, which method of inventory costing will the manager likely prefer?

Check (3) Ending inventory: FIFO, $18,400; LIFO, $18,000; WA, $17,760; (4) LIFO gross profit, $45,800

Refer to the **information** in Problem 5-3A and assume the periodic inventory system is used.

Problem 5-4A[A]
Periodic: Alternative cost flows
P1

Required

1. Compute cost of goods available for sale and the number of units available for sale.
2. Compute the number of units in ending inventory.
3. Compute the cost assigned to ending inventory using (*a*) FIFO, (*b*) LIFO, (*c*) weighted average, and (*d*) specific identification. (Round all amounts to cents.)
4. Compute gross profit earned by the company for each of the four costing methods in part 3.

Analysis Component

5. If the company's manager earns a bonus based on a percentage of gross profit, which method of inventory costing will the manager likely prefer?

A physical inventory of Liverpool Company taken at December 31 reveals the following.

Problem 5-5A
Lower of cost or market
P2

File Edit View Insert Format Tools Data Accounting Window Help

	Item	Units	Per Unit Cost	Per Unit Market
3	Audio equipment			
4	Receivers	345	$ 90	$ 98
5	CD players	260	111	100
6	MP3 players	326	86	95
7	Speakers	204	52	41
8	Video equipment			
9	Handheld LCDs	480	150	125
10	VCRs	291	93	84
11	Camcorders	212	310	322
12	Car audio equipment			
13	Satellite radios	185	70	84
14	CD/MP3 radios	170	97	105

Sheet1 / Sheet2 / Sheet3 /

Required

1. Calculate the lower of cost or market for the inventory applied separately to each item.
2. If the market amount is less than the recorded cost of the inventory, then record the LCM adjustment to the Merchandise Inventory account.

Check (1) $273,054

Problem 5-6A

Analysis of inventory errors

A2

mhhe.com/wildFAF4e

Navajo Company's financial statements show the following. The company recently discovered that in making physical counts of inventory, it had made the following errors: Inventory on December 31, 2012, is understated by $56,000, and inventory on December 31, 2013, is overstated by $20,000.

For Year Ended December 31		2012	2013	2014
(a)	Cost of goods sold	$ 615,000	$ 957,000	$ 780,000
(b)	Net income......................	230,000	285,000	241,000
(c)	Total current assets	1,255,000	1,365,000	1,200,000
(d)	Total equity	1,387,000	1,530,000	1,242,000

Required

1. For each key financial statement figure—(a), (b), (c), and (d) above—prepare a table similar to the following to show the adjustments necessary to correct the reported amounts.

Figure: _____	2012	2013	2014
Reported amount	_____	_____	_____
Adjustments for: 12/31/2012 error	_____	_____	_____
12/31/2013 error	_____	_____	_____
Corrected amount	_____	_____	_____

Check (1) Corrected net income: 2012, $286,000; 2013, $209,000; 2014, $261,000

Analysis Component

2. What is the error in total net income for the combined three-year period resulting from the inventory errors? Explain.

3. Explain why the understatement of inventory by $56,000 at the end of 2012 results in an understatement of equity by the same amount in that year.

Problem 5-7A[A]

Periodic: Alternative cost flows

P3

mhhe.com/wildFAF4e

Information: Seminole Company began year 2013 with 23,000 units of product in its January 1 inventory costing $15 each. It made successive purchases of its product in year 2013 as follows. The company uses a periodic inventory system. On December 31, 2013, a physical count reveals that 40,000 units of its product remain in inventory.

Mar. 7	30,000 units @ $18.00 each
May 25	39,000 units @ $20.00 each
Aug. 1	23,000 units @ $25.00 each
Nov. 10	35,000 units @ $26.00 each

Required

1. Compute the number and total cost of the units available for sale in year 2013.

2. Compute the amounts assigned to the 2013 ending inventory and the cost of goods sold using (a) FIFO, (b) LIFO, and (c) weighted average. (Round all amounts to cents.)

Check (2) Cost of goods sold: FIFO, $2,115,000; LIFO, $2,499,000; WA, $2,310,000

Problem 5-8A[A]

Periodic: Income comparisons and cost flows

A1 P3

Information: QP Corp. sold 4,000 units of its product at $50 per unit in year 2013 and incurred operating expenses of $5 per unit in selling the units. It began the year with 700 units in inventory and made successive purchases of its product as follows.

Jan. 1	Beginning inventory	700 units @ $18.00 per unit
Feb. 20	Purchase	1,700 units @ $19.00 per unit
May 16	Purchase	800 units @ $20.00 per unit
Oct. 3	Purchase	500 units @ $21.00 per unit
Dec. 11	Purchase	2,300 units @ $22.00 per unit
	Total	6,000 units

Required

1. Prepare comparative income statements similar to Exhibit 5.8 for the three inventory costing methods of FIFO, LIFO, and weighted average. (Round all amounts to cents.) Include a detailed cost of goods sold section as part of each statement. The company uses a periodic inventory system, and its income tax rate is 40%.

2. How would the financial results from using the three alternative inventory costing methods change if the Company had been experiencing declining costs in its purchases of inventory?

3. What advantages and disadvantages are offered by using (*a*) LIFO and (*b*) FIFO? Assume the continuing trend of increasing costs.

Check (1) Net income: FIFO, $61,200; LIFO, $57,180; WA, $59,196

The records of Alaska Company provide the following information for the year ended December 31.

Problem 5-9A[B]
Retail inventory method
P4

	At Cost	At Retail
January 1 beginning inventory	$ 469,010	$ 928,950
Cost of goods purchased	3,376,050	6,381,050
Sales		5,595,800
Sales returns		42,800

Required

1. Use the retail inventory method to estimate the company's year-end inventory at cost.

2. A year-end physical inventory at retail prices yields a total inventory of $1,686,900. Prepare a calculation showing the company's loss from shrinkage at cost and at retail.

Check (1) Inventory, $924,182 cost; (2) Inventory shortage at cost, $36,873

Wayward Company wants to prepare interim financial statements for the first quarter. The company wishes to avoid making a physical count of inventory. Wayward's gross profit rate averages 34%. The following information for the first quarter is available from its records.

Problem 5-10A[B]
Gross profit method
P4

January 1 beginning inventory	$ 302,580
Cost of goods purchased	941,040
Sales	1,211,160
Sales returns	8,410

Required

Use the gross profit method to estimate the company's first quarter ending inventory.

Check Estimated ending inventory, $449,805

Information: TDS Company uses a perpetual inventory system. It entered into the following purchases and sales transactions for April. (For specific identification, the April 9 sale consisted of 8 units from beginning inventory and 27 units from the April 6 purchase; the April 30 sale consisted of 12 units from beginning inventory 3 units from the April 6 purchase and 10 units from the April 25 purchase.)

PROBLEM SET B

Problem 5-1B
Perpetual: Alternative cost flows
P1

Date	Activities	Units Acquired at Cost	Units Sold at Retail
Apr. 1	Beginning inventory	20 units @ $3,000.00 per unit	
Apr. 6	Purchase	30 units @ $3,500.00 per unit	
Apr. 9	Sales		35 units @ $12,000.00 per unit
Apr. 17	Purchase	5 units @ $4,500.00 per unit	
Apr. 25	Purchase	10 units @ $4,800.00 per unit	
Apr. 30	Sales		25 units @ $14,000.00 per unit
	Total	65 units	60 units

Required

Check   (3) Ending inventory: FIFO, $24,000; LIFO, $15,000; WA, $20,000;

(4) LIFO gross profit, $549,500

1. Compute cost of goods available for sale and the number of units available for sale.
2. Compute the number of units in ending inventory.
3. Compute the cost assigned to ending inventory using (*a*) FIFO, (*b*) LIFO, (*c*) weighted average, and (*d*) specific identification. (Round all amounts to cents.)
4. Compute gross profit earned by the company for each of the four costing methods in part 3.

Problem 5-2B[A]
Periodic: Alternative cost flows

P1

Refer to the **information** in Problem 5-1B and assume the periodic inventory system is used.

Required

1. Compute cost of goods available for sale and the number of units available for sale.
2. Compute the number of units in ending inventory.
3. Compute the cost assigned to ending inventory using (*a*) FIFO, (*b*) LIFO, (*c*) weighted average, and (*d*) specific identification. (Round all amounts to cents.)
4. Compute gross profit earned by the company for each of the four costing methods in part 3.

Problem 5-3B
Perpetual: Alternative cost flows

P1

Information: Aloha Company uses a perpetual inventory system. It entered into the following calendar-year 2013 purchases and sales transactions. (For specific identification, the May 9 sale consisted of 80 units from beginning inventory and 100 units from the May 6 purchase; the May 30 sale consisted of 200 units from the May 6 purchase and 100 units from the May 25 purchase.)

Date	Activities	Units Acquired at Cost	Units Sold at Retail
May 1	Beginning inventory	150 units @ $300.00 per unit	
May 6	Purchase	350 units @ $350.00 per unit	
May 9	Sales		180 units @ $1,200.00 per unit
May 17	Purchase	80 units @ $450.00 per unit	
May 25	Purchase	100 units @ $458.00 per unit	
May 30	Sales	_____	300 units @ $1,400.00 per unit
	Total	680 units	480 units

Required

1. Compute cost of goods available for sale and the number of units available for sale.
2. Compute the number of units in ending inventory.

Check   (3) Ending inventory: FIFO, $88,800; LIFO, $62,500; WA, $75,600;

(4) LIFO gross profit, $449,200

3. Compute the cost assigned to ending inventory using (*a*) FIFO, (*b*) LIFO, (*c*) weighted average, and (*d*) specific identification. (Round all amounts to cents.)
4. Compute gross profit earned by the company for each of the four costing methods in part 3.

Analysis Component

5. If the company's manager earns a bonus based on a percent of gross profit, which method of inventory costing will the manager likely prefer?

Problem 5-4B[A]
Periodic: Alternative cost flows

P1

Refer to the **information** in Problem 5-3B and assume the periodic inventory system is used.

Required

1. Compute cost of goods available for sale and the number of units available for sale.
2. Compute the number of units in ending inventory.
3. Compute the cost assigned to ending inventory using (*a*) FIFO, (*b*) LIFO, (*c*) weighted average, and (*d*) specific identification. (Round all amounts to cents.)
4. Compute gross profit earned by the company for each of the four costing methods in part 3.

Analysis Component

5. If the company's manager earns a bonus based on a percentage of gross profit, which method of inventory costing will the manager likely prefer?

A physical inventory of Office Necessities taken at December 31 reveals the following.

Problem 5-5B
Lower of cost or market

P2

Item	Units	Per Unit Cost	Per Unit Market
Office furniture			
Desks	536	$261	$305
Credenzas	395	227	256
Chairs	687	49	43
Bookshelves	421	93	82
Filing cabinets			
Two-drawer	114	81	70
Four-drawer	298	135	122
Lateral	75	104	118
Office equipment			
Fax machines	370	168	200
Copiers	475	317	288
Telephones	302	125	117

Required

1. Compute the lower of cost or market for the inventory applied separately to each item.
2. If the market amount is less than the recorded cost of the inventory, then record the LCM adjustment to the Merchandise Inventory account.

Check   (1) $580,054

Hallam Company's financial statements show the following. The company recently discovered that in making physical counts of inventory, it had made the following errors: Inventory on December 31, 2012, is overstated by $18,000, and inventory on December 31, 2013, is understated by $26,000.

Problem 5-6B
Analysis of inventory errors

A2

For Year Ended December 31	2012	2013	2014
(a) Cost of goods sold	$207,200	$213,800	$197,030
(b) Net income	175,800	212,270	184,910
(c) Total current assets	276,000	277,500	272,950
(d) Total equity	314,000	315,000	346,000

Required

1. For each key financial statement figure—(a), (b), (c), and (d) above—prepare a table similar to the following to show the adjustments necessary to correct the reported amounts.

Figure: _____	2012	2013	2014
Reported amount			
Adjustments for: 12/31/2012 error			
12/31/2013 error			
Corrected amount			

Check   (1) Corrected net income:
2012, $157,800; 2013, $256,270;
2014, $158,910

Analysis Component

2. What is the error in total net income for the combined three-year period resulting from the inventory errors? Explain.
3. Explain why the overstatement of inventory by $18,000 at the end of 2012 results in an overstatement of equity by the same amount in that year.

Problem 5-7B[A]

Periodic: Alternative cost flows

P3

Information: Seneca Co. began year 2013 with 6,500 units of product in its January 1 inventory costing $35 each. It made successive purchases of its product in year 2013 as follows. The company uses a periodic inventory system. On December 31, 2013, a physical count reveals that 8,500 units of its product remain in inventory.

Jan. 4	11,500 units @ $33 each
May 18	13,400 units @ $32 each
July 9	11,000 units @ $29 each
Nov. 21	7,600 units @ $27 each

Required

Check   (2) Cost of goods sold:
FIFO, $1,328,700; LIFO, $1,266,500;
WA, $1,294,800

1. Compute the number and total cost of the units available for sale in year 2013.

2. Compute the amounts assigned to the 2013 ending inventory and the cost of goods sold using (*a*) FIFO, (*b*) LIFO, and (*c*) weighted average. (Round all amounts to cents.)

Problem 5-8B[A]

Periodic: Income comparisons and cost flows

A1   P3

Information: Shepard Company sold 4,000 units of its product at $100 per unit in year 2013 and incurred operating expenses of $15 per unit in selling the units. It began the year with 840 units in inventory and made successive purchases of its product as follows.

Jan. 1	Beginning inventory	840 units @ $58 per unit
April 2	Purchase	600 units @ $59 per unit
June 14	Purchase	1,205 units @ $61 per unit
Aug. 29	Purchase	700 units @ $64 per unit
Nov. 18	Purchase	1,655 units @ $65 per unit
	Total	5,000 units

Required

Check   (1) Net income: LIFO,
$52,896; FIFO, $57,000; WA, $55,200

1. Prepare comparative income statements similar to Exhibit 5.8 for the three inventory costing methods of FIFO, LIFO, and weighted average. (Round all amounts to cents.) Include a detailed cost of goods sold section as part of each statement. The company uses a periodic inventory system, and its income tax rate is 40%.

2. How would the financial results from using the three alternative inventory costing methods change if the company had been experiencing decreasing prices in its purchases of inventory?

3. What advantages and disadvantages are offered by using (*a*) LIFO and (*b*) FIFO? Assume the continuing trend of increasing costs.

Problem 5-9B[B]

Retail inventory method

P4

The records of Macklin Co. provide the following information for the year ended December 31.

	At Cost	At Retail
January 1 beginning inventory	$ 90,022	$115,610
Cost of goods purchased	502,250	761,830
Sales		782,300
Sales returns		3,460

Required

Check   (1) Inventory, $66,555 cost;
    (2) Inventory shortage at
    cost, $12,251.25

1. Use the retail inventory method to estimate the company's year-end inventory.

2. A year-end physical inventory at retail prices yields a total inventory of $80,450. Prepare a calculation showing the company's loss from shrinkage at cost and at retail.

Problem 5-10B[B]

Gross profit method

P4

Otingo Equipment Co. wants to prepare interim financial statements for the first quarter. The company wishes to avoid making a physical count of inventory. Otingo's gross profit rate averages 35%. The following information for the first quarter is available from its records.

January 1 beginning inventory	$ 802,880
Cost of goods purchased	2,209,636
Sales	3,760,260
Sales returns	79,300

2. b; LIFO perpetual

Date	Goods Purchased	Cost of Goods Sold	Inventory Balance
July 1			75 units @ $25 = $ 1,875
July 3	348 units @ $27 = $9,396		75 units @ $25 348 units @ $27 } = $ 11,271
July 8		300 units @ $27 = $ 8,100	75 units @ $25 48 units @ $27 } = $ 3,171
July 15	257 units @ $28 = $7,196		75 units @ $25 48 units @ $27 } = $ 10,367 257 units @ $28
July 23		257 units @ $28 18 units @ $27 } = $ 7,682 $15,782	75 units @ $25 30 units @ $27 } = $ 2,685

3. e; Specific identification (perpetual and periodic are identical for specific identification)—Ending inventory computation.

20 units @ $25	$ 500	
40 units @ $27	1,080	
45 units @ $28	1,260	
105 units	$2,840	

4. a; FIFO periodic. Ending inventory computation:
105 units @ $28 each = $2,940; The FIFO periodic inventory computation is identical to the FIFO perpetual inventory computation (see question 1).

5. a; FIFO periodic inventory = $(20 \times \$14) + (10 \times \$12)$
$$= \$400$$
a; LIFO periodic cost of goods sold $= (20 \times \$14) + (40 \times \$12) + (70 \times \$10)$
$$= \$1,460$$

6. d; Days' sales in inventory = (Ending inventory/Cost of goods sold $\times$ 365)
$$= (\$18,000/\$85,000) \times 365 = \underline{77.29 \text{ days}}$$

Accounting for Cash and Internal Controls

6

A Look Back

Chapters 4 and 5 focused on merchandising activities and accounting for inventory. We explained inventory systems, accounting for inventory transactions, and assigning costs to inventory.

A Look at This Chapter

This chapter extends our study of accounting to internal control and the analysis of cash. We describe procedures that are good for internal control. We also explain the control of and the accounting for cash, including control features of banking activities.

A Look Ahead

Chapter 7 focuses on receivables. We explain how to account and report on receivables and their related accounts. This includes estimating uncollectible receivables and computing interest earned.

Decision Insight

Cheese Wiz

"Entrepreneurship is the antithesis of stability."

—MICHAEL INWALD

BOSTON—Michael Inwald did his research: 2.2 billion grilled cheese sandwiches are consumed by Americans each year. His conclusion: The country is one big cheeseball! Given the cheese wiz he is, Michael, known to his friends as *Cheeseboy*, opened a fast-food grilled cheese take-out joint named **CHEESEBOY (CheeseBoy.com).** "I'm somewhat obsessed with cheese!" admits Michael. That obsession has led to several CHEESEBOY locations, and he is readying for a national franchise program.

"Giving our customers an amazing grilled cheese experience, all-around, is very critical to us," insists Michael. He currently offers customers a grilled cheese experience with four bread options, five cheese options, and a range of toppings. He also provides the classic tomato soup combo, along with other soup options. "The most challenging part of my business is . . . to create the perfect experience," explains Michael.

Although the grilled cheese experience is key to his success, Michael's management of internal controls and cash is equally impressive. Several control procedures monitor business activities and safeguard assets. An example is his inventory control system. Explains Michael, quality ingredients are crucial to

customer satisfaction, and monitoring controls ensure the quality of his ingredients. Similar controls are applied throughout his store. Michael explains that such controls raise productivity, cut expenses, and enhance the customer experience.

His store's cash management practices are equally impressive, including controls over cash receipts, disbursements, and petty cash. The use of bank reconciliations further helps with his store's control and management of cash. "Take basic accounting," explains Michael, "I was able to say, 'I'm going to need to know how to balance my books.'" Michael explains that he takes advantage of available banking services to enhance controls over cash.

Internal controls are crucial when on a busy day his stores bring in thousands of customers, and their cash. "We have put the infrastructure in place to ensure that (the growth) goes as smoothly as possible," explains Michael. "We're definitely going to be moving at what feels like light speed."

[Sources: *CHEESEBOY Website,* January 2013; *CNNMoney,* July 2011; *BOLDFACERS,* August 2011; *The Patriot Ledger,* November 2011; *Boston Business Journal,* December 2011; *The New Journal,* February 2012.]

We all are aware of theft and fraud. They affect us in several ways: We lock doors, chain bikes, review credit card statements, and acquire alarm systems. A company also takes actions to safeguard, control, and manage what it owns. Experience tells us that small companies are most vulnerable, usually due to weak internal controls. It is management's responsibility to set up policies and procedures to safeguard a company's assets, especially cash. To do so, management *and* employees must understand and apply principles of internal control. This chapter describes these principles and how to apply them. It focuses special attention on cash because it is easily transferable and is often at high risk of loss.

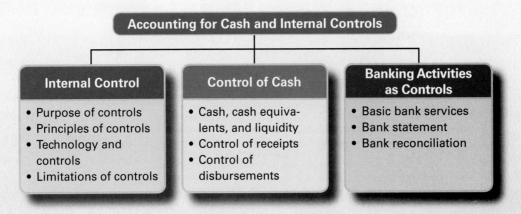

Accounting for Cash and Internal Controls

Internal Control
- Purpose of controls
- Principles of controls
- Technology and controls
- Limitations of controls

Control of Cash
- Cash, cash equivalents, and liquidity
- Control of receipts
- Control of disbursements

Banking Activities as Controls
- Basic bank services
- Bank statement
- Bank reconciliation

INTERNAL CONTROL

This section describes internal control and its fundamental principles. We also discuss the impact of technology on internal control and the limitations of control procedures.

Purpose of Internal Control

C1 Define internal control and identify its purpose and principles.

Managers (or owners) of small businesses often control the entire operation. These managers usually purchase all assets, hire and manage employees, negotiate all contracts, and sign all checks. They know from personal contact and observation whether the business is actually receiving the assets and services paid for. Most companies, however, cannot maintain this close personal supervision. They must delegate responsibilities and rely on formal procedures rather than personal contact in controlling business activities.

Internal Control System   Managers use an internal control system to monitor and control business activities. An **internal control system** consists of the policies and procedures managers use to

- Protect assets.
- Ensure reliable accounting.
- Promote efficient operations.
- Urge adherence to company policies.

A properly designed internal control system is a key part of systems design, analysis, and performance. Managers place a high priority on internal control systems because they can prevent avoidable losses, help managers plan operations, and monitor company and employee performance. For example, internal controls for health care must protect patient records and privacy. Internal controls do not provide guarantees, but they lower the company's risk of loss.

Sarbanes-Oxley Act (SOX)   The **Sarbanes-Oxley Act (SOX)** requires the managers and auditors of companies whose stock is traded on an exchange (called *public companies*) to document and certify the system of internal controls. Following are some of the specific requirements:

- Auditors must evaluate internal controls and issue an internal control report.
- Auditors of a client are restricted as to what consulting services they can provide that client.
- The person leading an audit can serve no more than seven years without a two-year break.
- Auditors' work is overseen by the *Public Company Accounting Oversight Board* (PCAOB).
- Harsh penalties exist for violators—sentences up to 25 years in prison with severe fines.

Decision Insight

Ball Control Ryan Braun of the Milwaukee Brewers won an appeal of a 50-game Major League Baseball (MLB) suspension for a positive drug test. Ryan maintained that MLB did not maintain control over his sample through the testing process and raised the risk that his sample was tainted. This control failure led to dismissal of that particular test result and him winning the appeal. Controls are crucial when people's livelihoods and reputations are on the line. ■

Quick Check
Answers — p. 285

1. Principles of internal control suggest that (choose one): (a) Responsibility for a series of related transactions (such as placing orders, receiving and paying for merchandise) should be assigned to one employee; (b) Responsibility for individual tasks should be shared by more than one employee so that one serves as a check on the other; or (c) Employees who handle considerable cash and easily transferable assets should be bonded.

2. What are some impacts of computing technology on internal control?

3. Many companies require each employee to take at least one week (five consecutive days) of vacation per year. Why is a "forced vacation" policy good for internal control?

CONTROL OF CASH

Cash is a necessary asset of every company. Most companies also own *cash equivalents* (defined below), which are assets similar to cash. Cash and cash equivalents are the most liquid of all assets and are easily hidden and moved. Cash is also the most desired asset as other assets must be *fenced* (sold in a secondary market). An effective system of internal controls protects cash assets and it should meet three basic guidelines:

1. Handling cash is separate from recordkeeping of cash.
2. Cash receipts are promptly deposited in a bank.
3. Cash disbursements are made by check.

The first guideline applies separation of duties to minimize errors and fraud. When duties are separated, two or more people must collude to steal cash and conceal this action in the accounting records. The second guideline uses immediate (say, daily) deposits of all cash receipts to produce a timely independent record of the cash received. It also reduces the likelihood of cash theft (or loss) and the risk that an employee could personally use the money before depositing it. The third guideline uses payments by check to develop an independent bank record of cash disbursements. This guideline also reduces the risk of cash theft (or loss).

This section begins with definitions of cash and cash equivalents. Discussion then focuses on controls and accounting for both cash receipts and disbursements. The exact procedures used to achieve control over cash vary across companies. They depend on factors such as company size, number of employees, volume of cash transactions, and sources of cash.

Cash, Cash Equivalents, and Liquidity

Good accounting systems help in managing the amount of cash and controlling who has access to it. Cash is the usual means of payment when paying for assets, services, or liabilities. **Liquidity** refers to a company's ability to pay for its near-term obligations. Cash and similar assets are called **liquid assets** because they can be readily used to settle such obligations. A company needs liquid assets to effectively operate.

Cash includes currency and coins along with the amounts on deposit in bank accounts, checking accounts (called *demand deposits*), and many savings accounts (called *time deposits*). Cash also

C2 Define cash and cash equivalents and explain how to report them.

Point: The most liquid assets are usually reported first on a balance sheet; the least liquid assets are reported last.

Point: Google reports cash and cash equivalents of $9,983 million in its balance sheet. This amount makes up nearly 15% of its total assets.

includes items that are acceptable for deposit in these accounts such as customer checks, cashier's checks, certified checks, and money orders. **Cash equivalents** are short-term, highly liquid investment assets meeting two criteria: (1) readily convertible to a known cash amount and (2) sufficiently close to their due date so that their market value is not sensitive to interest rate changes. Only investments purchased within three months of their due date usually satisfy these criteria. Examples of cash equivalents are short-term investments in assets such as U.S. Treasury bills and money market funds. To increase their return, many companies invest idle cash in cash equivalents. Most companies combine cash equivalents with cash as a single item on the balance sheet.

Cash Management

When companies fail, one of the most common causes is their inability to manage cash. Companies must plan both cash receipts and cash payments. The goals of cash management are twofold:

1. Plan cash receipts to meet cash payments when due.
2. Keep a minimum level of cash necessary to operate.

The *treasurer* of the company is responsible for cash management. Effective cash management involves applying the following cash management principles.

-   **Encourage collection of receivables.** The more quickly customers and others pay the company, the more quickly that company can use the money. Some companies have cash-only sales policies. Others might offer discounts for payments received early.
-   **Delay payment of liabilities.** The more delayed a company is in paying others, the more time it has to use the money. Some companies regularly wait to pay their bills until the last possible day allowed—although, a company must take care not to hurt its credit standing.
-   **Keep only necessary levels of assets.** The less money tied up in idle assets, the more money to invest in productive assets. Some companies maintain *just-in-time* inventory; meaning they plan inventory to be available at the same time orders are filled. Others might lease out excess warehouse space or rent equipment instead of buying it.
-   **Plan expenditures.** Money should be spent only when it is available. Companies must look at seasonal and business cycles to plan expenditures.
-   **Invest excess cash.** Excess cash earns no return and should be invested. Excess cash from seasonal cycles can be placed in a bank account or other short-term investment for income. Excess cash beyond what's needed for regular business should be invested in productive assets like factories and inventories.

Decision Insight

Days' Cash Expense Coverage The ratio of *cash (and cash equivalents) to average daily cash expenses* indicates the number of days a company can operate without additional cash inflows. It reflects on company liquidity and on the potential of excess cash.

Control of Cash Receipts

P1 Apply internal control to cash receipts and disbursements.

Internal control of cash receipts ensures that cash received is properly recorded and deposited. Cash receipts can arise from transactions such as cash sales, collections of customer accounts, receipts of interest earned, bank loans, sales of assets, and owner investments. This section explains internal control over two important types of cash receipts: over-the-counter and by mail.

Over-the-Counter Cash Receipts   For purposes of internal control, over-the-counter cash receipts from sales should be recorded on a cash register at the time of each sale. To help ensure that correct amounts are entered, each register should be located so customers can read the amounts entered. Clerks also should be required to enter each sale before wrapping merchandise and to give the customer a receipt for each sale. The design of each cash register should provide a permanent, locked-in record of each transaction. In many systems, the register is directly linked with computing and accounting services. Less advanced registers simply print a record of each transaction on a paper tape or electronic file locked inside the register.

Proper internal control prescribes that custody over cash should be separate from its recordkeeping. For over-the-counter cash receipts, this separation begins with the cash sale. The clerk who has access to cash in the register should not have access to its locked-in record. At the end of the clerk's work period, the clerk should count the cash in the register, record the amount, and turn over the cash and a record of its amount to the company cashier. The cashier, like the clerk, has access to the cash but should not have access to accounting records (or the register tape or file). A third employee, often a supervisor, compares the record of total register transactions (or the register tape or file) with the cash receipts reported by the cashier. This record is the basis for a journal entry recording over-the-counter cash receipts. The third employee has access to the records for cash but not to the actual cash. The clerk and the cashier have access to cash but not to the accounting records. None of them can make a mistake or divert cash without the difference being revealed—see the following diagram.

Point: Convenience stores sometimes display a sign: *Cashier has no access to cash in locked floor (or wall) safe.* Such signs help thwart theft and holdups because of lack of access to the floor (or wall) safe.

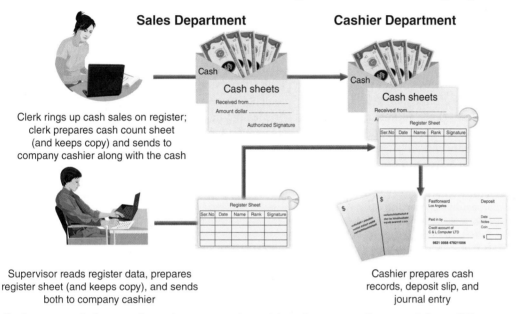

Cash over and short. Sometimes errors in making change are discovered from differences between the cash in a cash register and the record of the amount of cash receipts. Although a clerk is careful, one or more customers can be given too much or too little change. This means that at the end of a work period, the cash in a cash register might not equal the record of cash receipts. This difference is reported in the **Cash Over and Short** account, also called *Cash Short and Over,* which is an income statement account recording the income effects of cash overages and cash shortages. To illustrate, if a cash register's record shows $550 but the count of cash in the register is $555, the entry to record cash sales and its overage is

Point: Retailers often require cashiers to restrictively endorse checks immediately on receipt by stamping them "For deposit only."

Cash	555	
Cash Over and Short		5
Sales		550
To record cash sales and a cash overage.		

Assets = Liabilities + Equity
+555   + 5
                       +550

On the other hand, if a cash register's record shows $625 but the count of cash in the register is $621, the entry to record cash sales and its shortage is

Cash	621	
Cash Over and Short	4	
Sales		625
To record cash sales and a cash shortage.		

Assets = Liabilities + Equity
+621   − 4
                       +625

Since customers are more likely to dispute being shortchanged than being given too much change, the Cash Over and Short account usually has a debit balance at the end of an accounting period. A debit balance reflects an expense. It is reported on the income statement as part of general and administrative expenses. (Since the amount is usually small, it is often combined

Point: Merchants begin a business day with a *change fund* in their cash register. The accounting for a change fund is similar to that for petty cash, including that for cash shortages or overages.

with other small expenses and reported as part of *miscellaneous expenses*—or as part of *miscellaneous revenues* if it has a credit balance.)

Cash Receipts by Mail   Control of cash receipts that arrive through the mail starts with the person who opens the mail. Preferably, two people are assigned the task of, and are present for, opening the mail. In this case, theft of cash receipts by mail requires collusion between these two employees. Specifically, the person(s) opening the mail enters a list (in triplicate) of money received. This list should contain a record of each sender's name, the amount, and an explanation of why the money is sent. The first copy is sent with the money to the cashier. A second copy is sent to the recordkeeper in the accounting area. A third copy is kept by the clerk(s) who opened the mail. The cashier deposits the money in a bank, and the recordkeeper records the amounts received in the accounting records.

Point: Collusion implies that two or more individuals are knowledgeable or involved with the activities of the other(s).

This process reflects good internal control. That is, when the bank balance is reconciled by another person (explained later in the chapter), errors or acts of fraud by the mail clerks, the cashier, or the recordkeeper are revealed. They are revealed because the bank's record of cash deposited must agree with the records from each of the three. Moreover, if the mail clerks do not report all receipts correctly, customers will question their account balances. If the cashier does not deposit all receipts, the bank balance does not agree with the recordkeeper's cash balance. The recordkeeper and the person who reconciles the bank balance do not have access to cash and therefore have no opportunity to divert cash to themselves. This system makes errors and fraud highly unlikely. The exception is employee collusion.

Decision Insight

Perpetual Accounting   Walmart uses a network of information links with its point-of-sale cash registers to coordinate sales, purchases, and distribution. Its supercenters, for instance, ring up 15,000 separate sales on heavy days. By using cash register information, the company can fix pricing mistakes quickly and capitalize on sales trends. Interestingly, Sam Walton, the founder, was a self-described distruster of computers. ■

Control of Cash Disbursements

Control of cash disbursements is especially important as most large thefts occur from payment of fictitious invoices. One key to controlling cash disbursements is to require all expenditures to be made by check. The only exception is small payments made from petty cash. Another key is to deny access to the accounting records to anyone other than the owner who has the authority to sign checks. A small business owner often signs checks and knows from personal contact that the items being paid for are actually received. This arrangement is impossible in large businesses. Instead, internal control procedures must be substituted for personal contact. Such procedures are designed to assure the check signer that the obligations recorded are properly incurred and should be paid. This section describes these and other internal control procedures, including the voucher system and petty cash system. A method for management of cash disbursements for purchases is described in Appendix 6B.

Cash Budget   Projected cash receipts and cash disbursements are often summarized in a *cash budget.* Provided that sufficient cash exists for effective operations, companies wish to minimize the cash they hold because of its risk of theft and its low return versus other investment opportunities.

Decision Insight

Lock Box   Some companies do not receive cash in the mail but, instead, elect to have customers send deposits directly to the bank using a *lock box* system. Bank employees are charged with receipting the cash and depositing it in the correct business bank account. ■

Voucher System of Control   A **voucher system** is a set of procedures and approvals designed to control cash disbursements and the acceptance of obligations. The voucher system of control establishes procedures for

● Verifying, approving, and recording obligations for eventual cash disbursement.

● Issuing checks for payment of verified, approved, and recorded obligations.

A reliable voucher system follows standard procedures for every transaction. This applies even when multiple purchases are made from the same supplier.

A voucher system's control over cash disbursements begins when a company incurs an obligation that will result in payment of cash. A key factor in this system is that only approved departments and individuals are authorized to incur such obligations. The system often limits the type of obligations that a department or individual can incur. In a large retail store, for instance, only a purchasing department should be authorized to incur obligations for merchandise inventory. Another key factor is that procedures for purchasing, receiving, and paying for merchandise are divided among several departments (or individuals). These departments include the one requesting the purchase, the purchasing department, the receiving department, and the accounting department. To coordinate and control responsibilities of these departments, a company uses several different business documents. Exhibit 6.1 shows how documents are accumulated in a **voucher,** which is an internal document (or file) used to accumulate information to control cash disbursements and to ensure that a transaction is properly recorded. This specific example begins with a *purchase requisition* and concludes with a *check* drawn against cash. Appendix 6A describes the documentation and verification necessary for a voucher system of control. It also describes the internal control objective served by each document.

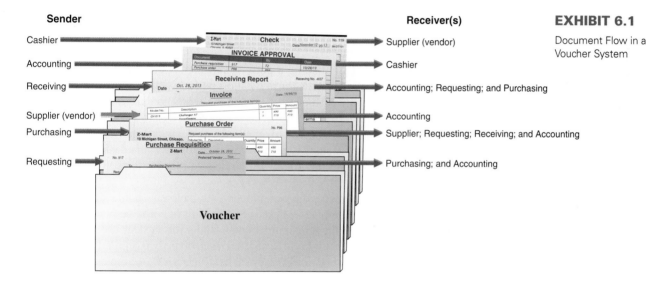

Sender		Receiver(s)
Cashier		Supplier (vendor)
Accounting		Cashier
Receiving		Accounting; Requesting; and Purchasing
Supplier (vendor)		Accounting
Purchasing		Supplier; Requesting; Receiving; and Accounting
Requesting		Purchasing; and Accounting

EXHIBIT 6.1

Document Flow in a Voucher System

A voucher system should be applied not only to purchases of inventory but to all expenditures. To illustrate, when a company receives a monthly telephone bill, it should review and verify the charges, prepare a voucher (file), and insert the bill. This transaction is then recorded with a journal entry. If the amount is currently due, a check is issued. If not, the voucher is filed for payment on its due date. If no voucher is prepared, verifying the invoice and its amount after several days or weeks can be difficult. Also, without records, a dishonest employee could collude with a dishonest supplier to get more than one payment for an obligation, payment for excessive amounts, or payment for goods and services not received. An effective voucher system helps prevent such frauds.

Point: MCI, formerly <u>WorldCom,</u> paid a whopping $500 million in SEC fines for accounting fraud. Among the charges were that it inflated earnings by as much as $10 billion. Its CEO, Bernard Ebbers, was sentenced to 25 years.

Point: A *voucher* is an internal document (or file).

Point: The basic purposes of paper and electronic documents are similar. However, the internal control system must change to reflect different risks, including confidential and competitive-sensitive information that is at greater risk in electronic systems.

■ **Decision** Insight ━━━━━━━━━━━━━━━━━━━━━━━━━━━━━━━━▶

Cyber Setup The FTC is on the cutting edge of cybersleuthing. Opportunists in search of easy money are lured to <u>WeMarket4U.net/SundaeStation</u> and <u>WeMarket4U.net/FatFoe</u>. Take the bait and you get warned. The top 5 fraud complaints as compiled by the Federal Trade Commission are shown to the right. ■

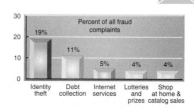

Quick Check   Answers — p. 285

4. Why must a company hold liquid assets?

5. Why does a company hold cash equivalent assets in addition to cash?

6. Identify at least two assets that are classified as cash equivalents.

7. Good internal control procedures for cash include which of the following? (*a*) All cash disbursements, other than those for very small amounts, are made by check; (*b*) One employee counts cash received from sales and promptly deposits cash receipts; or (*c*) Cash receipts by mail are opened by one employee who is then responsible for recording and depositing them.

8. Should all companies require a voucher system? At what point in a company's growth would you recommend a voucher system?

P2 Explain and record petty cash fund transactions.

Petty Cash System of Control   A basic principle for controlling cash disbursements is that all payments must be made by check. An exception to this rule is made for *petty cash disbursements,* which are the small payments required for items such as postage, courier fees, minor repairs, and low-cost supplies. To avoid the time and cost of writing checks for small amounts, a company sets up a petty cash fund to make small payments. (**Petty cash** activities are part of an *imprest system,* which designates advance money to establish the fund, to withdraw from the fund, and to reimburse the fund.)

Operating a petty cash fund.   Establishing a petty cash fund requires estimating the total amount of small payments likely to be made during a short period such as a week or month. A check is then drawn by the company cashier for an amount slightly in excess of this estimate. This check is recorded with a debit to the Petty Cash account (an asset) and a credit to Cash. The check is cashed, and the currency is given to an employee designated as the *petty cashier* or *petty cash custodian.* The petty cashier is responsible for keeping this cash safe, making payments from the fund, and keeping records of it in a secure place referred to as the *petty cashbox.*

Point: A petty cash fund is used only for business expenses.

When each cash disbursement is made, the person receiving payment should sign a prenumbered *petty cash receipt,* also called *petty cash ticket*—see Exhibit 6.2. The petty cash receipt is then placed in the petty cashbox with the remaining money. Under this system, the sum of all receipts plus the remaining cash equals the total fund amount. A $100 petty cash fund, for instance, contains any combination of cash and petty cash receipts that totals $100 (examples are $80 cash plus $20 in receipts, or $10 cash plus $90 in receipts). Each disbursement reduces cash and increases the amount of receipts in the petty cashbox.

EXHIBIT 6.2

Petty Cash Receipt

Z-Mart	No. 9
PETTY CASH RECEIPT	

For _Freight charges_
Date _November 5, 2013_   Approved by _JL Gull_
Charge to _Merchandise Inventory_
Amount _$6.75_   Received by _Dl. Fll_

Point: Petty cash receipts with either no signature or a forged signature usually indicate misuse of petty cash. Companies respond with surprise petty cash counts for verification.

The petty cash fund should be reimbursed when it is nearing zero and at the end of an accounting period when financial statements are prepared. For this purpose, the petty cashier sorts the paid receipts by the type of expense or account and then totals the receipts. The petty cashier presents all paid receipts to the company cashier, who stamps all receipts *paid* so they cannot be reused, files them for recordkeeping, and gives the petty cashier a check for their sum. When this check is cashed and the money placed in the cashbox, the total money in the cashbox is restored to its original amount. The fund is now ready for a new cycle of petty cash payments.

Illustrating a petty cash fund.   To illustrate, assume Z-Mart establishes a petty cash fund on November 1 and designates one of its office employees as the petty cashier. A $75 check is drawn, cashed, and the proceeds given to the petty cashier. The entry to record the setup of this petty cash fund is

Nov. 1	Petty Cash	75	
	Cash		75
	To establish a petty cash fund.		

Assets = Liabilities + Equity
+75
−75

After the petty cash fund is established, the Petty Cash account is not debited or credited again unless the amount of the fund is changed. (A fund should be increased if it requires reimbursement too frequently. On the other hand, if the fund is too large, some of its money should be redeposited in the Cash account.)

Next, assume that Z-Mart's petty cashier makes several November payments from petty cash. Each person who received payment is required to sign a receipt. On November 27, after making a $26.50 cash payment for tile cleaning, only $3.70 cash remains in the fund. The petty cashier then summarizes and totals the petty cash receipts as shown in Exhibit 6.3.

Point: Reducing or eliminating a petty cash fund requires a credit to Petty Cash.

Point: Although *individual* petty cash disbursements are not evidenced by a check, the initial petty cash fund is evidenced by a check, and later petty cash expenditures are evidenced by a check to replenish them *in total.*

EXHIBIT 6.3

Petty Cash Payments Report

Z-MART
Petty Cash Payments Report

Miscellaneous Expenses
| Nov. 2 | Cleaning of LCD panels .... | $20.00 | |
| Nov. 27 | Tile cleaning .... | 26.50 | $ 46.50 |

Merchandise Inventory (transportation-in)
| Nov. 5 | Transport of merchandise purchased .... | 6.75 | |
| Nov. 20 | Transport of merchandise purchased .... | 8.30 | 15.05 |

Delivery Expense
| Nov. 18 | Customer's package delivered .... | | 5.00 |

Office Supplies Expense
| Nov. 15 | Purchase of office supplies immediately used .... | | 4.75 |
| Total .... | | | $71.30 |

Point: This report can also include receipt number and names of those who approved and received cash payment (see Demo Problem 2).

The petty cash payments report and all receipts are given to the company cashier in exchange for a $71.30 check to reimburse the fund. The petty cashier cashes the check and puts the $71.30 cash in the petty cashbox. The company records this reimbursement as follows.

Nov. 27	Miscellaneous Expenses	46.50	
	Merchandise Inventory	15.05	
	Delivery Expense	5.00	
	Office Supplies Expense	4.75	
	Cash		71.30
	To reimburse petty cash.		

Assets = Liabilities + Equity
−71.30   −46.50
              −15.05
              − 5.00
              − 4.75

A petty cash fund is usually reimbursed at the end of an accounting period so that expenses are recorded in the proper period, even if the fund is not low on money. If the fund is not reimbursed at the end of a period, the financial statements would show both an overstated cash asset and understated expenses (or assets) that were paid out of petty cash. Some companies do not reimburse the petty cash fund at the end of each period under the notion that this amount is immaterial to users of financial statements.

Point: To avoid errors in recording petty cash reimbursement, follow these steps: (1) prepare payments report, (2) compute cash needed by subtracting cash remaining from total fund amount, (3) record entry, and (4) check "Dr. = Cr." in entry. Any difference is Cash Over and Short.

Increasing or decreasing a petty cash fund.   A decision to increase or decrease a petty cash fund is often made when reimbursing it. To illustrate, assume Z-Mart decides to *increase* its petty cash fund from $75 to $100 on November 27 when it reimburses the fund. The entries required are to (1) reimburse the fund as usual (see the preceding November 27 entry) and (2) increase the fund amount as follows.

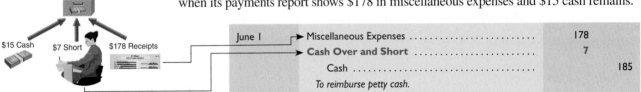

Nov. 27	Petty Cash	25	
	Cash		25
	To increase the petty cash fund amount.		

Alternatively, if Z-Mart *decreases* the petty cash fund from $75 to $55 on November 27, the entry is to (1) credit Petty Cash for $20 (decreasing the fund from $75 to $55) and (2) debit Cash for $20 (reflecting the $20 transfer from Petty Cash to Cash).

Cash over and short.   Sometimes a petty cashier fails to get a receipt for payment or overpays for the amount due. When this occurs and the fund is later reimbursed, the petty cash payments report plus the cash remaining will not total to the fund balance. This mistake causes the fund to be *short*. This shortage is recorded as an expense in the reimbursing entry with a debit to the Cash Over and Short account. (An overage in the petty cash fund is recorded with a credit to Cash Over and Short in the reimbursing entry.) To illustrate, prepare the June 1 entry to reimburse a $200 petty cash fund when its payments report shows $178 in miscellaneous expenses and $15 cash remains.

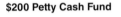

Summary of Petty Cash Accounting

Event	Petty Cash	Cash	Expenses
Set up fund	Dr.	Cr.	—
Reimburse fund..	—	Cr.	Dr.
Increase fund....	Dr.	Cr.	—
Decrease fund...	Cr.	Dr.	—

$200 Petty Cash Fund

$15 Cash $7 Short $178 Receipts

June 1	Miscellaneous Expenses	178	
	Cash Over and Short	7	
	Cash		185
	To reimburse petty cash.		

Decision Insight

Warning Signs   There are clues to internal control violations. Warning signs from accounting include (1) an increase in customer refunds—could be fake, (2) missing documents—could be used for fraud, (3) differences between bank deposits and cash receipts—could be cash embezzled, and (4) delayed recording—could reflect fraudulent records. Warning signs from employees include (1) lifestyle change—could be embezzlement, (2) too close with suppliers—could signal fraudulent transactions, and (3) failure to leave job, even for vacations—could conceal fraudulent activities. ∎

Quick Check   Answers — pp. 285–286

9. Why are some cash payments made from a petty cash fund and not by check?
10. Why should a petty cash fund be reimbursed at the end of an accounting period?
11. Identify at least two results of reimbursing a petty cash fund.
12. Assume that we are auditing a company for the first time. Our audit procedures for petty cash require a surprise audit of the petty cash fund. We approach the petty cash custodian to conduct the audit and she says: "I'm busy right now. Can we do this after lunch?" Do we accommodate the request?

BANKING ACTIVITIES AS CONTROLS

Banks (and other financial institutions) provide many services, including helping companies control cash. Banks safeguard cash, provide detailed and independent records of cash transactions, and are a source of cash financing. This section describes these services and the documents provided by banking activities that increase managers' control over cash.

Basic Bank Services

This section explains basic bank services—such as the bank account, the bank deposit, and checking—that contribute to the control of cash.

1. Identify the bank statement balance of the cash account (*balance per bank*). VideoBuster's bank balance is $2,050.

2. Identify and list any unrecorded deposits and any bank errors understating the bank balance. Add them to the bank balance. VideoBuster's $145 deposit placed in the bank's night depository on October 31 is not recorded on its bank statement.

3. Identify and list any outstanding checks and any bank errors overstating the bank balance. Deduct them from the bank balance. VideoBuster's comparison of canceled checks with its books shows two checks outstanding: No. 124 for $150 and No. 126 for $200.

4. Compute the *adjusted bank balance,* also called the *corrected* or *reconciled balance.*

5. Identify the company's book balance of the cash account (*balance per book*). VideoBuster's book balance is $1,404.58.

6. Identify and list any unrecorded credit memoranda from the bank, any interest earned, and errors understating the book balance. Add them to the book balance. VideoBuster's bank statement includes a credit memorandum showing the bank collected a note receivable for the company on October 23. The note's proceeds of $500 (minus a $15 collection fee) are credited to the company's account. VideoBuster's bank statement also shows a credit of $8.42 for interest earned on the average cash balance. There was no prior notification of this item, and it is not yet recorded.

7. Identify and list any unrecorded debit memoranda from the bank, any service charges, and errors overstating the book balance. Deduct them from the book balance. Debits on VideoBuster's bank statement that are not yet recorded include (a) a $23 charge for check printing and (b) an NSF check for $20 plus a related $10 processing fee. (The NSF check is dated October 16 and was included in the book balance.)

8. Compute the *adjusted book balance,* also called *corrected* or *reconciled balance.*

9. Verify that the two adjusted balances from steps 4 and 8 are equal. If so, they are reconciled. If not, check for accuracy and missing data to achieve reconciliation.

Point: Outstanding checks are identified by comparing canceled checks on the bank statement with checks recorded. This includes identifying any outstanding checks listed on the *previous* period's bank reconciliation that are not included in the canceled checks on this period's bank statement.

Point: Adjusting entries can be combined into one compound entry.

Adjusting Entries from a Bank Reconciliation   A bank reconciliation often identifies unrecorded items that need recording by the company. In VideoBuster's reconciliation, the adjusted balance of $1,845 is the correct balance as of October 31. But the company's accounting records show a $1,404.58 balance. We must prepare journal entries to adjust the book balance to the correct balance. It is important to remember that only the items reconciling the *book balance* require adjustment. A review of Exhibit 6.7 indicates that four entries are required for VideoBuster.

Collection of note.   The first entry is to record the proceeds of its note receivable collected by the bank less the expense of having the bank perform that service.

Oct. 31	Cash	485	
	Collection Expense	15	
	Notes Receivable		500
	To record the collection fee and proceeds		
	for a note collected by the bank.		

Assets = Liabilities + Equity
+485   −15
−500

Interest earned.   The second entry records interest credited to its account by the bank.

Oct. 31	Cash	8.42	
	Interest Revenue		8.42
	To record interest earned on the cash		
	balance in the checking account.		

Assets = Liabilities + Equity
+8.42   +8.42

Check printing.   The third entry records expenses for the check printing charge.

Oct. 31	Miscellaneous Expenses	23	
	Cash		23
	Check printing charge.		

Assets = Liabilities + Equity
−23   −23

NSF check.   The fourth entry records the NSF check that is returned as uncollectible. The $20 check was originally received from T. Woods in payment of his account and then deposited. The

Point: The company will try to collect the entire NSF amount of $30 from customer.

bank charged $10 for handling the NSF check and deducted $30 total from VideoBuster's account. This means the entry must reverse the effects of the original entry made when the check was received and must record (add) the $10 bank fee.

$$
\begin{array}{l}
\text{Assets} = \text{Liabilities} + \text{Equity} \\
+30 \\
-30
\end{array}
$$

Oct. 31	Accounts Receivable—T. Woods	30	
	Cash		30
	To charge Woods' account for $20 NSF check and $10 bank fee.		

Point: The Demo Problem 1 shows an adjusting entry for an error correction.

Cash			
Unadj. bal.	1,404.58		
⑥	485.00	⑦	23.00
⑥	8.42	⑦	30.00
Adj. bal.	1,845.00		

After these four entries are recorded, the book balance of cash is adjusted to the correct amount of $1,845 (computed as $1,404.58 + $485 + $8.42 − $23 − $30). The Cash T-account to the side shows the same computation, where entries are keyed to the numerical codes in Exhibit 6.7.

Decision Insight

Fraud   A survey reports that 74% of employees had 'personally seen' or had 'firsthand knowledge of' fraud or misconduct within the past year. Another survey found that fraudsters exploited weak internal controls in 74% of the frauds—up from 47% four years earlier—see graphic (KPMG 2011). ∎

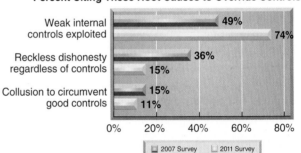

Percent Citing These Root Causes to Override Controls

	2007 Survey	2011 Survey
Weak internal controls exploited	49%	74%
Reckless dishonesty regardless of controls	36%	15%
Collusion to circumvent good controls	15%	11%

Quick Check   Answers — p. 286

13. What is a bank statement?

14. What is the meaning of the phrase *to reconcile a bank balance?*

15. Why do we reconcile the bank statement balance of cash and the depositor's book balance of cash?

16. List at least two items affecting the *bank balance* side of a bank reconciliation and indicate whether the items are added or subtracted.

17. List at least three items affecting the *book balance* side of a bank reconciliation and indicate whether the items are added or subtracted.

GLOBAL VIEW

This section discusses similarities and differences between U.S. GAAP and IFRS regarding internal controls and in the accounting and reporting of cash.

Internal Control Purposes, Principles, and Procedures   Both U.S. GAAP and IFRS aim for high-quality financial reporting. That aim translates into enhanced internal controls worldwide. Specifically, the purposes and principles of internal control systems are fundamentally the same across the globe. However, culture and other realities suggest different emphases on the mix of control procedures, and some sensitivity to different customs and environments when establishing that mix. Nevertheless, the discussion in this chapter applies internationally. **Nokia** provides the following description of its control activities.

NOKIA

Nokia has an internal audit function that acts as an independent appraisal function by examining and evaluating the adequacy and effectiveness of the company's system of internal control.

Control of Cash Accounting definitions for cash are similar for U.S. GAAP and IFRS. The need for control of cash is universal and applies globally. This means that companies worldwide desire to apply cash management procedures as explained in this chapter and aim to control both cash receipts and disbursements. Accordingly, systems that employ tools such as cash monitoring mechanisms, verification of documents, and petty cash processes are applied worldwide. The basic techniques explained in this chapter are part of those control procedures.

Banking Activities as Controls There is a global demand for banking services, bank statements, and bank reconciliations. To the extent feasible, companies utilize banking services as part of their effective control procedures. Further, bank statements are similarly used along with bank reconciliations to control and monitor cash.

 IFRS _____

Internal controls are crucial to companies that convert from U.S. GAAP to IFRS. Major risks include misstatement of financial information and fraud. Other risks are ineffective communication of the impact of this change for investors, creditors and others, and management's inability to certify the effectiveness of controls over financial reporting. ■

Days' Sales Uncollected **Decision Analysis**

An important part of cash management is monitoring the receipt of cash from receivables. If customers and others who owe money to a company are delayed in payment, then that company can find it difficult to pay its obligations when they are due. A company's customers are crucial partners in its cash management. Many companies attract customers by selling to them on credit. This means that cash receipts from customers are delayed until accounts receivable are collected.

A1 Compute the days' sales uncollected ratio and use it to assess liquidity.

One measure of how quickly a company can convert its accounts receivable into cash is the **days' sales uncollected,** also called *days' sales in receivables.* This measure is computed by dividing the current balance of receivables by net credit sales over the year just completed and then multiplying by 365 (number of days in a year). Since net credit sales usually are not reported to external users, the net sales (or revenues) figure is commonly used in the computation as in Exhibit 6.8.

$$\text{Days' sales uncollected} = \frac{\text{Accounts receivable}}{\text{Net sales}} \times 365$$

EXHIBIT 6.8

Days' Sales Uncollected

We use days' sales uncollected to estimate how much time is likely to pass before the current amount of accounts receivable is received in cash. For evaluation purposes, we need to compare this estimate to that for other companies in the same industry. We also make comparisons between current and prior periods.

To illustrate, we select data from the annual reports of two toy manufacturers, Hasbro and Mattel. Their days' sales uncollected figures are shown in Exhibit 6.9.

EXHIBIT 6.9

Analysis Using Days' Sales Uncollected

Company	Figure ($ millions)	2011	2010	2009	2008	2007
Hasbro	Accounts receivable	$1,035	$961	$1,039	$612	$655
	Net sales	$4,286	$4,002	$4,068	$4,022	$3,838
	Days' sales uncollected	88 days	88 days	93 days	56 days	62 days
Mattel	Accounts receivable	$1,247	$1,146	$749	$874	$991
	Net sales	$6,266	$5,856	$5,431	$5,918	$5,970
	Days' sales uncollected	73 days	71 days	50 days	54 days	61 days

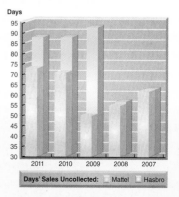

Days' sales uncollected for Hasbro in 2011 is computed as ($1,035/$4,286) × 365 days = 88 days. This means that it will take about 88 days to collect cash from ending accounts receivable. This number reflects one or more of the following factors: a company's ability to collect receivables, customer financial health, customer payment strategies, and discount terms. To further assess days' sales uncollected for Hasbro, we compare it to four prior years and to those of Mattel. We see that Hasbro's days' sales uncollected has worsened since 2008 as it takes much longer to collect its receivables relative to 2007 and 2008. In comparison, Mattel has also worsened from 50 days in 2009 up to 73 days in 2011. For all years, Mattel is superior to Hasbro on this measure of cash management. The less time that money is tied up in receivables often translates into increased profitability.

■ Decision Maker

Sales Representative   The sales staff is told to take action to help reduce days' sales uncollected for cash management purposes. What can you, a salesperson, do to reduce days' sales uncollected? ■   [Answer—p. 285]

DEMONSTRATION PROBLEM 1

Prepare a bank reconciliation for Jamboree Enterprises for the month ended November 30, 2013. The following information is available to reconcile Jamboree Enterprises' book balance of cash with its bank statement balance as of November 30, 2013:

a. After all posting is complete on November 30, the company's book balance of Cash has a $16,380 debit balance, but its bank statement shows a $38,520 balance.

b. Checks No. 2024 for $4,810 and No. 2026 for $5,000 are outstanding.

c. In comparing the canceled checks on the bank statement with the entries in the accounting records, it is found that Check No. 2025 in payment of rent is correctly drawn for $1,000 but is erroneously entered in the accounting records as $880.

> **Point:** Generally, the party that is not the initial recorder of an item, but is later informed, includes that item on its "book" of the bank reconciliation. For example, the bank records an NSF check and then informs the company. The company, as not the initial recorder of the item, reports it on the book side of its reconciliation.

d. The November 30 deposit of $17,150 was placed in the night depository after banking hours on that date, and this amount does not appear on the bank statement.

e. In reviewing the bank statement, a check written by Jumbo Enterprises in the amount of $160 was erroneously drawn against Jamboree's account.

f. A credit memorandum enclosed with the bank statement indicates that the bank collected a $30,000 note and $900 of related interest on Jamboree's behalf. This transaction was not recorded by Jamboree prior to receiving the statement.

g. A debit memorandum for $1,100 lists a $1,100 NSF check received from a customer, Marilyn Welch. Jamboree had not recorded the return of this check before receiving the statement.

h. Bank service charges for November total $40. These charges were not recorded by Jamboree before receiving the statement.

PLANNING THE SOLUTION

● Set up a bank reconciliation with a bank side and a book side (as in Exhibit 6.7). Leave room to both add and deduct items. Each column will result in a reconciled, equal balance.

● Examine each item *a* through *h* to determine whether it affects the book or the bank balance and whether it should be added or deducted from the bank or book balance.

● After all items are analyzed, complete the reconciliation and arrive at a reconciled balance between the bank side and the book side.

● For each reconciling item on the book side, prepare an adjusting entry. Additions to the book side require an adjusting entry that debits Cash. Deductions on the book side require an adjusting entry that credits Cash.

SOLUTION TO DEMONSTRATION PROBLEM 1

JAMBOREE ENTERPRISES					
Bank Reconciliation					
November 30, 2013					
Bank statement balance		$ 38,520	Book balance		$ 16,380
Add			Add		
Deposit of Nov. 30	$17,150		Collection of note	$30,000	
Bank error (Jumbo)	160	17,310	Interest earned	900	30,900
		55,830			47,280
Deduct			Deduct		
Outstanding checks			NSF check (M. Welch)	1,100	
No. 2024	4,810		Recording error (# 2025) ...	120	
No. 2026	5,000	9,810	Service charge	40	1,260
Adjusted bank balance ...		**$46,020**	**Adjusted book balance**		**$46,020**

^{A(B)} *Superscript letter A(B) denotes assignments based on Appendix 6A (6B).*

🛡 Icon denotes assignments that involve decision making.

Discussion Questions

1. List the seven broad principles of internal control.
2. 🛡 Internal control procedures are important in every business, but at what stage in the development of a business do they become especially critical?
3. 🛡 Why should responsibility for related transactions be divided among different departments or individuals?
4. 🛡 Why should the person who keeps the records of an asset not be the person responsible for its custody?
5. 🛡 When a store purchases merchandise, why are individual departments not allowed to directly deal with suppliers?
6. What are the limitations of internal controls?
7. Which of the following assets is most liquid? Which is least liquid? Inventory, building, accounts receivable, or cash.
8. What is a petty cash receipt? Who should sign it?
9. Why should cash receipts be deposited on the day of receipt?
10. **Polaris'** statement of cash flows in Appendix A **Polaris** describes changes in cash and cash equivalents for the year ended December 31, 2011. What total amount is

provided (used) by investing activities? What amount is provided (used) by financing activities?
11. Refer to **Arctic Cat's** financial statements in Appendix A. Identify Arctic Cat's net earnings (income) for the year ended March 31, 2011. Is its net earnings equal to the increase in cash and cash equivalents for the year? Explain the difference between net earnings and the increase in cash and cash equivalents. **Arctic Cat**
12. 🛡 Refer to **KTM's** balance sheet in Appendix A. How does its cash (titled "liquid assets") compare with its other current assets (both in amount and percent) as of December 31, 2011? Compare and assess its cash at December 31, 2011, with its cash at December 31, 2010. **KTM**
13. 🛡 **Piaggio's** balance sheet in Appendix A reports that cash and equivalents decreased during the year ended December 31, 2011. Identify the cash generated (or used) by operating activities, by investing activities, and by financing (funding) activities. **PIAGGIO**

connect

An internal control system consists of all policies and procedures used to protect assets, ensure reliable accounting, promote efficient operations, and urge adherence to company policies.

1. What is the main objective of internal control procedures? How is that objective achieved?
2. Why should recordkeeping for assets be separated from custody over those assets?
3. Why should the responsibility for a transaction be divided between two or more individuals or departments?

QUICK STUDY

QS 6-1
Internal control objectives
C1 🛡

Good accounting systems help in managing cash and controlling who has access to it.

1. What items are included in the category of cash?
2. What items are included in the category of cash equivalents?
3. What does the term *liquidity* refer to?

QS 6-2
Cash and equivalents
C2

A good system of internal control for cash provides adequate procedures for protecting both cash receipts and cash disbursements.

1. What are three basic guidelines that help achieve this protection?
2. Identify two control systems or procedures for cash disbursements.

QS 6-3
Internal control for cash
P1 🛡

---

1. For each of the following items, indicate whether its amount (i) affects the bank or book side of a bank reconciliation and (ii) represents an addition or a subtraction in a bank reconciliation.
   a. Interest on cash balance   d. Outstanding checks   g. Outstanding deposits
   b. Bank service charges   e. Credit memos
   c. Debit memos   f. NSF checks
2. Which of the items in part 1 require an adjusting journal entry?

QS 6-4
Bank reconciliation
P3

---

1. The petty cash fund of the Brooks Agency is established at $150. At the end of the current period, the fund contained $28 and had the following receipts: film rentals, $24, refreshments for meetings, $46 (both expenditures to be classified as Entertainment Expense); postage, $30; and printing, $22. Prepare journal entries to record (*a*) establishment of the fund and (*b*) reimbursement of the fund at the end of the current period.
2. Identify the two events that cause a Petty Cash account to be credited in a journal entry.

QS 6-5
Petty cash accounting
P2

QS 6-6
Bank reconciliation
P3

Nolan Company deposits all cash receipts on the day when they are received and it makes all cash payments by check. At the close of business on June 30, 2013, its Cash account shows an $22,352 debit balance. Nolan's June 30 bank statement shows $21,332 on deposit in the bank. Prepare a bank reconciliation for the Company using the following information.

a. Outstanding checks as of June 30 total $3,713.

b. The June 30 bank statement included a $41 debit memorandum for bank services; the company has not yet recorded the cost of these services.

c. In reviewing the bank statement, a $90 check written by the Company was mistakenly recorded in the company's books at $99.

d. June 30 cash receipts of $4,724 were placed in the bank's night depository after banking hours and were not recorded on the June 30 bank statement.

e. The bank statement included a $23 credit for interest earned on the cash in the bank.

QS 6-7
Reviewing bank statements
P3

An entrepreneur commented that a bank reconciliation may not be necessary as she regularly reviews her online bank statement for any unusual items and errors.

a. Describe how a bank reconciliation and an online review (or reading) of the bank statement are not equivalent.

b. Identify and explain at least two frauds or errors that would be uncovered through a bank reconciliation and that would *not* be uncovered through an online review of the bank statement.

QS 6-8
Days' sales uncollected
A1

The following annual account balances are taken from Armour Sports at December 31.

	2013	2012
Accounts receivable	$ 85,692	$ 80,485
Net sales	2,691,855	2,396,858

What is the change in the number of days' sales uncollected between years 2012 and 2013? (Round the number of days to one decimal.) According to this analysis, is the company's collection of receivables improving? Explain.

QS 6-9ᴬ
Documents in a voucher system
P4

Management uses a voucher system to help control and monitor cash disbursements. Identify and describe at least four key documents that are part of a voucher system of control.

QS 6-10ᴮ
Purchase discounts   **P5**

An important part of cash management is knowing when, and if, to take purchase discounts.

a. Which accounting method uses a Discounts Lost account?

b. What is the advantage of this method for management?

QS 6-11
International accounting and internal controls

C1 P1

Answer each of the following related to international accounting standards.

a. Explain how the purposes and principles of internal controls are different between accounting systems reporting under IFRS versus U.S. GAAP.

b. Cash presents special internal control challenges. How do internal controls for cash differ for accounting systems reporting under IFRS versus U.S. GAAP? How do the procedures applied differ across those two accounting systems?

EXERCISES

Exercise 6-1
Analyzing internal control

C1

Franco Company is a rapidly growing start-up business. Its recordkeeper, who was hired six months ago, left town after the company's manager discovered that a large sum of money had disappeared over the past three months. An audit disclosed that the recordkeeper had written and signed several checks made payable to her fiancé and then recorded the checks as salaries expense. The fiancé, who cashed the checks but never worked for the company, left town with the recordkeeper. As a result, the company incurred an uninsured loss of $184,000. Evaluate Franco's internal control system and indicate which principles of internal control appear to have been ignored.

Some of Crown Company's cash receipts from customers are received by the company with the regular mail. The company's recordkeeper opens these letters and deposits the cash received each day. (*a*) Identify any internal control problem(s) in this arrangement. (*b*) What changes to its internal control system do you recommend?

Exercise 6-2

Control of cash receipts by mail

P1

What internal control procedures would you recommend in each of the following situations?

1. A concession company has one employee who sells towels, coolers, and sunglasses at the beach. Each day, the employee is given enough towels, coolers, and sunglasses to last through the day and enough cash to make change. The money is kept in a box at the stand.

2. An antique store has one employee who is given cash and sent to garage sales each weekend. The employee pays cash for any merchandise acquired that the antique store resells.

Exercise 6-3

Internal control recommendations

C1

Good accounting systems help with the management and control of cash and cash equivalents.

1. Define and contrast the terms *liquid asset* and *cash equivalent.*

2. Why would companies invest their idle cash in cash equivalents?

3. Identify five principles of effective cash management.

Exercise 6-4

Cash, liquidity, and return

C2

Palmona Co. establishes a $200 petty cash fund on January 1. On January 8, the fund shows $38 in cash along with receipts for the following expenditures: postage, $74; transportation-in, $29; delivery expenses, $16; and miscellaneous expenses, $43. Palmona uses the perpetual system in accounting for merchandise inventory. Prepare journal entries to (1) establish the fund on January 1, (2) reimburse it on January 8, and (3) both reimburse the fund and increase it to $450 on January 8, assuming no entry in part 2. (*Hint*: Make two separate entries for part 3.)

Exercise 6-5

Petty cash fund accounting

P2

Check   (3) Cr. Cash $162 (total)

Waupaca Company establishes a $350 petty cash fund on September 9. On September 30, the fund shows $104 in cash along with receipts for the following expenditures: transportation-in, $40; postage expenses, $123; and miscellaneous expenses, $80. The petty cashier could not account for a $3 shortage in the fund. The company uses the perpetual system in accounting for merchandise inventory. Prepare (1) the September 9 entry to establish the fund, (2) the September 30 entry to reimburse the fund, and (3) an October 1 entry to increase the fund to $400.

Exercise 6-6

Petty cash fund with a shortage

P2

Check   (2) Cr. Cash $246 and (3) Cr. Cash $50

Prepare a table with the following headings for a monthly bank reconciliation dated September 30.

Exercise 6-7

Bank reconciliation and adjusting entries

P3

Bank Balance		Book Balance			Not Shown on the Reconciliation
Add	Deduct	Add	Deduct	Adjust	

For each item 1 through 12, place an *x* in the appropriate column to indicate whether the item should be added to or deducted from the book or bank balance, or whether it should not appear on the reconciliation. If the book balance is to be adjusted, place a *Dr.* or *Cr.* in the Adjust column to indicate whether the Cash balance should be debited or credited. At the left side of your table, number the items to correspond to the following list.

1. NSF check from customer is returned on September 25 but not yet recorded by this company.
2. Interest earned on the September cash balance in the bank.
3. Deposit made on September 5 and processed by the bank on September 6.
4. Checks written by another depositor but charged against this company's account.
5. Bank service charge for September.
6. Checks outstanding on August 31 that cleared the bank in September.
7. Check written against the company's account and cleared by the bank; erroneously not recorded by the company's recordkeeper.
8. Principal and interest on a note receivable to this company is collected by the bank but not yet recorded by the company.
9. Checks written and mailed to payees on October 2.
10. Checks written by the company and mailed to payees on September 30.
11. Night deposit made on September 30 after the bank closed.
12. Special bank charge for collection of note in part 8 on this company's behalf.

Exercise 6-8

Voucher system

P1

The voucher system of control is designed to control cash disbursements and the acceptance of obligations.

1. The voucher system of control establishes procedures for what two processes?
2. What types of expenditures should be overseen by a voucher system of control?
3. When is the voucher initially prepared? Explain.

Exercise 6-9

Bank reconciliation

P3

Wright Company deposits all cash receipts on the day when they are received and it makes all cash payments by check. At the close of business on May 31, 2013, its Cash account shows a $27,500 debit balance. The company's May 31 bank statement shows $25,800 on deposit in the bank. Prepare a bank reconciliation for the company using the following information.

a. The May 31 bank statement included a $100 debit memorandum for bank services; the company has not yet recorded the cost of these services.

b. Outstanding checks as of May 31 total $5,600.

c. May 31 cash receipts of $6,200 were placed in the bank's night depository after banking hours and were not recorded on the May 31 bank statement.

d. In reviewing the bank statement, a $400 check written by Smith Company was mistakenly drawn against Wright's account.

Check   Reconciled bal., $26,800

e. A debit memorandum for $600 refers to a $600 NSF check from a customer; the company has not yet recorded this NSF check.

Exercise 6-10

Bank reconciliation

P3

Del Gato Clinic deposits all cash receipts on the day when they are received and it makes all cash payments by check. At the close of business on June 30, 2013, its Cash account shows a $11,589 debit balance. Del Gato Clinic's June 30 bank statement shows $10,555 on deposit in the bank. Prepare a bank reconciliation for Del Gato Clinic using the following information:

a. Outstanding checks as of June 30 total $1,829.

b. The June 30 bank statement included a $16 debit memorandum for bank services.

c. Check No. 919, listed with the canceled checks, was correctly drawn for $467 in payment of a utility bill on June 15. Del Gato Clinic mistakenly recorded it with a debit to Utilities Expense and a credit to Cash in the amount of $476.

Check   Reconciled bal., $11,582

d. The June 30 cash receipts of $2,856 were placed in the bank's night depository after banking hours and were not recorded on the June 30 bank statement.

Exercise 6-11

Adjusting entries from bank reconciliation   **P3**

Prepare the adjusting journal entries that Del Gato Clinic must record as a result of preparing the bank reconciliation in Exercise 6-10.

Exercise 6-12

Liquid assets and accounts receivable

A1

Bargains Co. reported annual net sales for 2012 and 2013 of $665,000 and $747,000, respectively. Its year-end balances of accounts receivable follow: December 31, 2012, $61,000; and December 31, 2013, $93,000. (*a*) Calculate its days' sales uncollected at the end of each year. Round the number of days to one decimal. (*b*) Evaluate and comment on any changes in the amount of liquid assets tied up in receivables.

Exercise 6-13ᴬ

Documents in a voucher system

P4

Match each document in a voucher system in column one with its description in column two.

Document	**Description**
1. Purchase requisition	**A.** An itemized statement of goods prepared by the vendor listing the customer's name, items sold, sales prices, and terms of sale.
2. Purchase order	
3. Invoice	**B.** An internal file used to store documents and information to control cash disbursements and to ensure that a transaction is properly authorized and recorded.
4. Receiving report	
5. Invoice approval	
6. Voucher	**C.** A document used to place an order with a vendor that authorizes the vendor to ship ordered merchandise at the stated price and terms.
	D. A checklist of steps necessary for the approval of an invoice for recording and payment; also known as a check authorization.
	E. A document used by department managers to inform the purchasing department to place an order with a vendor.
	F. A document used to notify the appropriate persons that ordered goods have arrived, including a description of the quantities and condition of goods.

Piere Imports uses the perpetual system in accounting for merchandise inventory and had the following transactions during the month of October. Prepare entries to record these transactions assuming that Piere Imports records invoices (*a*) at gross amounts and (*b*) at net amounts.

Oct. 2 Purchased merchandise at a $3,000 price, invoice dated October 2, terms 2/10, n/30.
    10 Received a $500 credit memorandum (at full invoice price) for the return of merchandise that it purchased on October 2.
    17 Purchased merchandise at a $5,400 price, invoice dated October 17, terms 2/10, n/30.
    27 Paid for the merchandise purchased on October 17, less the discount.
    31 Paid for the merchandise purchased on October 2. Payment was delayed because the invoice was mistakenly filed for payment today. This error caused the discount to be lost.

Exercise 6-14[B]
Record invoices at gross or net amounts
P5

☰ connect

For each of these five separate cases, identify the principle(s) of internal control that is violated. Recommend what the business should do to ensure adherence to principles of internal control.

1. Chi Han records all incoming customer cash receipts for her employer and posts the customer payments to their respective accounts.
2. At Tico Company, Julia and Justine alternate lunch hours. Julia is the petty cash custodian, but if someone needs petty cash when he is at lunch, Jose fills in as custodian.
3. Nori Nozumi posts all patient charges and payments at the Hopeville Medical Clinic. Each night Nori backs up the computerized accounting system to a tape and stores the tape in a locked file at her desk.
4. Benedict Shales prides himself on hiring quality workers who require little supervision. As office manager, Benedict gives his employees full discretion over their tasks and for years has seen no reason to perform independent reviews of their work.
5. Carla Farah's manager has told her to reduce costs. Cala decides to raise the deductible on the plant's property insurance from $5,000 to $10,000. This cuts the property insurance premium in half. In a related move, she decides that bonding the plant's employees is a waste of money since the company has not experienced any losses due to employee theft. Cala saves the entire amount of the bonding insurance premium by dropping the bonding insurance.

PROBLEM SET A

Problem 6-1A
Analyzing internal control

C1

Nakashima Gallery had the following petty cash transactions in February of the current year.

Feb. 2 Wrote a $400 check, cashed it, and gave the proceeds and the petty cashbox to Chloe Addison, the petty cashier.
    5 Purchased bond paper for the copier for $14.15 that is immediately used.
    9 Paid $32.50 COD shipping charges on merchandise purchased for resale, terms FOB shipping point. Nakashima uses the perpetual system to account for merchandise inventory.
    12 Paid $7.95 postage to express mail a contract to a client.
    14 Reimbursed Adina Sharon, the manager, $68 for business mileage on her car.
    20 Purchased stationery for $67.77 that is immediately used.
    23 Paid a courier $20 to deliver merchandise sold to a customer, terms FOB destination.
    25 Paid $13.10 COD shipping charges on merchandise purchased for resale, terms FOB shipping point.
    27 Paid $54 for postage expenses.
    28 The fund had $120.42 remaining in the petty cash box. Sorted the petty cash receipts by accounts affected and exchanged them for a check to reimburse the fund for expenditures.
    28 The petty cash fund amount is increased by $100 to a total of $500.

Required

1. Prepare the journal entry to establish the petty cash fund.
2. Prepare a petty cash payments report for February with these categories: delivery expense, mileage expense, postage expense, merchandise inventory (for transportation-in), and office supplies expense. Sort the payments into the appropriate categories and total the expenditures in each category.
3. Prepare the journal entries (in dollars and cents) for part 2 to both (*a*) reimburse and (*b*) increase the fund amount.

Problem 6-2A
Establish, reimburse, and increase petty cash

P2

Check   (3a & 3b) Total Cr. to Cash $379.58

Problem 6-3A

Establish, reimburse, and adjust petty cash

P2 Sage 50

Kiona Co. set up a petty cash fund for payments of small amounts. The following transactions involving the petty cash fund occurred in May (the last month of the company's fiscal year).

May   1   Prepared a company check for $300 to establish the petty cash fund.
     15   Prepared a company check to replenish the fund for the following expenditures made since May 1.
        a.   Paid $88 for janitorial services.
        b.   Paid $53.68 for miscellaneous expenses.
        c.   Paid postage expenses of $53.50.
        d.   Paid $47.15 to *The County Gazette* (the local newspaper) for an advertisement.
        e.   Counted $62.15 remaining in the petty cash box.
     16   Prepared a company check for $200 to increase the fund to $500.
     31   The petty cashier reports that $288.20 cash remains in the fund. A company check is drawn to replenish the fund for the following expenditures made since May 15.
        f.   Paid postage expenses of $147.36.
        g.   Reimbursed the office manager for business mileage, $23.50.
        h.   Paid $34.75 to deliver merchandise to a customer, terms FOB destination.
     31   The company decides that the May 16 increase in the fund was too large. It reduces the fund by $100, leaving a total of $400.

Check   (1) Cr. to Cash: May 15, $237.85; May 16, $200.00

Required

1. Prepare journal entries (in dollars and cents) to establish the fund on May 1, to replenish it on May 15 and on May 31, and to reflect any increase or decrease in the fund balance on May 16 and May 31.

Analysis Component

2. Explain how the company's financial statements are affected if the petty cash fund is not replenished and no entry is made on May 31.

Problem 6-4A

Prepare a bank reconciliation and record adjustments

P3

mhhe.com/wildFAF4e

The following information is available to reconcile Branch Company's book balance of cash with its bank statement cash balance as of July 31, 2013.

a. On July 31, the company's Cash account has a $27,497 debit balance, but its July bank statement shows a $27,233 cash balance.

b. Check No. 3031 for $1,482 and Check No. 3040 for $558 were outstanding on the June 30 bank reconciliation. Check No. 3040 is listed with the July canceled checks, but Check No. 3031 is not. Also, Check No. 3065 for $382 and Check No. 3069 for $2,281, both written in July, are not among the canceled checks on the July 31 statement.

c. In comparing the canceled checks on the bank statement with the entries in the accounting records, it is found that Check No. 3056 for July rent was correctly written and drawn for $1,270 but was erroneously entered in the accounting records as $1,250.

d. A credit memorandum enclosed with the July bank statement indicates the bank collected $8,000 cash on a non-interest-bearing note for Branch, deducted a $45 collection fee, and credited the remainder to its account. Branch had not recorded this event before receiving the statement.

e. A debit memorandum for $805 lists a $795 NSF check plus a $10 NSF charge. The check had been received from a customer, Evan Shaw. Branch has not yet recorded this check as NSF.

f. Enclosed with the July statement is a $25 debit memorandum for bank services. It has not yet been recorded because no previous notification had been received.

g. Branch's July 31 daily cash receipts of $11,514 were placed in the bank's night depository on that date, but do not appear on the July 31 bank statement.

Required

1. Prepare the bank reconciliation for this company as of July 31, 2013.

Check   (1) Reconciled balance, $34,602; (2) Cr. Note Receivable $8,000

2. Prepare the journal entries necessary to bring the company's book balance of cash into conformity with the reconciled cash balance as of July 31, 2013.

Analysis Component

3. Assume that the July 31, 2013, bank reconciliation for this company is prepared and some items are treated incorrectly. For each of the following errors, explain the effect of the error on (i) the adjusted bank statement cash balance and (ii) the adjusted cash account book balance.

    a. The company's unadjusted cash account balance of $27,497 is listed on the reconciliation as $27,947.

    b. The bank's collection of the $8,000 note less the $45 collection fee is added to the bank statement cash balance on the reconciliation.

Chavez Company most recently reconciled its bank statement and book balances of cash on August 31 and it reported two checks outstanding, No. 5888 for $1,028.05 and No. 5893 for $494.25. The following information is available for its September 30, 2013, reconciliation.

Problem 6-5A

Prepare a bank reconciliation and record adjustments

P3

mhhe.com/wildFAF4e

Sage 50

From the September 30 Bank Statement

PREVIOUS BALANCE	TOTAL CHECKS AND DEBITS	TOTAL DEPOSITS AND CREDITS	CURRENT BALANCE
16,800.45	9,620.05	11,272.85	18,453.25

CHECKS AND DEBITS			DEPOSITS AND CREDITS		DAILY BALANCE	
Date	No.	Amount	Date	Amount	Date	Amount
09/03	5888	1,028.05	09/05	1,103.75	08/31	16,800.45
09/04	5902	719.90	09/12	2,226.90	09/03	15,772.40
09/07	5901	1,824.25	09/21	4,093.00	09/04	15,052.50
09/17		600.25 NSF	09/25	2,351.70	09/05	16,156.25
09/20	5905	937.00	09/30	12.50 IN	09/07	14,332.00
09/22	5903	399.10	09/30	1,485.00 CM	09/12	16,558.90
09/22	5904	2,090.00			09/17	15,958.65
09/28	5907	213.85			09/20	15,021.65
09/29	5909	1,807.65			09/21	19,114.65
					09/22	16,625.55
					09/25	18,977.25
					09/28	18,763.40
					09/29	16,955.75
					09/30	18,453.25

From Chavez Company's Accounting Records

Cash Receipts Deposited			
Date			Cash Debit
Sept.	5		1,103.75
	12		2,226.90
	21		4,093.00
	25		2,351.70
	30		1,682.75
			11,458.10

Cash Disbursements		
Check No.		Cash Credit
5901		1,824.25
5902		719.90
5903		399.10
5904		2,060.00
5905		937.00
5906		982.30
5907		213.85
5908		388.00
5909		1,807.65
		9,332.05

Cash						Acct. No. 101
Date		Explanation	PR	Debit	Credit	Balance
Aug.	31	Balance				15,278.15
Sept.	30	Total receipts	R12	11,458.10		26,736.25
	30	Total disbursements	D23		9,332.05	17,404.20

Additional Information

Check No. 5904 is correctly drawn for $2,090 to pay for computer equipment; however, the recordkeeper misread the amount and entered it in the accounting records with a debit to Computer Equipment and a credit to Cash of $2,060. The NSF check shown in the statement was originally received from a customer, S. Nilson, in payment of her account. Its return has not yet been recorded by the company. The credit memorandum is from the collection of a $1,500 note for Chavez Company by the bank. The bank deducted a $15 collection fee. The collection and fee are not yet recorded.

Check   (1) Reconciled balance, $18,271.45 (2) Cr. Note Receivable $1,500.00

Required

1. Prepare the September 30, 2013, bank reconciliation for this company.
2. Prepare the journal entries (in dollars and cents) to adjust the book balance of cash to the reconciled balance.

Analysis Component

3. The bank statement reveals that some of the prenumbered checks in the sequence are missing. Describe three situations that could explain this.

PROBLEM SET B

Problem 6-1B

Analyzing internal control

C1

For each of these five separate cases, identify the principle(s) of internal control that is violated. Recommend what the business should do to ensure adherence to principles of internal control.

1. Latisha Tally is the company's computer specialist and oversees its computerized payroll system. Her boss recently asked her to put password protection on all office computers. Latisha has put a password in place that allows only the boss access to the file where pay rates are changed and personnel are added or deleted from the payroll.
2. Marker Theater has a computerized order-taking system for its tickets. The system is active all week and backed up every Friday night.
3. Sutton Company has two employees handling acquisitions of inventory. One employee places purchase orders and pays vendors. The second employee receives the merchandise.
4. The owner of Super Pharmacy uses a check protector to perforate checks, making it difficult for anyone to alter the amount of the check. The check protector is on the owner's desk in an office that contains company checks and is normally unlocked.
5. Lavina Company is a small business that has separated the duties of cash receipts and cash disbursements. The employee responsible for cash disbursements reconciles the bank account monthly.

Problem 6-2B

Establish, reimburse, and increase petty cash

P2

Blues Music Center had the following petty cash transactions in March of the current year.

March 5	Wrote a $250 check, cashed it, and gave the proceeds and the petty cashbox to Jen Rouse, the petty cashier.
6	Paid $12.50 COD shipping charges on merchandise purchased for resale, terms FOB shipping point. Blues uses the perpetual system to account for merchandise inventory.
11	Paid $10.75 delivery charges on merchandise sold to a customer, terms FOB destination.
12	Purchased file folders for $14.13 that are immediately used.
14	Reimbursed Bob Geldof, the manager, $11.65 for office supplies purchased and used.
18	Purchased printer paper for $20.54 that is immediately used.
27	Paid $45.10 COD shipping charges on merchandise purchased for resale, terms FOB shipping point.
28	Paid postage expenses of $18.
30	Reimbursed Geldof $56.80 for business car mileage.
31	Cash of $61.53 remained in the fund. Sorted the petty cash receipts by accounts affected and exchanged them for a check to reimburse the fund for expenditures.
31	The petty cash fund amount is increased by $50 to a total of $300.

Required

1. Prepare the journal entry to establish the petty cash fund.

Check   (2) Total expenses $189.47

2. Prepare a petty cash payments report for March with these categories: delivery expense, mileage expense, postage expense, merchandise inventory (for transportation-in), and office supplies expense. Sort the payments into the appropriate categories and total the expenses in each category.

(3a & 3b) Total Cr. to Cash $238.47

3. Prepare the journal entries (in dollars and cents) for part 2 to both (*a*) reimburse and (*b*) increase the fund amount.

Problem 6-3B

Establishing, reimbursing, and adjusting petty cash

P2

Moya Co. establishes a petty cash fund for payments of small amounts. The following transactions involving the petty cash fund occurred in January (the last month of the company's fiscal year).

Jan. 3   A company check for $150 is written and made payable to the petty cashier to establish the petty cash fund.

14 A company check is written to replenish the fund for the following expenditures made since January 3.
    a. Purchased office supplies for $14.29 that are immediately used up.
    b. Paid $19.60 COD shipping charges on merchandise purchased for resale, terms FOB shipping point. Moya uses the perpetual system to account for inventory.
    c. Paid $38.57 to All-Tech for minor repairs to a computer.
    d. Paid $12.82 for items classified as miscellaneous expenses.
    e. Counted $62.28 remaining in the petty cash box.

15 Prepared a company check for $50 to increase the fund to $200.

31 The petty cashier reports that $17.35 remains in the fund. A company check is written to replenish the fund for the following expenditures made since January 14.
    f. Paid $50 to *The Smart Shopper* for an advertisement in January's newsletter.
    g. Paid $48.19 for postage expenses.
    h. Paid $78 to Smooth Delivery for delivery of merchandise, terms FOB destination.

31 The company decides that the January 15 increase in the fund was too little. It increases the fund by another $50, leaving a total of $250.

Required

1. Prepare journal entries (in dollars and cents) to establish the fund on January 3, to replenish it on January 14 and January 31, and to reflect any increase or decrease in the fund balance on January 15 and 31.

Check (1) Cr. to Cash: Jan. 14, $87.72; Jan. 31 (total), $232.65

Analysis Component

2. Explain how the company's financial statements are affected if the petty cash fund is not replenished and no entry is made on January 31.

The following information is available to reconcile Severino Co.'s book balance of cash with its bank statement cash balance as of December 31, 2013.

Problem 6-4B
Prepare a bank reconciliation and record adjustments

P3

a. The December 31 cash balance according to the accounting records is $32,878.30, and the bank statement cash balance for that date is $46,822.40.

b. Check No. 1273 for $4,589.30 and Check No. 1282 for $400, both written and entered in the accounting records in December, are not among the canceled checks. Two checks, No. 1231 for $2,289 and No. 1242 for $410.40, were outstanding on the most recent November 30 reconciliation. Check No. 1231 is listed with the December canceled checks, but Check No. 1242 is not.

c. When the December checks are compared with entries in the accounting records, it is found that Check No. 1267 had been correctly drawn for $3,456 to pay for office supplies but was erroneously entered in the accounting records as $3,465.

d. Two debit memoranda are enclosed with the statement and are unrecorded at the time of the reconciliation. One debit memorandum is for $762.50 and dealt with an NSF check for $745 received from a customer, Titus Industries, in payment of its account. The bank assessed a $17.50 fee for processing it. The second debit memorandum is a $99 charge for check printing. Severino did not record these transactions before receiving the statement.

e. A credit memorandum indicates that the bank collected $19,000 cash on a note receivable for the company, deducted a $20 collection fee, and credited the balance to the company's Cash account. Severino did not record this transaction before receiving the statement.

f. Severino's December 31 daily cash receipts of $9,583.10 were placed in the bank's night depository on that date, but do not appear on the December 31 bank statement.

Required

1. Prepare the bank reconciliation for this company as of December 31, 2013.
2. Prepare the journal entries (in dollars and cents) necessary to bring the company's book balance of cash into conformity with the reconciled cash balance as of December 31, 2013.

Check (1) Reconciled balance, $51,005.80; (2) Cr. Note Receivable $19,000.00

Analysis Component

3. Explain the nature of the communications conveyed by a bank when the bank sends the depositor (*a*) a debit memorandum and (*b*) a credit memorandum.

Problem 6-5B

Prepare a bank reconciliation and record adjustments

P3

Shamara Systems most recently reconciled its bank balance on April 30 and reported two checks outstanding at that time, No. 1771 for $781 and No. 1780 for $1,425.90. The following information is available for its May 31, 2013, reconciliation.

From the May 31 Bank Statement

PREVIOUS BALANCE	TOTAL CHECKS AND DEBITS	TOTAL DEPOSITS AND CREDITS	CURRENT BALANCE
18,290.70	13,094.80	16,566.80	21,762.70

CHECKS AND DEBITS			DEPOSITS AND CREDITS		DAILY BALANCE	
Date	No.	Amount	Date	Amount	Date	Amount
05/01	1771	781.00	05/04	2,438.00	04/30	18,290.70
05/02	1783	382.50	05/14	2,898.00	05/01	17,509.70
05/04	1782	1,285.50	05/22	1,801.80	05/02	17,127.20
05/11	1784	1,449.60	05/25	7,350.00 CM	05/04	18,279.70
05/18		431.80 NSF	05/26	2,079.00	05/11	16,830.10
05/25	1787	8,032.50			05/14	19,728.10
05/26	1785	63.90			05/18	19,296.30
05/29	1788	654.00			05/22	21,098.10
05/31		14.00 SC			05/25	20,415.60
					05/26	22,430.70
					05/29	21,776.70
					05/31	21,762.70

From Shamara Systems' Accounting Records

Cash Receipts Deposited				Cash Disbursements		
Date		Cash Debit		Check No.		Cash Credit
May	4	2,438.00		1782		1,285.50
	14	2,898.00		1783		382.50
	22	1,801.80		1784		1,449.60
	26	2,079.00		1785		63.90
	31	2,727.30		1786		353.10
		11,944.10		1787		8,032.50
				1788		644.00
				1789		639.50
						12,850.60

Cash						Acct. No. 101	
Date		Explanation	PR	Debit	Credit	Balance	
Apr.	30	Balance				16,083.80	
May	31	Total receipts	R7	11,944.10		28,027.90	
	31	Total disbursements	D8		12,850.60	15,177.30	

Additional Information

Check No. 1788 is correctly drawn for $654 to pay for May utilities; however, the recordkeeper misread the amount and entered it in the accounting records with a debit to Utilities Expense and a credit to Cash for $644. The bank paid and deducted the correct amount. The NSF check shown in the statement was originally received from a customer, W. Sox, in payment of her account. The company has not yet recorded its return. The credit memorandum is from a $7,400 note that the bank collected for the company.

The bank deducted a $50 collection fee and deposited the remainder in the company's account. The collection and fee have not yet been recorded.

Required

1. Prepare the May 31, 2013, bank reconciliation for Shamara Systems.

2. Prepare the journal entries (in dollars and cents) to adjust the book balance of cash to the reconciled balance.

Analysis Component

3. The bank statement reveals that some of the prenumbered checks in the sequence are missing. Describe three possible situations to explain this.

Check (1) Reconciled balance, $22,071.50; (2) Cr. Note Receivable $7,400.00

(This serial problem began in Chapter 1 and continues through most of the book. If previous chapter segments were not completed, the serial problem can begin at this point. It is helpful, but not necessary, to use the Working Papers that accompany the book.)

SP 6   Adria Lopez receives the March bank statement for Success Systems on April 11, 2014. The March 31 bank statement shows an ending cash balance of $77,354. A comparison of the bank statement with the general ledger Cash account, No. 101, reveals the following.

a. A. Lopez notices that the bank erroneously cleared a $500 check against her account in March that she did not issue. The check documentation included with the bank statement shows that this check was actually issued by a company named Sierra Systems.

b. On March 25, the bank issued a $50 debit memorandum for the safety deposit box that Success Systems agreed to rent from the bank beginning March 25.

c. On March 26, the bank issued a $102 debit memorandum for printed checks that Success Systems ordered from the bank.

d. On March 31, the bank issued a credit memorandum for $33 interest earned on Success Systems' checking account for the month of March.

e. A. Lopez notices that the check she issued for $128 on March 31, 2014, has not yet cleared the bank.

f. A. Lopez verifies that all deposits made in March do appear on the March bank statement.

g. The general ledger Cash account, No. 101, shows an ending cash balance per books of $77,845 as of March 31 (prior to any reconciliation).

Required

1. Prepare a bank reconciliation for Success Systems for the month ended March 31, 2014.

2. Prepare any necessary adjusting entries. Use Miscellaneous Expenses, No. 677, for any bank charges. Use Interest Revenue, No. 404, for any interest earned on the checking account for the month of March.

SERIAL PROBLEM
Success Systems

P3

Sage 50

Check (1) Adj. bank bal. $77,726

Beyond the Numbers

BTN 6-1   Refer to Polaris' financial statements in Appendix A to answer the following.

1. For both years ended December 31, 2011 and 2010, identify the total amount of cash and cash equivalents. Determine the percent (rounded to one decimal) that this amount represents of total current assets, total current liabilities, total shareholders' equity, and total assets for both years. Comment on any trends.

2. For years ended December 31, 2011 and 2010, use the information in the statement of cash flows to determine the percent change (rounded to one decimal) between the beginning and ending year amounts of cash and cash equivalents.

3. Compute the days' sales uncollected (rounded to two decimals) as of December 31, 2011 and 2010. Has the collection of receivables improved? Are accounts receivable an important asset for Polaris? Explain.

REPORTING IN ACTION

C2 A1

Polaris

Fast Forward

4. Access Polaris' financial statements for fiscal years ending after December 31, 2011, from its Website (Polaris.com) or the SEC's EDGAR database (www.sec.gov). Recompute its days' sales uncollected for years ending after December 31, 2011. Compare this to the days' sales uncollected for 2011 and 2010.

COMPARATIVE ANALYSIS

A1

Polaris

Arctic Cat

BTN 6-2   Key comparative figures for Polaris and Arctic Cat follow.

($ thousands)	Polaris		Arctic Cat	
	Current Year	Prior Year	Current Year	Prior Year
Accounts receivable	$ 115,302	$ 89,294	$ 23,732	$ 29,227
Net sales	2,656,949	1,991,139	363,015	350,871

Required

Compute days' sales uncollected (rounded to two decimals) for these companies for each of the two years shown. Comment on any trends for the companies. Which company has the largest percent change (rounded to two decimals) in days' sales uncollected?

ETHICS CHALLENGE

C1

BTN 6-3   Harriet Knox, Ralph Patton, and Marcia Diamond work for a family physician, Dr. Gwen Conrad, who is in private practice. Dr. Conrad is knowledgeable about office management practices and has segregated the cash receipt duties as follows. Knox opens the mail and prepares a triplicate list of money received. She sends one copy of the list to Patton, the cashier, who deposits the receipts daily in the bank. Diamond, the recordkeeper, receives a copy of the list and posts payments to patients' accounts. About once a month the office clerks have an expensive lunch they pay for as follows. First, Patton endorses a patient's check in Dr. Conrad's name and cashes it at the bank. Knox then destroys the remittance advice accompanying the check. Finally, Diamond posts payment to the customer's account as a miscellaneous credit. The three justify their actions by their relatively low pay and knowledge that Dr. Conrad will likely never miss the money.

Required

1. Who is the best person in Dr. Conrad's office to reconcile the bank statement?
2. Would a bank reconciliation uncover this office fraud?
3. What are some procedures to detect this type of fraud?
4. Suggest additional internal controls that Dr. Conrad could implement.

COMMUNICATING IN PRACTICE

P5

BTN 6-4[B]   Assume you are a business consultant. The owner of a company sends you an e-mail expressing concern that the company is not taking advantage of its discounts offered by vendors. The company currently uses the gross method of recording purchases. The owner is considering a review of all invoices and payments from the previous period. Due to the volume of purchases, however, the owner recognizes that this is time-consuming and costly. The owner seeks your advice about monitoring purchase discounts in the future. Provide a response in memorandum form.

TAKING IT TO THE NET

C1 P1

BTN 6-5   Visit the Association of Certified Fraud Examiners Website at <u>acfe.com</u>. Find and open the file "2010 Report to the Nation." Read the two-page Executive Summary and fill in the following blanks. (The report is under its *Fraud Resources* tab or under its *About the ACFE* tab [under Press Room]; we can also use the *Search* tab.)

1. The median loss caused by occupational frauds was $_____.
2. Nearly _____ of fraud cases involved losses of at least $1 million in losses.
3. Companies lose ___% of their annual revenues to fraud; this figure translates to a potential total fraud loss of more than $_____ trillion.
4. The typical length of fraud schemes was _____ months from the time the fraud began until it was detected.
5. Less than ___% of victim organizations conducted surprise audits, however these organizations have lower fraud losses and detect fraud more quickly than those without surprise audits.
6. Asset misappropriation schemes were most common at ___% of cases with a median loss of $_____.
7. Financial statement fraud schemes made up less than ___% of cases with a median loss of more than $_____ million.
8. Corruption schemes comprised ___% of cases with a median loss of $_____.
9. Less than ___% of the perpetrators had convictions prior to committing their frauds.

The general ledger continues to have a single Accounts Receivable account (called a *control account*) along with the other financial statement accounts, but a supplementary record is created to maintain a separate account for each customer. This supplementary record is called the *accounts receivable ledger* (or *accounts receivable subsidiary ledger*).

Exhibit 7.2 shows the relation between the Accounts Receivable account in the general ledger and its individual customer accounts in the accounts receivable ledger for TechCom, a small electronics wholesaler. This exhibit reports a $3,000 ending balance of TechCom's accounts receivable for June 30. TechCom's transactions are mainly in cash, but it has two major credit customers: CompStore and RDA Electronics. Its *schedule of accounts receivable* shows that the $3,000 balance of the Accounts Receivable account in the general ledger equals the total of its two customers' balances in the accounts receivable ledger.

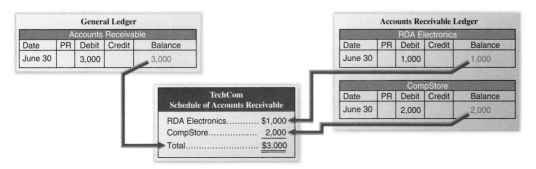

EXHIBIT 7.2

General Ledger and the Accounts Receivable Ledger (before July 1 transactions)

To see how accounts receivable from credit sales are recognized in the accounting records, we look at two transactions on July 1 between TechCom and its credit customers—see Exhibit 7.3. The first is a credit sale of $950 to CompStore. A credit sale is posted with both a debit to the Accounts Receivable account in the general ledger and a debit to the customer account in the accounts receivable ledger. The second transaction is a collection of $720 from RDA Electronics from a prior credit sale. Cash receipts from a credit customer are posted with a credit to the Accounts Receivable account in the general ledger and flow through to credit the customer account in the accounts receivable ledger. (Posting debits or credits to Accounts Receivable in two separate ledgers does not violate the requirement that debits equal credits. The equality of debits and credits is maintained in the general ledger. The accounts receivable ledger is a *supplementary* record providing information on each customer.)

EXHIBIT 7.3

Accounts Receivable Transactions

July 1	Accounts Receivable—CompStore	950	
	Sales		950
	*To record credit sales**		
July 1	Cash	720	
	Accounts Receivable—RDA Electronics		720
	To record collection of credit sales.		

Assets = Liabilities + Equity
+ 950   +950

Assets = Liabilities + Equity
+720
−720

* We omit the entry to Dr. Cost of Sales and Cr. Merchandise Inventory to focus on sales and receivables.

Exhibit 7.4 shows the general ledger and the accounts receivable ledger after recording the two July 1 transactions. The general ledger shows the effects of the sale, the collection, and the resulting balance of $3,230. These events are also reflected in the individual customer accounts:

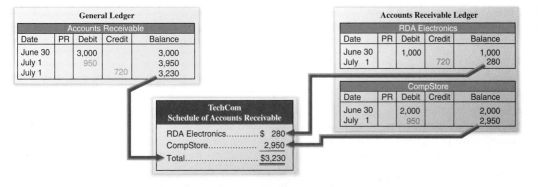

EXHIBIT 7.4

General Ledger and the Accounts Receivable Ledger (after July 1 transactions)

RDA Electronics has an ending balance of $280, and CompStore's ending balance is $2,950. The $3,230 sum of the individual accounts equals the debit balance of the Accounts Receivable account in the general ledger.

Like TechCom, many large retailers such as **Target** and **JCPenney** sell on credit. Many also maintain their own credit cards to grant credit to approved customers and to earn interest on any balance not paid within a specified period of time. This allows them to avoid the fee charged by credit card companies. The entries in this case are the same as those for TechCom except for the possibility of added interest revenue. If a customer owes interest on a bill, we debit Interest Receivable and credit Interest Revenue for that amount. (Many retailers require clerks to ask customers during checkout if they wish to apply for a store credit card—sweeteners are often used such as: *save 10% off today's purchases if you apply now.*)

Credit Card Sales Many companies allow their customers to pay for products and services using third-party credit cards such as **Visa**, **MasterCard**, or **American Express**, and debit cards (also called ATM or bank cards). This practice gives customers the ability to make purchases without cash or checks. Once credit is established with a credit card company or bank, the customer does not have to open an account with each store. Customers using these cards can make single monthly payments instead of several payments to different creditors and can defer their payments.

Many sellers allow customers to use third-party credit cards and debit cards instead of granting credit directly for several reasons. First, the seller does not have to evaluate each customer's credit standing or make decisions about who gets credit and how much. Second, the seller avoids the risk of extending credit to customers who cannot or do not pay. This risk is transferred to the card company. Third, the seller typically receives cash from the card company sooner than had it granted credit directly to customers. Fourth, a variety of credit options for customers offers a potential increase in sales volume. **Sears** historically offered credit only to customers using a Sears card but later changed its policy to permit customers to charge purchases to third-party credit card companies in a desire to increase sales. It reported: "SearsCharge increased its share of Sears retail sales even as the company expanded the payment options available to its customers with the acceptance . . . of Visa, MasterCard, and American Express in addition to the [Sears] Card."

There are guidelines in how companies account for credit card and debit card sales. Some credit cards, but nearly all debit cards, credit a seller's Cash account immediately upon deposit. In this case the seller deposits a copy of each card sales receipt in its bank account just as it deposits a customer's check. The majority of credit cards, however, require the seller to remit a copy (often electronically) of each receipt to the card company. Until payment is received, the seller has an account receivable from the card company. In both cases, the seller pays a fee for services provided by the card company, often ranging from 1% to 5% of card sales. This charge is deducted from the credit to the seller's account or the cash payment to the seller. (Many retailers accept MasterCard and Visa, but not American Express. The reason is that American Express usually charges retailers a higher percentage fee than other credit card companies.)

Point: Visa USA now transacts more than $1 trillion from its credit, debit, and prepaid cards.

Decision Insight

Debit Card vs. Credit Card A buyer's debit card purchase reduces the buyer's cash account balance at the card company, which is often a bank. Since the buyer's cash account balance is a liability (with a credit balance) for the card company to the buyer, the card company would debit that account for a buyer's purchase—hence, the term *debit card*. A credit card reflects authorization by the card company of a line of credit for the buyer with preset interest rates and payment terms—hence, the term *credit card*. Most card companies waive interest charges if the buyer pays its balance each month. ∎

Point: Web merchants pay twice as much in credit card association fees as other retailers because they suffer 10 times as much fraud.

The procedures used in accounting for credit card sales depend on whether cash is received immediately on deposit or cash receipt is delayed until the credit card company makes the payment.

Cash Received Immediately on Deposit   To illustrate, if TechCom has $100 of credit card sales with a 4% fee, and its $96 cash is received immediately on deposit, the entry is

July 15	Cash	96	
	Credit Card Expense	4	
	Sales		100
	*To record credit card sales less a 4% credit card expense.**		

Assets = Liabilities + Equity
+96   +100
                               −4

* We omit the entry to Dr. Cost of Sales and Cr. Merchandise Inventory to focus on credit card expense.

Cash Received Some Time after Deposit   However, if instead TechCom must remit electronically the credit card sales receipts to the credit card company and wait for the $96 cash payment, the entry on the date of sale is

July 15	**Accounts Receivable—Credit Card Co.**	96	
	Credit Card Expense	4	
	Sales		100
	*To record credit card sales less 4% credit card expense.**		

Assets = Liabilities + Equity
+96   +100
                               −4

* We omit the entry to Dr. Cost of Sales and Cr. Merchandise Inventory to focus on credit card expense.

When cash is later received from the credit card company, usually through electronic funds transfer, the entry is

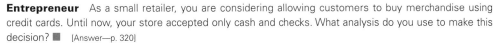

July 20	Cash	96	
	Accounts Receivable—Credit Card Co.		96
	To record cash receipt.		

Assets = Liabilities + Equity
+96
−96

Some firms report credit card expense in the income statement as a type of discount deducted from sales to get net sales. Other companies classify it as a selling expense or even as an administrative expense. Arguments can be made for each approach.

Point: Third-party credit card costs can be large. JCPenney reported third-party credit card costs exceeding $10 million.

 **Decision** Insight

Cabbie Credit Card Sales   Thirty New York cabs rolled out the first phase of a new mobile payment system for taxis. These 30 cabs are equipped with an iPad encased in a metal housing that includes a credit card reader. The iPad allows fares to swipe their card, sign their name on the screen with their finger, and then receive a receipt on their phone either by text or email. Taxi drivers are also able to interact with the system, dubbed "Checker," using their own iPhone app. ■

Installment Sales and Receivables   Many companies allow their credit customers to make periodic payments over several months. For example, Ford Motor Company reports more than $70 billion in installment receivables. The seller refers to such assets as *installment accounts* (or *finance*) *receivable,* which are amounts owed by customers from credit sales for which payment is required in periodic amounts over an extended time period. Source documents for installment accounts receivable include sales slips or invoices describing the sales transactions. The customer is usually charged interest. Although installment accounts receivable can have credit periods of more than one year, they are classified as current assets if the seller regularly offers customers such terms.

Decision Maker

Entrepreneur   As a small retailer, you are considering allowing customers to buy merchandise using credit cards. Until now, your store accepted only cash and checks. What analysis do you use to make this decision? ■   [Answer—p. 320]

Quick Check   Answers — p. 321

1. In recording credit card sales, when do you debit Accounts Receivable and when do you debit Cash?
2. A company accumulates sales receipts and remits them to the credit card company for payment. When are the credit card expenses recorded? When are these expenses incurred?

Valuing Accounts Receivable—Direct Write-Off Method

P1 Apply the direct write-off method to account for accounts receivable.

When a company directly grants credit to its customers, it expects that some customers will not pay what they promised. The accounts of these customers are *uncollectible accounts,* commonly called **bad debts.** The total amount of uncollectible accounts is an expense of selling on credit. Why do companies sell on credit if they expect some accounts to be uncollectible? The answer is that companies believe that granting credit will increase total sales and net income enough to offset bad debts. Companies use two methods to account for uncollectible accounts: (1) direct write-off method and (2) allowance method. We describe both.

Point: Managers realize that some portion of credit sales will be uncollectible, but which credit sales are uncollectible is unknown.

Recording and Writing Off Bad Debts   The **direct write-off method** of accounting for bad debts records the loss from an uncollectible account receivable when it is determined to be uncollectible. No attempt is made to predict bad debts expense. To illustrate, if TechCom determines on January 23 that it cannot collect $520 owed to it by its customer J. Kent, it recognizes the loss using the direct write-off method as follows:

Assets = Liabilities + Equity
−520   −520

Jan. 23	Bad Debts Expense	520	
	Accounts Receivable—J. Kent		520
	To write off an uncollectible account.		

The debit in this entry charges the uncollectible amount directly to the current period's Bad Debts Expense account. The credit removes its balance from the Accounts Receivable account in the general ledger (and its subsidiary ledger).

Point: If a customer fails to pay within the credit period, most companies send out repeated billings and make other efforts to collect.

Recovering a Bad Debt   Although uncommon, sometimes an account written off is later collected. This can be due to factors such as continual collection efforts or a customer's good fortune. If the account of J. Kent that was written off directly to Bad Debts Expense is later collected in full, the following two entries record this recovery:

Assets = Liabilities + Equity
+520   +520

Assets = Liabilities + Equity
+520
−520

Mar. 11	Accounts Receivable—J. Kent	520	
	Bad Debts Expense		520
	To reinstate account previously written off.		
Mar. 11	Cash	520	
	Accounts Receivable—J. Kent		520
	To record full payment of account.		

Assessing the Direct Write-Off Method   Examples of companies that use the direct write-off method include **Rand Medical Billing, Gateway Distributors, Microwave Satellite Technologies, First Industrial Realty, New Frontier Energy,** and **Sub Surface Waste Management.** The following disclosure by **Pharma-Bio Serv** is typical of the justification for this method: Bad debts are accounted for using the direct write-off method whereby an expense is recognized only when a specific account is determined to be uncollectible. The effect of using this method approximates that of the allowance method. Companies must weigh at least two accounting concepts when considering the use of the direct write-off method: the (1) matching principle and (2) materiality constraint.

Matching principle applied to bad debts.   The **matching (expense recognition) principle** requires expenses to be reported in the same accounting period as the sales they helped produce. This means that if extending credit to customers helped produce sales, the bad debts expense linked to those sales is matched and reported in the same period. The direct write-off method usually does *not* best match sales and expenses because bad debts expense is not recorded until an account becomes uncollectible, which often occurs in a period after that of the credit sale. To match bad debts expense with the sales it produces therefore requires a company to estimate future uncollectibles.

Point: Harley-Davidson reports $150 million of credit losses matched against $4,962 million of finance receivables.

Materiality constraint applied to bad debts.   The **materiality constraint** states that an amount can be ignored if its effect on the financial statements is unimportant to users' business decisions. The materiality constraint permits the use of the direct write-off method when bad debts expenses are very small in relation to a company's other financial statement items such as sales and net income.

Valuing Accounts Receivable—Allowance Method

The **allowance method** of accounting for bad debts matches the *estimated* loss from uncollectible accounts receivable against the sales they helped produce. We must use estimated losses because when sales occur, management does not know which customers will not pay their bills. This means that at the end of each period, the allowance method requires an estimate of the total bad debts expected to result from that period's sales. This method has two advantages over the direct write-off method: (1) it records estimated bad debts expense in the period when the related sales are recorded and (2) it reports accounts receivable on the balance sheet at the estimated amount of cash to be collected.

Point: Under direct write-off, expense is recorded each time an account is written off. Under the allowance method, expense is recorded with an adjusting entry equal to the total estimated uncollectibles for that period's sales.

Recording Bad Debts Expense   The allowance method estimates bad debts expense at the end of each accounting period and records it with an adjusting entry. TechCom, for instance, had credit sales of $300,000 during its first year of operations. At the end of the first year, $20,000 of credit sales remained uncollected. Based on the experience of similar businesses, TechCom estimated that $1,500 of its accounts receivable would be uncollectible. This estimated expense is recorded with the following adjusting entry:

	Bad Debts Expense Recognized in
Direct write-off method	The future when account is deemed uncollectible
Allowance method	Current period to yield realizable Accts. Rec. bal.

Dec. 31	Bad Debts Expense	1,500	
	Allowance for Doubtful Accounts		1,500
	To record estimated bad debts.		

Assets = Liabilities + Equity
−1,500   −1,500

The estimated Bad Debts Expense of $1,500 is reported on the income statement (as either a selling expense or an administrative expense) and offsets the $300,000 credit sales it helped produce. The **Allowance for Doubtful Accounts** is a contra asset account. A contra account is used instead of reducing accounts receivable directly because at the time of the adjusting entry, the company does not know which customers will not pay. After the bad debts adjusting entry is posted, TechCom's account balances (in T-account form) for Accounts Receivable and its Allowance for Doubtful Accounts are as shown in Exhibit 7.5.

Point: Credit approval is usually not assigned to the selling dept. because its goal is to increase sales, and it may approve customers at the cost of increased bad debts. Instead, approval is assigned to a separate credit-granting or administrative dept.

Accounts Receivable			**Allowance for Doubtful Accounts**		
Dec. 31	20,000			Dec. 31	1,500

EXHIBIT 7.5

General Ledger Entries after Bad Debts Adjusting Entry

The Allowance for Doubtful Accounts credit balance of $1,500 has the effect of reducing accounts receivable to its estimated realizable value. **Realizable value** refers to the expected proceeds from converting an asset into cash. Although credit customers owe $20,000 to TechCom, only $18,500 is expected to be realized in cash collections from these customers. In the balance sheet, the Allowance for Doubtful Accounts is subtracted from Accounts Receivable and is often reported as shown in Exhibit 7.6.

Point: Bad Debts Expense is also called *Uncollectible Accounts Expense.* The Allowance for Doubtful Accounts is also called *Allowance for Uncollectible Accounts.*

Current assets		
Accounts receivable	$20,000	
Less allowance for doubtful accounts	1,500	$18,500

EXHIBIT 7.6

Balance Sheet Presentation of the Allowance for Doubtful Accounts

Sometimes the Allowance for Doubtful Accounts is not reported separately. This alternative presentation is shown in Exhibit 7.7 (also see Appendix A).

Current assets	
Accounts receivable (net of $1,500 doubtful accounts)	$18,500

EXHIBIT 7.7

Alternative Presentation of the Allowance for Doubtful Accounts

Writing Off a Bad Debt   When specific accounts are identified as uncollectible, they are written off against the Allowance for Doubtful Accounts. To illustrate, TechCom decides that J. Kent's $520 account is uncollectible and makes the following entry to write it off.

Jan. 23	Allowance for Doubtful Accounts	520	
	Accounts Receivable—J. Kent		520
	To write off an uncollectible account.		

Assets = Liabilities + Equity
+520
−520

Point: The Bad Debts Expense account is not debited in the write-off entry because it was recorded in the period when sales occurred.

Posting this write-off entry to the Accounts Receivable account removes the amount of the bad debt from the general ledger (it is also posted to the accounts receivable subsidiary ledger). The general ledger accounts now appear as in Exhibit 7.8 (assuming no other transactions affecting these accounts).

EXHIBIT 7.8

General Ledger Entries after Write-Off

Accounts Receivable				Allowance for Doubtful Accounts			
Dec. 31	20,000						
		Jan. 23	520	Jan. 23	520	Dec. 31	1,500

Point: In posting a write-off, the ledger's Explanation column indicates the reason for this credit so it is not misinterpreted as payment in full.

The write-off does *not* affect the realizable value of accounts receivable as shown in Exhibit 7.9. Neither total assets nor net income is affected by the write-off of a specific account. Instead, both assets and net income are affected in the period when bad debts expense is predicted and recorded with an adjusting entry.

EXHIBIT 7.9

Realizable Value before and after Write-Off of a Bad Debt

	Before Write-Off	After Write-Off
Accounts receivable	$ 20,000	$ 19,480
Less allowance for doubtful accounts	1,500	980
Estimated realizable accounts receivable	$18,500	$18,500

Recovering a Bad Debt   When a customer fails to pay and the account is written off as uncollectible, his or her credit standing is jeopardized. To help restore credit standing, a customer sometimes volunteers to pay all or part of the amount owed. A company makes two entries when collecting an account previously written off by the allowance method. The first is to reverse the write-off and reinstate the customer's account. The second entry records the collection of the reinstated account. To illustrate, if on March 11 Kent pays in full his account previously written off, the entries are

Assets = Liabilities + Equity
+520
−520

Assets = Liabilities + Equity
+520
−520

Mar. 11	Accounts Receivable—J. Kent	520	
	Allowance for Doubtful Accounts		520
	To reinstate account previously written off.		
Mar. 11	Cash	520	
	Accounts Receivable—J. Kent		520
	To record full payment of account.		

Example: If TechCom used a collection agency and paid a 35% commission on $520 collected from Kent, how is this recorded? *Answer:*
Cash 338
Collection Expense 182
    Accts. Recble.—J. Kent 520

In this illustration, Kent paid the entire amount previously written off, but sometimes a customer pays only a portion of the amount owed. A question then arises as to whether the entire balance of the account or just the amount paid is returned to accounts receivable. This is a matter of judgment. If we believe this customer will later pay in full, we return the entire amount owed to accounts receivable, but if we expect no further collection, we return only the amount paid.

Decision Insight

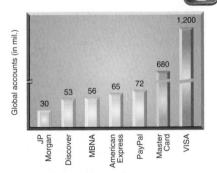

PayPal   PayPal is legally just a money transfer agent, but it is increasingly challenging big credit card brands—see chart. PayPal is successful because: (1) online credit card processing fees often exceed $0.15 per dollar, but PayPal's fees are under $0.10 per dollar. (2) PayPal's merchant fraud losses are under 0.2% of revenues, which compares to nearly 2% for online merchants using credit cards. ■

Estimating Bad Debts—Percent of Sales Method

P2   Apply the allowance method and estimate uncollectibles based on sales and accounts receivable.

The allowance method requires an estimate of bad debts expense to prepare an adjusting entry at the end of each accounting period. There are two common methods. One is based on the income statement relation between bad debts expense and sales. The second is based on the balance sheet relation between accounts receivable and the allowance for doubtful accounts.

The *percent of sales method,* also referred to as the *income statement method,* is based on the idea that a given percent of a company's credit sales for the period is uncollectible. To illustrate, assume that Musicland has credit sales of $400,000 in year 2013. Based on past experience, Musicland estimates 0.6% of credit sales to be uncollectible. This implies that Musicland expects $2,400 of bad debts expense from its sales (computed as $400,000 × 0.006). The adjusting entry to record this estimated expense is

Point: Focus is on *credit* sales because cash sales do not produce bad debts. If cash sales are a small or stable percent of credit sales, total sales can be used.

Dec. 31	Bad Debts Expense	2,400	
	Allowance for Doubtful Accounts		2,400
	To record estimated bad debts.		

Assets = Liabilities + Equity
−2,400   −2,400

The allowance account ending balance on the balance sheet for this method would rarely equal the bad debts expense on the income statement. This is so because unless a company is in its first period of operations, its allowance account has a zero balance only if the prior amounts written off as uncollectible *exactly* equal the prior estimated bad debts expenses. (When computing bad debts expense as a percent of sales, managers monitor and adjust the percent so it is not too high or too low.)

Point: When using the *percent of sales method* for estimating uncollectibles, the estimate of bad debts is the number used in the adjusting entry.

Estimating Bad Debts—Percent of Receivables Method

The *accounts receivable methods,* also referred to as *balance sheet methods,* use balance sheet relations to estimate bad debts—mainly the relation between accounts receivable and the allowance amount. The goal of the bad debts adjusting entry for these methods is to make the Allowance for Doubtful Accounts balance equal to the portion of accounts receivable that is estimated to be uncollectible. The estimated balance for the allowance account is obtained in one of two ways: (1) computing the percent uncollectible from the total accounts receivable or (2) aging accounts receivable.

The *percent of accounts receivable method* assumes that a given percent of a company's receivables is uncollectible. This percent is based on past experience and is impacted by current conditions such as economic trends and customer difficulties. The total dollar amount of all receivables is multiplied by this percent to get the estimated dollar amount of uncollectible accounts—reported in the balance sheet as the Allowance for Doubtful Accounts.

To illustrate, assume that Musicland has $50,000 of accounts receivable on December 31, 2013. Experience suggests 5% of its receivables is uncollectible. This means that *after* the adjusting entry is posted, we want the Allowance for Doubtful Accounts to show a $2,500 credit balance (5% of $50,000). We are also told that its beginning balance is $2,200, which is 5% of the $44,000 accounts receivable on December 31, 2012—see Exhibit 7.10.

Point: When using an accounts receivable method for estimating uncollectibles, the allowance account balance is adjusted to equal the estimate of uncollectibles.

EXHIBIT 7.10

Allowance for Doubtful Accounts after Bad Debts Adjusting Entry

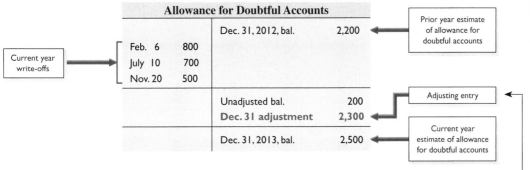

During 2013, accounts of customers are written off on February 6, July 10, and November 20. Thus, the account has a $200 credit balance *before* the December 31, 2013, adjustment. The adjusting entry to give the allowance account the estimated $2,500 balance is

Dec. 31	Bad Debts Expense	2,300	
	Allowance for Doubtful Accounts		2,300
	To record estimated bad debts.		

Assets = Liabilities + Equity
−2,300   −2,300

■ Decision Insight

Aging Pains Unlike wine, accounts receivable do not improve with age. Experience shows that the longer a receivable is past due, the lower is the likelihood of its collection. An *aging schedule* uses this knowledge to estimate bad debts. The chart here is from a survey that reported estimates of bad debts for receivables grouped by how long they were past their due dates. Each company sets its own estimates based on its customers and its experiences with those customers' payment patterns. ■

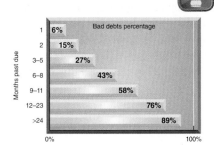

Estimating Bad Debts—Aging of Receivables Method

The **aging of accounts receivable** method uses both past and current receivables information to estimate the allowance amount. Specifically, each receivable is classified by how long it is past its due date. Then estimates of uncollectible amounts are made assuming that the longer an amount is past due, the more likely it is to be uncollectible. Classifications are often based on 30-day periods. After the amounts are classified (or aged), experience is used to estimate the percent of each uncollectible class. These percents are applied to the amounts in each class and then totaled to get the estimated balance of the Allowance for Doubtful Accounts. This computation is performed by setting up a schedule such as Exhibit 7.11.

EXHIBIT 7.11

Aging of Accounts Receivable

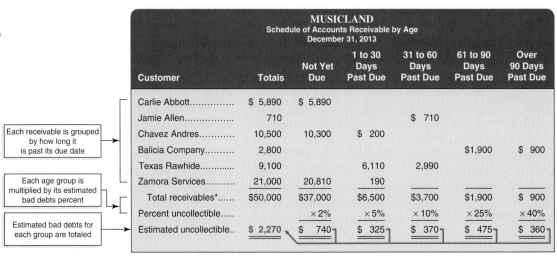

Customer	Totals	Not Yet Due	1 to 30 Days Past Due	31 to 60 Days Past Due	61 to 90 Days Past Due	Over 90 Days Past Due
Carlie Abbott...............	$ 5,890	$ 5,890				
Jamie Allen..................	710			$ 710		
Chavez Andres............	10,500	10,300	$ 200			
Balicia Company..........	2,800				$1,900	$ 900
Texas Rawhide.............	9,100		6,110	2,990		
Zamora Services..........	21,000	20,810	190			
Total receivables*......	$50,000	$37,000	$6,500	$3,700	$1,900	$ 900
Percent uncollectible.....		×2%	×5%	×10%	×25%	×40%
Estimated uncollectible..	$ 2,270	$ 740	$ 325	$ 370	$ 475	$ 360

MUSICLAND
Schedule of Accounts Receivable by Age
December 31, 2013

Each receivable is grouped by how long it is past its due date

Each age group is multiplied by its estimated bad debts percent

Estimated bad debts for each group are totaled

Exhibit 7.11 lists each customer's individual balances assigned to one of five classes based on its days past due. The amounts in each class are totaled and multiplied by the estimated percent of uncollectible accounts for each class. The percents used are regularly reviewed to reflect changes in the company and economy.

To explain, Musicland has $3,700 in accounts receivable that are 31 to 60 days past due. Its management estimates 10% of the amounts in this age class are uncollectible, or a total of $370 (computed as $3,700 × 10%). Similar analysis is done for each of the other four classes. The final total of $2,270 ($740 + $325 + 370 + $475 + $360) shown in the first column is the estimated balance for the Allowance for Doubtful Accounts. Exhibit 7.12 shows that since the allowance

EXHIBIT 7.12

Computation of the Required Adjustment for the Accounts Receivable Method

Unadjusted balance	$ 200 credit
Estimated balance	2,270 credit
Required adjustment	**$2,070 credit**

account has an unadjusted credit balance of $200, the required adjustment to the Allowance for Doubtful Accounts is $2,070. (We could also use a T-account for this analysis as shown in the margin.) This yields the following end-of-period adjusting entry:

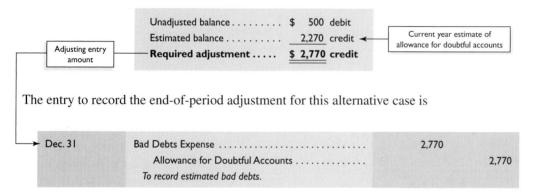

Alternatively, if the allowance account had an unadjusted *debit* balance of $500 (instead of the $200 credit balance), its required adjustment would be computed as follows. (Again, a T-account can be used for this analysis as shown in the margin.)

Point: A debit balance implies that write-offs for that period exceed the total allowance.

The entry to record the end-of-period adjustment for this alternative case is

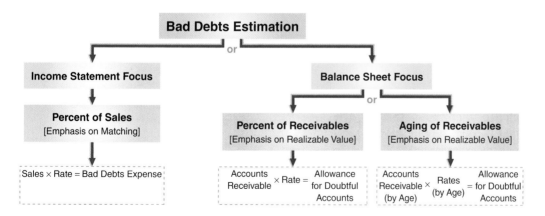

The aging of accounts receivable method is an examination of specific accounts and is usually the most reliable of the estimation methods.

Estimating Bad Debts—Summary of Methods   Exhibit 7.13 summarizes the principles guiding all three estimation methods and their focus of analysis. Percent of sales, with its income statement focus, does a good job at matching bad debts expense with sales. The accounts receivable methods, with their balance sheet focus, do a better job at reporting accounts receivable at realizable value.

EXHIBIT 7.13

Methods to Estimate Bad Debts

Bad Debts Estimation

or

Income Statement Focus

Balance Sheet Focus

or

Percent of Sales
[Emphasis on Matching]

Percent of Receivables
[Emphasis on Realizable Value]

Aging of Receivables
[Emphasis on Realizable Value]

Sales × Rate = Bad Debts Expense

Accounts Receivable × Rate = Allowance for Doubtful Accounts

Accounts Receivable (by Age) × Rates (by Age) = Allowance for Doubtful Accounts

■ **Decision** Maker

Labor Union Chief   One week prior to labor contract negotiations, financial statements are released showing no income growth. A 10% growth was predicted. Your analysis finds that the company increased its allowance for uncollectibles from 1.5% to 4.5% of receivables. Without this change, income would show a 9% growth. Does this analysis impact negotiations? ■   [Answer—p. 321]

3. Why must bad debts expense be estimated if such an estimate is possible?
4. What term describes the balance sheet valuation of Accounts Receivable less the Allowance for Doubtful Accounts?
5. Why is estimated bad debts expense credited to a contra account (Allowance for Doubtful Accounts) rather than to the Accounts Receivable account?
6. SnoBoard Company's year-end balance in its Allowance for Doubtful Accounts is a credit of $440. By aging accounts receivable, it estimates that $6,142 is uncollectible. Prepare SnoBoard's year-end adjusting entry for bad debts.
7. Record entries for these transactions assuming the allowance method is used:
   Jan. 10   The $300 account of customer Cool Jam is determined uncollectible.
   April 12   Cool Jam unexpectedly pays in full the account deemed uncollectible on Jan. 10.

NOTES RECEIVABLE

C2 Describe a note receivable, the computation of its maturity date, and the recording of its existence.

A **promissory note** is a written promise to pay a specified amount of money, usually with interest, either on demand or at a definite future date. Promissory notes are used in many transactions, including paying for products and services, and lending and borrowing money. Sellers sometimes ask for a note to replace an account receivable when a customer requests additional time to pay a past-due account. For legal reasons, sellers generally prefer to receive notes when the credit period is long and when the receivable is for a large amount. If a lawsuit is needed to collect from a customer, a note is the buyer's written acknowledgment of the debt, its amount, and its terms.

Exhibit 7.14 shows a simple promissory note dated July 10, 2013. For this note, Julia Browne promises to pay TechCom or to its order (according to TechCom's instructions) a specified amount of money ($1,000), called the **principal of a note,** at a definite future date (October 8, 2013). As the one who signed the note and promised to pay it at maturity, Browne is the **maker of the note.** As the person to whom the note is payable, TechCom is the **payee of the note.** To Browne, the note is a liability called a *note payable*. To TechCom, the same note is an asset called a *note receivable*. This note bears interest at 12%, as written on the note. **Interest** is the charge for using the money until its due date. To a borrower, interest is an expense. To a lender, it is revenue.

EXHIBIT 7.14

Promissory Note

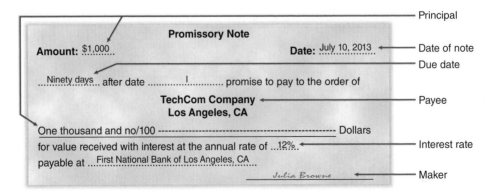

Computing Maturity and Interest

This section describes key computations for notes including the determination of maturity date, period covered, and interest computation.

Maturity Date and Period   The **maturity date of a note** is the day the note (principal and interest) must be repaid. The *period* of a note is the time from the note's (contract) date to its maturity date. Many notes mature in less than a full year, and the period they cover is often expressed in days. When the time of a note is expressed in days, its maturity date is the specified number of days after the note's date. As an example, a five-day note dated June 15 matures and is due on June 20. A 90-day note dated July 10 matures on October 8. This October 8 due date is computed as shown in Exhibit 7.15. The period of a note is sometimes expressed in months or years. When months are used, the note matures and is payable in the month of its maturity on the *same day of the month* as its original date. A nine-month note dated July 10, for instance, is payable on April 10. The same analysis applies when years are used.

Days in July	31
Minus the date of the note	10
Days remaining in July	21 ← July 11–31
Add days in August	31 ← Aug. 1–31
Add days in September	30 ← Sept. 1–30
Days to equal 90 days, or **maturity date of October 8**	8 ← Oct. 1–8
Period of the note in days	90

EXHIBIT 7.15

Maturity Date Computation

Interest Computation   *Interest* is the cost of borrowing money for the borrower or, alternatively, the profit from lending money for the lender. Unless otherwise stated, the rate of interest on a note is the rate charged for the use of the principal for one year. The formula for computing interest on a note is shown in Exhibit 7.16.

$$\begin{array}{ccccc} \text{Principal} \\ \text{of the note} \end{array} \times \begin{array}{c} \text{Annual} \\ \text{interest rate} \end{array} \times \begin{array}{c} \text{Time expressed} \\ \text{in fraction of year} \end{array} = \text{Interest}$$

EXHIBIT 7.16

Computation of Interest Formula

To simplify interest computations, a year is commonly treated as having 360 days (called the *banker's rule* in the business world and widely used in commercial transactions). **We treat a year as having 360 days for interest computations in the examples and assignments.** Using the promissory note in Exhibit 7.14 where we have a 90-day, 12%, $1,000 note, the total interest is computed as follows:

$$\$1,000 \times 12\% \times \frac{90}{360} = \$1,000 \times 0.12 \times 0.25 = \$30$$

Point: If the *banker's rule* is not followed, interest is computed as:

$1,000 × 12% × 90/365 = 29.589041

The *banker's rule* would yield $30, which is easier to account for than $29.589041.

Recognizing Notes Receivable

Notes receivable are usually recorded in a single Notes Receivable account to simplify record-keeping. The original notes are kept on file, including information on the maker, rate of interest, and due date. (When a company holds a large number of notes, it sometimes sets up a controlling account and a subsidiary ledger for notes. This is similar to the handling of accounts receivable.) To illustrate the recording for the receipt of a note, we use the $1,000, 90-day, 12% promissory note in Exhibit 7.14. TechCom received this note at the time of a product sale to Julia Browne. This transaction is recorded as follows:

July 10*	Notes Receivable	1,000	
	Sales		1,000
	Sold goods in exchange for a 90-day, 12% note.		

Assets = Liabilities + Equity
+1,000   +1,000

* We omit the entry to Dr. Cost of Sales and Cr. Merchandise Inventory to focus on sales and receivables.

When a seller accepts a note from an overdue customer as a way to grant a time extension on a past-due account receivable, it will often collect part of the past-due balance in cash. This partial payment forces a concession from the customer, reduces the customer's debt (and the seller's risk), and produces a note for a smaller amount. To illustrate, assume that Tech-Com agreed to accept $232 in cash along with a $600, 60-day, 15% note from Jo Cook to

Point: Notes receivable often are a major part of a company's assets. Likewise, notes payable often are a large part of a company's liabilities.

settle her $832 past-due account. TechCom made the following entry to record receipt of this cash and note:

Assets = Liabilities + Equity
+232
+600
−832

Oct. 5	Cash	232	
	Notes Receivable	600	
	Accounts Receivable—J. Cook		832
	Received cash and note to settle account.		

Valuing and Settling Notes

P3 Record the honoring and dishonoring of a note and adjustments for interest.

Recording an Honored Note The principal and interest of a note are due on its maturity date. The maker of the note usually *honors* the note and pays it in full. To illustrate, when J. Cook pays the note above on its due date, TechCom records it as follows:

Assets = Liabilities + Equity
+615   +15
−600

Dec. 4	Cash	615	
	Notes Receivable		600
	Interest Revenue		15
	Collect note with interest of $600 × 15% × 60/360.		

Interest Revenue, also called *Interest Earned,* is reported on the income statement.

Recording a Dishonored Note When a note's maker is unable or refuses to pay at maturity, the note is *dishonored.* The act of dishonoring a note does not relieve the maker of the obligation to pay. The payee should use every legitimate means to collect. How do companies report this event? The balance of the Notes Receivable account should include only those notes that have not matured. Thus, when a note is dishonored, we remove the amount of this note from the Notes Receivable account and charge it back to an account receivable from its maker. To illustrate, TechCom holds an $800, 12%, 60-day note of Greg Hart. At maturity, Hart dishonors the note. TechCom records this dishonoring of the note as follows:

Point: When posting a dishonored note to a customer's account, an explanation is included so as not to misinterpret the debit as a sale on account.

Assets = Liabilities + Equity
+816   +16
−800

Oct. 14	Accounts Receivable—G. Hart	816	
	Interest Revenue		16
	Notes Receivable		800
	To charge account of G. Hart for a dishonored note and interest of $800 × 12% × 60/360.		

Point: Reporting the details of notes is consistent with the **full disclosure principle,** which requires financial statements (including footnotes) to report all relevant information.

Charging a dishonored note back to the account of its maker serves two purposes. First, it removes the amount of the note from the Notes Receivable account and records the dishonored note in the maker's account. Second, and more important, if the maker of the dishonored note applies for credit in the future, his or her account will reveal all past dealings, including the dishonored note. Restoring the account also reminds the company to continue collection efforts from Hart for both principal and interest. The entry records the full amount, including interest, to ensure that it is included in collection efforts.

Recording End-of-Period Interest Adjustment When notes receivable are outstanding at the end of a period, any accrued interest earned is computed and recorded. To illustrate, on December 16, TechCom accepts a $3,000, 60-day, 12% note from a customer in granting an extension on a past-due account. When TechCom's accounting period ends on December 31, $15 of interest has accrued on this note ($3,000 × 12% × 15/360). The following adjusting entry records this revenue:

Assets = Liabilities + Equity
+15   +15

Dec. 31	Interest Receivable	15	
	Interest Revenue		15
	To record accrued interest earned.		

Interest Revenue appears on the income statement, and Interest Receivable appears on the balance sheet as a current asset. When the December 16 note is collected on February 14, TechCom's entry to record the cash receipt is

Feb. 14	Cash	3,060	
	Interest Revenue		45
	Interest Receivable		15
	Notes Receivable		3,000
	Received payment of note and its interest.		

Assets = Liabilities + Equity
+3,060   +45
−15
−3,000

Total interest earned on the 60-day note is $60. The $15 credit to Interest Receivable on February 14 reflects the collection of the interest accrued from the December 31 adjusting entry. The $45 interest earned reflects TechCom's revenue from holding the note from January 1 to February 14 of the current period.

Quick Check

Answers — p. 321

8. Irwin purchases $7,000 of merchandise from Stamford on December 16, 2013. Stamford accepts Irwin's $7,000, 90-day, 12% note as payment. Stamford's accounting period ends on December 31, and it does not make reversing entries. Prepare entries for Stamford on December 16, 2013, and December 31, 2013.

9. Using the information in Quick Check 8, prepare Stamford's March 16, 2014, entry if Irwin dishonors the note.

10. What is the maturity date of a 60-day note signed by the maker on September 15?

DISPOSAL OF RECEIVABLES

Companies can convert receivables to cash before they are due. Reasons for this include the need for cash or the desire not to be involved in collection activities. Converting receivables is usually done either by (1) selling them or (2) using them as security for a loan. A recent survey shows that about 20% of companies obtain cash from either selling receivables or pledging them as security. In some industries such as textiles, apparel and furniture, this is common practice.

C3 Explain how receivables can be converted to cash before maturity.

Selling Receivables

A company can sell all or a portion of its receivables to a finance company or bank. The buyer, called a *factor,* charges the seller a *factoring fee* and then the buyer takes ownership of the receivables and receives cash when they come due. By incurring a factoring fee, the seller receives cash earlier and can pass the risk of bad debts to the factor. The seller can also choose to avoid costs of billing and accounting for the receivables. To illustrate, if TechCom sells $20,000 of its accounts receivable and is charged a 4% factoring fee, it records this sale as follows:

Global: Firms in export sales increasingly sell their receivables to factors.

Aug. 15	Cash	19,200	
	Factoring Fee Expense	800	
	Accounts Receivable		20,000
	Sold accounts receivable for cash, less 4% fee.		

Assets = Liabilities + Equity
+19,200   −800
−20,000

The accounting for sales of notes receivable is similar to that for accounts receivable. The detailed entries are covered in advanced courses. Remember: When factoring receivables, the company selling receivables always receives less cash than the amount of receivables sold due to factoring fees.

Pledging Receivables

A company can raise cash by borrowing money and *pledging* its receivables as security for the loan. Pledging receivables does not transfer the risk of bad debts to the lender because the borrower retains ownership of the receivables. If the borrower defaults on the loan, the lender has a right to be paid from the cash receipts of the receivable when collected. To illustrate, when TechCom borrows $35,000 and pledges its receivables as security, it records this transaction as follows:

Assets = Liabilities + Equity
+35,000   +35,000

Aug. 20	Cash	35,000	
	Notes Payable		35,000
	Borrowed money with a note secured by pledging		
	receivables.		

Since pledged receivables are committed as security for a specific loan, the borrower's financial statements disclose the pledging of them. TechCom, for instance, includes the following note with its statements: **Accounts receivable of $40,000 are pledged as security for a $35,000 note payable.** Inventory and accounts receivable are two assets commonly demanded by bankers as collateral when making business loans.

Decision Maker

Analyst/Auditor: What's the Proper Allowance? You are reviewing accounts receivable. Over the past five years, the allowance account as a percentage of gross accounts receivable shows a steady downward trend. What does this finding suggest? ■   [Answer—p. 321]

GLOBAL VIEW

This section discusses similarities and differences between U.S. GAAP and IFRS regarding the recognition, measurement, and disposition of receivables.

Recognition of Receivables   Both U.S. GAAP and IFRS have similar asset criteria that apply to recognition of receivables. Further, receivables that arise from revenue-generating activities are subject to broadly similar criteria for U.S. GAAP and IFRS. Specifically, both refer to the realization principle and an earnings process. The realization principle under U.S. GAAP implies an *arm's-length transaction* occurs, whereas under IFRS this notion is applied in terms of reliable measurement and likelihood of economic benefits. Regarding U.S. GAAP's reference to an earnings process, IFRS instead refers to risk transfer and ownership reward. While these criteria are broadly similar, differences do exist, and they arise mainly from industry-specific guidance under U.S. GAAP, which is very limited under IFRS.

Valuation of Receivables   Both U.S. GAAP and IFRS require that receivables be reported net of estimated uncollectibles. Further, both systems require that the expense for estimated uncollectibles be recorded in the same period when any revenues from those receivables are recorded. This means that for accounts receivable, both U.S. GAAP and IFRS require the allowance method for uncollectibles (unless uncollectibles are immaterial). The allowance method using percent of sales, percent of receivables, and aging was explained in this chapter. Nokia reports the following for its allowance for uncollectibles:

NOKIA

> Management specifically analyzes accounts receivables and historical bad debt, customer concentrations, customer creditworthiness, current economic trends and changes in our customer payment terms when evaluating the adequacy of the allowance.

Disposition of Receivables   Both U.S. GAAP and IFRS apply broadly similar rules in recording dispositions of receivables. Those rules are discussed in this chapter. We should be aware of an important difference in terminology. Companies reporting under U.S. GAAP disclose Bad Debts Expense, which is also referred to as Provision for Bad Debts or the Provision for Uncollectible Accounts. For U.S. GAAP, *provision* here refers to expense. Under IFRS, the term *provision* usually refers to a liability whose amount or timing (or both) is uncertain.

Accounts Receivable Turnover   **Decision Analysis**

For a company selling on credit, we want to assess both the quality and liquidity of its accounts receivable. *Quality* of receivables refers to the likelihood of collection without loss. Experience shows that the longer receivables are outstanding beyond their due date, the lower the likelihood of collection. *Liquidity* of receivables refers to the speed of collection. **Accounts receivable turnover** is a measure of both the quality and liquidity of accounts receivable. It indicates how often, on average, receivables are received and collected during the period. The formula for this ratio is shown in Exhibit 7.17.

| A1 | Compute accounts receivable turnover and use it to help assess financial condition. |

$$\text{Accounts receivable turnover} = \frac{\text{Net sales}}{\text{Average accounts receivable, net}}$$

EXHIBIT 7.17

Accounts Receivable Turnover

We prefer to use net *credit* sales in the numerator because cash sales do not create receivables. However, since financial statements rarely report net credit sales, our analysis uses net sales. The denominator is the *average* accounts receivable balance, computed as (Beginning balance + Ending balance) ÷ 2. TechCom has an accounts receivable turnover of 5.1. This indicates its average accounts receivable balance is converted into cash 5.1 times during the period. Exhibit 7.18 shows graphically this turnover activity for TechCom.

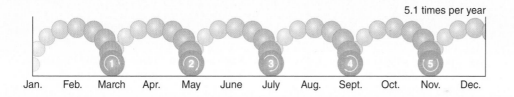

5.1 times per year

Jan.   Feb.   March   Apr.   May   June   July   Aug.   Sept.   Oct.   Nov.   Dec.

EXHIBIT 7.18

Rate of Accounts Receivable Turnover for TechCom

Accounts receivable turnover also reflects how well management is doing in granting credit to customers in a desire to increase sales. A high turnover in comparison with competitors suggests that management should consider using more liberal credit terms to increase sales. A low turnover suggests management should consider stricter credit terms and more aggressive collection efforts to avoid having its resources tied up in accounts receivable.

To illustrate, we take fiscal year data from two competitors: **Dell** and **Apple**. Exhibit 7.19 shows accounts receivable turnover for both companies.

Point: Credit risk ratio is computed by dividing the Allowance for Doubtful Accounts by Accounts Receivable. The higher this ratio, the higher is credit risk.

Company	Figure ($ millions)	2011	2010	2009	2008
Dell	Net sales	$ 61,494	$52,902	$61,101	$61,133
	Average accounts receivable, net	$ 6,165	$ 5,284	$ 5,346	$ 5,292
	Accounts receivable turnover	10.0	10.0	11.4	11.6
Apple	Net sales	$108,249	$65,225	$42,905	$37,491
	Average accounts receivable, net	$ 5,440	$ 4,436	$ 2,892	$ 2,030
	Accounts receivable turnover	19.9	14.7	14.8	18.5

EXHIBIT 7.19

Analysis Using Accounts Receivable Turnover

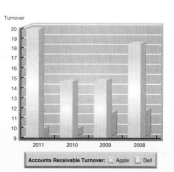

Dell's 2011 turnover is 10.0, computed as $61,494/$6,165 ($ millions). This means that Dell's average accounts receivable balance was converted into cash 10.0 times in 2011. Its turnover was flat in 2011, but it had been slightly declining in recent years. Apple's turnover exceeds that for Dell in each of the past 4 years. Is either company's turnover too high? Since sales are stable or markedly growing over this time period, each company's turnover rate does not appear to be too high. Instead, both Dell and Apple seem to be doing well in managing receivables. This is especially true given the recent recessionary period. Turnover for competitors is generally in the range of 7 to 12 for this same period.[1]

Decision Maker

Family Physician   Your medical practice is barely profitable, so you hire a health care analyst. The analyst highlights several points including the following: *"Accounts receivable turnover is too low. Tighter credit policies are recommended along with discontinuing service to those most delayed in payments."* How do you interpret these recommendations? What actions do you take? ■   [Answer—p. 321]

DEMONSTRATION PROBLEM

Clayco Company completes the following selected transactions during year 2013.

July 14   Writes off a $750 account receivable arising from a sale to Briggs Company that dates to 10 months ago. (Clayco Company uses the allowance method.)

   30   Clayco Company receives a $1,000, 90-day, 10% note in exchange for merchandise sold to Sumrell Company (the merchandise cost $600).

Aug. 15   Receives $2,000 cash plus a $10,000 note from JT Co. in exchange for merchandise that sells for $12,000 (its cost is $8,000). The note is dated August 15, bears 12% interest, and matures in 120 days.

Nov. 1   Completed a $200 credit card sale with a 4% fee (the cost of sales is $150). The cash is received immediately from the credit card company.

   3   Sumrell Company refuses to pay the note that was due to Clayco Company on October 28. Prepare the journal entry to charge the dishonored note plus accrued interest to Sumrell Company's accounts receivable.

   5   Completed a $500 credit card sale with a 5% fee (the cost of sales is $300). The payment from the credit card company is received on Nov. 9.

   15   Received the full amount of $750 from Briggs Company that was previously written off on July 14. Record the bad debts recovery.

Dec. 13   Received payment of principal plus interest from JT for the August 15 note.

Required

1. Prepare journal entries to record these transactions on Clayco Company's books.

2. Prepare an adjusting journal entry as of December 31, 2013, assuming the following:

   a. Bad debts are estimated to be $20,400 by aging accounts receivable. The unadjusted balance of the Allowance for Doubtful Accounts is $1,000 debit.

   b. Alternatively, assume that bad debts are estimated using the percent of sales method. The Allowance for Doubtful Accounts had a $1,000 debit balance before adjustment, and the company estimates bad debts to be 1% of its credit sales of $2,000,000.

PLANNING THE SOLUTION

● Examine each transaction to determine the accounts affected, and then record the entries.

● For the year-end adjustment, record the bad debts expense for the two approaches.

---

[1] As an estimate of *average days' sales uncollected,* we compute how many days (*on average*) it takes to collect receivables as follows: 365 days ÷ accounts receivable turnover. An increase in this *average collection period* can signal a decline in customers' financial condition.

SOLUTION TO DEMONSTRATION PROBLEM

1.

July 14	Allowance for Doubtful Accounts	750	
	Accounts Receivable—Briggs Co.		750
	Wrote off an uncollectible account.		
July 30	Notes Receivable—Sumrell Co.	1,000	
	Sales		1,000
	Sold merchandise for a 90-day, 10% note.		
July 30	Cost of Goods Sold	600	
	Merchandise Inventory		600
	To record the cost of July 30 sale.		
Aug. 15	Cash	2,000	
	Notes Receivable—JT Co.	10,000	
	Sales		12,000
	Sold merchandise to customer for $2,000 cash and $10,000 note.		
Aug. 15	Cost of Goods Sold	8,000	
	Merchandise Inventory		8,000
	To record the cost of Aug. 15 sale.		
Nov. 1	Cash	192	
	Credit Card Expense	8	
	Sales		200
	To record credit card sale less a 4% credit card expense.		
Nov. 1	Cost of Goods Sold	150	
	Merchandise Inventory		150
	To record the cost of Nov. 1 sale.		
Nov. 3	Accounts Receivable—Sumrell Co.	1,025	
	Interest Revenue		25
	Notes Receivable—Sumrell Co.		1,000
	To charge account of Sumrell Company for a $1,000 dishonored note and interest of $1,000 × 10% × 90/360.		
Nov. 5	Accounts Receivable—Credit Card Co.	475	
	Credit Card Expense	25	
	Sales		500
	To record credit card sale less a 5% credit card expense.		
Nov. 5	Cost of Goods Sold	300	
	Merchandise Inventory		300
	To record the cost of Nov. 5 sale.		
Nov. 9	Cash	475	
	Accounts Receivable—Credit Card Co.		475
	To record cash receipt from Nov. 5 sale.		
Nov. 15	Accounts Receivable—Briggs Co.	750	
	Allowance for Doubtful Accounts		750
	To reinstate the account of Briggs Company previously written off.		
Nov. 15	Cash	750	
	Accounts Receivable—Briggs Co.		750
	Cash received in full payment of account.		
Dec. 13	Cash	10,400	
	Interest Revenue		400
	Note Receivable—JT Co.		10,000
	Collect note with interest of $10,000 × 12% × 120/360.		

2a. Aging of accounts receivable method.

Dec. 31	Bad Debts Expense	21,400	
	Allowance for Doubtful Accounts		21,400
	To adjust allowance account from a $1,000		
	debit balance to a $20,400 credit balance.		

2b. Percent of sales method.*

Dec. 31	Bad Debts Expense	20,000	
	Allowance for Doubtful Accounts		20,000
	To provide for bad debts as 1% × $2,000,000		
	in credit sales.		

* For the income statement approach, which requires estimating bad debts as a percent of sales or credit sales, the Allowance account balance is *not* considered when making the adjusting entry.

Summary

C1 **Describe accounts receivable and how they occur and are recorded.** Accounts receivable are amounts due from customers for credit sales. A subsidiary ledger lists amounts owed by each customer. Credit sales arise from at least two sources: (1) sales on credit and (2) credit card sales. *Sales on credit* refers to a company's granting credit directly to customers. Credit card sales involve customers' use of third-party credit cards.

C2 **Describe a note receivable, the computation of its maturity date, and the recording of its existence.** A note receivable is a written promise to pay a specified amount of money at a definite future date. The maturity date is the day the note (principal and interest) must be repaid. Interest rates are normally stated in annual terms. The amount of interest on the note is computed by expressing time as a fraction of one year and multiplying the note's principal by this fraction and the annual interest rate. A note received is recorded at its principal amount by debiting the Notes Receivable account. The credit amount is to the asset, product, or service provided in return for the note.

C3 **Explain how receivables can be converted to cash before maturity.** Receivables can be converted to cash before maturity in three ways. First, a company can sell accounts receivable to a factor, who charges a factoring fee. Second, a company can borrow money by signing a note payable that is secured by pledging the accounts receivable. Third, notes receivable can be discounted at (sold to) a financial institution.

A1 **Compute accounts receivable turnover and use it to help assess financial condition.** Accounts receivable turnover is a measure of both the quality and liquidity of accounts receivable.

The accounts receivable turnover measure indicates how often, on average, receivables are received and collected during the period. Accounts receivable turnover is computed as net sales divided by average accounts receivable.

P1 **Apply the direct write-off method to account for accounts receivable.** The direct write-off method charges Bad Debts Expense when accounts are written off as uncollectible. This method is acceptable only when the amount of bad debts expense is immaterial.

P2 **Apply the allowance method and estimate uncollectibles based on sales and accounts receivable.** Under the allowance method, bad debts expense is recorded with an adjustment at the end of each accounting period that debits the Bad Debts Expense account and credits the Allowance for Doubtful Accounts. The uncollectible accounts are later written off with a debit to the Allowance for Doubtful Accounts. Uncollectibles are estimated by focusing on either (1) the income statement relation between bad debts expense and credit sales or (2) the balance sheet relation between accounts receivable and the allowance for doubtful accounts. The first approach emphasizes the matching principle using the income statement. The second approach emphasizes realizable value of accounts receivable using the balance sheet.

P3 **Record the honoring and dishonoring of a note and adjustments for interest.** When a note is honored, the payee debits the money received and credits both Notes Receivable and Interest Revenue. Dishonored notes are credited to Notes Receivable and debited to Accounts Receivable (to the account of the maker in an attempt to collect), and Interest Revenue is recorded for interest earned for the time the note is held.

Guidance Answers to Decision Maker and Decision Ethics

Entrepreneur Analysis of credit card sales should weigh the benefits against the costs. The primary benefit is the potential to increase sales by attracting customers who prefer the convenience of credit cards. The primary cost is the fee charged by the credit card company for providing this service. Analysis should therefore estimate the expected increase in dollar sales from allowing credit card sales and then subtract (1) the normal costs and expenses and (2) the credit card fees associated with this expected increase in dollar sales. If your analysis shows an increase in profit from allowing credit card sales, your store should probably accept them.

Labor Union Chief   Yes, this information is likely to impact your negotiations. The obvious question is why the company markedly increased this allowance. The large increase in this allowance means a substantial increase in bad debts expense *and* a decrease in earnings. This change (coming immediately prior to labor contract discussions) also raises concerns since it reduces the union's bargaining power for increased compensation. You want to ask management for supporting documentation justifying this increase. You also want data for two or three prior years and similar data from competitors. These data should give you some sense of whether the change in the allowance for uncollectibles is justified.

Analyst/Auditor   The downward trend suggests the company is reducing the relative amount charged to bad debts expense each year. This may reflect the company's desire to increase net income. On the other hand, it might be that collections have improved and the lower provision for bad debts is justified. If this is not the case, the lower allowances might be insufficient for bad debts.

Family Physician   The recommendations are twofold. First, the analyst suggests more stringent screening of patients' credit standing. Second, the analyst suggests dropping patients who are most overdue in payments. You are likely bothered by both suggestions. They are probably financially wise recommendations, but you are troubled by eliminating services to those less able to pay. One alternative is to follow the recommendations while implementing a care program directed at patients less able to pay for services. This allows you to continue services to patients less able to pay and lets you discontinue services to patients able but unwilling to pay.

Guidance Answers to Quick Checks

1. If cash is immediately received when credit card sales receipts are deposited, the company debits Cash at the time of sale. If the company does not receive payment until after it submits receipts to the credit card company, it debits Accounts Receivable at the time of sale. (Cash is later debited when payment is received from the credit card company.)

2. Credit card expenses are usually *recorded* and *incurred* at the time of their related sales, not when cash is received from the credit card company.

3. If possible, bad debts expense must be matched with the sales that gave rise to the accounts receivable. This requires that companies estimate future bad debts at the end of each period before they learn which accounts are uncollectible.

4. Realizable value (also called *net realizable value*).

5. The estimated amount of bad debts expense cannot be credited to the Accounts Receivable account because the specific customer accounts that will prove uncollectible cannot yet be identified and removed from the accounts receivable subsidiary ledger. Moreover, if only the Accounts Receivable account is credited, its balance would not equal the sum of its subsidiary account balances.

6.

| Dec. 31 | Bad Debts Expense | 5,702 | |
| | Allowance for Doubtful Accounts | | 5,702 |

7.

Jan. 10	Allowance for Doubtful Accounts	300	
	Accounts Receivable—Cool Jam		300
Apr. 12	Accounts Receivable—Cool Jam	300	
	Allowance for Doubtful Accounts		300
Apr. 12	Cash	300	
	Accounts Receivable—Cool Jam		300

8.

Dec. 16	Note Receivable—Irwin	7,000	
	Sales		7,000
Dec. 31	Interest Receivable	35	
	Interest Revenue		35
	($7,000 × 12% × 15/360)		

9.

Mar. 16	Accounts Receivable—Irwin	7,210	
	Interest Revenue		175
	Interest Receivable		35
	Notes Receivable—Irwin		7,000

10. The note matures on November 14, computed as follows:

Days in September	30
Minus the date of the note	(15)
Days remaining in September	15
Add days in October	31
Add days in November to equal 60 days	14
Period of the note in days	60

Key Terms

Accounts receivable (p. 302)

Accounts receivable turnover (p. 317)

Aging of accounts receivable (p. 310)

Allowance for Doubtful Accounts (p. 307)

Allowance method (p. 307)

Bad debts (p. 306)

Direct write-off method (p. 306)
Interest (p. 312)
Maker of the note (p. 312)
Matching (expense recognition) principle (p. 306)

Materiality constraint (p. 306)
Maturity date of a note (p. 312)
Payee of the note (p. 312)
Principal of a note (p. 312)

Promissory note (or **note**) (p. 312)
Realizable value (p. 307)

Multiple Choice Quiz
Answers on p. 333
mhhe.com/wildFAF4e

Additional Quiz Questions are available at the book's Website.

1. A company's Accounts Receivable balance at its December 31 year-end is $125,650, and its Allowance for Doubtful Accounts has a credit balance of $328 before year-end adjustment. Its net sales are $572,300. It estimates that 4% of outstanding accounts receivable are uncollectible. What amount of Bad Debts Expense is recorded at December 31?
   a. $5,354
   b. $328
   c. $5,026
   d. $4,698
   e. $34,338

2. A company's Accounts Receivable balance at its December 31 year-end is $489,300, and its Allowance for Doubtful Accounts has a debit balance of $554 before year-end adjustment. Its net sales are $1,300,000. It estimates that 6% of outstanding accounts receivable are uncollectible. What amount of Bad Debts Expense is recorded at December 31?
   a. $29,912
   b. $28,804
   c. $78,000
   d. $29,358
   e. $554

3. Total interest to be earned on a $7,500, 5%, 90-day note is
   a. $93.75
   b. $375.00
   c. $1,125.00
   d. $31.25
   e. $125.00

4. A company receives a $9,000, 8%, 60-day note. The maturity value of the note is
   a. $120
   b. $9,000
   c. $9,120
   d. $720
   e. $9,720

5. A company has net sales of $489,600 and average accounts receivable of $40,800. What is its accounts receivable turnover?
   a. 0.08
   b. 30.41
   c. 1,341.00
   d. 12.00
   e. 111.78

Icon denotes assignments that involve decision making.

Discussion Questions

1. How do sellers benefit from allowing their customers to use credit cards?

2. Why does the direct write-off method of accounting for bad debts usually fail to match revenues and expenses?

3. Explain the accounting constraint of materiality.

4. Why might a business prefer a note receivable to an account receivable?

5. Explain why writing off a bad debt against the Allowance for Doubtful Accounts does not reduce the estimated realizable value of a company's accounts receivable.

6. Why does the Bad Debts Expense account usually not have the same adjusted balance as the Allowance for Doubtful Accounts?

7. Refer to the financial statements and notes of **Polaris** in Appendix A. In its presentation of accounts receivable on the balance sheet, how does it title

accounts receivable? What does it report for its allowance as of December 31, 2011?

8. Refer to the balance sheet of **Arctic Cat** in Appendix A. Does it use the direct write-off method or allowance method in accounting for its accounts receivable? What is the realizable value of its receivable's balance as of March 31, 2011?

9. Refer to the financial statements of **KTM** in Appendix A. What does KTM title its accounts receivable on its consolidated balance sheet? What are KTM's accounts receivable at December 31, 2011?

10. Refer to the December 31, 2011, financial statements of **Piaggio** in Appendix A. What does it title its accounts receivable on its statement of financial position? Does Piaggio report its accounts receivable as current or non-current asset?

The accounting for plant assets reflects these two features. Since plant assets are used in operations, we try to match their costs against the revenues they generate. Also, since their useful lives extend over more than one period, our matching of costs and revenues must extend over several periods. Specifically, we value plant assets (balance sheet effect) and then, for many of them, we allocate their costs to periods benefiting from their use (income statement effect). An important exception is land; land cost is not allocated to expense when we expect it to have an indefinite life.

Exhibit 8.2 shows four main issues in accounting for plant assets: (1) computing the costs of plant assets, (2) allocating the costs of most plant assets (less any salvage amounts) against revenues for the periods they benefit, (3) accounting for expenditures such as repairs and improvements to plant assets, and (4) recording the disposal of plant assets. The following sections discuss these issues.

Point: It can help to view plant assets as prepaid expenses that benefit several future accounting periods.

EXHIBIT 8.2

Issues in Accounting for
Plant Assets

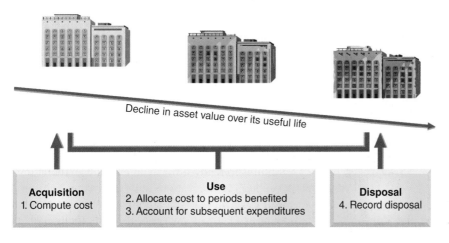

Decline in asset value over its useful life

| **Acquisition** | **Use** | **Disposal** |
| 1. Compute cost | 2. Allocate cost to periods benefited
3. Account for subsequent expenditures | 4. Record disposal |

COST DETERMINATION

Plant assets are recorded at cost when acquired. This is consistent with the *cost principle.* **Cost** includes all normal and reasonable expenditures necessary to get the asset in place and ready for its intended use. The cost of a factory machine, for instance, includes its invoice cost less any cash discount for early payment, plus any necessary freight, unpacking, assembling, installing, and testing costs. Examples are the costs of building a base or foundation for a machine, providing electrical hookups, and testing the asset before using it in operations.

C1 Explain the cost principle for computing the cost of plant assets.

To be recorded as part of the cost of a plant asset, an expenditure must be normal, reasonable, and necessary in preparing it for its intended use. If an asset is damaged during unpacking, the repairs are not added to its cost. Instead, they are charged to an expense account. Nor is a paid traffic fine for moving heavy machinery on city streets without a proper permit part of the machinery's cost; but payment for a proper permit is included in the cost of machinery. Charges are sometimes incurred to modify or customize a new plant asset. These charges are added to the asset's cost. We explain in this section how to determine the cost of plant assets for each of its four major classes.

Land

When land is purchased for a building site, its cost includes the total amount paid for the land, including any real estate commissions, title insurance fees, legal fees, and any accrued property taxes paid by the purchaser. Payments for surveying, clearing, grading, and draining also are included in the cost of land. Other costs include government assessments, whether incurred at the time of purchase or later, for items such as public roadways, sewers, and sidewalks. These assessments are included because they permanently add to the land's value. Land purchased as a building site sometimes includes structures that must be removed. In such cases, the total purchase price is charged to the Land account as is the cost of removing the structures, less any amounts recovered through sale of salvaged materials. To illustrate, assume that **Starbucks** paid $167,000 cash to acquire land for a retail store. This land had an old service garage that was removed at a net cost of

EXHIBIT 8.3

Computing Cost of Land

Cash price of land	$ 167,000
Net cost of garage removal	13,000
Closing costs	10,000
Cost of land	**$190,000**

$13,000 ($15,000 in costs less $2,000 proceeds from salvaged materials). Additional closing costs total $10,000, consisting of brokerage fees ($8,000), legal fees ($1,500), and title costs ($500). The cost of this land to Starbucks is $190,000 and is computed as shown in Exhibit 8.3.

Land Improvements

Land has an indefinite (unlimited) life and is not usually used up over time. **Land improvements** such as parking lot surfaces, driveways, fences, shrubs, and lighting systems, however, have limited useful lives and are used up. While the costs of these improvements increase the usefulness of the land, they are charged to a separate Land Improvement account so that their costs can be allocated to the periods they benefit.

Buildings

A Building account is charged for the costs of purchasing or constructing a building that is used in operations. When purchased, a building's costs usually include its purchase price, brokerage

fees, taxes, title fees, and attorney fees. Its costs also include all expenditures to ready it for its intended use, including any necessary repairs or renovations such as wiring, lighting, flooring, and wall coverings. When a company constructs a building or any plant asset for its own use, its costs include materials and labor plus a reasonable amount of indirect overhead cost. Overhead includes the costs of items such as heat, lighting, power, and depreciation on machinery used to construct the asset. Costs of construction also include design fees, building permits, and insurance during construction. However, costs such as insurance to cover the asset *after* it is placed in use are operating expenses.

Machinery and Equipment

The costs of machinery and equipment consist of all costs normal and necessary to purchase them and prepare them for their intended use. These include the purchase price, taxes, transportation charges, insurance while in transit, and the installing, assembling, and testing of the machinery and equipment.

Lump-Sum Purchase

Example: If appraised values in Exhibit 8.4 are land, $24,000; land improvements, $12,000; and building, $84,000, what cost is assigned to the building? *Answer:*
(1) $24,000 + $12,000 + $84,000
     = $120,000 (total appraisal)
(2) $84,000/$120,000 = 70%
     (building's percent of total)
(3) 70% × $90,000 = $63,000
     (building's apportioned cost)

Plant assets sometimes are purchased as a group in a single transaction for a lump-sum price. This transaction is called a *lump-sum purchase,* or *group, bulk,* or *basket purchase.* When this occurs, we allocate the cost of the purchase among the different types of assets acquired based on their *relative market values,* which can be estimated by appraisal or by using the tax-assessed valuations of the assets. To illustrate, assume **CarMax** paid $90,000 cash to acquire a group of items consisting of land appraised at $30,000, land improvements appraised at $10,000, and a building appraised at $60,000. The $90,000 cost is allocated on the basis of these appraised values as shown in Exhibit 8.4.

EXHIBIT 8.4

Computing Costs in a Lump-Sum Purchase

	Appraised Value	Percent of Total	Apportioned Cost
Land	$ 30,000	30% ($30,000/$100,000)	$27,000 ($90,000 × 30%)
Land improvements	10,000	10 ($10,000/$100,000)	9,000 ($90,000 × 10%)
Building	60,000	60 ($60,000/$100,000)	54,000 ($90,000 × 60%)
Totals	$100,000	100%	$ 90,000

1. Identify the asset class for each of the following: (*a*) supplies, (*b*) office equipment, (*c*) inventory, (*d*) land for future expansion, and (*e*) trucks used in operations.
2. Identify the account charged for each of the following: (*a*) the purchase price of a vacant lot to be used in operations and (*b*) the cost of paving that same vacant lot.
3. Compute the amount recorded as the cost of a new machine given the following payments related to its purchase: gross purchase price, $700,000; sales tax, $49,000; purchase discount taken, $21,000; freight cost—terms FOB shipping point, $3,500; normal assembly costs, $3,000; cost of necessary machine platform, $2,500; cost of parts used in maintaining machine, $4,200.

DEPRECIATION

Depreciation is the process of allocating the cost of a plant asset to expense in the accounting periods benefiting from its use. Depreciation does not measure the decline in the asset's market value each period, nor does it measure the asset's physical deterioration. Since depreciation reflects the cost of using a plant asset, depreciation charges are only recorded when the asset is actually in service. This section describes the factors we must consider in computing depreciation, the depreciation methods used, revisions in depreciation, and depreciation for partial periods.

Point: Depreciation is cost allocation, not asset valuation.

Factors in Computing Depreciation

Factors that determine depreciation are (1) cost, (2) salvage value, and (3) useful life.

Cost   The **cost** of a plant asset consists of all necessary and reasonable expenditures to acquire it and to prepare it for its intended use.

Salvage Value   The total amount of depreciation to be charged off over an asset's benefit period equals the asset's cost minus its salvage value. **Salvage value,** also called *residual value* or *scrap value,* is an estimate of the asset's value at the end of its benefit period. This is the amount the owner expects to receive from disposing of the asset at the end of its benefit period. If the asset is expected to be traded in on a new asset, its salvage value is the expected trade-in value.

Point: If we expect additional costs in preparing a plant asset for disposal, the salvage value equals the expected amount from disposal less any disposal costs.

Useful Life   The **useful life** of a plant asset is the length of time it is productively used in a company's operations. Useful life, also called *service life,* might not be as long as the asset's total productive life. For example, the productive life of a computer can be eight years or more. Some companies, however, trade in old computers for new ones every two years. In this case, these computers have a two-year useful life, meaning the cost of these computers (less their expected trade-in values) is charged to depreciation expense over a two-year period.

Point: Useful life and salvage value are estimates. Estimates require judgment based on all available information.

Several variables often make the useful life of a plant asset difficult to predict. A major variable is the wear and tear from use in operations. Two other variables, inadequacy and obsolescence, also require consideration. **Inadequacy** refers to the insufficient capacity of a company's plant assets to meet its growing productive demands. **Obsolescence** refers to the condition of a plant asset that is no longer useful in producing goods or services with a competitive advantage because of new inventions and improvements. Both inadequacy and obsolescence are difficult to predict because of demand changes, new inventions, and improvements. A company usually disposes of an inadequate or obsolete asset before it wears out.

A company is often able to better predict a new asset's useful life when it has past experience with a similar asset. When it has no such experience, a company relies on the experience of others or on engineering studies and judgment. In note 1 of its annual report, **Tootsie Roll**, a snack food manufacturer, reports the following useful lives:

Point: Land is recorded at cost but not depreciated because it normally retains its value over time.

Buildings	20–35 years
Machinery and Equipment	5–20 years

Decision Insight

Life Line   Life expectancy of plant assets is often in the eye of the beholder. For instance, **Hershey Foods** and **Tootsie Roll** are competitors and apply similar manufacturing processes, yet their equipment's life expectancies are different. Hershey depreciates equipment over 3 to 15 years, but Tootsie Roll depreciates them over 5 to 20 years. Such differences markedly impact financial statements. ■

Depreciation Methods

> **P1**   Compute and record depreciation using the straight-line, units-of-production, and declining-balance methods.

Depreciation methods are used to allocate a plant asset's cost over the accounting periods in its useful life. The most frequently used method of depreciation is the straight-line method. Another common depreciation method is the units-of-production method. We explain both of these methods in this section. This section also describes accelerated depreciation methods, with a focus on the declining-balance method.

The computations in this section use information about a machine that inspects athletic shoes before packaging. Manufacturers such as **Converse**, **Reebok**, **adidas**, and **Fila** use this machine. Data for this machine are in Exhibit 8.5.

EXHIBIT 8.5

Data for Athletic Shoe-Inspecting Machine

Cost	$10,000
Salvage value	1,000
Depreciable cost	$ 9,000
Useful life	
Accounting periods	5 years
Units inspected	36,000 shoes

Straight-Line Method   Straight-line depreciation charges the same amount of expense to each period of the asset's useful life. A two-step process is used. We first compute the *depreciable cost* of the asset, also called the *cost to be depreciated*. It is computed by subtracting the asset's salvage value from its total cost. Second, depreciable cost is divided by the number of accounting periods in the asset's useful life. The formula for straight-line depreciation, along with its computation for the inspection machine just described, is shown in Exhibit 8.6.

EXHIBIT 8.6

Straight-Line Depreciation Formula and Example

$$\frac{\text{Cost} - \text{Salvage value}}{\text{Useful life in periods}} = \frac{\$10,000 - \$1,000}{5 \text{ years}} = \$1,800 \text{ per year}$$

If this machine is purchased on December 31, 2012, and used throughout its predicted useful life of five years, the straight-line method allocates an equal amount of depreciation to each of the years 2013 through 2017. We make the following adjusting entry at the end of each of the five years to record straight-line depreciation of this machine.

Assets = Liabilities + Equity
−1,800   −1,800

Dec. 31	Depreciation Expense	1,800	
	Accumulated Depreciation—Machinery		1,800
	To record annual depreciation.		

Example: If the salvage value of the machine is $2,500, what is the annual depreciation? *Answer:* ($10,000 − $2,500)/5 years = $1,500

The $1,800 Depreciation Expense is reported on the income statement among operating expenses. The $1,800 Accumulated Depreciation is a contra asset account to the Machinery account in the balance sheet. The graph on the left in Exhibit 8.7 shows the $1,800 per year expenses reported in each of the five years. The graph on the right shows the amounts reported on each of the six December 31 balance sheets.

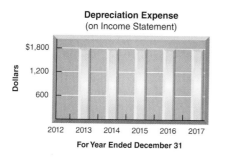

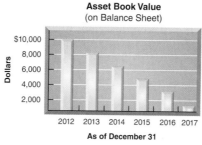

EXHIBIT 8.7

Financial Statement Effects of Straight-Line Depreciation

The net balance sheet amount is the **asset book value,** or simply *book value,* and is computed as the asset's total cost less its accumulated depreciation. For example, at the end of year 2 (December 31, 2014), its book value is $6,400 and is reported in the balance sheet as follows:

Book value = Cost − Accumulated depreciation

Machinery	$10,000
Less accumulated depreciation	3,600 $6,400 ◄— Book value

The book value of this machine declines by $1,800 each year due to depreciation. The left-side graphic in Exhibit 8.7 reveals why this method is called straight-line.

We also can compute the *straight-line depreciation rate,* defined as 100% divided by the number of periods in the asset's useful life. For the inspection machine, this rate is 20% (100% ÷ 5 years, or 1/5 per period). We use this rate, along with other information, to compute the machine's *straight-line depreciation schedule* shown in Exhibit 8.8. Note three points in this exhibit. First, depreciation expense is the same each period. Second, accumulated depreciation is the sum of current and prior periods' depreciation expense. Third, book value declines each period until it equals salvage value at the end of the machine's useful life.

Point: Depreciation requires estimates for salvage value and useful life. Ethics are relevant when managers might be tempted to choose estimates to achieve desired results on financial statements.

	Depreciation for the Period			End of Period	
Annual Period	Depreciable Cost*	Depreciation Rate	Depreciation Expense	Accumulated Depreciation	Book Value†
2012	—	—	—	—	$10,000
2013	$9,000	20%	$1,800	$1,800	8,200
2014	9,000	20	1,800	3,600	6,400
2015	9,000	20	1,800	5,400	4,600
2016	9,000	20	1,800	7,200	2,800
2017	9,000	20	1,800	9,000	1,000 ◄— Salvage value (not depreciated)

EXHIBIT 8.8

Straight-Line Depreciation Schedule

* $10,000 − $1,000.   † Book value is total cost minus accumulated depreciation.

Units-of-Production Method The straight-line method charges an equal share of an asset's cost to each period. If plant assets are used up in about equal amounts each accounting period, this method produces a reasonable matching of expenses with revenues. However, the use of some plant assets varies greatly from one period to the next. A builder, for instance, might use a piece of construction equipment for a month and then not use it again for several months. When equipment use varies from period to period, the units-of-production depreciation method can better match expenses with revenues. **Units-of-production depreciation** charges a varying amount to expense for each period of an asset's useful life depending on its *usage.*

A two-step process is used to compute units-of-production depreciation. We first compute *depreciation per unit* by subtracting the asset's salvage value from its total cost and then dividing by the total number of units expected to be produced during its useful life. Units of production can be expressed in product or other units such as hours used or miles driven. The second step is to compute depreciation expense for the period by multiplying the units produced in the period by the depreciation per unit. The formula for units-of-production depreciation, along with its computation for the machine described in Exhibit 8.5, is shown in Exhibit 8.9. (7,000 shoes are inspected and sold in its first year.)

EXHIBIT 8.9

Units-of-Production Depreciation Formula and Example

Step 1

$$\text{Depreciation per unit} = \frac{\text{Cost} - \text{Salvage value}}{\text{Total units of production}} = \frac{\$10,000 - \$1,000}{36,000 \text{ shoes}} = \$0.25 \text{ per shoe}$$

Step 2

Depreciation expense = Depreciation per unit × Units produced in period

$0.25 per shoe × 7,000 shoes = $1,750

Using data on the number of shoes inspected by the machine, we can compute the *units-of-production depreciation schedule* shown in Exhibit 8.10. For example, depreciation for the first year is $1,750 (7,000 shoes at $0.25 per shoe). Depreciation for the second year is $2,000 (8,000 shoes at $0.25 per shoe). Other years are similarly computed. Exhibit 8.10 shows that (1) depreciation expense depends on unit output, (2) accumulated depreciation is the sum of current and prior periods' depreciation expense, and (3) book value declines each period until it equals salvage value at the end of the asset's useful life. **Deltic Timber** is one of many companies using the units-of-production depreciation method. It reports that depreciation "is calculated over the estimated useful lives of the assets by using the units of production method for machinery and equipment."

Example: Refer to Exhibit 8.10. If the number of shoes inspected in 2017 is 5,500, what is depreciation for 2017? *Answer:* $1,250 (never depreciate below salvage value)

EXHIBIT 8.10

Units-of-Production Depreciation Schedule

Annual Period	Depreciation for the Period			End of Period	
	Number of Units	Depreciation per Unit	Depreciation Expense	Accumulated Depreciation	Book Value
2012	—	—	—	—	$10,000
2013	7,000	$0.25	$1,750	$1,750	8,250
2014	8,000	0.25	2,000	3,750	6,250
2015	9,000	0.25	2,250	6,000	4,000
2016	7,000	0.25	1,750	7,750	2,250
2017	5,000	0.25	1,250	9,000	1,000

Salvage value (not depreciated)

Declining-Balance Method An **accelerated depreciation method** yields larger depreciation expenses in the early years of an asset's life and less depreciation in later years. The most common accelerated method is the **declining-balance method** of depreciation, which uses a depreciation rate that is a multiple of the straight-line rate and applies it to the asset's beginning-of-period book value. The amount of depreciation declines each period because book value declines each period.

A common depreciation rate for the declining-balance method is double the straight-line rate. This is called the *double-declining-balance (DDB)* method. This method is applied in three steps: (1) compute the asset's straight-line depreciation rate, (2) double the straight-line rate, and (3) compute depreciation expense by multiplying this rate by the asset's beginning-of-period book value. To illustrate, let's return to the machine in Exhibit 8.5 and apply the double-declining-balance method to compute depreciation expense. Exhibit 8.11 shows the first-year depreciation computation for the machine. The three-step process is to (1) divide 100% by five years to determine the straight-line rate of 20%, or 1/5, per year, (2) double this 20% rate to get the

Point: In the DDB method, *double* refers to the rate and *declining balance* refers to book value. The rate is applied to beginning book value each period.

Ore Inventory, a current asset. To illustrate, and continuing with our example, assume that 40,000 tons are mined in the second year, but only 34,000 tons are sold. We record depletion of $68,000 (34,000 tons $\times$ $2 depletion per unit) and the remaining Ore Inventory of $12,000 (6,000 tons $\times$ $2 depletion per unit) as follows.

Dec. 31	Depletion Expense—Mineral Deposit	68,000	
	Ore Inventory	12,000	
	Accumulated Depletion—Mineral Deposit		80,000
	To record depletion and inventory of mineral deposit.		

Assets = Liabilities + Equity
−80,000   −68,000
+12,000

Plant Assets Used in Extracting

The conversion of natural resources by mining, cutting, or pumping usually requires machinery, equipment, and buildings. When the usefulness of these plant assets is directly related to the depletion of a natural resource, their costs are depreciated using the units-of-production method in proportion to the depletion of the natural resource. For example, if a machine is permanently installed in a mine and 10% of the ore is mined and sold in the period, then 10% of the machine's cost (less any salvage value) is allocated to depreciation expense. The same procedure is used when a machine is abandoned once resources have been extracted. If, however, a machine will be moved to and used at another site when extraction is complete, the machine is depreciated over its own useful life.

Decision Insight

Asset Control Long-term assets must be safeguarded against theft, misuse, and other damages. Controls take many forms depending on the asset, including use of security tags, the legal monitoring of rights infringements, and approvals of all asset disposals. A study reports that 43% of employees in operations and service areas witnessed the wasting, mismanaging, or abusing of assets in the past year (KPMG 2011). ■

Section 3—Intangible Assets

Intangible assets are nonphysical assets (used in operations) that confer on their owners long-term rights, privileges, or competitive advantages. Examples are patents, copyrights, licenses, leaseholds, franchises, goodwill, and trademarks. Lack of physical substance does not necessarily imply an intangible asset. Notes and accounts receivable, for instance, lack physical substance, but they are not intangibles. This section identifies the more common types of intangible assets and explains the accounting for them.

 Account for intangible assets.

Cost Determination and Amortization

An intangible asset is recorded at cost when purchased. Intangibles are then separated into those with limited lives or indefinite lives. If an intangible has a **limited life,** its cost is systematically allocated to expense over its estimated useful life through the process of **amortization.** If an intangible asset has an **indefinite life**—meaning that no legal, regulatory, contractual, competitive, economic, or other factors limit its useful life—it should not be amortized. (If an intangible with an indefinite life is later judged to have a limited life, it is amortized over that limited life.) Amortization of intangible assets is similar to depreciation of plant assets and the depletion of natural resources in that it is a process of cost allocation. However, only the straight-line method is used for amortizing intangibles *unless* the company can show that another method is preferred. The effects of amortization are recorded in a contra account (Accumulated Amortization). The gross acquisition cost of intangible assets is disclosed in the balance sheet along with their accumulated amortization (these disclosures are new). The eventual disposal of an intangible asset involves removing its book value, recording any other asset(s) received or given up, and recognizing any gain or loss for the difference.

Point: Depreciation, depletion, and amortization are related in that each describes cost allocation.

Point: The cost to acquire a Website address is an intangible asset.

Point: Goodwill is not amortized; instead, it is annually tested for impairment.

Many intangibles have limited lives due to laws, contracts, or other asset characteristics. Examples are patents, copyrights, and leaseholds. Other intangibles such as goodwill, trademarks, and trade names have lives that cannot be easily determined. The cost of intangible assets is amortized over the periods expected to benefit by their use, but in no case can this period be longer than the asset's legal existence. The values of some intangible assets such as goodwill continue indefinitely into the future and are not amortized. (An intangible asset that is not amortized is tested annually for **impairment**—if necessary, an impairment loss is recorded. Details for this test are in advanced courses.)

Intangible assets are often shown in a separate section of the balance sheet immediately after plant assets. **Callaway Golf**, for instance, follows this approach in reporting over $120 million of intangible assets in its balance sheet. Companies usually disclose their amortization periods for intangibles. The remainder of our discussion focuses on accounting for specific types of intangible assets.

Types of Intangibles

Patents The federal government grants patents to encourage the invention of new technology, mechanical devices, and production processes. A **patent** is an exclusive right granted to its owner to manufacture and sell a patented item or to use a process for 20 years. When patent rights are purchased, the cost to acquire the rights is debited to an account called Patents. If the owner engages in lawsuits to successfully defend a patent, the cost of lawsuits is debited to the Patents account. However, the costs of research and development leading to a new patent are expensed when incurred.

A patent's cost is amortized over its estimated useful life (not to exceed 20 years). If we purchase a patent costing $25,000 with a useful life of 10 years, we make the following adjusting entry at the end of each of the 10 years to amortize one-tenth of its cost.

Assets = Liabilities + Equity
−2,500   −2,500

Dec. 31	Amortization Expense—Patents	2,500	
	Accumulated Amortization—Patents		2,500
	To amortize patent costs over its useful life.		

The $2,500 debit to Amortization Expense appears on the income statement as a cost of the product or service provided under protection of the patent. The Accumulated Amortization—Patents account is a contra asset account to Patents.

Decision Insight

Mention "drug war" and most people think of illegal drug trade. But another drug war is under way: Brand-name drugmakers are fighting to stop generic copies of their products from hitting the market once patents expire. Delaying a generic rival can yield millions in extra sales. One way drugmakers fight patent expirations is to alter *drug delivery*. The first patent might require a patient to take a pill 4×/day. When that patent expires, the drugmaker can "improve" the drug's delivery release system to 2×/day, and then 1×/day, and so forth. ■

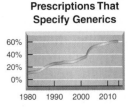

Prescriptions That Specify Generics

Copyrights A **copyright** gives its owner the exclusive right to publish and sell a musical, literary, or artistic work during the life of the creator plus 70 years, although the useful life of most copyrights is much shorter. The costs of a copyright are amortized over its useful life. The only identifiable cost of many copyrights is the fee paid to the Copyright Office of the federal government or international agency granting the copyright. If this fee is immaterial, it is charged directly to an expense account; but if the identifiable costs of a copyright are material, they are capitalized (recorded in an asset account) and periodically amortized by debiting an account called Amortization Expense—Copyrights.

Decision Insight

Mickey Mouse Protection Act The Walt Disney Company successfully lobbied Congress to extend copyright protection from the life of the creator plus 50 years to life of the creator plus 70 years. This extension allows the company to protect its characters for 20 additional years before the right to use them enters the public domain. Mickey Mouse is now protected by copyright law until 2023. The law is officially termed the Copyright Term Extension Act (CTEA) but it is also known as the Mickey Mouse Protection Act. ■

Franchises and Licenses Franchises and licenses are rights that a company or government grants an entity to deliver a product or service under specified conditions. Many organizations grant franchise and license rights—**McDonald's**, **Pizza Hut**, and **Major League Baseball** are just a few examples. The costs of franchises and licenses are debited to a Franchises and Licenses asset account and are amortized over the lives of the agreements. If an agreement is for an indefinite or perpetual period, those costs are not amortized.

Trademarks and Trade Names Companies often adopt unique symbols or select unique names and brands in marketing their products. A **trademark** or **trade (brand) name** is a symbol, name, phrase, or jingle identified with a company, product, or service. Examples are Nike swoosh, Marlboro Man, Big Mac, Coca-Cola, and Corvette. Ownership and exclusive right to use a trademark or trade name is often established by showing that one company used it before another. Ownership is best established by registering a trademark or trade name with the government's Patent Office. The cost of developing, maintaining, or enhancing the value of a trademark or trade name (such as advertising) is charged to expense when incurred. If a trademark or trade name is purchased, however, its cost is debited to an asset account and then amortized over its expected life. If the company plans to renew indefinitely its right to the trademark or trade name, the cost is not amortized.

Point: McDonald's "golden arches" are one of the world's most valuable trademarks, yet this asset is not shown on McDonald's balance sheet.

Goodwill Goodwill has a specific meaning in accounting. Goodwill is the amount by which a company's value exceeds the value of its individual assets and liabilities. This usually implies that the company as a whole has certain valuable attributes not measured among its individual assets and liabilities. These can include superior management, skilled workforce, good supplier or customer relations, quality products or services, good location, or other competitive advantages.

To keep accounting information from being too subjective, goodwill is not recorded unless an entire company or business segment is purchased. Purchased goodwill is measured by taking the purchase price of the company and subtracting the market value of its individual net assets (excluding goodwill). For instance, **Google** paid $1.19 billion to acquire **YouTube**; about $1.13 of the $1.19 billion was for goodwill.

Goodwill is measured as the excess of the cost of an acquired entity over the value of the acquired net assets. Goodwill is recorded as an asset, and it is *not* amortized. Instead, goodwill is annually tested for impairment. If the book value of goodwill does not exceed its fair (market) value, goodwill is not impaired. However, if the book value of goodwill does exceed its fair value, an impairment loss is recorded equal to that excess. (Details of this test are in advanced courses.)

Point: Amortization of goodwill is different for financial accounting and tax accounting. The IRS requires the amortization of goodwill over 15 years.

Example: Assume goodwill carries a book value of $500 and has an implied fair value of $475, *and* this $25 decline in value meets the 2-step impairment test. The entry to record this impairment is:
Impairment Loss $25
   Goodwill $25

Leaseholds Property is rented under a contract called a **lease.** The property's owner, called the **lessor,** grants the lease. The one who secures the right to possess and use the property is called the **lessee. A leasehold** refers to the rights the lessor grants to the lessee under the terms of the lease. A leasehold is an intangible asset for the lessee.

Certain leases require no advance payment from the lessee but require monthly rent payments. In this case, we do not set up a Leasehold account. Instead, the monthly payments are debited to a Rent Expense account. If a long-term lease requires the lessee to pay the final period's rent in advance when the lease is signed, the lessee records this advance payment with a debit to the Leasehold account. Since the advance payment is not used until the final period, the Leasehold account balance remains intact until that final period when its balance is transferred to Rent Expense. (Some long-term leases give the lessee essentially the same rights as a purchaser. This results in a tangible asset and a liability reported by the lessee. Chapter 10 describes these so-called *capital leases.*)

Point: A leasehold account implies existence of future benefits that the lessee controls because of a prepayment. It also meets the definition of an asset.

A long-term lease can increase in value when current rental rates for similar property rise while the required payments under the lease remain constant. This increase in value of a lease is not reported on the lessee's balance sheet. However, if the property is subleased and the new tenant makes a cash payment to the original lessee for the rights under the old lease, the new tenant debits this payment to a Leasehold account, which is amortized to Rent Expense over the remaining life of the lease.

Leasehold Improvements   A lessee sometimes pays for alterations or improvements to the leased property such as partitions, painting, and storefronts. These alterations and improvements are called **leasehold improvements,** and the lessee debits these costs to a Leasehold Improvements account. Since leasehold improvements become part of the property and revert to the lessor at the end of the lease, the lessee amortizes these costs over the life of the lease or the life of the improvements, whichever is shorter. The amortization entry debits Amortization Expense—Leasehold Improvements and credits Accumulated Amortization—Leasehold Improvements.

Other Intangibles   There are other types of intangible assets such as *software, noncompete covenants, customer lists,* and so forth. Our accounting for them is the same. First, we record the intangible asset's costs. Second, we determine whether the asset has a limited or indefinite life. If limited, we allocate its costs over that period. If indefinite, its costs are not amortized.

Quick Check   Answers — p. 361

12. Give an example of a natural resource and of an intangible asset.
13. A company pays $650,000 for an ore deposit. The deposit is estimated to have 325,000 tons of ore that will be mined over the next 10 years. During the first year, it mined, processed, and sold 91,000 tons. What is that year's depletion expense?
14. On January 6, 2013, a company pays $120,000 for a patent with a remaining 17-year legal life to produce a toy expected to be marketable for three years. Prepare entries to record its acquisition and the December 31, 2013, amortization entry.

GLOBAL VIEW

This section discusses similarities and differences between U.S. GAAP and IFRS in accounting and reporting for plant assets and intangible assets.

Accounting for Plant Assets   Issues involving cost determination, depreciation, additional expenditures, and disposals of plant assets are subject to broadly similar guidance for both U.S. GAAP and IFRS. Although differences exist, the similarities vastly outweigh the differences. Nokia describes its accounting for plant assets as follows:

NOKIA

> Property, plant and equipment are stated at cost less accumulated depreciation. Depreciation is recorded on a straight-line basis over the expected useful lives of the assets. Maintenance, repairs and renewals are generally charged to expense during the financial period in which they are incurred. However, major renovations are capitalized and included in the carrying amount of the asset . . . Major renovations are depreciated over the remaining useful life of the related asset.

One area where notable differences exist is in accounting for changes in the value of plant assets (between the time they are acquired and when disposed of). Namely, how does IFRS and U.S. GAAP treat decreases and increases in the value of plant assets subsequent to acquisition?

Decreases in the Value of Plant Assets   When the value of plant assets declines after acquisition, but before disposition, both U.S. GAAP and IFRS require companies to record those decreases as *impairment losses*. While the *test for impairment* uses a different base between U.S. GAAP and IFRS, a more fundamental difference is that U.S. GAAP revalues impaired plant assets to *fair value* whereas IFRS revalues them to a *recoverable amount* (defined as fair value less costs to sell).

Current Liabilities   **Current liabilities,** also called *short-term liabilities,* are obligations due within one year or the company's operating cycle, whichever is longer. They are expected to be paid using current assets or by creating other current liabilities. Common examples of current liabilities are accounts payable, short-term notes payable, wages payable, warranty liabilities, lease liabilities, taxes payable, and unearned revenues.

Point: Improper classification of liabilities can distort ratios used in financial statement analysis and business decisions.

Current liabilities differ across companies because they depend on the type of company operations. MGM Mirage, for instance, included the following current liabilities related to its gaming, hospitality and entertainment operations ($000s):

Advance deposits and ticket sales	$ 97,753
Casino outstanding chip liability	290,238
Casino front money deposits	111,763

Harley-Davidson reports a much different set of current liabilities. It discloses current liabilities made up of items such as warranty, recall, and dealer incentive liabilities.

Long-Term Liabilities   A company's obligations not expected to be paid within the longer of one year or the company's operating cycle are reported as **long-term liabilities.** They can include long-term notes payable, warranty liabilities, lease liabilities, and bonds payable. They are sometimes reported on the balance sheet in a single long-term liabilities total or in multiple categories. Domino's Pizza, for instance, reports long-term liabilities of $1,485 million. They are reported after current liabilities. A single liability also can be divided between the current and noncurrent sections if a company expects to make payments toward it in both the short and long term. Domino's reports long-term debt, $1,451,000,000; and current portion of long-term debt, $835,000, which is less than 1%. The second item is reported in current liabilities. We sometimes see liabilities that do not have a fixed due date but instead are payable on the creditor's demand. These are reported as current liabilities because of the possibility of payment in the near term. Exhibit 9.2 shows amounts of current liabilities and as a percent of total liabilities for selected companies.

Point: The current ratio is overstated if a company fails to classify any portion of long-term debt due next period as a current liability.

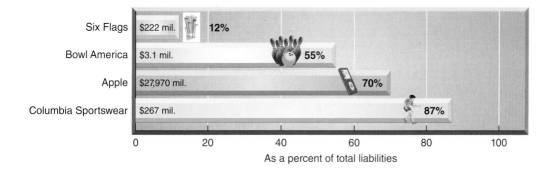

EXHIBIT 9.2

Current Liabilities of Selected Companies

Uncertainty in Liabilities

Accounting for liabilities involves addressing three important questions: Whom to pay? When to pay? How much to pay? Answers to these questions are often decided when a liability is incurred. For example, if a company has a $100 account payable to a specific individual, payable on March 15, the answers are clear. The company knows whom to pay, when to pay, and how much to pay. However, the answers to one or more of these questions are uncertain for some liabilities.

Uncertainty in Whom to Pay   Liabilities can involve uncertainty in whom to pay. For instance, a company can create a liability with a known amount when issuing a note that is payable to its holder. In this case, a specific amount is payable to the note's holder at a specified date, but the company does not know who the holder is until that date. Despite this uncertainty, the company reports this liability on its balance sheet.

Point: An *accrued expense* is an unpaid expense, and is also called an *accrued liability.*

Uncertainty in When to Pay   A company can have an obligation of a known amount to a known creditor but not know when it must be paid. For example, a legal services firm can accept fees in advance from a client who plans to use the firm's services in the future. This means that the firm has a liability that it settles by providing services at an unknown future date. Although this uncertainty exists, the legal firm's balance sheet must report this liability. These types of obligations are reported as current liabilities because they are likely to be settled in the short term.

Uncertainty in How Much to Pay   A company can be aware of an obligation but not know how much will be required to settle it. For example, a company using electrical power is billed only after the meter has been read. This cost is incurred and the liability created before a bill is received. A liability to the power company is reported as an estimated amount if the balance sheet is prepared before a bill arrives.

 IFRS _____

IFRS records a contingent liability when an obligation exists from a past event if there is a 'probable' outflow of resources and the amount can be estimated reliably. However, IFRS defines probable as 'more likely than not' while U.S. GAAP defines it as 'likely to occur.' ■

Quick Check   Answers — p. 403

1. What is a liability? Identify its crucial characteristics.

2. Is every expected future payment a liability?

3. If a liability is payable in 15 months, is it classified as current or long term?

KNOWN LIABILITIES

 C2 Identify and describe known current liabilities.

Most liabilities arise from situations with little uncertainty. They are set by agreements, contracts, or laws and are measurable. These liabilities are **known liabilities,** also called *definitely determinable liabilities.* Known liabilities include accounts payable, notes payable, payroll, sales taxes, unearned revenues, and leases. We describe how to account for these known liabilities in this section.

Accounts Payable

Accounts payable, or trade accounts payable, are amounts owed to suppliers, also called *vendors,* for products or services purchased on credit. Accounting for accounts payable is primarily explained and illustrated in our discussion of merchandising activities in Chapters 4 and 5.

Sales Taxes Payable

Nearly all states and many cities levy taxes on retail sales. Sales taxes are stated as a percent of selling prices. The seller collects sales taxes from customers when sales occur and remits these collections (often monthly) to the proper government agency. Since sellers currently owe these collections to the government, this amount is a current liability. **Home Depot**, for instance, reports sales taxes payable of $391 million in its recent annual report. To illustrate, if Home Depot sells materials on August 31 for $6,000 cash that are subject to a 5% sales tax, the revenue portion of this transaction is recorded as follows:

Assets = Liabilities + Equity
+6,300   +300   +6,000

Aug. 31	Cash	6,300	
	Sales		6,000
	Sales Taxes Payable ($6,000 × 0.05)		300
	To record cash sales and 5% sales tax.		

Sales Taxes Payable is debited and Cash credited when it remits these collections to the government. Sales Taxes Payable is not an expense. It arises because laws require sellers to collect this cash from customers for the government.[1]

Unearned Revenues

Unearned revenues (also called *deferred revenues, collections in advance,* and *prepayments*) are amounts received in advance from customers for future products or services. Advance ticket sales for sporting events or music concerts are examples. Rihanna, for instance, has "deferred revenues" from advance ticket sales. To illustrate, assume that Rihanna sells $5 million in tickets for eight concerts; the entry is

Point: To *defer* a revenue means to postpone recognition of a revenue collected in advance until it is earned. Sport teams must defer recognition of ticket sales until games are played.

June 30	Cash	5,000,000	
	Unearned Ticket Revenue		5,000,000
	To record sale of concert tickets.		

Assets = Liabilities + Equity
+5,000,000   +5,000,000

When a concert is played, Rihanna would record revenue for the portion earned.

Oct. 31	Unearned Ticket Revenue	625,000	
	Ticket Revenue		625,000
	To record concert ticket revenues earned.		

Assets = Liabilities + Equity
       −625,000   +625,000

Unearned Ticket Revenue is an unearned revenue account and is reported as a current liability. Unearned revenues also arise with airline ticket sales, magazine subscriptions, construction projects, hotel reservations, and custom orders.

▇ **Decision** Insight ▬▬▬▬▬▬▬▬▬▬▬▬▬▬▬▬▬▬▬▬▬▬▬▬▬▬▬▬▬▬

Reward Programs Gift card sales now exceed $100 billion annually, and reward (also called loyalty) programs are growing. There are no exact rules for how retailers account for rewards. When **Best Buy** launched its "Reward Zone," shoppers earned $5 on each $125 spent and had 90 days to spend it. Retailers make assumptions about how many reward program dollars will be spent and how to report it. Best Buy sets up a liability and reduces revenue by the same amount. **Talbots** does not reduce revenue but instead increases selling expense. **Men's Wearhouse** records rewards in cost of goods sold, whereas **Neiman Marcus** subtracts them from revenue. The FASB continues to review reward programs. ■

Short-Term Notes Payable

A **short-term note payable** is a written promise to pay a specified amount on a definite future date within one year or the company's operating cycle, whichever is longer. These promissory notes are negotiable (as are checks), meaning they can be transferred from party to party by endorsement. The written documentation provided by notes is helpful in resolving disputes and for pursuing legal actions involving these liabilities. Most notes payable bear interest to compensate for use of the money until payment is made. Short-term notes payable can arise from many transactions. A company that purchases merchandise on credit can sometimes extend the credit period by signing a note to replace an account payable. Such notes also can arise when money is borrowed from a bank. We describe both of these cases.

P1 Prepare entries to account for short-term notes payable.

Point: Required characteristics for negotiability of a note: (1) unconditional promise, (2) in writing, (3) specific amount, and (4) definite due date.

---

[1] Sales taxes can be computed from total sales receipts when sales taxes are not separately identified on the register. To illustrate, assume a 5% sales tax and $420 in total sales receipts (which includes sales taxes). Sales are computed as follows:

$$\text{Sales} = \text{Total sales receipts}/(1 + \text{Sales tax percentage}) = \$420/1.05 = \$400$$

Thus, the sales tax amount equals total sales receipts minus sales, or $420 − $400 = $20. Sellers are required to act as "agents" for the government and collect sales tax. This extra work can be offset by the sellers' ability to use or invest that cash until it must be paid to the government.

Note Given to Extend Credit Period   A company can replace an account payable with a note payable. A common example is a creditor that requires the substitution of an interest-bearing note for an overdue account payable that does not bear interest. A less common situation occurs when a debtor's weak financial condition motivates the creditor to accept a note, sometimes for a lesser amount, and to close the account to ensure that this customer makes no additional credit purchases.

To illustrate, let's assume that on August 23, Brady Company asks to extend its past-due $600 account payable to McGraw. After some negotiations, McGraw agrees to accept $100 cash and a 60-day, 12%, $500 note payable to replace the account payable. Brady records the transaction with this entry:

Assets = Liabilities + Equity
−100   −600
             +500

Aug. 23	Accounts Payable—McGraw	600	
	Cash		100
	Notes Payable—McGraw		500
	Gave $100 cash and a 60-day, 12% note for		
	payment on account.		

Point: Accounts payable are detailed in a subsidiary ledger, but notes payable are sometimes not. A file with copies of notes can serve as a subsidiary ledger.

Signing the note does not resolve Brady's debt. Instead, the form of debt is changed from an account payable to a note payable. McGraw prefers the note payable over the account payable because it earns interest and it is written documentation of the debt's existence, term, and amount. When the note comes due, Brady pays the note and interest by giving McGraw a check for $510. Brady records that payment with this entry:

Assets = Liabilities + Equity
−510   −500   −10

Oct. 22	Notes Payable—McGraw	500	
	Interest Expense	10	
	Cash		510
	Paid note with interest ($500 × 12% × 60/360).		

Point: Commercial companies commonly compute interest using a 360-day year. This is known as the *banker's rule.*

Interest expense is computed by multiplying the principal of the note ($500) by the annual interest rate (12%) for the fraction of the year the note is outstanding (60 days/360 days).

Note Given to Borrow from Bank   A bank nearly always requires a borrower to sign a promissory note when making a loan. When the note matures, the borrower repays the note with an amount larger than the amount borrowed. The difference between the amount borrowed and the amount repaid is *interest.* This section considers a type of note whose signer promises to pay *principal* (the amount borrowed) plus interest. In this case, the *face value* of the note equals principal. Face value is the value shown on the face (front) of the note. To illustrate, assume that a company needs $2,000 for a project and borrows this money from a bank at 12% annual interest. The loan is made on September 30, 2013, and is due in 60 days. Specifically, the borrowing company signs a note with a face value equal to the amount borrowed. The note includes a statement similar to this: *"I promise to pay $2,000 plus interest at 12% within 60 days after September 30."* This simple note is shown in Exhibit 9.3.

Point: When money is borrowed from a bank, the loan is reported as an asset (receivable) on the bank's balance sheet.

EXHIBIT 9.3

Note with Face Value Equal to Amount Borrowed

Promissory Note

$2,000   Sept. 30, 2013
Face Value   Date

Sixty days _____ after date, _____ I _____ promise to pay to the order of

National Bank
Boston, MA

Two thousand and no/100 ------------------------ **Dollars**

plus interest at the annual rate of __12%__.

Janet Lee

Required

1. Prepare journal entries to record these transactions and adjustments for 2012 and 2013.
2. How much warranty expense is reported for November 2012 and for December 2012?
3. How much warranty expense is reported for January 2013?
4. What is the balance of the Estimated Warranty Liability account as of December 31, 2012?
5. What is the balance of the Estimated Warranty Liability account as of January 31, 2013?

Check (3) $900
(4) $1,050 Cr.
(5) $950 Cr.

Shown here are condensed income statements for two different companies (both are organized as LLCs and pay no income taxes).

Problem 9-5A
Computing and analyzing times interest earned

A1

Miller Company	
Sales	$1,000,000
Variable expenses (80%)	800,000
Income before interest	200,000
Interest expense (fixed)	60,000
Net income	$ 140,000

Weaver Company	
Sales	$1,000,000
Variable expenses (60%)	600,000
Income before interest	400,000
Interest expense (fixed)	260,000
Net income	$ 140,000

Required

1. Compute times interest earned for Miller Company.
2. Compute times interest earned for Weaver Company.
3. What happens to each company's net income if sales increase by 30%?
4. What happens to each company's net income if sales increase by 50%?
5. What happens to each company's net income if sales increase by 80%?
6. What happens to each company's net income if sales decrease by 10%?
7. What happens to each company's net income if sales decrease by 20%?
8. What happens to each company's net income if sales decrease by 40%?

Check (3) Miller net income, $200,000 (43% increase)

(6) Weaver net income, $100,000 (29% decrease)

Analysis Component

9. Comment on the results from parts 3 through 8 in relation to the fixed-cost strategies of the two companies and the ratio values you computed in parts 1 and 2.

Francisco Company has 10 employees, each of whom earns $2,800 per month and is paid on the last day of each month. All 10 have been employed continuously at this amount since January 1. Francisco uses a payroll bank account and special payroll checks to pay its employees. On March 1, the following accounts and balances exist in its general ledger:

Problem 9-6A^A
Entries for payroll transactions
P2 P3 P5

a. FICA—Social Security Taxes Payable, $3,472; FICA—Medicare Taxes Payable, $812. (The balances of these accounts represent total liabilities for *both* the employer's and employees' FICA taxes for the February payroll only.)
b. Employees' Federal Income Taxes Payable, $4,000 (liability for February only).
c. Federal Unemployment Taxes Payable, $448 (liability for January and February together).
d. State Unemployment Taxes Payable, $2,240 (liability for January and February together).

During March and April, the company had the following payroll transactions.

Mar. 15 Issued check payable to Swift Bank, a federal depository bank authorized to accept employers' payments of FICA taxes and employee income tax withholdings. The $8,284 check is in payment of the February FICA and employee income taxes.
    31 Recorded the March payroll and transferred funds from the regular bank account to the payroll bank account. Issued checks payable to each employee in payment of the March payroll. The payroll register shows the following summary totals for the March pay period.

Check March 31: Salaries Payable, $21,858

Salaries				Federal	
Office Salaries	Shop Salaries	Gross Pay	FICA Taxes*	Income Taxes	Net Pay
$11,200	$16,800	$28,000	$1,736	$4,000	$21,858
			$ 406		

* FICA taxes are Social Security and Medicare, respectively.

March 31: Dr. Payroll Taxes
Expenses, $2,814

April 15: Cr. Cash, $8,284
(Swift Bank)

31 Recorded the employer's payroll taxes resulting from the March payroll. The company has a merit rating that reduces its state unemployment tax rate to 4.0% of the first $7,000 paid each employee. The federal rate is 0.8%.

Apr. 15 Issued check to Swift Bank in payment of the March FICA and employee income taxes.

15 Issued check to the State Tax Commission for the January, February, and March state unemployment taxes. Mailed the check and the first quarter tax return to the Commission.

30 Issued check payable to Swift Bank in payment of the employer's FUTA taxes for the first quarter of the year.

30 Mailed Form 941 to the IRS, reporting the FICA taxes and the employees' federal income tax withholdings for the first quarter.

Required

Prepare journal entries to record the transactions and events for both March and April.

PROBLEM SET B

Problem 9-1B
Short-term notes payable transactions and entries

P1

Warner Co. entered into the following transactions involving short-term liabilities in 2012 and 2013.

2012

Apr. 22 Purchased $5,000 of merchandise on credit from Fox Products, terms are 1/10, n/30. Warner uses the perpetual inventory system.

May 23 Replaced the April 22 account payable to Fox Products with a 60-day, $4,600 note bearing 15% annual interest along with paying $400 in cash.

July 15 Borrowed $12,000 cash from Spring Bank by signing a 120-day, 10% interest-bearing note with a face value of $12,000.

___?___ Paid the amount due on the note to Fox Products at maturity.

___?___ Paid the amount due on the note to Spring Bank at maturity.

Dec. 6 Borrowed $8,000 cash from City Bank by signing a 45-day, 9% interest-bearing note with a face value of $8,000.

31 Recorded an adjusting entry for accrued interest on the note to City Bank.

2013

___?___ Paid the amount due on the note to City Bank at maturity.

Required

1. Determine the maturity date for each of the three notes described.

Check (2) Fox, $115
          (3) $50
          (4) $40

2. Determine the interest due at maturity for each of the three notes. (Assume a 360-day year.)

3. Determine the interest expense to be recorded in the adjusting entry at the end of 2012.

4. Determine the interest expense to be recorded in 2013.

5. Prepare journal entries for all the preceding transactions and events for years 2012 and 2013.

Problem 9-2B
Payroll expenses, withholdings, and taxes

P2 P3

Fishing Guides Co. has four employees. FICA Social Security taxes are 6.2% of the first $110,100 paid to each employee, and FICA Medicare taxes are 1.45% of gross pay. Also, for the first $7,000 paid to each employee, the company's FUTA taxes are 0.8% and SUTA taxes are 1.75%. The company is preparing its payroll calculations for the week ended September 30. Payroll records show the following information for the company's four employees.

	File Edit View Insert Format Tools Data Accounting Window Help		
		Gross Pay	Current Week	
	Name	**Gross Pay through 9/23**	**Gross Pay**	**Income Tax Withholding**
3	Ahmed	$108,500	$2,500	$198
4	Carlos	36,650	1,515	182
5	June	6,650	475	32
6	Marie	22,200	1,000	68

In addition to gross pay, the company must pay one-half of the $50 per employee weekly health insurance; each employee pays the remaining one-half. The company also contributes an extra 5% of each employee's gross pay (at no cost to employees) to a pension fund.

Required

Compute the following for the week ended September 30 (round amounts to the nearest cent):

1. Each employee's FICA withholdings for Social Security.
2. Each employee's FICA withholdings for Medicare.
3. Employer's FICA taxes for Social Security.
4. Employer's FICA taxes for Medicare.
5. Employer's FUTA taxes.
6. Employer's SUTA taxes.
7. Each employee's net (take-home) pay.
8. Employer's total payroll-related expense for each employee.

Check (3) $284.58
(4) $79.61
(5) $2.80
(7) Total net pay, $4,545.81

Tavella Company's first weekly pay period of the year ends on January 8. On that date, the column totals in Tavella's payroll register indicate its sales employees earned $34,745, its office employees earned $21,225, and its delivery employees earned $1,030 in salaries. The employees are to have withheld from their salaries FICA Social Security taxes at the rate of 6.2%, FICA Medicare taxes at the rate of 1.45%, $8,625 of federal income taxes, $1,160 of medical insurance deductions, and $138 of union dues. No employee earned more than $7,000 in the first pay period.

Problem 9-3B
Entries for payroll transactions
P2 P3

Required

1. Calculate FICA Social Security taxes payable and FICA Medicare taxes payable. Prepare the journal entry to record Tavella Company's January 8 (employee) payroll expenses and liabilities. (Round amounts to cents.)

2. Prepare the journal entry to record Tavella's (employer) payroll taxes resulting from the January 8 payroll. Tavella's merit rating reduces its state unemployment tax rate to 3.4% of the first $7,000 paid each employee. The federal unemployment tax rate is 0.8%. (Round amounts to cents.)

Check (1) Cr. Salaries Payable, $42,716.50

(2) Dr. Payroll Taxes Expense, $6,754.50

On November 10, 2013, Lee Co. began operations by purchasing coffee grinders for resale. Lee uses the perpetual inventory method. The grinders have a 60-day warranty that requires the company to replace any nonworking grinder. When a grinder is returned, the company discards it and mails a new one from Merchandise Inventory to the customer. The company's cost per new grinder is $24 and its retail selling price is $50 in both 2013 and 2014. The manufacturer has advised the company to expect warranty costs to equal 10% of dollar sales. The following transactions and events occurred.

Problem 9-4B
Warranty expense and liability estimation
P4

2013

Nov. 16 Sold 50 grinders for $2,500 cash.
     30 Recognized warranty expense related to November sales with an adjusting entry.
Dec. 12 Replaced six grinders that were returned under the warranty.
     18 Sold 200 grinders for $10,000 cash.
     28 Replaced 17 grinders that were returned under the warranty.
     31 Recognized warranty expense related to December sales with an adjusting entry.

2014

Jan. 7 Sold 40 grinders for $2,000 cash.
     21 Replaced 36 grinders that were returned under the warranty.
     31 Recognized warranty expense related to January sales with an adjusting entry.

Required

1. Prepare journal entries to record these transactions and adjustments for 2013 and 2014.
2. How much warranty expense is reported for November 2013 and for December 2013?
3. How much warranty expense is reported for January 2014?
4. What is the balance of the Estimated Warranty Liability account as of December 31, 2013?
5. What is the balance of the Estimated Warranty Liability account as of January 31, 2014?

Check (3) $200
(4) $698 Cr.
(5) $34 Cr.

Shown here are condensed income statements for two different companies (both are organized as LLCs and pay no income taxes).

Problem 9-5B
Computing and analyzing times interest earned

A1

Ellis Company	
Sales	$240,000
Variable expenses (50%)	120,000
Income before interest	120,000
Interest expense (fixed)	90,000
Net income	$ 30,000

Seidel Company	
Sales	$240,000
Variable expenses (75%)	180,000
Income before interest	60,000
Interest expense (fixed)	30,000
Net income	$ 30,000

Required

1. Compute times interest earned for Ellis Company.
2. Compute times interest earned for Seidel Company.
3. What happens to each company's net income if sales increase by 10%?

Check (4) Ellis net income, $78,000 (160% increase)

(6) Seidel net income, $18,000 (40% decrease)

4. What happens to each company's net income if sales increase by 40%?
5. What happens to each company's net income if sales increase by 90%?
6. What happens to each company's net income if sales decrease by 20%?
7. What happens to each company's net income if sales decrease by 50%?
8. What happens to each company's net income if sales decrease by 80%?

Analysis Component

9. Comment on the results from parts 3 through 8 in relation to the fixed-cost strategies of the two companies and the ratio values you computed in parts 1 and 2.

Problem 9-6B[A]

Entries for payroll transactions

P2 P3 P5

MLS Company has five employees, each of whom earns $1,600 per month and is paid on the last day of each month. All five have been employed continuously at this amount since January 1. MLS uses a payroll bank account and special payroll checks to pay its employees. On June 1, the following accounts and balances exist in its general ledger:

a. FICA—Social Security Taxes Payable, $992; FICA—Medicare Taxes Payable, $232. (The balances of these accounts represent total liabilities for *both* the employer's and employees' FICA taxes for the May payroll only.)
b. Employees' Federal Income Taxes Payable, $1,050 (liability for May only).
c. Federal Unemployment Taxes Payable, $88 (liability for April and May together).
d. State Unemployment Taxes Payable, $440 (liability for April and May together).

During June and July, the company had the following payroll transactions.

June 15 Issued check payable to Security Bank, a federal depository bank authorized to accept employers' payments of FICA taxes and employee income tax withholdings. The $2,274 check is in payment of the May FICA and employee income taxes.

30 Recorded the June payroll and transferred funds from the regular bank account to the payroll bank account. Issued checks payable to each employee in payment of the June payroll. The payroll register shows the following summary totals for the June pay period.

Check June 30: Cr. Salaries Payable, $6,338

Salaries				Federal	
Office Salaries	Shop Salaries	Gross Pay	FICA Taxes*	Income Taxes	Net Pay
$3,800	$4,200	$8,000	$496	$1,050	$6,338
			$116		

* FICA taxes are Social Security and Medicare, respectively.

Check June 30: Dr. Payroll Taxes Expenses, $612

30 Recorded the employer's payroll taxes resulting from the June payroll. The company has a merit rating that reduces its state unemployment tax rate to 4.0% of the first $7,000 paid each employee. The federal rate is 0.8%.

July 15: Cr. Cash $2,274 (Security Bank)

July 15 Issued check payable to Security Bank in payment of the June FICA and employee income taxes.

15 Issued check to the State Tax Commission for the April, May and June state unemployment taxes. Mailed the check and the second quarter tax return to the State Tax Commission.

31 Issued check payable to Security Bank in payment of the employer's FUTA taxes for the first quarter of the year.

31 Mailed Form 941 to the IRS, reporting the FICA taxes and the employees' federal income tax withholdings for the second quarter.

Required

Prepare journal entries to record the transactions and events for both June and July.

(This serial problem began in Chapter 1 and continues through most of the book. If previous chapter segments were not completed, the serial problem can begin at this point. It is helpful, but not necessary, to use the Working Papers that accompany the book.)

SERIAL PROBLEM
Success Systems
P2 P3 C2

SP 9 Review the February 26 and March 25 transactions for Success Systems (SP 4) from Chapter 4.

Required

1. Assume that Lyn Addie is an unmarried employee. Her $1,000 of wages are subject to no deductions other than FICA Social Security taxes, FICA Medicare taxes, and federal income taxes. Her federal income taxes for this pay period total $159. Compute her net pay for the eight days' work paid on February 26. (Round amounts to the nearest cent.)

2. Record the journal entry to reflect the payroll payment to Lyn Addie as computed in part 1.

3. Record the journal entry to reflect the (employer) payroll tax expenses for the February 26 payroll payment. Assume Lyn Addie has not met earnings limits for FUTA and SUTA—the FUTA rate is 0.8% and the SUTA rate is 4% for Success Systems. (Round amounts to the nearest cent.)

4. Record the entry(ies) for the merchandise sold on March 25 if a 4% sales tax rate applies.

CP 9 Bug-Off Exterminators provides pest control services and sells extermination products manufactured by other companies. The following six-column table contains the company's unadjusted trial balance as of December 31, 2013.

COMPREHENSIVE PROBLEM
Bug-Off Exterminators
(Review of Chapters 1–9)

BUG-OFF EXTERMINATORS December 31, 2013					
	Unadjusted Trial Balance		Adjustments		Adjusted Trial Balance
Cash	$ 17,000				
Accounts receivable	4,000				
Allowance for doubtful accounts		$ 828			
Merchandise inventory	11,700				
Trucks	32,000				
Accum. depreciation—Trucks		0			
Equipment	45,000				
Accum. depreciation—Equipment		12,200			
Accounts payable		5,000			
Estimated warranty liability		1,400			
Unearned services revenue		0			
Interest payable		0			
Long-term notes payable		15,000			
Common stock		10,000			
Retained earnings		49,700			
Dividends	10,000				
Extermination services revenue		60,000			
Interest revenue		872			
Sales (of merchandise)		71,026			
Cost of goods sold	46,300				
Depreciation expense—Trucks	0				
Depreciation expense—Equipment	0				
Wages expense	35,000				
Interest expense	0				
Rent expense	9,000				
Bad debts expense	0				
Miscellaneous expense	1,226				
Repairs expense	8,000				
Utilities expense	6,800				
Warranty expense	0				
Totals	$226,026	$226,026			

The following information in *a* through *h* applies to the company at the end of the current year.

a. The bank reconciliation as of December 31, 2013, includes the following facts.

Cash balance per bank	$15,100
Cash balance per books	17,000
Outstanding checks.............................	1,800
Deposit in transit	2,450
Interest earned (on bank account)	52
Bank service charges (miscellaneous expense)	15

Reported on the bank statement is a canceled check that the company failed to record. (Information from the bank reconciliation allows you to determine the amount of this check, which is a payment on an account payable.)

b. An examination of customers' accounts shows that accounts totaling $679 should be written off as uncollectible. Using an aging of receivables, the company determines that the ending balance of the Allowance for Doubtful Accounts should be $700.

c. A truck is purchased and placed in service on January 1, 2013. Its cost is being depreciated with the straight-line method using the following facts and estimates.

Original cost	$32,000
Expected salvage value	8,000
Useful life (years)	4

d. Two items of equipment (a sprayer and an injector) were purchased and put into service in early January 2011. They are being depreciated with the straight-line method using these facts and estimates.

	Sprayer	Injector
Original cost	$27,000	$18,000
Expected salvage value	3,000	2,500
Useful life (years)	8	5

e. On August 1, 2013, the company is paid $3,840 cash in advance to provide monthly service for an apartment complex for one year. The company began providing the services in August. When the cash was received, the full amount was credited to the Extermination Services Revenue account.

f. The company offers a warranty for the services it sells. The expected cost of providing warranty service is 2.5% of the extermination services revenue of $57,760 for 2013. No warranty expense has been recorded for 2013. All costs of servicing warranties in 2013 were properly debited to the Estimated Warranty Liability account.

g. The $15,000 long-term note is an 8%, five-year, interest-bearing note with interest payable annually on December 31. The note was signed with First National Bank on December 31, 2013.

h. The ending inventory of merchandise is counted and determined to have a cost of $11,700. Bug-Off uses a perpetual inventory system.

Required

1. Use the preceding information to determine amounts for the following items.

Check (1*a*) Cash bal. $15,750
(1*b*) $551 credit

   a. Correct (reconciled) ending balance of Cash, and the amount of the omitted check.
   b. Adjustment needed to obtain the correct ending balance of the Allowance for Doubtful Accounts.
   c. Depreciation expense for the truck used during year 2013.
   d. Depreciation expense for the two items of equipment used during year 2013.
   e. The adjusted 2013 ending balances of the Extermination Services Revenue and Unearned Services Revenue accounts.

(1*f*) Estim. warranty
liability, $2,844 Cr.

   f. The adjusted 2013 ending balances of the accounts for Warranty Expense and Estimated Warranty Liability.
   g. The adjusted 2013 ending balances of the accounts for Interest Expense and Interest Payable. (Round amounts to nearest whole dollar.)

2. Use the results of part 1 to complete the six-column table by first entering the appropriate adjustments for items *a* through *g* and then completing the adjusted trial balance columns. (*Hint:* Item *b* requires two adjustments.)

(2) Adjusted trial balance totals, $238,207

3. Prepare journal entries to record the adjustments entered on the six-column table. Assume Bug-Off's adjusted balance for Merchandise Inventory matches the year-end physical count.

4. Prepare a single-step income statement, a statement of retained earnings (cash dividends during 2013 were $10,000), and a classified balance sheet.

(4) Net income, $9,274; Total assets, $82,771

Beyond the Numbers

BTN 9-1   Refer to the financial statements of Polaris in Appendix A to answer the following.

1. Compute times interest earned for the fiscal years ended 2011, 2010, and 2009. Comment on Polaris' ability to cover its interest expense for this period. Assume an industry average of 20 for times interest earned.

2. Polaris' current liabilities include "Sales promotions and incentives"; assume that this account reflects "Loyalty reward liabilities." Is this a known or an estimated liability? Explain how this liability is created.

3. Does Polaris have any commitments or contingencies? If yes, then briefly explain them.

Fast Forward

4. Access Polaris' financial statements for fiscal years ending after December 31, 2011, at its Website (Polaris.com) or the SEC's EDGAR database (www.sec.gov). Compute its times interest earned for years ending after December 31, 2011, and compare your results to those in part 1.

REPORTING IN ACTION

A1 P4

Polaris

BTN 9-2   Key figures for Polaris and Arctic Cat follow.

COMPARATIVE ANALYSIS

A1

Polaris
Arctic Cat

($ thousands)	Polaris			Arctic Cat		
	Current Year	One Year Prior	Two Years Prior	Current Year	One Year Prior	Two Years Prior
Net income	$227,575	$147,138	$101,017	$13,007	$1,875	$(9,508)
Income taxes	119,051	71,403	50,157	5,224	(777)	(6,247)
Interest expense	3,987	2,680	4,111	11	250	1,015

Required

1. Compute times interest earned for the three years' data shown for each company.

2. Comment on which company appears stronger in its ability to pay interest obligations if income should decline. Assume an industry average of 20.

BTN 9-3   Cameron Bly is a sales manager for an automobile dealership. He earns a bonus each year based on revenue from the number of autos sold in the year less related warranty expenses. Actual warranty expenses have varied over the prior 10 years from a low of 3% of an automobile's selling price to a high of 10%. In the past, Bly has tended to estimate warranty expenses on the high end to be conservative. He must work with the dealership's accountant at year-end to arrive at the warranty expense accrual for cars sold each year.

1. Does the warranty accrual decision create any ethical dilemma for Bly?

2. Since warranty expenses vary, what percent do you think Bly should choose for the current year? Justify your response.

ETHICS CHALLENGE

P4

BTN 9-4   Dusty Johnson is the accounting and finance manager for a manufacturer. At year-end, he must determine how to account for the company's contingencies. His manager, Tom Pretti, objects to Johnson's proposal to recognize an expense and a liability for warranty service on units of a new product introduced in the fourth quarter. Pretti comments, "There's no way we can estimate this warranty cost. We don't owe anyone anything until a product fails and it is returned. Let's report an expense if and when we do any warranty work."

COMMUNICATING IN PRACTICE

C3

Required

Prepare a one-page memorandum for Johnson to send to Pretti defending his proposal.

TAKING IT TO THE NET

C1 A1

BTN 9-5 Access the February 24, 2012, filing of the December 31, 2011, annual 10-K report of **McDonald's Corporation** (Ticker: MCD), which is available from www.SEC.gov.

Required

1. Identify the current liabilities on McDonald's balance sheet as of December 31, 2011.
2. What portion (in percent) of McDonald's long-term debt matures within the next 12 months?
3. Use the consolidated statement of income for the year ended December 31, 2011, to compute McDonald's times interest earned ratio. Comment on the result. Assume an industry average of 15.0.

TEAMWORK IN ACTION

C2 P1

BTN 9-6 Assume that your team is in business and you must borrow $6,000 cash for short-term needs. You have been shopping banks for a loan, and you have the following two options.

A. Sign a $6,000, 90-day, 10% interest-bearing note dated June 1.
B. Sign a $6,000, 120-day, 8% interest-bearing note dated June 1.

Required

1. Discuss these two options and determine the best choice. Ensure that all teammates concur with the decision and understand the rationale.
2. Each member of the team is to prepare *one* of the following journal entries.
   a. Option A—at date of issuance.
   b. Option B—at date of issuance.
   c. Option A—at maturity date.
   d. Option B—at maturity date.
3. In rotation, each member is to explain the entry he or she prepared in part 2 to the team. Ensure that all team members concur with and understand the entries.
4. Assume that the funds are borrowed on December 1 (instead of June 1) and your business operates on a calendar-year reporting period. Each member of the team is to prepare *one* of the following entries.
   a. Option A—the year-end adjustment.
   b. Option B—the year-end adjustment.
   c. Option A—at maturity date.
   d. Option B—at maturity date.
5. In rotation, each member is to explain the entry he or she prepared in part 4 to the team. Ensure that all team members concur with and understand the entries.

ENTREPRENEURIAL DECISION

A1

BTN 9-7 Review the chapter's opening feature about Karen Cooper, and her start-up company, SmartIT Staffing. Assume that she is considering expanding her business to open an office in Europe. Assume her current income statement is as follows.

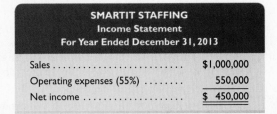

SMARTIT STAFFING	
Income Statement	
For Year Ended December 31, 2013	
Sales	$1,000,000
Operating expenses (55%)	550,000
Net income	$ 450,000

SmartIT Staffing currently has no interest-bearing debt. If it expands to open a European location, it will require a $300,000 loan. SmartIT Staffing has found a bank that will loan it the money on a 7% note payable. The company believes that, at least for the first few years, sales at its European location will be $250,000, and that all expenses will follow the same patterns as its current locations.

Required

1. Prepare an income statement (showing three separate columns for current operations, European, and total) for the company assuming that it borrows the funds and expands to Europe. Annual revenues for current operations are expected to remain at $1,000,000.

2. Compute the company's times interest earned under the expansion assumptions in part 1.

3. Assume sales at its European location are $400,000. Prepare an income statement (with columns for current operations, European, and total) for the company and compute times interest earned.

4. Assume sales at its European location are $100,000. Prepare an income statement (with columns for current operations, European, and total) for the company and compute times interest earned.

5. Comment on your results from parts 1 through 4.

BTN 9-8 Check your phone book or the Social Security Administration Website (www.ssa.gov) to locate the Social Security office near you. Visit the office to request a personal earnings and estimate form. Fill out the form and mail according to the instructions. You will receive a statement from the Social Security Administration regarding your earnings history and future Social Security benefits you can receive. (Formerly the request could be made online. The online service has been discontinued and is now under review by the Social Security Administration due to security concerns.) It is good to request an earnings and benefit statement every 5 to 10 years to make sure you have received credit for all wages earned and for which you and your employer have paid taxes into the system.

HITTING THE ROAD

P2

BTN 9-9 KTM, Polaris, and Arctic Cat are all competitors in the global marketplace. Comparative figures for KTM (www.KTM.com), along with selected figures from Polaris and Arctic Cat, follow.

GLOBAL DECISION

A1

KTM
Polaris
Arctic Cat

Key Figures	KTM (EUR thousands) Current Year	KTM (EUR thousands) Prior Year	Polaris Current Year	Polaris Prior Year	Arctic Cat Current Year	Arctic Cat Prior Year
Net income	20,818	2,660	—	—	—	—
Income taxes	1,709*	(229)	—	—	—	—
Interest expense	9,693	4,256	—	—	—	—
Times interest earned	?	?	87.9	82.5	1,658.4	5.4

*KTM's income taxes is a "positive" for the current year, which is not normal and occurs because of tax loss carryforwards that are explained in advanced courses.

Required

1. Compute the times interest earned ratio for the most recent two years for KTM using the data shown.

2. Which company of the three presented provides the best coverage of interest expense? Explain.

ANSWERS TO MULTIPLE CHOICE QUIZ

1. b; $6,000 × 0.05 × 30/360 = $25
2. e; $50,000 × (.062 + .0145) = $3,825
3. b; $7,000 × (.008 + .054) = $434

4. c; 10,000 television sets × .01 × $250 = $25,000
5. a; 150 employees × $175 per day × 1 vacation day earned = $26,250

Accounting for Long-Term Liabilities

A Look Back

Chapter 9 focused on how current liabilities are identified, computed, recorded, and reported. Attention was directed at notes, payroll, sales taxes, warranties, employee benefits, and contingencies.

A Look at This Chapter

This chapter describes the accounting for and analysis of bonds and notes. We explain their characteristics, payment patterns, interest computations, retirement, and reporting requirements. An appendix to this chapter introduces leases and pensions.

A Look Ahead

Chapter 11 focuses on corporate equity transactions, including stock issuances and dividends. We also explain how to report and analyze income, earnings per share, and retained earnings.

Learning Objectives

CONCEPTUAL

C1 Explain the types and payment patterns of notes. (p. 432)

C2 *Appendix 10A*—Explain and compute the present value of an amount(s) to be paid at a future date(s). (p. 440)

C3 *Appendix 10C*—Describe interest accrual when bond payment periods differ from accounting periods. (p. 444)

C4 *Appendix 10D*—Describe accounting for leases and pensions. (p. 446)

ANALYTICAL

A1 Compare bond financing with stock financing. (p. 422)

A2 Assess debt features and their implications. (p. 436)

A3 Compute the debt-to-equity ratio and explain its use. (p. 436)

PROCEDURAL

P1 Prepare entries to record bond issuance and interest expense. (p. 424)

P2 Compute and record amortization of bond discount using straight-line method. (p. 425)

P3 Compute and record amortization of bond premium using straight-line method. (p. 428)

P4 Record the retirement of bonds. (p. 431)

P5 Prepare entries to account for notes. (p. 434)

P6 *Appendix 10B*—Compute and record amortization of bond discount using effective interest method. (p. 442)

P7 *Appendix 10B*—Compute and record amortization of bond premium using effective interest method. (p. 443)

Decision Insight

Hippie Biz

"I really enjoy the concept of being a modern hippie."
—KYLE SMITLEY

WASHINGTON, DC—"Being a modern hippie is knowing when, where, and how to let both your hippie and modern sides come forth," declares Kyle Smitley. "The eco-friendly world is full of spontaneity and tree-hugging." The hippie in her led Kyle to launch **barley & birch (barleyandbirch.com),** an American-made 100% certified organic clothing line, which pledges to give much of its profits to environmental and social causes. "I started barley & birch to make a difference," insists Kyle. "I wanted to . . . make every single facet of the line carbon neutral."

Kyle is driven to make her business a success. "As a young entrepreneur with no experience, I was a sitting duck," admits Kyle. "There were people that either didn't take me seriously or wanted to take my money." Launching her fledgling business presented challenges. She especially focused on the important task of managing liabilities to suppliers, shippers, and others in the supply chain.

Kyle insists that effective management of liabilities, especially long-term financing from sources such as bonds and notes, is crucial to success. In her case, she launched barley & birch with a loan, or notes payable, from ACCION. "I obtained a $10,000 business loan," explains Kyle. Interest payments, principal repayments, and operating expenses had to be controlled. "The best advice I ever received was from my father, an accountant," says Kyle. "He told me to be realistic about my budget and that it is easy to spend all of your money on lots of little things that have the risk of killing your business."

Kyle continues to monitor liabilities and their payment patterns, and she is not shy about striving to better learn the accounting side. "I am never done working," says Kyle. "I am always frantically catching up!" She insists that accounting for and monitoring liabilities of long-term financing are important ingredients to a successful start-up. Her company now generates sufficient income to pay for interest and principal on long-term debt and is on target for a goal of $2 million in sales this year.

Still, the larger message of barley & birch is about eco-friendly products and carbon neutrality. "Money only makes me excited if I can give it away," explains Kyle. "The business is only a tool. It is the car, and philanthropy is the engine."

[Sources: *barley & birch Website,* January 2013; *Modern Hippie Mag,* January 2010; *Ladies Who Launch,* June 2010; *YHP Website,* November 2009; *DePauw University News,* March 2011; *The Toledo Times,* May 2012]

Individuals, companies, and governments issue bonds to finance their activities. In return for financing, bonds promise to repay the lender with interest. This chapter explains the basics of bonds and the accounting for their issuance and retirement. The chapter also describes long-term notes as another financing source. We explain how present value concepts impact both the accounting for and reporting of bonds and notes. Appendixes to this chapter discuss present value concepts applicable to liabilities, effective interest amortization, and the accounting for leases and pensions.

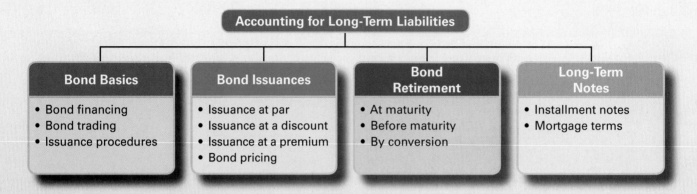

Accounting for Long-Term Liabilities			
Bond Basics	**Bond Issuances**	**Bond Retirement**	**Long-Term Notes**
• Bond financing • Bond trading • Issuance procedures	• Issuance at par • Issuance at a discount • Issuance at a premium • Bond pricing	• At maturity • Before maturity • By conversion	• Installment notes • Mortgage terms

BASICS OF BONDS

This section explains the basics of bonds and a company's motivation for issuing them.

Bond Financing

A1 Compare bond financing with stock financing.

Projects that demand large amounts of money often are funded from bond issuances. (Both for-profit and nonprofit companies, as well as governmental units, such as nations, states, cities, and school districts, issue bonds.) A **bond** is its issuer's written promise to pay an amount identified as the par value of the bond with interest. The **par value of a bond,** also called the *face amount* or *face value,* is paid at a specified future date known as the bond's *maturity date.* Most bonds also require the issuer to make semiannual interest payments. The amount of interest paid each period is determined by multiplying the par value of the bond by the bond's contract rate of interest for that same period. This section explains both advantages and disadvantages of bond financing.

Advantages of Bonds   There are three main advantages of bond financing:

1. *Bonds do not affect owner control.* Equity financing reflects ownership in a company, whereas bond financing does not. A person who contributes $1,000 of a company's $10,000 equity financing typically controls one-tenth of all owner decisions. A person who owns a $1,000, 11%, 20-year bond has no ownership right. This person, or bondholder, is to receive from the bond issuer 11% interest, or $110, each year the bond is outstanding and $1,000 when it matures in 20 years.

2. *Interest on bonds is tax deductible.* Bond interest payments are tax deductible for the issuer, but equity payments (distributions) to owners are not. To illustrate, assume that a corporation with no bond financing earns $15,000 in income *before* paying taxes at a 40% tax rate, which amounts to $6,000 ($15,000 × 40%) in taxes. If a portion of its financing is in bonds, however, the resulting bond interest is deducted in computing taxable income. That is, if bond interest expense is $10,000, the taxes owed would be $2,000 ([$15,000 − $10,000] × 40%), which is less than the $6,000 owed with no bond financing.

3. *Bonds can increase return on equity.* A company that earns a higher return with borrowed funds than it pays in interest on those funds increases its return on equity. This process is called *financial leverage* or *trading on the equity.*

Point: Financial leverage reflects issuance of bonds, notes, or preferred stock.

To illustrate the third point, consider Magnum Co., which has $1 million in equity and is planning a $500,000 expansion to meet increasing demand for its product. Magnum predicts the

$500,000 expansion will yield $125,000 in additional income before paying any interest. It currently earns $100,000 per year and has no interest expense. Magnum is considering three plans. Plan A is to not expand. Plan B is to expand and raise $500,000 from equity financing. Plan C is to expand and issue $500,000 of bonds that pay 10% annual interest ($50,000). Exhibit 10.1 shows how these three plans affect Magnum's net income, equity, and return on equity (net income/equity). The owner(s) will earn a higher return on equity if expansion occurs. Moreover, the preferred expansion plan is to issue bonds. Projected net income under Plan C ($175,000) is smaller than under Plan B ($225,000), but the return on equity is larger because of less equity investment. Plan C has another advantage if income is taxable. This illustration reflects a general rule: *Return on equity increases when the expected rate of return from the new assets is higher than the rate of interest expense on the debt financing.*

Example: Compute return on equity for all three plans if Magnum currently earns $150,000 instead of $100,000.
Answer ($ 000s):
Plan A = 15%   ($150/$1,000)
Plan B = 18.3%   ($275/$1,500)
Plan C = 22.5%   ($225/$1,000)

EXHIBIT 10.1

Financing with Bonds versus Equity

	Plan A: Do Not Expand	Plan B: Equity Financing	Plan C: Bond Financing
Income before interest expense	$ 100,000	$ 225,000	$ 225,000
Interest expense	—	—	(50,000)
Net income	$ 100,000	$ 225,000	$ 175,000
Equity	$1,000,000	$1,500,000	$1,000,000
Return on equity	10.0%	15.0%	17.5%

Disadvantages of Bonds   The two main disadvantages of bond financing are these:

1. *Bonds can decrease return on equity.* When a company earns a lower return with the borrowed funds than it pays in interest, it decreases its return on equity. This downside risk of financial leverage is more likely to arise when a company has periods of low income or net losses.

2. *Bonds require payment of both periodic interest and the par value at maturity.* Bond payments can be especially burdensome when income and cash flow are low. Equity financing, in contrast, does not require any payments because cash withdrawals (dividends) are paid at the discretion of the owner (or board).

A company must weigh the risks and returns of the disadvantages and advantages of bond financing when deciding whether to issue bonds to finance operations.

Point: Debt financing is desirable when interest is tax deductible, when owner control is preferred, and when return on equity exceeds the debt's interest rate.

Point: The phrase: *debt is cheaper than equity,* refers in part to interest expense on bonds being tax deductible whereas dividends on stock are not.

Bond Trading

Bonds are securities that can be readily bought and sold. A large number of bonds trade on both the New York Exchange and the American Exchange. A bond *issue* consists of a number of bonds, usually in denominations of $1,000 or $5,000, and is sold to many different lenders. After bonds are issued, they often are bought and sold by investors, meaning that any particular bond probably has a number of owners before it matures. Since bonds are exchanged (bought and sold) in the market, they have a market value (price). For convenience, bond market values are expressed as a percent of their par (face) value. For example, a company's bonds might be trading at 103½, meaning they can be bought or sold for 103.5% of their par value. Bonds can also trade below par value. For instance, if a company's bonds are trading at 95, they can be bought or sold at 95% of their par value.

Decision Insight

Quotes   The **IBM** bond quote here is interpreted (left to right) as **Bonds,** issuer name; **Rate,** contract interest rate (5.7%); **Mat,** matures in year 2017 when principal is paid; **Yld,** yield rate (4.7%) of bond at current price; **Vol,** daily dollar worth ($130,000) of trades (in 1,000s); **Close,** closing price (121.18) for the day as percentage of par value; **Chg,** change (+0.24%) in closing price from prior day's close. ∎

Bonds	Rate	Mat	Yld	Vol	Close	Chg
IBM	5.7	17	4.7	130	121.18	+0.24%

Bond-Issuing Procedures

State and federal laws govern bond issuances. Bond issuers also want to ensure that they do not violate any of their existing contractual agreements when issuing bonds. Authorization of bond issuances includes the number of bonds authorized, their par value, and the contract interest rate. The legal document identifying the rights and obligations of both the bondholders and the issuer is called the **bond indenture,** which is the legal contract between the issuer and the bondholders (and specifies how often interest is paid). A bondholder may also receive a bond certificate as evidence of the company's debt. A **bond certificate,** such as that shown in Exhibit 10.2, includes specifics such as the issuer's name, the par value, the contract interest rate, and the maturity date. Many companies reduce costs by not issuing paper certificates to bondholders.[1]

EXHIBIT 10.2

Bond Certificate

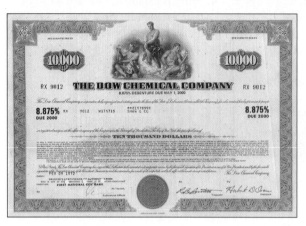

Point: *Indenture* refers to a bond's legal contract; *debenture* refers to an unsecured bond.

BOND ISSUANCES

This section explains accounting for bond issuances at par, below par (discount), and above par (premium). It also describes how to amortize a discount or premium and record bonds issued between interest payment dates.

Issuing Bonds at Par

P1 Prepare entries to record bond issuance and interest expense.

To illustrate an issuance of bonds at par value, suppose a company receives authorization to issue $800,000 of 9%, 20-year bonds dated January 1, 2013, that mature on December 31, 2032, and pay interest semiannually on each June 30 and December 31. After accepting the bond indenture on behalf of the bondholders, the trustee can sell all or a portion of the bonds to an underwriter. If all bonds are sold at par value, the issuer records the sale as follows.

Assets   = Liabilities + Equity
+800,000   +800,000

2013			
Jan. 1	Cash..	800,000	
	Bonds Payable		800,000
	Sold bonds at par.		

This entry reflects increases in the issuer's cash *and* long-term liabilities.

The issuer records the first semiannual interest payment as follows.

Assets   = Liabilities + Equity
−36,000   −36,000

2013			
June 30	Bond Interest Expense	36,000	
	Cash.......................................		36,000
	Paid semiannual interest (9% × $800,000 × ½ year).		

Point: The *spread* between the dealer's cost and what buyers pay can be huge. Dealers earn more than $25 billion in annual spread revenue.

Global: In the United Kingdom, government bonds are called *gilts*— short for gilt-edged investments.

[1] The issuing company normally sells its bonds to an investment firm called an *underwriter,* which resells them to the public. An issuing company can also sell bonds directly to investors. When an underwriter sells bonds to a large number of investors, a *trustee* represents and protects the bondholders' interests. The trustee monitors the issuer to ensure that it complies with the obligations in the bond indenture. Most trustees are large banks or trust companies. The trustee writes and accepts the terms of a bond indenture before it is issued. When bonds are offered to the public, called *floating an issue,* they must be registered with the Securities and Exchange Commission (SEC). SEC registration requires the issuer to file certain financial information. Most company bonds are issued in par value units of $1,000 or $5,000. *A baby bond* has a par value of less than $1,000, such as $100.

The issuer pays and records its semiannual interest obligation every six months until the bonds mature. When they mature, the issuer records its payment of principal as follows.

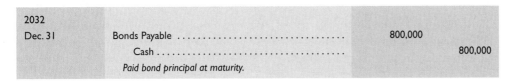

2032			
Dec. 31	Bonds Payable	800,000	
	Cash		800,000
	Paid bond principal at maturity.		

Assets = Liabilities + Equity
−800,000   −800,000

Bond Discount or Premium

The bond issuer pays the interest rate specified in the indenture, the **contract rate**, also referred to as the *coupon rate, stated rate,* or *nominal rate*. The annual interest paid is determined by multiplying the bond par value by the contract rate. The contract rate is usually stated on an annual basis, even if interest is paid semiannually. For example, if a company issues a $1,000, 8% bond paying interest semiannually, it pays annual interest of $80 (8% × $1,000) in two semiannual payments of $40 each.

The contract rate sets the amount of interest the issuer pays in *cash,* which is not necessarily the *bond interest expense* actually incurred by the issuer. Bond interest expense depends on the bond's market value at issuance, which is determined by market expectations of the risk of lending to the issuer. The bond's **market rate** of interest is the rate that borrowers are willing to pay and lenders are willing to accept for a particular bond and its risk level. As the risk level increases, the rate increases to compensate purchasers for the bonds' increased risk. Also, the market rate is generally higher when the time period until the bond matures is longer due to the risk of adverse events occurring over a longer time period.

Many bond issuers try to set a contract rate of interest equal to the market rate they expect as of the bond issuance date. When the contract rate and market rate are equal, a bond sells at par value, but when they are not equal, a bond does not sell at par value. Instead, it is sold at a *premium* above par value or at a *discount* below par value. Exhibit 10.3 shows the relation between the contract rate, market rate, and a bond's issue price.

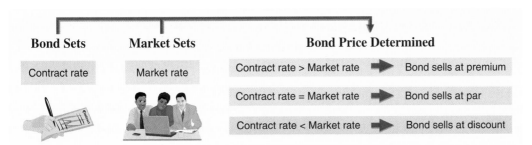

EXHIBIT 10.3

Relation between Bond Issue Price, Contract Rate, and Market Rate

Quick Check   Answers — p. 449

1. A company issues $10,000 of 9%, 5-year bonds dated January 1, 2013, that mature on December 31, 2017, and pay interest semiannually on each June 30 and December 31. Prepare the entry to record this bond issuance and the first semiannual interest payment.
2. How do you compute the amount of interest a bond issuer pays in cash each year?
3. When the contract rate is above the market rate, do bonds sell at a premium or a discount? Do purchasers pay more or less than the par value of the bonds?

Issuing Bonds at a Discount

A **discount on bonds payable** occurs when a company issues bonds with a contract rate less than the market rate. This means that the issue price is less than par value. To illustrate, assume that Fila announces an offer to issue bonds with a $100,000 par value, an 8% annual contract rate (paid semiannually), and a two-year life. Also assume that the market rate for Fila bonds is

P2 Compute and record amortization of bond discount.

Point: The difference between the contract rate and the market rate of interest on a new bond issue is usually a fraction of a percent. We use a difference of 2% to emphasize the effects.

10%. These bonds then will sell at a discount since the contract rate is less than the market rate. The exact issue price for these bonds is stated as 96.454 (implying 96.454% of par value, or $96,454); we show how to compute this issue price later in the chapter. These bonds obligate the issuer to pay two separate types of future cash flows:

1. Par value of $100,000 cash at the end of the bonds' two-year life.
2. Cash interest payments of $4,000 (4% × $100,000) at the end of each semiannual period during the bonds' two-year life.

The exact pattern of cash flows for the Fila bonds is shown in Exhibit 10.4.

EXHIBIT 10.4

Cash Flows for Fila Bonds

				$100,000
	$4,000	$4,000	$4,000	$4,000
0	6 mo.	12 mo.	18 mo.	24 mo.

When Fila accepts $96,454 cash for its bonds on the issue date of December 31, 2013, it records the sale as follows.

Assets = Liabilities + Equity
+96,454   +100,000
          −3,546

Dec. 31	Cash	96,454	
	Discount on Bonds Payable	3,546	
	Bonds Payable		100,000
	Sold bonds at a discount on their issue date.		

Point: Book value at issuance always equals the issuer's cash borrowed.

These bonds are reported in the long-term liability section of the issuer's December 31, 2013, balance sheet as shown in Exhibit 10.5. A discount is deducted from the par value of bonds to yield the **carrying (book) value of bonds.** Discount on Bonds Payable is a contra liability account.

EXHIBIT 10.5

Balance Sheet Presentation of Bond Discount

Long-term liabilities		
Bonds payable, 8%, due December 31, 2015	$100,000	
Less discount on bonds payable	3,546	$96,454 ← carrying (book) value

Amortizing a Bond Discount   Fila receives $96,454 for its bonds; in return it must pay bondholders $100,000 after two years (plus semiannual interest payments). The $3,546 discount is paid to bondholders at maturity and is part of the cost of using the $96,454 for two years. The upper portion of panel A in Exhibit 10.6 shows that total bond interest expense of $19,546 is the difference between the total amount repaid to bondholders ($116,000) and the amount borrowed from bondholders ($96,454). Alternatively, we can compute total bond interest expense as the sum of the four interest payments and the bond discount. This alternative computation is shown in the lower portion of panel A.

Point: *Zero-coupon bonds* do not pay periodic interest (contract rate is zero). These bonds always sell at a discount because their 0% contract rate is always below the market rate.

The total $19,546 bond interest expense must be allocated across the four semiannual periods in the bonds' life, and the bonds' carrying value must be updated at each balance sheet date. This is accomplished using the straight-line method (or the effective interest method in Appendix 10B). Both methods systematically reduce the bond discount to zero over the two-year life. This process is called *amortizing a bond discount.*

> *The following section on discount amortization uses the straight-line method. Appendix 10B uses the effective interest method. An instructor can choose to cover either one or both methods. If the straight-line method is skipped, then read Appendix 10B and return to the section (on page 428) titled "Issuing Bonds at a Premium."*

Straight-Line Method   The **straight-line bond amortization** method allocates an equal portion of the total bond interest expense to each interest period. To apply the straight-line method to Fila's bonds, we divide the total bond interest expense of $19,546 by 4 (the number of semiannual periods in the bonds' life). This gives a bond interest expense of $4,887 per period, which is $4,886.5 rounded to the nearest dollar per period (all computations, including those for assignments, are rounded to the nearest whole dollar). Alternatively, we can find this

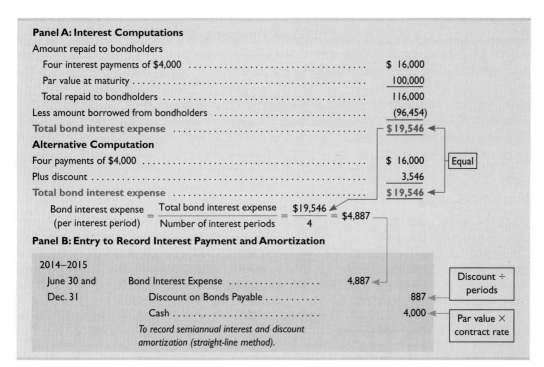

EXHIBIT 10.6

Interest Computation and Entry for Bonds Issued at a Discount

number by first dividing the $3,546 discount by 4, which yields the $887 amount of discount to be amortized each interest period. When the $887 is added to the $4,000 cash payment, the bond interest expense for each period is $4,887. Panel B of Exhibit 10.6 shows how the issuer records bond interest expense and updates the balance of the bond liability account at the end of *each* of the four semiannual interest periods (June 30, 2014, through December 31, 2015).

Exhibit 10.7 shows the pattern of decreases in the Discount on Bonds Payable account and the pattern of increases in the bonds' carrying value. The following points summarize the discount bonds' straight-line amortization:

1. At issuance, the $100,000 par value consists of the $96,454 cash received by the issuer plus the $3,546 discount.

2. During the bonds' life, the (unamortized) discount decreases each period by the $887 amortization ($3,546/4), and the carrying value (par value less unamortized discount) increases each period by $887.

EXHIBIT 10.7

Straight-Line Amortization of Bond Discount

Semiannual Period-End		Unamortized Discount*	Carrying Value†
(0)	12/31/2013	$3,546	$ 96,454
(1)	6/30/2014	2,659	97,341
(2)	12/31/2014	1,772	98,228
(3)	6/30/2015	885	99,115
(4)	12/31/2015	0‡	100,000

* Total bond discount (of $3,546) less accumulated periodic amortization ($887 per semiannual interest period).

† Bond par value (of $100,000) less unamortized discount.

‡ Adjusted for rounding.

The two columns always sum to par value for a discount bond.

3. At maturity, the unamortized discount equals zero, and the carrying value equals the $100,000 par value that the issuer pays the holder.

We see that the issuer incurs a $4,887 bond interest expense each period but pays only $4,000 cash. The $887 unpaid portion of this expense is added to the bonds' carrying value. (The total $3,546 unamortized discount is "paid" when the bonds mature; $100,000 is paid at maturity but only $96,454 was received at issuance.)

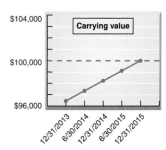

Decision Insight

Ratings Game   Many bond buyers rely on rating services to assess bond risk. The best known are **Standard & Poor's**, **Moody's**, and **Fitch**. These services focus on the issuer's financial statements and other factors in setting ratings. Standard & Poor's ratings, from best quality to default, are AAA, AA, A, BBB, BB, B, CCC, CC, C, and D. Ratings can include a plus (+) or minus (−) to show relative standing within a category. Bonds rated in the A and B range are referred to as *investment grade;* lower-rated bonds are considered much riskier. ■

Quick Check
Answers — p. 449

Five-year, 6% bonds with a $100,000 par value are issued at a price of $91,893. Interest is paid semiannually, and the bonds' market rate is 8% on the issue date. Use this information to answer the following questions:

4. Are these bonds issued at a discount or a premium? Explain your answer.
5. What is the issuer's journal entry to record the issuance of these bonds?
6. What is the amount of bond interest expense recorded at the first semiannual period using the straight-line method?

Issuing Bonds at a Premium

P3 Compute and record amortization of bond premium.

When the contract rate of bonds is higher than the market rate, the bonds sell at a price higher than par value. The amount by which the bond price exceeds par value is the **premium on bonds.** To illustrate, assume that **Adidas** issues bonds with a $100,000 par value, a 12% annual contract rate, semiannual interest payments, and a two-year life. Also assume that the market rate for Adidas bonds is 10% on the issue date. The Adidas bonds will sell at a premium because the contract rate is higher than the market rate. The issue price for these bonds is stated as 103.546 (implying 103.546% of par value, or $103,546); we show how to compute this issue price later in the chapter. These bonds obligate the issuer to pay out two separate future cash flows:

1. Par value of $100,000 cash at the end of the bonds' two-year life.
2. Cash interest payments of $6,000 (6% × $100,000) at the end of each semiannual period during the bonds' two-year life.

The exact pattern of cash flows for the Adidas bonds is shown in Exhibit 10.8.

EXHIBIT 10.8

Cash Flows for Adidas Bonds

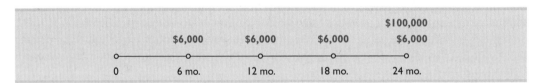

When Adidas accepts $103,546 cash for its bonds on the issue date of December 31, 2013, it records this transaction as follows.

Assets	=	Liabilities	+	Equity
+103,546		+100,000		
		+3,546		

Dec. 31	Cash	103,546	
	Premium on Bonds Payable		3,546
	Bonds Payable		100,000
	Sold bonds at a premium on their issue date.		

These bonds are reported in the long-term liability section of the issuer's December 31, 2013, balance sheet as shown in Exhibit 10.9. A premium is added to par value to yield the carrying (book) value of bonds. Premium on Bonds Payable is an adjunct (also called *accretion*) liability account.

EXHIBIT 10.9

Balance Sheet Presentation of Bond Premium

Long-term liabilities		
Bonds payable, 12%, due December 31, 2015	$100,000	
Plus premium on bonds payable	3,546	$103,546

Amortizing a Bond Premium   Adidas receives $103,546 for its bonds; in return, it pays bondholders $100,000 after two years (plus semiannual interest payments). The $3,546 premium not repaid to issuer's bondholders at maturity goes to reduce the issuer's expense of using the $103,546 for two years. The upper portion of panel A of Exhibit 10.10 shows that total bond interest expense of $20,454 is the difference between the total amount repaid to bondholders ($124,000) and the amount borrowed from bondholders ($103,546). Alternatively, we can compute total bond

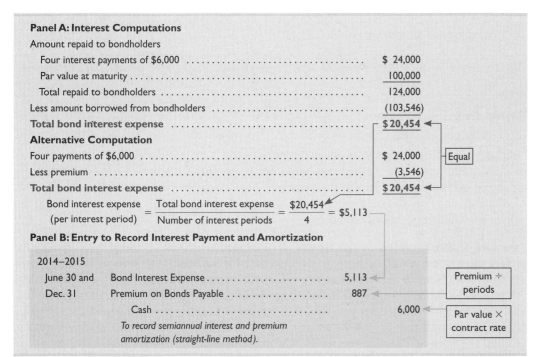

Panel A: Interest Computations

Amount repaid to bondholders

Four interest payments of $6,000	$ 24,000	
Par value at maturity	100,000	
Total repaid to bondholders	124,000	
Less amount borrowed from bondholders	(103,546)	
Total bond interest expense	**$20,454** ◄	
Alternative Computation		
Four payments of $6,000	$ 24,000	Equal
Less premium	(3,546)	
Total bond interest expense	**$20,454** ◄	

$$\text{Bond interest expense} \atop \text{(per interest period)} = \frac{\text{Total bond interest expense}}{\text{Number of interest periods}} = \frac{\$20,454}{4} = \$5,113$$

Panel B: Entry to Record Interest Payment and Amortization

2014–2015			
June 30 and	Bond Interest Expense	5,113 ◄	Premium ÷ periods
Dec. 31	Premium on Bonds Payable	887 ◄	
	Cash		6,000 ◄ Par value × contract rate
	To record semiannual interest and premium		
	amortization (straight-line method).		

EXHIBIT 10.10

Interest Computation and Entry for Bonds Issued at a Premium

interest expense as the sum of the four interest payments less the bond premium. The premium is subtracted because it will not be paid to bondholders when the bonds mature; see the lower portion of panel A. Total bond interest expense must be allocated over the four semiannual periods using the straight-line method (or the effective interest method in Appendix 10B).

Point: The phrase: *ability to service debt,* refers to making interest and principal payments on time.

> *The following section on premium amortization uses the straight-line method. Appendix 10B uses the effective interest method. An instructor can choose to cover either one or both methods. If the straight-line method is skipped, then read Appendix 10B and return to the section (next page) titled "Bond Pricing."*

Straight-Line Method The straight-line method allocates an equal portion of total bond interest expense to each of the bonds' semiannual interest periods. To apply this method to Adidas bonds, we divide the two years' total bond interest expense of $20,454 by 4 (the number of semiannual periods in the bonds' life). This gives a total bond interest expense of $5,113 per period, which is $5,113.5 rounded down so that the journal entry balances and for simplicity in presentation (alternatively, one could carry cents). Panel B of Exhibit 10.10 shows how the issuer records bond interest expense and updates the balance of the bond liability account for *each* semiannual period (June 30, 2014, through December 31, 2015).

Point: A premium decreases Bond Interest Expense; a discount increases it.

EXHIBIT 10.11

Straight-Line Amortization of Bond Premium

Semiannual Period-End	Unamortized Premium*	Carrying Value[†]
(0) 12/31/2013	$3,546	$103,546
(1) 6/30/2014	2,659	102,659
(2) 12/31/2014	1,772	101,772
(3) 6/30/2015	885	100,885
(4) 12/31/2015	0[‡]	100,000

* Total bond premium (of $3,546) less accumulated periodic amortization ($887 per semiannual interest period).

[†] Bond par value (of $100,000) plus unamortized premium.

[‡] Adjusted for rounding.

During the bond life, carrying value is adjusted to par and the amortized premium to zero.

Exhibit 10.11 shows the pattern of decreases in the unamortized Premium on Bonds Payable account and in the bonds' carrying value. The following points summarize straight-line amortization of the premium bonds:

1. At issuance, the $100,000 par value plus the $3,546 premium equals the $103,546 cash received by the issuer.

2. During the bonds' life, the (unamortized) premium decreases each period by the $887 amortization ($3,546/4), and the carrying value decreases each period by the same $887.

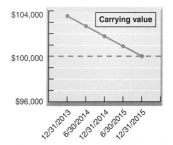

Point: There are nearly 5 million individual U.S. bond issues, ranging from huge treasuries to tiny municipalities. This compares to about 12,000 individual U.S. stocks that are traded.

3. At maturity, the unamortized premium equals zero, and the carrying value equals the $100,000 par value that the issuer pays the holder.

> *The next section describes bond pricing. An instructor can choose to cover bond pricing or not. Assignments requiring the next section are Quick Study 10-4 and Exercises 10-9 and 10-10.*

Bond Pricing

Point: InvestingInBonds.com is a bond research and learning source.

Prices for bonds traded on an organized exchange are often published in newspapers and through online services. This information normally includes the bond price (called *quote*), its contract rate, and its current market (called *yield*) rate. However, only a fraction of bonds are traded on organized exchanges. To compute the price of a bond, we apply present value concepts. This section explains how to use *present value concepts* to price the Fila discount bond and the Adidas premium bond described earlier.

Point: A bond's market value (price) at issuance equals the present value of its future cash payments, where the interest (discount) rate used is the bond's market rate.

Present Value of a Discount Bond The issue price of bonds is found by computing the present value of the bonds' cash payments, discounted at the bonds' market rate. When computing the present value of the Fila bonds, we work with *semiannual* compounding periods because this is the time between interest payments; the annual market rate of 10% is considered a semiannual rate of 5%. Also, the two-year bond life is viewed as four semiannual periods. The price computation is twofold: (1) Find the present value of the $100,000 par value paid at maturity and (2) find the present value of the series of four semiannual payments of $4,000 each; see Exhibit 10.4. These present values can be found by using *present value tables*. Appendix B at the end of this book shows present value tables and describes their use. Table B.1 at the end of Appendix B is used for the single $100,000 maturity payment, and Table B.3 in Appendix B is used for the $4,000 series of interest payments. Specifically, we go to Table B.1, row 4, and across to the 5% column to identify the present value factor of 0.8227 for the maturity payment. Next, we go to Table B.3, row 4, and across to the 5% column, where the present value factor is 3.5460 for the series of interest payments. We compute bond price by multiplying the cash flow payments by their corresponding present value factors and adding them together; see Exhibit 10.12.

Point: Many calculators have present value functions for computing bond prices.

EXHIBIT 10.12

Computing Issue Price for the Fila Discount Bonds

Calculator	
N = 4	PMT = 4,000
I/Yr = 5	FV = 100,000
	PV = 96,454

Cash Flow	Table	Present Value Factor	Amount	Present Value
$100,000 par (maturity) value	B.1	0.8227	× $100,000 =	$ 82,270
$4,000 interest payments	B.3	3.5460	× 4,000 =	14,184
Price of bond				$96,454

Point: Calculator inputs defined:
N   Number of semiannual periods
I/Yr Market rate per semiannual period
FV   Future (maturity) value
PMT Payment (interest) per semiannual period
PV   Price (present value)

Present Value of a Premium Bond We find the issue price of the Adidas bonds by using the market rate to compute the present value of the bonds' future cash flows. When computing the present value of these bonds, we again work with *semiannual* compounding periods because this is the time between interest payments. The annual 10% market rate is applied as a semiannual rate of 5%, and the two-year bond life is viewed as four semiannual periods. The computation is twofold: (1) Find the present value of the $100,000 par value paid at maturity and (2) find the present value of the series of four payments of $6,000 each; see Exhibit 10.8. These present values can be found by using present value tables. First, go to Table B.1, row 4, and across to the 5% column where the present value factor is 0.8227 for the maturity payment. Second, go to Table B.3, row 4, and across to the 5% column, where the present value factor is 3.5460 for the series of interest payments. The bonds' price is computed by multiplying the cash flow payments by their corresponding present value factors and adding them together; see Exhibit 10.13.

EXHIBIT 10.13

Computing Issue Price for the Adidas Premium Bonds

Calculator	
N = 4	PMT = 6,000
I/Yr = 5	FV = 100,000
	PV = 103,546

Cash Flow	Table	Present Value Factor	Amount	Present Value
$100,000 par (maturity) value	B.1	0.8227	× $100,000 =	$ 82,270
$6,000 interest payments	B.3	3.5460	× 6,000 =	21,276
Price of bond				$103,546

■ **Decision** Insight

Unreported Liabilities Drove U.S. Financial Crisis? Many argue that unreported liabilities were a major cause of the financial crisis. They assert that "off-balance-sheet accounting" encouraged bad loans, securitizations, and derivatives that drove much of the crisis. It is argued that balance sheets failed to report many of these liabilities. For example, because bank liabilities used to finance assets were not transparent, the markets failed to penalize banks that used derivatives and variable interest entities (VIEs) to take excessive risks. Arguably, such accounting is fraudulent. ■

Quick Check   Answers — p. 449

On December 31, 2012, a company issues 16%, 10-year bonds with a par value of $100,000. Interest is paid on June 30 and December 31. The bonds are sold to yield a 14% annual market rate at an issue price of $110,592. Use this information to answer questions 7 through 9:

7. Are these bonds issued at a discount or a premium? Explain your answer.

8. Using the straight-line method to allocate bond interest expense, the issuer records the second interest payment (on December 31, 2013) with a debit to Premium on Bonds Payable in the amount of (a) $7,470, (b) $530, (c) $8,000, or (d) $400.

9. How are these bonds reported in the long-term liability section of the issuer's balance sheet as of December 31, 2013?

BOND RETIREMENT

This section describes the retirement of bonds (1) at maturity, (2) before maturity, and (3) by conversion to stock.

P4 Record the retirement of bonds.

Bond Retirement at Maturity

The carrying value of bonds at maturity always equals par value. For example, both Exhibits 10.7 (a discount) and 10.11 (a premium) show that the carrying value of bonds at the end of their lives equals par value ($100,000). The retirement of these bonds at maturity, assuming interest is already paid and entered, is recorded as follows:

2015			
Dec. 31	Bonds Payable	100,000	
	Cash		100,000
	To record retirement of bonds at maturity.		

Assets = Liabilities + Equity
−100,000   −100,000

Bond Retirement before Maturity

Issuers sometimes wish to retire some or all of their bonds prior to maturity. For instance, if interest rates decline greatly, an issuer may wish to replace high-interest-paying bonds with new low-interest bonds. Two common ways to retire bonds before maturity are to (1) exercise a call option or (2) purchase them on the open market. In the first instance, an issuer can reserve the right to retire bonds early by issuing callable bonds. The bond indenture can give the issuer an option to *call* the bonds before they mature by paying the par value plus a *call premium* to bondholders. In the second case, the issuer retires bonds by repurchasing them on the open market at their current price. Whether bonds are called or repurchased, the issuer is unlikely to pay a price that exactly equals their carrying value. When a difference exists between the bonds' carrying value and the amount paid, the issuer records a gain or loss equal to the difference.

To illustrate the accounting for retiring callable bonds, assume that a company issued callable bonds with a par value of $100,000. The call option requires the issuer to pay a call premium of $3,000 to bondholders in addition to the par value. Next, assume that after the June 30, 2013, interest payment, the bonds have a carrying value of $104,500. Then on July 1, 2013, the issuer calls these bonds and pays $103,000 to bondholders. The issuer recognizes a $1,500 gain from

Point: Bond retirement is also referred to as *bond redemption*.

Point: Gains and losses from retiring bonds were *previously* reported as extraordinary items. New standards require that they now be judged by the "unusual and infrequent" criteria for reporting purposes.

the difference between the bonds' carrying value of $104,500 and the retirement price of $103,000. The issuer records this bond retirement as follows.

Assets	=	Liabilities	+	Equity
−103,000		−100,000		+1,500
		−4,500		

July 1	Bonds Payable	100,000	
	Premium on Bonds Payable	4,500	
	Gain on Bond Retirement		1,500
	Cash		103,000
	To record retirement of bonds before maturity.		

An issuer usually must call all bonds when it exercises a call option. However, to retire as many or as few bonds as it desires, an issuer can purchase them on the open market. If it retires less than the entire class of bonds, it recognizes a gain or loss for the difference between the carrying value of those bonds retired and the amount paid to acquire them.

Bond Retirement by Conversion

Holders of convertible bonds have the right to convert their bonds to stock. When conversion occurs, the bonds' carrying value is transferred to equity accounts and no gain or loss is recorded. (We further describe convertible bonds in the Decision Analysis section of this chapter.)

To illustrate, assume that on January 1 the $100,000 par value bonds of **Converse**, with a carrying value of $100,000, are converted to 15,000 shares of $2 par value common stock. The entry to record this conversion follows (the market prices of the bonds and stock are *not* relevant to this entry; the material in Chapter 11 is helpful in understanding this transaction):

Convertible Bond

Assets	=	Liabilities	+	Equity
		−100,000		+30,000
				+70,000

Jan. 1	Bonds Payable	100,000	
	Common Stock		30,000
	Paid-In Capital in Excess of Par Value		70,000
	To record retirement of bonds by conversion.		

Decision Insight

Junk Bonds   Junk bonds are company bonds with low credit ratings due to a higher than average likelihood of default. On the upside, the high risk of junk bonds can yield high returns if the issuer survives and repays its debt. ■

Quick Check   Answer — p. 449

10. Six years ago, a company issued $500,000 of 6%, eight-year bonds at a price of 95. The current carrying value is $493,750. The company decides to retire 50% of these bonds by buying them on the open market at a price of 102½. What is the amount of gain or loss on the retirement of these bonds?

LONG-TERM NOTES PAYABLE

 C1 Explain the types and payment patterns of notes.

Like bonds, notes are issued to obtain assets such as cash. Unlike bonds, notes are typically transacted with a *single* lender such as a bank. An issuer initially records a note at its selling price—that is, the note's face value minus any discount or plus any premium. Over the note's life, the amount of interest expense allocated to each period is computed by multiplying the market rate (at issuance of the note) by the beginning-of-period note balance. The note's carrying (book) value at any time equals its face value minus any unamortized discount or plus any unamortized premium; carrying value is also computed as the present value of all remaining payments, discounted using the market rate at issuance.

Installment Notes

An **installment note** is an obligation requiring a series of payments to the lender. Installment notes are common for franchises and other businesses when lenders and borrowers agree to spread payments over several periods. To illustrate, assume that Foghog borrows $60,000 from a bank to purchase equipment. It signs an 8% installment note requiring six annual payments of principal plus interest and it records the note's issuance at January 1, 2013, as follows.

Point: Banks sometimes reject loans when risk of default by borrowers is high. Then, bonds can serve as another way borrowers can finance operations or expansion.

Jan. 1	Cash	60,000
	Notes Payable	60,000
	Borrowed $60,000 by signing an 8%, six-year installment note.	

Assets = Liabilities + Equity
+60,000   +60,000

Payments on an installment note normally include the accrued interest expense plus a portion of the amount borrowed (the *principal*). This section describes an installment note with equal payments.

The equal total payments pattern consists of changing amounts of both interest and principal. To illustrate, assume that Foghog borrows $60,000 by signing a $60,000 note that requires six *equal payments* of $12,979 at the end of each year. (The present value of an annuity of six annual payments of $12,979, discounted at 8%, equals $60,000; we show this computation in footnote 2 on the next page.) The $12,979 includes both interest and principal, the amounts of which change with each payment. Exhibit 10.14 shows the pattern of equal total payments and its two parts, interest and principal. Column A shows the note's beginning balance. Column B shows accrued

Years

2013 2014 2015 2016 2017 2018

Point: Most consumer notes are installment notes that require equal total payments.

EXHIBIT 10.14

Installment Note: Equal Total Payments

	(A)	Payments		(D)	(E)
		(B)	(C)	Credit	
Period Ending Date	Beginning Balance	Debit Interest Expense 8% × (A)	Debit Notes Payable (D) − (B)	Cash (computed)	Ending Balance (A) − (C)
(1) 12/31/2013	$60,000	$ 4,800	$ 8,179	$12,979	$51,821
(2) 12/31/2014	51,821	4,146	8,833	12,979	42,988
(3) 12/31/2015	42,988	3,439	9,540	12,979	33,448
(4) 12/31/2016	33,448	2,676	10,303	12,979	23,145
(5) 12/31/2017	23,145	1,852	11,127	12,979	12,018
(6) 12/31/2018	12,018	961	12,018	12,979	0
		$17,874	$60,000	$77,874	

☐ Interest ☐ Principal

Decreasing Accrued Interest

Increasing Principal Component

Equal Total Payments

End of Year		
2013	$4,800	$8,179
2014	$4,146	$8,833
2015	$3,439	$9,540
2016	$2,676	$10,303
2017	$1,852	$11,127
2018	$961	$12,018

0   $2,500 $5,000 $7,500 $10,000 $12,500 $15,000

Cash Payment Pattern

interest for each year at 8% of the beginning note balance. Column C shows the impact on the note's principal, which equals the difference between the total payment in column D and the interest expense in column B. Column E shows the note's year-end balance.

Although the six cash payments are equal, accrued interest decreases each year because the principal balance of the note declines. As the amount of interest decreases each year, the portion of each payment applied to principal increases. This pattern is graphed in the lower part of Exhibit 10.14. Foghog uses the amounts in Exhibit 10.14 to record its first two payments (for years 2013 and 2014) as follows:

| **P5** | Prepare entries to account for notes. |

Assets   = Liabilities + Equity
−12,979   −8,179   −4,800

2013		
Dec. 31	Interest Expense	4,800	
	Notes Payable	8,179	
	Cash		12,979
	To record first installment payment.		

Assets   = Liabilities + Equity
−12,979   −8,833   −4,146

2014		
Dec. 31	Interest Expense	4,146	
	Notes Payable	8,833	
	Cash		12,979
	To record second installment payment.		

Foghog records similar entries but with different amounts for each of the remaining four payments. After six years, the Notes Payable account balance is zero.[2]

Decision Insight

Missing Debt A study reports that 13% of employees in finance and accounting witnessed the falsifying or manipulating of accounting information in the past year (KPMG 2009). This includes nondisclosure of special concern with long-term liabilities. Another study reports that most people committing fraud (36%) work in the finance function of their firm (KPMG 2011). For example, Enron violated GAAP to keep debt off its balance sheet. ■

Mortgage Notes and Bonds

Point: The Truth-in-Lending Act requires lenders to provide information about loan costs including finance charges and interest rate.

A **mortgage** is a legal agreement that helps protect a lender if a borrower fails to make required payments on notes or bonds. A mortgage gives the lender a right to be paid from the cash proceeds of the sale of a borrower's assets identified in the mortgage. A legal document, called a *mortgage contract,* describes the mortgage terms.

Global: Countries vary in the preference given to debtholders vs. stockholders when a company is in financial distress. Some countries such as Germany, France, and Japan give preference to stockholders over debtholders.

Mortgage notes carry a mortgage contract pledging title to specific assets as security for the note. Mortgage notes are especially popular in the purchase of homes and the acquisition of plant assets. Less common *mortgage bonds* are backed by the issuer's assets. Accounting for mortgage notes and bonds is similar to that for unsecured notes and bonds, except that the mortgage agreement must be disclosed. For example, **TIBCO Software** reports that its "mortgage note payable . . . is collateralized by the commercial real property acquired [corporate headquarters]."

Example: Suppose the $60,000 installment loan has an 8% interest rate with eight equal annual payments. What is the annual payment? *Answer* (using Table B.3): $60,000/5.7466 = $10,441

---

[2] Table B.3 in Appendix B is used to compute the dollar amount of the six payments that equal the initial note balance of $60,000 at 8% interest. We go to Table B.3, row 6, and across to the 8% column, where the present value factor is 4.6229. The dollar amount is then computed by solving this relation:

Table	Present Value Factor		Dollar Amount		Present Value
B.3	4.6229	×	?	=	$60,000

The dollar amount is computed by dividing $60,000 by 4.6229, yielding $12,979.

c. Straight-line amortization table for premium bonds.

Semiannual Period-End	Unamortized Premium	Carrying Value
(0) 1/1/2013	$30,881	$430,881
(1) 6/30/2013	27,793	427,793
(2) 12/31/2013	24,705	424,705
(3) 6/30/2014	21,617	421,617
(4) 12/31/2014	18,529	418,529
(5) 6/30/2015	15,441	415,441
(6) 12/31/2015	12,353	412,353
(7) 6/30/2016	9,265	409,265
(8) 12/31/2016	6,177	406,177
(9) 6/30/2017	3,089	403,089
(10) 12/31/2017	0*	400,000

* Adjusted for rounding.

d. Journal entry for June 30, 2013, bond payment.

June 30	Bond Interest Expense	20,912	
	Premium on Bonds Payable	3,088	
	Cash		24,000
	Paid semiannual interest on bonds.		

e. Journal entry for January 1, 2015, bond retirement.

Jan. 1	Bonds Payable	400,000	
	Premium on Bonds Payable	18,529	
	Cash		416,000
	Gain on Retirement of Bonds		2,529
	To record bond retirement (carrying value as of Dec. 31, 2014).		

Part 3: Bonds (Effective Interest Amortization)[B]

c. The effective interest amortization table for premium bonds.

Semiannual Interest Period	(A) Cash Interest Paid 6% × $400,000	(B) Interest Expense 5% × Prior (E)	(C) Premium Amortization (A) − (B)	(D) Unamortized Premium Prior (D) − (C)	(E) Carrying Value $400,000 + (D)
(0) 1/1/2013				$30,881	$430,881
(1) 6/30/2013	$ 24,000	$ 21,544	$ 2,456	28,425	428,425
(2) 12/31/2013	24,000	21,421	2,579	25,846	425,846
(3) 6/30/2014	24,000	21,292	2,708	23,138	423,138
(4) 12/31/2014	24,000	21,157	2,843	20,295	420,295
(5) 6/30/2015	24,000	21,015	2,985	17,310	417,310
(6) 12/31/2015	24,000	20,866	3,134	14,176	414,176
(7) 6/30/2016	24,000	20,709	3,291	10,885	410,885
(8) 12/31/2016	24,000	20,544	3,456	7,429	407,429
(9) 6/30/2017	24,000	20,371	3,629	3,800	403,800
(10) 12/31/2017	24,000	20,200*	3,800	0	400,000
	$240,000	$209,119	$30,881		

* Adjusted for rounding

d. Journal entry for June 30, 2013, bond payment.

June 30	Bond Interest Expense	21,544	
	Premium on Bonds Payable	2,456	
	Cash		24,000
	Paid semiannual interest on bonds.		

e. Journal entry for January 1, 2015, bond retirement.

Jan. 1	Bonds Payable	400,000	
	Premium on Bonds Payable	20,295	
	Cash		416,000
	Gain on Retirement of Bonds		4,295
	To record bond retirement (carrying value as of December 31, 2014).		

APPENDIX

10A   Present Values of Bonds and Notes

This appendix explains how to apply present value techniques to measure a long-term liability when it is created and to assign interest expense to the periods until it is settled. Appendix B at the end of the book provides additional discussion of present value concepts.

C2 Explain and compute the present value of an amount(s) to be paid at a future date(s).

Present Value Concepts   The basic present value concept is that cash paid (or received) in the future has less value now than the same amount of cash paid (or received) today. To illustrate, if we must pay $1 one year from now, its present value is less than $1. To see this, assume that we borrow $0.9259 today that must be paid back in one year with 8% interest. Our interest expense for this loan is computed as $0.9259 × 8%, or $0.0741. When the $0.0741 interest is added to the $0.9259 borrowed, we get the $1 payment necessary to repay our loan with interest. This is formally computed in Exhibit 10A.1. The $0.9259 borrowed is the present value of the $1 future payment. More generally, an amount borrowed equals the present value of the future payment. (This same interpretation applies to an investment. If $0.9259 is invested at 8%, it yields $0.0741 in revenue after one year. This amounts to $1, made up of principal and interest.)

EXHIBIT 10A.1

Components of a One-Year Loan

Amount borrowed	$0.9259
Interest for one year at 8%	0.0741
Amount owed after 1 year	$ 1.0000

Point: Benjamin Franklin is said to have described compounding as "the money, money makes, makes more money."

To extend this example, assume that we owe $1 two years from now instead of one year, and the 8% interest is compounded annually. *Compounded* means that interest during the second period is based on the total of the amount borrowed plus the interest accrued from the first period. The second period's interest is then computed as 8% multiplied by the sum of the amount borrowed plus interest earned in the first period. Exhibit 10A.2 shows how we compute the present value of $1 to be paid in two years. This amount is $0.8573. The first year's interest of $0.0686 is added to the principal so that the second year's interest is based on $0.9259. Total interest for this two-year period is $0.1427, computed as $0.0686 plus $0.0741.

EXHIBIT 10A.2

Components of a Two-Year Loan

Amount borrowed	$0.8573
Interest for first year ($0.8573 × 8%)	0.0686
Amount owed after 1 year	0.9259
Interest for second year ($0.9259 × 8%)	0.0741
Amount owed after 2 years	$ 1.0000

Present Value Tables   The present value of $1 that we must repay at some future date can be computed by using this formula: $1/(1 + i)^n$. The symbol i is the interest rate per period and n is the number of periods until the future payment must be made. Applying this formula to our two-year loan, we get $1/(1.08)^2$, or $0.8573. This is the same value shown in Exhibit 10A.2. We can use this formula to find any present value. However, a simpler method is to use a *present value table,* which lists present values computed with this formula for various interest rates and time periods. Many people find it helpful in learning present value concepts to first work with the table and then move to using a calculator.

Exhibit 10A.3 shows a present value table for a future payment of 1 for up to 10 periods at three different interest rates. Present values in this table are rounded to four decimal places. This table is drawn from the larger and more complete Table B.1 in Appendix B at the end of the book. Notice that the first value in the 8% column is 0.9259, the value we computed earlier for the present value of a $1 loan for one year at 8% (see Exhibit 10A.1). Go to the second row in the same 8% column and find the present value of 1 discounted at 8% for two years, or 0.8573. This $0.8573 is the present value of our obligation to repay $1 after two periods at 8% interest (see Exhibit 10A.2).

EXHIBIT 10A.3

Present Value of 1

Periods	Rate 6%	Rate 8%	Rate 10%
1	0.9434	**0.9259**	0.9091
2	0.8900	**0.8573**	0.8264
3	0.8396	0.7938	0.7513
4	0.7921	0.7350	0.6830
5	0.7473	0.6806	0.6209
6	0.7050	0.6302	0.5645
7	0.6651	0.5835	0.5132
8	0.6274	0.5403	0.4665
9	0.5919	0.5002	0.4241
10	0.5584	0.4632	0.3855

Example: Use Exhibit 10A.3 to find the present value of $1 discounted for 2 years at 6%. *Answer:* $0.8900

Applying a Present Value Table   To illustrate how to measure a liability using a present value table, assume that a company plans to borrow cash and repay it as follows: $2,000 after one year, $3,000 after two years, and $5,000 after three years. How much does this company receive today if the interest rate on this loan is 10%? To answer, we need to compute the present value of the three future payments, discounted at 10%. This computation is shown in Exhibit 10A.4 using present values from Exhibit 10A.3. The company can borrow $8,054 today at 10% interest in exchange for its promise to make these three payments at the scheduled dates.

EXHIBIT 10A.4

Present Value of a Series of Unequal Payments

Periods	Payments	Present Value of 1 at 10%	Present Value of Payments
1	$2,000	0.9091	$ 1,818
2	3,000	0.8264	2,479
3	5,000	0.7513	3,757
Present value of all payments			**$8,054**

Present Value of an Annuity   The $8,054 present value for the loan in Exhibit 10A.4 equals the sum of the present values of the three payments. When payments are not equal, their combined present value is best computed by adding the individual present values as shown in Exhibit 10A.4. Sometimes payments follow an **annuity,** which is a series of *equal* payments at equal time intervals. The present value of an annuity is readily computed.

To illustrate, assume that a company must repay a 6% loan with a $5,000 payment at each year-end for the next four years. This loan amount equals the present value of the four payments discounted at 6%. Exhibit 10A.5 shows how to compute this loan's present value of $17,326 by multiplying each payment by its matching present value factor taken from Exhibit 10A.3.

However, the series of $5,000 payments is an annuity, so we can compute its present value with either of two shortcuts. First, the third column of Exhibit 10A.5 shows that the sum of the present values of 1 at 6% for periods 1 through 4 equals 3.4651. One shortcut is to multiply this total of 3.4651 by the $5,000 annual payment to get the combined present value of $17,326. It requires one multiplication instead of four.

EXHIBIT 10A.5

Present Value of a Series of Equal Payments (Annuity) by Discounting Each Payment

Periods	Payments	Present Value of 1 at 6%	Present Value of Payments
1	$5,000	0.9434	$ 4,717
2	5,000	0.8900	4,450
3	5,000	0.8396	4,198
4	5,000	0.7921	3,961
Present value of all payments		**3.4651**	**$17,326**

EXHIBIT 10A.6

Present Value of an Annuity of 1

Periods	Rate		
	6%	8%	10%
1	0.9434	0.9259	0.9091
2	1.8334	1.7833	1.7355
3	2.6730	2.5771	2.4869
4	**3.4651**	3.3121	3.1699
5	4.2124	3.9927	3.7908
6	4.9173	4.6229	4.3553
7	5.5824	5.2064	4.8684
8	6.2098	5.7466	5.3349
9	6.8017	6.2469	5.7590
10	7.3601	6.7101	6.1446

Example: Use Exhibit 10A.6 to find the present value of an annuity of eight $15,000 payments with an 8% interest rate. *Answer:* $15,000 × 5.7466 = $86,199

Example: If this borrower makes five semiannual payments of $8,000, what is the present value of this annuity at a 12% rate? *Answer:* 4.2124 × $8,000 = $33,699

The second shortcut uses an *annuity table* such as the one shown in Exhibit 10A.6, which is drawn from the more complete Table B.3 in Appendix B. We go directly to the annuity table to get the present value factor for a specific number of payments and interest rate. We then multiply this factor by the amount of the payment to find the present value of the annuity. Specifically, find the row for four periods and go across to the 6% column, where the factor is 3.4651. This factor equals the present value of an annuity with four payments of 1, discounted at 6%. We then multiply 3.4651 by $5,000 to get the $17,326 present value of the annuity.

Compounding Periods Shorter Than a Year   The present value examples all involved periods of one year. In many situations, however, interest is compounded over shorter periods. For example, the interest rate on bonds is usually stated as an annual rate but interest is often paid every six months (semiannually). This means that the present value of interest payments from such bonds must be computed using interest periods of six months.

Assume that a borrower wants to know the present value of a series of 10 *semiannual payments* of $4,000 made over five years at an *annual interest rate* of 12%. The interest rate is stated as an annual rate of 12%, but it is actually a rate of 6% per semiannual interest period. To compute the present value of this series of $4,000 payments, go to row 10 of Exhibit 10A.6 and across to the 6% column to find the factor 7.3601. The present value of this annuity is $29,440 (7.3601 × $4,000).

Appendix B further describes present value concepts and includes more complete present value tables and assignments.

Quick Check   Answers — p. 449

14. A company enters into an agreement to make four annual year-end payments of $1,000 each, starting one year from now. The annual interest rate is 8%. The present value of these four payments is (*a*) $2,923, (*b*) $2,940, or (*c*) $3,312.

15. Suppose a company has an option to pay either (*a*) $10,000 after one year or (*b*) $5,000 after six months and another $5,000 after one year. Which choice has the lower present value?

APPENDIX

10B

Effective Interest Amortization

P6 *Appendix 10B*—Compute and record amortization of bond discount using effective interest method.

Point: The effective interest method computes bond interest expense using the market rate at issuance. This rate is applied to a changing carrying value.

Effective Interest Amortization of a Discount Bond   The straight-line method yields changes in the bonds' carrying value while the amount for bond interest expense remains constant. This gives the impression of a changing interest rate when users divide a constant bond interest expense over a changing carrying value. As a result, accounting standards allow use of the straight-line method only when its results do not differ materially from those obtained using the effective interest method. The **effective interest method,** or simply *interest method,* allocates total bond interest expense over the bonds' life in a way that yields a constant rate of interest. This constant rate of interest is the market rate at the issue date. Thus, bond interest expense for a period equals the carrying value of the bond at the beginning of that period multiplied by the market rate when issued.

Exhibit 10B.1 shows an effective interest amortization table for the Fila bonds (as described in Exhibit 10.4). The key difference between the effective interest and straight-line methods lies in computing bond interest expense. Instead of assigning an equal amount of bond interest expense to each option or purchasing them in the market. Bondholders can also retire bonds early by exercising a conversion feature on convertible bonds. The issuer recognizes a gain or loss for the difference between the amount paid and the bond carrying value.

P5 **Prepare entries to account for notes.** Interest is allocated to each period in a note's life by multiplying its beginning-period carrying value by its market rate at issuance. If a note is repaid with equal payments, the payment amount is computed by dividing the borrowed amount by the present value of an annuity factor (taken from a present value table) using the market rate and the number of payments.

P6^B **Compute and record amortization of bond discount using effective interest method.** Bonds are issued at a discount

when the contract rate is less than the market rate, making the issue (selling) price less than par. The amount of bond interest expense assigned to each period, including amortization of the discount, is computed using the effective interest method.

P7^B **Compute and record amortization of bond premium using effective interest method.** Bonds are issued at a premium when the contract rate is higher than the market rate, making the issue (selling) price greater than par. The amount of bond interest expense assigned to each period, including amortization of the premium, is computed using the effective interest method.

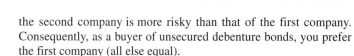

Guidance Answers to Decision Maker

Entrepreneur This is a "present value" question. The market interest rate (10%) and present value ($3,000) are known, but the payment required two years later is unknown. This amount ($3,630) can be computed as $3,000 \times 1.10 \times 1.10$. Thus, the sale price is $3,630 when no payments are received for two years. The $3,630 received two years from today is equivalent to $3,000 cash today.

Bond Investor The debt-to-equity ratio for the first company is 0.2 ($350,000/$1,750,000) and for the second company is 1.2 ($1,200,000/$1,000,000), suggesting that the financing structure of

the second company is more risky than that of the first company. Consequently, as a buyer of unsecured debenture bonds, you prefer the first company (all else equal).

Bond Rater Bonds with longer repayment periods (life) have higher risk. Also, bonds issued by companies in financial difficulties or facing higher than normal uncertainties have higher risk. Moreover, companies with higher than normal debt and large fluctuations in earnings are considered of higher risk. Discount bonds are more risky on one or more of these factors.

Guidance Answers to Quick Checks

1.

2013			
Jan. 1	Cash	10,000	
	Bonds Payable		10,000
June 30	Bond Interest Expense	450	
	Cash		450

2. Multiply the bond's par value by its contract rate of interest.

3. Bonds sell at a premium when the contract rate exceeds the market rate and the purchasers pay more than their par value.

4. The bonds are issued at a discount, meaning that issue price is less than par value. A discount occurs because the bond contract rate (6%) is less than the market rate (8%).

5.

Cash	91,893	
Discount on Bonds Payable	8,107	
Bonds Payable		100,000

6. $3,811 (total bond interest expense of $38,107 divided by 10 periods; or the $3,000 semiannual cash payment plus the $8,107 discount divided by 10 periods).

7. The bonds are issued at a premium, meaning issue price is higher than par value. A premium occurs because the bonds' contract rate (16%) is higher than the market rate (14%).

8. (*b*) For each semiannual period: $10,592/20 periods = $530 premium amortization.

9.

Bonds payable, 16%, due 12/31/2022	$100,000
Plus premium on bonds payable	9,532* $109,532

* Original premium balance of $10,592 less $530 and $530 amortized on 6/30/2013 and 12/31/2013, respectively.

10. $9,375 loss, computed as the difference between the repurchase price of $256,250 [50% of ($500,000 × 102.5%)] and the carrying value of $246,875 (50% of $493,750).

11. (*c*)

12. The interest portion of an installment payment equals the period's beginning loan balance multiplied by the market interest rate at the time of the note's issuance.

13. On the balance sheet, the account balances of the related liability (note payable) and asset (cash) accounts are decreased. On the income statement, interest expense is recorded.

14. (*c*), computed as 3.3121 × $1,000 = $3,312.

15. The option of paying $10,000 after one year has a lower present value. It postpones paying the first $5,000 by six months. More generally, the present value of a further delayed payment is always lower than a less delayed payment.

16. (*a*) Reflects payment of accrued interest recorded back on May 1; $500,000 × 9% × 1/12 = $15,000.

Key Terms

Annuity (p. 441)	Debt-to-equity ratio (p. 437)	Pension plan (p. 448)
Bearer bonds (p. 436)	Discount on bonds payable (p. 425)	Premium on bonds (p. 428)
Bond (p. 422)	Effective interest method (p. 442)	Registered bonds (p. 436)
Bond certificate (p. 424)	Fair value option (p. 435)	Secured bonds (p. 436)
Bond indenture (p. 424)	Installment note (p. 433)	Serial bonds (p. 436)
Callable bonds (p. 436)	Lease (p. 446)	Sinking fund bonds (p. 436)
Capital leases (p. 446)	Market rate (p. 425)	Straight-line bond amortization (p. 426)
Carrying (book) value of bonds (p. 426)	Mortgage (p. 434)	Term bonds (p. 436)
Contract rate (p. 425)	Off-balance-sheet financing (p. 447)	Unsecured bonds (p. 436)
Convertible bonds (p. 436)	Operating leases (p. 446)	
Coupon bonds (p. 436)	Par value of a bond (p. 422)	

Multiple Choice Quiz   Answers on p. 463   mhhe.com/wildFAF4e

Additional Quiz Questions are available at the book's Website.

1. A bond traded at 97½ means that
   a. The bond pays 97½% interest.
   b. The bond trades at $975 per $1,000 bond.
   c. The market rate of interest is below the contract rate of interest for the bond.
   d. The bonds can be retired at $975 each.
   e. The bond's interest rate is 2½%.

2. A bondholder that owns a $1,000, 6%, 15-year bond has
   a. The right to receive $1,000 at maturity.
   b. Ownership rights in the bond issuing entity.
   c. The right to receive $60 per month until maturity.
   d. The right to receive $1,900 at maturity.
   e. The right to receive $600 per year until maturity.

3. A company issues 8%, 20-year bonds with a par value of $500,000. The current market rate for the bonds is 8%. The amount of interest owed to the bondholders for each semiannual interest payment is
   a. $40,000.
   b. $0.
   c. $20,000.
   d. $800,000.
   e. $400,000.

4. A company issued 5-year, 5% bonds with a par value of $100,000. The company received $95,735 for the bonds. Using the straight-line method, the company's interest expense for the first semiannual interest period is
   a. $2,926.50.
   b. $5,853.00.
   c. $2,500.00.
   d. $5,000.00.
   e. $9,573.50.

5. A company issued 8-year, 5% bonds with a par value of $350,000. The company received proceeds of $373,745. Interest is payable semiannually. The amount of premium amortized for the first semiannual interest period, assuming straight-line bond amortization, is
   a. $2,698.
   b. $23,745.
   c. $8,750.
   d. $9,344.
   e. $1,484.

B(C,D) *Superscript letter B(C, D) denotes assignments based on Appendix 10B (10C, 10D).*
🔲 Icon denotes assignments that involve decision making.

Discussion Questions

1. What is the main difference between notes payable and bonds payable?
2. What is the main difference between a bond and a share of stock?
3. 🔲 What is the advantage of issuing bonds instead of obtaining financing from the company's owners?
4. What is a bond indenture? What provisions are usually included in it?
5. What are the duties of a trustee for bondholders?
6. What are the *contract* rate and the *market* rate for bonds?
7. 🔲 What factors affect the market rates for bonds?
8.B 🔲 Does the straight-line or effective interest method produce an interest expense allocation that yields a constant rate of interest over a bond's life? Explain.

Braun Company signs a five-year capital lease with Verdi Company for office equipment. The annual lease payment is $20,000 (due at the end of each year), and the interest rate is 10%.

Required

1. Compute the present value of Braun's lease payments.
2. Prepare the journal entry to record Braun's capital lease at its inception.
3. Complete a lease payment schedule for the five years of the lease with the following headings. Assume that the beginning balance of the lease liability (present value of lease payments) is $75,816. (*Hint:* To find the amount allocated to interest in year 1, multiply the interest rate by the beginning-of-year lease liability. The amount of the annual lease payment not allocated to interest is allocated to principal. Reduce the lease liability by the amount allocated to principal to update the lease liability at each year-end.)

Period Ending Date	Beginning Balance of Lease Liability	Interest on Lease Liability	Reduction of Lease Liability	Cash Lease Payment	Ending Balance of Lease Liability

4. Use straight-line depreciation and prepare the journal entry to depreciate the leased asset at the end of year 1. Assume zero salvage value and a five-year life for the office equipment.

Problem 10-11B[D]
Capital lease accounting
C4

Check (1) $75,816

(3) Year 3 ending balance, $34,712

(*This serial problem began in Chapter 1 and continues through most of the book. If previous chapter segments were not completed, the serial problem can begin at this point. It is helpful, but not necessary, to use the Working Papers that accompany the book.*)

SP 10 Adria Lopez has consulted with her local banker and is considering financing an expansion of her business by obtaining a long-term bank loan. Selected account balances at March 31, 2014, for Success Systems follow.

Total assets	$129,909	Total liabilities	$875	Total equity	$129,034

Required

1. The bank has offered a long-term secured note to Success Systems. The bank's loan procedures require that a client's debt-to-equity ratio not exceed 0.8. As of March 31, 2014, what is the maximum amount that Success Systems could borrow from this bank (rounded to nearest dollar)?
2. If Success Systems borrows the maximum amount allowed from the bank, what percentage of assets would be financed (*a*) by debt and (*b*) by equity?
3. What are some factors Adria Lopez should consider before borrowing the funds?

SERIAL PROBLEM
Success Systems
A1 A3

Check (1) $102,352

Beyond the Numbers

BTN 10-1 Refer to Polaris' financial statements in Appendix A to answer the following.

1. Identify the items, if any, that make up Polaris' long-term debt as reported on its balance sheet at December 31, 2011.
2. Assume that Polaris has $100,000 thousand in convertible debentures that carry a 4.25% contract rate of interest. How much annual cash interest must be paid on those convertible debentures?
3. How much cash did it generate from issuance of debt for the year-ended December 31, 2011? How much cash did it use for repayments of debt for that same year?

REPORTING IN ACTION
A1 A2
Polaris

Fast Forward

4. Access Polaris' financial statements for the years ending after December 31, 2011, from its Website (Polaris.com) or the SEC's EDGAR database (www.sec.gov). Has it issued additional long-term debt since the year-end December 31, 2011? If yes, identify the amount(s).

COMPARATIVE ANALYSIS

A3

Polaris

Arctic Cat

BTN 10-2   Key figures for **Polaris** and **Arctic Cat** follow.

($ thousands)	Polaris		Arctic Cat	
	Current Year	**Prior Year**	**Current Year**	**Prior Year**
Total assets	$1,228,024	$1,061,647	$272,906	$246,084
Total liabilities	727,968	690,656	89,870	78,745
Total equity	500,056	370,991	183,036	167,339

Required

1. Compute the debt-to-equity ratios for Polaris and Arctic Cat for both the current year and the prior year.
2. Use the ratios you computed in part 1 to determine which company's financing structure is least risky. Assume an industry average of 0.64 for debt-to-equity.

ETHICS CHALLENGE

C4   A1

BTN 10-3   Traverse County needs a new county government building that would cost $10 million. The politicians feel that voters will not approve a municipal bond issue to fund the building since it would increase taxes. They opt to have a state bank issue $10 million of tax-exempt securities to pay for the building construction. The county then will make yearly lease payments (of principal and interest) to repay the obligation. Unlike conventional municipal bonds, the lease payments are not binding obligations on the county and, therefore, require no voter approval.

Required

1. Do you think the actions of the politicians and the bankers in this situation are ethical?
2. How do the tax-exempt securities used to pay for the building compare in risk to a conventional municipal bond issued by Traverse County?

COMMUNICATING IN PRACTICE

P3

BTN 10-4   Your business associate mentions that she is considering investing in corporate bonds currently selling at a premium. She says that since the bonds are selling at a premium, they are highly valued and her investment will yield more than the going rate of return for the risk involved. Reply with a memorandum to confirm or correct your associate's interpretation of premium bonds.

TAKING IT TO THE NET

A2

BTN 10-5   Access the March 22, 2012, filing of the 10-K report of **Home Depot** for the year ended January 31, 2012, from **www.sec.gov** (Ticker: HD). Refer to Home Depot's balance sheet, including its note 4 (on debt).

Required

1. Identify Home Depot's long-term liabilities and the amounts for those liabilities from Home Depot's balance sheet at January 31, 2012.
2. Review Home Depot's note 4. The note reports that as of January 31, 2012, it had $2.961 billion of "5.875% Senior Notes; due December 16, 2036; interest payable semiannually on June 16 and December 16." These notes have a face value of $3.0 billion and were originally issued at $2.958 billion.
   a. Why would Home Depot issue $3.0 billion of its notes for only $2.958 billion?
   b. How much cash interest must Home Depot pay each June 16 and December 16 on these notes?

TEAMWORK IN ACTION

P2   P3

BTN 10-6^B   Break into teams and complete the following requirements related to *effective interest* amortization for a premium bond.

1. Each team member is to independently prepare a blank table with proper headings for amortization of a bond premium. When all have finished, compare tables and ensure that all are in agreement.

Parts 2 and 3 require use of these facts: On January 1, 2013, McElroy issues $100,000, 9%, five-year bonds at 104.1. The market rate at issuance is 8%. McElroy pays interest semiannually on June 30 and December 31.

2. In rotation, *each* team member must explain how to complete *one* line of the bond amortization table, including all computations for his or her line. (Round amounts to the nearest dollar.) All members are to fill in their tables during this process. You need not finish the table; stop after all members have explained a line.

Disadvantages of Corporate Characteristics

- **Government regulation:** A corporation must meet requirements of a state's incorporation laws, which subject the corporation to state regulation and control. Proprietorships and partnerships avoid many of these regulations and governmental reports.

- **Corporate taxation:** Corporations are subject to the same property and payroll taxes as proprietorships and partnerships plus *additional* taxes. The most burdensome of these are federal and state income taxes that together can take 40% or more of corporate pretax income. Moreover, corporate income is usually taxed a second time as part of stockholders' personal income when they receive cash distributed as dividends. This is called *double taxation.* (The usual dividend tax is 15%; however, it is less than 15% for lower income taxpayers, and in some cases zero.)

Point: Proprietorships and partnerships are not subject to income taxes. Their income is taxed as the personal income of their owners.

Point: Double taxation is less severe when a corporation's owner-manager collects a salary that is taxed only once as part of his or her personal income.

Decision Insight

Stock Financing   Mark Zuckerberg took his company, **Facebook**, public by issuing its first shares on the Nasdaq exchange in 2012. This initial public offering (IPO) of Facebook shares raised billions in equity financing. It also raised the importance of accounting reports versus market hype. The IPO of Facebook shares comes 8 years after the company was founded by Zuckerberg in his college dorm room. ■

Corporate Organization and Management

This section describes the incorporation, costs, and management of corporate organizations.

Incorporation   A corporation is created by obtaining a charter from a state government. A charter application usually must be signed by the prospective stockholders called *incorporators* or *promoters* and then filed with the proper state official. When the application process is complete and fees paid, the charter is issued and the corporation is formed. Investors then purchase the corporation's stock, meet as stockholders, and elect a board of directors. Directors oversee a corporation's affairs.

Point: A corporation is not required to have an office in its state of incorporation. Delaware is viewed as having favorable corporate laws and about half of all corporations listed on the NYSE are incorporated there.

Organization Expenses   Organization expenses (also called *organization costs*) are the costs to organize a corporation; they include legal fees, promoters' fees, and amounts paid to obtain a charter. The corporation records (debits) these costs to an expense account called *Organization Expenses.* Organization costs are expensed as incurred because it is difficult to determine the amount and timing of their future benefits.

Management of a Corporation   The ultimate control of a corporation rests with stockholders who control a corporation by electing its *board of directors,* or simply, *directors.* Each stockholder usually has one vote for each share of stock owned. This control relation is shown in Exhibit 11.1. Directors are responsible for and have final authority for managing corporate activities. A board can act only as a collective body and usually limits its actions to setting general policy.

A corporation usually holds a stockholder meeting at least once a year to elect directors and transact business as its bylaws require. A group of stockholders owning or controlling votes of more than a 50% share of a corporation's stock can elect the board and control the corporation. Stockholders who do not attend stockholders' meetings must have an opportunity to delegate their voting rights to an agent by signing a **proxy,** a document that gives a designated agent the right to vote the stock.

Day-to-day direction of corporate business is delegated to executive officers appointed by the board. A corporation's chief executive officer (CEO) is often its president. Several vice presidents, who report to the president, are commonly assigned specific areas of management responsibility such as finance, production, and marketing. One person often has the dual role of chairperson of the board of directors and CEO. In this case, the president is usually designated the chief operating officer (COO).

EXHIBIT 11.1

Corporate Structure

Stockholders

↓

Board of Directors

↓

President, Vice President, and Other Officers

↓

Employees of the Corporation

Corporate governance is the system by which companies are directed and controlled.

Point: *Bylaws* are guidelines that govern the behavior of individuals employed by and managing the corporation.

Global: Some corporate labels are:

Country	Label
United States	Inc.
France	SA
United Kingdom	
Public	PLC
Private	Ltd
Germany & Austria	
Public	AG
Private	GmbH
Sweden & Finland	AB
Italy	SpA
Netherlands	NV
Australia	AG
Mexico	SA
Bahamas	IBC

■ Decision Insight

Seed Money　Sources for start-up money include (1) "angel" investors such as family, friends, or anyone who believes in a company, (2) employees, investors, and even suppliers who can be paid with stock, and (3) venture capitalists (investors) who have a record of entrepreneurial success. See the National Venture Capital Association (**NVCA.org**) for information. ■

Stockholders of Corporations

This section explains stockholder rights, stock purchases and sales, and the role of registrar and transfer agents.

Rights of Stockholders　When investors buy stock, they acquire all *specific* rights the corporation's charter grants to stockholders. They also acquire *general* rights granted stockholders by the laws of the state in which the company is incorporated. When a corporation has only one class of stock, it is identified as **common stock.** State laws vary, but common stockholders usually have the general right to

1. Vote at stockholders' meetings (or register proxy votes electronically).
2. Sell or otherwise dispose of their stock.
3. Purchase their proportional share of any common stock later issued by the corporation. This **preemptive right** protects stockholders' proportionate interest in the corporation. For example, a stockholder who owns 25% of a corporation's common stock has the first opportunity to buy 25% of any new common stock issued.
4. Receive the same dividend, if any, on each common share of the corporation.
5. Share in any assets remaining after creditors and preferred stockholders are paid when, and if, the corporation is liquidated. Each common share receives the same amount.

Stockholders also have the right to receive timely financial reports.

Stock Certificates and Transfer　Investors who buy a corporation's stock, sometimes receive a *stock certificate* as proof of share ownership. Many corporations issue only one cer-

EXHIBIT 11.2

Stock Certificate

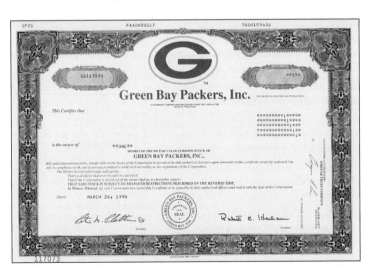

tificate for each block of stock purchased. A certificate can be for any number of shares. Exhibit 11.2 shows a stock certificate of the **Green Bay Packers.** A certificate shows the company name, stockholder name, number of shares, and other crucial information. Issuance of certificates is becoming less common. Instead, many stockholders maintain accounts with the corporation or their stockbrokers and never receive actual certificates.

Point: The Green Bay Packers is the only nonprofit, community-owned major league professional sports team. The NFL now prohibits any other teams from becoming community-owned.

Registrar and Transfer Agents　If a corporation's stock is traded on a major stock exchange, the corporation must have a registrar and a transfer agent. A *registrar* keeps stockholder records and prepares official lists of stockholders for stockholder meetings and dividend payments. A *transfer agent* assists with purchases and sales of shares by receiving and issuing certificates as necessary. Registrars and transfer agents are usually large banks or trust companies with computer facilities and staff to do this work.

Decision Insight

Pricing Stock   A prospectus accompanies a stock's initial public offering (IPO), giving financial information about the company issuing the stock. A prospectus should help answer these questions to price an IPO:
(1) Is the underwriter reliable? (2) Is there growth in revenues, profits, and cash flows? (3) What is management's view of operations? (4) Are current owners selling? (5) What are the risks? ■

Basics of Capital Stock

Capital stock is a general term that refers to any shares issued to obtain capital (owner financing). This section introduces terminology and accounting for capital stock.

Subcategories of Authorized Stock

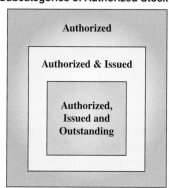

The inner-most box shows that shares issued decline
if a company buys back its stock previously issued.

Authorized Stock   **Authorized stock** is the number of shares that a corporation's charter
allows it to sell. The number of authorized shares usually exceeds the number of shares issued
(and outstanding), often by a large amount. (*Outstanding stock* refers to issued stock held by
stockholders.) No formal journal entry is required for stock authorization. A corporation must
apply to the state for a change in its charter if it wishes to issue more shares than previously
authorized. A corporation discloses the number of shares authorized in the equity section of its
balance sheet or notes. Apple's balance sheet reports 1.8 billion common shares authorized as
of the start of its 2012 fiscal year.

Selling (Issuing) Stock   A corporation can sell stock directly or indirectly. To *sell
directly*, it advertises its stock issuance to potential buyers. This type of issuance is most
common with privately held corporations. To *sell indirectly*, a corporation pays a brokerage
house (investment banker) to issue its stock. Some brokerage houses *underwrite* an indirect
issuance of stock; that is, they buy the stock from the corporation and take all gains or losses
from its resale.

Market Value of Stock   **Market value per share** is the price at which a stock is bought
and sold. Expected future earnings, dividends, growth, and other company and economic factors
influence market value. Traded stocks' market values are available daily in newspapers such as
The Wall Street Journal and online. The current market value of previously issued shares (for
example, the price of stock in trades between investors) does not impact the issuing corporation's
stockholders' equity.

Classes of Stock   When all authorized shares have the same rights and characteristics, the
stock is called *common stock*. A corporation is sometimes authorized to issue more than one
class of stock, including preferred stock and different classes of common stock. American
Greetings, for instance, has two types of common stock: Class A stock has 1 vote per share and
Class B stock has 10 votes per share.

Par Value Stock   **Par value stock** is stock that is assigned a **par value,** which is an amount
assigned per share by the corporation in its charter. For example, Monster Worldwide, Inc.'s
common stock has a par value of $0.001. Other commonly assigned par values are $10, $5, $1 and
$0.01. There is no restriction on the assigned par value. In many states, the par value of a stock
establishes **minimum legal capital,** which refers to the least amount that the buyers of stock must
contribute to the corporation or be subject to paying at a future date. For example, if a corporation
issues 1,000 shares of $10 par value stock, the corporation's minimum legal capital in these states
would be $10,000. Minimum legal capital is intended to protect a corporation's creditors. Since
creditors cannot demand payment from stockholders' personal assets, their claims are limited to
the corporation's assets and any minimum legal capital. At liquidation, creditor claims are paid
before any amounts are distributed to stockholders.

Point: Managers are motivated to set a
low par value when minimum legal capital
or state issuance taxes are based on par
value.

Point: Minimum legal capital was
intended to protect creditors by
requiring a minimum level of net assets.

No-Par Value Stock   **No-par value stock,** or simply *no-par stock,* is stock *not* assigned a
value per share by the corporate charter. Its advantage is that it can be issued at any price without the possibility of a minimum legal capital deficiency.

Point: Par, no-par, and stated value
do *not* set the stock's market value.

EXHIBIT 11.3

Equity Composition

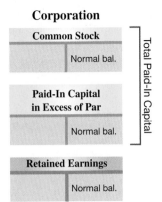

Corporation

Stated Value Stock   Stated value stock is no-par stock to which the directors assign a "stated" value per share. Stated value per share becomes the minimum legal capital per share in this case.

Stockholders' Equity   A corporation's equity is known as **stockholders' equity,** also called *shareholders' equity* or *corporate capital.* Stockholders' equity consists of (1) paid-in (or contributed) capital and (2) retained earnings; see Exhibit 11.3. **Paid-in capital** is the total amount of cash and other assets the corporation receives from its stockholders in exchange for its stock. **Retained earnings** is the cumulative net income (and loss) not distributed as dividends to its stockholders.

Point: Paid-in capital comes from stock-related transactions, whereas retained earnings comes from operations; if retained earnings has a debit balance, it is often titled Accumulated Deficit.

Decision Insight

Stock Quote   The **Target** stock quote is interpreted as (left to right): **Hi,** highest price in past 52 weeks; **Lo,** lowest price in past 52 weeks;

52 Weeks				Yld		Vol				Net
Hi	Lo	Sym	Div	%	PE	mil.	Hi	Lo	Close	Chg
58.95	45.28	TGT	1.20	2.07	13.5	668	58.06	57.40	57.63	−0.30

Sym, company exchange symbol; **Div,** dividends paid per share in past year; **Yld %,** dividend divided by closing price; **PE,** stock price per share divided by earnings per share; **Vol mil.,** number (in millions) of shares traded; **Hi,** highest price for the day; **Lo,** lowest price for the day; **Close,** closing price for the day; **Net Chg,** change in closing price from prior day. ■

Quick Check   Answers — p. 491

1. Which of the following is *not* a characteristic of the corporate form of business? (*a*) Ease of capital accumulation, (*b*) Stockholder responsibility for corporate debts, (*c*) Ease in transferability of ownership rights, or (*d*) Double taxation.
2. Why is a corporation's income said to be taxed twice?
3. Is it more common for a company to issue common stock with a par value of $10 or $.001? Explain why.

COMMON STOCK

 P1   Record the issuance of corporate stock.

Accounting for the issuance of common stock affects only paid-in (contributed) capital accounts; no retained earnings accounts are affected.

Issuing Par Value Stock

Par value stock can be issued at par, at a premium (above par), or at a discount (below par). In each case, stock can be exchanged for either cash or noncash assets.

Issuing Par Value Stock at Par   When common stock is issued at par value, we record amounts for both the asset(s) received and the par value stock issued. To illustrate, the entry to record Dillon Snowboards' issuance of 30,000 shares of $10 par value stock for $300,000 cash on June 5, 2013, follows:

Assets   = Liabilities +   Equity
+300,000   +300,000

$10 par value × 30,000 shares

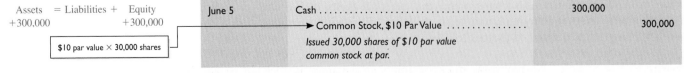

June 5	Cash	300,000	
	Common Stock, $10 Par Value		300,000
	Issued 30,000 shares of $10 par value common stock at par.		

Exhibit 11.4 shows the stockholders' equity of Dillon Snowboards at year-end 2013 (its first year of operations) after income of $65,000 and no dividend payments.

Stockholders' Equity

Preferred stock—$100 par value, 7% cumulative, 2,000 shares authorized, 1,000 shares issued and outstanding	$100,000
Common stock—$25 par value, 12,000 shares authorized, 10,000 shares issued and outstanding	250,000
Paid-in capital in excess of par value, common stock	15,000
Retained earnings	82,000
Total stockholders' equity	$447,000

EXHIBIT 11.23

Stockholders' Equity with Preferred and Common Stock

The book value computations are in Exhibit 11.24. Equity is first allocated to preferred shares before the book value of common shares is computed.

Total stockholders' equity		$447,000
Less equity applicable to preferred shares		
Call price (1,000 shares × $108)	$108,000	
Dividends in arrears ($100,000 × 7% × 2 years)	14,000	(122,000)
Equity applicable to common shares		$325,000
Book value per preferred share ($122,000/1,000 shares)		**$122.00**
Book value per common share ($325,000/10,000 shares)		**$ 32.50**

EXHIBIT 11.24

Computing Book Value per Preferred and Common Share

Book value per share reflects the value per share if a company is liquidated at balance sheet amounts. Book value is also the starting point in many stock valuation models, merger negotiations, price setting for public utilities, and loan contracts. The main limitation in using book value is the potential difference between recorded value and market value for assets and liabilities. Investors often adjust their analysis for estimates of these differences.

 Decision Maker

Investor   You are considering investing in **BMX**, whose book value per common share is $4 and price per common share on the stock exchange is $7. From this information, are BMX's net assets priced higher or lower than its recorded values? ■   [Answer—p. 491]

DEMONSTRATION PROBLEM 1

Barton Corporation began operations on January 1, 2012. The following transactions relating to stockholders' equity occurred in the first two years of the company's operations.

2012

Jan. 1   Authorized the issuance of 2 million shares of $5 par value common stock and 100,000 shares of $100 par value, 10% cumulative, preferred stock.

Jan. 2   Issued 200,000 shares of common stock for $12 cash per share.

Jan. 3   Issued 100,000 shares of common stock in exchange for a building valued at $820,000 and merchandise inventory valued at $380,000.

Jan. 4   Paid $10,000 cash to the company's founders for organization activities.

Jan. 5   Issued 12,000 shares of preferred stock for $110 cash per share.

2013

June 4   Issued 100,000 shares of common stock for $15 cash per share.

Required

1. Prepare journal entries to record these transactions.

2. Prepare the stockholders' equity section of the balance sheet as of December 31, 2012, and December 31, 2013, based on these transactions.

3. Prepare a table showing dividend allocations and dividends per share for 2012 and 2013 assuming Barton declares the following cash dividends: 2012, $50,000, and 2013, $300,000.

4. Prepare the January 2, 2012, journal entry for Barton's issuance of 200,000 shares of common stock for $12 cash per share assuming

    a. Common stock is no-par stock without a stated value.

    b. Common stock is no-par stock with a stated value of $10 per share.

PLANNING THE SOLUTION

- Record journal entries for the transactions for 2012 and 2013.
- Determine the balances for the 2012 and 2013 equity accounts for the balance sheet.
- Prepare the contributed capital portion of the 2012 and 2013 balance sheets.
- Prepare a table similar to Exhibit 11.11 showing dividend allocations for 2012 and 2013.
- Record the issuance of common stock under both specifications of no-par stock.

SOLUTION TO DEMONSTRATION PROBLEM 1

1. Journal entries.

2012			
Jan. 2	Cash	2,400,000	
	Common Stock, $5 Par Value		1,000,000
	Paid-In Capital in Excess of Par Value,		
	Common Stock		1,400,000
	Issued 200,000 shares of common stock.		
Jan. 3	Building	820,000	
	Merchandise Inventory	380,000	
	Common Stock, $5 Par Value		500,000
	Paid-In Capital in Excess of Par Value,		
	Common Stock		700,000
	Issued 100,000 shares of common stock.		
Jan. 4	Organization Expenses	10,000	
	Cash		10,000
	Paid founders for organization costs.		
Jan. 5	Cash	1,320,000	
	Preferred Stock, $100 Par Value		1,200,000
	Paid-In Capital in Excess of Par Value,		
	Preferred Stock		120,000
	Issued 12,000 shares of preferred stock.		
2013			
June 4	Cash	1,500,000	
	Common Stock, $5 Par Value		500,000
	Paid-In Capital in Excess of Par Value,		
	Common Stock		1,000,000
	Issued 100,000 shares of common stock.		

2. Balance sheet presentations (at December 31 year-end).

	2013	2012
Stockholders' Equity		
Preferred stock—$100 par value, 10% cumulative, 100,000		
shares authorized, 12,000 shares issued and outstanding	$1,200,000	$1,200,000
Paid-in capital in excess of par value, preferred stock	120,000	120,000
Total paid-in capital by preferred stockholders	1,320,000	1,320,000
Common stock—$5 par value, 2,000,000 shares authorized,		
300,000 shares issued and outstanding in 2012, and		
400,000 shares issued and outstanding in 2013	2,000,000	1,500,000
Paid-in capital in excess of par value, common stock	3,100,000	2,100,000
Total paid-in capital by common stockholders	5,100,000	3,600,000
Total paid-in capital	$6,420,000	$4,920,000

3. A company has 5,000 shares of $100 par preferred stock and 50,000 shares of $10 par common stock outstanding. Its total stockholders' equity is $2,000,000. Its book value per common share is:
  a. $100.00
  b. $ 10.00
  c. $ 40.00
  d. $ 30.00
  e. $ 36.36

4. A company paid cash dividends of $0.81 per share. Its earnings per share is $6.95 and its market price per share is $45.00. Its dividend yield is:
  a. 1.8%
  b. 11.7%

  c. 15.4%
  d. 55.6%
  e. 8.6%

5. A company's shares have a market value of $85 per share. Its net income is $3,500,000, and its weighted-average common shares outstanding is 700,000. Its price-earnings ratio is:
  a. 5.9
  b. 425.0
  c. 17.0
  d. 10.4
  e. 41.2

[I] Icon denotes assignments that involve decision making.

Discussion Questions

1. What are organization expenses? Provide examples.

2. How are organization expenses reported?

3. [I] Who is responsible for directing a corporation's affairs?

4. What is the difference between authorized shares and outstanding shares?

5. What is the preemptive right of common stockholders?

6. List the general rights of common stockholders.

7. What is the difference between the market value per share and the par value per share?

8. What is the difference between the par value and the call price of a share of preferred stock?

9. [I] Why would an investor find convertible preferred stock attractive?

10. Identify and explain the importance of the three dates relevant to corporate dividends.

11. Why is the term *liquidating dividend* used to describe cash dividends debited against paid-in capital accounts?

12. [I] How does declaring a stock dividend affect the corporation's assets, liabilities, and total equity? What are the effects of the eventual distribution of that stock?

13. [I] What is the difference between a stock dividend and a stock split?

14. [I] Courts have ruled that a stock dividend is not taxable income to stockholders. What justifies this decision?

15. How does the purchase of treasury stock affect the purchaser's assets and total equity?

16. [I] Why do laws place limits on treasury stock purchases?

17. How are EPS results computed for a corporation with a simple capital structure?

18. What is a stock option?

19. How is book value per share computed for a corporation with no preferred stock? What is the main limitation of using book value per share to value a corporation?

20. Refer to Polaris' 2011 balance sheet in Appendix A. How many shares of common stock are authorized? How many shares of voting common stock are issued?   **Polaris**

21. [I] Refer to the 2011 balance sheet for Arctic Cat in Appendix A. What is the par value per share of its common stock? Suggest a rationale for the amount of par value it assigned.   **Arctic Cat**

22. [I] Refer to the financial statements for Piaggio in Appendix A. How much were its cash payments for treasury stock purchases for the year ended December 31, 2011?   **PIAGGIO**

[McGraw] **connect**

Of the following statements, which are true for the corporate form of organization?

1. Ownership rights cannot be easily transferred.

2. Owners have unlimited liability for corporate debts.

3. Capital is more easily accumulated than with most other forms of organization.

4. Corporate income that is distributed to shareholders is usually taxed twice.

5. It is a separate legal entity.

6. It has a limited life.

7. Owners are not agents of the corporation.

QUICK STUDY

QS 11-1
Characteristics of corporations
C1

QS 11-2
Issuance of no-par
common stock
P1

Prepare the journal entry to record Autumn Company's issuance of 63,000 shares of no-par value common stock assuming the shares:

a. Sell for $29 cash per share.

b. Are exchanged for land valued at $1,827,000.

QS 11-3
Issuance of common stock
P1

Prepare the journal entry to record Zende Company's issuance of 75,000 shares of $5 par value common stock assuming the shares sell for:

a. $5 cash per share.

b. $6 cash per share.

QS 11-4
Issuance of par and stated
value common stock
P1

Prepare the journal entry to record Jevonte Company's issuance of 36,000 shares of its common stock assuming the shares have a:

a. $2 par value and sell for $18 cash per share.

b. $2 stated value and sell for $18 cash per share.

QS 11-5
Issuance of common stock
P1

Prepare the issuer's journal entry for each separate transaction. (*a*) On March 1, Atlantic Co. issues 42,500 shares of $4 par value common stock for $297,500 cash. (*b*) On April 1, OP Co. issues no-par value common stock for $70,000 cash. (*c*) On April 6, MPG issues 2,000 shares of $25 par value common stock for $45,000 of inventory, $145,000 of machinery, and acceptance of an $94,000 note payable.

QS 11-6
Issuance of preferred stock
P1 P2

a. Prepare the journal entry to record Tamasine Company's issuance of 5,000 shares of $100 par value 7% cumulative preferred stock for $102 cash per share.

b. Assuming the facts in part 1, if Tamasine declares a year-end cash dividend, what is the amount of dividend paid to preferred shareholders? (Assume no dividends in arrears.)

QS 11-7
Accounting for cash dividends
P2

Prepare journal entries to record the following transactions for Emerson Corporation.

July 15   Declared a cash dividend payable to common stockholders of $165,000.
August 15   Date of record is August 15 for the cash dividend declared on July 15.
August 31   Paid the dividend declared on July 15.

QS 11-8
Accounting for small
stock dividend
P2

The stockholders' equity section of Jun Company's balance sheet as of April 1 follows. On April 2, Jun declares and distributes a 10% stock dividend. The stock's per share market value on April 2 is $20 (prior to the dividend). Prepare the stockholders' equity section immediately after the stock dividend.

Common stock—$5 par value, 375,000 shares authorized, 200,000 shares issued and outstanding	$1,000,000
Paid-in capital in excess of par value, common stock	600,000
Retained earnings	833,000
Total stockholders' equity	$2,433,000

QS 11-9
Dividend allocation between
classes of shareholders
C2

Stockholders' equity of Ernst Company consists of 80,000 shares of $5 par value, 8% cumulative preferred stock and 250,000 shares of $1 par value common stock. Both classes of stock have been outstanding since the company's inception. Ernst did not declare any dividends in the prior year, but it now declares and pays a $110,000 cash dividend at the current year-end. Determine the amount distributed to each class of stockholders for this two-year-old company.

QS 11-10
Purchase and sale of
treasury stock P3

On May 3, Zirbal Corporation purchased 4,000 shares of its own stock for $36,000 cash. On November 4, Zirbal reissued 850 shares of this treasury stock for $8,500. Prepare the May 3 and November 4 journal entries to record Zirbal's purchase and reissuance of treasury stock.

QS 11-11
Accounting for changes in
estimates; error adjustments
C3

Answer the following questions related to a company's activities for the current year:

1. A review of the notes payable files discovers that three years ago the company reported the entire amount of a payment (principal and interest) on an installment note payable as interest expense. This mistake had a material effect on the amount of income in that year. How should the correction be reported in the current year financial statements?

2. After using an expected useful life of seven years and no salvage value to depreciate its office equipment over the preceding three years, the company decided early this year that the equipment will last only two more years. How should the effects of this decision be reported in the current year financial statements?

Murray Company reports net income of $770,000 for the year. It has no preferred stock, and its weighted-average common shares outstanding is 280,000 shares. Compute its basic earnings per share.

QS 11-12
Basic earnings per share A1

Epic Company earned net income of $900,000 this year. The number of common shares outstanding during the entire year was 400,000, and preferred shareholders received a $20,000 cash dividend. Compute Epic Company's basic earnings per share.

QS 11-13
Basic earnings per share A1

Compute Topp Company's price-earnings ratio if its common stock has a market value of $20.54 per share and its EPS is $3.95. Would an analyst likely consider this stock potentially overpriced- or underpriced or neither? Explain.

QS 11-14
Price-earnings ratio A2

Foxburo Company expects to pay a $2.34 per share cash dividend this year on its common stock. The current market value of Foxburo stock is $32.50 per share. Compute the expected dividend yield on the Foxburo stock. Would you classify the Foxburo stock as a growth or an income stock? Explain.

QS 11-15
Dividend yield A3

The stockholders' equity section of Montel Company's balance sheet follows. The preferred stock's call price is $40. Determine the book value per share of the common stock.

QS 11-16
Book value per common share

A4

Preferred stock—5% cumulative, $10 par value, 20,000 shares authorized, issued and outstanding	$ 200,000
Common stock—$5 par value, 200,000 shares authorized, 150,000 shares issued and outstanding	750,000
Retained earnings	900,000
Total stockholders' equity	$1,850,000

Air France-KLM reports the following equity information for its fiscal year ended March 31, 2012 (euros in millions). Prepare its journal entry, using its account titles, to record the issuance of capital stock assuming that its entire par value stock was issued on March 31, 2012, for cash.

QS 11-17
International equity disclosures

P1

March 31	2012
Issued capital	€ 300
Additional paid-in capital	2,971

---

connect

Describe how each of the following characteristics of organizations applies to corporations.

EXERCISES

Exercise 11-1
Characteristics of corporations

C1

1. Owner authority and control	5. Duration of life
2. Ease of formation	6. Owner liability
3. Transferability of ownership	7. Legal status
4. Ability to raise large capital amounts	8. Tax status of income

---

Rodriguez Corporation issues 19,000 shares of its common stock for $152,000 cash on February 20. Prepare journal entries to record this event under each of the following separate situations.

1. The stock has a $2 par value.

2. The stock has neither par nor stated value.

3. The stock has an $5 stated value.

Exercise 11-2
Accounting for par, stated, and no-par stock issuances

P1

Exercise 11-3
Recording stock issuances
P1

Prepare journal entries to record the following four separate issuances of stock.

1. A corporation issued 4,000 shares of $5 par value common stock for $35,000 cash.

2. A corporation issued 2,000 shares of no-par common stock to its promoters in exchange for their efforts, estimated to be worth $40,000. The stock has a $1 per share stated value.

3. A corporation issued 2,000 shares of no-par common stock to its promoters in exchange for their efforts, estimated to be worth $40,000. The stock has no stated value.

4. A corporation issued 1,000 shares of $50 par value preferred stock for $60,000 cash.

Exercise 11-4
Stock issuance for noncash assets
P1

Sudoku Company issues 7,000 shares of $7 par value common stock in exchange for land and a building. The land is valued at $45,000 and the building at $85,000. Prepare the journal entry to record issuance of the stock in exchange for the land and building.

Exercise 11-5
Identifying characteristics of preferred stock
C2

Match each description 1 through 6 with the characteristic of preferred stock that it best describes by writing the letter of that characteristic in the blank next to each description.

A. Callable   **B.** Convertible   **C.** Cumulative

D. Noncumulative   **E.** Nonparticipating   **F.** Participating

_____ **1.** Holders of the stock are entitled to receive current and all past dividends before common stockholders receive any dividends.

_____ **2.** The issuing corporation can retire the stock by paying a prespecified price.

_____ **3.** Holders of the stock can receive dividends exceeding the stated rate under certain conditions.

_____ **4.** Holders of the stock are not entitled to receive dividends in excess of the stated rate.

_____ **5.** Holders of this stock can exchange it for shares of common stock.

_____ **6.** Holders of the stock lose any dividends that are not declared in the current year.

Exercise 11-6
Stock dividends and splits
P2

On June 30, 2013, Sharper Corporation's common stock is priced at $62 per share before any stock dividend or split, and the stockholders' equity section of its balance sheet appears as follows.

Common stock—$10 par value, 120,000 shares authorized, 50,000 shares issued and outstanding	$ 500,000
Paid-in capital in excess of par value, common stock	200,000
Retained earnings	660,000
Total stockholders' equity	$1,360,000

1. Assume that the company declares and immediately distributes a 50% stock dividend. This event is recorded by capitalizing retained earnings equal to the stock's par value. Answer these questions about stockholders' equity as it exists *after* issuing the new shares.

a. What is the retained earnings balance?

Check (1*b*) $1,360,000

b. What is the amount of total stockholders' equity?

c. How many shares are outstanding?

2. Assume that the company implements a 3-for-2 stock split instead of the stock dividend in part 1. Answer these questions about stockholders' equity as it exists *after* issuing the new shares.

(2*a*) $660,000

a. What is the retained earnings balance?

b. What is the amount of total stockholders' equity?

c. How many shares are outstanding?

3. Explain the difference, if any, to a stockholder from receiving new shares distributed under a large stock dividend versus a stock split.

Exercise 11-7
Stock dividends and per share book values
P2

The stockholders' equity of TVX Company at the beginning of the day on February 5 follows:

Common stock—$10 par value, 150,000 shares authorized, 60,000 shares issued and outstanding	$ 600,000
Paid-in capital in excess of par value, common stock	425,000
Retained earnings	550,000
Total stockholders' equity	$1,575,000

that amount increased during the period. To see this it is helpful to use *account analysis*. This usually involves setting up a T-account and reconstructing its major entries to compute cash receipts or payments. The following reconstructed Accounts Receivable T-account reveals that cash receipts are less than sales:

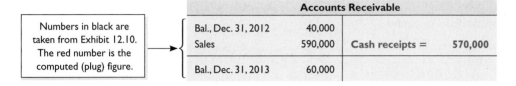

Accounts Receivable			
Bal., Dec. 31, 2012	40,000		
Sales	590,000	Cash receipts =	570,000
Bal., Dec. 31, 2013	60,000		

Numbers in black are taken from Exhibit 12.10. The red number is the computed (plug) figure.

We see that sales are $20,000 greater than cash receipts. This $20,000—as reflected in the $20,000 increase in Accounts Receivable—is subtracted from net income when computing cash provided by operating activities (see Exhibit 12.11).

Merchandise inventory. Merchandise inventory *increases* by $14,000, from a $70,000 beginning balance to an $84,000 ending balance. This increase implies that Genesis had greater cash purchases than cost of goods sold. This larger amount of cash purchases is in the form of inventory, as reflected in the following account analysis:

Merchandise Inventory			
Bal., Dec. 31, 2012	70,000		
Purchases =	314,000	Cost of goods sold	300,000
Bal., Dec. 31, 2013	84,000		

EXHIBIT 12.11

Statement of Cash Flows—Indirect Method

GENESIS Statement of Cash Flows For Year Ended December 31, 2013		
Cash flows from operating activities		
Net income	$ 38,000	
Adjustments to reconcile net income to net cash provided by operating activities		
① Increase in accounts receivable	(20,000)	
Increase in merchandise inventory	(14,000)	
Increase in prepaid expenses	(2,000)	
Decrease in accounts payable	(5,000)	
Decrease in interest payable	(1,000)	
Increase in income taxes payable	10,000	
② Depreciation expense	24,000	
③ Loss on sale of plant assets	6,000	
Gain on retirement of notes	(16,000)	
Net cash provided by operating activities		$20,000
Cash flows from investing activities		
Cash received from sale of plant assets	12,000	
Cash paid for purchase of plant assets	(10,000)	
Net cash provided by investing activities		2,000
Cash flows from financing activities		
Cash received from issuing stock	15,000	
Cash paid to retire notes	(18,000)	
Cash paid for dividends	(14,000)	
Net cash used in financing activities		(17,000)
Net increase in cash		$ 5,000
Cash balance at prior year-end		12,000
Cash balance at current year-end		$17,000

Point: Refer to Exhibit 12.10 and identify the $5,000 change in cash. This change is what the statement of cash flows explains; it serves as a check.

Point: The statement of cash flows is usually the last prepared of the four required financial statements.

The amount by which purchases exceed cost of goods sold—as reflected in the $14,000 increase in inventory—is subtracted from net income when computing cash provided by operating activities (see Exhibit 12.11).

Prepaid expenses. Prepaid Expenses *increase* $2,000, from a $4,000 beginning balance to a $6,000 ending balance, implying that Genesis's cash payments exceed its recorded prepaid expenses. These higher cash payments increase the amount of Prepaid Expenses, as reflected in its reconstructed T-account:

Prepaid Expenses			
Bal., Dec. 31, 2012	4,000		
Cash payments =	218,000	Wages and other operating exp.	216,000
Bal., Dec. 31, 2013	6,000		

The amount by which cash payments exceed the recorded operating expenses—as reflected in the $2,000 increase in Prepaid Expenses—is subtracted from net income when computing cash provided by operating activities (see Exhibit 12.11).

Adjustments for changes in current liabilities. Changes in current liabilities normally result from operating activities. An example is a purchase that affects accounts payable. Increases in current liabilities yield the following adjustment to net income when computing operating cash flows:

Increases in current liabilities are added to net income.

To see the logic for this adjustment, consider that an increase in the Accounts Payable account suggests that cash payments are less than the related (cost of goods sold) expense. As another example, an increase in wages payable implies that cash paid for wages is less than the recorded wages expense. Since the recorded expense is greater than the cash paid, we add the increase in wages payable to net income to compute net cash flow from operations.

Conversely, when current liabilities decrease, the following adjustment is required:

Decreases in current liabilities are subtracted from net income.

To illustrate, these adjustments are applied to the current liabilities in Exhibit 12.10.

Accounts payable. Accounts payable *decrease* $5,000, from a beginning balance of $40,000 to an ending balance of $35,000. This decrease implies that cash payments to suppliers exceed purchases by $5,000 for the period, which is reflected in the reconstructed Accounts Payable T-account:

Accounts Payable			
		Bal., Dec. 31, 2012	40,000
Cash payments =	319,000	Purchases	314,000
		Bal., Dec. 31, 2013	35,000

The amount by which cash payments exceed purchases—as reflected in the $5,000 decrease in Accounts Payable—is subtracted from net income when computing cash provided by operating activities (see Exhibit 12.11).

Interest payable. Interest payable *decreases* $1,000, from a $4,000 beginning balance to a $3,000 ending balance. This decrease indicates that cash paid for interest exceeds interest expense by $1,000, which is reflected in the Interest Payable T-account:

Interest Payable			
		Bal., Dec. 31, 2012	4,000
Cash paid for interest =	8,000	Interest expense	7,000
		Bal., Dec. 31, 2013	3,000

The amount by which cash paid exceeds recorded expense—as reflected in the $1,000 decrease in Interest Payable—is subtracted from net income (see Exhibit 12.11).

Income taxes payable. Income taxes payable *increase* $10,000, from a $12,000 beginning balance to a $22,000 ending balance. This increase implies that reported income taxes exceed the cash paid for taxes, which is reflected in the Income Taxes Payable T-account:

Income Taxes Payable			
		Bal., Dec. 31, 2012	12,000
Cash paid for taxes =	5,000	Income taxes expense	15,000
		Bal., Dec. 31, 2013	22,000

The amount by which cash paid falls short of the reported taxes expense—as reflected in the $10,000 increase in Income Taxes Payable—is added to net income when computing cash provided by operating activities (see Exhibit 12.11).

② **Adjustments for Operating Items Not Providing or Using Cash**   The income statement usually includes some expenses that do not reflect cash outflows in the period. Examples are depreciation, amortization, depletion, and bad debts expense. The indirect method for reporting operating cash flows requires that

Expenses with no cash outflows are added back to net income.

To see the logic of this adjustment, recall that items such as depreciation, amortization, depletion, and bad debts originate from debits to expense accounts and credits to noncash accounts. These entries have *no* cash effect, and we add them back to net income when computing net cash flows from operations. Adding them back cancels their deductions.

Similarly, when net income includes revenues that do not reflect cash inflows in the period, the indirect method for reporting operating cash flows requires that

Revenues with no cash inflows are subtracted from net income.

We apply these adjustments to the Genesis operating items that do not provide or use cash.

Depreciation.   Depreciation expense is the only Genesis operating item that has no effect on cash flows in the period. We must add back the $24,000 depreciation expense to net income when computing cash provided by operating activities. (We later explain that any cash outflow to acquire a plant asset is reported as an investing activity.)

③ **Adjustments for Nonoperating Items**   Net income often includes losses that are not part of operating activities but are part of either investing or financing activities. Examples are a loss from the sale of a plant asset and a loss from retirement of notes payable. The indirect method for reporting operating cash flows requires that

Nonoperating losses are added back to net income.

To see the logic, consider that items such as a plant asset sale and a notes retirement are normally recorded by recognizing the cash, removing all plant asset or notes accounts, and recognizing any loss or gain. The cash received or paid is not part of operating activities but is part of either investing or financing activities. *No* operating cash flow effect occurs. However, because the nonoperating loss is a deduction in computing net income, we need to add it back to net income when computing cash flow from operations. Adding it back cancels the deduction.

Similarly, when net income includes gains not part of operating activities, the indirect method for reporting operating cash flows requires that

Nonoperating gains are subtracted from net income.

To illustrate these adjustments, we consider the nonoperating items of Genesis.

Summary Adjustments for Changes in Current Assets and Current Liabilities		
Account	**Increases**	**Decreases**
Noncash current assets	Deduct from NI	Add to NI
Current liabilities.	Add to NI	Deduct from NI

Point: An income statement reports revenues, gains, expenses, and losses on an accrual basis. The statement of cash flows reports cash received and cash paid for operating, financing, and investing activities.

Point: By adding back nonoperating items such as 'Loss on sale of plant assets' to net income, we get operating income, which is the starting point for the operating section of the statement of cash flows.

Loss on sale of plant assets.   Genesis reports a $6,000 loss on sale of plant assets as part of net income. This loss is a proper deduction in computing income, but it is *not part of operating activities*. Instead, a sale of plant assets is part of investing activities. Thus, the $6,000 nonoperating loss is added back to net income (see Exhibit 12.11). Adding it back cancels the loss. We later explain how to report the cash inflow from the asset sale in investing activities.

Gain on retirement of debt.   A $16,000 gain on retirement of debt is properly included in net income, but it is *not part of operating activities*. This means the $16,000 nonoperating gain must be subtracted from net income to obtain net cash provided by operating activities (see Exhibit 12.11). Subtracting it cancels the recorded gain. We later describe how to report the cash outflow to retire debt.

Summary of Adjustments for Indirect Method

Exhibit 12.12 summarizes the most common adjustments to net income when computing net cash provided or used by operating activities under the indirect method.

EXHIBIT 12.12

Summary of Selected Adjustments for Indirect Method

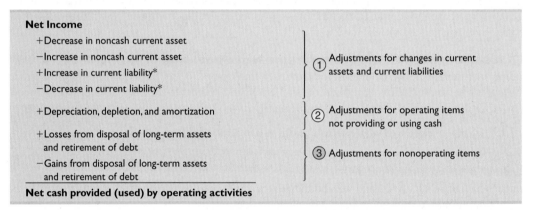

Net Income

+Decrease in noncash current asset

−Increase in noncash current asset

+Increase in current liability*

−Decrease in current liability*

  ① Adjustments for changes in current assets and current liabilities

+Depreciation, depletion, and amortization

  ② Adjustments for operating items not providing or using cash

+Losses from disposal of long-term assets and retirement of debt

−Gains from disposal of long-term assets and retirement of debt

  ③ Adjustments for nonoperating items

Net cash provided (used) by operating activities

* Excludes current portion of long-term debt and any (nonsales-related) short-term notes payable—both are financing activities.

The computations in determining cash provided or used by operating activities are different for the indirect and direct methods, but the result is identical. Both methods yield the same $20,000 figure for cash from operating activities for Genesis; see Exhibits 12.7 and 12.11.

Decision Insight

Cash or Income   The difference between net income and operating cash flows can be large and sometimes reflects on the quality of earnings. This bar chart shows the net income and operating cash flows of three companies. Operating cash flows can be either higher or lower than net income. ∎

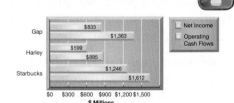

Quick Check

Answers — p. 540

4. Determine the net cash provided or used by operating activities using the following data: net income, $74,900; decrease in accounts receivable, $4,600; increase in inventory, $11,700; decrease in accounts payable, $1,000; loss on sale of equipment, $3,400; payment of cash dividends, $21,500.

5. Why are expenses such as depreciation and amortization added to net income when cash flow from operating activities is computed by the indirect method?

6. A company reports net income of $15,000 that includes a $3,000 gain on the sale of plant assets. Why is this gain subtracted from net income in computing cash flow from operating activities using the indirect method?

[continued from previous page]

(5)ᴮ Cost of goods sold	....	$ 222,300
	Plus increase in merchandise inventory	9,525
	Purchases	231,825
	Plus decrease in accounts payable	4,950
	Cash paid for merchandise	$236,775
(6)ᴮ Other operating expenses	....	$ 120,300
	Plus increase in prepaid expenses	1,950
	Cash paid for other operating expenses	$122,250
(7)ᴮ Income taxes expense	....	$ 13,725
	Less increase in income taxes payable	(675)
	Cash paid for income taxes	$ 13,050

* Supporting T-account analysis for part 1 follows:

Equipment				
Bal., Dec. 31, 2012	146,700			
Cash purchase	10,500	Sale		21,375
Bal., Dec. 31, 2013	135,825			

Accumulated Depreciation—Equipment				
			Bal., Dec. 31, 2012	47,550
Sale		11,100	Depr. expense	25,500
			Bal., Dec. 31, 2013	61,950

UMLAUF COMPANY
Statement of Cash Flows (Indirect Method)
For Year Ended December 31, 2013

Cash flows from operating activities		
Net income	$60,150	
Adjustments to reconcile net income to net cash provided by operating activities		
Decrease in accounts receivable	5,700	
Increase in merchandise inventory	(9,525)	
Increase in prepaid expenses	(1,950)	
Decrease in accounts payable	(4,950)	
Increase in income taxes payable	675	
Depreciation expense	25,500	
Loss on sale of plant assets	3,300	
Loss on retirement of bonds	825	
Net cash provided by operating activities		$79,725
Cash flows from investing activities		
Cash received from sale of equipment	6,975	
Cash paid for equipment	(10,500)	
Net cash used in investing activities		(3,525)
Cash flows from financing activities		
Cash paid to retire bonds payable	(38,325)	
Cash paid for dividends	(18,750)	
Net cash used in financing activities		(57,075)
Net increase in cash		$19,125
Cash balance at prior year-end		23,925
Cash balance at current year-end		$43,050

UMLAUF COMPANY
Statement of Cash Flows (Direct Method)
For Year Ended December 31, 2013

Cash flows from operating activities		
Cash received from customers	$451,800	
Cash paid for merchandise	(236,775)	
Cash paid for other operating expenses	(122,250)	
Cash paid for income taxes	(13,050)	
Net cash provided by operating activities		$79,725
Cash flows from investing activities		
Cash received from sale of equipment	6,975	
Cash paid for equipment	(10,500)	
Net cash used in investing activities		(3,525)
Cash flows from financing activities		
Cash paid to retire bonds payable	(38,325)	
Cash paid for dividends	(18,750)	
Net cash used in financing activities		(57,075)
Net increase in cash		$19,125
Cash balance at prior year-end		23,925
Cash balance at current year-end		$43,050

APPENDIX

12A

Spreadsheet Preparation of the Statement of Cash Flows

This appendix explains how to use a spreadsheet to prepare the statement of cash flows under the indirect method.

P4   Illustrate use of a spreadsheet to prepare a statement of cash flows.

Preparing the Indirect Method Spreadsheet   Analyzing noncash accounts can be challenging when a company has a large number of accounts and many operating, investing, and financing transactions. A *spreadsheet,* also called *work sheet* or *working paper,* can help us organize the information needed to prepare a statement of cash flows. A spreadsheet also makes it easier to check the accuracy of our work. To illustrate, we return to the comparative balance sheets and income statement shown in Exhibit 12.10. We use the following identifying letters *a* through *g* to code changes in accounts, and letters *h* through *m* for additional information, to prepare the statement of cash flows:

    a. Net income is $38,000.

    b. Accounts receivable increase by $20,000.

    c. Merchandise inventory increases by $14,000.

    d. Prepaid expenses increase by $2,000.

    e. Accounts payable decrease by $5,000.

    f. Interest payable decreases by $1,000.

    g. Income taxes payable increase by $10,000.

    h. Depreciation expense is $24,000.

    i. Plant assets costing $30,000 with accumulated depreciation of $12,000 are sold for $12,000 cash. This yields a loss on sale of assets of $6,000.

    j. Notes with a book value of $34,000 are retired with a cash payment of $18,000, yielding a $16,000 gain on retirement.

k. Plant assets costing $70,000 are purchased with a cash payment of $10,000 and an issuance of notes payable for $60,000.

l. Issued 3,000 shares of common stock for $15,000 cash.

m. Paid cash dividends of $14,000.

Exhibit 12A.1 shows the indirect method spreadsheet for Genesis. We enter both beginning and ending balance sheet amounts on the spreadsheet. We also enter information in the Analysis of Changes columns (keyed to the additional information items *a* through *m*) to explain changes in the accounts and determine the cash flows for operating, investing, and financing activities. Information about noncash investing and financing activities is reported near the bottom.

EXHIBIT 12A.1

Spreadsheet for Preparing Statement of Cash Flows—Indirect Method

File Edit View Insert Format Tools Data Accounting Window Help

GENESIS
Spreadsheet for Statement of Cash Flows—Indirect Method
For Year Ended December 31, 2013

	Dec. 31, 2012		Analysis of Changes Debit		Credit	Dec. 31, 2013
Balance Sheet—Debit Bal. Accounts						
Cash	$ 12,000					$ 17,000
Accounts receivable	40,000	(b)	$ 20,000			60,000
Merchandise inventory	70,000	(c)	14,000			84,000
Prepaid expenses	4,000	(d)	2,000			6,000
Plant assets	210,000	(k1)	70,000	(i)	$ 30,000	250,000
	$336,000					$417,000
Balance Sheet—Credit Bal. Accounts						
Accumulated depreciation	$ 48,000	(i)	12,000	(h)	24,000	$ 60,000
Accounts payable	40,000	(e)	5,000			35,000
Interest payable	4,000	(f)	1,000			3,000
Income taxes payable	12,000			(g)	10,000	22,000
Notes payable	64,000	(j)	34,000	(k2)	60,000	90,000
Common stock, $5 par value	80,000			(l)	15,000	95,000
Retained earnings	88,000	(m)	14,000	(a)	38,000	112,000
	$336,000					$417,000
Statement of Cash Flows						
Operating activities						
Net income		(a)	38,000			
Increase in accounts receivable				(b)	20,000	
Increase in merchandise inventory				(c)	14,000	
Increase in prepaid expenses				(d)	2,000	
Decrease in accounts payable				(e)	5,000	
Decrease in interest payable				(f)	1,000	
Increase in income taxes payable		(g)	10,000			
Depreciation expense		(h)	24,000			
Loss on sale of plant assets		(i)	6,000			
Gain on retirement of notes				(j)	16,000	
Investing activities						
Receipts from sale of plant assets		(i)	12,000			
Payment for purchase of plant assets				(k1)	10,000	
Financing activities						
Payment to retire notes				(j)	18,000	
Receipts from issuing stock		(l)	15,000			
Payment of cash dividends				(m)	14,000	
Noncash Investing and Financing Activities						
Purchase of plant assets with notes		(k2)	60,000	(k1)	60,000	
			$337,000		$337,000	

Sheet1 / Sheet2 / Sheet3 /

Entering the Analysis of Changes on the Spreadsheet   The following sequence of procedures is used to complete the spreadsheet after the beginning and ending balances of the balance sheet accounts are entered:

① Enter net income as the first item in the Statement of Cash Flows section for computing operating cash inflow (debit) and as a credit to Retained Earnings.

② In the Statement of Cash Flows section, adjustments to net income are entered as debits if they increase cash flows and as credits if they decrease cash flows. Applying this same rule, adjust net income for the change in each noncash current asset and current liability account related to operating activities. For each adjustment to net income, the offsetting debit or credit must help reconcile the beginning and ending balances of a current asset or current liability account.

③ Enter adjustments to net income for income statement items not providing or using cash in the period. For each adjustment, the offsetting debit or credit must help reconcile a noncash balance sheet account.

④ Adjust net income to eliminate any gains or losses from investing and financing activities. Because the cash from a gain must be excluded from operating activities, the gain is entered as a credit in the operating activities section. Losses are entered as debits. For each adjustment, the related debit and/or credit must help reconcile balance sheet accounts and involve reconstructed entries to show the cash flow from investing or financing activities.

⑤ After reviewing any unreconciled balance sheet accounts and related information, enter the remaining reconciling entries for investing and financing activities. Examples are purchases of plant assets, issuances of long-term debt, stock issuances, and dividend payments. Some of these may require entries in the noncash investing and financing section of the spreadsheet (reconciled).

⑥ Check accuracy by totaling the Analysis of Changes columns and by determining that the change in each balance sheet account has been explained (reconciled).

Point: Analysis of the changes on the spreadsheet are summarized here:

1. Cash flows from operating activities generally affect net income, current assets, and current liabilities.

2. Cash flows from investing activities generally affect noncurrent asset accounts.

3. Cash flows from financing activities generally affect noncurrent liability and equity accounts.

We illustrate these steps in Exhibit 12A.1 for Genesis:

Step	Entries
①	(a)
②	(b) through (g)
③	(h)
④	(i) through (j)
⑤	(k) through (m)

Since adjustments *i*, *j*, and *k* are more challenging, we show them in the following debit and credit format. These entries are for purposes of our understanding; they are *not* the entries actually made in the journals. Changes in the Cash account are identified as sources or uses of cash.

i.	Loss from sale of plant assets	6,000	
	Accumulated depreciation	12,000	
	Receipt from sale of plant assets **(source of cash)**	12,000	
	Plant assets		30,000
	To describe sale of plant assets.		
j.	Notes payable	34,000	
	Payments to retire notes **(use of cash)**		18,000
	Gain on retirement of notes		16,000
	To describe retirement of notes.		
k1.	Plant assets	70,000	
	Payment to purchase plant assets **(use of cash)**		10,000
	Purchase of plant assets financed by notes		60,000
	To describe purchase of plant assets.		
k2.	Purchase of plant assets financed by notes	60,000	
	Notes payable		60,000
	To issue notes for purchase of assets.		

Direct Method of Reporting Operating Cash Flows

12B

We compute cash flows from operating activities under the direct method by adjusting accrual-based income statement items to the cash basis. The usual approach is to adjust income statement accounts related to operating activities for changes in their related balance sheet accounts as follows:

P5 Compute cash flows from operating activities using the direct method.

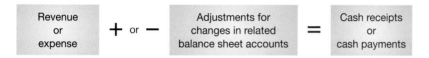

| Revenue or expense | + or − | Adjustments for changes in related balance sheet accounts | = | Cash receipts or cash payments |

The framework for reporting cash receipts and cash payments for the operating section of the cash flow statement under the direct method follows. We consider cash receipts first and then cash payments.

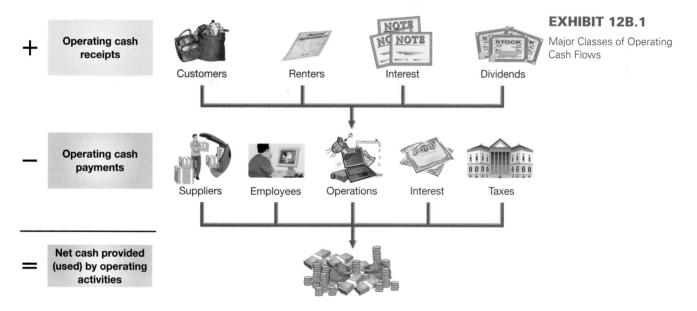

EXHIBIT 12B.1

Major Classes of Operating Cash Flows

Operating Cash Receipts   A review of Exhibit 12.10 and the additional information reported by Genesis suggests only one potential cash receipt: sales to customers. This section, therefore, starts with sales to customers as reported on the income statement and then adjusts it as necessary to obtain cash received from customers to report on the statement of cash flows.

Cash Received from Customers   If all sales are for cash, the amount received from customers equals the sales reported on the income statement. When some or all sales are on account, however, we must adjust the amount of sales for the change in Accounts Receivable. It is often helpful to use *account analysis* to do this. This usually involves setting up a T-account and reconstructing its major entries, with emphasis on cash receipts and payments. To illustrate, we use a T-account that includes accounts receivable balances for Genesis on December 31, 2012 and 2013. The beginning balance is $40,000 and the ending balance is $60,000. Next, the income statement shows sales of $590,000, which we enter on the debit side of this account. We now can reconstruct the Accounts Receivable account to determine the amount of cash received from customers as follows:

Point: An accounts receivable increase implies that cash received from customers is less than sales (the converse is also true).

Accounts Receivable			
Bal., Dec. 31, 2012	40,000		
Sales	590,000	Cash receipts =	570,000
Bal., Dec. 31, 2013	60,000		

Example: If the ending balance of accounts receivable is $20,000 (instead of $60,000), what is cash received from customers? *Answer:* $610,000

This T-account shows that the Accounts Receivable balance begins at $40,000 and increases to $630,000 from sales of $590,000, yet its ending balance is only $60,000. This implies that cash receipts from customers are $570,000, computed as $40,000 + $590,000 − [?] = $60,000. This computation can be rearranged to express cash received as equal to sales of $590,000 minus a $20,000 increase in accounts receivable. This computation is summarized as a general rule in Exhibit 12B.2. The statement of cash flows in Exhibit 12.7 reports the $570,000 cash received from customers as a cash inflow from operating activities.

EXHIBIT 12B.2

Formula to Compute Cash Received from Customers—Direct Method

$$\text{Cash received from customers} = \text{Sales} \begin{cases} + \text{ Decrease in accounts receivable} \\ \text{or} \\ - \text{ Increase in accounts receivable} \end{cases}$$

Other Cash Receipts   While Genesis's cash receipts are limited to collections from customers, we often see other types of cash receipts, most commonly cash receipts involving rent, interest, and dividends. We compute cash received from these items by subtracting an increase in their respective receivable or adding a decrease. For instance, if rent receivable increases in the period, cash received from renters is less than rent revenue reported on the income statement. If rent receivable decreases, cash received is more than reported rent revenue. The same logic applies to interest and dividends. The formulas for these computations are summarized later in this appendix.

Point: Net income is measured using accrual accounting. Cash flows from operations are measured using cash basis accounting.

Operating Cash Payments   A review of Exhibit 12.10 and the additional Genesis information shows four operating expenses: cost of goods sold; wages and other operating expenses; interest expense; and taxes expense. We analyze each expense to compute its cash amounts for the statement of cash flows. (We then examine depreciation and the other losses and gains.)

Cash Paid for Merchandise   We compute cash paid for merchandise by analyzing both cost of goods sold and merchandise inventory. If all merchandise purchases are for cash and the ending balance of Merchandise Inventory is unchanged from the beginning balance, the amount of cash paid for merchandise equals cost of goods sold—an uncommon situation. Instead, there normally is some change in the Merchandise Inventory balance. Also, some or all merchandise purchases are often made on credit, and this yields changes in the Accounts Payable balance. When the balances of both Merchandise Inventory and Accounts Payable change, we must adjust the cost of goods sold for changes in both accounts to compute cash paid for merchandise. This is a two-step adjustment.

First, we use the change in the account balance of Merchandise Inventory, along with the cost of goods sold amount, to compute cost of purchases for the period. An increase in merchandise inventory implies that we bought more than we sold, and we add this inventory increase to cost of goods sold to compute cost of purchases. A decrease in merchandise inventory implies that we bought less than we sold, and we subtract the inventory decrease from cost of goods sold to compute purchases. We illustrate the *first step* by reconstructing the Merchandise Inventory account of Genesis:

Merchandise Inventory			
Bal., Dec. 31, 2012	70,000		
Purchases =	314,000	Cost of goods sold	300,000
Bal., Dec. 31, 2013	84,000		

The beginning balance is $70,000, and the ending balance is $84,000. The income statement shows that cost of goods sold is $300,000, which we enter on the credit side of this account. With this information, we determine the amount for cost of purchases to be $314,000. This computation can be rearranged to express cost of purchases as equal to cost of goods sold of $300,000 plus the $14,000 increase in inventory.

The second step uses the change in the balance of Accounts Payable, and the amount of cost of purchases, to compute cash paid for merchandise. A decrease in accounts payable implies that we paid for more goods than we acquired this period, and we would then add the accounts payable decrease to cost of purchases to compute cash paid for merchandise. An increase in accounts payable implies that we paid for less than the amount of goods acquired, and we would subtract the accounts payable increase from purchases to compute cash paid for merchandise. The *second step* is applied to Genesis by reconstructing its Accounts Payable account:

Accounts Payable			
		Bal., Dec. 31, 2012	40,000
Cash payments =	319,000	Purchases	314,000
		Bal., Dec. 31, 2013	35,000

Its beginning balance of $40,000 plus purchases of $314,000 minus an ending balance of $35,000 yields cash paid of $319,000 (or $40,000 + $314,000 − [?] = $35,000). Alternatively, we can express cash paid for merchandise as equal to purchases of $314,000 plus the $5,000 decrease in accounts payable. The $319,000 cash paid for merchandise is reported on the statement of cash flows in Exhibit 12.7 as a cash outflow under operating activities.

Example: If the ending balances of Inventory and Accounts Payable are $60,000 and $50,000, respectively (instead of $84,000 and $35,000), what is cash paid for merchandise? *Answer:* $280,000

We summarize this two-step adjustment to cost of goods sold to compute cash paid for merchandise inventory in Exhibit 12B.3.

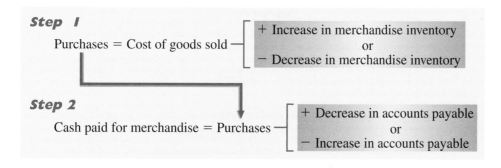

EXHIBIT 12B.3

Two Steps to Compute Cash Paid for Merchandise—Direct Method

Cash Paid for Wages and Operating Expenses (Excluding Depreciation)   The income statement of Genesis shows wages and other operating expenses of $216,000 (see Exhibit 12.10). To compute cash paid for wages and other operating expenses, we adjust this amount for any changes in their related balance sheet accounts. We begin by looking for any prepaid expenses and accrued liabilities related to wages and other operating expenses in the balance sheets of Genesis in Exhibit 12.10. The balance sheets show prepaid expenses but no accrued liabilities. Thus, the adjustment is limited to the change in prepaid expenses. The amount of adjustment is computed by assuming that all cash paid for wages and other operating expenses is initially debited to Prepaid Expenses. This assumption allows us to reconstruct the Prepaid Expenses account:

Prepaid Expenses			
Bal., Dec. 31, 2012	4,000		
Cash payments =	218,000	Wages and other operating exp.	216,000
Bal., Dec. 31, 2013	6,000		

Prepaid Expenses increase by $2,000 in the period, meaning that cash paid for wages and other operating expenses exceeds the reported expense by $2,000. Alternatively, we can express cash paid for wages and other operating expenses as equal to its reported expenses of $216,000 plus the $2,000 increase in prepaid expenses.[1]

Point: A decrease in prepaid expenses implies that reported expenses include an amount(s) that did not require a cash outflow in the period.

Exhibit 12B.4 summarizes the adjustments to wages (including salaries) and other operating expenses. The Genesis balance sheet did not report accrued liabilities, but we include them in the formula to explain the adjustment to cash when they do exist. A decrease in accrued liabilities implies that we paid cash for more goods or services than received this period, so we add the decrease in accrued liabilities to the expense amount to obtain cash paid for these goods or services. An increase in accrued liabilities implies that we paid cash for less than what was acquired, so we subtract this increase in accrued liabilities from the expense amount to get cash paid.

---

[1] The assumption that all cash payments for wages and operating expenses are initially debited to Prepaid Expenses is not necessary for our analysis to hold. If cash payments are debited directly to the expense account, the total amount of cash paid for wages and other operating expenses still equals the $216,000 expense plus the $2,000 increase in Prepaid Expenses (which arise from end-of-period adjusting entries).

EXHIBIT 12B.4

Formula to Compute Cash Paid for Wages and Operating Expenses—Direct Method

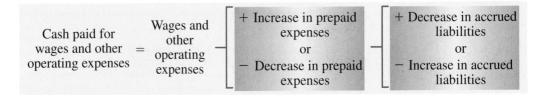

Cash paid for interest and income taxes   Computing operating cash flows for interest and taxes is similar to that for operating expenses. Both require adjustments to their amounts reported on the income statement for changes in their related balance sheet accounts. We begin with the Genesis income statement showing interest expense of $7,000 and income taxes expense of $15,000. To compute the cash paid, we adjust interest expense for the change in interest payable and then the income taxes expense for the change in income taxes payable. These computations involve reconstructing both liability accounts:

Interest Payable			
		Bal., Dec. 31, 2012	4,000
Cash paid for interest =	8,000	Interest expense	7,000
		Bal., Dec. 31, 2013	3,000

Income Taxes Payable			
		Bal., Dec. 31, 2012	12,000
Cash paid for taxes =	5,000	Income taxes expense	15,000
		Bal., Dec. 31, 2013	22,000

These accounts reveal cash paid for interest of $8,000 and cash paid for income taxes of $5,000. The formulas to compute these amounts are in Exhibit 12B.5. Both of these cash payments are reported as operating cash outflows on the statement of cash flows in Exhibit 12.7.

EXHIBIT 12B.5

Formulas to Compute Cash Paid for Both Interest and Taxes—Direct Method

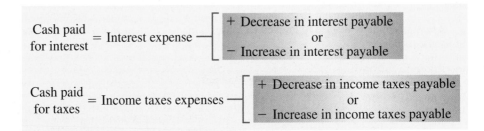

Analysis of Additional Expenses, Gains, and Losses   Genesis has three additional items reported on its income statement: depreciation, loss on sale of assets, and gain on retirement of debt. We must consider each for its potential cash effects.

Depreciation Expense   Depreciation expense is $24,000. It is often called a *noncash expense* because depreciation has no cash flows. Depreciation expense is an allocation of an asset's depreciable cost. The cash outflow with a plant asset is reported as part of investing activities when it is paid for. Thus, depreciation expense is *never* reported on a statement of cash flows using the direct method; nor is depletion or amortization expense.

Loss on Sale of Assets   Sales of assets frequently result in gains and losses reported as part of net income, but the amount of recorded gain or loss does *not* reflect any cash flows in these transactions. Asset sales result in cash inflow equal to the cash amount received, regardless of whether the asset was sold at a gain or a loss. This cash inflow is reported under investing activities. Thus, the loss or gain on a sale of assets is *never* reported on a statement of cash flows using the direct method.

Gain on Retirement of Debt   Retirement of debt usually yields a gain or loss reported as part of net income, but that gain or loss does *not* reflect cash flow in this transaction. Debt retirement results in cash outflow equal to the cash paid to settle the debt, regardless of whether the debt is retired at a gain or loss.

Point: The direct method is usually viewed as *user friendly* because less accounting knowledge is required to understand and use it.

The following selected information is from Ellerby Company's comparative balance sheets.

QS 12-4
Computing cash from asset sales
P3

At December 31	2013	2012
Furniture	$132,000	$184,500
Accumulated depreciation—Furniture	(88,700)	(110,700)

The income statement reports depreciation expense for the year of $18,000. Also, furniture costing $52,500 was sold for its book value. Compute the cash received from the sale of furniture.

The following selected information is from the Princeton Company's comparative balance sheets.

QS 12-5
Computing financing cash flows
P3

At December 31	2013	2012
Common stock, $10 par value	$105,000	$100,000
Paid-in capital in excess of par	567,000	342,000
Retained earnings	313,500	287,500

The company's net income for the year ended December 31, 2013, was $48,000.
1. Compute the cash received from the sale of its common stock during 2013.
2. Compute the cash paid for dividends during 2013.

Use the following balance sheets and income statement to answer QS 12-6 through QS 12-11.

QS 12-6
Indirect: Computing cash from operations P2

CRUZ, INC.
Comparative Balance Sheets
December 31, 2013

	2013	2012
Assets		
Cash	$ 94,800	$ 24,000
Accounts receivable, net	41,000	51,000
Inventory	85,800	95,800
Prepaid expenses	5,400	4,200
Furniture	109,000	119,000
Accum. depreciation—Furniture	(17,000)	(9,000)
Total assets	$319,000	$285,000
Liabilities and Equity		
Accounts payable	$ 15,000	$ 21,000
Wages payable	9,000	5,000
Income taxes payable	1,400	2,600
Notes payable (long-term)	29,000	69,000
Common stock, $5 par value	229,000	179,000
Retained earnings	35,600	8,400
Total liabilities and equity	$319,000	$285,000

CRUZ, INC.
Income Statement
For Year Ended December 31, 2013

Sales		$488,000
Cost of goods sold		314,000
Gross profit		174,000
Operating expenses		
Depreciation expense	$37,600	
Other expenses	89,100	126,700
Income before taxes		47,300
Income taxes expense		17,300
Net income		$ 30,000

Required

Use the indirect method to prepare the cash provided or used from operating activities section only of the statement of cash flows for this company.

Refer to the data in QS 12-6.
Furniture costing $55,000 is sold at its book value in 2013. Acquisitions of furniture total $45,000 cash, on which no depreciation is necessary because it is acquired at year-end. What is the cash inflow related to the sale of furniture?

QS 12-7
Computing cash from asset sales
P3

QS 12-8

Computing financing cash outflows **P3**

Refer to the data in QS 12-6.

1. Assume that all common stock is issued for cash. What amount of cash dividends is paid during 2013?
2. Assume that no additional notes payable are issued in 2013. What cash amount is paid to reduce the notes payable balance in 2013?

QS 12-9[B]

Direct: Computing cash received from customers **P5**

Refer to the data in QS 12-6.

1. How much cash is received from sales to customers for year 2013?
2. What is the net increase or decrease in cash for year 2013?

QS 12-10[B]

Direct: Computing operating cash outflows **P5**

Refer to the data in QS 12-6.

1. How much cash is paid to acquire merchandise inventory during year 2013?
2. How much cash is paid for operating expenses during year 2013?

QS 12-11[B]

Direct: Computing cash from operations **P5**

Refer to the data in QS 12-6.

Use the direct method to prepare the cash provided or used from operating activities section only of the statement of cash flows for this company.

QS 12-12

Analyses of sources and uses of cash **A1**

Financial data from three competitors in the same industry follow.

1. Which of the three competitors is in the strongest position as shown by its statement of cash flows?
2. Analyze and compare the strength of Moore's cash flow on total assets ratio to that of Sykes.

($ thousands)	Moore	Sykes	Kritch
Cash provided (used) by operating activities	$ 70,000	$ 60,000	$ (24,000)
Cash provided (used) by investing activities			
Proceeds from sale of operating assets			26,000
Purchase of operating assets	(28,000)	(34,000)	
Cash provided (used) by financing activities			
Proceeds from issuance of debt			23,000
Repayment of debt	(6,000)		
Net increase (decrease) in cash	$ 36,000	$ 26,000	$ 25,000
Average total assets	$ 790,000	$ 625,000	$ 300,000

QS 12-13[A]

Noncash accounts on a spreadsheet **P4**

When a spreadsheet for a statement of cash flows is prepared, all changes in noncash balance sheet accounts are fully explained on the spreadsheet. Explain how these noncash balance sheet accounts are used to fully account for cash flows on a spreadsheet.

QS 12-14

Indirect: Computing cash flows from operations

P2

For each of the following separate cases, compute cash flows from operations. The list includes all balance sheet accounts related to operating activities.

	Case X	Case Y	Case Z
Net income	$ 4,000	$100,000	$72,000
Depreciation expense	30,000	8,000	24,000
Accounts receivable increase (decrease)	40,000	20,000	(4,000)
Inventory increase (decrease)	(20,000)	(10,000)	10,000
Accounts payable increase (decrease)	24,000	(22,000)	14,000
Accrued liabilities increase (decrease)	(44,000)	12,000	(8,000)

Compute cash flows from investing activities using the following company information.

Sale of short-term investments	$ 6,000
Cash collections from customers	16,000
Purchase of used equipment	5,000
Depreciation expense	2,000

QS 12-15
Computing cash flows from investing
P3

Compute cash flows from financing activities using the following company information.

Additional short-term borrowings	$20,000
Purchase of short-term investments	5,000
Cash dividends paid	16,000
Interest paid	8,000

QS 12-16
Computing cash flows from financing
P3

Use the following financial statements and additional information to (1) prepare a statement of cash flows for the year ended December 31, 2014, using the *indirect method,* and (2) analyze and briefly discuss the statement prepared in part 1 with special attention to operating activities and to the company's cash level.

QS 12-17
Indirect: Preparation of statement of cash flows
P1

MONTGOMERY INC.
Comparative Balance Sheets
December 31, 2014 and 2013

	2014	2013
Assets		
Cash	$ 30,400	$ 30,550
Accounts receivable, net	10,050	12,150
Inventory	90,100	70,150
Equipment	49,900	41,500
Accum. depreciation—Equipment	(22,500)	(15,300)
Total assets	$157,950	$139,050
Liabilities and Equity		
Accounts payable	$ 23,900	$ 25,400
Salaries payable	500	600
Common stock, no par value	110,000	100,000
Retained earnings	23,550	13,050
Total liabilities and equity	$157,950	$139,050

MONTGOMERY INC.
Income Statement
For Year Ended December 31, 2014

Sales		$45,575
Cost of goods sold		(18,950)
Gross profit		26,625
Operating expenses		
Depreciation expense	$7,200	
Other expenses	5,550	
Total operating expense		12,750
Income before taxes		13,875
Income tax expense		3,375
Net income		$10,500

Additional Information

a. No dividends are declared or paid in 2014.

b. Issued additional stock for $10,000 cash in 2014.

c. Purchased equipment for cash in 2014; no equipment was sold in 2014.

Answer each of the following related to international accounting standards.

1. Which method, indirect or direct, is acceptable for reporting operating cash flows under IFRS?

2. For each of the following four cash flows, identify whether it is reported under the operating, investing, or financing section (or some combination) within the indirect format of the statement of cash flows reported under IFRS and under U.S. GAAP.

QS 12-18
International cash flow disclosures
C1

Cash Flow Source	US GAAP Reporting	IFRS Reporting
a. Interest paid		
b. Dividends paid		
c. Interest received		
d. Dividends received		

EXERCISES

Exercise 12-1

Indirect: Cash flow classification

C1

The following transactions and events occurred during the year. Assuming that this company uses the *indirect method* to report cash provided by operating activities, indicate where each item would appear on its statement of cash flows by placing an *x* in the appropriate column.

	Operating Activities	Investing Activities	Financing Activities	Noncash Investing and Financing Activities	Not Reported on Statement or in Notes
	Statement of Cash Flows				
a. Declared and paid a cash dividend	___	___	___	___	___
b. Recorded depreciation expense	___	___	___	___	___
c. Paid cash to settle long-term note payable	___	___	___	___	___
d. Prepaid expenses increased in the year	___	___	___	___	___
e. Accounts receivable decreased in the year	___	___	___	___	___
f. Purchased land by issuing common stock	___	___	___	___	___
g. Paid cash to purchase inventory	___	___	___	___	___
h. Sold equipment for cash, yielding a loss	___	___	___	___	___
i. Accounts payable decreased in the year	___	___	___	___	___
j. Income taxes payable increased in the year	___	___	___	___	___

Exercise 12-2^B

Direct: Cash flow classification

C1   P5

The following transactions and events occurred during the year. Assuming that this company uses the *direct method* to report cash provided by operating activities, indicate where each item would appear on the statement of cash flows by placing an *x* in the appropriate column.

	Operating Activities	Investing Activities	Financing Activities	Noncash Investing and Financing Activities	Not Reported on Statement or in Notes
	Statement of Cash Flows				
a. Retired long-term notes payable by issuing common stock	___	___	___	___	___
b. Paid cash toward accounts payable	___	___	___	___	___
c. Sold inventory for cash	___	___	___	___	___
d. Paid cash dividend that was declared in a prior period	___	___	___	___	___
e. Accepted six-month note receivable in exchange for plant assets	___	___	___	___	___
f. Recorded depreciation expense	___	___	___	___	___
g. Paid cash to acquire treasury stock	___	___	___	___	___
h. Collected cash from sales	___	___	___	___	___
i. Borrowed cash from bank by signing a nine-month note payable	___	___	___	___	___
j. Paid cash to purchase a patent	___	___	___	___	___

Exercise 12-3

Indirect: Cash flows from operating activities

P2

Fitzpatrick Company's calendar-year 2013 income statement shows the following: Net Income, $374,000; Depreciation Expense, $44,000; Amortization Expense, $7,200; Gain on Sale of Plant Assets, $6,000. An examination of the company's current assets and current liabilities reveals the following changes (all from operating activities): Accounts Receivable decrease, $17,100; Merchandise Inventory decrease, $42,000; Prepaid Expenses increase, $4,700; Accounts Payable decrease, $8,200; Other Payables increase, $1,200. Use the *indirect method* to compute cash flow from operating activities.

The following summarized Cash T-account reflects the total debits and total credits to the Cash account of Thomas Corporation for calendar year 2013.

(1) Use this information to prepare a complete statement of cash flows for year 2013. The cash provided or used by operating activities should be reported using the *direct method*.

(2) Refer to the statement of cash flows prepared for part 1 to answer the following questions *a* through *d*: (*a*) Which section—operating, investing, or financing—shows the largest cash (i) inflow and (ii) outflow? (*b*) What is the largest individual item among the investing cash outflows? (*c*) Are the cash proceeds larger from issuing notes or issuing stock? (*d*) Does the company have a net cash inflow or outflow from borrowing activities?

Exercise 12-16[B]

Direct: Preparation of statement of cash flows from Cash T-account

P1

```
Accounting System:                                                    _ □ x
File  Edit  Maintain  Tasks  Analysis  Options  Reports  Window  Help
┌────────────────────────────────Cash──────────────────────────────_□x┐
│ Balance, Dec. 31, 2012 ...............    333,000                              │
│ Receipts from customers ...........  5,000,000 │ Payments for merchandise .............  2,590,000 │
│ Receipts from dividends ...........     208,400 │ Payments for wages .......................    550,000 │
│ Receipts from land sale ............     220,000 │ Payments for rent .........................    320,000 │
│ Receipts from machinery sale .....     710,000 │ Payments for interest ....................    218,000 │
│ Receipts from issuing stock ......   1,540,000 │ Payments for taxes ......................    450,000 │
│ Receipts from borrowing ..........   3,600,000 │ Payments for machinery ...............  2,236,000 │
│                                                 │ Payments for long-term investments ....  1,260,000 │
│                                                 │ Payments for note payable .............    386,000 │
│                                                 │ Payments for dividends ................    500,000 │
│                                                 │ Payments for treasury stock ...........    218,000 │
│ Balance, Dec. 31, 2013 ..........  $     ?       │                                           │
└───────────────────────────────────────────────────────────────────┘
 Sales    Purchases    General    Payroll    Inventory    Company    Analysis
                       Ledger
```

A company reported average total assets of $1,240,000 in 2012 and $1,510,000 in 2013. Its net operating cash flow in 2012 was $102,920 and $138,920 in 2013. Calculate its cash flow on total assets ratio for both years. Comment on the results and any change in performance.

Exercise 12-17

Analyses of cash flow on total assets   A1

Peugeot S.A. reports the following financial information for the year ended December 31, 2011 (euros in millions). Prepare its statement of cash flows under the indirect method.

Exercise 12-18

Indirect: Statement of cash flows under IFRS

P1

Net income	€ 784	Cash paid for purchase of treasury stock and other...	€ (199)
Depreciation and amortization	3,037	Cash paid for other financing activities.............	(2,282)
Gains on disposals and other	(883)	Cash from disposal of plant assets and intangibles	189
Net decrease in working capital ...	(1,183)	Cash paid for plant assets and intangibles	(3,921)
Cash paid for dividends	(290)	Cash and cash equivalents, December 31, 2010	10,442

≡ connect

Forten Company, a merchandiser, recently completed its calendar-year 2013 operations. For the year, (1) all sales are credit sales, (2) all credits to Accounts Receivable reflect cash receipts from customers, (3) all purchases of inventory are on credit, (4) all debits to Accounts Payable reflect cash payments for inventory, and (5) Other Expenses are paid in advance and are initially debited to Prepaid Expenses. The company's balance sheets and income statement follow.

PROBLEM SET A

Problem 12-1A

Indirect: Statement of cash flows

A1 P1 P2 P3

FORTEN COMPANY
Comparative Balance Sheets
December 31, 2013 and 2012

	2013	2012
Assets		
Cash	$ 49,800	$ 73,500
Accounts receivable	65,810	50,625
Merchandise inventory	275,656	251,800
Prepaid expenses	1,250	1,875
Equipment	157,500	108,000
Accum. depreciation—Equipment	(36,625)	(46,000)
Total assets	$513,391	$439,800
Liabilities and Equity		
Accounts payable	$ 53,141	$114,675
Short-term notes payable	10,000	6,000
Long-term notes payable	65,000	48,750
Common stock, $5 par value	162,750	150,250
Paid-in capital in excess of par, common stock	37,500	0
Retained earnings	185,000	120,125
Total liabilities and equity	$513,391	$439,800

FORTEN COMPANY
Income Statement
For Year Ended December 31, 2013

Sales		$582,500
Cost of goods sold		285,000
Gross profit		297,500
Operating expenses		
Depreciation expense	$ 20,750	
Other expenses.................	132,400	153,150
Other gains (losses)		
Loss on sale of equipment		(5,125)
Income before taxes		139,225
Income taxes expense		24,250
Net income		$114,975

Additional Information on Year 2013 Transactions

a. The loss on the cash sale of equipment was $5,125 (details in *b*).

b. Sold equipment costing $46,875, with accumulated depreciation of $30,125, for $11,625 cash.

c. Purchased equipment costing $96,375 by paying $30,000 cash and signing a long-term note payable for the balance.

d. Borrowed $4,000 cash by signing a short-term note payable.

e. Paid $50,125 cash to reduce the long-term notes payable.

f. Issued 2,500 shares of common stock for $20 cash per share.

g. Declared and paid cash dividends of $50,100.

Required

Check Cash from operating
activities, $40,900

1. Prepare a complete statement of cash flows; report its operating activities using the *indirect method.* Disclose any noncash investing and financing activities in a note.

Analysis Component

2. Analyze and discuss the statement of cash flows prepared in part 1, giving special attention to the wisdom of the cash dividend payment.

Problem 12-2A[A]
Indirect: Cash flows
spreadsheet

P1 P2 P3 P4

Refer to the information reported about Forten Company in Problem 12-1A.

Required

Prepare a complete statement of cash flows using a spreadsheet as in Exhibit 12A.1; report its operating activities using the indirect method. Identify the debits and credits in the Analysis of Changes columns with letters that correspond to the following list of transactions and events.

a. Net income was $114,975.

b. Accounts receivable increased.

c. Merchandise inventory increased.

d. Prepaid expenses decreased.

e. Accounts payable decreased.

f. Depreciation expense was $20,750.

g. Sold equipment costing $46,875, with accumulated depreciation of $30,125, for $11,625 cash. This yielded a loss of $5,125.

h. Purchased equipment costing $96,375 by paying $30,000 cash and **(i.)** by signing a long-term note payable for the balance.

j. Borrowed $4,000 cash by signing a short-term note payable.

k. Paid $50,125 cash to reduce the long-term notes payable.

l. Issued 2,500 shares of common stock for $20 cash per share.

m. Declared and paid cash dividends of $50,100.

Check Analysis of Changes column totals, $600,775

Refer to Forten Company's financial statements and related information in Problem 12-1A.

Problem 12-3A^B — rendered: **Problem 12-3A**[B]

Direct: Statement of cash flows P1 P3 P5

Required

Prepare a complete statement of cash flows; report its operating activities according to the *direct method.* Disclose any noncash investing and financing activities in a note.

Check Cash used in financing activities, $(46,225)

Golden Corp., a merchandiser, recently completed its 2013 operations. For the year, (1) all sales are credit sales, (2) all credits to Accounts Receivable reflect cash receipts from customers, (3) all purchases of inventory are on credit, (4) all debits to Accounts Payable reflect cash payments for inventory, (5) Other Expenses are all cash expenses, and (6) any change in Income Taxes Payable reflects the accrual and cash payment of taxes. The company's balance sheets and income statement follow.

Problem 12-4A

Indirect: Statement of cash flows

P1 P2 P3

mhhe.com/wildFAF4e

GOLDEN CORPORATION
Comparative Balance Sheets
December 31, 2013 and 2012

	2013	2012
Assets		
Cash	$ 164,000	$107,000
Accounts receivable	83,000	71,000
Merchandise inventory	601,000	526,000
Equipment	335,000	299,000
Accum. depreciation—Equipment	(158,000)	(104,000)
Total assets	$1,025,000	$899,000
Liabilities and Equity		
Accounts payable	$ 87,000	$ 71,000
Income taxes payable	28,000	25,000
Common stock, $2 par value	592,000	568,000
Paid-in capital in excess of par value, common stock	196,000	160,000
Retained earnings	122,000	75,000
Total liabilities and equity	$1,025,000	$899,000

GOLDEN CORPORATION
Income Statement
For Year Ended December 31, 2013

Sales		$1,792,000
Cost of goods sold		1,086,000
Gross profit		706,000
Operating expenses		
Depreciation expense	$ 54,000	
Other expenses	494,000	548,000
Income before taxes		158,000
Income taxes expense		22,000
Net income		$ 136,000

Additional Information on Year 2013 Transactions

a. Purchased equipment for $36,000 cash.

b. Issued 12,000 shares of common stock for $5 cash per share.

c. Declared and paid $89,000 in cash dividends.

Required

Prepare a complete statement of cash flows; report its cash inflows and cash outflows from operating activities according to the *indirect method.*

Check Cash from operating activities, $122,000

Refer to the information reported about Golden Corporation in Problem 12-4A.

Problem 12-5A^A — rendered: **Problem 12-5A**[A]

Indirect: Cash flows spreadsheet

P1 P2 P3 P4

mhhe.com/wildFAF4e

Required

Prepare a complete statement of cash flows using a spreadsheet as in Exhibit 12A.1; report operating activities under the indirect method. Identify the debits and credits in the Analysis of Changes columns with letters that correspond to the following list of transactions and events.

a. Net income was $136,000.

b. Accounts receivable increased.

[continued on next page]

   c. Merchandise inventory increased.
   d. Accounts payable increased.
   e. Income taxes payable increased.
   f. Depreciation expense was $54,000.
   g. Purchased equipment for $36,000 cash.
   h. Issued 12,000 shares at $5 cash per share.
   i. Declared and paid $89,000 of cash dividends.

Check   Analysis of Changes column totals, $481,000

Problem 12-6A[B]
Direct: Statement of cash flows   P1   P3   P5

mhhe.com/wildFAF4e

Check   Cash used in financing activities, $(29,000)

Refer to Golden Corporation's financial statements and related information in Problem 12-4A.

Required

Prepare a complete statement of cash flows; report its cash flows from operating activities according to the *direct method*.

Problem 12-7A
Indirect: Computing cash flows from operations

P2

Lansing Company's 2013 income statement and selected balance sheet data at December 31, 2012 and 2013, follow.

LANSING COMPANY Selected Balance Sheet Accounts		
At December 31	**2013**	**2012**
Accounts receivable	$5,600	$5,800
Inventory	1,980	1,540
Accounts payable........	4,400	4,600
Salaries payable	880	700
Utilities payable	220	160
Prepaid insurance	260	280
Prepaid rent	220	180

LANSING COMPANY Income Statement For Year Ended December 31, 2013	
Sales revenue	$97,200
Expenses	
Cost of goods sold	42,000
Depreciation expense	12,000
Salaries expense	18,000
Rent expense	9,000
Insurance expense	3,800
Interest expense	3,600
Utilities expense	2,800
Net income	$ 6,000

Check   Cash from operating activities, $17,780

Required

Prepare the cash flows from operating activities section only of the company's 2013 statement of cash flows using the indirect method.

Problem 12-8A[B]
Direct: Computing cash flows from operations

P5

Refer to the information in Problem 12-7A.

Required

Prepare the cash flows from operating activities section only of the company's 2013 statement of cash flows using the direct method.

PROBLEM SET B

Problem 12-1B
Indirect: Statement of cash flows

A1 P1 P2 P3

Gazelle Corporation, a merchandiser, recently completed its calendar-year 2013 operations. For the year, (1) all sales are credit sales, (2) all credits to Accounts Receivable reflect cash receipts from customers, (3) all purchases of inventory are on credit, (4) all debits to Accounts Payable reflect cash payments for inventory, and (5) Other Expenses are paid in advance and are initially debited to Prepaid Expenses. The company's balance sheets and income statement follow.

GAZELLE CORPORATION
Comparative Balance Sheets
December 31, 2013 and 2012

	2013	2012
Assets		
Cash	$123,450	$ 61,550
Accounts receivable	77,100	80,750
Merchandise inventory	240,600	250,700
Prepaid expenses	15,100	17,000
Equipment	262,250	200,000
Accum. depreciation—Equipment	(110,750)	(95,000)
Total assets	$607,750	$515,000
Liabilities and Equity		
Accounts payable	$ 17,750	$102,000
Short-term notes payable	15,000	10,000
Long-term notes payable	100,000	77,500
Common stock, $5 par	215,000	200,000
Paid-in capital in excess		
of par, common stock	30,000	0
Retained earnings	230,000	125,500
Total liabilities and equity	$607,750	$515,000

GAZELLE CORPORATION
Income Statement
For Year Ended December 31, 2013

Sales		$1,185,000
Cost of goods sold		595,000
Gross profit		590,000
Operating expenses		
Depreciation expense	$ 38,600	
Other expenses	362,850	
Total operating expenses		401,450
		188,550
Other gains (losses)		
Loss on sale of equipment		(2,100)
Income before taxes		186,450
Income taxes expense		28,350
Net income		$ 158,100

Additional Information on Year 2013 Transactions

a. The loss on the cash sale of equipment was $2,100 (details in *b*).

b. Sold equipment costing $51,000, with accumulated depreciation of $22,850, for $26,050 cash.

c. Purchased equipment costing $113,250 by paying $43,250 cash and signing a long-term note payable for the balance.

d. Borrowed $5,000 cash by signing a short-term note payable.

e. Paid $47,500 cash to reduce the long-term notes payable.

f. Issued 3,000 shares of common stock for $15 cash per share.

g. Declared and paid cash dividends of $53,600.

Required

1. Prepare a complete statement of cash flows; report its operating activities using the *indirect method*. Disclose any noncash investing and financing activities in a note.

Check Cash from operating activities, $130,200

Analysis Component

2. Analyze and discuss the statement of cash flows prepared in part 1, giving special attention to the wisdom of the cash dividend payment.

Refer to the information reported about Gazelle Corporation in Problem 12-1B.

Required

Prepare a complete statement of cash flows using a spreadsheet as in Exhibit 12A.1; report its operating activities using the *indirect method*. Identify the debits and credits in the Analysis of Changes columns with letters that correspond to the following list of transactions and events.

Problem 12-2B[A]
Indirect: Cash flows spreadsheet

P1 P2 P3 P4

a. Net income was $158,100.

b. Accounts receivable decreased.

c. Merchandise inventory decreased.

d. Prepaid expenses decreased.

e. Accounts payable decreased.

f. Depreciation expense was $38,600.

[continued on next page]

g. Sold equipment costing $51,000, with accumulated depreciation of $22,850, for $26,050 cash. This yielded a loss of $2,100.

h. Purchased equipment costing $113,250 by paying $43,250 cash and **(i.)** by signing a long-term note payable for the balance.

j. Borrowed $5,000 cash by signing a short-term note payable.

k. Paid $47,500 cash to reduce the long-term notes payable.

l. Issued 3,000 shares of common stock for $15 cash per share.

Check Analysis of Changes column totals, $681,950

m. Declared and paid cash dividends of $53,600.

Problem 12-3B^B

Direct: Statement of cash flows   P1   P3   P5

Check Cash used in financing activities, $(51,100)

Refer to Gazelle Corporation's financial statements and related information in Problem 12-1B.

Required

Prepare a complete statement of cash flows; report its operating activities according to the *direct method*. Disclose any noncash investing and financing activities in a note.

Problem 12-4B

Indirect: Statement of cash flows

P1   P2   P3

Satu Company, a merchandiser, recently completed its 2013 operations. For the year, (1) all sales are credit sales, (2) all credits to Accounts Receivable reflect cash receipts from customers, (3) all purchases of inventory are on credit, (4) all debits to Accounts Payable reflect cash payments for inventory, (5) Other Expenses are cash expenses, and (6) any change in Income Taxes Payable reflects the accrual and cash payment of taxes. The company's balance sheets and income statement follow.

SATU COMPANY
Comparative Balance Sheets
December 31, 2013 and 2012

	2013	2012
Assets		
Cash	$ 58,750	$ 28,400
Accounts receivable	20,222	25,860
Merchandise inventory	165,667	140,320
Equipment	107,750	77,500
Accum. depreciation—Equipment	(46,700)	(31,000)
Total assets	$305,689	$241,080
Liabilities and Equity		
Accounts payable	$ 20,372	$157,530
Income taxes payable	2,100	6,100
Common stock, $5 par value	40,000	25,000
Paid-in capital in excess		
of par, common stock	68,000	20,000
Retained earnings	175,217	32,450
Total liabilities and equity	$305,689	$241,080

SATU COMPANY
Income Statement
For Year Ended December 31, 2013

Sales		$750,800
Cost of goods sold		269,200
Gross profit		481,600
Operating expenses		
Depreciation expense	$ 15,700	
Other expenses	173,933	189,633
Income before taxes		291,967
Income taxes expense		89,200
Net income		$202,767

Additional Information on Year 2013 Transactions

a. Purchased equipment for $30,250 cash.

b. Issued 3,000 shares of common stock for $21 cash per share.

c. Declared and paid $60,000 of cash dividends.

Required

Check Cash from operating activities, $57,600

Prepare a complete statement of cash flows; report its cash inflows and cash outflows from operating activities according to the *indirect method*.

Refer to the information reported about Satu Company in Problem 12-4B.

Required

Prepare a complete statement of cash flows using a spreadsheet as in Exhibit 12A.1; report operating activities under the *indirect method*. Identify the debits and credits in the Analysis of Changes columns with letters that correspond to the following list of transactions and events.

a. Net income was $202,767.

b. Accounts receivable decreased.

c. Merchandise inventory increased.

d. Accounts payable decreased.

e. Income taxes payable decreased.

f. Depreciation expense was $15,700.

g. Purchased equipment for $30,250 cash.

h. Issued 3,000 shares at $21 cash per share.

i. Declared and paid $60,000 of cash dividends.

Problem 12-5B[A]

Indirect: Cash flows spreadsheet

P1 P2 P3 P4

Check Analysis of Changes column totals, $543,860

Refer to Satu Company's financial statements and related information in Problem 12-4B.

Required

Prepare a complete statement of cash flows; report its cash flows from operating activities according to the *direct method.*

Problem 12-6B[B]

Direct: Statement of cash flows

P1 P3 P5

Check Cash provided by financing activities, $3,000

Salt Lake Company's 2013 income statement and selected balance sheet data at December 31, 2012 and 2013, follow.

Problem 12-7B

Indirect: Computing cash flows from operations

P2

SALT LAKE COMPANY Income Statement For Year Ended December 31, 2013	
Sales revenue	$156,000
Expenses	
Cost of goods sold	72,000
Depreciation expense	32,000
Salaries expense	20,000
Rent expense	5,000
Insurance expense	2,600
Interest expense	2,400
Utilities expense	2,000
Net income	$ 20,000

SALT LAKE COMPANY Selected Balance Sheet Accounts		
At December 31	2013	2012
Accounts receivable	$3,600	$3,000
Inventory	860	980
Accounts payable	2,400	2,600
Salaries payable	900	600
Utilities payable	200	0
Prepaid insurance	140	180
Prepaid rent	100	200

Required

Prepare the cash flows from operating activities section only of the company's 2013 statement of cash flows using the indirect method.

Check Cash from operating activities, $51,960

Refer to the information in Problem 12-7B.

Required

Prepare the cash flows from operating activities section only of the company's 2013 statement of cash flows using the direct method.

Problem 12-8B[B]

Direct: Computing cash flows from operations

P5

SERIAL PROBLEM
Success Systems **(Indirect)**

P1 P2 P3

(This serial problem began in Chapter 1 and continues through most of the book. If previous chapter segments were not completed, the serial problem can begin at this point. It is helpful, but not necessary, to use the Working Papers that accompany the book.)

SP 12   Adria Lopez, owner of Success Systems, decides to prepare a statement of cash flows for her business. (Although the serial problem allowed for various ownership changes in earlier chapters, we will prepare the statement of cash flows using the following financial data.)

SUCCESS SYSTEMS Comparative Balance Sheets December 31, 2013, and March 31, 2014		
	2014	**2013**
Assets		
Cash	$ 77,845	$58,160
Accounts receivable	22,720	5,668
Merchandise inventory	704	0
Computer supplies	2,005	580
Prepaid insurance	1,110	1,665
Prepaid rent	825	825
Office equipment	8,000	8,000
Accumulated depreciation—Office equipment	(800)	(400)
Computer equipment	20,000	20,000
Accumulated depreciation— Computer equipment	(2,500)	(1,250)
Total assets	$129,909	$93,248
Liabilities and Equity		
Accounts payable	$ 0	$ 1,100
Wages payable	875	500
Unearned computer service revenue	0	1,500
Common stock	108,000	83,000
Retained earnings	21,034	7,148
Total liabilities and equity	$129,909	$93,248

SUCCESS SYSTEMS Income Statement For Three Months Ended March 31, 2014		
Computer services revenue		$25,160
Net sales		18,693
Total revenue		43,853
Cost of goods sold	$14,052	
Depreciation expense— Office equipment	400	
Depreciation expense— Computer equipment	1,250	
Wages expense	3,250	
Insurance expense	555	
Rent expense	2,475	
Computer supplies expense	1,305	
Advertising expense	600	
Mileage expense	320	
Repairs expense—Computer	960	
Total expenses		25,167
Net income		$18,686

Check Cash flows used by operations: $(515)

Required

Prepare a statement of cash flows for Success Systems using the *indirect method* for the three months ended March 31, 2014. Recall that the owner Adria Lopez contributed $25,000 to the business in exchange for additional stock in the first quarter of 2014 and has received $4,800 in cash dividends.

Beyond the Numbers

REPORTING IN ACTION

A1

Polaris

BTN 12-1   Refer to Polaris' financial statements in Appendix A to answer the following.

1. Is Polaris' statement of cash flows prepared under the direct method or the indirect method? How do you know?
2. For each year 2011, 2010, and 2009, is the amount of cash provided by operating activities more or less than the cash paid for dividends?
3. What is the largest amount in reconciling the difference between net income and cash flow from operating activities in 2011? In 2010? In 2009?
4. Identify the largest cash inflow and outflow for investing *and* for financing activities in 2012 and in 2010.

Fast Forward

5. Obtain Polaris' financial statements for a year ending after December 31, 2011, from either its Website (Polaris.com) or the SEC's database (www.sec.gov). Since December 31, 2011, what are Polaris' largest cash outflows and cash inflows in the investing and in the financing sections of its statement of cash flows?

BTN 12-2 Key figures for Polaris and Arctic Cat follow.

($ thousands)	Polaris			Arctic Cat		
	Current Year	I Year Prior	2 Years Prior	Current Year	I Year Prior	2 Years Prior
Operating cash flows	$ 302,530	$ 297,619	$193,201	$ (5,123)	$ 29,315	$ 19,591
Total assets	1,228,024	1,061,647	763,653	272,906	246,084	251,165

COMPARATIVE
ANALYSIS

A1

Polaris

Arctic Cat

Required

1. Compute the recent two years' cash flow on total assets ratios for Polaris and Arctic Cat.
2. What does the cash flow on total assets ratio measure?
3. Which company has the highest cash flow on total assets ratio for the periods shown?
4. Does the cash flow on total assets ratio reflect on the quality of earnings? Explain.

BTN 12-3 Katie Murphy is preparing for a meeting with her banker. Her business is finishing its fourth year of operations. In the first year, it had negative cash flows from operations. In the second and third years, cash flows from operations were positive. However, inventory costs rose significantly in year 4, and cash flows from operations will probably be down 25%. Murphy wants to secure a line of credit from her banker as a financing buffer. From experience, she knows the banker will scrutinize operating cash flows for years 1 through 4 and will want a projected number for year 5. Murphy knows that a steady progression upward in operating cash flows for years 1 through 4 will help her case. She decides to use her discretion as owner and considers several business actions that will turn her operating cash flow in year 4 from a decrease to an increase.

ETHICS CHALLENGE

C1 A1

Required

1. Identify two business actions Murphy might take to improve cash flows from operations.
2. Comment on the ethics and possible consequences of Murphy's decision to pursue these actions.

BTN 12-4 Your friend, Diana Wood, recently completed the second year of her business and just received annual financial statements from her accountant. Wood finds the income statement and balance sheet informative but does not understand the statement of cash flows. She says the first section is especially confusing because it contains a lot of additions and subtractions that do not make sense to her. Wood adds, "The income statement tells me the business is more profitable than last year and that's most important. If I want to know how cash changes, I can look at comparative balance sheets."

COMMUNICATING
IN PRACTICE

C1

Required

Write a half-page memorandum to your friend explaining the purpose of the statement of cash flows. Speculate as to why the first section is so confusing and how it might be rectified.

BTN 12-5 Access the March 30, 2012, filing of the 10-K report (for year ending December 31, 2011) of Mendocino Brewing Company, Inc., at www.sec.gov.

TAKING IT TO
THE NET

A1

Required

1. Does Mendocino Brewing use the direct or indirect method to construct its consolidated statement of cash flows?
2. For the year ended December 31, 2011, what is the largest item in reconciling the net income to net cash provided by operating activities?
3. In the recent two years, has the company been more successful in generating operating cash flows or in generating net income? Identify the figures to support the answer.
4. In the year ended December 31, 2011, what was the largest cash outflow for investing activities *and* for financing activities?
5. What item(s) does Mendocino Brewing report as supplementary cash flow information?
6. Does Mendocino Brewing report any noncash financing activities for 2011? Identify them, if any.

TEAMWORK IN ACTION

C1 A1 P2 P5

BTN 12-6   Team members are to coordinate and independently answer one question within each of the following three sections. Team members should then report to the team and confirm or correct teammates' answers.

1. Answer *one* of the following questions about the statement of cash flows.
    a. What are this statement's reporting objectives?
    b. What two methods are used to prepare it? Identify similarities and differences between them.
    c. What steps are followed to prepare the statement?
    d. What types of analyses are often made from this statement's information?

2. Identify and explain the adjustment from net income to obtain cash flows from operating activities using the indirect method for *one* of the following items.
    a. Noncash operating revenues and expenses.
    b. Nonoperating gains and losses.
    c. Increases and decreases in noncash current assets.
    d. Increases and decreases in current liabilities.

3.^BIdentify and explain the formula for computing cash flows from operating activities using the direct method for *one* of the following items.
    a. Cash receipts from sales to customers.
    b. Cash paid for merchandise inventory.
    c. Cash paid for wages and operating expenses.
    d. Cash paid for interest and taxes.

Note: For teams of more than four, some pairing within teams is necessary. Use as an in-class activity or as an assignment. If used in class, specify a time limit on each part. Conclude with reports to the entire class, using team rotation. Each team can prepare responses on a transparency.

ENTREPRENEURIAL DECISION

C1 A1

BTN 12-7   Review the chapter's opener involving TOMS and its young entrepreneurial owner, Blake Mycoskie.

Required

1. In a business such as TOMS, monitoring cash flow is always a priority. Even though TOMS now has thousands in annual sales and earns a positive net income, explain how cash flow can lag behind net income.

2. TOMS is a privately owned corporation. What are potential sources of financing for its future expansion?

C1 A1

BTN 12-8   Jenna and Matt Wilder are completing their second year operating Mountain High, a downhill ski area and resort. Mountain High reports a net loss of $(10,000) for its second year, which includes an $85,000 extraordinary loss from fire. This past year also involved major purchases of plant assets for renovation and expansion, yielding a year-end total asset amount of $800,000. Mountain High's net cash outflow for its second year is $(5,000); a summarized version of its statement of cash flows follows:

Net cash flow provided by operating activities	$295,000
Net cash flow used by investing activities	(310,000)
Net cash flow provided by financing activities	10,000

Required

Write a one-page memorandum to the Wilders evaluating Mountain High's current performance and assessing its future. Give special emphasis to cash flow data and their interpretation.

HITTING THE ROAD

C1

BTN 12-9   Visit The Motley Fool's Website (Fool.com). Enter the *Fool's School* (at *Fool.com/School*). Identify and select the link *How to Value Stocks.* (Please note the site may ask you to register with your email address. Registration is free and grants access to full articles on the site.)

Required

1. Click on *Introduction to Valuation Methods,* and then *Cash-Flow-Based Valuations.* How does the Fool's school define cash flow? What is the school's reasoning for this definition?

2. Per the school's instruction, why do analysts focus on earnings before interest and taxes (EBIT)?

3. Visit other links at this Website that interest you such as "How to Read a Balance Sheet," or find out what the "Fool's Ratio" is. Write a half-page report on what you find.

figures from Polaris's financial statements, this section explains how to compute dollar changes and percent changes for comparative statements.

Computation of Dollar Changes and Percent Changes   Comparing financial statements over relatively short time periods—two to three years—is often done by analyzing changes in line items. A change analysis usually includes analyzing absolute dollar amount changes and percent changes. Both analyses are relevant because dollar changes can yield large percent changes inconsistent with their importance. For instance, a 50% change from a base figure of $100 is less important than the same percent change from a base amount of $100,000 in the same statement. Reference to dollar amounts is necessary to retain a proper perspective and to assess the importance of changes. We compute the *dollar change* for a financial statement item as follows:

> **Dollar change = Analysis period amount − Base period amount**

Analysis period is the point or period of time for the financial statements under analysis, and *base period* is the point or period of time for the financial statements used for comparison purposes. The prior year is commonly used as a base period. We compute the *percent change* by dividing the dollar change by the base period amount and then multiplying this quantity by 100 as follows:

$$\text{Percent change (\%)} = \frac{\text{Analysis period amount} - \text{Base period amount}}{\text{Base period amount}} \times 100$$

We can always compute a dollar change, but we must be aware of a few rules in working with percent changes. To illustrate, look at four separate cases in this chart:

Case	Analysis Period	Base Period	Change Analysis Dollar	Change Analysis Percent
A	$ 1,500	$(4,500)	$ 6,000	—
B	(1,000)	2,000	(3,000)	—
C	8,000	—	8,000	—
D	0	10,000	(10,000)	(100%)

When a negative amount appears in the base period and a positive amount in the analysis period (or vice versa), we cannot compute a meaningful percent change; see cases A and B. Also, when no value is in the base period, no percent change is computable; see case C. Finally, when an item has a value in the base period and zero in the analysis period, the decrease is 100 percent; see case D.

It is common when using horizontal analysis to compare amounts to either average or median values from prior periods (average and median values smooth out erratic or unusual fluctuations).[1] We also commonly round percents and ratios to one or two decimal places, but practice on this matter is not uniform. Computations are as detailed as necessary, which is judged by whether rounding potentially affects users' decisions. Computations should not be excessively detailed so that important relations are lost among a mountain of decimal points and digits.

Comparative Balance Sheets   Comparative balance sheets consist of balance sheet amounts from two or more balance sheet dates arranged side by side. Its usefulness is often improved by showing each item's dollar change and percent change to highlight large changes.

Analysis of comparative financial statements begins by focusing on items that show large dollar or percent changes. We then try to identify the reasons for these changes and, if possible, determine whether they are favorable or unfavorable. We also follow up on items with small changes when we expected the changes to be large.

---

[1] *Median* is the middle value in a group of numbers. For instance, if five prior years' incomes are (in 000s) $15, $19, $18, $20, and $22, the median value is $19. When there are two middle numbers, we can take their average. For instance, if four prior years' sales are (in 000s) $84, $91, $96, and $93, the median is $92 (computed as the average of $91 and $93).

Example: What is a more significant change, a 70% increase on a $1,000 expense or a 30% increase on a $400,000 expense? *Answer:* The 30% increase.

Example: When there is a value in the base period and zero in the analysis period, the decrease is 100%. Why isn't the reverse situation an increase of 100%? *Answer:* A 100% increase of zero is still zero.

Point: Spreadsheet programs can help with horizontal, vertical, and ratio analyses, including graphical depictions of financial relations.

EXHIBIT 13.1

Comparative Balance Sheets

Polaris

POLARIS INDUSTRIES INC. Comparative Balance Sheets December 31, 2011 and 2010				
(in thousands)	2011	2010	Dollar Change	Percent Change
Assets				
Cash and cash equivalents	$ 325,336	$ 393,927	$ (68,591)	(17.4)%
Trade receivables, net	115,302	89,294	26,008	29.1
Inventories, net	298,042	235,927	62,115	26.3
Prepaid expenses and other	37,608	21,628	15,980	73.9
Income taxes receivable........................	24,723	—	24,723	—
Deferred tax assets	77,665	67,369	10,296	15.3
Total current assets	878,676	808,145	70,531	8.7
Property, plant and equipment, net	213,778	184,011	29,767	16.2
Investments in finance and other affiliates	47,251	38,178	9,073	23.8
Deferred tax assets	10,601	—	10,601	—
Goodwill and other intangible assets, net	77,718	31,313	46,405	148.2
Total assets	$1,228,024	$1,061,647	$166,377	15.7
Liabilities				
Current portion of long-term liablities.............	$ 2,653	$ 100,000	$ (97,347)	(97.3)%
Accounts payable.............................	146,743	113,248	33.495	29.6
Accrued liabilities.............................	465,496	368,358	97,138	26.4
Income taxes payable..........................	639	2,604	(1,965)	(75.5)
Total current liabilities	615,531	584,210	31,321	5.4
Long term income taxes payable..................	7,837	5,509	2,328	42.3
Deferred income tax liability.....................	—	937	(937)	(100.0)
Capital lease obligations	4,600	—	4,600	—
Long-term debt	100,000	100,000	0	0.0
Total liabilities................................	727,968	690,656	37,312	5.4
Stockholders' Equity				
Common stock	684	685	(1)	(0.1)
Additional paid-in capital	165,518	79,239	86,279	108.9
Retained earnings	321,831	285,169	36,662	12.9
Accumulated other comprehensive income	12,023	5,898	6,125	103.8
Total stockholders' equity	500,056	370,991	129,065	34.8
Total liabilities and stockholders' equity	$1,228,024	$1,061,647	$166,377	15.7

Point: Business consultants use comparative statement analysis to provide management advice.

Exhibit 13.1 shows comparative balance sheets for Polaris Industries, Inc. (PII). A few items stand out. Accounts receivable and inventories are asset categories showing substantial increases. The inventory build up and accounts receivable increase are likely reflective of the recession. Cash and cash equivalents have decreased substantially. Some of these resources were applied to pay off the long-term debt that came due in 2011. Polaris added property, plant, and equipment, and the increase in Goodwill reflects acquisition activity. Of course, its sizable total asset growth of 15.7% must be accompanied by future income to validate Polaris's growth strategy.

We likewise see substantial increases on the financing side, the most notable ones (in amount) being accounts payable and accrued liabilities totaling $130,633 thousand. The increase in these items is probably related to the recessionary period covering this report. Polaris also reinvested much of its income as reflected in the $36,622 thousand increase in retained earnings. Again, we must monitor these increases in investing and financing activities to be sure they are reflected in increased operating performance.

Comparative Income Statements   Comparative income statements are prepared similarly to comparative balance sheets. Amounts for two or more periods are placed side by side, with additional columns for dollar and percent changes. Exhibit 13.2 shows Polaris's comparative income statements.

POLARIS INDUSTRIES INC. Comparative Income Statements For Years Ended December 31, 2011 and 2010				
(in thousands, except per share)	2011	2010	Dollar Change	Percent Change
Sales.................................	$2,656,949	$1,991,139	$665,810	33.4%
Cost of sales	1,916,366	1,460,926	455,440	31.2
Gross profit	740,583	530,213	210,370	39.7
Selling and marketing	178,725	142,353	36,372	25.6
Research and development...........	105,631	84,940	20,691	24.4
General and administrative...........	130,395	99,055	31,340	31.6
Total operating expenses	414,751	326,348	88,403	27.1
Income from financial services	24,092	16,856	7,236	42.9
Operating income	349,924	220,721	129,203	58.5
Non-operating expense, net	3,298	2,180	1,118	51.3
Income before income taxes	346,626	218,541	128,085	58.6
Provision for income taxes	119,051	71,403	47,648	66.7
Net income........................	$ 227,575	$ 147,138	$ 80,437	54.7
Basic net income per share	$ 3.31	$ 2.20	$ 1.11	50.5
Diluted net income per share	$ 3.20	$ 2.14	$ 1.06	49.5

EXHIBIT 13.2

Comparative Income Statements

Polaris

Polaris has substantial revenue growth of 33.4% in 2011. This finding helps support management's growth strategy as reflected in the comparative balance sheets. Polaris evidences an ability to control cost of goods sold (31.2% increase) and other operating expenses, which all increased but at lower rates than the growth in revenues. Polaris's net income growth of 54.7% on revenue growth of 33.4% is very good.

Point: Percent change can also be computed by dividing the current period by the prior period and subtracting 1.0. For example, the 33.4% revenue increase of Exhibit 13.2 is computed as: ($2,656,949/$1,991,139) − 1.

Trend Analysis

Trend analysis, also called *trend percent analysis* or *index number trend analysis,* is a form of horizontal analysis that can reveal patterns in data across successive periods. It involves computing trend percents for a series of financial numbers and is a variation on the use of percent changes. The difference is that trend analysis does not subtract the base period amount in the numerator. To compute trend percents, we do the following:

1. Select a *base period* and assign each item in the base period a weight of 100%.
2. Express financial numbers as a percent of their base period number.

Specifically, a *trend percent,* also called an *index number,* is computed as follows:

$$\text{Trend percent (\%)} = \frac{\text{Analysis period amount}}{\text{Base period amount}} \times 100$$

To illustrate trend analysis, we use the Polaris data shown in Exhibit 13.3.

Point: *Index* refers to the comparison of the analysis period to the base period. Percents determined for each period are called *index numbers.*

(in thousands)	2011	2010	2009	2008	2007
Sales	$2,656,949	$1,991,139	$1,565,887	$1,948,254	$1,780,009
Cost of sales	1,916,366	1,460,926	1,172,668	1,502,546	1,386,989
Operating expenses	414,751	326,348	245,320	284,114	262,269

EXHIBIT 13.3

Revenue and Expenses

These data are from Polaris's current and prior financial statements. The base period is 2007 and the trend percent is computed in each subsequent year by dividing that year's amount by its 2007 amount. For instance, the revenue trend percent for 2011 is 149.3%, computed as $2,656,949/$1,780,009. The trend percents—using the data from Exhibit 13.3—are shown in Exhibit 13.4.

EXHIBIT 13.4

Trend Percents for Revenue and Expenses

	2011	2010	2009	2008	2007
Sales	149.3%	111.9%	88.0%	109.5%	100.0%
Cost of sales	138.2	105.3	84.5	108.3	100.0
Operating expenses	158.1	124.4	93.5	108.3	100.0

Point: Trend analysis expresses a percent of base, not a percent of change.

Graphical depictions often aid analysis of trend percents. Exhibit 13.5 shows the trend percents from Exhibit 13.4 in a *line graph,* which can help us identify trends and detect changes in direction or magnitude. It reveals that the trend line for revenue consistently falls short of that for operating expenses. Moreover, the magnitude of that difference has grown. This result does not bode well for Polaris because profitability of the company will suffer if operating expenses cannot be controlled. Management must try to better control these costs in future years. The trend line for cost of goods sold is much more encouraging since revenue growth outpaces the growth in cost of goods sold for each year from 2008–2011. This trend shows that Polaris is able to increase its gross profit margin in each of these years.

EXHIBIT 13.5

Trend Percent Lines for Revenue and Expenses of Polaris

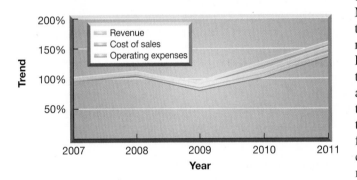

Exhibit 13.6 compares Polaris's revenue trend line to that of Arctic Cat and KTM for this same period. Polaris is able to grow its revenue in each year relative to its base year except for 2008. In this respect Polaris soundly outperforms its competitors, as Arctic Cat's and KTM's revenues fall sharply each year from 2008–2010 before rebounding in 2011. These data indicate that Polaris's products and services have met with greater consumer acceptance.

EXHIBIT 13.6

Trend Percent Lines—Polaris, Arctic Cat and KTM

Polaris

Arctic Cat

KTM

Trend analysis of financial statement items can include comparisons of relations between items on different financial statements. For instance, Exhibit 13.7 compares Polaris's revenue and total assets. The rate of increase in total assets (159.5%) is less than the increase in revenues (723.8%) since 2007. Is this result favorable or not? The answer is that Polaris was *less* efficient in using its assets in 2011. Management has not generated revenues sufficient to compensate for this asset growth.

EXHIBIT 13.7

Revenue and Asset Data for Polaris

(in thousands)	2011	2007	Trend Percent (2011 vs. 2007)
Sales	$2,656,949	$1,780,009	149.3%
Total assets	1,228,024	769,881	159.5

A ratio expresses a mathematical relation between two quantities. It can be expressed as a percent, rate, or proportion. For instance, a change in an account balance from $100 to $250 can be expressed as (1) 150% increase, (2) 2.5 times, or (3) 2.5 to 1 (or 2.5:1). Computation of a ratio is a simple arithmetic operation, but its interpretation is not. To be meaningful, a ratio must refer to an economically important relation. For example, a direct and crucial relation exists between an item's sales price and its cost. Accordingly, the ratio of cost of goods sold to sales is meaningful. In contrast, no obvious relation exists between freight costs and the balance of long-term investments.

This section describes an important set of financial ratios and its application. The selected ratios are organized into the four building blocks of financial statement analysis: (1) liquidity and efficiency, (2) solvency, (3) profitability, and (4) market prospects. All of these ratios were explained at relevant points in prior chapters. The purpose here is to organize and apply them under a summary framework. We use four common standards, in varying degrees, for comparisons: intracompany, competitor, industry, and guidelines.

Point: Some sources for industry norms are *Annual Statement Studies* by Robert Morris Associates, *Industry Norms & Key Business Ratios* by Dun & Bradstreet, *Standard & Poor's Industry Surveys,* and Reuters.com/finance.

Liquidity and Efficiency

Liquidity refers to the availability of resources to meet short-term cash requirements. It is affected by the timing of cash inflows and outflows along with prospects for future performance. Analysis of liquidity is aimed at a company's funding requirements. *Efficiency* refers to how productive a company is in using its assets. Efficiency is usually measured relative to how much revenue is generated from a certain level of assets.

Both liquidity and efficiency are important and complementary. If a company fails to meet its current obligations, its continued existence is doubtful. Viewed in this light, all other measures of analysis are of secondary importance. Although accounting measurements assume the company's continued existence, our analysis must always assess the validity of this assumption using liquidity measures. Moreover, inefficient use of assets can cause liquidity problems. A lack of liquidity often precedes lower profitability and fewer opportunities. It can foretell a loss of owner control. To a company's creditors, lack of liquidity can yield delays in collecting interest and principal payments or the loss of amounts due them. A company's customers and suppliers of goods and services also are affected by short-term liquidity problems. Implications include a company's inability to execute contracts and potential damage to important customer and supplier relationships. This section describes and illustrates key ratios relevant to assessing liquidity and efficiency.

Working Capital and Current Ratio   The amount of current assets less current liabilities is called **working capital,** or *net working capital.* A company needs adequate working capital to meet current debts, to carry sufficient inventories, and to take advantage of cash discounts. A company that runs low on working capital is less likely to meet current obligations or to continue operating. When evaluating a company's working capital, we must not only look at the dollar amount of current assets less current liabilities, but also at their ratio. The *current ratio* is defined as follows (see Chapter 3 for additional explanation):

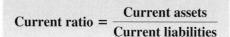

$$\text{Current ratio} = \frac{\text{Current assets}}{\text{Current liabilities}}$$

Drawing on information in Exhibit 13.1, Polaris's working capital and current ratio for both 2011 and 2010 are shown in Exhibit 13.14. Also, Arctic Cat (2.65), KTM (1.77), and the Industry's current ratio (7) are shown in the margin. Polaris's 2011 ratio (1.43) is between the competitors' ratios, and it does not appear in danger of defaulting on loan payments. A high current ratio suggests a strong liquidity position and an ability to meet current obligations. A company can, however, have a current ratio that is too high. An excessively high current ratio means that the company has invested too much in current assets compared to its current

(in thousands)	2011	2010
Current assets	$878,676	$808,145
Current liabilities	615,531	584,210
Working capital	**$263,145**	**$223,935**
Current ratio		
$878,676/$615,531 =	1.43 to 1	
$808,145/$584,210 =		1.38 to 1

EXHIBIT 13.14

Polaris's Working Capital and Current Ratio

Current ratio
Arctic Cat = 2.65
KTM = 1.77
Industry = 1.9

obligations. An excessive investment in current assets is not an efficient use of funds because current assets normally generate a low return on investment (compared with long-term assets).

Many users apply a guideline of 2:1 (or 1.5:1) for the current ratio in helping evaluate a company's debt-paying ability. A company with a 2:1 or higher current ratio is generally thought to be a good credit risk in the short run. Such a guideline or any analysis of the current ratio must recognize at least three additional factors: (1) type of business, (2) composition of current assets, and (3) turnover rate of current asset components.

Type of business.   A service company that grants little or no credit and carries few inventories can probably operate on a current ratio of less than 1:1 if its revenues generate enough cash to pay its current liabilities. On the other hand, a company selling high-priced clothing or furniture requires a higher ratio because of difficulties in judging customer demand and cash receipts. For instance, if demand falls, inventory may not generate as much cash as expected. Accordingly, analysis of the current ratio should include a comparison with ratios from successful companies in the same industry and from prior periods. We must also recognize that a company's accounting methods, especially choice of inventory method, affect the current ratio. For instance, when costs are rising, a company using LIFO tends to report a smaller amount of current assets than when using FIFO.

Point: When a firm uses LIFO in a period of rising costs, the standard for an adequate current ratio usually is lower than if it used FIFO.

Composition of current assets.   The composition of a company's current assets is important to an evaluation of short-term liquidity. For instance, cash, cash equivalents, and short-term investments are more liquid than accounts and notes receivable. Also, short-term receivables normally are more liquid than inventory. Cash, of course, can be used to immediately pay current debts. Items such as accounts receivable and inventory, however, normally must be converted into cash before payment is made. An excessive amount of receivables and inventory weakens a company's ability to pay current liabilities. The acid-test ratio (see below) can help with this assessment.

Turnover rate of assets.   Asset turnover measures a company's efficiency in using its assets. One relevant measure of asset efficiency is the revenue generated. A measure of total asset turnover is revenues divided by total assets, but evaluation of turnover for individual assets is also useful. We discuss both receivables turnover and inventory turnover on the next page.

■ Decision Maker

Banker   A company requests a one-year, $200,000 loan for expansion. This company's current ratio is 4:1, with current assets of $160,000. Key competitors carry a current ratio of about 1.9:1. Using this information, do you approve the loan application? Does your decision change if the application is for a 10-year loan? ■   [Answer—p. 591]

Acid-Test Ratio   Quick assets are cash, short-term investments, and current receivables. These are the most liquid types of current assets. The *acid-test ratio,* also called *quick ratio,* and introduced in Chapter 4, reflects on a company's short-term liquidity.

$$\text{Acid-test ratio} = \frac{\text{Cash + Short-term investments + Current receivables}}{\text{Current liabilities}}$$

Polaris's acid-test ratio is computed in Exhibit 13.15. Polaris's 2011 acid-test ratio (0.72) is between that for Arctic Cat (1.70) and KTM (0.63), but less than the 1:1 common guideline for

EXHIBIT 13.15

Acid-Test Ratio

Acid-test ratio
Arctic Cat = 1.70
KTM = 0.63
Industry = 0.9

(in thousands)	2011	2010
Cash and equivalents	$325,336	$393,927
Current receivables	115,302	89,294
Total quick assets	$440,638	$483,221
Current liabilities	$615,531	$584,210
Acid-test ratio		
$440,638/$615,531	0.72 to 1	
$483,221/$584,210		0.83 to 1

an acceptable acid-test ratio. The ratio for Arctic Cat exceeds the 0.9 industry norm. As with analysis of the current ratio, we need to consider other factors. For instance, the frequency with which a company converts its current assets into cash affects its working capital requirements. This implies that analysis of short-term liquidity should also include an analysis of receivables and inventories, which we consider next.

Global: Ratio analysis helps overcome currency translation problems, but it does *not* overcome differences in accounting principles.

Accounts Receivable Turnover We can measure how frequently a company converts its receivables into cash by computing the *accounts receivable turnover*. This ratio is defined as follows (see Chapter 7 for additional explanation):

$$\text{Accounts receivable turnover} = \frac{\text{Net sales}}{\text{Average accounts receivable, net}}$$

Short-term receivables from customers are often included in the denominator along with accounts receivable. Also, accounts receivable turnover is more precise if credit sales are used for the numerator, but external users generally use net sales (or net revenues) because information about credit sales is typically not reported. Polaris's 2011 accounts receivable turnover is computed as follows ($ millions).

Point: Some users prefer using gross accounts receivable (before subtracting the allowance for doubtful accounts) to avoid the influence of a manager's bad debts estimate.

$$\frac{\$2,656,949}{(\$89,294 + \$115,302)/2} = 26.0 \text{ times}$$

Accounts receivable turnover
Arctic Cat = 17.5
KTM = 9.5
Industry = 15.0

Polaris's value of 26.0 exceeds that of Arctic Cat's 17.5 and KTM's 9.5. Accounts receivable turnover is high when accounts receivable are quickly collected. A high turnover is favorable because it means the company need not commit large amounts of funds to accounts receivable. However, an accounts receivable turnover can be too high; this can occur when credit terms are so restrictive that they negatively affect sales volume.

Point: Ending accounts receivable can be substituted for the average balance in computing accounts receivable turnover if the difference between ending and average receivables is small.

Inventory Turnover How long a company holds inventory before selling it will affect working capital requirements. One measure of this effect is *inventory turnover,* also called *merchandise turnover* or *merchandise inventory turnover,* which is defined as follows (see Chapter 5 for additional explanation):

$$\text{Inventory turnover} = \frac{\text{Cost of goods sold}}{\text{Average inventory}}$$

Using Polaris's cost of goods sold and inventories information, we compute its inventory turnover for 2011 as follows (if the beginning and ending inventories for the year do not represent the usual inventory amount, an average of quarterly or monthly inventories can be used).

Inventory turnover
Arctic Cat = 5.08
KTM = 3.34
Industry = 4.0

$$\frac{\$1,916,366}{(\$235,927 + \$298,042)/2} = 7.18 \text{ times}$$

Polaris's inventory turnover of 7.18 is more than Arctic Cat's 5.08 and KTM's 3.34, and the industry's 4.0. A company with a high turnover requires a smaller investment in inventory than one producing the same sales with a lower turnover. Inventory turnover can be too high, however, if the inventory a company keeps is so small that it restricts sales volume.

Days' Sales Uncollected Accounts receivable turnover provides insight into how frequently a company collects its accounts. Days' sales uncollected is one measure of this activity, which is defined as follows (Chapter 6 provides additional explanation):

$$\text{Days' sales uncollected} = \frac{\text{Accounts receivable, net}}{\text{Net sales}} \times 365$$

Any short-term notes receivable from customers are normally included in the numerator.

Polaris's 2011 days' sales uncollected follows.

Day's sales uncollected
Arctic Cat = 18.6
KTM = 37.1

$$\frac{\$115,302}{\$2,656,949} \times 365 = 15.8 \text{ days}$$

Both Arctic Cat's days' sales uncollected of 18.6 days and KTM's 37.1 days are more than the 15.8 days for Polaris. Days' sales uncollected is more meaningful if we know company credit terms. A rough guideline states that days' sales uncollected should not exceed $1\frac{1}{3}$ times the days in its (1) credit period, *if* discounts are not offered or (2) discount period, *if* favorable discounts are offered.

Days' Sales in Inventory   *Days' sales in inventory* is a useful measure in evaluating inventory liquidity. Days' sales in inventory is linked to inventory in a way that days' sales uncollected is linked to receivables. We compute days' sales in inventory as follows (Chapter 5 provides additional explanation).

$$\text{Days' sales in inventory} = \frac{\text{Ending inventory}}{\text{Cost of goods sold}} \times 365$$

Polaris's days' sales in inventory for 2011 follows.

Days' sales in inventory
Arctic Cat = 61.8
KTM = 111.9
Industry = 75

$$\frac{\$298,042}{\$1,916,366} \times 365 = 56.8 \text{ days}$$

Point: *Average collection period* is estimated by dividing 365 by the accounts receivable turnover ratio. For example, 365 divided by an accounts receivable turnover of 6.1 indicates a 60-day average collection period.

If the products in Polaris's inventory are in demand by customers, this formula estimates that its inventory will be converted into receivables (or cash) in 56.8 days. If all of Polaris's sales were credit sales, the conversion of inventory to receivables in 56.8 days *plus* the conversion of receivables to cash in 15.8 days implies that inventory will be converted to cash in about 72.6 days (56.8 + 15.8).

Total Asset Turnover   *Total asset turnover* reflects a company's ability to use its assets to generate sales and is an important indication of operating efficiency. The definition of this ratio follows (Chapter 8 offers additional explanation).

$$\text{Total asset turnover} = \frac{\text{Net sales}}{\text{Average total assets}}$$

Polaris's total asset turnover for 2011 follows and is greater than that for both Arctic Cat (1.79) and KTM (1.13).

Total asset turnover
Arctic Cat = 1.79
KTM = 1.13
Industry = 1.3

$$\frac{\$2,656,949}{(\$1,061,647 + \$1,228,024)/2} = 2.32 \text{ times}$$

Quick Check   Answers – p. 591

8. Information from Paff Co. at Dec. 31, 2012, follows: cash, $820,000; accounts receivable, $240,000; inventories, $470,000; plant assets, $910,000; accounts payable, $350,000; and income taxes payable, $180,000. Compute its (a) current ratio and (b) acid-test ratio.

9. On Dec. 31, 2013, Paff Company (see question 8) had accounts receivable of $290,000 and inventories of $530,000. During 2013, net sales amounted to $2,500,000 and cost of goods sold was $750,000. Compute (a) accounts receivable turnover, (b) days' sales uncollected, (c) inventory turnover, and (d) days' sales in inventory.

Selected year-end financial statements of Overton Corporation follow. (All sales were on credit; selected balance sheet amounts at December 31, 2012, were inventory, $17,400; total assets, $94,900; common stock, $35,500; and retained earnings, $18,800.)

Problem 13-4B
Calculation of financial statement ratios

P3

OVERTON CORPORATION Income Statement For Year Ended December 31, 2013	
Sales	$315,500
Cost of goods sold	236,100
Gross profit	79,400
Operating expenses	49,200
Interest expense	2,200
Income before taxes	28,000
Income taxes	4,200
Net income	$ 23,800

OVERTON CORPORATION
Balance Sheet
December 31, 2013

Assets		Liabilities and Equity	
Cash	$ 6,100	Accounts payable	$ 11,500
Short-term investments	6,900	Accrued wages payable	3,300
Accounts receivable, net	12,100	Income taxes payable	2,600
Notes receivable (trade)*	3,000	Long-term note payable, secured	
Merchandise inventory	13,500	by mortgage on plant assets	30,000
Prepaid expenses	2,000	Common stock, $5 par value	35,000
Plant assets, net	73,900	Retained earnings	35,100
Total assets	$117,500	Total liabilities and equity	$117,500

* These are short-term notes receivable arising from customer (trade) sales.

Required

Compute the following: (1) current ratio, (2) acid-test ratio, (3) days' sales uncollected, (4) inventory turnover, (5) days' sales in inventory, (6) debt-to-equity ratio, (7) times interest earned, (8) profit margin ratio, (9) total asset turnover, (10) return on total assets, and (11) return on common stockholders' equity. Round to one decimal place, except for part 6 round to two decimals.

Check Acid-test ratio, 1.6 to 1; Inventory turnover, 15.3

Summary information from the financial statements of two companies competing in the same industry follows.

Problem 13-5B
Comparative ratio analysis

A1 P3

	Fargo Company	Ball Company		Fargo Company	Ball Company
Data from the current year-end balance sheets			**Data from the current year's income statement**		
Assets			Sales	$393,600	$667,500
Cash	$ 20,000	$ 36,500	Cost of goods sold	290,600	480,000
Accounts receivable, net	77,100	70,500	Interest expense	5,900	12,300
Current notes receivable (trade)	11,600	9,000	Income tax expense	5,700	12,300
Merchandise inventory	86,800	82,000	Net income	33,850	61,700
Prepaid expenses	9,700	10,100	Basic earnings per share	1.27	2.19
Plant assets, net	176,900	252,300			
Total assets	$382,100	$460,400			
			Beginning-of-year balance sheet data		
Liabilities and Equity			Accounts receivable, net	$ 72,200	$ 73,300
Current liabilities	$ 90,500	$ 97,000	Current notes receivable (trade)	0	0
Long-term notes payable	93,000	93,300	Merchandise inventory	105,100	80,500
Common stock, $5 par value	133,000	141,000	Total assets	383,400	443,000
Retained earnings	65,600	129,100	Common stock, $5 par value	133,000	141,000
Total liabilities and equity	$382,100	$460,400	Retained earnings	49,100	109,700

Required

Check (1) Fargo: Accounts
receivable turnover, 4.9; Inventory
turnover, 3.0

        (2) Ball: Profit margin,
9.2%; PE, 11.4

1. For both companies compute the (*a*) current ratio, (*b*) acid-test ratio, (*c*) accounts (including notes) receivable turnover, (*d*) inventory turnover, (*e*) days' sales in inventory, and (*f*) days' sales uncollected. Identify the company you consider to be the better short-term credit risk and explain why. Round to one decimal place.

2. For both companies compute the (*a*) profit margin ratio, (*b*) total asset turnover, (*c*) return on total assets, and (*d*) return on common stockholders' equity. Assuming that each company paid cash dividends of $1.50 per share and each company's stock can be purchased at $25 per share, compute their (*e*) price-earnings ratios and (*f*) dividend yields. Round to one decimal place, except for part *b* round to two decimals. Identify which company's stock you would recommend as the better investment and explain why.

Problem 13-6B[A]
Income statement computations
and format

A2

Selected account balances from the adjusted trial balance for Harbor Corp. as of its calendar year-end December 31, 2013, follow.

	Debit	Credit
a. Accumulated depreciation—Buildings		$ 400,000
b. Interest revenue		20,000
c. Net sales		2,640,000
d. Income taxes expense	$?	
e. Loss on hurricane damage (pretax and extraordinary)	64,000	
f. Accumulated depreciation—Equipment		220,000
g. Other operating expenses	328,000	
h. Depreciation expense—Equipment	100,000	
i. Loss from settlement of lawsuit	36,000	
j. Gain from settlement of lawsuit		68,000
k. Loss on sale of equipment	24,000	
l. Loss from operating a discontinued segment (pretax)	120,000	
m. Depreciation expense—Buildings	156,000	
n. Correction of overstatement of prior year's expense (pretax)		48,000
o. Cost of goods sold	1,040,000	
p. Loss on sale of discontinued segment's assets (pretax)	180,000	
q. Accounts payable		132,000

Required

Answer each of the following questions by providing supporting computations.

1. Assume that the company's income tax rate is 25% for all items. Identify the tax effects and after-tax amounts of the four items labeled pretax.

2. What is the amount of income from continuing operations before income taxes? What is the amount of income taxes expense? What is the amount of income from continuing operations?

Check (3) $(225,000)

       (4) $558,000

       (5) $510,000

3. What is the total amount of after-tax income (loss) associated with the discontinued segment?

4. What is the amount of income (loss) before the extraordinary items?

5. What is the amount of net income for the year?

SERIAL PROBLEM
Success Systems

P3

(This serial problem began in Chapter 1 and continues through most of the book. If previous chapter segments were not completed, the serial problem can begin at this point. It is helpful, but not necessary, to use the Working Papers that accompany the book.)

SP 13 Use the following selected data from Success Systems' income statement for the three months ended March 31, 2014, and from its March 31, 2014, balance sheet to complete the requirements below: computer services revenue, $25,160; net sales (of goods), $18,693; total sales and revenue, $43,853; cost of goods sold, $14,052; net income, $18,686; quick assets, $100,205; current assets, $105,209; total assets, $129,909; current liabilities, $875; total liabilities, $875; and total equity, $129,034.

Required

1. Compute the gross margin ratio (both with and without services revenue) and net profit margin ratio (round the percent to one decimal).

2. Compute the current ratio and acid-test ratio (round to one decimal).

3. Compute the debt ratio and equity ratio (round the percent to one decimal).

4. What percent of its assets are current? What percent are long term (round the percent to one decimal)?

POLARIS INDUSTRIES INC.
CONSOLIDATED STATEMENTS OF CASH FLOWS

For the Year Ended December 31 (In thousands)	2011	2010	2009
Operating Activities			
Net income	$ 227,575	$147,138	$ 101,017
Adjustments to reconcile net income to net cash provided by operating activities:			
(Gain) loss on securities available for sale	—	(825)	8,952
Depreciation and amortization	66,390	66,519	64,593
Noncash compensation	20,548	18,052	10,226
Noncash income from financial services	(4,444)	(4,574)	(4,021)
Noncash expense from other affiliates	133	1,376	382
Deferred income taxes	(16,946)	(16,888)	13,573
Tax effect of share-based compensation exercises	(23,120)	(10,610)	410
Changes in current operating items:			
Trade receivables	(23,115)	1,111	8,192
Inventories	(49,973)	(56,612)	42,997
Accounts payable	27,232	37,580	(40,329)
Accrued expenses	80,668	107,363	(24,759)
Income taxes payable/receivable	(1,343)	7,033	7,325
Prepaid expenses and others, net	(1,075)	956	4,643
Net cash provided by operating activities	302,530	297,619	193,201
Investing Activities			
Purchase of property and equipment	(84,484)	(55,718)	(43,932)
Investments in finance affiliate	(12,588)	(9,173)	(3,007)
Distributions from finance affiliate	11,950	17,910	17,261
Investment in other affiliates	(5,000)	—	—
Proceeds from sale of investments	876	9,061	—
Acquisition of businesses, net of cash acquired	(51,899)	(4,738)	—
Net cash used for investment activities	(141,145)	(42,118)	(29,678)
Financing Activities			
Borrowings under credit agreement / senior notes	100,000	—	364,000
Repayments under credit agreement	(202,333)	—	(364,000)
Repurchase and retirement of common shares	(132,372)	(27,486)	(4,556)
Cash dividends to shareholders	(61,585)	(53,043)	(50,177)
Tax effect of proceeds from share-based compensation exercises	23,120	10,610	(410)
Proceeds from stock issuances under employee plans	45,654	68,105	4,733
Net cash used for financing activities	(227,516)	(1,814)	(50,410)
Impact of currency exchange rates on cash balances	(2,460)	—	—
Net increase (decrease) in cash and cash equivalents	(68,591)	253,687	113,113
Cash and cash equivalents at beginning of period	393,927	140,240	27,127
Cash and cash equivalents at end of period	$ 325,336	$393,927	$ 140,240
Supplemental Cash Flow Information:			
Interest paid on debt borrowings	$ 3,350	$ 2,813	$ 3,966
Income taxes paid	$ 132,088	$ 81,142	$ 29,039

POLARIS

POLARIS INDUSTRIES INC.
SELECTED NOTES TO CONSOLIDATED FINANCIAL STATEMENTS

Note 1.   Organization and Significant Accounting Policies

Polaris Industries Inc. ("Polaris" or the "Company") a Minnesota corporation, and its subsidiaries, are engaged in the design, engineering, manufacturing and marketing of innovative, high-quality, high-performance Off-Road Vehicles ("ORV"), Snowmobiles, and On-Road Vehicles, including motorcycles and Small Electric Vehicles. Polaris products, together with related parts, garments and accessories are sold worldwide through a network of dealers, distributors and its subsidiaries located in the United States, Canada, France, the United Kingdom, Australia, Norway, Sweden, Germany, Spain, China, India and Brazil.

Basis of presentation: The accompanying consolidated financial statements include the accounts of Polaris and its wholly-owned subsidiaries. All inter-company transactions and balances have been eliminated in consolidation. Income from financial services is reported as a component of operating income to better reflect income from ongoing operations, of which financial services has a significant impact.

During the 2011 third quarter, the Board of Directors declared a two-for-one split of the Company's outstanding shares of Common Stock. On September 12, 2011, Polaris shareholders received one additional share of Common Stock for each share they held of record at the close of business on September 2, 2011. All amounts, including shares and per share information, have been adjusted to give effect to the two-for-one stock split.

Investment in finance affiliate: The caption Investment in finance affiliate in the consolidated balance sheets represents Polaris' 50 percent equity interest in Polaris Acceptance, a partnership agreement between GE Commercial Distribution Finance Corporation ("GECDF") and one of Polaris' wholly-owned subsidiaries. Polaris Acceptance provides floor plan financing to Polaris dealers in the United States. Polaris' investment in Polaris Acceptance is accounted for under the equity method, and is recorded as investments in finance affiliate in the consolidated balance sheets.

Investment in other affiliates: The caption Investments in other affiliates in the consolidated balance sheets for the period ended December 31, 2011 represents the Company's October 2011 investment in Brammo, Inc., a privately held manufacturer of electric motorcycles. This investment represents a minority interest in Brammo and is accounted for under the cost method.

(Gain) Loss on Securities Available for Sale: The net gain of $825,000 in 2010 on securities available for sale resulted from a $1,594,000 gain on the sale of our remaining investment in KTM during the 2010 third quarter offset by a related non-cash impairment charge of $769,000 during the 2010 second quarter. In the first quarter 2009, we recorded a non-cash impairment charge on securities held for sales of $8,952,000 from the decline in the fair value of the KTM shares owned by Polaris as of March 31, 2009, when it was determined that the decline in the fair value of the KTM shares owned by the Company was other than temporary.

Use of estimates: The preparation of financial statements in conformity with accounting principles generally accepted in the United States requires management to make estimates and assumptions that affect the reported amounts of assets and liabilities and disclosure of contingent assets and liabilities at the date of the financial statements and the reported amounts of revenues and expenses during the reporting period. Ultimate results could differ from those estimates.

Cash equivalents: Polaris considers all highly liquid investments purchased with an original maturity of 90 days or less to be cash equivalents. Cash equivalents are stated at cost, which approximates fair value. Such investments consist principally of money market mutual funds.

Allowance for doubtful accounts: Polaris' financial exposure to collection of accounts receivable is limited due to its agreements with certain finance companies. For receivables not serviced through these finance companies, the Company provides a reserve for doubtful accounts based on historical rates and trends. This reserve is adjusted periodically as information about specific accounts becomes available.

Inventories: Inventories are stated at the lower of cost (first-in, first-out method) or market. The major components of inventories are as follows (in thousands):

December 31	2011	2010
Raw materials and purchased components	$ 61,296	$ 35,580
Service parts, garments and accessories	77,437	60,813
Finished goods.........................	175,252	155,744
Less: reserves.........................	(15,943)	(16,210)
Inventories	$298,042	$235,927

Property and equipment: Property and equipment is stated at cost. Depreciation is provided using the straight-line method over the estimated useful life of the respective assets, ranging from 10–40 years for buildings and improvements and from 1–7 years for equipment and tooling. Fully depreciated tooling is eliminated from the accounting records annually.

Research and Development Expenses: Polaris records research and development expenses in the period in which they are incurred as a component of operating expenses. In the years ended December 31, 2011, 2010, and 2009, Polaris incurred $105,631,000, $84,940,000, and $62,999,000, respectively.

Advertising Expenses: Polaris records advertising expenses as a component of selling and marketing expenses in the period in which they are incurred. In the years ended December 31, 2011, 2010, and 2009, Polaris incurred $48,877,000, $40,833,000 and $37,433,000, respectively.

Shipping and Handling Costs: Polaris records shipping and handling costs as a component of cost of sales at the time the product is shipped.

Product warranties: Polaris provides a limited warranty for its ORVs for a period of six months and for a period of one year for its snowmobiles and motorcycles and a two year period for SEVs. Polaris provides longer warranties in certain geographical markets as determined by local regulations and market conditions and may provide longer warranties related to certain promotional programs.

ARCTIC CAT INC.

CONSOLIDATED STATEMENTS OF OPERATIONS

Years ended March 31	2011	2010	2009
Net sales			
Snowmobile & ATV units	$363,015,000	$350,871,000	$454,589,000
Parts, garments, & accessories	101,636,000	99,857,000	109,024,000
Total net sales	464,651,000	450,728,000	563,613,000
Cost of goods sold			
Snowmobile & ATV units	302,783,000	309,217,000	411,776,000
Parts, garments, & accessories	60,359,000	58,275,000	68,665,000
Total cost of goods sold	363,142,000	367,492,000	480,441,000
Gross profit	101,509,000	83,236,000	83,172,000
Operating expenses			
Selling & marketing	33,540,000	33,929,000	43,971,000
Research & development	15,029,000	12,926,000	18,404,000
General & administrative	34,805,000	35,045,000	33,904,000
Goodwill impairment charge	—	—	1,750,000
Total operating expenses	83,374,000	81,900,000	98,029,000
Operating profit (loss)	18,135,000	1,336,000	(14,857,000)
Other income (expense)			
Interest income	107,000	12,000	117,000
Interest expense	(11,000)	(250,000)	(1,015,000)
Total other income (expense)	96,000	(238,000)	(898,000)
Earnings (loss) before incomes taxes	18,231,000	1,098,000	(15,755,000)
Income tax expense (benefit)	5,224,000	(777,000)	(6,247,000)
Net earnings (loss)	$ 13,007,000	$ 1,875,000	$ (9,508,000)
Net earnings (loss) per share			
Basic	$ 0.71	$ 0.10	$ (0.53)
Diluted	$ 0.70	$ 0.10	$ (0.53)
Weighted average share outstanding			
Basic	18,232,000	18,220,000	18,070,000
Diluted	18,539,000	18,291,000	18,070,000

ARCTIC CAT

ARCTIC CAT INC.

CONSOLIDATED STATEMENTS OF SHAREHOLDERS' EQUITY

Years ended March 31	Common Stock		Class B Common Stock		Additional Paid-in Capital	Accumulated Other Comprehensive Income (Loss)	Retained Earnings	Total
	Shares	Amount	Shares	Amount				
Balances at March 31, 2008	11,833,485	$118,000	6,102,000	$61,000	$ —	$ 4,768,000	$175,915,000	$180,862,000
Restricted stock awards	163,500	2,000	—	—	(2,000)	—	—	—
Restricted stock forfeited	(9,500)	—	—	—	—	—	—	—
Stock based compensation expense	—	—	—	—	2,570,000	—	—	2,570,000
Comprehensive loss:								
Net loss	—	—	—	—	—	—	(9,508,000)	(9,508,000)
Unrealized loss on derivative instruments, net of tax	—	—	—	—	—	(133,000)	—	(133,000)
Foreign currency adjustment	—	—	—	—	—	(5,147,000)	—	(5,147,000)
Total comprehensive loss								(14,788,000)
Dividends ($.21 per share)	—	—	—	—	—	—	(3,796,000)	(3,796,000)
Balances at March 31, 2009	11,987,485	120,000	6,102,000	61,000	2,568,000	(512,000)	162,611,000	164,848,000
Restricted stock awards	140,500	1,000	—	—	(1,000)	—	—	—
Restricted stock forfeited	(2,000)	—	—	—	—	—	—	—
Stock based compensation expense	—	—	—	—	2,486,000	—	—	2,486,000
Comprehensive income:								
Net earnings	—	—	—	—	—	—	1,875,000	1,875,000
Unrealized gain on derivative instruments, net of tax	—	—	—	—	—	244,000	—	244,000
Foreign currency adjustment	—	—	—	—	—	(2,114,000)	—	(2,114,000)
Total comprehensive income								5,000
Balances at March 31, 2010	12,125,985	121,000	6,102,000	61,000	5,053,000	(2,382,000)	164,486,000	167,339,000
Exercise of stock options	184,869	2,000	—	—	726,000	—	—	728,000
Tax benefits from stock options exercised	—	—	—	—	745,000	—	—	745,000
Repurchase of common stock	(183,953)	(2,000)	—	—	(2,417,000)	—	—	(2,419,000)
Restricted stock awards	78,500	1,000	—	—	(1,000)	—	—	—
Restricted stock forfeited	(6,130)	—	—	—	—	—	—	—
Stock based compensation expense	—	—	—	—	3,174,000	—	—	3,174,000
Comprehensive income:								
Net earnings	—	—	—	—	—	—	13,007,000	13,007,000
Unrealized loss on derivative instruments, net of tax	—	—	—	—	—	(1,147,000)	—	(1,147,000)
Foreign currency adjustment	—	—	—	—	—	1,609,000	—	1,609,000
Total comprehensive income								13,469,000
Balances at March 31, 2011	12,199,271	$122,000	6,102,000	$61,000	$ 7,280,000	$(1,920,000)	$177,493,000	$183,036,000

ARCTIC CAT INC.

CONSOLIDATED STATEMENTS OF CASH FLOWS

Years ended March 31	2011	2010	2009
Cash flows from operating activities			
Net earnings (loss)	**$ 13,007,000**	$ 1,875,000	$ (9,508,000)
Adjustments to reconcile net earnings to net cash provided by (used in) operating activities			
Depreciation and amortization	**15,816,000**	22,779,000	28,981,000
Loss on the disposal of assets	**105,000**	144,000	252,000
Impairment of goodwill	**—**	—	1,750,000
Deferred income taxes benefit	**(3,194,000)**	(3,577,000)	(6,379,000)
Stock based compensation expense	**3,174,000**	2,486,000	2,570,000
Changes in operating assets and liabilities			
Trading securities	**(71,162,000)**	(39,082,000)	24,837,000
Accounts receivable, less allowances	**5,543,000**	9,400,000	(437,000)
Inventories	**20,587,000**	40,003,000	2,798,000
Prepaid expenses	**345,000**	205,000	(1,246,000)
Accounts payable	**2,879,000**	(7,668,000)	(29,615,000)
Accrued expenses	**9,238,000**	(585,000)	(3,392,000)
Income taxes	**(1,461,000)**	3,335,000	8,980,000
Net cash provided by (used in) operating activities	**(5,123,000)**	29,315,000	19,591,000
Cash flows from investing activities			
Purchases of property and equipment	**(11,761,000)**	(6,540,000)	(14,226,000)
Proceeds from the sale of assets	**87,000**	—	—
Net cash used in investing activities	**(11,674,000)**	(6,540,000)	(14,226,000)
Cash flows from financing activities			
Checks written in excess of bank balance	**—**	221,000	—
Proceeds from short-term borrowings	**1,012,000**	73,429,000	227,230,000
Payments on short-term borrowings	**(1,012,000)**	(73,429,000)	(227,230,000)
Proceeds from issuance of common stock	**728,000**	—	—
Tax benefit from stock option exercises	**745,000**	—	—
Repurchase of common stock	**(2,419,000)**	—	—
Dividends paid	**—**	—	(3,796,000)
Net cash provided by (used in) financing activities	**(946,000)**	221,000	(3,796,000)
Effect of exchange rate changes on cash and cash equivalents	**632,000**	(2,429,000)	(382,000)
Net increase (decrease) in cash and cash equivalents	**(17,111,000)**	20,567,000	1,187,000
Cash and cash equivalents at beginning of year	**31,811,000**	11,244,000	10,057,000
Cash and cash equivalents at end of year	**$ 14,700,000**	$ 31,811,000	$ 11,244,000
Supplemental disclosure of cash payments for:			
Income taxes	**$ 9,179,000**	$ 1,935,000	$ 409,000
Interest	**$ 11,000**	$ 250,000	$ 987,000

Supplemental disclosure of non-cash investing and financing activities:

As of March 31, 2011 and 2010, the unrealized gain (loss) on derivative instruments, net of tax was ($1,147,000) and $244,000.

KTM POWER SPORTS AG
CONSOLIDATED INCOME STATEMENT
FOR BUSINESS YEAR 2011

(In thousands of Euro)	2011
Net sales	526,801
Cost of goods sold	(371,752)
Gross margin	155,049
Selling and sport-activity expenses	(71,952)
R&D expenses	(23,099)
Infrastructure and administration expenses	(20,870)
Other operating expenses	(9,206)
Other operating Income	1,088
Operating result	31,009
Interest income	768
Interest expenses	(9,693)
Other financial and participation result	(2,975)
Pre-tax result	19,109
Tax on income and earnings	1,709
NET RESULT	20,818
Thereof net result to owners	*20,719*
Thereof net result to non-controlling shareholders	*99*
EARNINGS PER SHARE (EUR)	
Basic	2.003
Diluted	1.968

KTM POWER SPORTS AG
CONSOLIDATED STATEMENT OF COMPREHENSIVE INCOME
FOR BUSINESS YEAR 2011

(In thousands of Euro)	2011
Net result of the business year	20,818
Currency conversion	107
Valuation of cash flow hedges	11,393
Deferred tax on the valuation of cash flow hedges	(2,848)
Other income	8,652
TOTAL INCOME	29,470
Thereof net result to owners	*29,371*
Thereof net result to non-controlling shareholders	*99*

KTM

KTM POWER SPORTS AG
CONSOLIDATED BALANCE SHEET
AS AT DECEMBER 31

ASSETS

(In thousands of Euro)	12/31/2011	12/31/2010
SHORT-TERM ASSETS		
Liquid assets	14,962	8,946
Accounts receivable — trade to third parties	49,924	53,087
Accounts receivable — trade to affiliated companies	1,443	1,040
Accounts receivable — trade to associated companies	2,227	3,130
Inventory	113,979	108,910
Prepayments	1,649	1,169
Other short-term assets	9,701	7,231
	193,885	**183,513**
LONG-TERM ASSETS		
Financial fixed assets	7,458	6,222
Tangible fixed assets	84,256	63,204
Goodwill	78,793	78,492
Intangible fixed assets	118,202	110,118
Deferred taxes	3,132	3,725
Other long-term assets	49	51
	291,890	**261,812**
ASSETS	**485,775**	**445,325**

EQUITY AND LIABILITIES

(In thousands of Euro)	12/31/2011	12/31/2010
SHORT-TERM LIABILITIES		
Bank loans	5,415	14,061
Accounts payable — trade to third parties	54,578	37,725
Accounts payable — trade to affiliated companies	11,062	7,979
Accounts payable — trade to associated companies	2,600	2,895
Provisions	4,238	3,993
Liabilities — corporate tax	1,470	33
Prepayments	735	1,614
Other short-term liabilities	29,256	33,926
	109,353	**102,226**
LONG-TERM LIABILITIES		
Interest-bearing loans	132,898	129,957
Liabilities for personnel	7,699	6,479
Liabilities from deferred taxes	14,560	15,851
Liabilities to affiliated companies	0	13,021
Other long-term liabilities	1,490	1,005
	156,648	**166,313**
SHAREHOLDER'S EQUITY		
Share capital	10,509	10,109
Reserves including retained earnings	208,987	166,593
Non-controlling shares	279	84
	219,775	**176,786**
EQUITY AND LIABILITIES	**485,775**	**445,325**

KTM

KTM POWER SPORTS AG
CONSOLIDATED CASH FLOW STATEMENT
FOR BUSINESS YEAR 2011

(In thousands of Euro)	2011
CONSOLIDATED CASH FLOW FROM OPERATING ACTIVITIES	
+(−) Profit (loss) of the business year	20,818
+(−) Profit (loss) of non-controlling shareholders	(99)
+(−) Depreciation (write-up) of fixed assets	33,368
+(−) Depreciation (write-up) to financial assets	118
+(−) Deferred taxes	(3,352)
− Results from consolidation not affecting income	(649)
− Results from companies validated at-equity not affecting income	(657)
+(−) Addition (disposal) of liabilities for personnel	1,432
−(+) Profit (loss) from the sale of fixed assets	(59)
Consolidated cash flow from earnings	**50,919**
−(+) Increase (decrease) in inventories including prepayments	(5,069)
−(+) Increase (decrease) in accounts receiveable − trade, prepayments, other short- and longterm assets	831
−(+) Increase (decrease) in accounts receivable − trade from affiliated companies	430
−(+) Increase (decrease) in accounts receivable − trade from associated companies	903
(+)− Increase (decrease) in accounts payable − trade, prepayments and other short-term and long-term liabilities	16,346
(+)− Increase (decrease) in accounts payable − trade from affiliated companies	3,083
(+)− Increase (decrease) in accounts payable − trade from associated companies	(295)
(+)− Increase (decrease) from corporate taxes, deferred taxes and other provisions	3,201
	19,429
Cash flow from operating activities	**70,348**
CONSOLIDATED CASH FLOW FROM INVESTMENT ACTIVITIES	
− Investments in fixed assets (outflow of funds for investments)	(37,705)
− Investments in financial assets	(697)
(+)− Changes from first/final consolidation	273
+ Disposal of fixed assets (inflow of funds from sales: book value + profit (− loss) from the disposal of fixed assets)	871
(+)− Currency rate differences from fixed assets	(13)
Consolidated cash flow from investment activities	**(37,271)**
CONSOLIDATED CASH FLOW FROM FINANCING ACTIVITIES	
(+)− Currency rate differences	33
+ Capital increase	1,095
(+)− Increase (decrease) of short-term bank loans	(8,646)
(+)− Change in liabilities to affiliated and associated companies	(259)
(+)− Increase (decrease) in long-term interest bearing loans	(19,479)
+(−) Changes in non-controlling interests	196
+(−) Change deconsolidation Cost Plus subsidiaries	0
Consolidated cash flow from financing activities	**(27,060)**
CONSOLIDATED CASH FLOW	
+(−) Consolidated cash flow from operating activities	70,348
+(−) Consolidated cash flow from investment activities	(37,271)
+(−) Consolidated cash flow from financing activities	(27,060)
Change in the liquidity of the group	**6,017**
+ Starting cash and cash equivalents of the group	8,946
CASH AND CASH EQUIVALENTS OF THE GROUP AS AT DECEMBER 31	**14,962**
Consisting of cash in hand. cheques, cash at bank and term deposits	*14,962*
Interest paid	10,052
Taxes paid	547

The concepts of present and future values are important to modern business, including the preparation and analysis of financial statements. The purpose of this appendix is to explain, illustrate, and compute present and future values. This appendix applies these concepts with reference to both business and everyday activities.

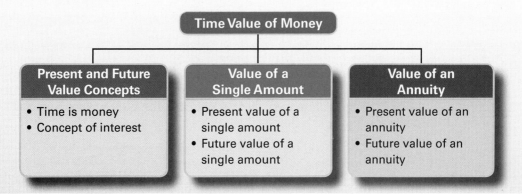

Time Value of Money

Present and Future Value Concepts
- Time is money
- Concept of interest

Value of a Single Amount
- Present value of a single amount
- Future value of a single amount

Value of an Annuity
- Present value of an annuity
- Future value of an annuity

PRESENT AND FUTURE VALUE CONCEPTS

The old saying "Time is money" reflects the notion that as time passes, the values of our assets and liabilities change. This change is due to *interest,* which is a borrower's payment to the owner of an asset for its use. The most common example of interest is a savings account asset. As we keep a balance of cash in the account, it earns interest that the financial institution pays us. An example of a liability is a car loan. As we carry the balance of the loan, we accumulate interest costs on it. We must ultimately repay this loan with interest.

Present and future value computations enable us to measure or estimate the interest component of holding assets or liabilities over time. The present value computation is important when we want to know the value of future-day assets *today.* The future value computation is important when we want to know the value of present-day assets *at a future date.* The first section focuses on the present value of a single amount. The second section focuses on the future value of a single amount. Then both the present and future values of a series of amounts (called an *annuity*) are defined and explained.

C1 Describe the earning of interest and the concepts of present and future values.

Decision Insight

Working for Lotto Winnings   Lottery winners often never work again. Kenny Dukes, a recent Georgia lottery winner, doesn't have that option. He is serving parole for burglary charges, and Georgia requires its parolees to be employed (or in school). For his lottery winnings, Dukes had to choose between $31 million in 30 annual payments or $16 million in one lump sum ($10.6 million after-tax); he chose the latter. ■

PRESENT VALUE OF A SINGLE AMOUNT

We graphically express the present value, called p, of a single future amount, called f, that is received or paid at a future date in Exhibit B.1.

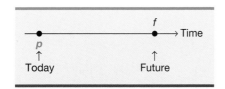

EXHIBIT B.1

Present Value of a Single Amount Diagram

The formula to compute the present value of a single amount is shown in Exhibit B.2, where p = present value; f = future value; i = rate of interest per period; and n = number of periods. (Interest is also called the *discount,* and an interest rate is also called the *discount rate.*)

EXHIBIT B.2

Present Value of a Single
Amount Formula

$$p = \frac{f}{(1 + i)^n}$$

To illustrate present value concepts, assume that we need $220 one period from today. We want to know how much we must invest now, for one period, at an interest rate of 10% to provide for this $220. For this illustration, the p, or present value, is the unknown amount—the specifics are shown graphically as follows:

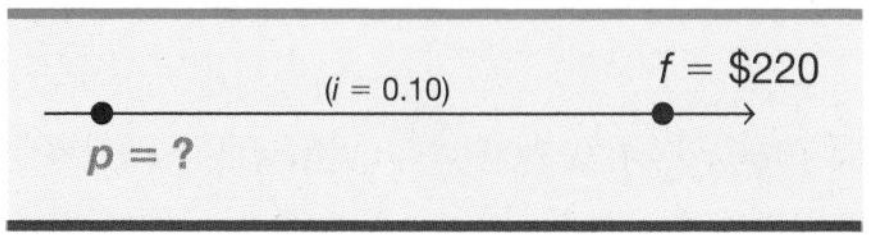

$$(i = 0.10) \qquad f = \$220$$
$$p = ?$$

Conceptually, we know p must be less than $220. This is obvious from the answer to this question: Would we rather have $220 today or $220 at some future date? If we had $220 today, we could invest it and see it grow to something more than $220 in the future. Therefore, we would prefer the $220 today. This means that if we were promised $220 in the future, we would take less than $220 today. But how much less? To answer that question, we compute an estimate of the present value of the $220 to be received one period from now using the formula in Exhibit B.2 as follows:

$$p = \frac{f}{(1 + i)^n} = \frac{\$220}{(1 + 0.10)^1} = \$200$$

We interpret this result to say that given an interest rate of 10%, we are indifferent between $200 today or $220 at the end of one period.

We can also use this formula to compute the present value for *any number of periods.* To illustrate, consider a payment of $242 at the end of two periods at 10% interest. The present value of this $242 to be received two periods from now is computed as follows:

$$p = \frac{f}{(1 + i)^n} = \frac{\$242}{(1 + 0.10)^2} = \$200$$

I will pay your allowance at the end of the month. Do you want to wait or receive its present value today?

Together, these results tell us we are indifferent between $200 today, or $220 one period from today, or $242 two periods from today given a 10% interest rate per period.

The number of periods (n) in the present value formula does not have to be expressed in years. Any period of time such as a day, a month, a quarter, or a year can be used. Whatever period is used, the interest rate (i) must be compounded for the same period. This means that if a situation expresses n in months and i equals 12% per year, then i is transformed into interest earned per month (or 1%). In this case, interest is said to be *compounded monthly.*

A present value table helps us with present value computations. It gives us present values (factors) for a variety of both interest rates (i) and periods (n). Each present value in a present value table assumes that the future value (f) equals 1. When the future value (f) is different from 1, we simply multiply the present value (p) from the table by that future value to give us the estimate. The formula used to construct a table of present values for a single future amount of 1 is shown in Exhibit B.3.

EXHIBIT B.3

Present Value of 1 Formula

$$p = \frac{1}{(1 + i)^n}$$

This formula is identical to that in Exhibit B.2 except that f equals 1. Table B.1 at the end of this appendix is such a present value table. It is often called a **present value of 1 table**. A present value table involves three factors: p, i, and n. Knowing two of these three factors allows us to compute the third. (A fourth is f, but as already explained, we need only multiply the 1 used in the formula by f.) To illustrate the use of a present value table, consider three cases.

> **P1** Apply present value concepts to a single amount by using interest tables.

Case I   (solve for p when knowing i and n). To show how we use a present value table, let's look again at how we estimate the present value of $220 (the f value) at the end of one period ($n = 1$) where the interest rate (i) is 10%. To solve this case, we go to the present value table (Table B.1) and look in the row for 1 period and in the column for 10% interest. Here we find a present value (p) of 0.9091 based on a future value of 1. This means, for instance, that $1 to be received one period from today at 10% interest is worth $0.9091 today. Since the future value in this case is not $1 but $220, we multiply the 0.9091 by $220 to get an answer of $200.

Case 2   (solve for n when knowing p and i). To illustrate, assume a $100,000 future value ($f$) that is worth $13,000 today ($p$) using an interest rate of 12% (i) but where n is unknown. In particular, we want to know how many periods (n) there are between the present value and the future value. To put this in context, it would fit a situation in which we want to retire with $100,000 but currently have only $13,000 that is earning a 12% return and we will be unable to save any additional money. How long will it be before we can retire? To answer this, we go to Table B.1 and look in the 12% interest column. Here we find a column of present values (p) based on a future value of 1. To use the present value table for this solution, we must divide $13,000 ($p$) by $100,000 ($f$), which equals 0.1300. This is necessary because *a present value table defines* f *equal to 1, and* p *as a fraction of 1.* We look for a value nearest to 0.1300 (p), which we find in the row for 18 periods (n). This means that the present value of $100,000 at the end of 18 periods at 12% interest is $13,000; alternatively stated, we must work 18 more years.

Case 3   (solve for i when knowing p and n). In this case, we have, say, a $120,000 future value ($f$) worth $60,000 today ($p$) when there are nine periods (n) between the present and future values, but the interest rate is unknown. As an example, suppose we want to retire with $120,000, but we have only $60,000 and we will be unable to save any additional money, yet we hope to retire in nine years. What interest rate must we earn to retire with $120,000 in nine years? To answer this, we go to the present value table (Table B.1) and look in the row for nine periods. To use the present value table, we must divide $60,000 ($p$) by $120,000 ($f$), which equals 0.5000. Recall that this step is necessary because a present value table defines f equal to 1 and p as a fraction of 1. We look for a value in the row for nine periods that is nearest to 0.5000 (p), which we find in the column for 8% interest (i). This means that the present value of $120,000 at the end of nine periods at 8% interest is $60,000 or, in our example, we must earn 8% annual interest to retire in nine years.

Quick Check   Answer – p. B-7

1. A company is considering an investment expected to yield $70,000 after six years. If this company demands an 8% return, how much is it willing to pay for this investment?

FUTURE VALUE OF A SINGLE AMOUNT

We must modify the formula for the present value of a single amount to obtain the formula for the future value of a single amount. In particular, we multiply both sides of the equation in Exhibit B.2 by $(1 + i)^n$ to get the result shown in Exhibit B.4.

$$f = p \times (1 + i)^n$$

EXHIBIT B.4

Future Value of a Single Amount Formula

The future value (f) is defined in terms of p, i, and n. We can use this formula to determine that $200 ($p$) invested for 1 ($n$) period at an interest rate of 10% (i) yields a future value of $220 as follows:

$$f = p \times (1 + i)^n$$
$$= \$200 \times (1 + 0.10)^1$$
$$= \$220$$

P2 Apply future value concepts to a single amount by using interest tables.

This formula can also be used to compute the future value of an amount for *any number of periods* into the future. To illustrate, assume that $200 is invested for three periods at 10%. The future value of this $200 is $266.20, computed as follows:

$$f = p \times (1 + i)^n$$
$$= \$200 \times (1 + 0.10)^3$$
$$= \$266.20$$

A future value table makes it easier for us to compute future values (f) for many different combinations of interest rates (i) and time periods (n). Each future value in a future value table assumes the present value (p) is 1. As with a present value table, if the future amount is something other than 1, we simply multiply our answer by that amount. The formula used to construct a table of future values (factors) for a single amount of 1 is in Exhibit B.5.

EXHIBIT B.5

Future Value of 1 Formula

$$f = (1 + i)^n$$

Table B.2 at the end of this appendix shows a table of future values for a current amount of 1. This type of table is called a **future value of 1 table**.

There are some important relations between Tables B.1 and B.2. In Table B.2, for the row where $n = 0$, the future value is 1 for each interest rate. This is so because no interest is earned when time does not pass. We also see that Tables B.1 and B.2 report the same information but in a different manner. In particular, one table is simply the *inverse* of the other. To illustrate this inverse relation, let's say we invest $100 for a period of five years at 12% per year. How much do we expect to have after five years? We can answer this question using Table B.2 by finding the future value (f) of 1, for five periods from now, compounded at 12%. From that table we find $f = 1.7623$. If we start with $100, the amount it accumulates to after five years is $176.23 ($100 $\times$ 1.7623). We can alternatively use Table B.1. Here we find that the present value (p) of 1, discounted five periods at 12%, is 0.5674. Recall the inverse relation between present value and future value. This means that $p = 1/f$ (or equivalently, $f = 1/p$). We can compute the future value of $100 invested for five periods at 12% as follows: $f = \$100 \times (1/0.5674) = \$176.24$ (which equals the $176.23 just computed, except for a 1 cent rounding difference).

A future value table involves three factors: f, i, and n. Knowing two of these three factors allows us to compute the third. To illustrate, consider these three possible cases.

Case 1 (solve for f when knowing i and n). Our preceding example fits this case. We found that $100 invested for five periods at 12% interest accumulates to $176.24.

Case 2 (solve for n when knowing f and i). In this case, we have, say, $2,000 ($p$) and we want to know how many periods (n) it will take to accumulate to $3,000 ($f$) at 7% ($i$) interest. To answer this, we go to the future value table (Table B.2) and look in the 7% interest column. Here we find a column of future values (f) based on a present value of 1. To use a future value table, we must divide $3,000 ($f$) by $2,000 ($p$), which equals 1.500. This is necessary because *a future value table defines* p *equal to 1, and* f *as a multiple of 1*. We look for a value nearest to 1.50 (f), which we find in the row for six periods (n). This means that $2,000 invested for six periods at 7% interest accumulates to $3,000.

Case 3 (solve for i when knowing f and n). In this case, we have, say, $2,001 ($p$), and in nine years ($n$) we want to have $4,000 ($f$). What rate of interest must we earn to accomplish this? To answer that, we go to Table B.2 and search in the row for nine periods. To use a future value table, we must divide $4,000 ($f$) by $2,001 ($p$), which equals 1.9990. Recall that this is necessary because a future value table defines p equal to 1 and f as a multiple of 1. We look for a value nearest to 1.9990 (f), which we find in the column for 8% interest (i). This means that $2,001 invested for nine periods at 8% interest accumulates to $4,000.

Quick Check   Answer – p. B-7

> **2.** Assume that you win a $150,000 cash sweepstakes. You decide to deposit this cash in an account earning 8% annual interest, and you plan to quit your job when the account equals $555,000. How many years will it be before you can quit working?

PRESENT VALUE OF AN ANNUITY

An *annuity* is a series of equal payments occurring at equal intervals. One example is a series of three annual payments of $100 each. An *ordinary annuity* is defined as equal end-of-period payments at equal intervals. An ordinary annuity of $100 for three periods and its present value (p) are illustrated in Exhibit B.6.

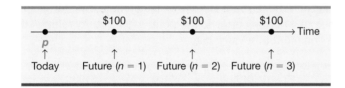

EXHIBIT B.6

Present Value of an Ordinary Annuity Diagram

One way to compute the present value of an ordinary annuity is to find the present value of each payment using our present value formula from Exhibit B.3. We then add each of the three present values. To illustrate, let's look at three $100 payments at the end of each of the next three periods with an interest rate of 15%. Our present value computations are

P3 Apply present value concepts to an annuity by using interest tables.

$$p = \frac{\$100}{(1 + 0.15)^1} + \frac{\$100}{(1 + 0.15)^2} + \frac{\$100}{(1 + 0.15)^3} = \$228.32$$

This computation is identical to computing the present value of each payment (from Table B.1) and taking their sum or, alternatively, adding the values from Table B.1 for each of the three payments and multiplying their sum by the $100 annuity payment.

A more direct way is to use a present value of annuity table. Table B.3 at the end of this appendix is one such table. This table is called a **present value of an annuity of 1 table**. If we look at Table B.3 where $n = 3$ and $i = 15\%$, we see the present value is 2.2832. This means that the present value of an annuity of 1 for three periods, with a 15% interest rate, equals 2.2832.

A present value of an annuity formula is used to construct Table B.3. It can also be constructed by adding the amounts in a present value of 1 table. To illustrate, we use Tables B.1 and B.3 to confirm this relation for the prior example:

From Table B.1		From Table B.3	
$i = 15\%, n = 1$	0.8696		
$i = 15\%, n = 2$	0.7561		
$i = 15\%, n = 3$	0.6575		
Total	2.2832	$i = 15\%, n = 3$	2.2832

We can also use business calculators or spreadsheet programs to find the present value of an annuity.

■ **Decision** Insight

Blessed Winnings   "I don't have good luck—I'm blessed," proclaimed Andrew "Jack" Whittaker, 55, a sewage treatment contractor, after winning the largest ever undivided jackpot in a U.S. lottery. Whittaker had to choose between $315 million in 30 annual installments or $170 million in one lump sum ($112 million after-tax). ■

Quick Check   Answer — p. B-7

3. A company is considering an investment paying $10,000 every six months for three years. The first payment would be received in six months. If this company requires an 8% annual return, what is the maximum amount it is willing to pay for this investment?

FUTURE VALUE OF AN ANNUITY

The future value of an *ordinary annuity* is the accumulated value of each annuity payment with interest as of the date of the final payment. To illustrate, let's consider the earlier annuity of three annual payments of $100. Exhibit B.7 shows the point in time for the future value (f). The first payment is made two periods prior to the point when future value is determined, and the final payment occurs on the future value date.

EXHIBIT B.7

Future Value of an Ordinary
Annuity Diagram

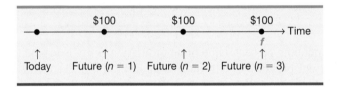

One way to compute the future value of an annuity is to use the formula to find the future value of *each* payment and add them. If we assume an interest rate of 15%, our calculation is

$$f = \$100 \times (1 + 0.15)^2 + \$100 \times (1 + 0.15)^1 + \$100 \times (1 + 0.15)^0 = \$347.25$$

This is identical to using Table B.2 and summing the future values of each payment, or adding the future values of the three payments of 1 and multiplying the sum by $100.

P4 Apply future value concepts to an annuity by using interest tables.

A more direct way is to use a table showing future values of annuities. Such a table is called a **future value of an annuity of 1 table**. Table B.4 at the end of this appendix is one such table. Note that in Table B.4 when $n = 1$, the future values equal 1 ($f = 1$) for all rates of interest. This is so because such an annuity consists of only one payment and the future value is determined on the date of that payment—no time passes between the payment and its future value. The future value of an annuity formula is used to construct Table B.4. We can also construct it by adding the amounts from a future value of 1 table. To illustrate, we use Tables B.2 and B.4 to confirm this relation for the prior example:

From Table B.2		From Table B.4	
$i = 15\%, n = 0$	1.0000		
$i = 15\%, n = 1$	1.1500		
$i = 15\%, n = 2$	1.3225		
Total	3.4725	$i = 15\%, n = 3$	3.4725

Note that the future value in Table B.2 is 1.0000 when $n = 0$, but the future value in Table B.4 is 1.0000 when $n = 1$. Is this a contradiction? No. When $n = 0$ in Table B.2, the future value is determined on the date when a single payment occurs. This means that no interest is earned because no time has passed, and the future value equals the payment. Table B.4 describes annuities with equal payments occurring at the end of each period. When $n = 1$, the annuity has one payment, and its future value equals 1 on the date of its final and only payment. Again, no time passes between the payment and its future value date.

Quick Check   Answer — p. B-7

4. A company invests $45,000 per year for five years at 12% annual interest. Compute the value of this annuity investment at the end of five years.

Summary

C1 **Describe the earning of interest and the concepts of present and future values.** Interest is payment by a borrower to the owner of an asset for its use. Present and future value computations are a way for us to estimate the interest component of holding assets or liabilities over a period of time.

P1 **Apply present value concepts to a single amount by using interest tables.** The present value of a single amount received at a future date is the amount that can be invested now at the specified interest rate to yield that future value.

P2 **Apply future value concepts to a single amount by using interest tables.** The future value of a single amount invested

at a specified rate of interest is the amount that would accumulate by the future date.

P3 **Apply present value concepts to an annuity by using interest tables.** The present value of an annuity is the amount that can be invested now at the specified interest rate to yield that series of equal periodic payments.

P4 **Apply future value concepts to an annuity by using interest tables.** The future value of an annuity invested at a specific rate of interest is the amount that would accumulate by the date of the final payment.

Guidance Answers to Quick Checks

1. $70,000 \times 0.6302 = $44,114$ (use Table B.1, $i = 8\%$, $n = 6$).

2. $555,000/$150,000 = 3.7000$; Table B.2 shows this value is not achieved until after 17 years at 8% interest.

3. $10,000 \times 5.2421 = $52,421$ (use Table B.3, $i = 4\%$, $n = 6$).

4. $45,000 \times 6.3528 = $285,876$ (use Table B.4, $i = 12\%$, $n = 5$).

---

connect

Assume that you must make future value estimates using the *future value of 1 table* (Table B.2). Which interest rate column do you use when working with the following rates?

1. 8% annual rate, compounded quarterly

2. 12% annual rate, compounded annually

3. 6% annual rate, compounded semiannually

4. 12% annual rate, compounded monthly

Ken Francis is offered the possibility of investing $2,745 today and in return to receive $10,000 after 15 years. What is the annual rate of interest for this investment? (Use Table B.1.)

Megan Brink is offered the possibility of investing $6,651 today at 6% interest per year in a desire to accumulate $10,000. How many years must Brink wait to accumulate $10,000? (Use Table B.1.)

Flaherty is considering an investment that, if paid for immediately, is expected to return $140,000 five years from now. If Flaherty demands a 9% return, how much is she willing to pay for this investment?

CII, Inc., invests $630,000 in a project expected to earn a 12% annual rate of return. The earnings will be reinvested in the project each year until the entire investment is liquidated 10 years later. What will the cash proceeds be when the project is liquidated?

Beene Distributing is considering a project that will return $150,000 annually at the end of each year for the next six years. If Beene demands an annual return of 7% and pays for the project immediately, how much is it willing to pay for the project?

QS B-7 Future value of an annuity P4	Claire Fitch is planning to begin an individual retirement program in which she will invest $1,500 at the end of each year. Fitch plans to retire after making 30 annual investments in the program earning a return of 10%. What is the value of the program on the date of the last payment (30 years from the present)?

━━━ connect

EXERCISES

Exercise B-1 Number of periods of an investment P2	Bill Thompson expects to invest $10,000 at 12% and, at the end of a certain period, receive $96,463. How many years will it be before Thompson receives the payment? (Use Table B.2.)
Exercise B-2 Interest rate on an investment P2	Ed Summers expects to invest $10,000 for 25 years, after which he wants to receive $108,347. What rate of interest must Summers earn? (Use Table B.2.)
Exercise B-3 Interest rate on an investment P3	Jones expects an immediate investment of $57,466 to return $10,000 annually for eight years, with the first payment to be received one year from now. What rate of interest must Jones earn? (Use Table B.3.)
Exercise B-4 Number of periods of an investment P3	Keith Riggins expects an investment of $82,014 to return $10,000 annually for several years. If Riggins earns a return of 10%, how many annual payments will he receive? (Use Table B.3.)
Exercise B-5 Interest rate on an investment P4	Algoe expects to invest $1,000 annually for 40 years to yield an accumulated value of $154,762 on the date of the last investment. For this to occur, what rate of interest must Algoe earn? (Use Table B.4.)
Exercise B-6 Number of periods of an investment P4	Kate Beckwith expects to invest $10,000 annually that will earn 8%. How many annual investments must Beckwith make to accumulate $303,243 on the date of the last investment? (Use Table B.4.)
Exercise B-7 Present value of an annuity P3	Sam Weber finances a new automobile by paying $6,500 cash and agreeing to make 40 monthly payments of $500 each, the first payment to be made one month after the purchase. The loan bears interest at an annual rate of 12%. What is the cost of the automobile?
Exercise B-8 Present value of bonds P1 P3	Spiller Corp. plans to issue 10%, 15-year, $500,000 par value bonds payable that pay interest semiannually on June 30 and December 31. The bonds are dated December 31, 2013, and are issued on that date. If the market rate of interest for the bonds is 8% on the date of issue, what will be the total cash proceeds from the bond issue?
Exercise B-9 Present value of an amount P1	McAdams Company expects to earn 10% per year on an investment that will pay $606,773 six years from now. Use Table B.1 to compute the present value of this investment. (Round the amount to the nearest dollar.)
Exercise B-10 Present value of an amount and of an annuity P1 P3	Compute the amount that can be borrowed under each of the following circumstances: **1.** A promise to repay $90,000 seven years from now at an interest rate of 6%. **2.** An agreement made on February 1, 2013, to make three separate payments of $20,000 on February 1 of 2014, 2015, and 2016. The annual interest rate is 10%.
Exercise B-11 Present value of an amount P1	On January 1, 2013, a company agrees to pay $20,000 in three years. If the annual interest rate is 10%, determine how much cash the company can borrow with this agreement.
Exercise B-12 Practical applications of the time value of money P1 P2 P3 P4	**a.** How much would you have to deposit today if you wanted to have $60,000 in 4 years? Annual interest rate is 9%. **b.** Assume that you are saving up for a trip around the world when you graduate in 2 years. If you can earn 8% on your investments, how much would you have to deposit today to have $15,000 when you graduate?

c. Would you rather have $463 now or $1,000 ten years from now? Assume that you can earn 9% on your investments.

d. Assume that a college parking sticker today costs $90. If the cost of parking is increasing at the rate of 5% per year, how much will the college parking sticker cost in 8 years?

e. Assume that the average price of a new home is $158,500. If new homes are increasing at a rate of 10% per year, how much will a new home cost in 8 years?

f. An investment will pay you $10,000 in 10 years, and it will also pay you $400 at the end of *each* of the next 10 years (years 1 thru 10). If the annual interest rate is 6%, how much would you be willing to pay today for this type of investment?

g. A college student is reported in the newspaper as having won $10,000,000 in the Kansas State Lottery. However, as is often the custom with lotteries, she does *not* actually receive the entire $10 million now. Instead she will receive $500,000 at the end of the year for *each* of the next 20 years. If the annual interest rate is 6%, what is the present value (today's amount) that she won? (Ignore taxes.)

C&H Ski Club recently borrowed money and agrees to pay it back with a series of six annual payments of $5,000 each. C&H subsequently borrows more money and agrees to pay it back with a series of four annual payments of $7,500 each. The annual interest rate for both loans is 6%.

1. Use Table B.1 to find the present value of these two separate annuities. (Round amounts to the nearest dollar.)

2. Use Table B.3 to find the present value of these two separate annuities. (Round amounts to the nearest dollar.)

Exercise B-13
Present values of annuities
P3

Otto Co. borrows money on April 30, 2013, by promising to make four payments of $13,000 each on November 1, 2013; May 1, 2014; November 1, 2014; and May 1, 2015.

1. How much money is Otto able to borrow if the interest rate is 8%, compounded semiannually?

2. How much money is Otto able to borrow if the interest rate is 12%, compounded semiannually?

3. How much money is Otto able to borrow if the interest rate is 16%, compounded semiannually?

Exercise B-14
Present value with semiannual compounding
C1 P3

Mark Welsch deposits $7,200 in an account that earns interest at an annual rate of 8%, compounded quarterly. The $7,200 plus earned interest must remain in the account 10 years before it can be withdrawn. How much money will be in the account at the end of 10 years?

Exercise B-15
Future value
of an amount P2

Kelly Malone plans to have $50 withheld from her monthly paycheck and deposited in a savings account that earns 12% annually, compounded monthly. If Malone continues with her plan for two and one-half years, how much will be accumulated in the account on the date of the last deposit?

Exercise B-16
Future value
of an annuity P4

Starr Company decides to establish a fund that it will use 10 years from now to replace an aging production facility. The company will make a $100,000 initial contribution to the fund and plans to make quarterly contributions of $50,000 beginning in three months. The fund earns 12%, compounded quarterly. What will be the value of the fund 10 years from now?

Exercise B-17
Future value of
an amount plus
an annuity P2 P4

Catten, Inc., invests $163,170 today earning 7% per year for nine years. Use Table B.2 to compute the future value of the investment nine years from now. (Round the amount to the nearest dollar.)

Exercise B-18
Future value of an amount P2

For each of the following situations, identify (1) the case as either (*a*) a present or a future value and (*b*) a single amount or an annuity, (2) the table you would use in your computations (but do not solve the problem), and (3) the interest rate and time periods you would use.

a. You need to accumulate $10,000 for a trip you wish to take in four years. You are able to earn 8% compounded semiannually on your savings. You plan to make only one deposit and let the money accumulate for four years. How would you determine the amount of the one-time deposit?

b. Assume the same facts as in part (*a*) except that you will make semiannual deposits to your savings account.

c. You want to retire after working 40 years with savings in excess of $1,000,000. You expect to save $4,000 a year for 40 years and earn an annual rate of interest of 8%. Will you be able to retire with more than $1,000,000 in 40 years? Explain.

d. A sweepstakes agency names you a grand prize winner. You can take $225,000 immediately or elect to receive annual installments of $30,000 for 20 years. You can earn 10% annually on any investments you make. Which prize do you choose to receive?

Exercise B-19
Using present and future
value tables
C1 P1 P2 P3 P4

TABLE B.1

Present Value of 1

$$p = 1/(1 + i)^n$$

	Rate											
Periods	1%	2%	3%	4%	5%	6%	7%	8%	9%	10%	12%	15%
1	0.9901	0.9804	0.9709	0.9615	0.9524	0.9434	0.9346	0.9259	0.9174	0.9091	0.8929	0.8696
2	0.9803	0.9612	0.9426	0.9246	0.9070	0.8900	0.8734	0.8573	0.8417	0.8264	0.7972	0.7561
3	0.9706	0.9423	0.9151	0.8890	0.8638	0.8396	0.8163	0.7938	0.7722	0.7513	0.7118	0.6575
4	0.9610	0.9238	0.8885	0.8548	0.8227	0.7921	0.7629	0.7350	0.7084	0.6830	0.6355	0.5718
5	0.9515	0.9057	0.8626	0.8219	0.7835	0.7473	0.7130	0.6806	0.6499	0.6209	0.5674	0.4972
6	0.9420	0.8880	0.8375	0.7903	0.7462	0.7050	0.6663	0.6302	0.5963	0.5645	0.5066	0.4323
7	0.9327	0.8706	0.8131	0.7599	0.7107	0.6651	0.6227	0.5835	0.5470	0.5132	0.4523	0.3759
8	0.9235	0.8535	0.7894	0.7307	0.6768	0.6274	0.5820	0.5403	0.5019	0.4665	0.4039	0.3269
9	0.9143	0.8368	0.7664	0.7026	0.6446	0.5919	0.5439	0.5002	0.4604	0.4241	0.3606	0.2843
10	0.9053	0.8203	0.7441	0.6756	0.6139	0.5584	0.5083	0.4632	0.4224	0.3855	0.3220	0.2472
11	0.8963	0.8043	0.7224	0.6496	0.5847	0.5268	0.4751	0.4289	0.3875	0.3505	0.2875	0.2149
12	0.8874	0.7885	0.7014	0.6246	0.5568	0.4970	0.4440	0.3971	0.3555	0.3186	0.2567	0.1869
13	0.8787	0.7730	0.6810	0.6006	0.5303	0.4688	0.4150	0.3677	0.3262	0.2897	0.2292	0.1625
14	0.8700	0.7579	0.6611	0.5775	0.5051	0.4423	0.3878	0.3405	0.2992	0.2633	0.2046	0.1413
15	0.8613	0.7430	0.6419	0.5553	0.4810	0.4173	0.3624	0.3152	0.2745	0.2394	0.1827	0.1229
16	0.8528	0.7284	0.6232	0.5339	0.4581	0.3936	0.3387	0.2919	0.2519	0.2176	0.1631	0.1069
17	0.8444	0.7142	0.6050	0.5134	0.4363	0.3714	0.3166	0.2703	0.2311	0.1978	0.1456	0.0929
18	0.8360	0.7002	0.5874	0.4936	0.4155	0.3503	0.2959	0.2502	0.2120	0.1799	0.1300	0.0808
19	0.8277	0.6864	0.5703	0.4746	0.3957	0.3305	0.2765	0.2317	0.1945	0.1635	0.1161	0.0703
20	0.8195	0.6730	0.5537	0.4564	0.3769	0.3118	0.2584	0.2145	0.1784	0.1486	0.1037	0.0611
25	0.7798	0.6095	0.4776	0.3751	0.2953	0.2330	0.1842	0.1460	0.1160	0.0923	0.0588	0.0304
30	0.7419	0.5521	0.4120	0.3083	0.2314	0.1741	0.1314	0.0994	0.0754	0.0573	0.0334	0.0151
35	0.7059	0.5000	0.3554	0.2534	0.1813	0.1301	0.0937	0.0676	0.0490	0.0356	0.0189	0.0075
40	0.6717	0.4529	0.3066	0.2083	0.1420	0.0972	0.0668	0.0460	0.0318	0.0221	0.0107	0.0037

TABLE B.2

Future Value of 1

$$f = (1 + i)^n$$

	Rate											
Periods	1%	2%	3%	4%	5%	6%	7%	8%	9%	10%	12%	15%
0	1.0000	1.0000	1.0000	1.0000	1.0000	1.0000	1.0000	1.0000	1.0000	1.0000	1.0000	1.0000
1	1.0100	1.0200	1.0300	1.0400	1.0500	1.0600	1.0700	1.0800	1.0900	1.1000	1.1200	1.1500
2	1.0201	1.0404	1.0609	1.0816	1.1025	1.1236	1.1449	1.1664	1.1881	1.2100	1.2544	1.3225
3	1.0303	1.0612	1.0927	1.1249	1.1576	1.1910	1.2250	1.2597	1.2950	1.3310	1.4049	1.5209
4	1.0406	1.0824	1.1255	1.1699	1.2155	1.2625	1.3108	1.3605	1.4116	1.4641	1.5735	1.7490
5	1.0510	1.1041	1.1593	1.2167	1.2763	1.3382	1.4026	1.4693	1.5386	1.6105	1.7623	2.0114
6	1.0615	1.1262	1.1941	1.2653	1.3401	1.4185	1.5007	1.5869	1.6771	1.7716	1.9738	2.3131
7	1.0721	1.1487	1.2299	1.3159	1.4071	1.5036	1.6058	1.7138	1.8280	1.9487	2.2107	2.6600
8	1.0829	1.1717	1.2668	1.3686	1.4775	1.5938	1.7182	1.8509	1.9926	2.1436	2.4760	3.0590
9	1.0937	1.1951	1.3048	1.4233	1.5513	1.6895	1.8385	1.9990	2.1719	2.3579	2.7731	3.5179
10	1.1046	1.2190	1.3439	1.4802	1.6289	1.7908	1.9672	2.1589	2.3674	2.5937	3.1058	4.0456
11	1.1157	1.2434	1.3842	1.5395	1.7103	1.8983	2.1049	2.3316	2.5804	2.8531	3.4785	4.6524
12	1.1268	1.2682	1.4258	1.6010	1.7959	2.0122	2.2522	2.5182	2.8127	3.1384	3.8960	5.3503
13	1.1381	1.2936	1.4685	1.6651	1.8856	2.1329	2.4098	2.7196	3.0658	3.4523	4.3635	6.1528
14	1.1495	1.3195	1.5126	1.7317	1.9799	2.2609	2.5785	2.9372	3.3417	3.7975	4.8871	7.0757
15	1.1610	1.3459	1.5580	1.8009	2.0789	2.3966	2.7590	3.1722	3.6425	4.1772	5.4736	8.1371
16	1.1726	1.3728	1.6047	1.8730	2.1829	2.5404	2.9522	3.4259	3.9703	4.5950	6.1304	9.3576
17	1.1843	1.4002	1.6528	1.9479	2.2920	2.6928	3.1588	3.7000	4.3276	5.0545	6.8660	10.7613
18	1.1961	1.4282	1.7024	2.0258	2.4066	2.8543	3.3799	3.9960	4.7171	5.5599	7.6900	12.3755
19	1.2081	1.4568	1.7535	2.1068	2.5270	3.0256	3.6165	4.3157	5.1417	6.1159	8.6128	14.2318
20	1.2202	1.4859	1.8061	2.1911	2.6533	3.2071	3.8697	4.6610	5.6044	6.7275	9.6463	16.3665
25	1.2824	1.6406	2.0938	2.6658	3.3864	4.2919	5.4274	6.8485	8.6231	10.8347	17.0001	32.9190
30	1.3478	1.8114	2.4273	3.2434	4.3219	5.7435	7.6123	10.0627	13.2677	17.4494	29.9599	66.2118
35	1.4166	1.9999	2.8139	3.9461	5.5160	7.6861	10.6766	14.7853	20.4140	28.1024	52.7996	133.1755
40	1.4889	2.2080	3.2620	4.8010	7.0400	10.2857	14.9745	21.7245	31.4094	45.2593	93.0510	267.8635

notes, bonds, and certificates of deposit; they are issued by governments, companies, and individuals. *Equity securities* reflect an owner relationship such as shares of stock issued by companies.

Classification and Reporting

Accounting for investments in securities depends on three factors: (1) security type, either debt or equity, (2) the company's intent to hold the security either short term or long term, and (3) the company's (investor's) percent ownership in the other company's (investee's) equity securities. Exhibit C.2 identifies five classes of securities using these three factors. It describes each of these five classes of securities and the standard reporting required under each class.

EXHIBIT C.2

Investments in Securities

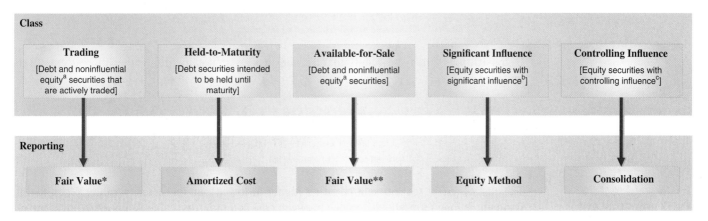

Class				
Trading [Debt and noninfluential equity[a] securities that are actively traded]	**Held-to-Maturity** [Debt securities intended to be held until maturity]	**Available-for-Sale** [Debt and noninfluential equity[a] securities]	**Significant Influence** [Equity securities with significant influence[b]]	**Controlling Influence** [Equity securities with controlling influence[c]]

Reporting				
Fair Value*	**Amortized Cost**	**Fair Value****	**Equity Method**	**Consolidation**

[a] Holding less than 20% of voting stock (equity securities only).   [b] Holding 20% or more, but not more than 50%, of voting stock.   [c] Holding more than 50% of voting stock.

* Unrealized gains and losses reported on the income statement.

** Unrealized gains and losses reported in the equity section of the balance sheet and in comprehensive income.

Debt Securities: Accounting Basics

This section explains the accounting basics for *debt securities,* including that for acquisition, disposition, and any interest.

Acquisition.   Debt securities are recorded at cost when purchased. To illustrate, assume that Music City paid $29,500 plus a $500 brokerage fee on September 1, 2012, to buy Dell's 7%, two-year bonds payable with a $30,000 par value. The bonds pay interest semiannually on August 31 and February 28. Music City intends to hold the bonds until they mature on August 31, 2014; consequently, they are classified as held-to-maturity (HTM) securities. The entry to record this purchase follows. (If the maturity of the securities was short term, and management's intent was to hold them until they mature, then they would be classified as Short-Term Investments—HTM.)

2012			
Sept. 1	Long-Term Investments—HTM (Dell)	30,000	
	Cash		30,000
	Purchased bonds to be held to maturity.		

Assets = Liabilities + Equity
+30,000
−30,000

Interest earned.   Interest revenue for investments in debt securities is recorded when earned. To illustrate, on December 31, 2012, at the end of its accounting period, Music City accrues interest receivable as follows.

Dec. 31	Interest Receivable	700	
	Interest Revenue		700
	Accrued interest earned ($30,000 × 7% × ⁴⁄₁₂).		

Assets = Liabilities + Equity
+700   +700

The $700 reflects 4/6 of the semiannual cash receipt of interest—the portion Music City earned as of December 31. Relevant sections of Music City's financial statements at December 31, 2012, are shown in Exhibit C.3.

EXHIBIT C.3

Financial Statement Presentation
of Debt Securities

On the income statement for year 2012:	
Interest revenue	**$ 700**
On the December 31, 2012, balance sheet:	
Long-term investments—Held-to-maturity securities (at amortized cost)	**$30,000**

On February 28, 2013, Music City records receipt of semiannual interest.

Assets = Liabilities + Equity
+1,050   +350
−700

Feb. 28	Cash	1,050	
	Interest Receivable		700
	Interest Revenue		350
	Received six months' interest on Dell bonds.		

Disposition. When the bonds mature, the proceeds (not including the interest entry) are recorded as:

Assets = Liabilities + Equity
+30,000
−30,000

2014			
Aug. 31	Cash	30,000	
	Long-Term Investments—HTM (Dell)..........		30,000
	Received cash from matured bonds.		

The cost of a debt security can be either higher or lower than its maturity value. When the investment is long term, the difference between cost and maturity value is amortized over the remaining life of the security. We assume for ease of computations that the cost of a long-term debt security equals its maturity value.

Example: What is cost per share?
Answer: Cost per share is the total cost of acquisition, including broker fees, divided by number of shares acquired.

Equity Securities: Accounting Basics

This section explains the accounting basics for *equity securities,* including that for acquisition, dividends, and disposition.

Acquisition. Equity securities are recorded at cost when acquired, including commissions or brokerage fees paid. To illustrate, assume that Music City purchases 1,000 shares of Intex common stock at par value for $86,000 on October 10, 2012. It records this purchase of available-for-sale (AFS) securities as follows.

Assets = Liabilities + Equity
+86,000
−86,000

Oct. 10	Long-Term Investments—AFS (Intex)	86,000	
	Cash		86,000
	Purchased 1,000 shares of Intex.		

Dividend earned. Any cash dividends received are credited to Dividend Revenue and reported in the income statement. To illustrate, on November 2, Music City receives a $1,720 quarterly cash dividend on the Intex shares, which it records as:

Assets = Liabilities + Equity
+1,720   +1,720

Nov. 2	Cash	1,720	
	Dividend Revenue		1,720
	Received dividend of $1.72 per share.		

Disposition. When the securities are sold, sale proceeds are compared with the cost, and any gain or loss is recorded. To illustrate, on December 20, Music City sells 500 of the Intex shares for $45,000 cash and records this sale as:

Assets = Liabilities + Equity
+45,000   +2,000
−43,000

Dec. 20	Cash	45,000	
	Long-Term Investments—AFS (Intex)		43,000
	Gain on Sale of Long-Term Investments		2,000
	Sold 500 Intex shares ($86,000 × 500/1,000).		

Micron's account balance on January 9, 2013, for its investment in Star is $73,650. This is the investment's cost *plus* Micron's equity in Star's earnings since its purchase *less* Micron's equity in Star's cash dividends since its purchase. When an investment in equity securities is sold, the gain or loss is computed by comparing proceeds from the sale with the book value of the investment on the date of sale. If Micron sells its Star stock for $80,000 on January 10, 2013, it records the sale as:

Point: Security prices are sometimes listed in fractions. For example, a debt security with a price of $22\frac{1}{4}$ is the same as $22.25.

Jan. 10	Cash	80,000	
	Long-Term Investments—Star		73,650
	Gain on Sale of Investment		6,350
	Sold 3,000 shares of stock for $80,000.		

Assets = Liabilities + Equity
+80,000   +6,350
−73,650

Investment in Securities with Controlling Influence

A long-term investment classified as **equity securities with controlling influence** implies that the investor can exert a controlling influence over the investee. An investor who owns more than 50% of a company's voting stock has control over the investee. This investor can dominate all other shareholders in electing the corporation's board of directors and has control over the investee's management. In some cases, controlling influence can extend to situations of less than 50% ownership. Exhibit C.7 summarizes the accounting for investments in equity securities based on an investor's ownership in the stock.

C2 Describe how to report equity securities with controlling influence.

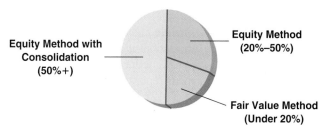

EXHIBIT C.7

Accounting for Equity Investments by Percent of Ownership

The *equity method with consolidation* is used to account for long-term investments in equity securities with controlling influence. The investor reports *consolidated financial statements* when owning such securities. The controlling investor is called the **parent,** and the investee is called the **subsidiary.** Many companies are parents with subsidiaries. Examples are (1) Gap, Inc., the parent of Gap, Old Navy, and Banana Republic; and (2) Brunswick, the parent of Mercury Marine, Sea Ray, and U.S. Marine. A company owning all the outstanding stock of a subsidiary can, if it desires, take over the subsidiary's assets, retire the subsidiary's stock, and merge the subsidiary into the parent. However, there often are financial, legal, and tax advantages if a business operates as a parent controlling one or more subsidiaries. When a company operates as a parent with subsidiaries, each entity maintains separate accounting records. From a legal viewpoint, the parent and each subsidiary are separate entities with all rights, duties, and responsibilities of individual companies.

Consolidated financial statements show the financial position, results of operations, and cash flows of all entities under the parent's control, including all subsidiaries. These statements are prepared as if the business were organized as one entity. The parent uses the equity method in its accounts, but the investment account is *not* reported on the parent's financial statements. Instead, the individual assets and liabilities of the parent and its subsidiaries are combined on one balance sheet. Their revenues and expenses also are combined on one income statement, and their cash flows are combined on one statement of cash flows. The procedures for preparing consolidated financial statements are in advanced courses.

 IFRS _____

Unlike U.S. GAAP, IFRS requires uniform accounting policies be used throughout the group of consolidated subsidiaries. Also, unlike U.S. GAAP, IFRS offers no detailed guidance on valuation procedures. ■

Accounting Summary for Investments in Securities

Exhibit C.8 summarizes the standard accounting for investments in securities. Recall that many investment securities are classified as either short term or long term depending on management's intent and ability to convert them in the future. Understanding the accounting for these investments enables us to draw better conclusions from financial statements in making business decisions.

EXHIBIT C.8

Accounting for Investments
in Securities

Classification	Accounting
Short-Term Investment in Securities	
Held-to-maturity (debt) securities	Cost (without any discount or premium amortization)
Trading (debt and equity) securities	Fair value (with fair value adjustment to income)
Available-for-sale (debt and equity) securities	Fair value (with fair value adjustment to equity)
Long-Term Investment in Securities	
Held-to-maturity (debt) securities	Cost (with any discount or premium amortization)
Available-for-sale (debt and equity) securities	Fair value (with fair value adjustment to equity)
Equity securities with significant influence	Equity method
Equity securities with controlling influence	Equity method (with consolidation)

Comprehensive Income   Comprehensive income is defined as all changes in equity during a period except those from owners' investments and dividends. Specifically, comprehensive income is computed by adding or subtracting *other comprehensive income* to net income:

Net income	$ #
Other comprehensive income	#
Comprehensive income	$ #

Point: Some users believe that since AFS securities are not actively traded, reporting fair value changes in income would unnecessarily increase income variability and decrease usefulness.

Other comprehensive income includes unrealized gains and losses on available-for-sale securities, foreign currency translation adjustments, and certain pension adjustments. (*Accumulated other comprehensive income* is defined as the cumulative impact of *other comprehensive income*.)

Comprehensive income is reported in financial statements in one of two ways (which reflects new FASB guidance as of 2012):

1. On a separate *statement of comprehensive income* that immediately follows the income statement.
2. On the lower section of the income statement (as a single continuous *statement of income and comprehensive income*).

Option 1 is the most common. **KTM**, for example, reports a statement of comprehensive income following its income statement in Appendix A near the end of the book (Piaggio also applies this same presentation in Appendix A). Following is an abbreviated version of the KTM statement using language more common for U.S. GAAP:

KTM

Net income	20,818
Foreign currency conversion.	107
Valuation of cash flow hedges, net of tax	8,545
Other comprehensive income	8,652
Total comprehensive income	29,470

Other comprehensive income

Option 2 adds the components of other comprehensive income to net income on the bottom of the income statement to compute a continuous statement of income and comprehensive income. There is no difference in the numbers; it is simply a matter of how those numbers are presented. A third option, which is no longer acceptable, was to include the components of other comprehensive income and its total along with the total of comprehensive income in the statement of equity. Polaris and Arctic Cat show examples of this presentation, which is no longer acceptable for future years.

Quick Check
Answers — p. C-19

6. Give at least two examples of assets classified as long-term investments.
7. What are the requirements for an equity security to be listed as a long-term investment?
8. Identify similarities and differences in accounting for long-term investments in debt securities that are held-to-maturity versus those available-for-sale.
9. What are the three possible classifications of long-term equity investments? Describe the criteria for each class and the method used to account for each.

GLOBAL VIEW

This section discusses similarities and differences for the accounting and reporting of investments when financial statements are prepared under U.S. GAAP vis-à-vis IFRS.

Accounting for Noninfluential Securities   The accounting for noninfluential securities is broadly similar between U.S. GAAP and IFRS. *Trading securities* are accounted for using fair values with unrealized gains and losses reported in net income as fair values change. *Available-for-sale securities* are accounted for using fair values with unrealized gains and losses reported in other comprehensive income as fair values change (and later in net income when realized). *Held-to-maturity securities* are accounted for using amortized cost. Similarly, companies have the option under both systems to apply the fair value option for available-for-sale and held-to-maturity securities. Also, both systems review held-to-maturity securities for impairment. There are some differences in terminology under IFRS: (1) trading securities are commonly referred to as *financial assets at fair value through profit and loss,* and (2) available-for-sale securities are commonly referred to as *available-for-sale financial assets.* NOKIA reports the following categories for noninfluential securities: (1) ***Financial assets at fair value through profit or loss,*** consisting of financial assets held for trading and financial assets designated upon initial recognition as at fair value through profit or loss, (2) ***Available-for-sale financial assets,*** which are measured at fair value.

NOKIA

Accounting for Influential Securities   The accounting for influential securities is broadly similar across U.S. GAAP and IFRS. Specifically, under the *equity method,* the share of investee's net income is reported in the investor's income in the same period the investee earns that income; also, the investment account equals the acquisition cost plus the share of investee income less the share of investee dividends (minus amortization of excess on purchase price above fair value of identifiable, limited-life assets). Under the *consolidation method,* investee and investor revenues and expenses are combined, absent intercompany transactions, and subtracting noncontrolling interests. Also, nonintercompany assets and liabilities are similarly combined (eliminating the need for an investment account), and noncontrolling interests are subtracted from equity. There are some differences in terminology: (1) U.S. GAAP companies commonly refer to earnings from long-term investments as *equity in earnings of affiliates* whereas IFRS companies commonly use *equity in earnings of associated (or associate) companies,* (2) U.S. GAAP companies commonly refer to noncontrolling interests in consolidated subsidiaries as *minority interests* whereas IFRS companies commonly use *noncontrolling interests.*

Components of Return on Total Assets   **Decision Analysis**

A company's **return on total assets** (or simply *return on assets*) is important in assessing financial performance. The return on total assets can be separated into two components, profit margin and total asset turnover, for additional analyses. Exhibit C.9 shows how these two components determine return on total assets.

> **A1** Compute and analyze the components of return on total assets.

$$\text{Return on total assets} = \text{Profit margin} \times \text{Total asset turnover}$$

$$\frac{\text{Net income}}{\text{Average total assets}} = \frac{\text{Net income}}{\text{Net sales}} \times \frac{\text{Net sales}}{\text{Average total assets}}$$

EXHIBIT C.9

Components of Return on Total Assets

Profit margin reflects the percent of net income in each dollar of net sales. Total asset turnover reflects a company's ability to produce net sales from total assets. All companies desire a high return on total assets. By considering these two components, we can often discover strengths and weaknesses not revealed by return on total assets alone. This improves our ability to assess future performance and company strategy.

To illustrate, consider return on total assets and its components for **Gap Inc.** in Exhibit C.10.

EXHIBIT C.10

Gap's Components of Return on Total Assets

Fiscal Year	Return on Total Assets	=	Profit Margin	×	Total Asset Turnover
2012	11.5%	=	5.7%	×	2.01
2011	16.0*	=	8.2	×	1.95
2010	14.1*	=	7.7	×	1.83
2009	12.6	=	6.66	×	1.89
2008	10.2*	=	5.28	×	1.92

* Differences due to rounding.

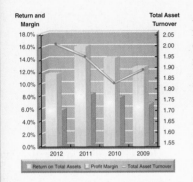

At least three findings emerge. First, Gap's return on total assets improved from 10.2% in 2008 to 11.5% in 2012. Second, total asset turnover has slightly improved over this period, from 1.92 to 2.01. Third, Gap's profit margin steadily increased over this period, from 2008's level of 5.28%. These components reveal the dual role of profit margin and total asset turnover in determining return on total assets. They also reveal that the driver of Gap's recent improvement in return on total assets is not total asset turnover but profit margin.

Generally, if a company is to maintain or improve its return on total assets, it must meet any decline in either profit margin or total asset turnover with an increase in the other. If not, return on assets will decline. Companies consider these components in planning strategies. A component analysis can also reveal where a company is weak and where changes are needed, especially in a competitor analysis. If asset turnover is lower than the industry norm, for instance, a company should focus on raising asset turnover at least to the norm. The same applies to profit margin.

■ **Decision Maker** ═══════════════════════════════════════

Retailer   You are an entrepreneur and owner of a retail sporting goods store. The store's recent annual performance reveals (industry norms in parentheses): return on total assets = 11% (11.2%); profit margin = 4.4% (3.5%); and total asset turnover = 2.5 (3.2). What does your analysis of these figures reveal? ■   [Answer—p. C-19]

DEMONSTRATION PROBLEM—1

Garden Company completes the following selected transactions related to its short-term investments during 2013.

May   8   Purchased 300 shares of FedEx stock as a short-term investment in available-for-sale securities at $40 per share plus $975 in broker fees.

Sept. 2   Sold 100 shares of its investment in FedEx stock at $47 per share and held the remaining 200 shares; broker's commission was $225.

Oct.   2   Purchased 400 shares of Ajay stock for $60 per share plus $1,600 in commissions. The stock is held as a short-term investment in available-for-sale securities.

Required

1. Prepare journal entries for the above transactions of Garden Company for 2013.

2. Prepare an adjusting journal entry as of December 31, 2013, if the fair values of the equity securities held by Garden Company are $48 per share for FedEx and $55 per share for Ajay. (Year 2013 is the first year Garden Company acquired short-term investments.)

SOLUTION TO DEMONSTRATION PROBLEM—1

1.

May 8	Short-Term Investments—AFS (FedEx)	12,975	
	Cash		12,975
	Purchased 300 shares of FedEx stock		
	(300 × $40) + $975.		

[continued on next page]

[continued from previous page]

Sept. 2	Cash	4,475	
	Gain on Sale of Short-Term Investment		150
	Short-Term Investments—AFS (FedEx)		4,325
	Sold 100 shares of FedEx for $47 per share less		
	a $225 commission. The original cost is		
	($12,975 × 100/300).		
Oct. 2	Short-Term Investments—AFS (Ajay)	25,600	
	Cash		25,600
	Purchased 400 shares of Ajay for $60 per share		
	plus $1,600 in commissions.		

2. Computation of unrealized gain or loss follows.

Short-Term Investments in Available-for-Sale Securities	Shares	Cost per Share	Total Cost	Fair Value per Share	Total Fair Value	Unrealized Gain (Loss)
FedEx	200	$43.25	$ 8,650	$48.00	$ 9,600	
Ajay	400	64.00	25,600	55.00	22,000	
Totals			$34,250		$31,600	$(2,650)

The adjusting entry follows:

Dec. 31	Unrealized Loss—Equity	2,650	
	Fair Value Adjustment—Available-for-Sale (ST)		2,650
	To reflect an unrealized loss in fair values		
	of available-for-sale securities.		

DEMONSTRATION PROBLEM—2

The following transactions relate to Brown Company's long-term investments during 2012 and 2013. Brown did not own any long-term investments prior to 2012. Show (1) the appropriate journal entries and (2) the relevant portions of each year's balance sheet and income statement that reflect these transactions for both 2012 and 2013.

2012

Sept. 9 Purchased 1,000 shares of Packard, Inc., common stock for $80,000 cash. These shares represent 30% of Packard's outstanding shares.

Oct. 2 Purchased 2,000 shares of AT&T common stock for $60,000 cash as a long-term investment. These shares represent less than a 1% ownership in AT&T.

17 Purchased as a long-term investment 1,000 shares of Apple Computer common stock for $40,000 cash. These shares are less than 1% of Apple's outstanding shares.

Nov. 1 Received $5,000 cash dividend from Packard.

30 Received $3,000 cash dividend from AT&T.

Dec. 15 Received $1,400 cash dividend from Apple.

31 Packard's net income for this year is $70,000.

31 Fair values for the investments in equity securities are Packard, $84,000; AT&T, $48,000; and Apple Computer, $45,000.

31 For preparing financial statements, note the following post-closing account balances: Common Stock, $500,000, and Retained Earnings, $350,000.

2013

Jan. 1 Sold Packard, Inc., shares for $108,000 cash.

May 30 Received $3,100 cash dividend from AT&T.

June 15 Received $1,600 cash dividend from Apple.

Aug. 17   Sold the AT&T stock for $52,000 cash.
     19   Purchased 2,000 shares of Coca-Cola common stock for $50,000 cash as a long-term invest-
          ment. The stock represents less than a 5% ownership in Coca-Cola.
Dec. 15   Received $1,800 cash dividend from Apple.
     31   Fair values of the investments in equity securities are Apple, $39,000, and Coca-Cola, $48,000.
     31   For preparing financial statements, note the following post-closing account balances: Common
          Stock, $500,000, and Retained Earnings, $410,000.

PLANNING THE SOLUTION

- Account for the investment in Packard under the equity method.
- Account for the investments in AT&T, Apple, and Coca-Cola as long-term investments in available-for-sale securities.
- Prepare the information for the two years' balance sheets by including the relevant asset and equity accounts, and the two years' income statements by identifying the relevant revenues, earnings, gains, and losses.

SOLUTION TO DEMONSTRATION PROBLEM—2

1. Journal entries for 2012.

Sept. 9	Long-Term Investments—Packard	80,000	
	Cash		80,000
	Acquired 1,000 shares, representing a 30% equity in Packard.		
Oct. 2	Long-Term Investments—AFS (AT&T)	60,000	
	Cash		60,000
	Acquired 2,000 shares as a long-term investment in available-for-sale securities.		
Oct. 17	Long-Term Investments—AFS (Apple)	40,000	
	Cash		40,000
	Acquired 1,000 shares as a long-term investment in available-for-sale securities.		
Nov. 1	Cash	5,000	
	Long-Term Investments—Packard		5,000
	Received dividend from Packard.		
Nov. 30	Cash	3,000	
	Dividend Revenue		3,000
	Received dividend from AT&T.		
Dec. 15	Cash	1,400	
	Dividend Revenue		1,400
	Received dividend from Apple.		
Dec. 31	Long-Term Investments—Packard	21,000	
	Earnings from Investment (Packard)		21,000
	To record 30% share of Packard's annual earnings of $70,000.		
Dec. 31	Unrealized Loss—Equity	7,000	
	Fair Value Adjustment—Available-for-Sale (LT)* . . .		7,000
	To record change in fair value of long-term available-for-sale securities.		

* Fair value adjustment computations:

	Cost	Fair Value	Unrealized Gain (Loss)
AT&T	$ 60,000	$48,000	$(12,000)
Apple	40,000	45,000	5,000
Total	$100,000	$93,000	$ (7,000)

Required balance of the Fair Value
  Adjustment—Available-for-Sale
  (LT) account (credit) . . . . $(7,000)
Existing balance   0
Necessary adjustment (credit) . . . . . . $(7,000)

2. The December 31, 2012, selected balance sheet items appear as follows.

Assets	
Long-term investments	
Available-for-sale securities (at fair value; cost is $100,000)	$ 93,000
Investment in equity securities	96,000
Total long-term investments	189,000
Stockholders' Equity	
Common stock	500,000
Retained earnings	350,000
Unrealized loss—Equity	(7,000)

The relevant income statement items for the year ended December 31, 2012, follow.

Dividend revenue	$ 4,400
Earnings from investment	21,000

1. Journal entries for 2013.

Jan. 1	Cash	108,000	
	Long-Term Investments—Packard		96,000
	Gain on Sale of Long-Term Investments		12,000
	Sold 1,000 shares for cash.		
May 30	Cash	3,100	
	Dividend Revenue		3,100
	Received dividend from AT&T.		
June 15	Cash	1,600	
	Dividend Revenue		1,600
	Received dividend from Apple.		
Aug. 17	Cash	52,000	
	Loss on Sale of Long-Term Investments	8,000	
	Long-Term Investments—AFS (AT&T)		60,000
	Sold 2,000 shares for cash.		
Aug. 19	Long-Term Investments—AFS (Coca-Cola)	50,000	
	Cash		50,000
	Acquired 2,000 shares as a long-term *investment in available-for-sale securities.*		
Dec. 15	Cash	1,800	
	Dividend Revenue		1,800
	Received dividend from Apple.		
Dec. 31	Fair Value Adjustment—Available-for-Sale (LT)*	4,000	
	Unrealized Loss—Equity		4,000
	To record change in fair value of long-term *available-for-sale securities.*		

* Fair value adjustment computations:

	Cost	Fair Value	Unrealized Gain (Loss)
Apple	$40,000	$39,000	$(1,000)
Coca-Cola	50,000	48,000	(2,000)
Total	$90,000	$87,000	$(3,000)

Required balance of the Fair Value Adjustment—Available-for-Sale (LT) account (credit)	$(3,000)
Existing balance (credit)	(7,000)
Necessary adjustment (debit)	$ 4,000

2. The December 31, 2013, balance sheet items appear as follows.

Assets	
Long-term investments	
Available-for-sale securities (at fair value; cost is $90,000)	$ 87,000
Stockholders' Equity	
Common stock	500,000
Retained earnings	410,000
Unrealized loss—Equity	(3,000)

The relevant income statement items for the year ended December 31, 2013, follow.

Dividend revenue	$ 6,500
Gain on sale of long-term investments.	12,000
Loss on sale of long-term investments	(8,000)

APPENDIX

C-A   Investments in International Operations

Many entities from small entrepreneurs to large corporations conduct business internationally. Some entities' operations occur in so many different countries that the companies are called **multinationals.** Many of us think of **Coca-Cola** and **McDonald's,** for example, as primarily U.S. companies, but most of their sales occur outside the United States. Exhibit C-A.1 shows the percent of international sales and income for selected U.S. companies. Managing and accounting for multinationals present challenges. This section describes some of these challenges and how to account for and report these activities.

EXHIBIT C-A.1

International Sales and Income as a Percent of Their Totals

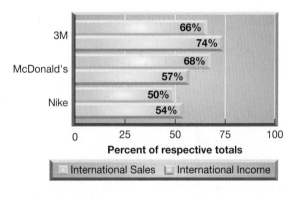

Two major accounting challenges that arise when companies have international operations relate to transactions that involve more than one currency. The first is to account for sales and purchases listed in a foreign currency. The second is to prepare consolidated financial statements with international subsidiaries. For ease in this discussion, we use companies with a U.S. base of operations and assume the need to prepare financial statements in U.S. dollars. This means the *reporting currency* of these companies is the U.S. dollar.

Point: Transactions *listed* or *stated* in a foreign currency are said to be *denominated* in that currency.

Explain foreign exchange rates and record transactions listed in a foreign currency.

Point: To convert currency, see XE.com

Exchange Rates between Currencies   Markets for the purchase and sale of foreign currencies exist all over the world. In these markets, U.S. dollars can be exchanged for Canadian dollars, British pounds, Japanese yen, Euros, or any other legal currencies. The price of one currency stated in terms of another currency is called a **foreign exchange rate.** Exhibit C-A.2 lists recent exchange rates for selected currencies. The exchange rate for British pounds and U.S. dollars is $1.8980, meaning 1 British pound could be purchased for $1.8980. On that same day, the exchange rate between Mexican pesos and U.S. dollars is $0.0925, or 1 Mexican peso can be purchased for $0.0925. Exchange rates fluctuate due to changing economic and political conditions, including the supply and demand for currencies and expectations about future events.

> ■ **Decision** Insight ━━━━━━━━━━━━━━━━━━━━━━━━━━━━━
>
> **Greek Haircut**   Investors in government debt securities in the Euro-zone must be careful of the heightened default risk associated with securities issued by certain Eurozone member nations. For example, in 2012, buyers of certain Greek bonds were repaid only 30% of principal because of the government's inability to honor its full obligation on the bonds. ■

Source (unit)	Price in $U.S.	Source (unit)	Price in $U.S.
Britain (pound)	$1.8980	Canada (dollar)	$0.9793
Mexico (peso)	0.0925	Japan (yen)	0.0090
Taiwan (dollar)	0.0305	Europe (Euro)	1.2920

* Rates will vary over time based on economic, political, and other changes.

EXHIBIT C-A.2

Foreign Exchange Rates for
Selected Currencies*

Sales and Purchases Listed in a Foreign Currency
When a U.S. company makes a credit sale to an international customer, accounting for the sale and the account receivable is straightforward if sales terms require the international customer's payment in U.S. dollars. If sale terms require (or allow) payment in a foreign currency, however, the U.S. company must account for the sale and the account receivable in a different manner.

Sales in a Foreign Currency   To illustrate, consider the case of the U.S.-based manufacturer Boston Company, which makes credit sales to London Outfitters, a British retail company. A sale occurs on December 12, 2012, for a price of £10,000 with payment due on February 10, 2013. Boston Company keeps its accounting records in U.S. dollars. To record the sale, Boston Company must translate the sales price from pounds to dollars. This is done using the exchange rate on the date of the sale. Assuming the exchange rate on December 12, 2012, is $1.80, Boston records this sale as follows.

Dec. 12	Accounts Receivable—London Outfitters	18,000	
	Sales*		18,000
	To record a sale at £10,000, when the exchange rate equals $1.80.* (£10,000 × $1.80/£)		

Assets = Liabilities + Equity
+18,000   +18,000

When Boston Company prepares its annual financial statements on December 31, 2012, the current exchange rate is $1.84. Thus, the current dollar value of Boston Company's receivable is $18,400 (£10,000 × $1.84/£). This amount is $400 higher than the amount recorded on December 12. Accounting principles require a receivable to be reported in the balance sheet at its current dollar value. Thus, Boston Company must make the following entry to record the increase in the dollar value of this receivable at year-end.

Dec. 31	Accounts Receivable—London Outfitters	400	
	Foreign Exchange Gain		400
	To record the increased value of the British pound for the receivable.		

Assets = Liabilities + Equity
+400   +400

On February 10, 2013, Boston Company receives London Outfitters' payment of £10,000. It immediately exchanges the pounds for U.S. dollars. On this date, the exchange rate for pounds is $1.78. Thus, Boston Company receives only $17,800 (£10,000 × $1.78/£). It records the cash receipt and the loss associated with the decline in the exchange rate as follows.

Point: Foreign exchange gains are credits, and foreign exchange losses are debits.

Feb. 10	Cash	17,800	
	Foreign Exchange Loss	600	
	Accounts Receivable—London Outfitters		18,400
	Received foreign currency payment of an account and converted it into dollars.		

Assets = Liabilities + Equity
+17,800   −600
−18,400

Gains and losses from foreign exchange transactions are accumulated in the Foreign Exchange Gain (or Loss) account. After year-end adjustments, the balance in the Foreign Exchange Gain (or Loss) account is reported on the income statement and closed to the Income Summary account.

Purchases in a Foreign Currency   Accounting for credit purchases from an international seller is similar to the case of a credit sale to an international customer. In particular, if the U.S. company is required to make payment in a foreign currency, the account payable must be translated into dollars before the U.S. company can record it. If the exchange rate is different when preparing financial statements and when paying for the purchase, the U.S. company must recognize a foreign exchange gain or loss at those dates. To illustrate, assume NC Imports, a U.S. company, purchases products costing €20,000 (euros) from

Example: Assume that a U.S. company makes a credit purchase from a British company for £10,000 when the exchange rate is $1.62. At the balance sheet date, this rate is $1.72. Does this imply a gain or loss for the U.S. company? *Answer:* A loss.

Hamburg Brewing on January 15, when the exchange rate is $1.20 per euro. NC records this transaction as follows.

Assets = Liabilities + Equity
+24,000   +24,000

Jan. 15	Inventory	24,000	
	Accounts Payable—Hamburg Brewing		24,000
	To record a €20,000 purchase when exchange rate		
	is $1.20 (€20,000 × $1.20/€)		

NC Imports makes payment in full on February 14 when the exchange rate is $1.25 per euro, which is recorded as follows.

Assets = Liabilities + Equity
−25,000   −24,000   −1,000

Feb. 14	Accounts Payable—Hamburg Brewing	24,000	
	Foreign Exchange Loss	1,000	
	Cash		25,000
	To record cash payment towards €20,000 account		
	when exchange rate is $1.25 (€20,000 × $1.25/€).		

Decision Insight

Global Greenback What do changes in foreign exchange rates mean? A decline in the price of the U.S. dollar against other currencies usually yields increased international sales for U.S. companies, without hiking prices or cutting costs, and puts them on a stronger competitive footing abroad. At home, they can raise prices without fear that foreign rivals will undercut them. ■

Consolidated Statements with International Subsidiaries A second challenge in accounting for international operations involves preparing consolidated financial statements when the parent company has one or more international subsidiaries. Consider a U.S.-based company that owns a controlling interest in a French subsidiary. The reporting currency of the U.S. parent is the dollar. The French subsidiary maintains its financial records in euros. Before preparing consolidated statements, the parent must translate financial statements of the French company into U.S. dollars. After this translation is complete (including that for accounting differences), it prepares consolidated statements the same as for domestic subsidiaries. Procedures for translating an international subsidiary's account balances depend on the nature of the subsidiary's operations. The process requires the parent company to select appropriate foreign exchange rates and to apply those rates to the foreign subsidiary's account balances. This is described in advanced courses.

Global: A weaker U.S. dollar often increases global sales for U.S. companies.

Decision Maker

Entrepreneur Assume that Ben and Jerry's purchases milk from dairies in both the U.S. and Canada. The price of the Canadian dollar in terms of the U.S. dollar jumps from US$0.70 to US$0.80. Is the ice cream maker now more or less likely to buy milk from Canadian or U.S. suppliers? ■   [Answer—p. C-19]

Summary

C1   **Distinguish between debt and equity securities and between short-term and long-term investments.** *Debt securities* reflect a creditor relationship and include investments in notes, bonds, and certificates of deposit. *Equity securities* reflect an owner relationship and include shares of stock issued by other companies. Short-term investments in securities are current assets that meet two criteria: (1) They are expected to be converted into cash within one year or the current operating cycle of the business, whichever is longer and (2) they are readily convertible to cash, or *marketable*. All other investments in securities are long-term. Long-term investments also include assets not used in operations and those held for special purposes, such as land for expansion. Investments in securities are classified into one of five groups: (1) trading securities, which are always short-term, (2) debt securi-

ties held-to-maturity, (3) debt and equity securities available-for-sale, (4) equity securities in which an investor has a significant influence over the investee, and (5) equity securities in which an investor has a controlling influence over the investee.

C2   **Describe how to report equity securities with controlling influence.** If an investor owns more than 50% of another company's voting stock and controls the investee, the investor's financial reports are prepared on a consolidated basis. These reports are prepared as if the company were organized as one entity.

C3A   **Explain foreign exchange rates and record transactions listed in a foreign currency.** A foreign exchange rate is the price of one currency stated in terms of another. An entity with transactions in a foreign currency when the exchange rate changes between the transaction dates and their settlement will experience exchange gains or losses. When a company makes a credit sale to a foreign customer and sales terms call for payment in a foreign currency, the company must translate the foreign currency into dollars to record the receivable. If the exchange rate changes before payment is received, exchange gains or losses are recognized in the year they occur. The same treatment is used when a company makes a credit purchase from a foreign supplier and is required to make payment in a foreign currency.

A1 **Compute and analyze the components of return on total assets.** Return on total assets has two components: profit margin and total asset turnover. A decline in one component must be met with an increase in another if return on assets is to be maintained. Component analysis is helpful in assessing company performance compared to that of competitors and its own past.

P1 **Account for trading securities.** Investments are initially recorded at cost, and any dividend or interest from these investments is recorded in the income statement. Investments classified as trading securities are reported at fair value. Unrealized gains and losses on trading securities are reported in income. When investments are sold, the difference between the

net proceeds from the sale and the cost of the securities is recognized as a gain or loss.

P2 **Account for held-to-maturity securities.** Debt securities held-to-maturity are reported at cost when purchased. Interest revenue is recorded as it accrues. The cost of long-term held-to-maturity securities is adjusted for the amortization of any difference between cost and maturity value.

P3 **Account for available-for-sale securities.** Debt and equity securities available-for-sale are recorded at cost when purchased. Available-for-sale securities are reported at their fair values on the balance sheet with unrealized gains or losses shown in the equity section. Gains and losses realized on the sale of these investments are reported in the income statement.

P4 **Account for equity securities with significant influence.** The equity method is used when an investor has a significant influence over an investee. This usually exists when an investor owns 20% or more of the investee's voting stock but not more than 50%. The equity method means an investor records its share of investee earnings with a debit to the investment account and a credit to a revenue account. Dividends received reduce the investment account balance.

Guidance Answers to Decision Maker

Money Manager If you have investments in fixed-rate bonds and notes when interest rates fall, the value of your investments increases. This is so because the bonds and notes you hold continue to pay the same (high) rate while the market is demanding a new lower interest rate. Your strategy is to continue holding your investments in bonds and notes, and, potentially, to increase these holdings through additional purchases.

Retailer Your store's return on assets is 11%, which is similar to the industry norm of 11.2%. However, disaggregation of return on assets reveals that your store's profit margin of 4.4% is much higher than the norm of 3.5%, but your total asset turnover of 2.5 is much lower than the norm of 3.2. These results suggest that, as compared with competitors, you are less efficient in using assets. You need to

focus on increasing sales or reducing assets. You might consider reducing prices to increase sales, provided such a strategy does not reduce your return on assets. For instance, you could reduce your profit margin to 4% to increase sales. If total asset turnover increases to more than 2.75 when profit margin is lowered to 4%, your overall return on assets is improved.

Entrepreneur You are now less likely to buy Canadian milk products because it takes more U.S. money to buy a Canadian dollar (and milk). For instance, the purchase of milk from a Canadian dairy with a $1,000 (Canadian dollars) price would have cost the U.S. company $700 (U.S. dollars, computed as C$1,000 × US$0.70) before the rate change, and $800 (US dollars, computed as C$1,000 × US$0.80) after the rate change.

Guidance Answers to Quick Checks

1. Short-term held-to-maturity securities are reported at cost.
2. Trading securities are reported at fair value.
3. The equity section of the balance sheet (and in comprehensive income).
4. The income statement.
5. The Fair Value Adjustment account does not have a normal balance. Its balance is a function of market values for securities which move up or down. The balance of this valuation account is determined by market conditions.
6. Long-term investments include (1) long-term funds earmarked for a special purpose, (2) debt and equity securities that do not meet current asset requirements, and (3) long-term assets not used in the regular operations of the business.
7. An equity investment is classified as long term if it is not marketable or, if marketable, it is not held as an available source of cash to meet the needs of current operations.
8. Debt securities held-to-maturity and debt securities available-for-sale are both recorded at cost. Also, interest on both is accrued as earned. However, only long-term securities held-to-maturity require amortization of the difference between cost and maturity value. In addition, only securities available-for-sale require a period-end adjustment to fair value.
9. Long-term equity investments are placed in one of three categories and accounted for as follows: (a) **available-for-sale** (noninfluential, less than 20% of outstanding stock)—fair value; (b) **significant influence** (20% to 50% of outstanding stock)—equity method; and (c) **controlling influence** (holding more than 50% of outstanding stock)—equity method with consolidation.

Key Terms

Available-for-sale (AFS) securities (p. C-6)	Equity securities with significant influence (p. C-8)	Other comprehensive income (p. C-10)
Comprehensive income (p. C-10)	Foreign exchange rate (p. C-16)	Parent (p. C-9)
Consolidated financial statements (p. C-9)	Held-to-maturity (HTM) securities (p. C-6)	Return on total assets (p. C-11)
Equity method (p. C-8)		Short-term investments (p. C-2)
Equity securities with controlling influence (p. C-9)	Long-term investments (p. C-2)	Subsidiary (p. C-9)
	Multinational (p. C-16)	Trading securities (p. C-5)
		Unrealized gain (loss) (p. C-5)

Multiple Choice Quiz   Answers on p. C-35   mhhe.com/wildFAF4e

1. A company purchased $30,000 of 5% bonds for investment purposes on May 1. The bonds pay interest on February 1 and August 1. The amount of interest revenue accrued at December 31 (the company's year-end) is:
   a. $1,500
   b. $1,375
   c. $1,000
   d. $625
   e. $300

2. Earlier this period, Amadeus Co. purchased its only available-for-sale investment in the stock of Bach Co. for $83,000. The period-end fair value of this stock is $84,500. Amadeus records a:
   a. Credit to Unrealized Gain—Equity for $1,500.
   b. Debit to Unrealized Loss—Equity for $1,500.
   c. Debit to Investment Revenue for $1,500.
   d. Credit to Fair Value Adjustment—Available-for-Sale for $3,500.
   e. Credit to Cash for $1,500.

3. Mozart Co. owns 35% of Melody Inc. Melody pays $50,000 in cash dividends to its shareholders for the period. Mozart's entry to record the Melody dividend includes a:
   a. Credit to Investment Revenue for $50,000.
   b. Credit to Long-Term Investments for $17,500.

   c. Credit to Cash for $17,500.
   d. Debit to Long-Term Investments for $17,500.
   e. Debit to Cash for $50,000.

4. A company has net income of $300,000, net sales of $2,500,000, and total assets of $2,000,000. Its return on total assets equals:
   a. 6.7%
   b. 12.0%
   c. 8.3%
   d. 80.0%
   e. 15.0%

5. A company had net income of $80,000, net sales of $600,000, and total assets of $400,000. Its profit margin and total asset turnover are:

	Profit Margin	Total Asset Turnover
a.	1.5%	13.3
b.	13.3%	1.5
c.	13.3%	0.7
d.	7.0%	13.3
e.	10.0%	26.7

[A] Superscript A denotes assignments based on Appendix C-A.

[I] Icon denotes assignments that involve decision making.

Discussion Questions

1. Under what two conditions should investments be classified as current assets?

2. [I] On a balance sheet, what valuation must be reported for short-term investments in trading securities?

3. If a short-term investment in available-for-sale securities costs $10,000 and is sold for $12,000, how should the difference between these two amounts be recorded?

4. Identify the three classes of noninfluential and two classes of influential investments in securities.

5. Under what conditions should investments be classified as current assets? As long-term assets?

6. For investments in available-for-sale securities, how are unrealized (holding) gains and losses reported?

7. If a company purchases its only long-term investments in available-for-sale debt securities this period and their fair value is below cost at the balance sheet date, what entry is required to recognize this unrealized loss?

Information regarding Carperk Company's individual investments in securities during its calendar-year 2013, along with the December 31, 2013, fair values, follows.

a. Investment in Brava Company bonds: $420,500 cost, $457,000 fair value. Carperk intends to hold these bonds until they mature in 2018.

b. Investment in Baybridge common stock: 29,500 shares; $362,450 cost; $391,375 fair value. Carperk owns 32% of Baybridge's voting stock and has a significant influence over Baybridge.

c. Investment in Buffa common stock: 12,000 shares; $165,500 cost; $178,000 fair value. This investment amounts to 3% of Buffa's outstanding shares, and Carperk's goal with this investment is to earn dividends over the next few years.

d. Investment in Newton common stock: 3,500 shares; $90,300 cost; $88,625 fair value. Carperk's goal with this investment is to reap an increase in fair value of the stock over the next three to five years. Newton has 30,000 common shares outstanding.

e. Investment in Farmers common stock: 16,300 shares; $100,860 cost; $111,210 fair value. This stock is marketable and is held as an investment of cash available for operations.

Required

1. Identify whether each investment should be classified as a short-term or long-term investment. For each long-term investment, indicate in which of the long-term investment classifications it should be placed.

2. Prepare a journal entry dated December 31, 2013, to record the fair value adjustment of the long-term investments in available-for-sale securities. Carperk had no long-term investments prior to year 2013.

Exercise C-12
Classifying investments in securities; recording fair values
C1 P2 P3 P4

Check   (2) Unrealized gain, $10,825

Prepare journal entries to record the following transactions and events of Kodax Company.

2013

Jan.   2   Purchased 30,000 shares of Grecco Co. common stock for $408,000 cash plus a broker's fee of $3,000 cash. Bushtex has 90,000 shares of common stock outstanding and its policies will be significantly influenced by Kodax.

Sept. 1   Grecco declared and paid a cash dividend of $1.50 per share.

Dec. 31   Grecco announced that net income for the year is $486,900.

2014

June   1   Grecco declared and paid a cash dividend of $2.10 per share.

Dec. 31   Grecco announced that net income for the year is $702,750.

Dec. 31   Kodax sold 10,000 shares of Grecco for $320,000 cash.

Exercise C-13
Securities transactions; equity method
P4

The following information is available from the financial statements of Regae Industries. Compute Regae's return on total assets for 2013 and 2014. (Round returns to one-tenth of a percent.) Comment on the company's efficiency in using its assets in 2013 and 2014.

Exercise C-14
Return on total assets
A1

File Edit View Insert Format Tools Data Window Help			
	2012	**2013**	**2014**
Total assets, December 31	$210,000	$340,000	$770,000
Net income	30,200	38,400	60,300

Leigh of New York sells its products to customers in the United States and the United Kingdom. On December 16, 2013, Leigh sold merchandise on credit to Bronson Ltd. of London at a price of 17,000 pounds. The exchange rate on that day for £1 was $1.4583. On December 31, 2013, when Leigh prepared its financial statements, the rate was £1 for $1.4382. Bronson paid its bill in full on January 15, 2014, at which time the exchange rate was £1 for $1.4482. Leigh immediately exchanged the 17,000 pounds for U.S. dollars. Prepare Leigh's journal entries on December 16, December 31, and January 15 (round to the nearest dollar).

Exercise C-15ᴬ
Foreign currency transactions
C3

Exercise C-16[A]

Computing foreign exchange
gains and losses on receivables

C3

On May 8, 2013, Jett Company (a U.S. company) made a credit sale to Lopez (a Mexican company). The
terms of the sale required Lopez to pay 800,000 pesos on February 10, 2014. Jett prepares quarterly
financial statements on March 31, June 30, September 30, and December 31. The exchange rates for pesos
during the time the receivable is outstanding follow.

May 8, 2013	$0.1323
June 30, 2013	0.1352
September 30, 2013	0.1368
December 31, 2013	0.1335
February 10, 2014	0.1386

Compute the foreign exchange gain or loss that Jett should report on each of its quarterly income statements for the last three quarters of 2013 and the first quarter of 2014. Also compute the amount reported on
Jett's balance sheets at the end of each of its last three quarters of 2013.

Exercise C-17

International accounting
for investments

P3

The **Carrefour Group** reports the following description of its financial assets available-for-sale.

> Assets available for sale are . . . valued at fair value. Unrealized . . . gains or losses are recorded as shareholders'
> equity until they are sold.

Note 10 to Carrefour's 2010 financial statements reports €18 million in *net* unrealized losses (net of unrealized gains) for 2010, which is included in the fair value of its available-for-sale securities reported on the
balance sheet.

1. What amount of the €18 million net unrealized losses, if any, is reported in its 2010 income statement? Explain.

2. If the €18 million net unrealized losses are not reported in the income statement, in which statement
are they reported, if any? Explain.

McGraw Hill connect

PROBLEM SET A

Problem C-1A

Recording transactions and
fair value adjustments for
trading securities

P1

Sage 50 QB

Carlsville Company, which began operations in 2013, invests its idle cash in trading securities. The following transactions are from its short-term investments in its trading securities.

2013

Jan. 20   Purchased 800 shares of Ford Motor Co. at $26 per share plus a $125 commission.
Feb. 9   Purchased 2,200 shares of Lucent at $44.25 per share plus a $578 commission.
Oct. 12   Purchased 750 shares of Z-Seven at $7.50 per share plus a $200 commission.

2014

Apr. 15   Sold 800 shares of Ford Motor Co. at $29 per share less a $285 commission.
July   5   Sold 750 shares of Z-Seven at $10.25 per share less a $102.50 commission.
July 22   Purchased 1,600 shares of Hunt Corp. at $30 per share plus a $444 commission.
Aug. 19   Purchased 1,800 shares of Donna Karan at $18.25 per share plus a $290 commission.

2015

Feb. 27   Purchased 3,400 shares of HCA at $34 per share plus a $420 commission.
Mar. 3   Sold 1,600 shares of Hunt at $25 per share less a $250 commission.
June 21   Sold 2,200 shares of Lucent at $42 per share less a $420 commission.
June 30   Purchased 1,200 shares of Black & Decker at $47.50 per share plus a $595 commission.
Nov. 1   Sold 1,800 shares of Donna Karan at $18.25 per share less a $309 commission.

Required

1. Prepare journal entries to record these short-term investment activities for the years shown. (Ignore
any year-end adjusting entries.)

Check (2) Dr. Fair Value
Adjustment—Trading $985

2. On December 31, 2015, prepare the adjusting entry to record any necessary fair value adjustment for
the portfolio of trading securities when HCA's share price is $36 and Black & Decker's share price is
$43.50. (Assume the Fair Value Adjustment—Trading account had an unadjusted balance of zero.)

Rose Company had no short-term investments prior to year 2013. It had the following transactions involving short-term investments in available-for-sale securities during 2013.

Problem C-2A

Recording, adjusting, and reporting short-term available-for-sale securities

P3

Apr. 16   Purchased 4,000 shares of Gem Co. stock at $24.25 per share plus a $180 brokerage fee.
May   1   Paid $100,000 to buy 90-day U.S. Treasury bills (debt securities): $100,000 principal amount, 6% interest, securities dated May 1.
July   7   Purchased 2,000 shares of PepsiCo stock at $49.25 per share plus a $175 brokerage fee.
       20   Purchased 1,000 shares of Xerox stock at $16.75 per share plus a $205 brokerage fee.
Aug. 3   Received a check for principal and accrued interest on the U.S. Treasury bills that matured on July 29.
       15   Received an $0.85 per share cash dividend on the Gem Co. stock.
       28   Sold 2,000 shares of Gem Co. stock at $30 per share less a $225 brokerage fee.
Oct.   1   Received a $1.90 per share cash dividend on the PepsiCo shares.
Dec. 15   Received a $1.05 per share cash dividend on the remaining Gem Co. shares.
       31   Received a $1.30 per share cash dividend on the PepsiCo shares.

Required

1. Prepare journal entries to record the preceding transactions and events.

2. Prepare a table to compare the year-end cost and fair values of Rose's short-term investments in available-for-sale securities. The year-end fair values per share are: Gem Co., $26.50; PepsiCo, $46.50; and Xerox, $13.75.

3. Prepare an adjusting entry, if necessary, to record the year-end fair value adjustment for the portfolio of short-term investments in available-for-sale securities.

Check   (2) Cost = $164,220

(3) Dr. Unrealized Loss— Equity $4,470

Analysis Component

4. Explain the balance sheet presentation of the fair value adjustment for Rose's short-term investments.

5. How do these short-term investments affect Rose's (*a*) income statement for year 2013 and (*b*) the equity section of its balance sheet at year-end 2013?

Grass Security, which began operations in 2013, invests in long-term available-for-sale securities. Following is a series of transactions and events determining its long-term investment activity.

Problem C-3A

Recording, adjusting, and reporting long-term available-for-sale securities

P3

Sage 50

2013

Jan. 20   Purchased 1,000 shares of Johnson & Johnson at $20.50 per share plus a $240 commission.
Feb.   9   Purchased 1,200 shares of Sony at $46.20 per share plus a $225 commission.
June 12   Purchased 1,500 shares of Mattel at $27.00 per share plus an $195 commission.
Dec. 31   Per share fair values for stocks in the portfolio are Johnson & Johnson, $21.50; Mattel, $30.90; Sony, $38.

2014

Apr. 15   Sold 1,000 shares of Johnson & Johnson at $23.50 per share less a $525 commission.
July   5   Sold 1,500 shares of Mattel at $23.90 per share less a $235 commission.
July 22   Purchased 600 shares of Sara Lee at $22.50 per share plus a $480 commission.
Aug. 19   Purchased 900 shares of Eastman Kodak at $17 per share plus a $198 commission.
Dec. 31   Per share fair values for stocks in the portfolio are: Kodak, $19.25; Sara Lee, $20.00; Sony, $35.00.

2015

Feb. 27   Purchased 2,400 shares of Microsoft at $67.00 per share plus a $525 commission.
June 21   Sold 1,200 shares of Sony at $48.00 per share less a $880 commission.
June 30   Purchased 1,400 shares of Black & Decker at $36.00 per share plus a $435 commission.
Aug.   3   Sold 600 shares of Sara Lee at $16.25 per share less a $435 commission.
Nov.   1   Sold 900 shares of Eastman Kodak at $22.75 per share less a $625 commission.
Dec. 31   Per share fair values for stocks in the portfolio are: Black & Decker, $39.00; Microsoft, $69.00.

Required

1. Prepare journal entries to record these transactions and events and any year-end fair value adjustments to the portfolio of long-term available-for-sale securities.

[continued on next page]

Check (2b) Fair Value Adjustment bal.:
12/31/13, $(3,650); 12/31/14; $(13,818)

(3b) Unrealized Gain at
12/31/2015, $8,040

2. Prepare a table that summarizes the (a) total cost, (b) total fair value adjustment, and (c) total fair value of the portfolio of long-term available-for-sale securities at each year-end.

3. Prepare a table that summarizes (a) the realized gains and losses and (b) the unrealized gains or losses for the portfolio of long-term available-for-sale securities at each year-end.

Problem C-4A
Long-term investment transactions; unrealized and realized gains and losses

C2 P3 P4

Stoll Co.'s long-term available-for-sale portfolio at December 31, 2012, consists of the following.

Available-for-Sale Securities	Cost	Fair Value
40,000 shares of Company A common stock	$535,300	$490,000
7,000 shares of Company B common stock	159,380	154,000
17,500 shares of Company C common stock	662,750	640,938

Stoll enters into the following long-term investment transactions during year 2013.

Jan. 29 Sold 3,500 shares of Company B common stock for $79,188 less a brokerage fee of $1,500.
Apr. 17 Purchased 10,000 shares of Company W common stock for $197,500 plus a brokerage fee of $2,400. The shares represent a 30% ownership in Company W.
July 6 Purchased 4,500 shares of Company X common stock for $126,562 plus a brokerage fee of $1,750. The shares represent a 10% ownership in Company X.
Aug. 22 Purchased 50,000 shares of Company Y common stock for $375,000 plus a brokerage fee of $1,200. The shares represent a 51% ownership in Company Y.
Nov. 13 Purchased 8,500 shares of Company Z common stock for $267,900 plus a brokerage fee of $2,450. The shares represent a 5% ownership in Company Z.
Dec. 9 Sold 40,000 shares of Company A common stock for $515,000 less a brokerage fee of $4,100.

The fair values of its investments at December 31, 2013, are: B, $81,375; C, $610,312; W, $191,250; X, $118,125; Y, $531,250; and Z, $278,800.

Required

1. Determine the amount Stoll should report on its December 31, 2013, balance sheet for its long-term investments in available-for-sale securities.

Check (2) Cr. Unrealized Loss—
Equity, $20,002

2. Prepare any necessary December 31, 2013, adjusting entry to record the fair value adjustment for the long-term investments in available-for-sale securities.

3. What amount of gains or losses on transactions relating to long-term investments in available-for-sale securities should Stoll report on its December 31, 2013, income statement?

Problem C-5A
Accounting for long-term investments in securities; with and without significant influence

P3 P4

Selk Steel Co., which began operations on January 4, 2013, had the following subsequent transactions and events in its long-term investments.

2013

Jan. 5 Selk purchased 60,000 shares (20% of total) of Kildaire's common stock for $1,560,000.
Oct. 23 Kildaire declared and paid a cash dividend of $3.20 per share.
Dec. 31 Kildaire's net income for 2013 is $1,164,000, and the fair value of its stock at December 31 is $30.00 per share.

2014

Oct. 15 Kildaire declared and paid a cash dividend of $2.60 per share.
Dec. 31 Kildaire's net income for 2014 is $1,476,000, and the fair value of its stock at December 31 is $32.00 per share.

2015

Jan. 2 Selk sold all of its investment in Kildaire for $1,894,000 cash.

Part 1

Assume that Selk has a significant influence over Kildaire with its 20% share of stock.

Required

1. Prepare journal entries to record these transactions and events for Selk.

Check (2) Carrying value per share,
$29

2. Compute the carrying (book) value per share of Selk's investment in Kildaire common stock as reflected in the investment account on January 1, 2015.

3. Compute the net increase or decrease in Selk's equity from January 5, 2013, through January 2, 2015, resulting from its investment in Kildaire.

evaluate its system of internal controls, including the resulting reports. *External auditors* are independent of a company and are hired to assess and evaluate the "fairness" of financial statements (or to perform other contracted financial services). *(p. 13)*

Authorized stock Total amount of stock that a corporation's charter authorizes it to issue. *(p. 469)*

Available-for-sale (AFS) securities Investments in debt and equity securities that are not classified as trading securities or held-to-maturity securities. *(p. C-6)*

Average cost See *weighted average*.

Bad debts Accounts of customers who do not pay what they have promised to pay; an expense of selling on credit; also called *uncollectible accounts*. *(p. 306)*

Balance column account Account with debit and credit columns for recording entries and another column for showing the balance of the account after each entry. *(p. 60)*

Balance sheet Financial statement that lists types and dollar amounts of assets, liabilities, and equity at a specific date. *(p. 20)*

Balance sheet equation (See *accounting equation*.)

Bank reconciliation Report that explains the difference between the book (company) balance of cash and the cash balance reported on the bank statement. *(p. 273)*

Bank statement Bank report on the depositor's beginning and ending cash balances, and a listing of its changes, for a period. *(p. 272)*

Basic earnings per share Net income less any preferred dividends and then divided by weighted-average common shares outstanding. *(p. 485)*

Batch processing Accumulating source documents for a period of time and then processing them all at once such as once a day, week, or month. *(p. E-16)*

Bearer bonds Bonds made payable to whoever holds them (the *bearer*); also called *unregistered bonds*. *(p. 436)*

Betterments Expenditures to make a plant asset more efficient or productive; also called *improvements*. *(p. 347)*

Bond Written promise to pay the bond's par (or face) value and interest at a stated contract rate; often issued in denominations of $1,000. *(p. 422)*

Bond certificate Document containing bond specifics such as issuer's name, bond par value, contract interest rate, and maturity date. *(p. 424)*

Bond indenture Contract between the bond issuer and the bondholders; identifies the parties' rights and obligations. *(p. 424)*

Book value Asset's acquisition costs less its accumulated depreciation (or depletion, or amortization); also sometimes used synonymously as the *carrying value* of an account. *(pp. 104 & 341)*

Book value per common share Recorded amount of equity applicable to common shares divided by the number of common shares outstanding. *(p. 486)*

Book value per preferred share Equity applicable to preferred shares (equals its call price [or par value if it is not callable] plus any cumulative dividends in arrears) divided by the number of preferred shares outstanding. *(p. 486)*

Bookkeeping (See *recordkeeping*.)

Business An organization of one or more individuals selling products and/or services for profit.

Business entity assumption Principle that requires a business to be accounted for separately from its owner(s) and from any other entity. *(p. 12)*

Business segment Part of a company that can be separately identified by the products or services that it provides or by the geographic markets that it serves; also called *segment*. *(p. 588)*

C corporation Corporation that does not qualify for nor elect to be treated as a proprietorship or partnership for income tax purposes and therefore is subject to income taxes; also called *C corp*. *(p. 12)*

Call price Amount that must be paid to call and retire a callable preferred stock or a callable bond. *(p. 479)*

Callable bonds Bonds that give the issuer the option to retire them at a stated amount prior to maturity. *(p. 436)*

Callable preferred stock Preferred stock that the issuing corporation, at its option, may retire by paying the call price plus any dividends in arrears. *(p. 479)*

Canceled checks Checks that the bank has paid and deducted from the depositor's account. *(p. 272)*

Capital expenditures Additional costs of plant assets that provide material benefits extending beyond the current period; also called *balance sheet expenditures*. *(p. 346)*

Capital leases Long-term leases in which the lessor transfers substantially all risk and rewards of ownership to the lessee. *(p. 446)*

Capital stock General term referring to a corporation's stock used in obtaining capital (owner financing). *(p. 469)*

Capitalize Record the cost as part of a permanent account and allocate it over later periods.

Carrying (book) value of bonds Net amount at which bonds are reported on the balance sheet; equals the par value of the bonds less any unamortized discount or plus any unamortized premium; also called *carrying amount or book value*. *(p. 426)*

Cash Includes currency, coins, and amounts on deposit in bank checking or savings accounts. *(p. 263)*

Cash basis accounting Accounting system that recognizes revenues when cash is received and records expenses when cash is paid. *(p. 99)*

Cash budget Plan that shows expected cash inflows and outflows during the budget period, including receipts from loans needed to maintain a minimum cash balance and repayments of such loans. *(p. 266)*

Cash disbursements journal Special journal normally used to record all payments of cash; also called *cash payments journal*. *(p. E-14)*

Cash discount Reduction in the price of merchandise granted by a seller to a buyer when payment is made within the discount period. *(p. 165)*

Cash equivalents Short-term, investment assets that are readily convertible to a known cash amount or sufficiently close to their maturity date (usually within 90 days) so that market value is not sensitive to interest rate changes. *(p. 264)*

Cash flow on total assets Ratio of operating cash flows to average total assets; not sensitive to income recognition and measurement; partly reflects earnings quality. *(p. 528)*

Cash Over and Short Income statement account used to record cash overages and cash shortages arising from errors in cash receipts or payments. *(p. 265)*

Cash receipts journal Special journal normally used to record all receipts of cash. *(p. E-11)*

Change in an accounting estimate Change in an accounting estimate that results from new information, subsequent developments, or improved judgment that impacts current and future periods. *(pp. 345 & 483)*

Chart of accounts List of accounts used by a company; includes an identification number for each account. *(p. 54)*

Check Document signed by a depositor instructing the bank to pay a specified amount to a designated recipient. *(p. 271)*

Check register Another name for a cash disbursements journal when the journal has a column for check numbers. *(pp. 282 & E-14)*

Classified balance sheet Balance sheet that presents assets and liabilities in relevant subgroups, including current and noncurrent classifications. *(p. 117)*

Closing entries Entries recorded at the end of each accounting period to transfer end-of-period balances in revenue, gain, expense, loss, and withdrawal (dividend for a corporation) accounts to the capital account (to retained earnings for a corporation). *(p. 112)*

Closing process Necessary end-of-period steps to prepare the accounts for recording the transactions of the next period. *(p. 112)*

Columnar journal Journal with more than one column. *(p. E-8)*

Committee of Sponsoring Organizations (COSO) Committee of Sponsoring Organizations of the Treadway Commission (or COSO) is a joint initiative of five private sector organizations and is dedicated to providing thought leadership through the development of frameworks and guidance on enterprise risk management, internal control, and fraud deterrence. *(p. 259)*

Common stock Corporation's basic ownership share; also generically called *capital stock.* *(pp. 13 & 468)*

Common-size financial statement Statement that expresses each amount as a percent of a base amount. In the balance sheet, total assets is usually the base and is expressed as 100%. In the income statement, net sales is usually the base. *(p. 571)*

Comparative financial statement Statement with data for two or more successive periods placed in side-by-side columns, often with changes shown in dollar amounts and percents. *(p. 566)*

Compatibility principle Information system principle that prescribes an accounting system to conform with a company's activities, personnel, and structure. *(p. E-3)*

Complex capital structure Capital structure that includes outstanding rights or options to purchase common stock, or securities that are convertible into common stock. *(p. 485)*

Components of accounting systems Five basic components of accounting systems are source documents, input devices, information processors, information storage, and output devices. *(p. E-3)*

Compound journal entry Journal entry that affects at least three accounts. *(p. 63)*

Comprehensive income Net change in equity for a period, excluding owner investments and distributions. *(p. C-10)*

Computer hardware Physical equipment in a computerized accounting information system.

Computer network Linkage giving different users and different computers access to common databases and programs. *(p. E-16)*

Computer software Programs that direct operations of computer hardware.

Conceptual framework The basic concepts that underlie the preparation and presentation of financial statements for external users; can serve as a guide in developing future standards and to resolve accounting issues that are not addressed directly in current standards using the definitions, recognition criteria, and measurement concepts for assets, liabilities, revenues, and expenses. *(p. 10)*

Conservatism constraint Principle that prescribes the less optimistic estimate when two estimates are about equally likely. *(p. 220)*

Consignee Receiver of goods owned by another who holds them for purposes of selling them for the owner. *(p. 210)*

Consignor Owner of goods who ships them to another party who will sell them for the owner. *(p. 210)*

Consistency concept Principle that prescribes use of the same accounting method(s) over time so that financial statements are comparable across periods. *(p. 219)*

Consolidated financial statements Financial statements that show all (combined) activities under the parent's control, including those of any subsidiaries. *(p. C-9)*

Contingent liability Obligation to make a future payment if, and only if, an uncertain future event occurs. *(p. 390)*

Contra account Account linked with another account and having an opposite normal balance; reported as a subtraction from the other account's balance. *(p. 103)*

Contract rate Interest rate specified in a bond indenture (or note); multiplied by the par value to determine the interest paid each period; also called *coupon rate, stated rate,* or *nominal rate.* *(p. 425)*

Contributed capital Total amount of cash and other assets received from stockholders in exchange for stock; also called *paid-in capital.* *(p. 15)*

Contributed capital in excess of par value Difference between the par value of stock and its issue price when issued at a price above par.

Control principle Information system principle that prescribes an accounting system to aid managers in controlling and monitoring business activities. *(p. E-2)*

Controlling account General ledger account, the balance of which (after posting) equals the sum of the balances in its related subsidiary ledger. *(p. E-7)*

Convertible bonds Bonds that bondholders can exchange for a set number of the issuer's shares. *(p. 436)*

Convertible preferred stock Preferred stock with an option to exchange it for common stock at a specified rate. *(p. 478)*

Copyright Right giving the owner the exclusive privilege to publish and sell musical, literary, or artistic work during the creator's life plus 70 years. *(p. 352)*

Corporation Business that is a separate legal entity under state or federal laws with owners called *shareholders* or *stockholders.* *(pp. 12 & 466)*

Cost All normal and reasonable expenditures necessary to get an asset in place and ready for its intended use. *(pp. 337 & 339)*

Cost accounting system Accounting system for manufacturing activities based on the perpetual inventory system. *(p. 654)*

Cost-benefit constraint The notion that the benefit of a disclosure exceeds the cost of that disclosure. *(p. 13)*

Cost-benefit principle Information system principle that prescribes the benefits from an activity in an accounting system to outweigh the costs of that activity. *(pp. 262 & E-3)*

Cost of goods available for sale Consists of beginning inventory plus net purchases of a period.

Cost of goods sold Cost of inventory sold to customers during a period; also called *cost of sales. (p. 162)*

Cost principle Accounting principle that prescribes financial statement information to be based on actual costs incurred in business transactions. *(p. 11)*

Coupon bonds Bonds with interest coupons attached to their certificates; bondholders detach coupons when they mature and present them to a bank or broker for collection. *(p. 436)*

Credit Recorded on the right side; an entry that decreases asset and expense accounts, and increases liability, revenue, and most equity accounts; abbreviated Cr. *(p. 57)*

Credit memorandum Notification that the sender has credited the recipient's account in the sender's records. *(p. 171)*

Credit period Time period that can pass before a customer's payment is due. *(p. 165)*

Credit terms Description of the amounts and timing of payments that a buyer (debtor) agrees to make in the future. *(p. 165)*

Creditors Individuals or organizations entitled to receive payments. *(p. 54)*

Cumulative preferred stock Preferred stock on which undeclared dividends accumulate until paid; common stockholders cannot receive dividends until cumulative dividends are paid. *(p. 477)*

Current assets Cash and other assets expected to be sold, collected, or used within one year or the company's operating cycle, whichever is longer. *(p. 118)*

Current liabilities Obligations due to be paid or settled within one year or the company's operating cycle, whichever is longer. *(pp. 119 & 379)*

Current portion of long-term debt Portion of long-term debt due within one year or the operating cycle, whichever is longer; reported under current liabilities. *(p. 387)*

Current ratio Ratio used to evaluate a company's ability to pay its short-term obligations, calculated by dividing current assets by current liabilities. *(p. 121)*

Date of declaration Date the directors vote to pay a dividend. *(p. 473)*

Date of payment Date the corporation makes the dividend payment. *(p. 473)*

Date of record Date directors specify for identifying stockholders to receive dividends. *(p. 473)*

Days' sales in inventory Estimate of number of days needed to convert inventory into receivables or cash; equals ending inventory divided by cost of goods sold and then multiplied by 365; also called *days' stock on hand. (p. 223)*

Days' sales uncollected Measure of the liquidity of receivables computed by dividing the current balance of receivables by the annual credit (or net) sales and then multiplying by 365; also called *days' sales in receivables. (p. 277)*

Debit Recorded on the left side; an entry that increases asset and expense accounts, and decreases liability, revenue, and most equity accounts; abbreviated Dr. *(p. 57)*

Debit memorandum Notification that the sender has debited the recipient's account in the sender's records. *(p. 166)*

Debt ratio Ratio of total liabilities to total assets; used to reflect risk associated with a company's debts. *(p. 71)*

Debt-to-equity ratio Defined as total liabilities divided by total equity; shows the proportion of a company financed by non-owners (creditors) in comparison with that financed by owners. *(p. 437)*

Debtors Individuals or organizations that owe money. *(p. 51)*

Declining-balance method Method that determines depreciation charge for the period by multiplying a depreciation rate (often twice the straight-line rate) by the asset's beginning-period book value. *(p. 342)*

Deferred income tax liability Corporation income taxes that are deferred until future years because of temporary differences between GAAP and tax rules. *(p. 402)*

Departmental accounting system Accounting system that provides information useful in evaluating the profitability or cost effectiveness of a department.

Depletion Process of allocating the cost of natural resources to periods when they are consumed and sold. *(p. 350)*

Deposit ticket Lists items such as currency, coins, and checks deposited and their corresponding dollar amounts. *(p. 271)*

Deposits in transit Deposits recorded by the company but not yet recorded by its bank. *(p. 274)*

Depreciable cost Cost of a plant asset less its salvage value. *(p. 340)*

Depreciation Expense created by allocating the cost of plant and equipment to periods in which they are used; represents the expense of using the asset. *(pp. 103 & 339)*

Diluted earnings per share Earnings per share calculation that requires dilutive securities be added to the denominator of the basic EPS calculation. *(p. 485)*

Dilutive securities Securities having the potential to increase common shares outstanding; examples are options, rights, convertible bonds, and convertible preferred stock. *(p. 485)*

Direct method Presentation of net cash from operating activities for the statement of cash flows that lists major operating cash receipts less major operating cash payments. *(p. 516)*

Direct write-off method Method that records the loss from an uncollectible account receivable at the time it is determined to be uncollectible; no attempt is made to estimate bad debts. *(p. 306)*

Discount on bonds payable Difference between a bond's par value and its lower issue price or carrying value; occurs when the contract rate is less than the market rate. *(p. 425)*

Discount on note payable Difference between the face value of a note payable and the (lesser) amount borrowed; reflects the added interest to be paid on the note over its life.

Discount on stock Difference between the par value of stock and its issue price when issued at a price below par value. *(p. 471)*

Discount period Time period in which a cash discount is available and the buyer can make a reduced payment. *(p. 165)*

Discount rate Expected rate of return on investments; also called *cost of capital, hurdle rate,* or *required rate of return.* *(p. B-2)*

Discounts lost Expenses resulting from not taking advantage of cash discounts on purchases. *(p. 283)*

Dividend in arrears Unpaid dividend on cumulative preferred stock; must be paid before any regular dividends on preferred stock and before any dividends on common stock. *(p. 477)*

Dividend yield Ratio of the annual amount of cash dividends distributed to common shareholders relative to the common stock's market value (price). *(p. 486)*

Dividends Corporation's distributions of assets to its owners. *(p. 15)*

Dodd-Frank Wall Street Reform and Consumer Protection Act *(p. 14)*

Double-declining-balance (DDB) depreciation Depreciation equals beginning book value multiplied by 2 times the straight-line rate. *(p. 342)*

Double-entry accounting Accounting system in which each transaction affects at least two accounts and has at least one debit and one credit. *(p. 57)*

Double taxation Corporate income is taxed and then its later distribution through dividends is normally taxed again for shareholders. *(p. 13)*

Earnings (See *net income.*)

Earnings per share (EPS) Amount of income earned by each share of a company's outstanding common stock; also called *net income per share.* *(p. 485)*

Effective interest method Allocates interest expense over the bond life to yield a constant rate of interest; interest expense for a period is found by multiplying the balance of the liability at the beginning of the period by the bond market rate at issuance; also called *interest method.* *(p. 442)*

Efficiency Company's productivity in using its assets; usually measured relative to how much revenue a certain level of assets generates. *(p. 565)*

Efficiency variance Difference between the actual quantity of an input and the standard quantity of that input. *(p. 916)*

Electronic funds transfer (EFT) Use of electronic communication to transfer cash from one party to another. *(p. 271)*

Employee benefits Additional compensation paid to or on behalf of employees, such as premiums for medical, dental, life, and disability insurance, and contributions to pension plans. *(p. 387)*

Employee earnings report Record of an employee's net pay, gross pay, deductions, and year-to-date payroll information. *(p. 398)*

Enterprise resource planning (ERP) software Programs that manage a company's vital operations, which range from order taking to production to accounting. *(p. E-17)*

Entity Organization that, for accounting purposes, is separate from other organizations and individuals.

EOM Abbreviation for *end of month;* used to describe credit terms for credit transactions. *(p. 165)*

Equity Owner's claim on the assets of a business; equals the residual interest in an entity's assets after deducting liabilities; also called *net assets.* *(p. 15)*

Equity method Accounting method used for long-term investments when the investor has "significant influence" over the investee. *(p. C-8)*

Equity ratio Portion of total assets provided by equity, computed as total equity divided by total assets. *(p. 579)*

Equity securities with controlling influence Long-term investment when the investor is able to exert controlling influence over the investee; investors owning 50% or more of voting stock are presumed to exert controlling influence. *(p. C-9)*

Equity securities with significant influence Long-term investment when the investor is able to exert significant influence over the investee; investors owning 20 percent or more (but less than 50 percent) of voting stock are presumed to exert significant influence. *(p. C-8)*

Estimated liability Obligation of an uncertain amount that can be reasonably estimated. *(p. 387)*

Ethics Codes of conduct by which actions are judged as right or wrong, fair or unfair, honest or dishonest. *(p. 7)*

Events Happenings that both affect an organization's financial position and can be reliably measured. *(p. 16)*

Expanded accounting equation Assets = Liabilities + Equity; Equity equals [Owner capital − Owner withdrawals + Revenues − Expenses] for a noncorporation; Equity equals [Contributed capital + Retained earnings + Revenues − Expenses] for a corporation where dividends are subtracted from retained earnings. *(p. 15)*

Expense recognition (or matching) principle (See *matching principle.*)

Expenses Outflows or using up of assets as part of operations of a business to generate sales. *(p. 15)*

External transactions Exchanges of economic value between one entity and another entity. *(p. 16)*

External users Persons using accounting information who are not directly involved in running the organization. *(p. 5)*

Extraordinary gains or losses Gains or losses reported separately from continuing operations because they are both unusual and infrequent. *(p. 588)*

Extraordinary repairs Major repairs that extend the useful life of a plant asset beyond prior expectations; treated as a capital expenditure. *(p. 347)*

Fair value option Fair Value Option (FVO) refers to an option to measure eligible items at fair value; eligible items include *financial assets,* such as HTM, AFS, and equity method investments, and *financial liabilities.* FVO is applied "instrument by instrument" and is elected when the eligible item is "first recognized"; once FVO is elected the decision is "irrevocable." When FVO is elected, it is measured at "fair value" and unrealized gains and losses are recognized in earnings. *(p. 435)*

Federal depository bank Bank authorized to accept deposits of amounts payable to the federal government. *(p. 395)*

Federal Insurance Contributions Act (FICA) Taxes Taxes assessed on both employers and employees; for Social Security and Medicare programs. *(p. 384)*

Federal Unemployment Taxes (FUTA) Payroll taxes on employers assessed by the federal government to support its unemployment insurance program. *(p. 386)*

FIFO method (See *first-in, first-out.*)

Financial accounting Area of accounting aimed mainly at serving external users. *(p. 5)*

Financial Accounting Standards Board (FASB) Independent group of full-time members responsible for setting accounting rules. *(p. 9)*

Posting reference (PR) column A column in journals in which individual ledger account numbers are entered when entries are posted to those ledger accounts. *(p. 60)*

Preemptive right Stockholders' right to maintain their proportionate interest in a corporation with any additional shares issued. *(p. 468)*

Preferred stock Stock with a priority status over common stockholders in one or more ways, such as paying dividends or distributing assets. *(p. 476)*

Premium on bonds Difference between a bond's par value and its higher carrying value; occurs when the contract rate is higher than the market rate; also called *bond premium. (p. 428)*

Premium on stock (See *contributed capital in excess of par value.) (p. 471)*

Prepaid expenses Items paid for in advance of receiving their benefits; classified as assets. *(p. 101)*

Price-earnings (PE) ratio Ratio of a company's current market value per share to its earnings per share; also called *price-to-earnings. (p. 485)*

Principal of a note Amount that the signer of a note agrees to pay back when it matures, not including interest. *(p. 312)*

Principles of internal control Principles prescribing management to establish responsibility, maintain records, insure assets, separate recordkeeping from custody of assets, divide responsibility for related transactions, apply technological controls, and perform reviews. *(p. 259)*

Prior period adjustment Correction of an error in a prior year that is reported in the statement of retained earnings (or statement of stockholders' equity) net of any income tax effects. *(p. 483)*

Pro forma financial statements Statements that show the effects of proposed transactions and events as if they had occurred. *(p. 128)*

Profit (See *net income.)*

Profit margin Ratio of a company's net income to its net sales; the percent of income in each dollar of revenue; also called *net profit margin. (p. 121)*

Promissory note (or **note**) Written promise to pay a specified amount either on demand or at a definite future date; is a *note receivable* for the lender but a *note payable* for the lendee. *(p. 312)*

Proprietorship (See *sole proprietorship.)*

Proxy Legal document giving a stockholder's agent the power to exercise the stockholder's voting rights. *(p. 467)*

Purchase discount Term used by a purchaser to describe a cash discount granted to the purchaser for paying within the discount period. *(p. 165)*

Purchase order Document used by the purchasing department to place an order with a seller (vendor). *(p. 280)*

Purchase requisition Document listing merchandise needed by a department and requesting it be purchased. *(p. 280)*

Purchases journal Journal normally used to record all purchases on credit. *(p. E-13)*

Ratio analysis Determination of key relations between financial statement items as reflected in numerical measures. *(p. 566)*

Realizable value Expected proceeds from converting an asset into cash. *(p. 307)*

Receiving report Form used to report that ordered goods are received and to describe their quantity and condition. *(p. 281)*

Recordkeeping Part of accounting that involves recording transactions and events, either manually or electronically; also called *bookkeeping. (p. 4)*

Registered bonds Bonds owned by investors whose names and addresses are recorded by the issuer; interest payments are made to the registered owners. *(p. 436)*

Relevance principle Information system principle prescribing that its reports be useful, understandable, timely, and pertinent for decision making. *(p. E-2)*

Report form balance sheet Balance sheet that lists accounts vertically in the order of assets, liabilities, and equity. *(p. 22)*

Restricted retained earnings Retained earnings not available for dividends because of legal or contractual limitations. *(p. 482)*

Retail inventory method Method for estimating ending inventory based on the ratio of the amount of goods for sale at cost to the amount of goods for sale at retail. *(p. 234)*

Retailer Intermediary that buys products from manufacturers or wholesalers and sells them to consumers. *(p. 162)*

Retained earnings Cumulative income less cumulative losses and dividends. *(pp. 15 & 470)*

Retained earnings deficit Debit (abnormal) balance in Retained Earnings; occurs when cumulative losses and dividends exceed cumulative income; also called *accumulated deficit. (p. 473)*

Return Monies received from an investment; often in percent form. *(p. 27)*

Return on assets (See *return on total assets.)*

Return on equity Ratio of net income to average equity for the period.

Return on total assets Ratio reflecting operating efficiency; defined as net income divided by average total assets for the period; also called *return on assets* or *return on investment. (pp. 24 & C-11)*

Revenue expenditures Expenditures reported on the current income statement as an expense because they do not provide benefits in future periods. *(p. 346)*

Revenue recognition principle The principle prescribing that revenue is recognized when earned. *(p. 11)*

Revenues Gross increase in equity from a company's business activities that earn income; also called *sales. (p. 15)*

Reverse stock split Occurs when a corporation calls in its stock and replaces each share with less than one new share; increases both market value per share and any par or stated value per share. *(p. 476)*

Reversing entries Optional entries recorded at the beginning of a period that prepare the accounts for the usual journal entries as if adjusting entries had not occurred in the prior period. *(p. 129)*

Risk Uncertainty about an expected return. *(p. 27)*

S corporation Corporation that meets special tax qualifications so as to be treated like a partnership for income tax purposes. *(p. D-3)*

Sales (See *revenues.)*

Sales discount Term used by a seller to describe a cash discount granted to buyers who pay within the discount period. *(p. 165)*

Sales journal Journal normally used to record sales of goods on credit.

Salvage value Estimate of amount to be recovered at the end of an asset's useful life; also called *residual value* or *scrap value*. *(p. 339)*

Sarbanes-Oxley Act (SOX) Created the *Public Company Accounting Oversight Board,* regulates analyst conflicts, imposes corporate governance requirements, enhances accounting and control disclosures, impacts insider transactions and executive loans, establishes new types of criminal conduct, and expands penalties for violations of federal securities laws. *(pp. 13 & 258)*

Schedule of accounts payable List of the balances of all accounts in the accounts payable ledger and their totals. *(p. E-14)*

Schedule of accounts receivable List of the balances of all accounts in the accounts receivable ledger and their totals. *(p. E-9)*

Section 404 (of SOX) Section 404 of SOX requires management and the external auditor to report on the adequacy of the company's internal control on financial reporting, which is the most costly aspect of SOX for companies to implement as documenting and testing important financial manual and automated controls require enormous efforts. Section 404 also requires management to produce an "internal control report" as part of each annual SEC report that affirms "the responsibility of management for establishing and maintaining an adequate internal control structure and procedures for financial reporting." *(p. 259)*

Secured bonds Bonds that have specific assets of the issuer pledged as collateral. *(p. 436)*

Securities and Exchange Commission (SEC) Federal agency Congress has charged to set reporting rules for organizations that sell ownership shares to the public. *(p. 9)*

Segment return on assets Segment operating income divided by segment average (identifiable) assets for the period.

Selling expenses Expenses of promoting sales, such as displaying and advertising merchandise, making sales, and delivering goods to customers. *(p. 175)*

Serial bonds Bonds consisting of separate amounts that mature at different dates. *(p. 436)*

Service company Organization that provides services instead of tangible products.

Shareholders Owners of a corporation; also called *stockholders*. *(p. 13)*

Shares Equity of a corporation divided into ownership units; also called *stock*. *(p. 13)*

Short-term investments Debt and equity securities that management expects to convert to cash within the next 3 to 12 months (or the operating cycle if longer); also called *temporary investments* or *marketable securities*. *(p. C-2)*

Short-term note payable Current obligation in the form of a written promissory note. *(p. 381)*

Shrinkage Inventory losses that occur as a result of theft or deterioration. *(p. 172)*

Signature card Includes the signatures of each person authorized to sign checks on the bank account. *(p. 271)*

Simple capital structure Capital structure that consists of only common stock and nonconvertible preferred stock; consists of no dilutive securities. *(p. 485)*

Single-step income statement Income statement format that includes cost of goods sold as an expense and shows only one subtotal for total expenses. *(p. 176)*

Sinking fund bonds Bonds that require the issuer to make deposits to a separate account; bondholders are repaid at maturity from that account. *(p. 436)*

Small stock dividend Stock dividend that is 25% or less of a corporation's previously outstanding shares. *(p. 474)*

Social responsibility Being accountable for the impact that one's actions might have on society. *(p. 8)*

Sole proprietorship Business owned by one person that is not organized as a corporation; also called *proprietorship*. *(p. 12)*

Solvency Company's long-run financial viability and its ability to cover long-term obligations. *(p. 565)*

Source documents Source of information for accounting entries that can be in either paper or electronic form; also called *business papers*. *(p. 52)*

Special journal Any journal used for recording and posting transactions of a similar type. *(p. E-6)*

Specific identification Method for assigning cost to inventory when the purchase cost of each item in inventory is identified and used to compute cost of inventory. *(pp. 213 & 230)*

Spreadsheet Computer program that organizes data by means of formulas and format; also called *electronic work sheet*. *(pp. 123 & 532)*

State Unemployment Taxes (SUTA) State payroll taxes on employers to support its unemployment programs. *(p. 386)*

Stated value stock No-par stock assigned a stated value per share; this amount is recorded in the stock account when the stock is issued. *(p. 470)*

Statement of cash flows A financial statement that lists cash inflows (receipts) and cash outflows (payments) during a period; arranged by operating, investing, and financing. *(pp. 20 & 510)*

Statement of owner's equity Report of changes in equity over a period; adjusted for increases (owner investment and net income) and for decreases (withdrawals and net loss). *(p. 20)*

Statement of partners' equity Financial statement that shows total capital balances at the beginning of the period, any additional investment by partners, the income or loss of the period, the partners' withdrawals, and the partners' ending capital balances; also called *statement of partners' capital*. *(p. D-7)*

Statement of retained earnings Report of changes in retained earnings over a period; adjusted for increases (net income), for decreases (dividends and net loss), and for any prior period adjustment. *(p. 20)*

Statement of stockholders' equity Financial statement that lists the beginning and ending balances of each major equity account and describes all changes in those accounts. *(p. 483)*

Statements of Financial Accounting Standards (SFAS) FASB publications that establish U.S. GAAP.

Stock (See *shares*) *(p. 13)*

Stock dividend Corporation's distribution of its own stock to its stockholders without the receipt of any payment. *(p. 474)*

Stock options Rights to purchase common stock at a fixed price over a specified period of time. *(p. 483)*

Stock split Occurs when a corporation calls in its stock and replaces each share with more than one new share; decreases both the market value per share and any par or stated value per share. *(p. 476)*

Stock subscription Investor's contractual commitment to purchase unissued shares at future dates and prices.

Stockholders (See *shareholders.*) *(p. 13)*

Stockholders' equity A corporation's equity; also called *shareholders' equity* or *corporate capital*. *(p. 470)*

Straight-line depreciation Method that allocates an equal portion of the depreciable cost of plant asset (cost minus salvage) to each accounting period in its useful life. *(pp. 103 & 341)*

Straight-line bond amortization Method allocating an equal amount of bond interest expense to each period of the bond life. *(p. 426)*

Subsidiary Entity controlled by another entity (parent) in which the parent owns more than 50% of the subsidiary's voting stock. *(p. C-9)*

Subsidiary ledger List of individual subaccounts and amounts with a common characteristic; linked to a controlling account in the general ledger. *(p. E-6)*

Supplementary records Information outside the usual accounting records; also called *supplemental records*. *(p. 168)*

Supply chain Linkages of services or goods extending from suppliers, to the company itself, and on to customers.

T-account Tool used to show the effects of transactions and events on individual accounts. *(p. 57)*

Temporary accounts Accounts used to record revenues, expenses, and withdrawals (dividends for a corporation); they are closed at the end of each period; also called *nominal accounts*. *(p. 112)*

Term bonds Bonds scheduled for payment (maturity) at a single specified date. *(p. 436)*

Throughput time (See *cycle time.*)

Time period assumption Assumption that an organization's activities can be divided into specific time periods such as months, quarters, or years. *(pp. 12 & 98)*

Times interest earned Ratio of income before interest expense (and any income taxes) divided by interest expense; reflects risk of covering interest commitments when income varies. *(p. 392)*

Total asset turnover Measure of a company's ability to use its assets to generate sales; computed by dividing net sales by average total assets. *(p. 355)*

Trade discount Reduction from a list or catalog price that can vary for wholesalers, retailers, and consumers. *(p. 164)*

Trademark or **trade (brand) name** Symbol, name, phrase, or jingle identified with a company, product, or service. *(p. 353)*

Trading on the equity (See *financial leverage.*)

Trading securities Investments in debt and equity securities that the company intends to actively trade for profit. *(p. C-5)*

Transaction Exchange of economic consideration affecting an entity's financial position that can be reliably measured. *(p. 16)*

Treasury stock Corporation's own stock that it reacquired and still holds. *(p. 480)*

Trial balance List of accounts and their balances at a point in time; total debit balances equal total credit balances. *(p. 67)*

Unadjusted trial balance List of accounts and balances prepared before accounting adjustments are recorded and posted. *(p. 110)*

Unclassified balance sheet Balance sheet that broadly groups assets, liabilities, and equity accounts. *(p. 117)*

Unearned revenue Liability created when customers pay in advance for products or services; earned when the products or services are later delivered. *(pp. 55 & 104)*

Units-of-production depreciation Method that charges a varying amount to depreciation expense for each period of an asset's useful life depending on its usage. *(p. 341)*

Unlimited liability Legal relationship among general partners that makes each of them responsible for partnership debts if the other partners are unable to pay their shares. *(p. D-3)*

Unrealized gain (loss) Gain (loss) not yet realized by an actual transaction or event such as a sale. *(p. C-5)*

Unsecured bonds Bonds backed only by the issuer's credit standing; almost always riskier than secured bonds; also called *debentures*. *(p. 436)*

Unusual gain or loss Gain or loss that is abnormal or unrelated to the company's ordinary activities and environment. *(p. 588)*

Useful life Length of time an asset will be productively used in the operations of a business; also called *service life* or *limited life*. *(pp. 339 & 351)*

Vendee Buyer of goods or services. *(p. 281)*

Vendor Seller of goods or services. *(p. 280)*

Vertical analysis Evaluation of each financial statement item or group of items in terms of a specific base amount. *(p. 566)*

Voucher Internal file used to store documents and information to control cash disbursements and to ensure that a transaction is properly authorized and recorded. *(p. 267)*

Voucher register Journal (referred to as *book of original entry*) in which all vouchers are recorded after they have been approved. *(p. 282)*

Voucher system Procedures and approvals designed to control cash disbursements and acceptance of obligations. *(p. 266)*

Wage bracket withholding table Table of the amounts of income tax withheld from employees' wages. *(p. 400)*

Warranty Agreement that obligates the seller to correct or replace a product or service when it fails to perform properly within a specified period. *(p. 388)*

Weighted average Method for assigning inventory cost to sales; the cost of available-for-sale units is divided by the number of units available to determine per unit cost prior to each sale that is then multiplied by the units sold to yield the cost of that sale. *(pp. 216 & 232)*

Weighted-average method   (See *weighted average.*)

Wholesaler Intermediary that buys products from manufacturers or other wholesalers and sells them to retailers or other wholesalers. *(p. 162)*

Work sheet Spreadsheet used to draft an unadjusted trial balance, adjusting entries, adjusted trial balance, and financial statements. *(p. 123)*

Working capital Current assets minus current liabilities at a point in time. *(p. 575)*

Working papers Analyses and other informal reports prepared by accountants and managers when organizing information for formal reports and financial statements. *(p. 127)*

Chart of Accounts

Following is a typical chart of accounts, which is used in several assignments. Every company has its own unique accounts and numbering system.

Assets

Current Assets

101 Cash
102 Petty cash
103 Cash equivalents
104 Short-term investments
105 Fair value adjustment, _____ securities (S-T)
106 Accounts receivable
107 Allowance for doubtful accounts
108 Legal fees receivable
109 Interest receivable
110 Rent receivable
111 Notes receivable
119 Merchandise inventory
120 _____ inventory
121 _____ inventory
124 Office supplies
125 Store supplies
126 _____ supplies
128 Prepaid insurance
129 Prepaid interest
131 Prepaid rent
132 Raw materials inventory
133 Goods in process inventory, _____
134 Goods in process inventory, _____
135 Finished goods inventory

Long-Term Investments

141 Long-term investments
142 Fair value adjustment, _____ securities (L-T)
144 Investment in _____
145 Bond sinking fund

Plant Assets

151 Automobiles
152 Accumulated depreciation—Automobiles
153 Trucks
154 Accumulated depreciation—Trucks
155 Boats
156 Accumulated depreciation—Boats
157 Professional library
158 Accumulated depreciation—Professional library
159 Law library
160 Accumulated depreciation—Law library
161 Furniture
162 Accumulated depreciation—Furniture
163 Office equipment
164 Accumulated depreciation—Office equipment
165 Store equipment

166 Accumulated depreciation—Store equipment
167 _____ equipment
168 Accumulated depreciation—_____ equipment
169 Machinery
170 Accumulated depreciation—Machinery
173 Building _____
174 Accumulated depreciation—Building _____
175 Building _____
176 Accumulated depreciation—Building _____
179 Land improvements _____
180 Accumulated depreciation—Land improvements _____
181 Land improvements _____
182 Accumulated depreciation—Land improvements _____
183 Land

Natural Resources

185 Mineral deposit
186 Accumulated depletion—Mineral deposit

Intangible Assets

191 Patents
192 Leasehold
193 Franchise
194 Copyrights
195 Leasehold improvements
196 Licenses
197 Accumulated amortization—_____

Liabilities

Current Liabilities

201 Accounts payable
202 Insurance payable
203 Interest payable
204 Legal fees payable
207 Office salaries payable
208 Rent payable
209 Salaries payable
210 Wages payable
211 Accrued payroll payable
214 Estimated warranty liability
215 Income taxes payable
216 Common dividend payable
217 Preferred dividend payable
218 State unemployment taxes payable
219 Employee federal income taxes payable
221 Employee medical insurance payable

222 Employee retirement program payable
223 Employee union dues payable
224 Federal unemployment taxes payable
225 FICA taxes payable
226 Estimated vacation pay liability

Unearned Revenues

230 Unearned consulting fees
231 Unearned legal fees
232 Unearned property management fees
233 Unearned _____ fees
234 Unearned _____ fees
235 Unearned janitorial revenue
236 Unearned _____ revenue
238 Unearned rent

Notes Payable

240 Short-term notes payable
241 Discount on short-term notes payable
245 Notes payable
251 Long-term notes payable
252 Discount on long-term notes payable

Long-Term Liabilities

253 Long-term lease liability
255 Bonds payable
256 Discount on bonds payable
257 Premium on bonds payable
258 Deferred income tax liability

Equity

Owner's Equity

301 _____, Capital
302 _____, Withdrawals
303 _____, Capital
304 _____, Withdrawals
305 _____, Capital
306 _____, Withdrawals

Paid-In Capital

307 Common stock, $ _____ par value
308 Common stock, no-par value
309 Common stock, $ _____ stated value
310 Common stock dividend distributable
311 Paid-in capital in excess of par value, Common stock

312 Paid-in capital in excess of stated value,
    No-par common stock
313 Paid-in capital from retirement of common stock
314 Paid-in capital, Treasury stock
315 Preferred stock
316 Paid-in capital in excess of par value,
    Preferred stock

Retained Earnings

318 Retained earnings
319 Cash dividends (or Dividends)
320 Stock dividends

Other Equity Accounts

321 Treasury stock, Common
322 Unrealized gain—Equity
323 Unrealized loss—Equity

Revenues

401 _____ fees earned
402 _____ fees earned
403 _____ services revenue
404 _____ services revenue
405 Commissions earned
406 Rent revenue (or Rent earned)
407 Dividends revenue (or Dividend earned)
408 Earnings from investment in _____
409 Interest revenue (or Interest earned)
410 Sinking fund earnings
413 Sales
414 Sales returns and allowances
415 Sales discounts

Cost of Sales

Cost of Goods Sold

502 Cost of goods sold
505 Purchases
506 Purchases returns and allowances
507 Purchases discounts
508 Transportation-in

Manufacturing

520 Raw materials purchases
521 Freight-in on raw materials
530 Factory payroll
531 Direct labor
540 Factory overhead
541 Indirect materials
542 Indirect labor
543 Factory insurance expired
544 Factory supervision
545 Factory supplies used
546 Factory utilities
547 Miscellaneous production costs
548 Property taxes on factory building
549 Property taxes on factory equipment
550 Rent on factory building
551 Repairs, factory equipment
552 Small tools written off
560 Depreciation of factory equipment
561 Depreciation of factory building

Standard Cost Variance

580 Direct material quantity variance
581 Direct material price variance
582 Direct labor quantity variance
583 Direct labor price variance
584 Factory overhead volume variance
585 Factory overhead controllable variance

Expenses

Amortization, Depletion, and Depreciation

601 Amortization expense—_____
602 Amortization expense—_____
603 Depletion expense—_____
604 Depreciation expense—Boats
605 Depreciation expense—Automobiles
606 Depreciation expense—Building _____
607 Depreciation expense—Building _____
608 Depreciation expense—Land
    improvements _____
609 Depreciation expense—Land
    improvements _____
610 Depreciation expense—Law library
611 Depreciation expense—Trucks
612 Depreciation expense—_____ equipment
613 Depreciation expense—_____ equipment
614 Depreciation expense—_____
615 Depreciation expense—_____

Employee-Related Expenses

620 Office salaries expense
621 Sales salaries expense
622 Salaries expense
623 _____ wages expense
624 Employees' benefits expense
625 Payroll taxes expense

Financial Expenses

630 Cash over and short
631 Discounts lost
632 Factoring fee expense
633 Interest expense

Insurance Expenses

635 Insurance expense—Delivery equipment
636 Insurance expense—Office equipment
637 Insurance expense—_____

Rental Expenses

640 Rent expense
641 Rent expense—Office space
642 Rent expense—Selling space
643 Press rental expense
644 Truck rental expense
645 _____ rental expense

Supplies Expenses

650 Office supplies expense
651 Store supplies expense
652 _____ supplies expense
653 _____ supplies expense

Miscellaneous Expenses

655 Advertising expense
656 Bad debts expense
657 Blueprinting expense
658 Boat expense
659 Collection expense
661 Concessions expense
662 Credit card expense
663 Delivery expense
664 Dumping expense
667 Equipment expense
668 Food and drinks expense
671 Gas and oil expense
672 General and administrative expense
673 Janitorial expense
674 Legal fees expense
676 Mileage expense
677 Miscellaneous expenses
678 Mower and tools expense
679 Operating expense
680 Organization expense
681 Permits expense
682 Postage expense
683 Property taxes expense
684 Repairs expense—_____
685 Repairs expense—_____
687 Selling expense
688 Telephone expense
689 Travel and entertainment expense
690 Utilities expense
691 Warranty expense
695 Income taxes expense

Gains and Losses

701 Gain on retirement of bonds
702 Gain on sale of machinery
703 Gain on sale of investments
704 Gain on sale of trucks
705 Gain on _____
706 Foreign exchange gain or loss
801 Loss on disposal of machinery
802 Loss on exchange of equipment
803 Loss on exchange of _____
804 Loss on sale of notes
805 Loss on retirement of bonds
806 Loss on sale of investments
807 Loss on sale of machinery
808 Loss on _____
809 Unrealized gain—Income
810 Unrealized loss—Income
811 Impairment gain
812 Impairment loss

Clearing Accounts

901 Income summary
902 Manufacturing summary

SELECTED TRANSACTIONS AND RELATIONS

① Merchandising Transactions Summary

Merchandising Transactions		Merchandising Entries	Dr.	Cr.
Purchases	Purchasing merchandise for resale.	• Merchandise Inventory	#	
		Cash or Accounts Payable		#
	Paying freight costs on purchases; FOB shipping point.	• Merchandise Inventory	#	
		Cash		#
	Paying within discount period.	• Accounts Payable	#	
		Merchandise Inventory		#
		Cash		#
	Recording purchase returns or allowances.	• Cash or Accounts Payable	#	
		Merchandise Inventory		#
Sales	Selling merchandise.	• Cash or Accounts Receivable	#	
		Sales............................		#
		• Cost of Goods Sold..................	#	
		Merchandise Inventory		#
	Receiving payment within discount period.	• Cash	#	
		Sales Discounts	#	
		Accounts Receivable		#
	Granting sales returns or allowances.	• Sales Returns and Allowances.........	#	
		Cash or Accounts Receivable		#
		• Merchandise Inventory	#	
		Cost of Goods Sold		#
	Paying freight costs on sales; FOB destination.	• Delivery Expense	#	
		Cash		#

Merchandising Events		Adjusting and Closing Entries	Dr.	Cr.
Adjusting	Adjusting due to shrinkage (occurs when recorded amount larger than physical inventory).	Cost of Goods Sold	#	
		Merchandise Inventory		#
Closing	Closing temporary accounts with credit balances.	Sales	#	
		Income Summary		#
	Closing temporary accounts with debit balances.	Income Summary	#	
		Sales Returns and Allowances		#
		Sales Discounts		#
		Cost of Goods Sold		#
		Delivery Expense		#
		"Other Expenses"		#

② Merchandising Cost Flows

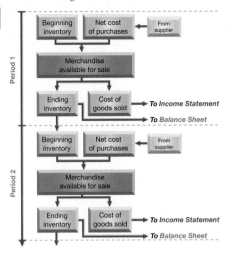

③ Credit Terms and Amounts

*Discount refers to a purchase discount for a buyer and a sales discount for a seller.

④ Bad Debts Estimation

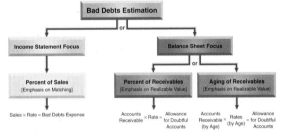

⑤ Bond Valuation

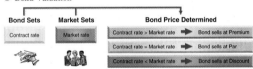

Bond Sets	Market Sets	Bond Price Determined
Contract rate	Market rate	Contract rate > Market rate ➡ Bond sells at Premium
		Contract rate = Market rate ➡ Bond sells at Par
		Contract rate < Market rate ➡ Bond sells at Discount

⑦ Dividend Transactions

Account Affected	Type of Dividend		
	Cash Dividend	Stock Dividend	Stock Split
Cash	Decrease	—	—
Common Stock	—	Increase	—
Retained Earnings ..	Decrease	Decrease	—

⑥ Stock Transactions Summary

Stock Transactions		Stock Entries	Dr.	Cr.
Issue Common Stock	Issue par value common stock at par (par stock recorded at par).	Cash	#	
		Common Stock		#
	Issue par value common stock at premium (par stock recorded at par).	Cash	#	
		Common Stock		#
		Paid-In Capital in Excess of Par Value, Common Stock		#
	Issue no-par value common stock (no-par stock recorded at amount received).	Cash	#	
		Common Stock		#
	Issue stated value common stock at stated value (stated stock recorded at stated value).	Cash	#	
		Common stock		#
	Issue stated value common stock at premium (stated stock recorded at stated value).	Cash	#	
		Common stock		#
		Paid-In Capital in Excess of Stated Value, Common Stock		#
Issue Preferred Stock	Issue par value preferred stock at par (par stock recorded at par).	Cash	#	
		Preferred Stock		#
	Issue par value preferred stock at premium (par stock recorded at par).	Cash	#	
		Preferred Stock		#
		Paid-In Capital in Excess of Par Value, Preferred Stock		#
Reacquire Common Stock	Reacquire its own common stock (treasury stock recorded at cost).	Treasury Stock, Common	#	
		Cash		#
Reissue Common Stock	Reissue its treasury stock at cost (treasury stock removed at cost).	Cash	#	
		Treasury Stock, Common		#
	Reissue its treasury stock above cost (treasury stock removed at cost).	Cash	#	
		Treasury Stock, Common		#
		Paid-In Capital, Treasury		#
	Reissue its treasury stock below cost (treasury stock removed at cost; if paid-in capital is insufficient to cover amount below cost, retained earnings is debited for remainder).	Cash	#	
		Paid-In Capital, Treasury	#	
		Retained Earnings (if necessary)	#	
		Treasury Stock, Common		#

⑧ A Rose by Any Other Name

The same financial statement sometimes receives different titles. Following are some of the more common aliases.*

Balance Sheet	Statement of Financial Position Statement of Financial Condition
Income Statement	Statement of Income Operating Statement Statement of Operations Statement of Operating Activity Earnings Statement Statement of Earnings Profit and Loss (P&L) Statement
Statement of Cash Flows	Statement of Cash Flow Cash Flows Statement Statement of Changes in Cash Position Statement of Changes in Financial Position
Statement of Stockholders' Equity	Statement of Shareholders' Equity Statement of Changes in Shareholders' Equity Statement of Stockholders' Equity and Comprehensive Income Statement of Changes in Owner's Equity Statement of Changes in Owner's Capital Statement of Changes in Capital Accounts

*The term **Consolidated** often precedes or follows these statement titles to reflect the combination of different entities, such as a parent company and its subsidiaries.